Brean Down excavations 1983–1987

English # Heritage

Archaeological Report no 15

Brean Down excavations 1983–1987

Martin Bell

with major contributions by
M Allen, A Clark, K Crabtree, J Evans, J Foster, R Harrison, S Johnson, A K Jones, B Levitan,
R Macphail, C O'Mahoney, S Needham, J E Robinson, S Ross, A Saville, V Straker, A Walker,
D Williams, A Woodward

Historic Buildings and Monuments Commission for England
1990

Copyright © 1990 English Heritage (Historic Buildings and Monuments Commission for England)

Published by English Heritage, Fortress House, 23 Savile Row, London W1X 2HE

Printed in England by Stephen Austin/Hertford

British Library Cataloguing in Publication Data
Bell, Martin, 1953–
 Brean Down excavations 1983–1987. – (Historic Buildings and Monuments Commission for England, Archaeological Report; no 15).
 1. Somerset. Antiquities. Sites
 I. Title II. English Heritage III. Series
 936.2381

ISBN 1-85074-268-5

Contents

List of illustrations.. viii
List of tables.. x
Microfiche contents xi
Colour microfiche contents xii
Acknowledgements.. xv

A Site investigations 1

1 Introduction to the site, research methods, and stratigraphy... 1
Topography... 1
Superficial geology.. 1
Natural history and archaeology of Brean Down 1
The history of archaeological work on the sandcliff.. 3
Gold bracelet discovery in 1983........................... 6
Survey, Easter 1984 6
Coastal retreat 7
Excavations 1985–6 and their research objectives 8
  Research methods in the main trench 1985 9
  Further excavation 1986............................... 14
  Auger and soil pit survey 15
The stratigraphic sequence and sections 15
Structure of the report.................................... 18
  Relationship between the text, illustrations, and archive 18

2 Beaker and earlier activity in Units 8a and 7 19
Description of Unit 8a 19
Excavation and sieving of Unit 8a 19
  Features in Unit 8a..................................... 19
  Artefact distribution in Unit 8a 23
Unit 7: the 'Beaker sand' 23
Beaker activity conclusions 24

3 Early/middle Bronze Age, Unit 6................... 28
The stratigraphy 28
Excavation and sieving of Units 6a and 6b........... 28
  Features in Unit 6a: Contexts 285–7 28
  Structure 57... 28
  A possible earlier structure, Context 181 31
  Sedimentary sequence postdating Structure 57... 31
  Interpretation of Structure 57 32
Dating, artefact distributions, and activity areas 34

4 Middle Bronze Age structures in Unit 5b 37
The stratigraphy 37
Excavation and sieving................................... 37
Structure 59 39
  Features below the floor of Structure 59 39
  Contexts relating to Structure 59 41
Structure 95 42
  Features below the floor of Structure 95 43
  Contexts contemporary with the floor 45
  Gullies 49
  Contexts south of Structure 95 50
  Sediments postdating Structure 95 50
Discussion and interpretation of the structures in Unit 5b... 51
  Structure 95... 51
  Structure 59... 52
The date of Unit 5b.. 54

Artefact distributions and activity areas in Unit 5b 54
  Structure 95.. 54
  The area outside the structures...................... 60
  Structure 59.. 60
Comparison of the structures and conclusions 62

5 Late Bronze Age occupation, Unit 4 63
The stratigraphy 63
Excavation and sieving................................... 63
  Features at the base of Context 16 63
  Interpretation of Contexts 26, 55, and 276.......... 63
  Features within Context 16 66
Finds and their distribution in Unit 4.................. 70
Conclusions... 71

6 The sub-Roman cemetery and Iron Age to medieval stratigraphy..................................... 73
The stratigraphy 73
Excavation of the cemetery and the human bone evidence *by Bruce Levitan*................................. 74
Dating and conclusions 77
  Iron Age and medieval small finds 80
  Settlement pattern 82

7 The post-medieval period *by Martin Bell and Cathy O'Mahoney*.. 84
The stratigraphy 84
Post-medieval pottery 84
Other finds.. 84
Artefact distributions..................................... 86
Conclusions and historical evidence 89

8 The auger survey, soil pits, and intertidal archaeology... 90
Introduction... 90
The auger survey *by Keith Crabtree*..................... 90
  The stratigraphy, as evidenced from the auger survey... 92
The soil pits... 94
  Soil Pit II... 94
  Soil Pit III.. 94
  Soil Pit XII... 96
  Soil Pit IV.. 96
  Soil Pit I.. 99
  Soil Pit V... 99
  Soil Pit VI.. 101
Intertidal archaeology 103
  Soil Pit VII... 103
  Intertidal peat 103
  Other aspects of the intertidal zone 104
Correlation and conclusions............................. 104

B The Bronze Age cultural evidence................. 107

9 Scientific dating....................................... 107
Radiocarbon dating *by Jill Walker* 107
  Measurement technique 107
  Pretreatment 107
  Chemical processing 107
  Counting 107
  Estimation of errors 107
  Calibration... 107
  Interpretation of the data 111
  Conclusions 111

Comments on the radiocarbon dates *by Martin Bell* 112
    Conclusions 113
Archaeomagnetic measurements *by Anthony Clark* 113
    Hearth (Context 134) in Structure 95, Unit 5b ... 114
    Sediment column from Soil Pit VI, north section 114

10 Bell Beaker pottery *by Richard Harrison* 117
Catalogue of sherds.. 117
    Primary contexts 117
    Secondary contexts 119
Conclusions... 119
A note on the petrology of two Beaker sherds *by David Williams* 120

11 The Bronze Age pottery *by Ann Woodward* 121
Introduction.. 121
Fabrics *by David Williams and Ann Woodward* 121
    Macroscopic descriptions 121
    Microscopic descriptions............................. 122
Biconical vessels largely from Unit 6..................... 123
    Assemblage characteristics 124
Trevisker-related vessels from Unit 5b.................. 126
    Context 112, within Structure 95..................... 126
    Context 53, above Structure 95 129
    Context 112, within Structure 95..................... 129
    Other contexts 129
    Unit 5a 131
    Assemblage characteristics 131
The plain ware assemblage from Unit 4 133
    Vessels in Fabric 481 from Context 16 133
    Vessels in Fabric 481 from features at the base of Context 16... 137
    Vessels in Fabric 481 from features within Context 16... 137
    1983 finds of Fabric 481 137
    Vessels in fabrics other than 481 from Context 16... 138
    Assemblage characteristics 138
Fragmentation.. 140
Form and function.. 140
Distribution in relation to structures and features 144

12 Bronze Age metalwork 146
The gold bracelets and Class B1 bracelets in Britain *by Stuart Needham* 146
Copper alloy objects *by Jennifer Foster* 150
Gold-coloured metal spheres.................................. 151
    Analysis *by Duncan Hook* 151

13 The flint and chert artefacts *by Alan Saville* 152
Raw material... 152
Technology.. 152
Context and typology 152
    Unit 8a 154
    Unit 7 154
    Unit 6 156
    Unit 5b 156
    Unit 4 156
    Modern, residual, and unstratified material..... 157
Conclusions... 157

14 Other Bronze Age artefacts *by Jennifer Foster* .. 158
Introduction.. 158

Pottery spindle whorl 158
Stone object 158
Shale objects 159
    X-ray fluorescence analysis of the shale objects *by Michael Heyworth* 160
Bone objects.. 160
    Pins 160
    Awls... 160
    Gouges and 'chisels' 162
    Smoothers 162
    Miscellaneous bone objects 162
Briquetage objects 165
    Pedestals 165
    Evaporation trays 169
    Conclusions 170
    Petrological examination of Bronze Age briquetage *by David Williams* 173
    Analysis of briquetage fragments *by John Evans* 173
Fired clay objects.. 174
    Possible loomweight fragments.................... 174
    Slabs 174
    Miscellaneous fired clay objects................... 175
Geological specimens *by Reg Bradshaw* 175

C Environmental and economic evidence......... 176

15 Physical and chemical characteristics of the stratigraphy *by Sheila M Ross* 176
Introduction.. 176
Analytical methods 176
Results of stratigraphic analyses............................ 176
    Particle size analysis of the sediments............ 176
    Forms of carbon in the sediments 179
    Forms of iron and phosphorus in the sediments.. 179
Chemical analysis of Unit 5b.................................. 182
    Structure 95... 182
    Structure 59... 183

16 Soil history and micromorphology *by Richard I Macphail* 187
Introduction.. 187
Samples and methods.. 187
Results.. 187
Discussion... 187
    The Pleistocene deposits 187
    Post-glacial soil formation and Beaker occupation 188
    Colluvial deposits of Units 8a and 6............... 191
    The early Bronze Age occupation deposits, Unit 6a 193
    Middle Bronze Age, Units 5b and 5a.............. 194
    Late Bronze Age, Unit 4 195
    Iron Age to Roman colluvium, Unit 4a 196
Conclusions... 196

17 Magnetic susceptibility *by Michael J Allen* 197
Introduction.. 197
Materials and methods... 197
Sampling.. 197
    Stratigraphic sequence 197
    Unit 5b, Context 53...................................... 198
Results.. 198
    Programme 1: stratigraphy........................... 198
    Programme 2: Unit 5b.................................. 201

Comparison 201
Summary 202

18 Pollen analysis, diatoms, ostracods, and the foreshore peat 203
Pollen analysis of the foreshore peat *by Keith Crabtree* 203
Macroscopic plant remains from the foreshore peat *by Vanessa Straker* 205
Discussion *by Keith Crabtree* 206
Pollen analysis of sandcliff samples and marine silts *by Keith Crabtree* 206
    The sandcliff 206
    The marine silts 207
Diatoms *by Keith Crabtree* 207
Ostracods *by Eric Robinson* 208
    Sandcliff sequence 208
    Soil Pit VI 209

19 Charred plant macrofossils *by Vanessa Straker* 211
Charcoal from the buried soil (Unit 8a) 211
Other plant macrofossils 211
    Cultivated plants 213
    Wild plants 213
    Unit 8a 216
    Unit 7 216
    Unit 6b 216
    Unit 6a 217
    Unit 6α 217
    Unit 5b 217
    Unit 4 218
    Plant impressions in briquetage 218
Discussion 219

20 The vertebrate remains *by Bruce Levitan* 220
Introduction 220
i The Pleistocene material 221
ii The 'Beaker sand' and basal palaeosol deposits 221
iii Comparison of the deposits in the middle and early Bronze Age structures 221
    General comparison between the structures 223
    Relative frequencies of cattle, sheep, and pig ... 225
iv The character of the late Bronze Age deposits ... 233
    The major mammals 233
    Distribution of bones 233
    Other mammals 235
    Other animals 235
v Ageing, butchery, and measurements: Units 4–8 236
    Cattle and sheep: summary 237
vi Ecological considerations 237
vii Human bones from Bronze Age contexts 238
viii Intrusions and disturbances 238
Conclusions 239

21 Coprolites and faecal concretions *by Andrew K G Jones* 242
Introduction 242
Results 242
Discussion 245
    Coprolites 245
    Possible coprolites 245
    Amorphous concretions 245
Conclusions 245

22 Mollusca and other zoological evidence 246
Non-marine Mollusca *by Martin Bell and Su Johnson* 246
    Introduction and aims 246
    Methods 246
    The molluscan sequence on the sandcliff 247
    Mollusca from Soil Pit VI 249
Marine Mollusca *by Su Johnson* 250
    Introduction 250
    Variation in the shell shape of *Nucella lapillus* ... 251
    Discussion 251
Notes on other zoological evidence *by Martin Bell* 252
    Barnacles 252
    Crabs 252
    Birds' eggs 252

D 23 Conclusions 253

Post-depositional processes 253
The cultural sequence and its dating 253
Settlement pattern 255
Burial practice 255
Palaeoenvironment 257
Palaeoeconomy 260
Archaeological Resource Management 262

Summary/Résumé/Zusammenfassung 264
Bibliography 268
Index 275

List of illustrations

Fig 1   Location map: (a) in relation to southern Britain; (b) in relation to Mendip, the Somerset Levels, and post-glacial sediments
Fig 2   View of the sandcliff from the sea, May 1959
Fig 3   Brean Down relict landscape
Fig 4   Sandcliff section 1954–9 reproduced from ApSimon *et al* 1961
Fig 5   The gold bracelets *in situ*, 6 May 1983
Fig 6   Section a–b of the irregular sandcliff face drawn in 1984
Fig 7   Section c–d of the irregular sandcliff face drawn in 1984
Fig 8   Section drawing exercise, Easter 1984, stones of Feature G (Structure 57) overlain by Unit 5b surface
Fig 9   Plan of the sandcliff showing coastal retreat and the relative positions of the sections in 1955–60 and 1985
Fig 10   Plan showing the progress of the excavation and the areas of each stratigraphic unit excavated in plan and on Sections 13 and 14
Fig 11   View of the excavation trench from Brean Down
Fig 12   Three-dimensional artefact recording: (a) the method of artefact measurement and (b) the format of data on the computer archive
Fig 13   Survey of the sandcliff showing contours and excavated areas
Fig 14   Location of the chief sections
Fig 15   The main section, 1985
Fig 16   Section of the sandcliff north of the main trench
Fig 17   Section 16 excavated in 1985 at 23m on the A-axis
Fig 18   Sections 13 and 21 excavated in 1985 at 10m and 998.7m respectively on the A-axis
Fig 19   Contour plans showing the areas of Units 8a and 7 excavated
Fig 20   (a) Plan of Unit 8a; (b) artefact distributions in Unit 8a; (c) section of gully 191
Fig 21   Basal palaeosol Unit 8a under excavation showing possible gully 191
Fig 22   Possible cultivation marks on the surface of Unit 8a
Fig 23   Sandcliff section showing the distribution of Beaker pottery in all contexts
Fig 24   Section showing basal palaeosol (Unit 8a) overlain by sand (Unit 7) and colluvium (Unit 6)
Fig 25   Palaeosol (Unit 8a) exposed in the foreground in Soil Pit VII on the beach and in the background at the base of the sandcliff sequence
Fig 26   Plan of Unit 6
Fig 27   Sections 5, 120, and 59
Fig 28   Plan of Structure 57
Fig 29   Structure 57 from the west
Fig 30   Structure 57 from the east showing possible earlier Structure 181 and the deep sounding
Fig 31   Artefact distributions (a) from the floor level of Structure 57 and (b) from Unit 6 contexts postdating Structure 57
Fig 32   The excavation of Structures 59 (left) and 95 (right) in Unit 5b
Fig 33   Contoured plan of the surface of Unit 5b
Fig 34   Plan of structures in Unit 5b and cut features at the base of Unit 5b
Fig 35   Structure 59
Fig 36   Plan of Structure 59
Fig 37   Sections relating to Structure 59
Fig 38   Plan of Structure 95
Fig 39   Sections relating to Structure 95
Fig 40   Structure 95 from the south-east during the early stages of excavation
Fig 41   Structure 95 showing wall trench, stormwater gully, hearth, and terrace wall
Fig 42   Plan of the wall trench of Structure 95
Fig 43   Wall trench (139) of Structure 95 showing silty clay patches
Fig 44   Sections of the stormwater gully and terrace fill of Structure 95
Fig 45   Hypothetical reconstruction of Structure 95 in cross-section
Fig 46   Unit 5b structures: distribution of (a) pottery (for the distribution of different fabrics see Fig 102b) and (b) briquetage
Fig 47   Unit 5b structures: distribution of (a) bone and metal artefacts and (b) flint and stone artefacts
Fig 48   Unit 5b structures: distribution of (a) coprolites and (b) bones
Fig 49   Unit 5b structures: distribution of (a) marine Mollusca and (b) hearth debris
Fig 50   Reconstruction drawing of the structures and activities in Unit 5b
Fig 51   Plan of Unit 4: (a) features at the base of Unit 4; (b) the surface of Unit 4
Fig 52   Sections of features in Unit 4
Fig 53   Plans of the northern part of Unit 4: (a) the base of the unit; (b) surface of the unit after the removal of 0.1m
Fig 54   Ditch (88) section from west
Fig 55   Unit 4, Structure 50
Fig 56   Structure 50 at an early stage of excavation
Fig 57   Structure 50 after removal of smaller stones
Fig 58   The north part of the excavation trench showing the surface of Unit 4 in plan and Units 4a and above in section
Fig 59   Plan of Unit 4a showing positions of overlying sub-Roman burials in the main (1985) excavation trench and Trench IX (1986)
Fig 60   Sub-Roman burials in the northern end of the main excavation trench (1985) and Trench IX (1986)
Fig 61   Infant burial 3 with stone grave lining round feet
Fig 62   Skeleton 4
Fig 63   Plan of (a) skeleton 8, (b) skeleton 7 and wall to north, and (c) the large boulder covering skeleton 7
Fig 64   Skeleton 7
Fig 65   Distribution plots of human bones not associated with specific skeletons
Fig 66   Artefacts of probable Roman to early medieval date
Fig 67   Post-medieval pottery nos 1–15
Fig 68   Spanish oil jars 16 and 17
Fig 69   Post-medieval small finds
Fig 70   Artefact distributions: (a) prehistoric pottery in Units 1–4a with key to pottery fabrics; (b) sixteenth- and seventeenth-century pottery; (c) later sixteenth- to twentieth-century pottery

Fig 71 Distribution of sherds of a single Donyatt cistern
Fig 72 Plan of sandcliff showing the relationship between the main trench and the soil pits and auger holes; also shown is the extent of late Bronze Age Unit 4 and the approximate outcrop of the basal palaeosol Unit 8a on the beach
Fig 73 Three-dimensional diagram of the auger survey
Fig 74 Sections along the line of auger borings
Fig 75 Soil Pit II: (a) section with auger hole 25/980, 0.5m south; (b) plan of Unit 4
Fig 76 Section of Soil Pit III showing auger hole 30/960, 2m to the south
Fig 77 View from the south along the soil pit transect; from foreground to background Pits VI, V, IV, and XII
Fig 78 Soil pit and auger transect along the 900m coordinate, from the top of Brean Down (left) to the estuarine flats (right) showing the stratigraphy in Pits XII, I, and IV
Fig 79 Soil Pit V: (a) section and (b) plan of stone feature (220) on surface of Unit 6
Fig 80 Soil Pit V: section showing stone feature (Context 220) on the surface of Unit 6
Fig 81 Soil Pit VI: section showing archaeomagnetic dating column
Fig 82 Calibrated radiocarbon dates at one and two standard deviations
Fig 83 Magnetic measurements on the Brean Down sediment column compared with the declination and inclination curves of Turner and Thompson (1982)
Fig 84 Bell Beaker pottery from primary contexts
Fig 85 Bell Beaker pottery from secondary contexts
Fig 86 Vertical distribution of all sherds by fabric
Fig 87 The occurrence of stratified prehistoric pottery fabrics by major unit
Fig 88 Pottery largely from Unit 6
Fig 89 Trevisker-related vessels from Unit 5b, Context 112
Fig 90 Trevisker-related vessels from Unit 5b, Context 112
Fig 91 Trevisker-related vessels from Unit 5b, Context 53
Fig 92 Trevisker-related vessels from Unit 5b
Fig 93 Vessels in Fabric 481 from Context 16
Fig 94 Vessels in Fabric 481 from Context 16
Fig 95 Vessels in Fabric 481 from Context 16 and from features within Context 16
Fig 96 1983 finds in Fabric 481
Fig 97 Vessels in fabrics other than 481 from Context 16
Fig 98 Distribution of rim types in Unit 4
Fig 99 Sherd weight categories showing distribution of sherd weight
Fig 100 The occurrence of rim diameters in selected south-western Bronze Age pottery assemblages
Fig 101 Rim size ranges for selected Bronze Age assemblages and assemblage groups
Fig 102 Distribution of prehistoric pottery fabrics (a) in Unit 6 in relation to Structure 57 and (b) in Unit 5b in relation to Structures 59 and 95
Fig 103 Distribution in Unit 5b: (a) of reconstructed vessels and selected ceramic traits; (b) detailed distribution of reconstructed vessels in grid square 16/8
Fig 104 Distribution of prehistoric pottery fabrics in Unit 4 in relation to features
Fig 105 Gold bracelets from Unit 4
Fig 106 Bronze Age metalwork
Fig 107 The distribution of Class B late Bronze Age bracelets
Fig 108 Flints from Units 8a, 7, and 6
Fig 109 Flints from Units 6, 5b, and 4
Fig 110 Flints from modern, residual, and unstratified contexts
Fig 111 Pottery spindle whorl and stone object
Fig 112 Shale objects
Fig 113 Bone pins and awls
Fig 114 Bone gouges, 'chisel', and smoothers
Fig 115 Miscellaneous bone objects
Fig 116 Briquetage pedestals
Fig 117 Briquetage pedestals
Fig 118 Briquetage trays
Fig 119 Briquetage pedestal
Fig 120 Reconstruction of tray 97 and pedestal 70
Fig 121 Fired clay artefacts
Fig 122 Particle size distribution for sediments of 12 of the major stratigraphic contexts
Fig 123 Distribution of loss on ignition, organic carbon, calcium carbonate, crystalline and mobile iron, and phosphate in sediments of 12 of the major stratigraphic contexts
Fig 124a Plan (A) and spatial distribution of (B) phosphorus, (C) crystalline iron, and (D) mobile iron in sediments of Structure 95, Unit 5b
Fig 124b Spatial distribution of (E) loss on ignition, (F) organic carbon, and (G) total nitrogen in sediments of Structure 95, Unit 5b
Fig 125a Plan (A) and spatial distribution of (B) phosphorus, (C) crystalline iron, and (D) mobile iron in sediments of Structure 59, Unit 5b
Fig 125b Spatial distribution of (E) loss on ignition, (F) organic carbon, and (G) total nitrogen in sediments of Structure 59, Unit 5b
Fig 126 Stages in the soil history of Unit 8a
Fig 127 Palaeosol (Unit 8a), thin section B
Fig 128 Schematic section of the basal palaeosol Unit 8a, showing typical microfabrics of the main soil horizons
Fig 129 Palaeosol (Unit 8a), thin section C
Fig 130 Layered occupation deposit (Unit 6a), thin section O
Fig 131 Summary diagram of magnetic susceptibility variation through the stratigraphic sequence at Brean Down
Fig 132 Magnetic and chemical distributions viewed isometrically at 45° over Structure 95, Unit 5b
Fig 133 Block of sediment from the intertidal zone
Fig 134 Pollen analysis of the foreshore peat
Fig 135 Macroscopic plant remains from the foreshore peat
Fig 136 Habitat groups represented by plant macrofossils from the main stratigraphic units
Fig 137 A breakdown of the types of cultivated plants in the main stratigraphic units
Fig 138 Pie diagrams showing the relative importance of the main plant habitat groups in Units 6α, 5b, and 4

Fig 139 Distribution of animal bone in Units 7 and 8a
Fig 140 Distribution of animal bone in Structure 57, Unit 6α
Fig 141 Distribution of animal bone in Unit 5b: (a) cattle and cattle-sized bone; (b) sheep and sheep-sized bone
Fig 142 Animal bone in Unit 5b; species other than cattle and sheep
Fig 143 The relative frequencies of mammals in Bronze Age Structures 95, 59, and 57
Fig 144 The relative frequencies of mammals in Units 5b and 6
Fig 145 Anatomical representation of cattle bones in (a) Unit 5b and (b) Unit 6
Fig 146 Cumulative frequency graph showing the anatomical representation of cattle and sheep in (a) Unit 5b and (b) Unit 6
Fig 147 Anatomical representation of sheep bones in (a) Unit 5b and (b) Unit 6
Fig 148 Anatomical representation of (a) cattle and (b) sheep in Unit 4; (c) anatomical representation of cattle and sheep using cumulative frequency graph
Fig 149 Distribution of cattle and sheep bones in Unit 4
Fig 150 Distribution of species other than cattle and sheep in Unit 4
Fig 151 Mandible wear stages for Units 4–8a
Fig 152 Distribution of rabbit bones
Fig 153 Coprolites
Fig 154 Coprolites
Fig 155 General view of the excavation showing mollusc sampling columns
Fig 156 Land mollusc diagram
Fig 157 Marine mollusc diagram showing the number of shells per unit
Fig 158 Summary of the Brean pottery sequence
Fig 159 The archaeological and environmental context of Brean Down
Fig 160 (a) Predicted high tide levels on OD scale for Burnham-on-Sea for 1989; (b) correlation chart on the same scale as 160a showing certain tidal levels at Brean, the heights of coastal protection works, and and the silty clay surface; (c) the number of days when the rivers Brue, Parrett, and Tone reached flood stage between 1952 and 1965
Fig 161 Records of tides at Avonmouth above HAT (8m OD) since the early seventeenth century
Fig 162 Comparison between the height of Mean High Water Spring Tides and the Brean saltmarsh surface in the last six millennia

List of tables

1 Comparison of the stratigraphy reported in 1961 with that of 1985
2 Pottery fabrics in Unit 6
3 Radiocarbon dates listed by stratigraphic unit
4 Radiocarbon dates – full calibration data
5 Groupings of radiocarbon dates
6 Number of decorated Beaker sherds by stratigraphic unit
7 The occurrence of Bronze Age pottery by phase unit
8 Dimensions and weight of the gold bracelets
9 Typological analysis of all struck flint and chert artefacts
10 Typological analysis of flint artefacts from stratified contexts
11 Variation between briquetage pedestals
12 Chemical analysis of briquetage
13 Numbers of pollen grains in two samples from Unit 8a, Context 61
14 Charcoal from the buried soil (Unit 8a)
15 Carbonised plant remains
16 Carbonised plant remains: taxa from Table 15 assigned to groups as shown in Figs 136 and 138
17 Summary of vertebrate fauna
18 Summary of animals from Structures 95, 59, and 57
19 Summary of bird and fish species by stratigraphic unit
20 Summary of small mammals, reptiles, and amphibians
21 Frequency of rabbits by stratigraphic unit
22 The stratigraphic occurrence of coprolites, possible coprolites, and amorphous concretions
23 Results of parasitological investigation of coprolites, possible coprolites, and amorphous concretions
24 Dimensions of *Trichuris* ova
25 Estimates of coastal retreat based on two rates calculated for the recent past

Microfiche contents

1:A5 The distribution of Bronze Age small finds in Unit 4, by M Bell (Chapter 5)
1:A6 Possible Iron Age pottery, by M Bell (Chapter 6)
1:A7–8 The Roman pottery, by P Leach (Chapter 6)
1:A9–10 Small finds of probable Roman or early medieval date, by J Foster (Chapter 6)
1:A11–B4 Post-medieval pottery, by C O'Mahoney (Chapter 7)
1:B5 Summary of the number of post-medieval sherds in each context, by C O'Mahoney (Chapter 7)
1:B6–7 Catalogue of all post-medieval sherds correlating illustration numbers with artefact numbers and context, by C O'Mahoney (Chapter 7)
1:B8–9 Post-medieval metalwork and small finds, by J Foster (Chapter 7)
1:B9 Clay tobacco pipes, by S Minnett (Chapter 7)
1:B10 Distribution of post-medieval non-ceramic artefact types, by M Bell and C O'Mahoney (Chapter 7)
1:B11–C4 Diagrams showing the auger transects, by K Crabtree (Chapter 8)
1:C5 List of prehistoric pottery fabrics in each soil pit context, by A Woodward (Chapter 8)
1:C6 Inventory and concordance for illustrated flint and chert artefacts, by A Saville (Chapter 13)
1:C7 Table of briquetage, clay objects, and daub by context, by J Foster (Chapter 14)
1:C8–10 Table of geological specimens, by R Bradshaw (Chapter 14)
1:C11 Particle size analysis for sediments of twelve of the major stratigraphic contexts, by S M Ross (Chapter 15)
1:C12 Chemical analysis of sediments from twelve of the major stratigraphic contexts, by S M Ross (Chapter 15)
1:C13 Particle size analysis for selected micromorphological thin section samples, by R I Macphail (Chapter 16)
1:C14 Analytical data relating to calcium carbonate, organic matter, loss on ignition, forms of iron, and magnetic susceptibility for selected micromorphological thin section samples, by R I Macphail (Chapter 16)
1:D1–3 Soil profile descriptions, by R I Macphail (Chapter 16)
1:D4–E3 Micromorphological description and preliminary interpretation, by R I Macphail (Chapter 16)
1:E4 Introduction to magnetic susceptibility results, by M J Allen (Chapter 17)
1:E5 Graphs of magnetic susceptibility in Units 8, 7, and 6, by M J Allen (Chapter 17)
1:E6 Graphs of magnetic susceptibility in Units 5d to 1, by M J Allen (Chapter 17)
1:E7 Graph of magnetic susceptibility from the stratigraphic sequence in Soil Pit VI, by M J Allen (Chapter 17)
1:E8 Wire diagram of Structure 95, Unit 5b showing the variation in (a) magnetic susceptibility and (b) phosphate, by M J Allen (Chapter 17)
1:E9 Wire diagram of Structure 95, Unit 5b showing the variation in (a) dithionite iron (Fe_d) and (b) pyrophosphate iron (Fe_p), by M J Allen (Chapter 17)
1:E10 Wire diagram of Structure 95, Unit 5b showing the variation in (a) organic carbon and (b) loss on ignition, by M J Allen (Chapter 17)
1:E11 Wire diagram of Structure 95, Unit 5b showing the variation in (a) nitrogen and (b) carbon/nitrogen ratios, by M J Allen (Chapter 17)
1:E12 Wire diagram of Structure 59, Unit 5b showing the variation in (a) magnetic susceptibility and (b) phosphate, by M J Allen (Chapter 17)
1:E13 Wire diagram of Structure 59, Unit 5b showing the variation in (a) dithionite iron (Fe_d) and (b) pyrophosphate iron (Fe_p), by M J Allen (Chapter 17)
1:E14 Wire diagram of Structure 59, Unit 5b showing the variation in (a) organic carbon and (b) loss on ignition, by M J Allen (Chapter 17)
1:F1 Wire diagram of Structure 59, Unit 5b showing the variation in (a) nitrogen and (b) carbon/nitrogen ratios, by M J Allen (Chapter 17)
1:F2 Tables of magnetic susceptibility data from mollusc columns 1 and 2, by M J Allen (Chapter 17)
1:F3 Tables of magnetic susceptibility data from mollusc columns 3 to 5, by M J Allen (Chapter 17)
1:F4 Tables of magnetic susceptibility data from Soil Pit VI and other stratigraphically related samples from the sandcliff sequence, by M J Allen (Chapter 17)
1:F5 Context variability of magnetic susceptibility results from data tabulated on MF1:F2–4, by M J Allen (Chapter 17)
1:F6–7 Magnetic susceptibility and chemical data from the grid over Structure 95, Unit 5b and additional magnetic susceptibility samples from Structure 95, by M J Allen (Chapter 17)
1:F8 Magnetic susceptibility and chemical data from a grid over Structure 59, Unit 5b and a table showing the correction applied to magnetic susceptibility samples from Structures 59 and 95 which weighed less than 100g, by M J Allen (Chapter 17)
1:F9 Table of pollen from samples through the sandcliff stratigraphy based on a subjective assessment, by K Crabtree (Chapter 18)
1:F10 Table showing contexts sieved for charred plant macrofossils, by V Straker (Chapter 19)
1:F11 Sketch diagram showing the approximate locations of bones in Pleistocene layers, by B Levitan (Chapter 20)
1:F12 Table showing anatomical representation of cattle and sheep in Unit 5b, by B Levitan (Chapter 20)
1:F13 Table showing anatomical representation of cattle and sheep in Unit 6, by B Levitan (Chapter 20)
1:F14 Table showing anatomical representation of cattle and sheep in Unit 4, by B Levitan (Chapter 20)
1:G1 Selected measurements of cattle, sheep, pig, horse, red deer, and sturgeon bones compared to those from Runnymede and Potterne with a diagram showing the measurement points for the sturgeon skull plate, by B Levitan (Chapter 20)
1:G2 Summary of unarticulated human bones from Unit 3 and prehistoric layers, by B Levitan (Chapter 20)
1:G3–5 Catalogue of samples selected for parasitological investigation, by A K G Jones (Chapter 21)
1:G6 Catalogue of unexamined coprolites and

samples which were not of faecal origin, by A K G Jones (Chapter 21)

1:G7 Table of non-marine Mollusca from the sandcliff sequence, by M Bell and S Johnson (Chapter 22)

1:G8 Table showing the number of shells of four species of land mollusc recovered by hand-picking and site-sieving, compared to the numbers of rabbit bones, all listed by stratigraphic unit, by M Bell and S Johnson (Chapter 22)

1:G9 Table of Mollusca from Soil Pit VI, by M Bell and S Johnson (Chapter 22)

1:G10 Table of marine Mollusca in each context, by S Johnson (Chapter 22)

1:G11 Diagram of the ratio between the length and the aperture height of *Nucella lapillus* by stratigraphic unit compared to the ratios of Crothers relating to modern populations at Brean, by S Johnson (Chapter 22)

Colour microfiche contents

The colour microfiche, which relates to Chapter 16, is available as an optional extra; see p 18. Bracketed numbers are microfiche frame numbers.

Colour MF 1 (A7) Brean Down sandcliff from left to right. Carboniferous Limestone of the Down promontory; Pleistocene deposits (dune, Unit 9: breccia, Unit 8b); top of prehistoric catena

Colour MF 2 (A7) Brean Down sandcliff showing, from the base upwards: breccia (Unit 8b); palaeosol (Unit 8a), thickening downslope to below the high spring tide level; the wedge of blown sand (Unit 7); Middle Bronze Age colluvium and occupation deposits (Units 6 and 5); blown sand and late Bronze Age occupation deposits (Unit 4); reddish stony colluvium (Unit 4a); and Early Christian blown sand (Unit 3)

Colour MF 3 (A8) Profile 1, upwards – thin section B, C, and D in palaeosol (Unit 8a) above stony breccia (Unit 8b)

Colour MF 4 (A9) Profile 2, upwards – thin sections G (Unit 8a/'Beaker sand' Unit 7), H, and I (MBA colluvium Unit 6b/6c), L and M (MBA occupation Unit 6a)

Colour MF 5 (A10) Position of thin section O, sample 146 (early Bronze Age Unit 6a)

Colour MF 6 (A10) Position of thin section N, sample 149 (middle Bronze Age Unit 5b)

Colour MF 7 (A11) Profile 3, greyish stony LBA occupation (Unit 4) overlain by reddish stony colluvium (Unit 4a) and Early Christian (Unit 3) sediments; modern soil above

Colour MF 8 (A12) Field, profile 3, thin section P in moderately stone-free soil at top of Unit 4; hole above in Unit 4a locates thin section R

Colour MF 9 (A13) Photomicrograph; Dr Cornwall's Unit 13 (Pleistocene) sample; probable mixed windblown and water deposited colluvium of fine sand to medium sand size soil fragments (papules) of reddish *terra fusca* clay (right centre), very common dark brown silt and clay granules (probably from cryogenic soils) and probable strong red rubified silt and clay soil (top right); silt and sand size quartz also present. Plane polarised light, frame length 3.3mm

Colour MF 10 (A13) As Colour MF 9. Crossed polarised light; note poorly birefringent granules

Colour MF 11 (A14) As Colour MF 9 and 10. Oblique incident light

Colour MF 12 (B1) Dr Cornwall's Unit 12a (Pleistocene) sample; well-sorted silts and fine sand size soil fragments, possibly wind transported but water lain; probable meltwater has washed clay down profile to form a link capping micropan. Plane polarised light, frame length 5.255mm

Colour MF 13 (B1) As Colour MF 12. Crossed polarised light

Colour MF 14 (B2) Dr Cornwall's Unit 9 (Pleistocene dune) sample; windblown fine sand size deposit of quartz, shell, and soil fragments. Plane polarised light, frame length 5.225mm

Colour MF 15 (B2) As Colour MF 14. Crossed polarised light

Colour MF 16 (B3) Palaeosol (Unit 8a) thin section B; fragments of ferruginous beta B *terra fusca* clay. Plane polarised light, frame length 3.3mm

Colour MF 17 (B3) As Colour MF 16. Crossed polarised light; note pure clay content

Colour MF 18 (B4) Dr Cornwall's Unit 8a sample; base of the palaeosol, mixture of *terra fusca* beta B clay, blown sand, and silt. Plane polarised light, frame length 5.225mm

Colour MF 19 (B4) As Colour MF 18. Crossed polarised light

Colour MF 20 (B5) Gully in palaeosol (Unit 8a), thin section A; manganese impregnated fragment of humic Ah horizon material; note fine structure. Plane polarised light, frame length 3.3mm

Colour MF 21 (B5) As Colour MF 20; note birefringent clay coatings around voids and peds. Crossed polarised light

Colour MF 22 (B6) Palaeosol (Unit 8a), thin section B; soil fragments of reddish beta B clay, yellowish brown silty B(t) horizon and blackish, fine charcoal rich burned soil material, all separated by reddish dusty clay infilling and coating void space (as Colour MF 18), anomalous mixture of various soil horizon material and the infilling of voids by dusty clay to produce a closed vughy porosity, indicates soil disruption, probably through woodland clearance – the presence of burned soil possibly also suggesting contemporaneous burning; slight rounding of fragments may be the result of small downslope movement under gravity. Plane polarised light, frame length 3.3mm

Colour MF 23 (B7) As Colour MF 22; note birefringent clay infills and poorly birefringent burned soil. Crossed polarised light

Colour MF 24 (B7) As Colour MF 22; note variations in soil types and infills. Oblique incident light

Colour MF 25 (B8) Palaeosol (Unit 8a), thin section C; soil is a homogenised yellowish brown loam containing charcoal; coarse peds with diffuse boundaries, within-ped and between-ped textural features (intercalations and very dusty clay void coatings) all suggest physical mixing and slaking; interpreted as a cultivated fabric. Plane polarised light, frame length 3.3mm

Colour MF 26 (B8) As Colour MF 25; note birefringent coatings and intercalations. Crossed polarised light

Colour MF 27 (B9) Palaeosol (Unit 8a), thin section D; totally homogenised yellowish brown loam with mammilated mineral excrements and open vughy porosity, all indicating reworking of soil by earthworms. Plane polarised light, frame length 3.3mm

Colour MF 28 (B10) Palaeosol (Unit 8a), thin section J; probable turf (Ah) material, pseudomorphically replaced by iron-manganese impregnation; this layer possibly represents grassland stabilisation of the Beaker palaeosol. Plane polarised light, frame length 0.33mm

Colour MF 29 (B10) As Colour MF 28; note post turf-line birefringent dusty clay coatings washed-in from the overlying ploughsoil colluvium (Unit 6). Crossed polarised light

Colour MF 30 (B11) Soil Pit V; thin section E (Unit 6b); mixture of yellowish brown loam and pale yellow silt containing high quantitites of dark brown amorphous organic matter; layer represents the interdigitation of terrestrial colluvium and estuarine/marine peaty silts. Plane polarised light, frame length 0.33mm

Colour MF 31 (B11) As Colour MF 30; note high birefringent silt. Crossed polarised light

Colour MF 32 (B12) Detail of Colour MF 30; peaty silts contain abundant phytoliths from aquatic plants with occasional diatoms. Plane polarised light, frame length 0.116mm

Colour MF 33 (B12) Palaeosol, thin section F (Unit 8a), Soil Pit VII on the foreshore; coarse wood charcoal set in yellowish brown silt loam containing many phytoliths; layer probably represents the homogenisation, under saturated conditions, of colluvial loam and estuarine/marine silt. Plane polarised light, frame length 0.33mm

Colour MF 34 (B13) Colluvium (Unit 6b), thin section J; sand and speckled brown clay containing fine charcoal; closed vughy porosity with abundant dusty clay coatings; layer interpreted as the result of cultivation mixing of the eroding palaeosol (Unit 8a) and blown sand, slaked soil forming textural features. Plane polarised light, frame length 0.33mm

Colour MF 35 (B13) As Colour MF 33; note birefringent void coatings. Crossed polarised light

Colour MF 36 (B14) Colluvium (Unit 6b), thin section H; a mixture of sand and patchy fine material commonly displaying textural features, which suggests the layer is a colluvial ploughsoil. Plane polarised light, frame length c 8mm

Colour MF 37 (C1) Occupation deposits (Unit 6a), thin section L; rather dense speckled yellowish brown, silty and organic stained fine fabric and sand with included coarse phytoliths; layer interpreted as purposeful dump of estuarine/marine silts and peat for constructional purposes; activities such as trampling have incorporated blown sand. Plane polarised light, frame length 3.3mm

Colour MF 38 (C1) As Colour MF 37; moderate birefringence suggest the inclusion of ash material; note non-birefringent nature of phytoliths. Crossed polarised light

Colour MF 39 (C2) Detail of Colour MF 38; coarse phytolith of probable aquatic plant material imported alongside silt into this layer. Plane polarised light, frame length 0.33mm

Colour MF 40 (C3) Occupation deposits (Unit 6a), thin section M; the vertical boundary between occupation sediments (as in Colour MF 37) and similar deposits stained and infilled by yellowish amorphous material which is tentatively interpreted as a weakly ferruginous organic and phosphate rich complex; this may represent a weathered surface where ash has become decalcified liberating phosphate. Plane polarised light, frame length 3.3mm

Colour MF 41 (C3) As Colour MF 40; note difference in birefringence of the still ashy horizon above; the amorphous infills may be pseudomorphic of plant (algal) material growing in ash rich horizons and contributing to its weathering. Crossed polarised light

Colour MF 42 (C4) Deeper in the occupation deposits (Unit 6a), thin section L; compact sediments containing 1mm size nodules; material as in Colour MF 37 is weathered and compacted and has been affected by secondary nodular formation. Plane polarised light, frame length 8mm

Colour MF 43 (C4) As Colour MF 42; detail of nodule showing concentric nature and possible associated vivianite. Plane polarised light, frame length 3.3mm

Colour MF 44 (C5) As Colour MF 42; note birefringent nature of nodule suggesting it is not purely comprised of amorphous iron. Crossed polarised light

Colour MF 45 (C5) As Colour MF 42; ferruginous nature is apparent, but nodule is suspected of including phosphate and also calcium. Oblique incident light

Colour MF 46 (C6) Layered occupation deposits (Unit 6a), thin section O; here two layers containing charcoal; one rich in ash whereas the other contains brown amorphous organic matter, suggesting peat (some of which is charred) is present. Plane polarised light, frame length 3.3mm

Colour MF 47 (C6) As Colour MF 46. Crossed polarised light

Colour MF 48 (C7) As Colour MF 46; unweathered (protected) probable low temperature hearth layers comprising coarse wood charcoal, well sorted fine bone fragments and pure ash of calcium carbonate crystals. Plane polarised light, frame length 3.3mm

Colour MF 49 (C7) As Colour MF 48; note poorly birefringent weakly burned bone and the highly birefringent ash layer. Crossed polarised light

Colour MF 50 (C8) Occupation deposits (Unit 5b), thin section N; detail of amorphous peaty organic matter and layered phytoliths set in a thin matrix containing phytoliths. Plane polarised light, frame length 0.116mm

Colour MF 51 (C8) As Colour MF 50, but under ultra violet light; note fluorescent phytolith and specks of ash

Colour MF 52 (C9) As Colour MF 50; area of dark occupation material; in the left centre vessicular vitrified ash containing no charcoal is present, whereas elsewhere finely fragmented charcoal has become fused into ash residues weakly pseudomorphic of plant material; high temperature burning has apparently destroyed any calcium carbonate crystals while silica from phytoliths has melted; the lack of charcoal in places indicates complete combustion. Plane polarised light, frame length 3.3mm

Colour MF 53 (C9)   As Colour MF 52; note non-birefringent nature of heavily burned ash residues. Crossed polarised light

Colour MF 54 (C10)   As Colour MF 52; note pure grey colour of vessicular ash residues. Oblique incident light

Colour MF 55 (C10)   As Colour MF 52; other evidence of high temperature or industrial use of this part of the site is probable fragments of briquetage; here clay from the palaeosol has been strongly reddened and a heavily charred plant fragment is evidence of plant tempering. Plane polarised light, frame length 3.3mm

Colour MF 56 (C11)   Occupation deposits (Unit 4), thin section P in Late Bronze Age soil above very stony sediments; mixture of sand and pale yellowish matrix with textural features. Plane polarised light, frame length 3.3mm

Colour MF 57 (C11)   As Colour MF 56; detail shows matrix to contain phytoliths and charred material of occupation deposits in part derived from imported estuarine silts; textural features such as this very dusty void coating indicate slaking of the horizon perhaps through cultivation. Plane polarised light, frame length 0.33mm

Acknowledgements

Many people contributed to the successful completion of the Brean Down project and I am glad of the opportunity to place on permanent record my gratitude to them. The National Trust gave permission to excavate and provided much active support through the Trust's Archaeological Adviser, David Thackray, and regional Land Agent, Paul Kendrick. Bob Fells, the Trust's Warden, kindly provided practical help and the Trust's MSC teams assisted with backfilling and coastal protection work. Martin Vowles of Brean Down Farm was most kind in allowing us to camp and excavate on his land and I would also like to acknowledge the hospitality of the successive owners of the Brean Bird Garden, Mr Reg Paine and Mr and Mrs Fisher.

The project was largely funded by the Historic Buildings and Monuments Commission (English Heritage) whose regional inspector, Paul Gosling, has been a valued source of advice. Other financial contributions came from the Maltwood Fund of the Royal Society of Arts, the National Trust, and Somerset County Council; the last two also provided help in kind. As archaeological advisers to the project we were fortunate in having Arthur ApSimon, Richard Harrison, and Ann Woodward, who have contributed many useful ideas throughout. In this regard it is also important to acknowledge the part played in the planning and fieldwork of the project by several of those who are also contributors to this volume. Mike Allen was assistant director and took responsibility for photography, while Keith Crabtree organised the auger survey, Vanessa Straker the sieving programme, and Bruce Levitan the on-site computer artefact recording facility.

Finds processing was organised by Julie Jones and Su Johnson and the site planners were Hazel Riley and Nick Watson. Other supervisory responsibilities were undertaken by Helen Smith, Rachel Seager-Smith, Kit Watson, Nancy Walling, and Kerry York. The following played a major part in the excavation: Peter Boyer, Nick Branch, Ian Clewes, Stuart Ellinson, Jenni Heathcote, Andy Josephs, Philip Markham, Joanne McDade, Rachel Smith, Chris Sharp, David Trevarthen, Toby Whitty, Bridget Wilson, and Humphrey Woods. We remember with particular gratitude and sadness the late Bruce Muir who shifted more sand than anybody on the excavation and tragically died in a car accident a few weeks after the 1985 season.

The most difficult and testing time of any archaeological project is the post-excavation stage and I am grateful to all those who have contributed to this volume for their efficiency and help. Mike Allen and Su Johnson have successively worked as post-excavation assistants and have done much towards completion of this report. I am also particularly grateful to my wife, Jennifer Foster, who has greatly eased the post-excavation burden by her work on the finds; she reconstructed and drew the pottery and drew and reported on many of the other prehistoric finds as well as contributing in many other ways to the project as a whole. The flints were drawn by Sue Rouillard and the post-medieval pottery by Cathy O'Mahoney. Toby Whitty was responsible for final drawings of many of the plans and sections. Peter Dunn was responsible for the reconstruction drawings, Figures 45 and 50. I am particularly grateful to Richard Harrison, an anonymous referee, and several members of the team for their comments on an earlier version of the text. I, of course, remain responsible for errors.

The Department of Geography, Bristol University, helped during the excavation with the loan of equipment and transport through the good offices of Keith Crabtree and John Thornes. That Department's cartographer, Simon Godden, drew some diagrams and photographic help was provided by Tony Philpott.

Considerable help with computing aspects during the post-excavation stage was provided by Alan Rogers, Computer Manager at Lampeter. The report was word processed by Maureen Hunwicks with customary efficiency. The project as a whole was organised within the Archaeology Unit, Department of Geography at Lampeter, and I am grateful to the College for facilities and support.

Martin Bell

A Site investigations

1 Introduction to the site, research methods, and stratigraphy

Topography (Fig 1)

Brean Down is a Carboniferous Limestone promontory which projects 1.6km into the Bristol Channel and forms a western extension of the Mendip Hills. To the north lie Weston Bay and Weston-Super-Mare, and to the south lies Bridgwater Bay which forms the seaward edge of the Somerset Levels. The River Axe debouches on the east end of Brean Down into Weston Bay. The enormous tidal range of the Bristol Channel (c 11m at Brean), together with the gently sloping flats to the south and north of the Down, mean that low water is c 1.5km from the sea wall and at low tide a vast expanse of mud is exposed.

The long thin promontory of Brean Down has two summits: the western summit rises to 97m, the eastern summit to 79m. To the north the Down slopes to low cliffs, while to the south the slope is much steeper and ends in cliffs up to c 50m high. The present cliff line is a multi-phase landform of ancient origin. Inland it is buried by a thick sequence of Quaternary sediments. Coastal erosion is cutting into these and exhuming the fossil cliff.

Superficial geology

The fine coastal section through the Quaternary sequence (Fig 2) is known as Brean Down sandcliff; this was fully described in a seminal paper by Ap-Simon *et al* (1961). The sequence consists of a great triangular section up to 30m thick against the former limestone cliff. The greater part of this sequence (c 20m) is blown sand but there are also breccia deposits derived from the south side of the Down by physical weathering and solifluction. Against the cliff all but the top 1m of sediment is Pleistocene.

South towards the base of the slope are up to 5m of post-glacial blown sands, slope deposits, and occupation horizons which form the main subject of this report.

Inland the extent of the sandcliff is delimited by surface topography (Figs 3 and 13). In plan the deposits are roughly the shape of an extremely attenuated isosceles triangle, the base being represented by the coast where in 1985 the exposure was c 80m across. The north side is marked by craggy limestone outcrops marking the top of the former degraded cliff. Here the sandcliff deposits rise to a maximum height of c 33m OD. The south side is marked by a break of slope between the 7 and 8m contours where the sloping sandcliff deposits give way to coastal flats. By 200–300m inland the sandcliff has tapered to a very narrow strip. The sandcliff forms the northern limit of a much more extensive coastal sandbar which extends to the south for 10km as far as Burnham-on-Sea and the mouth of the River Parrett (Fig 1). Inland of this bar are thick deposits of Flandrian silty clays constituting the Somerset Silt Levels which extend up to 9km inland and cover some 180 sq km south of Brean Down. There are further substantial tracts of silty clays on the other side of the River Axe to the north. Several major studies have examined the stratigraphic sequence of the Somerset Levels and its relationship to Flandrian sea level rise (eg Kidson and Heyworth 1973; Heyworth and Kidson 1982; Hawkins 1971; 1973). The present project examined, on a very local scale, the stratigraphic relationship between the well-dated sandcliff sequence and the silts. In the coastal belt there are, within the silts, peat bands which in places are exposed on the foreshore as at Stolford. A thin exposure of *Phragmites* peat occurs on the foreshore 400m south of Brean Down and is discussed in the present report. Inland of the silt levels the peat deposits thicken to form the Somerset peat levels, the ecological history and archaeology of which, particularly in the peatlands between the Poldens and Wedmore Ridge, has been very intensively studied for many years (Coles and Coles 1986).

Natural history and archaeology of Brean Down

The Down, including the seaward end of the sandcliff, is a National Trust property and a Site of Special Scientific Interest (SSSI). It is a classic example of a small relict landscape containing both rare plant and animal species and much evidence of former activity by man (Fig 3). The rare plants occur on the rocky slopes on the south side of the Down; the most notable member is the white rockrose, *Helianthemum appenninum*, which is only known from two other sites in Britain and is regarded as a Pleistocene relict species. It occurs in a dwarf sedge grassland community with a number of very rare biota including other plants, ground bugs, flea beetles, and ants. Altogether eight species of plants and animals found on the Down are listed in the British Red Data Books which identify biota of extreme national rarity (National Trust 1982).

The Quaternary sandcliff sequence is designated as an SSSI for geological reasons. The archaeological evidence in the post-glacial part of this sequence forms the main subject of this volume. In addition there is much other evidence for past human activity on the Down. Nine tumuli or clearance cairns are sited on top of the Down. Near the east end the defences of a small Iron Age hillfort were sectioned by Burrow (1976). Beside the eastern summit is a fourth-century Romano-Celtic temple excavated by ApSimon (1964–5), and recently an inscribed lead curse has been found on the beach just west of the sandcliff (Hassall and Tomlin 1986). On both summits of the Down are extensive areas of celtic fields which are marked on Figure 3 after an original survey by David Thackray for the National Trust. Fowler (1975, 131) suggests a late Roman or later date though he notes that there is no specific dating evidence. The most recent activity is military and consists of a Palmerstonian fort at the west end which, together

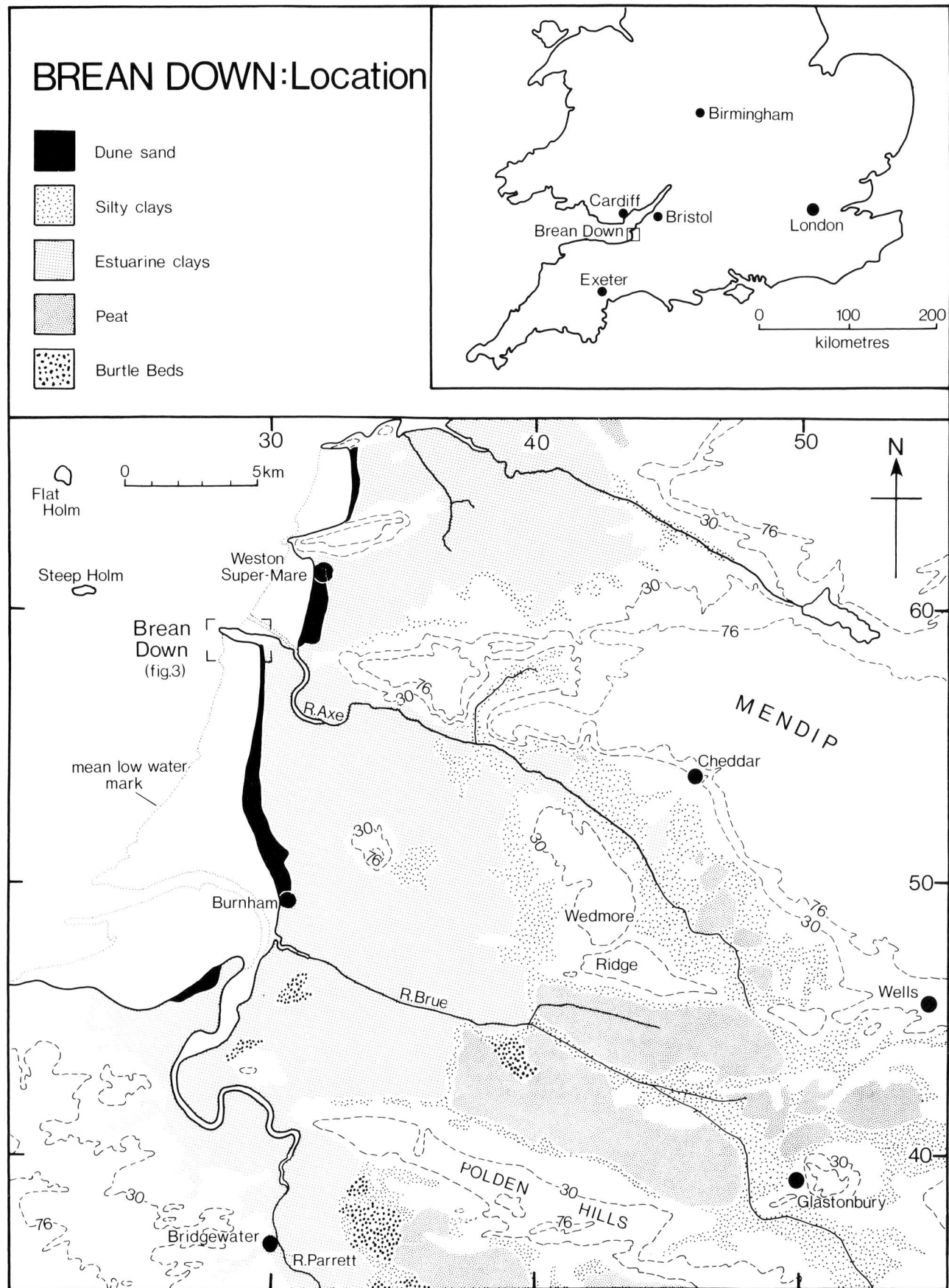

Fig 1 Location map: (a) in relation to southern Britain; (b) in relation to Mendip, the Somerset Levels, and post-glacial sediments

Fig 2   View of the sandcliff from the sea, May 1959 (photo: H Taylor)

with an area round the Iron Age hillfort, was also fortified during the Second World War.

The history of archaeological work on the sandcliff

Since at least the turn of the century human bones have been weathering from the sandcliff (Knight 1902). Many amateur archaeologists, mostly members of the University of Bristol Spelaeological Society, have visited the site and collected artefacts exposed by erosion. In 1961 the discoveries were brought together and assessed in their stratigraphic context (ApSimon *et al* 1961). That paper discussed both the Pleistocene and post-glacial stratigraphy and drew on finds and notebooks largely in the Spelaeological Society Museum. The basis of the paper was a meticulous record of the sandcliff section as exposed between 1954 and 1959; their summary section is reproduced here as Figure 4. During this work excavation of the post-glacial sediments was very limited, being restricted to clarifying stratigraphy in places and obtaining additional artefacts from certain horizons. It was demonstrated that the Pleistocene sandcliff stratigraphy (Fig 4.8b–13) could be dated to the last glaciation and there was important associated faunal evidence particularly from the 'bone bed' (Fig 4.11). Three pieces of bone showed evidence of possible working by man but no other artefacts were found in the Pleistocene deposits.

An outline of the post-glacial sequence is given in Figure 4 and can be summarised as follows (after ApSimon *et al* 1961, 72):

1   Turf and humus
2   Modern pebble bed and blown sand
3   Grey stony sand with cemetery
4   Iron Age sand
5   Blown sand
6   Bronze Age sand (and clay)
7   'Beaker sand'
8a Red loam

This numbering scheme has been retained in the present report to make it as easy as possible to correlate the two accounts. Here these major stratigraphic divisions are referred to not as layers, since many of them comprise several separate layers, but as *Units*. In the light of the recent work it has been necessary to create a number of further subdivisions within the original scheme. Four main prehistoric occupation layers were identified in 1961: 8a and 7 – Beaker; 6 – middle Bronze Age; and 4, then dated to the early Iron Age. Separating these layers were sterile sands. The prehistoric sequence was overlain by a cemetery assigned to the early Christian period and a post-medieval building.

Following publication of the 1961 paper the sandcliff continued to erode and further finds, particularly of human bone (eg Burrow 1985), were regularly made. Normal tides do not touch the sandcliff since the mean high water spring tide level is 6m and the base of the sandcliff is just above 7m. Erosion is

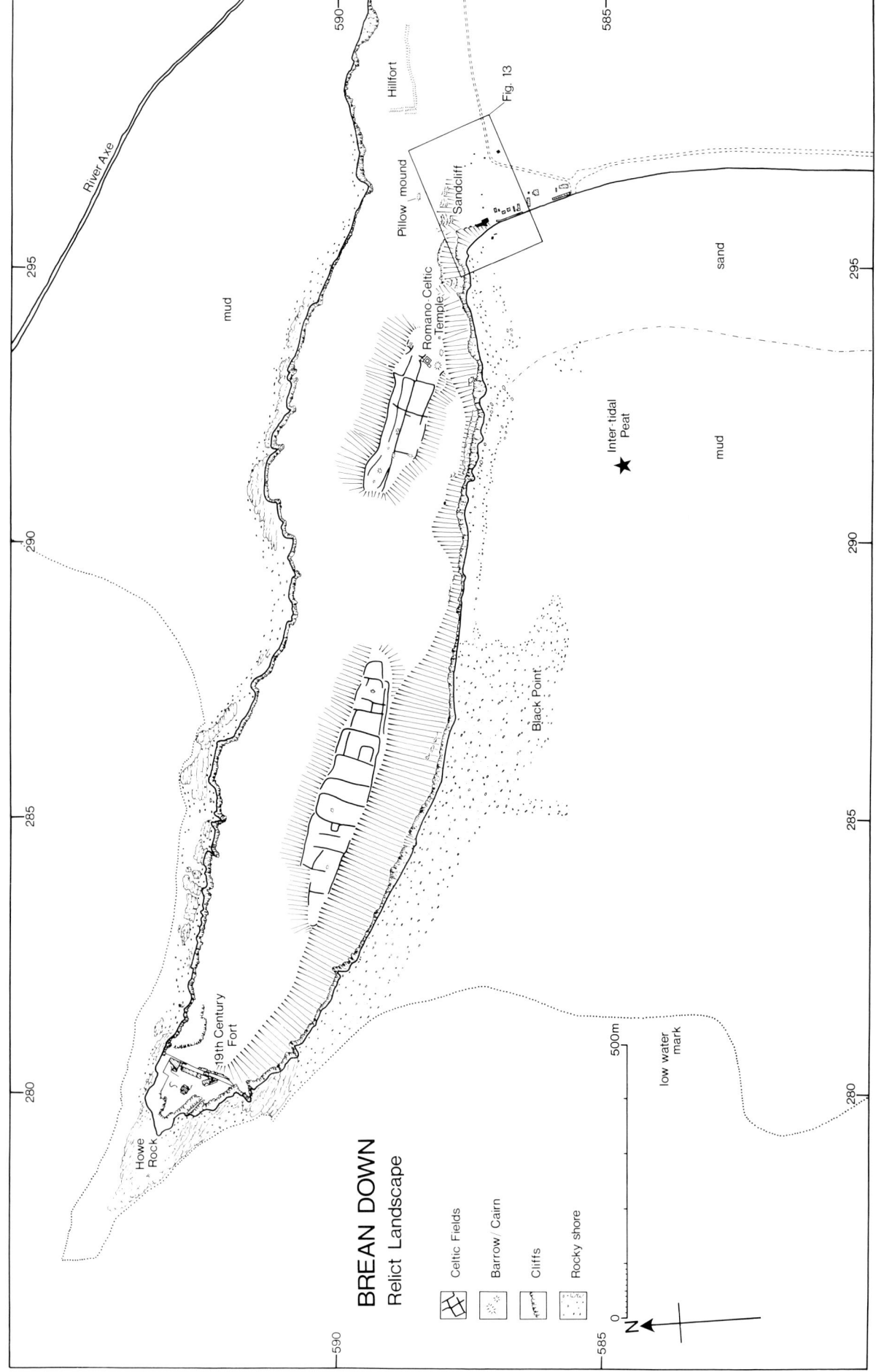

Fig 3 Brean Down relict landscape

INTRODUCTION TO THE SITE, RESEARCH METHODS, AND STRATIGRAPHY

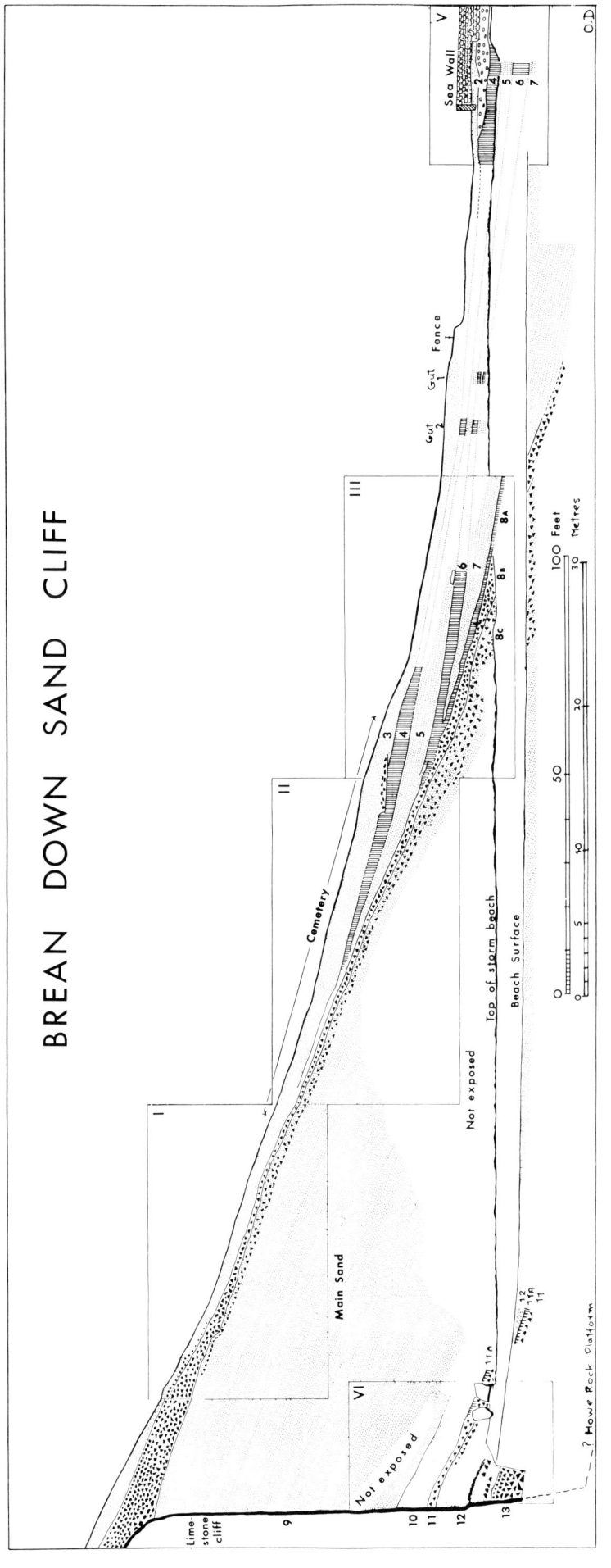

Fig 4 Sandcliff section 1954–9 reproduced from ApSimon et al 1961

Fig 5 The gold bracelets in situ, 6 May 1983 (photo: K Crabtree)

concentrated during major storm events, one of the most dramatic of which occurred on 13 December 1981. This storm surge constituted a tide with an estimated recurrence interval of 72 years and a 1 to 2 year wave height (Duncan 1986b). The water overtopped the coast c 50m south of the sandcliff, destroyed two holiday cottages, damaged much other property, and flooded a considerable area.

Wessex Water responded by building 50m of concrete wave return structure which linked the surviving old sea wall to the south with the rising ground of the sandcliff. Unfortunately the sandcliff itself remained unprotected and no regular archaeological watching brief was maintained during this work which would have provided valuable information about the extent and nature of the southern part of the sandcliff sequence, only small areas of which have ever been recorded (Fig 4). Occasional visits were made by archaeologists and in c April 1983 Arthur ApSimon (pers comm) found a complete cylindrical Bronze Age loomweight in slumped sand just north of the steps which form the northern end of the wave return structure. Photographs of the site (Taylor 1984; L Durston, Wessex Water, pers comm) show that particularly pronounced changes to the topography of the sandcliff occurred between about December 1981 and early spring 1983. A pronounced bluff, the foundations of which were formed by the Pleistocene breccia (8b), developed as a result of erosion of unconsolidated sand to the south. This bluff was subject to slump and erosion as a result of which several finds of pottery and human bone were made.

Gold bracelet discovery in 1983

On 6 May 1983 Keith Crabtree of Bristol University took his Quaternary Geography class to see Brean sandcliff as he had done for 20 years. He was in the process of explaining to the class that the post-glacial deposits sometimes produced archaeological material when he noticed two Bronze Age gold bracelets on the section. Figure 5 shows his discovery *in situ*. The two bracelets were linked together and there was no evidence of any container. On 10 and 25 May a small team from Bristol University, including Keith Crabtree, Richard Harrison, and Nick Watson, and the writer drew part of the section where the bracelets had been found in order to establish as exactly as possible how the find related to the sequence published by ApSimon *et al* (1961). On the first visit the impression left by the bracelets was still visible in the sand and could be marked on the section (Fig 6). It was clear that the bracelets had come from a slumped block. The stratigraphy of this block showed that it had slumped down c 0.85m from the base of Unit 4. During the section drawing exercise a possible ditch was noted 1m to the south of the bracelet find near the base of Unit 4, and c 0.7m to the north was a feature consisting of two occupation layers each c 0.1m thick separated by sterile sand. It is considered likely that the bracelets derive from one of these features.

Whilst the section was being drawn, a number of pieces of pottery, bone, and shell were recorded. Of particular interest was a rim sherd (Fig 96.118) found in association with the bracelets. Derivation of the slumped block from Unit 4 is confirmed both by the form of the rim and by David Williams' thin section report which shows that the main inclusion is calcite, a fabric characteristic of the pottery in Unit 4. During the recording operation the block of sand containing the impressions of the bracelets was removed for subsequent examination of any biological evidence. When this block was sieved in the laboratory by Nick Watson, a further scrap of sheet gold was found. In November 1983 the coroner's court declared that all three of the gold objects were Treasure Trove and they were subsequently purchased by Somerset County Museum, Taunton. A brief report on the discovery was published in *Antiquity* (Crabtree 1984).

Survey, Easter 1984

The limited work in spring 1983 suggested that it was desirable to prepare a new section drawing of the southern part of the post-glacial section to put the bracelet find in a wider context and for comparison with the sections drawn in 1954–9. Between 24 April and 1 May 1984 a 27m length of section was drawn (Fig 6) and an assessment report on the site's future was prepared (Bell and Straker 1984). No excavation

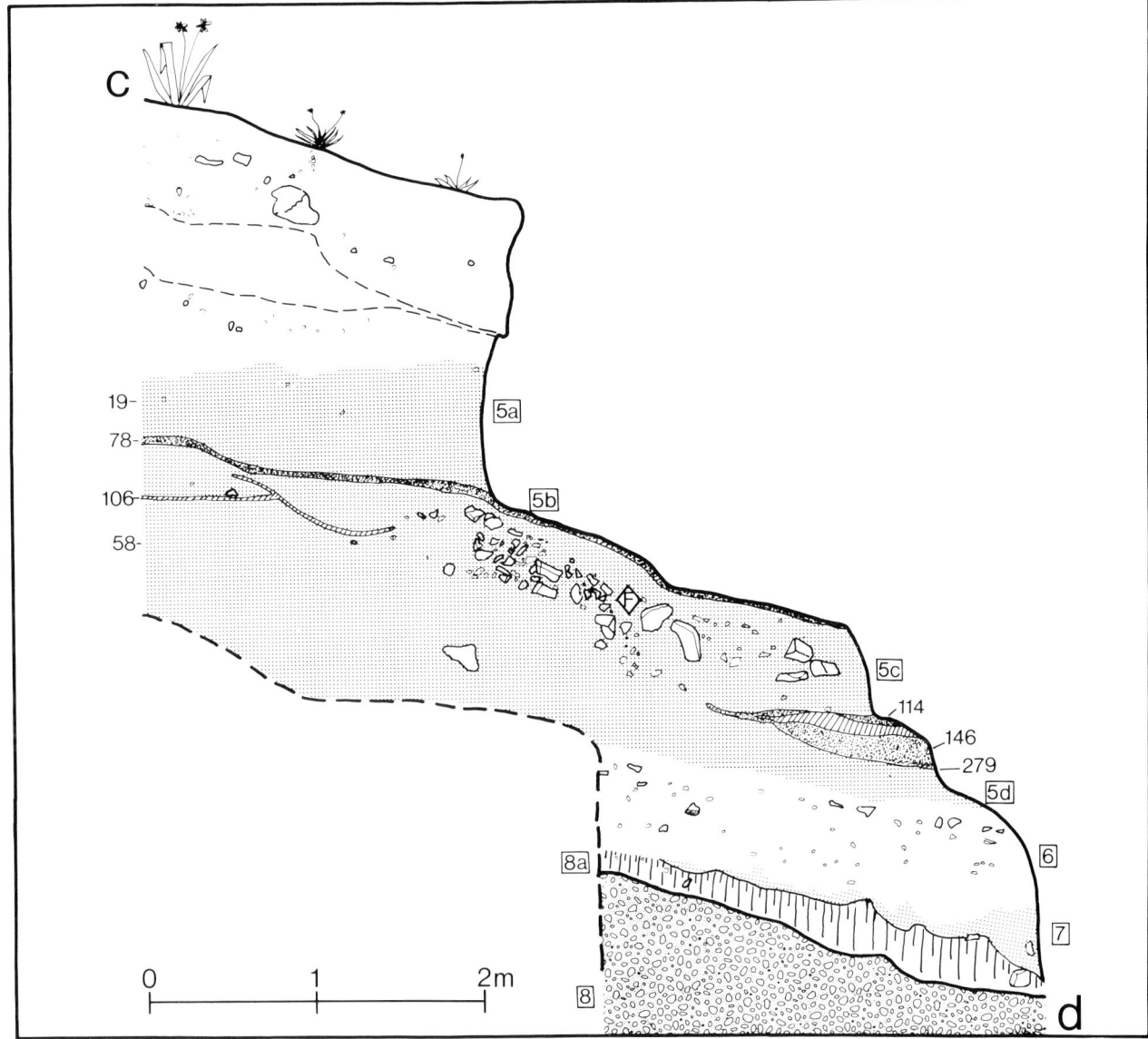

Fig 7 Section c–d of the irregular sandcliff face drawn in 1984

was done – the eroding face was simply cleaned back to *in situ* sediments except where these were obscured by large slumps or vegetation. Quite large areas, particularly of Units 1 and 3, were obscured and a further consequence of the non-destructive methodology employed was that the section was far from straight. In particular there was a projecting bluff near the middle of the section. The change in orientation of the section at this point is marked by a heavy broken line, c–d, on Figure 6. A subsidiary section (Fig 7) illustrates the stratigraphy on the north side of this bluff. The relationship of the two sections to the plan of the sandcliff and to sections revealed by later excavation is shown in Figure 14.

The most important features identified on the section were two concentrations of large limestone blocks (Fig 6.F, G, and Fig 8) which were interpreted as possible stone structures. They occurred within Unit 5 and were associated with a marked stabilisation layer and a group of pottery of probable middle Bronze Age date. This layer, which has been distinguished as Unit 5b, was not recorded in the 1961 paper because at that time this part of the section was badly obscured by slump (ApSimon *et al* 1961, fig 19). With that exception the sequence recorded in 1984 was closely comparable to the sequence reported in 1961. The section drawing exercise also confirmed the presence of a ditch (B) just to the south of the bracelet findspot and the pelvis of a human burial (A) was recorded at the base of Unit 3. Whilst drawing the section 299 artefacts were also recorded.

Coastal retreat

It was important to establish the relationship between the section drawn in 1955–9 and its position in the mid 1980s. This would also help to provide information on coastal retreat which was needed in order to establish whether the site should be protected from the sea.

Comparison of the Ordnance Survey maps of 1887 and 1971 suggested that some 7m were lost in 84

Fig 8 Section drawing exercise, Easter 1984, stones of Feature G (Structure 57) overlain by Unit 5b surface (photo: A Philpott)

years, giving an average rate of 80mm per year. The 1887 map shows a sea wall of which only fragments survived in front of the sandcliff by the 1930s. The stump of this wall south of the sandcliff is shown on several illustrations in the 1961 report. Whilst it survived this wall is likely to have greatly reduced erosion and there is evidence that over the last 30 years much higher erosion rates have obtained. This evidence comes from a comparison of the survey prepared in 1955 (ApSimon *et al* 1961, fig 15) and the survey of 1984–5. Arthur ApSimon kindly provided copies of the original surveys; these included fixed points which are not shown on the published version and which fortunately can still be traced on the ground.

Reference to Figure 9, which compares the two surveys, shows considerable variation in the extent of erosion on different parts of the sandcliff. Against the limestone cliff the Pleistocene strata, Units 10–13, have only retreated about 4m (130mm per year). The upper breccia (Unit 8b) on the other hand has retreated a maximum of 10m (330mm per year) and the cliff top has retreated an average of 6.6m (220mm per year). The last figure agrees well with the erosion rate at the toe of the slope calculated by Duncan (1985); he calculated that between 1970 and 1985 erosion occurred at an average rate of 233mm per year. Thus erosion of the cemented limestone breccia, which forms a projecting 'nose' on the front of the sandcliff, has been particularly severe in the last 30 years and has given rise to a significant loss of the overlying archaeological deposits for which the breccias form a foundation. It follows that, in the area of the archaeological deposits investigated in the 1980s, the basal post-glacial units (eg 8a–6) are *c* 10m inland of the cliff face where they were exposed in 1955, the upper units (eg 1 and 3) are *c* 6.6m inland, and Units 4 and 5 are intermediate between these two extremes.

Excavations 1985–6 and their research objectives

Threats to the site were manifest: apart from coastal erosion, significant damage was also being done by visitors clambering up the face and there had also been some illegal digging into the section by treasure hunters after the inquest on the bracelet discovery was reported in the press. Equally clear from the 1983 and 1984 surveys was the site's potential, especially with the discovery of possible stone buildings. Bronze Age settlements are remarkably few in Somerset, and such evidence is badly needed to complement the important trackway and environmental record from the Somerset Levels. The potential of dune sands for preserving settlement sequences had been clearly demonstrated in the south-west by earlier excavations at Gwithian (Megaw *et al* 1961) and

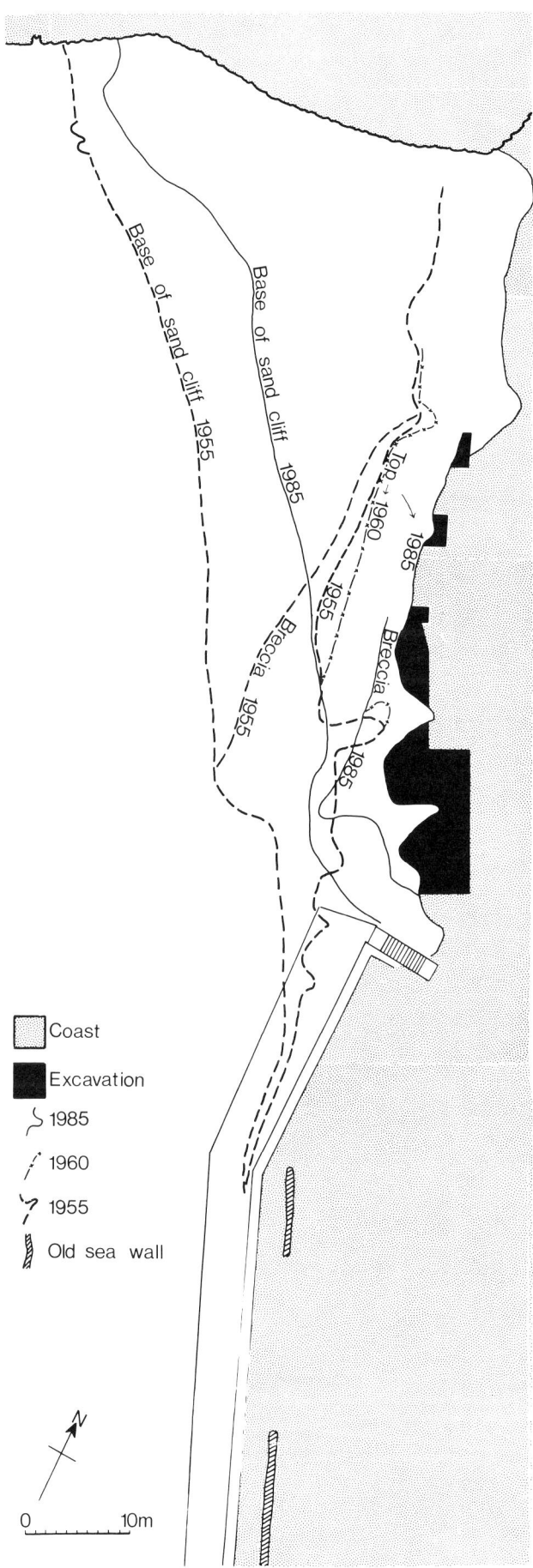

Fig 9 *Plan of the sandcliff showing coastal retreat and the relative positions of the sections in 1955–60 and 1985*

Nornour (Butcher 1978). The Prehistoric Society (1984), in its *Prehistory, priorities and society*, emphasised the need for further work on dune sequences and a recent survey of environmental archaeology in the south-west (Bell 1984) highlighted the particular potential of such sites for the recovery of environmental data. Such factors led to the mounting of a rescue excavation which was largely funded by English Heritage with contributions from several other bodies (see acknowledgements). The main excavation took place from 22 July to 29 September 1985, and was followed by smaller-scale work between 26 July and 20 August 1986. There were also two periods of watching brief and survey supervised by Michael Allen in October 1985 and February 1987 whilst the site was being protected from the sea. The specific aims of the excavation and survey project were defined at the outset as follows:

i   Archaeological resource management, to establish the extent and importance of the site so that if necessary proposals could be formulated for its long term protection and management
ii To obtain stratified groups of Bronze Age artefacts, particularly pottery, associated with radiocarbon dates from the main occupation layers
iii To recover palaeoenvironmental and palaeoeconomic sequences from the Bronze Age stratigraphy by means of a sieving and sampling programme
iv To carry out a limited investigation of the sub-Roman cemetery
v   To investigate the potential for *in situ* artefact assemblages within aeolian sands and the effect of post-depositional processes such as winnowing and bioturbation (mixing by animals or plants) on artefact or ecofact movement

Research methods in the main trench 1985

A trench was excavated back from the sandcliff face centred on ST 29575 58725. It was 24.3m long. On the seaward side it was of irregular shape following the eroding cliff face. Inland the trench was L-shaped at the outset; the northern half was 2–3m wide and the southern part 7–9m wide. The depth of post-glacial stratigraphy varied from 3.6m at the northern end to 5.6m at the southern end. It would have been impossible and dangerous to produce a free-standing section through this depth of unconsolidated sand. Nor was this desirable because it would certainly have led to accelerated erosion. Accordingly the trench was excavated in a series of steps corresponding to the main stratigraphic units and giving a profile at the end of the excavation which roughly corresponded to the pre-excavation profile. One consequence of the stepped trench, together with the limited time available, was that a much larger area was excavated in the upper Units 1–5 compared to the lower Units 6–8a. In the case of Unit 7, in particular, it was only possible to excavate a very small area. Figure 10 summarises the progress of the excavation, showing in plan and section the extent and location of the area of each stratigraphic unit containing occupation evidence.

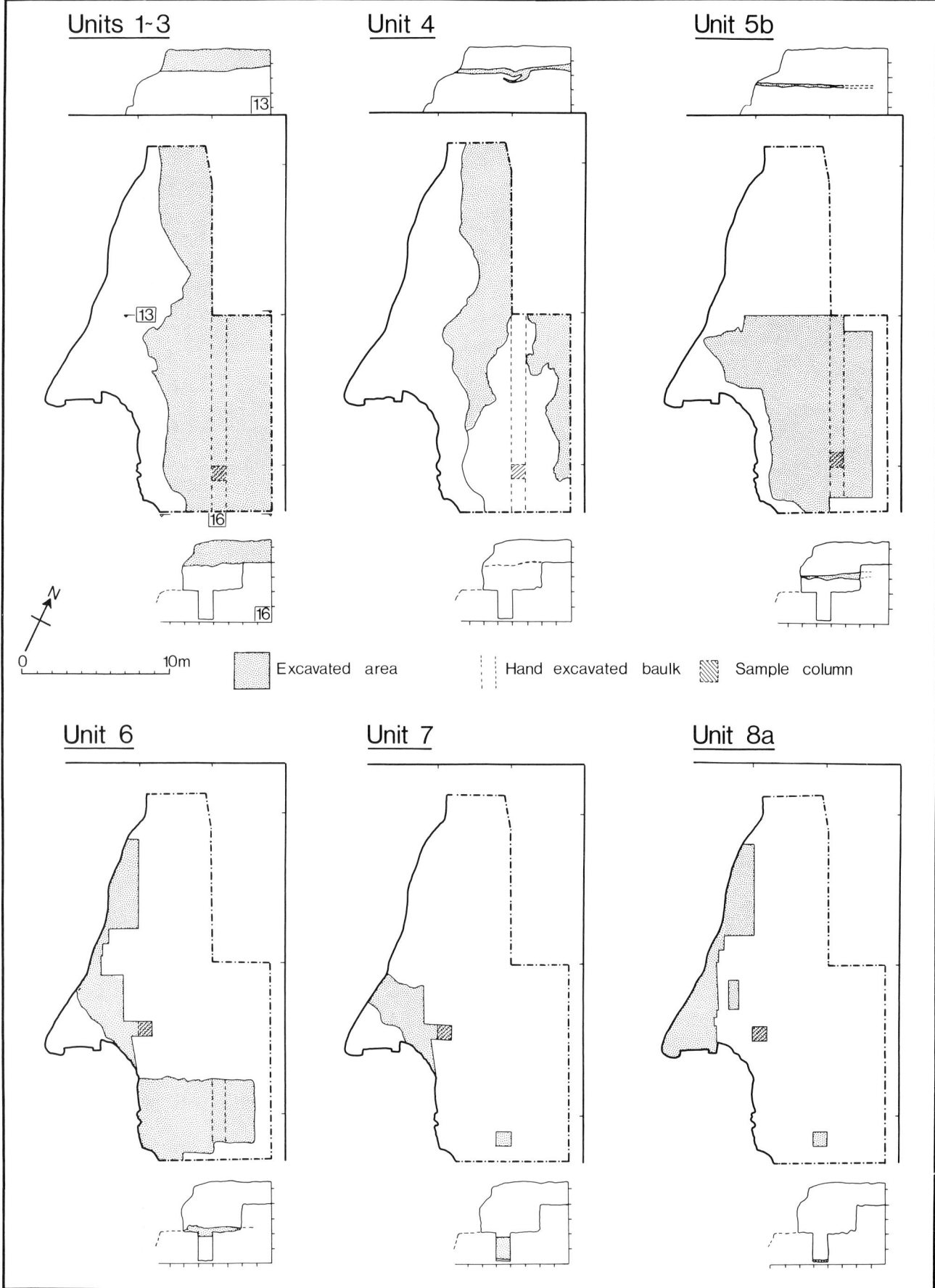

Fig 10 Plan showing the progress of the excavation and the areas of each stratigraphic unit excavated in plan and on Sections 13 and 14

Fig 11 View of the excavation trench from Brean Down (photo: A Philpott)

Sampling

The trench (Fig 11) was excavated entirely by hand. Layers such as topsoil, some colluvial layers, and the virtually sterile sand layers were removed by pick and shovel. Occupation horizons were carefully excavated by trowel. In addition a baulk was excavated using a uniform trowelling technique for all layers. This strip was 1m wide and 13m long down as far as the base of Unit 5b, below which its length decreased to 4m in Units 5d and 6 and 1m in Units 7 and 8a. In order to maximise the recovery of artefacts and biota the occupation layers were almost entirely dry sieved. The equipment used was designed by Richard Harrison and consisted of a tent-shaped scaffold frame with wooden sided sieve boxes of mesh size 5.6mm suspended from a ridge pole by wires. In addition, an extensive programme of wet sieving was carried out using a modified Siraf type device (Williams 1973). One or more sacks of sediment, each of three buckets' volume, were taken for sieving from every square metre in the main occupation horizons examined – Units 4, 5b, and 8a. In addition, samples from a metre square column of sediment were water sieved through the entire stratigraphy and the rest of this column was dry sieved.

Three-dimensional artefact recording

Several studies of prehistoric settlement have demonstrated the importance of artefact distributions in helping to reconstruct activity patterns, the function of structures, and even such elusive aspects as the status and gender of those occupying different parts of a settlement (D L Clarke 1972; Ellison 1978; Drewett 1982a). Blown sands offer particular potential for the preservation of distinct, sometimes very brief, activity episodes which, even in the space of a few hours, can be sealed by a considerable thickness of blown sand. This contrasts with poorly sealed sites where we may find several superimposed, perhaps quite different, activity patterns of various dates. Furthermore, in dune deposits studies of the artefact content of the intervening sand layers provide some measure of the degree of post-depositional movement affecting the archaeological record. For these reasons it was decided to three-dimensionally record all types of artefact. The methods of three-dimensional recording used in the trench were based on those employed in earlier studies of lynchets and dry valley colluvial sediments (Bell 1977; 1983a).

The position of each find was marked by a plastic garden label, with a unique number, held in place by

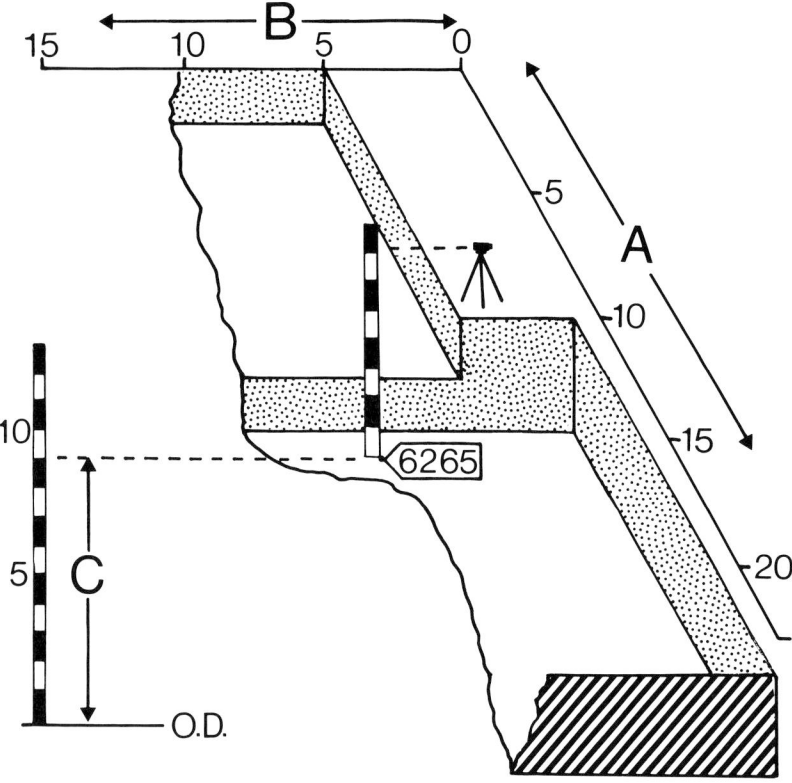

BEAKER POTTERY IN ALL CONTEXTS

Artefact No	Co-ord A	Co-ord B	Co-ord C	Context	Type code
587	17.22	2.23	12.49	13	356
5903	-1.00	-1.00	-1.00	157	356
5926	-1.00	-1.00	-1.00	162	355
5926	-1.00	-1.00	-1.00	162	356
5991	-1.00	-1.00	-1.00	61	355
5991	-1.00	-1.00	-1.00	61	356
6097	20.28	6.83	9.28	163	355
6097	20.28	6.83	9.28	163	356
6110	-1.00	-1.00	-1.00	66	356
6134	-1.00	-1.00	-1.00	163	355
6134	-1.00	-1.00	-1.00	163	356
6145	-1.00	-1.00	-1.00	163	355
6145	-1.00	-1.00	-1.00	163	356
6242	12.94	12.86	9.77	62	356
6265	15.51	10.69	9.41	62	355
6265	15.51	10.69	9.41	62	356
6401	12.19	12.71	9.45	63	355
6410	14.78	14.70	8.66	63	355
6414	5.75	11.40	11.68	63	356
6426	11.75	12.49	9.64	63	355
6435	6.41	11.88	11.55	63	355
6440	10.92	12.95	9.95	63	356
6444	3.36	11.07	12.43	63	356
6456	8.14	12.32	10.93	63	355
6457	6.54	11.93	11.39	63	355
6458	5.23	10.47	11.92	63	355
6464	8.40	12.50	10.91	63	355
6465	8.24	12.54	10.92	63	355
6468	8.85	12.73	10.59	63	356
6472	8.52	12.54	10.83	63	355
6474	6.70	11.11	11.39	63	355
6492	13.10	12.60	9.03	63	356

Fig 12   Three-dimensional artefact recording: (a) the method of artefact measurement and (b) the format of data on the computer archive (-1 signifies missing data, eg finds from sieving); a plot of these data is given in Fig 23

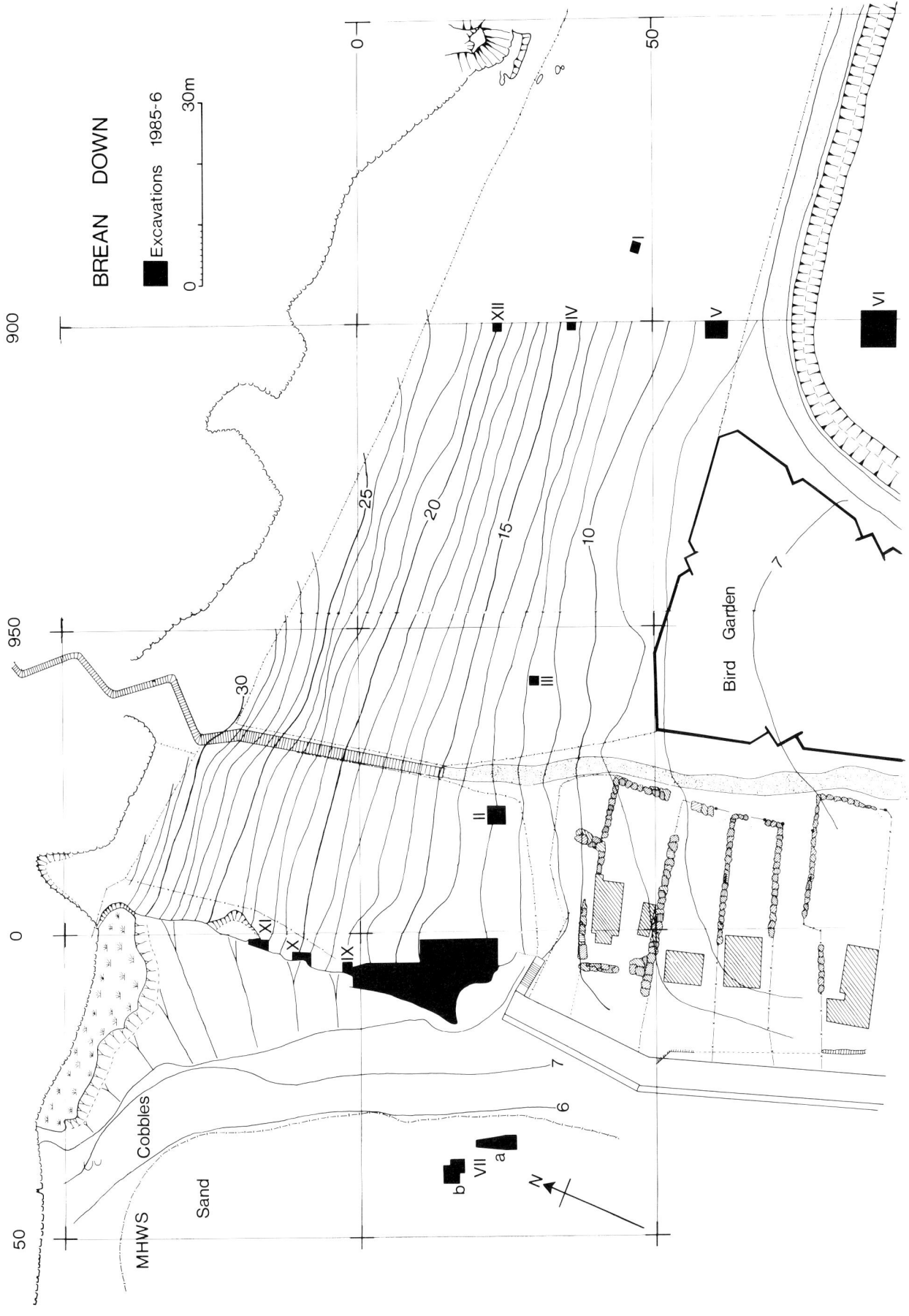

Fig 13 Survey of the sandcliff showing contours and excavated areas

a nail. The find itself was placed in a plastic margarine tub marked with the same number. Then the object was sent away for washing, marking, and identification. At regular intervals the positions of the labels were measured, as illustrated in Figure 12a. The A (site north–south) and B (site east–west) coordinates were recorded by measuring horizontal distance on the ground; the C coordinate (height above OD) was obtained with a level. These coordinates were written on pre-printed lists. At the end of each day all the artefacts which had been washed and marked during the day were provisionally identified using a numerical typecode list which was drawn up in outline at the beginning of the excavation and added to as the work progressed.

Because of the number of artefacts involved (6634) it would have been impossible to manipulate all the data about them manually. In particular, previous research projects had identified the problems of updating and correcting such an archive manually. Fortunately Bruce Levitan was on site for the duration of the excavation and each day put the data on to a Comart Communicator microcomputer which manipulated the data entirely by the use of commercially available software, as described in more detail elsewhere (Levitan 1986). The data were input in the form of six fields, as illustrated in Figure 12b. It was possible to draw up lists of artefact types, finds from each context, and coordinates very quickly during the excavation. Of especial importance was the facility to plot horizontal (coordinate A against B) or vertical (coordinate A against C) diagrams of artefact distributions whilst digging was actually in progress.

In several instances the availability of this information fed back directly into the excavation strategy because hypotheses suggested by artefact distribution could be explicitly tested during the next day's excavation. Furthermore the computer data base was complete and ready for use the day after digging stopped. During the post-excavation stage the data were copied on to the VAX mainframe computer at Saint David's University College. Alan Rogers, Head of the Computer Unit, was responsible for this stage of the work. The provisional field identifications of artefacts were updated in the light of specialist studies reported in this volume. It was then possible to produce laser-printed distribution diagrams, several of which are reproduced directly in this report. In the case of distribution drawings which required artefact numbers or the outlines of excavated features, the laser-printed distributions have been redrawn for publication.

Unfortunately it was not possible to three-dimensionally record every single find in all parts of the site. Sometimes, of course, an exact findspot could not be identified in a pile of loosened sand. Sometimes, for logistical reasons, it was decided to restrict the recording of certain artefact types to the 1m wide trowel-excavated strip. Rabbit bones and coke in Units 1 and 3 were only recorded in this strip. It was also found that three-dimensional recording of some features and parts of the site made their excavation impossibly slow. Where these unfortunate compromises affect the artefact diagrams they are noted in the relevant section of the report. When three-

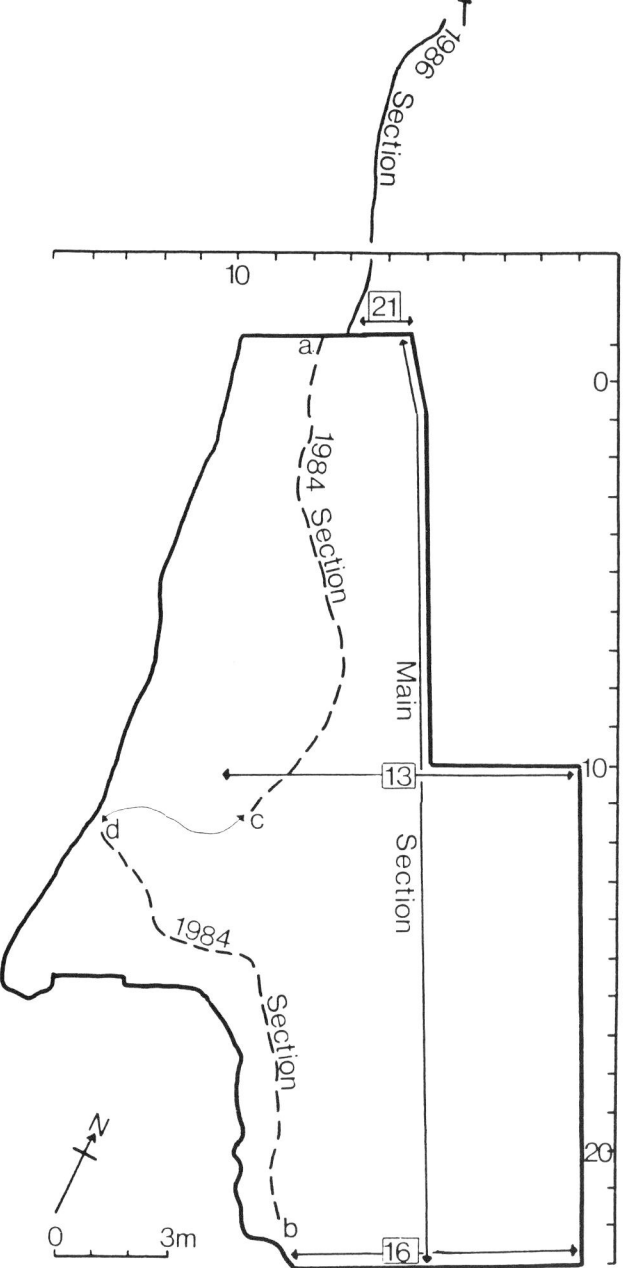

Fig 14 Location of the chief sections

dimensional recording was not possible finds were assigned to general trays for that context in the traditional way.

Further excavation 1986

Following excavation the 1985 trench was backfilled and the National Trust placed stone-filled wire baskets in front of the most vulnerable part of the section as a temporary erosion control measure. Fortunately the basal palaeosol (Unit 8a), of which it was possible to excavate only a small area in 1985, was still exposed in front of the wire baskets so further excavation was possible in this area during 1986. At the same time the post-glacial cliff section to the north of the main trench was drawn (Fig 16) and three

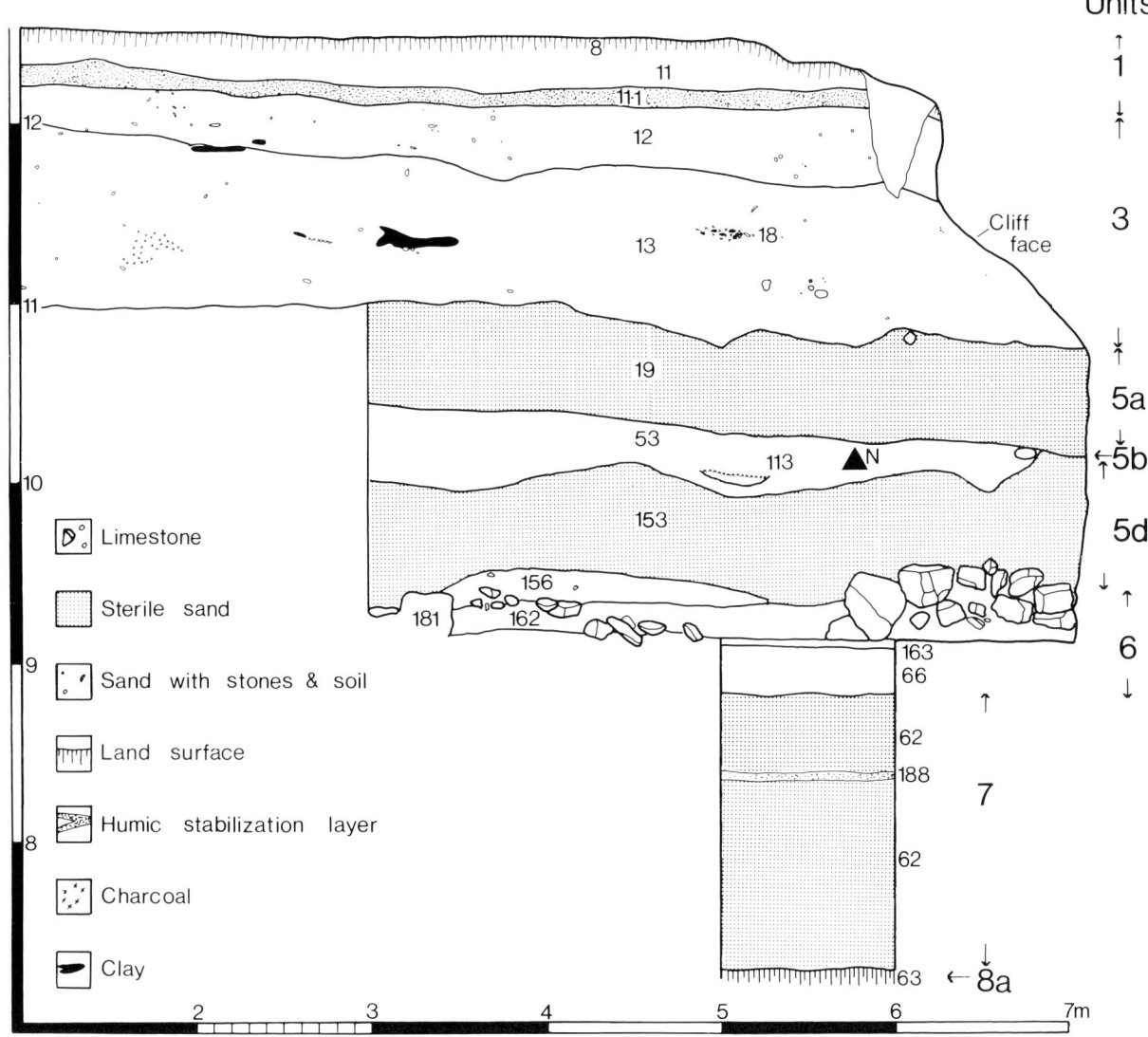

Fig 17 Section 16 excavated in 1985 at 23m on the A-axis

burials which were eroding from the face were excavated by means of small trenches (Fig 13.IX, X, XI).

Auger and soil pit survey

As previously noted, one objective of the project was to establish the extent of the archaeological site inland. It was also important to establish to what extent the stratigraphic sequence changed inland. Accordingly, between 1985 and 1987 a soil pit and auger survey was conducted of the sandcliff deposits within *c* 100m of the coast. Seven soil pits were excavated (Fig 13), six on the sandcliff and one (VI) to the south on the alluvial flats. In addition 96 auger holes were put down under the supervision of Keith Crabtree, who discusses the methods and results in Chapter 8. During 1986–7 there was also some limited investigation of deposits on the foreshore where a pit (VII) was opened up some 26m west of the main excavation trench and a peat bed 0.5km offshore was investigated.

The stratigraphic sequence and sections

Before embarking on discussion of the individual occupation horizons it is necessary to present the sequence in outline and identify some differences between the 1961 and 1985 stratigraphies. The basic 1985 sequence is outlined on four main sections (Figs 15, 17, and 18), the relative positions of which are marked on Figure 14. The whole sequence is shown on the main section (Fig 15) which is to some extent a composite drawing because Unit 6 and below have been projected on to the section from up to 6m to the west. In preparing this composite section no correction has been introduced to account for the dip of deposits in a westerly direction; had this been done the artefact coordinates would also have required recalculation since it is important to be able to make a precise comparison between artefact distributions and sections. In fact only the relatively small areas excavated of Units 6–8c had a marked dip on the B-axis, 5° in the case of 8a, 2½° in the case of 6.

Figure 17 shows the full sequence at the south end of the site where it was possible to maintain a single vertical face. This figure gives an impression of the stepped profile of the excavation. Figure 18 shows Section 13 in the middle of the trench; it is very much a partial profile since part of the upper sequence had been removed before this section was drawn and because the stepped profile of the trench meant that at no single point was a complete column of the whole sequence exposed. Also on Figure 18 is Section 21 which shows part of the north wall of the trench; this only goes down to the top of Unit 5a where excavation stopped in this area. The stratigraphy of the sandcliff face north of the 1985 trench was drawn in 1986 and is shown in Figure 16 which illustrates the way in which the post-glacial stratigraphy becomes increasingly compressed as one by one the layers fade out approaching the limestone cliff.

As noted earlier, the basic stratigraphy revealed in 1985 is comparable to that reported in 1961. Clearly no dramatic changes have been brought to light by coastal retreat of between 10 and 6.6m. There are, however, some significant differences between these two sequences; these are outlined in Table 1 and noted in the following brief review of the sequence:

Unit 1   Turf and topsoil, defined in this report as deposits of demonstrable twentieth-century date.
Unit 2   Reported in 1961 from a pit c 32m south of the 1985 section; this area was covered by the wave return wall built in 1983.
Unit 3   Excavation and artefact plotting have made it necessary to subdivide this unit:

Table 1   Comparison of the stratigraphy reported in 1961 with that of 1985

Layer	ApSimon et al 1961		Unit	This report		Main contexts
1	turf and humus		1		turf, humus, and twentieth-century sand	8, 10, 9, 11
2	A – yellow blown sand B – modern beach shingle C – grey marine clay		–		not exposed in 1983–87	
3	grey stony sand A – dirty brown sand B – mass of stones C – stoneless grey sand locally passing into yellow blown sand – burials		3	3a 3b1 3b2 3c 3c2	yellow blown sand, few stones – mainly in southern half of trench blown sand with limestone blocks – post-medieval deposit blown sand with limestone – medieval sub-Roman cemetery stoneless yellow sand predating cemetery	12, 13 ?18 23 many 31
4	4A reddish stony loam 4B greyish yellow sand with stones 4C reddish brown stony sand	=4D reddish brown sand and limestone 4E dark grey brown clayey soil 4F clean yellow sand 4G hearth 4H ash 4J muddy brown sand	4	4a 4	reddish brown stony colluvium greyish silty sand with stones – occupation layer not present in 1983–7	25 16
5	blown sand – no subdivisions		5	5a 5b (5c 5d	yellow sterile sand olive green/brown stained occupation layer with stone structures and hearth debris previously identified in 1984 but now shown to be part of Unit 5b; not used in this report) yellow sterile sand	19 53, 59, 95 58, 153
6			6	6α 6a 6b	stone structure and occupation horizon grey silty clay reddish colluvium	57 61 66
	6A grey green stony clay 6C hearth 6B reddish loamy sand with limestone blocks					
7	yellow 'Beaker sand'		7		yellow 'Beaker sand'	62
8A 8Z 8B	red loam – soil weathered surface of Unit 8b on north end of sandcliff – Pleistocene angular limestone breccia – Pleistocene		8a 8z 8b		basal palaeosol weathered surface of Unit 8b on north end of sandcliff – Pleistocene angular limestone breccia – Pleistocene	63 126

INTRODUCTION TO THE SITE, RESEARCH METHODS, AND STRATIGRAPHY

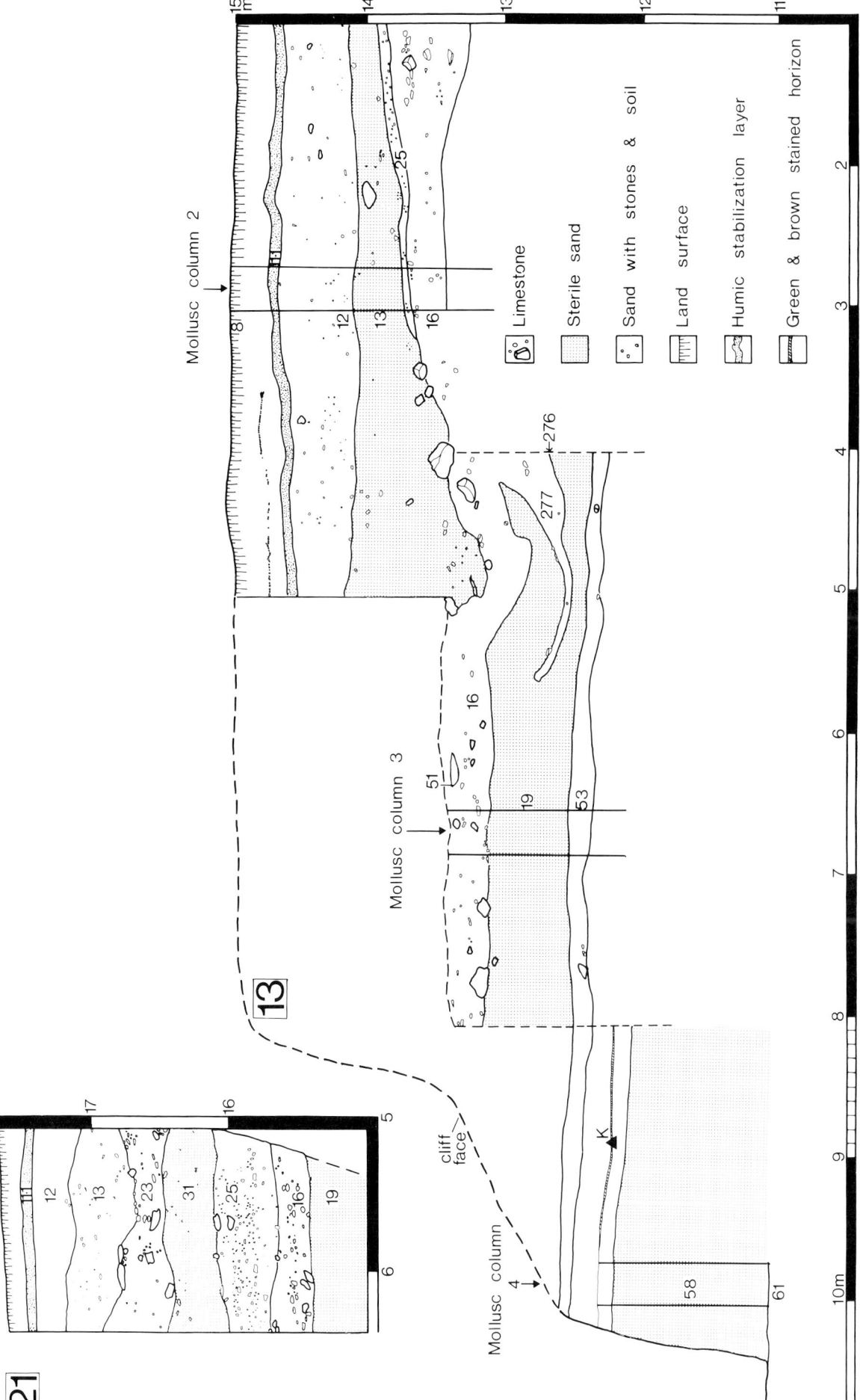

Fig 18 Sections 13 and 21 excavated in 1985 at 10m and 998.7m respectively on the A-axis

3a Yellowish brown sand with some stones and post-medieval artefacts; this unit is largely in the southern half of the trench

3b This has now been subdivided to take account of the fact that limestone blocks recorded in 1961 relate to a post-medieval building (Unit 3b1) whereas blown sand with limestone blocks on the northern part of the site is of medieval date (Unit 3b2)

3c This unit has also been subdivided to take account of the fact that the sub-Roman graves (Unit 3c1) postdate a thin layer of sterile sand (Unit 3c2)

Unit 4 As reported here Unit 4 has a very simple stratigraphy of reddish silty colluvium (Unit 4a) overlying grey silty sand (Unit 4); seven further subdivisions reported in 1961 were not present in the 1985 excavation.

Unit 5 In 1961 this unit was represented only by sterile undifferentiated sand. Work in 1984–5 showed that two layers of sterile sand (Units 5a and 5d) were separated by the most important occupation horizon investigated in the present study (Unit 5b) in which two structures were found. The part of the section where this horizon is present was badly obscured by slump in the 1950s.

Unit 6 An additional unit (Unit 6α) has been inserted at the top of this sequence to include a stone structure and its destruction debris. Otherwise the stratigraphy is as reported in 1961: grey silty clay (6a) overlying reddish colluvium (6b).

Unit 7 Yellow sand as in 1961.

Unit 8a Palaeosol at the base of post-glacial sequence.

Structure of the report

In Chapters 2–7 the main post-glacial occupation horizons are discussed in turn beginning with the earliest and ending with the most recent. Chapter 8 outlines evidence from the soil pits and auger survey. Specialist discussion of the prehistoric artefacts is reserved for Section B of the report. The environmental and economic evidence is discussed by specialists in Section C. Certain of the conclusions from Sections B and C which relate to individual units of stratigraphy are incorporated with cross-reference in the discussion sections of Chapters 2–8. The concluding Section D of the report looks at the sequence as a whole and the wider cultural and environmental issues. The text report is supported by a microfiche archive which provides detailed artefact reports on post-Bronze Age material and other information, and tables of data which are necessary to substantiate some of the points made in the main text. Where this is the case reference is given as, eg, MF1:A7, ie microfiche 1, frame A7. The colour microfiche which illustrates the soil samples discussed in Chapter 16 is an optional extra purchase; details are available from the publishers. Indexes of both microfiches are given in the contents pages.

Relationship between the text, illustrations, and archive

As far as possible the numbers assigned to contexts, artefacts, and sections in the field have been retained in this report in order to make correlation of the report and the archive (including the objects) as straightforward as possible. Sometimes the numbering could be confusing; for instance Structure 95 does not imply the existence of 95 structures, but is simply the unique number given to that context. Where description of a context (eg layer, floor, posthole, etc) is followed by a number in brackets, then that is the unique number for that context.

On the same principle, sections are not numbered in text sequence but retain their original field drawing number. In the text this is preceded by a figure number, eg (Fig 14.13). On the drawings section numbers are in boxes.

A basic principle in constructing the report has been to relate artefacts as closely and clearly as possible to the exact positions in which they were found. To this end discussion of the excavated contexts concludes with an outline of the main finds, usually those which are illustrated. So far as possible we have also marked on the distribution drawings the positions in which artefacts were found. Both in the text and on the distribution drawings the numbers refer to the illustration number *for the type of find in question*. For instance flint 16 in the text or a symbol for flint with 16 beside it both refer to flint drawing no 16. If that is appreciated then readers should not be confused by the fact that there is also a pottery illustration no 16. In cases where confusion may arise we have added a figure number.

In the case of illustrated finds the original numbers given to these finds in the field are included after the illustration number in discussions of the finds. Objects which are not illustrated retain their original field record number. Field record numbers were allocated on the following basis:

1–6634 Main excavation trench
50,000 Finds from the soil pits and auger surveys
60,000 Finds from sieving
70,000 Unstratified finds

The site archive, including all the field records and finds, will be deposited in the Somerset County Museum, Taunton. The computer based 3D artefact record could of course be used to draw up a wide variety of distribution diagrams in addition to those used to illustrate this report. To facilitate such future work, copies of the data on floppy disc have been deposited, together with paper copies, at Taunton Museum and the National Monuments Record; they are also available at cost price from the Department of Archaeology, Saint David's University College, University of Wales, Lampeter, Dyfed SA48 7ED.

2 Beaker and earlier activity in Units 8a and 7

Description of Unit 8a

A clearly defined palaeosol marked the base of the post-glacial stratigraphy. This had developed on the upper unit of Pleistocene sediments, an earthy breccia (Unit 8b). The palaeosol (Context 63; Unit 8a) was exposed at *c* 8.4m OD just above the level of the beach; it sloped uphill for some 31m and faded out at 19.4m OD. Its surface had a direction of dip of north 166° south and the angle of dip was 21°; the soil is therefore formed on what the Soil Survey (Hodgson 1974) would classify as a steep slope. The palaeosol surface was a reddish brown (5YR 4/3) sandy clay loam (particle size, stone size, and other soil descriptive classes follow Hodgson 1974 throughout). The lower part of the palaeosol profile was a dark reddish brown (2.5YR 3/4) clay. As Richard Macphail's micromorphological report (Chapter 16) explains, the clay is largely derived from underlying Pleistocene breccia and is the eroded product of pre-Flandrian weathering cycles. Charcoal fragments occurred throughout the palaeosol and were particularly concentrated in its upper part. The palaeosol surface contained few stones although there were occasional large examples. Stonyness increased with depth: all the stones were Carboniferous Limestone and were rounded by chemical weathering; most are likely to be derived from the underlying breccia. At the base of the slope the palaeosol depth was 0.2 to 0.3m, but it thinned upslope to as little as 50mm where limestone pieces from the underlying breccia projected through its surface. It is evident from the sections (Figs 15 and 16) that the gradual thinning of 8a and its disappearance at 19.4m OD is the result of erosion, one product of which is a colluvial deposit Unit 6b. Near the base of the slope, between 10 and 12m OD, this colluvium rests directly on the palaeosol but below 10m OD a wedge of blown sand (Unit 7) separates the two units.

Excavation and sieving of Unit 8a

During the main excavation season in summer 1985 it only proved possible to excavate about 4 sq m of Unit 8a at points where deeper soundings and sampling columns penetrated the basal stratigraphy. This was because of shortage of time brought about by the discovery of so much Bronze Age structural evidence in overlying units. Fortunately, however, a significant area of the basal palaeosol projected to seaward of the 1985 backfill and the stone-filled wire gabion baskets which were emplaced to prevent its erosion. Consequently it was possible to excavate another 6 sq m during the watching brief in October 1985 when the gabions were being emplaced, and then a further 20 sq m in summer 1986, by which time all the still exposed palaeosol had been excavated (Fig 19) in advance of its burial by immense boulders forming a permanent coastal protection. The total volume of Unit 8a excavated, 4 cu m, is, however, relatively modest by comparison with the volumes of material examined in some of the overlying units. Excavation was entirely by trowel and all finds spotted were three-dimensionally recorded. The palaeosol was divided into 1m grid squares to facilitate sieving. A total of 123 buckets of sediment were wet sieved: above 9m on the A-axis, where the palaeosol was thinner, one three-bucket sack was sieved per grid square; below 9m two sacks were sieved per square, one from the upper part of the profile and one from the lower part. All the remaining sediment (200 buckets) was dry sieved.

Features in Unit 8a (Fig 20)

Context 191

A curving gully (Fig 21) truncated at either end by the cliff face, 0.6m wide, 0.22m deep, with a fill (127) of dark reddish brown clay (5YR 4/3) similar to that forming the basal part of Unit 8a elsewhere. The gully was not visible on the palaeosol surface and seems likely to relate to a period significantly predating the final pedological development of this surface. The gully contained scattered charcoal, two bones, a leaf-shaped flint arrowhead (7), an unretouched flake with edge gloss (9), and an unillustrated flake.

Contexts 221 and 283

Within the general scatter of charcoal which characterised Unit 8a two particular concentrations were noted. Context 283 was on the palaeosol surface in grid squares 14/12 and 13. Context 221 was at the surface of the clay horizon which formed the lower part of the palaeosol profile. Neither patch was associated with a concentration of other finds, and they seem to represent two chronologically distinct burning episodes.

Context 189

A slight oval depression in the palaeosol surface 0.4m in diameter and 40mm deep. Filled by sand (190) from the overlying Unit 7. It contained no finds and may be the result of animal activity.

Possible cultivation marks, Context 284

Upslope of the main area of excavated palaeosol a small area, 1.3 sq m, of overlying sand was removed to expose the palaeosol surface, thus revealing faint traces (Figs 19 and 22) of linear marks running roughly along the contours. They were slight sand-filled depressions in the palaeosol surface and were also marked by darker brown staining. Unfortunately it was not possible to expose a larger area of these marks; to have done so could have reduced the stability of the sandcliff. Probably the marks are the result of cultivation but the area examined is too small for certainty, and equally uncertain is the type of implement with which they were made. The marks occurred on a part of the slope which was demonstrably truncated by erosion and was only buried by

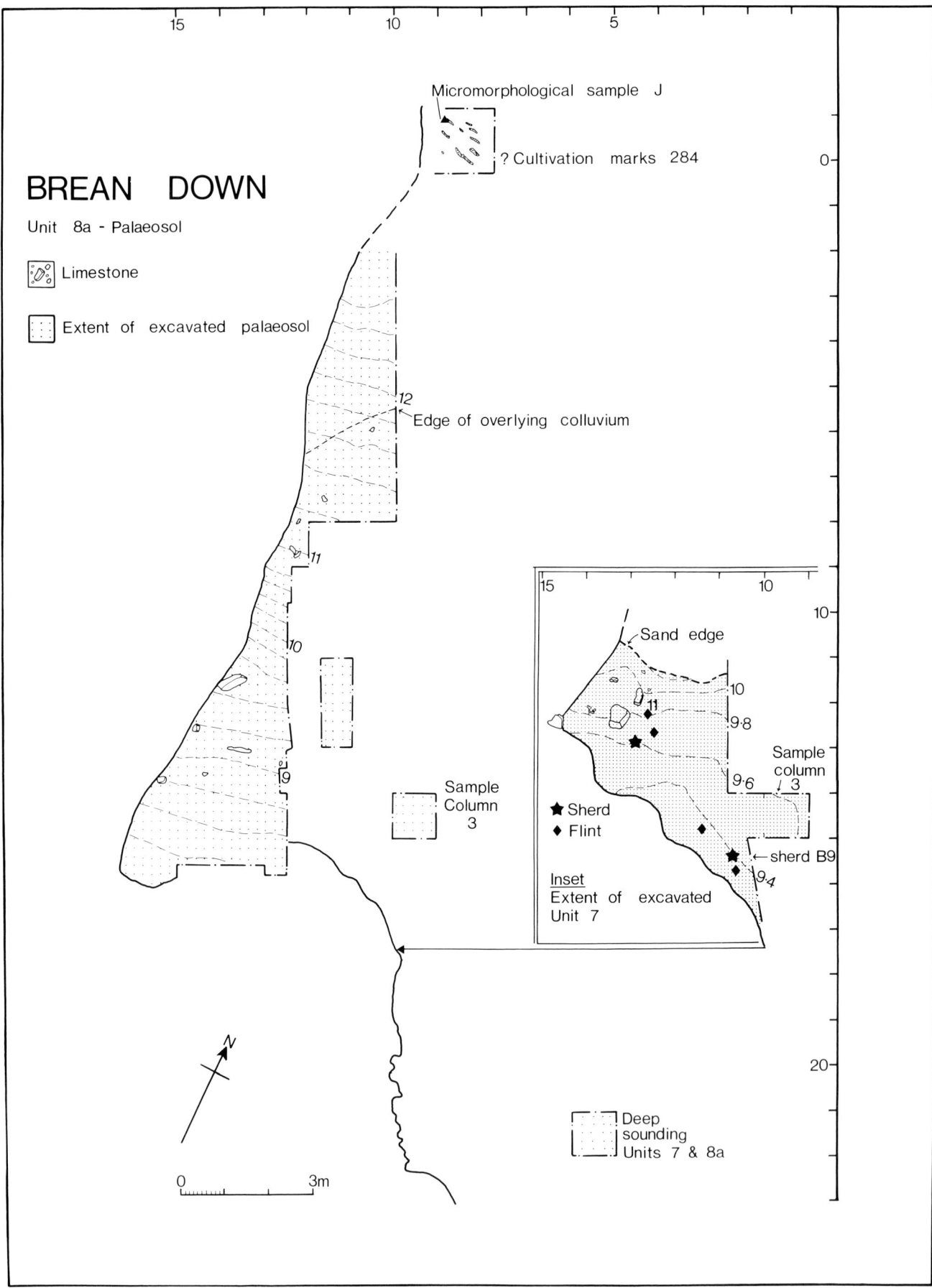

Fig 19 Contour plans showing the areas of Units 8a and 7 excavated; the numbers on the inset refer to illustrated finds of the relevant artefact type

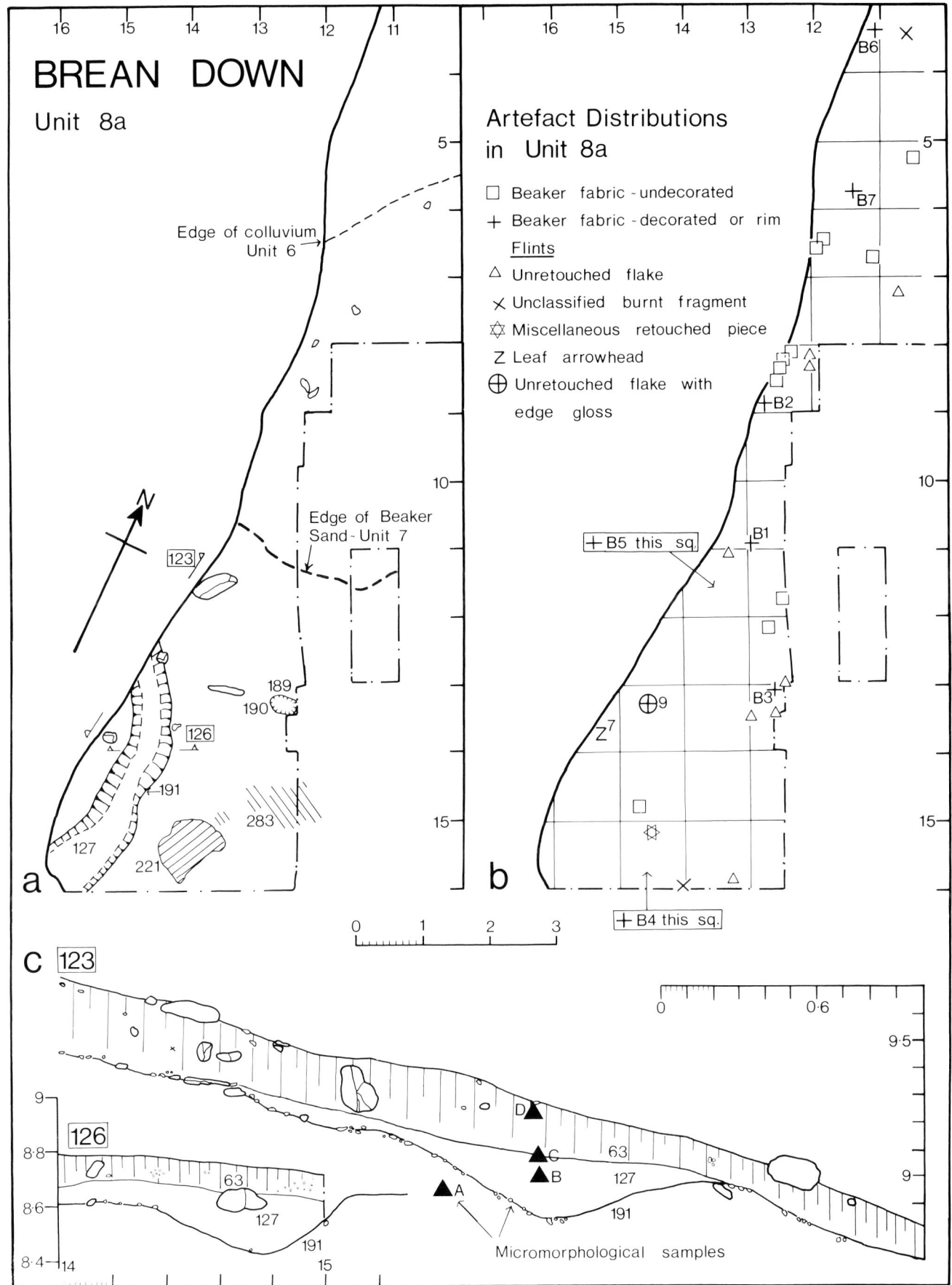

Fig 20 (a) Plan of Unit 8a; (b) artefact distributions in Unit 8a (the numbers refer to illustrated artefacts); (c) section of gully 191

Fig 21   Basal palaeosol Unit 8a under excavation showing possible gully 191 (photo: M J Allen)

Fig 22 Possible cultivation marks on the surface of Unit 8a (photo: M J Allen)

blown sand sometime in the middle to late Bronze Age. The possible cultivation marks can probably be associated with the truncation episode which led to the deposition of Unit 6b at the base of the slope; in which case they are early/middle Bronze Age, significantly later than the cultural material recovered from the palaeosol surface lower down the slope.

Artefact distribution in Unit 8a

The generally diffuse scatter of charcoal in this layer is mirrored by that of artefacts (Fig 20b). There were seven decorated Beaker sherds (Fig 84.B1–7) and 19 minute plain body sherds. A distribution diagram of Beaker sherds in all contexts (Fig 23) shows that they are particularly concentrated in the basal palaeosol. Among the 27 flint artefacts, three of which were from soil pits inland, the tools were a leaf-shaped arrowhead (8) and three miscellaneous and unillustrated retouched pieces, of which one is from Soil Pit V. The distributions of bones (Fig 139) and pottery (Fig 20) suggest that there is rather more material on the steeper slope between c 11 and 12.5m OD. The explanation may be that this area was exposed for a longer period, in fact during two distinct episodes of Beaker activity.

Unit 7: the 'Beaker sand'

This context (62) was a wedge of yellow (10YR 5/6) sand overlying the basal palaeosol below c 10m OD (Fig 24). The maximum depth of sand was 1.5m in the deep sounding (Fig 19). Between 0.2 and 0.4m from the top of the unit was a 20mm thick band of brown (10YR 5/3) sand (188) with fine charcoal and limpet shells (Fig 27). Land molluscan evidence (Chapter 22) indicates that this was a vegetated surface. The presence of five large limestone blocks in the upper part of Unit 7 is unlikely to be natural and probably results from human activity, though there was certainly no evidence for a structure or focus of activity. The cleaned surface of Unit 7 was mottled by probable animal burrows about 60mm in diameter; they were clearly not recent and no rabbit bones were found this far down. Presumably we must look to

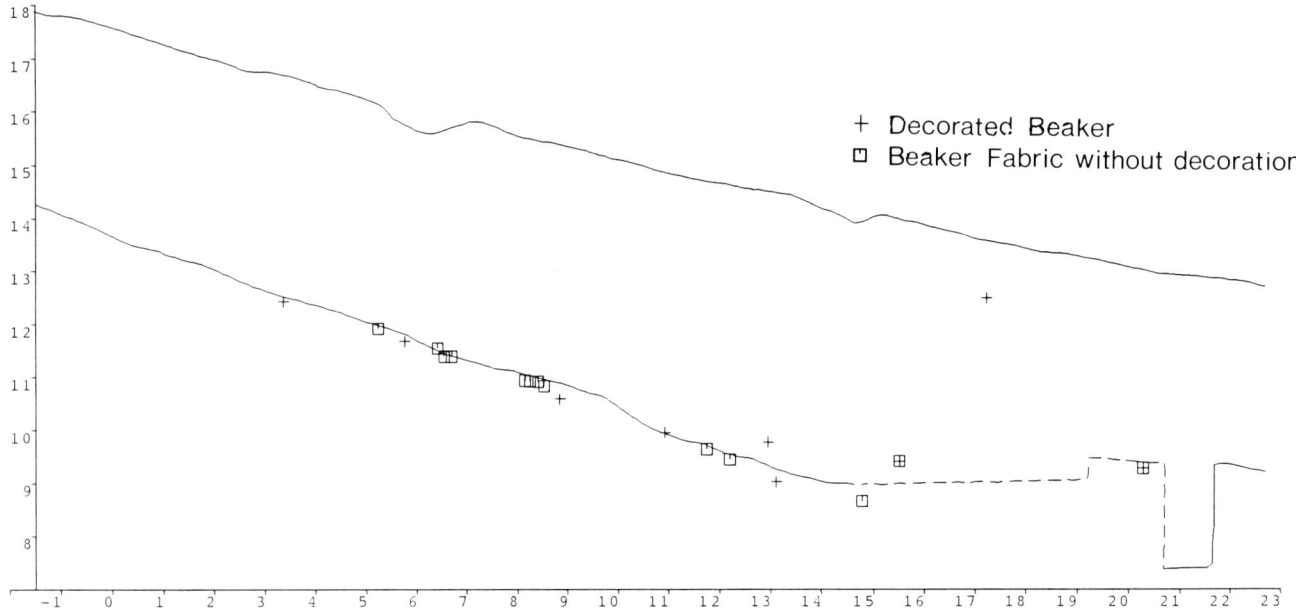

Fig 23 Sandcliff section showing the distribution of Beaker pottery in all contexts

native small mammals of which mole, water vole, and wood mouse are represented by bones in Unit 7.

The volume of Unit 7 examined was limited to 6 cu m. This was trowel excavated and dry sieved apart from 18 buckets of Context 62 and 3 buckets of Context 188 which were wet sieved. Artefacts were few and confined to the burnt band (188) and above. Context 188 produced five flint flakes. Context 62 had eight flints including a core (12), an edge trimmed flake (6240, not illustrated), and two scrapers (10 and 11), one piece of worked bone (69), two decorated Beaker sherds (B8 and B9), and a plain body sherd of Beaker fabric. There was also one sherd of coarsely gritted pottery (Fabric 361) which was almost certainly intrusive from an overlying occupation horizon.

Beaker activity conclusions

The palaeosol (8a) is a fine example of a diachronous surface, ie one which was buried at different dates at various points on the catenary sequence upslope. On the foreshore the surface dips steeply below the present beach and has been observed in Soil Pit VII at 4m OD, some 3m below the present highest astronomical tides (Fig 25). Inland in Soil Pit VI the palaeosol is present at 0m OD below 7m of estuarine silt. This evidence, further discussed in Chapter 8, shows that the palaeosol was an active surface at a time of much lower sea level. In particular, archaeomagnetic dating of the Soil Pit VI sequence shows that here the palaeosol was buried during or before the seventh millennium BP. In the main excavation trench at the base of the slope between 8.4 and 10m OD the palaeosol was sealed (Fig 15) early in the second millennium bc by blown sand (Unit 7). Above c 10m OD where this sand faded out against the slope the palaeosol was still exposed and was subsequently truncated by an erosion episode, perhaps associated with the possible cultivation marks, which led to the deposition of Unit 6b colluvium. Further upslope above 14m OD, Unit 8a was buried by blown sand constituting Unit 5a early in the first millennium BC. Thus the number of phases of human activity to which the palaeosol has been subjected increases upslope.

At the base of the slope where the palaeosol is buried by the 'Beaker sand' there is archaeological evidence for at least two periods of activity. The earliest is represented by the curving gully (191). It may be significant that ApSimon et al (1961, fig 19) show a feature in the same stratigraphic position near the base of the palaeosol and, like 191, almost certainly predating its final pedogenic development. The two diagnostic artefacts from 191, a leaf-shaped arrowhead and an unretouched flake with edge gloss, would both be acceptable in a Neolithic context. Activity during this period is confirmed by an earlier Neolithic radiocarbon date. All of the pottery from the recent excavation of Unit 8a is likely to be half a millennium to a millennium younger since it is all of Beaker type. Other ceramic types are, however, represented among the earlier finds. Arthur ApSimon has recently re-examined the pottery he published in 1961 and concludes (pers comm, 25.7.88) that Grooved Ware is represented by ApSimon et al 1961, fig 25:3 and 5. Gibson (1982, 115–16) has also noted some Grooved Ware among the published assemblage as well as Peterborough Ware, although it should be noted that the one definite Peterborough sherd he illustrates comes from the temple not the sandcliff.

The radiocarbon dates from Unit 8a support the notion of at least two distinct periods of activity. One charcoal sample gave an earlier Neolithic date of 4720±140 BP (HAR-7023). This is earlier than Grooved Ware dates from southern Britain (Smith 1974, fig 13; Darvill 1987a, 88) and seems likely to relate to a preceding phase of activity, possibly woodland clearance. Three other Unit 8a dates are within the range of determinations for contexts elsewhere

Fig 24 *Section showing basal palaeosol (Unit 7) and colluvium (Unit 6); micromorphological samples G, H, I, L, and M are marked and mollusc column 5 is on the right (photo: M J Allen)*

Fig 25 Palaeosol (Unit 8a) exposed in the foreground in Soil Pit VII on the beach and in the background at the base of the sandcliff sequence (photo: M J Allen)

with Beakers (Gibson 1982, fig 2). One, 3810±90 BP (HAR-8990), is about the middle of that range whereas two dates are late in the range: 3460±80 BP (HAR-8547) and 3390±90 BP (HAR-8993). The last two are both from areas of the palaeosol which were buried by blown sand of Unit 7 and show that activity on Unit 8a persisted until about the middle of the second millennium BC in radiocarbon years.

HAR-8547 is from a pit discovered on the foreshore after a gale in 1936. The pit lay at c 4.5m OD and upon excavation (Taylor and Taylor 1949) was found to contain a fine Maritime Beaker and a Beaker with fingernail decoration. Charcoal from this pit survived clearly labelled in the collections of the University of Bristol Spelaeological Society and was, together with H Taylor's manuscript notes on the find, kindly made available by Arthur ApSimon. The survival of this charcoal is despite a statement by Taylor and Taylor (1949, 90) to the effect that it had been destroyed during the war. The date of 3460±80 BP (HAR-8547) seems very late for a Maritime Beaker which are generally regarded as early in the series: steps 1 and 2 of Lanting and van der Waals (1972). The paucity of radiocarbon dates for steps 1 and 2 has been noted by both Gibson (1982, fig 2) and Burgess (1980, 68), so this new date may cast doubt on accepted views of Beaker development. Harrison (1988) has, however, emphasised that wiggles on the calibration curve mean that radiocarbon provides a very imprecise chronology for Beakers. It is also possible that, despite the association implied by the original report (Taylor and Taylor 1949) and Taylor's manuscript notes, the charcoal and pots were not derived from a single event. The pit with its two beakers has generally been interpreted as a burial where the bones have been lost by decalcification. The 1985–6 excavations showed that there was some decalcification of the palaeosol; the few molluscs which survived were very fragmentary, but on the other hand some bone was present, so the burial hypothesis cannot be accepted with absolute certainty.

The relatively small number of artefacts in the palaeosol and their scattered distribution does not suggest intensive activity on the old land surface during either the Neolithic or Beaker phases. As to the nature of that activity it is most clearly demonstrated by Richard Macphail's micromorphological studies (Chapter 16). A former tree cover is indicated; there is evidence of tree-throw and burning, the latter probably to be correlated with the earliest dated charcoal. A phase of cultivation followed. Of special significance is the evidence for cultivation where Unit 8a was sealed by Unit 7, showing that cultivation and some erosion of the soil profile took place on the site during or before the episode represented by the Beaker sherds as well as subsequently during the early Bronze Age when the upper part of the slope was eroded to produce Unit 6b. After the first cultivation phase and before burial by the 'Beaker sands' there was a phase of biological working suggesting that cultivation had been abandoned for at least several seasons. A possible implication of the micromorphological evidence is that the diffuse scatter of Beaker artefacts represents not so much *in situ* settlement as secondary refuse distributed on the fields with manure.

It seems possible that the main focus of Beaker activity was seaward. The 1955 cliff face was between 6 and 10m to the west and the finds reported in 1961 suggest that Beaker material may have been more abundant here. However, it should be noted that ApSimon *et al* (1961, 81) emphasised that pottery and flint were rare compared to charcoal, bone, and limpet shell. Assuming that the sandcliff erosion rates calculated between 1955 and 1985 are broadly applicable to the 19 years between 1936 and 1955, then the Beaker pit lay between 24 and 29m west of the 1985–6 excavations.

Clearly, however, Beaker activity does not fade out completely inland. Individual decorated Beaker sherds were recovered from the relatively tiny areas exposed in Soil Pits II, IV, and I (Chapter 8) indicating that the scatter of Beaker material extends at least 130m inland and up onto the steeper parts of the sandcliff slope where Soil Pits I and IV were located. The implication might be that the whole of the sandcliff area was cultivated from a lost settlement to seaward but it is equally possible that other foci of Beaker activity exist inland.

We know that there was more than one phase of Beaker activity because in the main trench there was a quite separate episode in the upper part of Unit 7. This has a radiocarbon date of 3560±90 (HAR-9156) which overlaps with the two latest dates in Unit 8a. Thus most of Unit 7 was laid down relatively quickly in the mid fourth millennium BP in radiocarbon years. Beaker activity in the upper part of Unit 7 was originally identified by ApSimon *et al* (1961) whose section drawings and an archive photograph taken in 1956 show a more extensive exposure of 'Beaker sands' with their top edge lying 0.5m OD higher, suggesting perhaps that their upper edge may dip inland.

3 Early/middle Bronze Age, Unit 6

The stratigraphy

The lower part (6b) of this unit consists of eroded soil; the upper part contains a high proportion of anthropogenically introduced material (6a) and includes a substantial stone structure (6α, Fig 26). In the south part of the excavation this unit overlies the 'Beaker sand' (Unit 7) but when this gives out against the slope (Fig 15) it rests directly on the basal palaeosol (Unit 8a) from which, as micromorphological examination (Chapter 16) confirms, its lower portion has been derived by erosion. Unit 6 itself fades out against the slope between 11.4 and 12m OD.

The lower part of the unit (6b, Context 66) consists of reddish brown (5YR 4/3) sandy loam with rare medium stones. It is up to 0.4m thick and contains abundant scattered charcoal; the proportion of sand increases upwards through the unit. Near the top of Context 66 (Fig 27, Section 120) are two very thin (10mm) lenses of ash and charcoal and above these is a discontinuous lens 20mm thick of yellow sand which was also noted by ApSimon *et al* (1961, 81) and, though thin, is clearly extensive.

Overlying this is Unit 6a (Context 61), a layer of grey (2.5Y 5/0) silty clay up to 0.4m thick. It is, however, a heterogeneous deposit with in places multiple lenses of ash 10–40mm thick (Fig 27, Section 59) as well as lenses of reddish brown (5YR 5/3) sandy loam and sand. Micromorphological examination (Chapter 16) reveals that 6a includes a component of marine silt rich in phytoliths, diatoms, and organic matter. The surface of the layer was iron-stained (5YR 4/6) and below this was an olive green (2.5Y 5/6) stained band; the cause of this staining is discussed in Chapters 15 and 16. The top of the unit dipped at 10° in the direction north 165° south. Generally 6a contained just a few medium and coarse stones but in places it was extremely stony and this stone was almost entirely of structural origin.

Excavation and sieving of Units 6a and 6b

The excavated area of Unit 6 can be divided into two parts (Fig 26): a strip along the cliff edge, and the area of Structure 57. Beginning with the cliff edge strip, 14 sq m between 10 and 17m on the A-axis were somewhat hastily excavated in 1985; only some of the finds could be three-dimensionally recorded and sieving had to be restricted to column 3. Subsequently in 1986 it was possible to examine 5 sq m north of 9m on the A-axis more carefully. Here Unit 6 was 0.2m or less thick; all finds were three-dimensionally recorded and three buckets were wet sieved from each grid square with the remainder being dry sieved. In total 4 cu m of Unit 6a were excavated and 42 buckets wet sieved whilst 5 cu m of Unit 6b were excavated but only 6 buckets wet sieved.

During excavation the surfaces of Units 6a and 6b and the component lenses within them were carefully examined for any evidence of cultivation marks, but none was found. It has already been noted, however, in Chapter 2 that possible cultivation marks were present in the surface of Unit 8a 6m north of the edge of Unit 6 (Fig 26); these were tentatively correlated with the erosion episode which gave rise to Unit 6b.

Illustrated artefacts in Unit 6b (Context 66) are sherds 1 and 2, Beaker sherd B10, miscellaneous retouched flint 18, and rod 15. Illustrated artefacts in Unit 6a (Context 61) are sherds 3–6, a flint knife (13), a miscellaneous retouched flint (17), an edge trimmed flake (19), and a bone gouge (58).

Features in Unit 6a: Contexts 285–7

Three pits or postholes in the surface of Unit 6a (Fig 26), 0.4m in diameter and 0.3m deep, were filled with sterile yellow sand of the overlying Unit 5d (Fig 27, Section 59). The three holes are aligned and may represent a fence line on the surface of Unit 6a. It should however be noted that they were close to the cliff edge and not well sealed by overlying deposits, so it is possible that they are the result of recent disturbance.

Structure 57

The section drawing exercise over Easter 1984 revealed a major concentration of stone in the southern part of the excavated area (Figs 6 and 8). At that time the base of the section was covered with slump so it was unclear whether the stones were within or below Unit 5d. Detailed excavation in 1985 established that it was part of Unit 6 and postdated at least the lower part of that unit. Because this episode was not clearly represented in the 1961 scheme a separate stratigraphic designation (Unit 6α) has been given to Structure 57 and its associated layers.

By the time complex structures in the overlying Unit 5b had been investigated there was only about one week available for the excavation of this structure. Accordingly 34 sq m were excavated with the objective of uncovering the probable building in plan but not dissecting the structure itself. This strategy was decided in consultation with the Ancient Monuments Inspector for the region, Paul Gosling, because it was already clear by this stage that the site was sufficiently important to warrant protection from the sea.

The stone concentration proved to be an oval structure (Figs 28, 29, and 30), two-thirds of which lay in the excavated area. Coastal erosion had already removed the south-west portion and a further portion lay beyond the excavation trench to the south-east. The walls were about 1.5m thick; no clear outer wall face was identified. There was an inner wall face of very large stones up to 0.6m in maximum dimension with a second course of smaller blocks surviving in places. Behind the face was an infill of smaller limestone blocks which survived to a height of up to 1.3m above the floor level. There appears to have

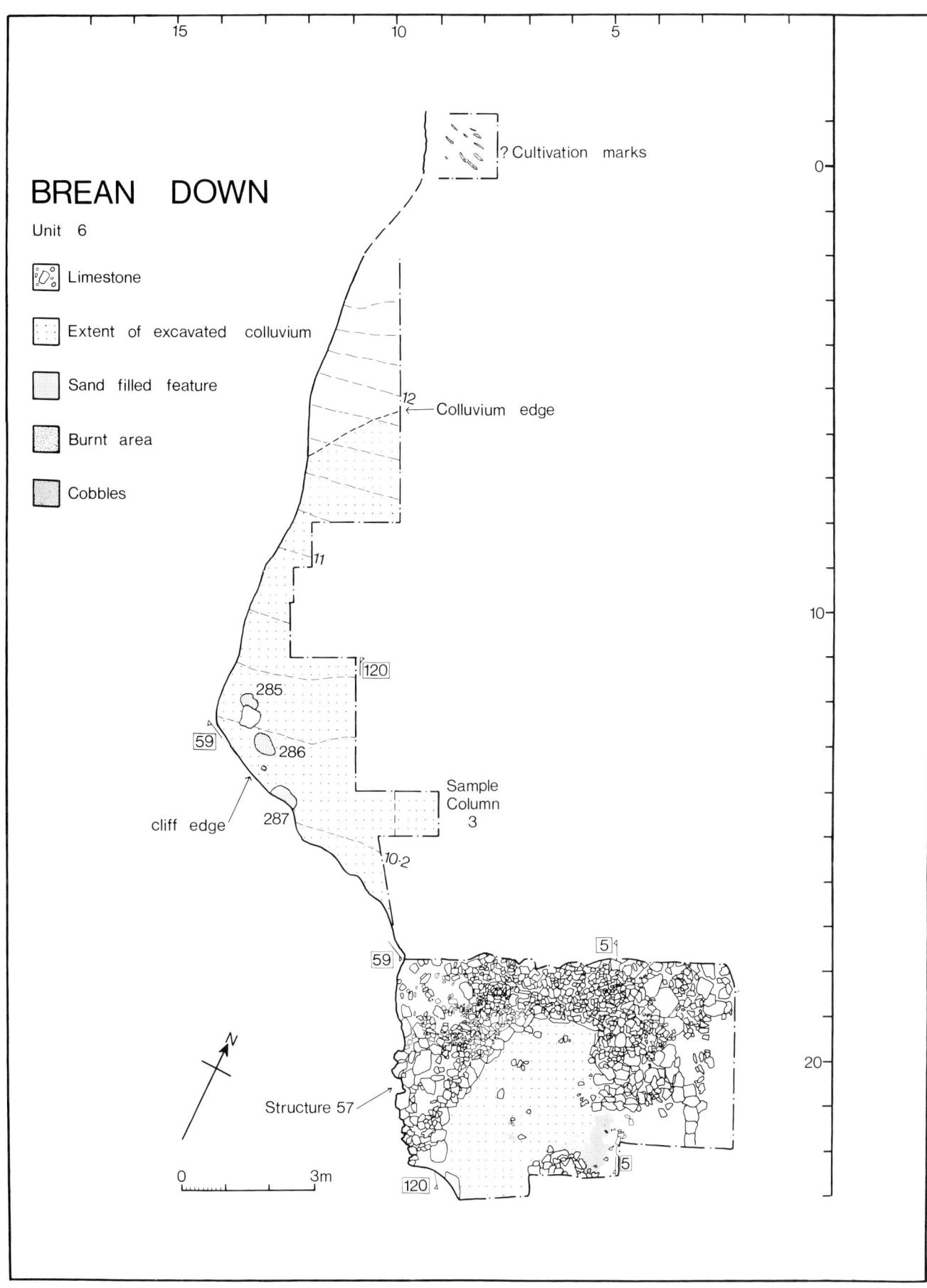

Fig 26 Plan of Unit 6

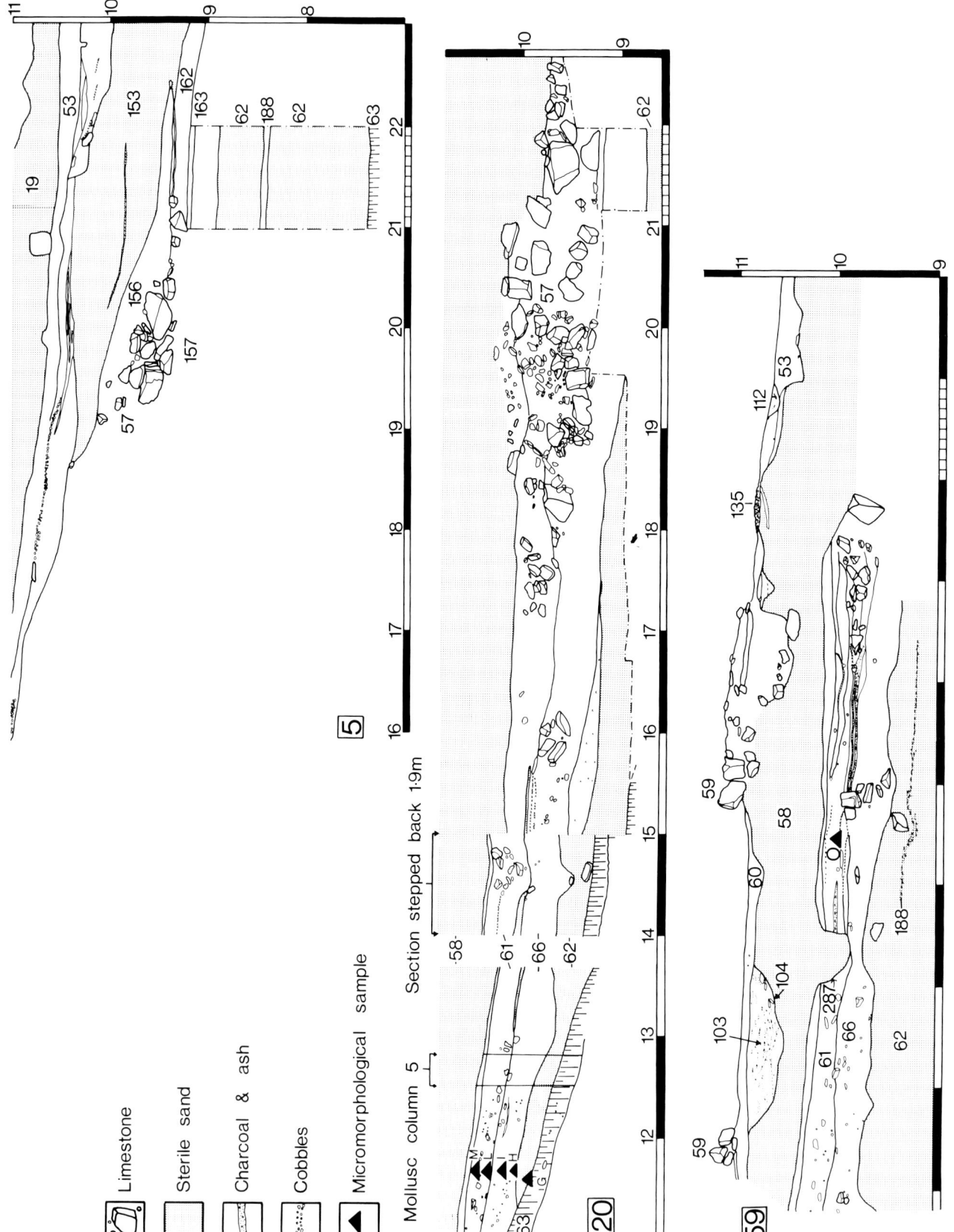

Fig 27 Sections 5, 120, and 59

BREAN DOWN
Unit 6: Structure 57

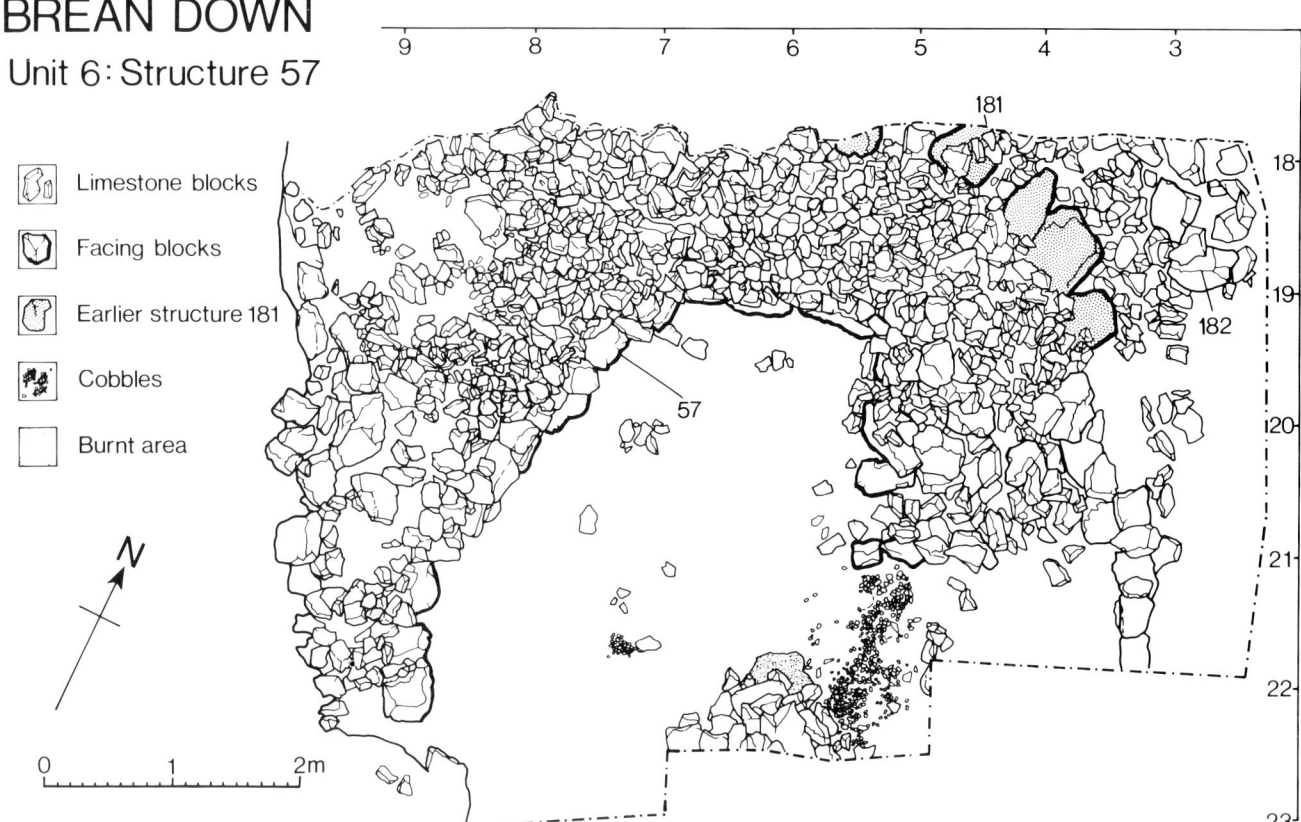

Fig 28   Plan of Structure 57

been a funnel-shaped entrance about 1m wide facing south-east marked by a gap in the wall and cobbling (177). South of the probable entrance was a pile of large stones which may represent either the wall itself, though no certain facing blocks were evident, or collapse from the wall. It was not possible to remove any of these stones because they supported a 3m vertical section (Fig 17).

The floor was a surface (163) between 9.2 and 9.4m sloping to the south; it comprised sandy loams of Unit 6 on to which the structure had been erected. There was no overall evidence of distinctive flooring material introduced to the site for the purpose, although there were tiny areas of cobbling, ash, and silt. Just inside the entrance was a lens of burning and laminated ash (178). No evidence was found of internal arrangements. The floor area was divided into 1m squares which were excavated in spits of 0.05m. Four squares were taken down to a depth of 0.3m, the others to a depth of 0.05 or 0.1m. A three bucket sack was sieved from each 0.05m spit, a total of 54 buckets being sieved. Illustrated artefacts from the floor area of Structure 57 (Context 163) are sherds 7–13 and 14 (from entrance cobbling 177), Beaker sherds B13–16, flints – scraper (21), knife (20), and piercer (22), coprolites (Fig 153.11 and 14), and four fragments of briquetage trays (109–112) and a possible fragment of briquetage pedestal (6079, not illustrated).

Because the walls of Structure 57 were not dissected it was not possible to resolve fully its stratigraphic relationship to Units 6a and 6b. Comparison of the cliff face section outside the structure with that revealed by excavation within the structure (Fig 27, Sections 120 and 5 respectively) does, however, clarify the problem. Units 6a and 6b were both present within the structure but both, especially 6a, were much thinner: 6a – 0.05m within the structure and 0.4m outside; 6b – 0.25m within the structure and 0.6m outside.

Clearly Structure 57 postdates at least the lower part of Unit 6b. Less clear is to what extent it was terraced into Units 6b and 6a or alternatively to what extent these units accumulated against its outer wall. Unit 6a was rich in ash and sediment of estuarine origin and may partly consist of material associated with occupation of the structure.

A possible earlier structure, Context 181

Within the wall of Structure 57 was an area of substantial blocks averaging 0.4m square (Fig 28.181 and Fig 30). The faces of these blocks were so aligned as to suggest that they did not form an outer wall face for Structure 57 but formed the *inner* face of an earlier structure. Two other large blocks (182) could represent part of the outer face of this wall. If this structure was circular it would have been 8 to 10m in diameter. It looks therefore as if Structure 57 was built within the shell of an earlier virtually unexamined structure.

Sedimentary sequence postdating Structure 57

The stratigraphy overlying Structure 57 is illustrated in Figure 27, Section 5. Overlying the floor in the

Fig 29   Structure 57 from the west (photo: M J Allen)

centre of the structure was 0.3m of light brown (10YR 6/4) sand (162); this was virtually sterile of finds (Beaker sherd B12, two other sherds) and is likely to reflect a period of abandonment. Round the edge of the structure was a mass of limestone from wall collapse (157) which produced illustrated sherds 15 and 16 and Beaker sherd B11. Then there was a layer of relatively humic brown (5YR 4/2) silty sand (156) with charcoal and the following illustrated artefacts: sherd 17, flint scraper (14), miscellaneous retouched flint (16), bone point (45), and miscellaneous fired clay object (123). Succeeding this and entirely filling the collapsed structure was up to 0.8m of brownish yellow (10YR 6/6) sand (153) which was part of a much more extensive blanket of sterile sand (5d) which completely separated the occupation surfaces 5b and 6.

Interpretation of Structure 57

We seem to be dealing with an oval structure with an interior 3m by at least 4.5m, the south end being partly destroyed and partly outside the excavated area. There was less stone towards the southern end of the building but that area may have been robbed just as, presumably, the wall facing blocks were

Fig 30 Structure 57 from the east showing possible earlier Structure 181 and the deep sounding (photo: M J Allen)

robbed above the first or second courses. The substantial nature of the walls, together with the fact that the wall core survived up to 1.3m above the floor, indicates that it was basically a stone structure. No evidence was found for postholes or other timber elements. It was perhaps similar to the later Structure 59 in Unit 5b which seems to have been largely stone-built, but quite different from Structure 95, also in 5b, which, though it had stone elements, is interpreted as largely wooden.

In looking elsewhere for parallels it is necessary to anticipate subsequent discussion by noting that Unit 6 is dated to the early/middle Bronze Age. There is a general similarity to the Bronze Age stone-built round houses of the south-west though most of these are more or less round and have an internal ring of roof supports, as for instance at Shaugh Moor (Wainwright and Smith 1980) and Stannon Down (Mercer 1970). The closest comparanda seem to be the stone houses of Scilly. Here the Nornour structures are comparable, particularly Building 9 which is an irregular oval c 4.2m by 2.4m and is dated to the second half of the second millennium BC (Butcher 1978). Many of the other oval stone structures relating to probably second-millennium activity on the Scillies are also comparable (Ashbee 1974), particularly those on Par Beach and Little Bay, the internal dimensions of which are respectively 6m by 2.8m and 7m by 3.5m. If we look more widely, we find oval or U-shaped stone structures in the second and third millennia BC on the Scottish islands, eg Northton on Harris (Simpson 1976), Rosinish, Benbecula (Shepherd 1976), the Scord of Brouster (Whittle *et al* 1986), and elsewhere on Shetland (Calder 1955–6), but nearly all of these are much larger than Brean Structure 57.

Dating, artefact distributions, and activity areas

Five radiocarbon dates are available from Unit 6. Unit 6b contained much scattered charcoal of which a sample gave a date of 3890±130 BP (HAR-7022). It was originally noted by ApSimon *et al* (1961, 81) that the basal part of Unit 6b produced Beaker pottery and the remainder contained middle Bronze Age sherds. The radiocarbon date from Unit 6b supports the interpretation that this layer may have started to form at the time of Beaker activity. An element of uncertainty must remain, however, because Unit 8a contains so much charcoal that some of it is likely to have survived erosion and therefore become included in Unit 6b. In fact, as Table 2 shows, the recent excavations produced only single sherds of Beaker pottery in Units 6a and 6b but seven sherds were found in Unit 6α. It is also clear from Table 2 that nearly all the pottery in Unit 6b is in fabrics characteristic of subsequent early and middle Bronze Age activity at Brean.

The first radiocarbon date obtained for Unit 6a was 2600±90 BP (HAR-7021). The sample came from what was regarded as a securely stratified context, one of the discrete lenses of burning sealed by silty clay. Even so, it is at least four centuries later than we would anticipate from the ceramic evidence and from

Table 2 Pottery fabrics in Unit 6

	Unit 6b, Cont 66	Unit 6a, Cont 61	Unit 6α, Str 57	Unit 6α, post Str 57	Total Unit 6
Beaker fabrics					
355, 356	1	1	5	2	9
Early and middle Bronze Age fabrics					
361	16	19	43	12	90
363	15	9	2	3	29
364	-	-	4	1	5
365	26	-	43	-	69
521	1	-	-	2	3
Total					205

HAR-8991 and HAR-7020, and furthermore is sealed by a good group of earlier dates in Unit 5b. No satisfactory hypothesis can be advanced to explain this conflict; the date has been confirmed by a second date from half of the original sample: 2770±90 BP (HAR-8992).

Another charcoal sample from Unit 6a gave a date of 3120±90 BP (HAR-8991) and charcoal from Context 163 gave a date of 3310±80 BP (HAR-7020). Both dates are broadly in line with the pottery dating suggested for Unit 6. They imply some duration for Units 6a and 6α and suggest that Unit 6a may have continued to accumulate after the life of Structure 57.

Attempts to consider the activities associated with Structure 57 are made more difficult by the fact that the floor essentially comprised an earlier colluvial deposit. The possibility of earlier material being incorporated within the floor was further exacerbated by the apparent existence of an earlier, largely uninvestigated, structure (181) on the site. However, most of the artefacts were in the top part of the floor layer rather than the underlying colluvium which seems to have contained only sparse finds. Figure 31a plots the artefacts within a 0.2m band corresponding to the floor level. The first point to emphasise, by comparison for instance with structures in overlying Unit 5b, is the relative scarcity of artefacts: just 117 pot sherds, for instance, from all contexts in Unit 6α. The second point which emerges is the concentration of artefacts, particularly pottery and bone, in the northern 1.5m of the structure. There was no indication in the field that this represented a specific dump of material, but it might represent some sort of internal subdivision which acted as a trap for artefacts.

The presence of four fragments of briquetage trays and a possible fragment of briquetage pedestal in the floor layer is of particular interest, since this is stratigraphically the earliest context to produce briquetage at Brean, which is in turn one of the earliest briquetage sites in the British Isles (Chapter 14). The quantity of briquetage, when compared, for instance, to its distribution in Unit 5b structures, makes it unlikely that activities associated with briquetage were occurring in Structure 57. There is no indication that the production of flint tools took place in the structure or indeed anywhere in the excavated area of Unit 6; the ratio of tools to unretouched flakes from the unit as a whole is 15 to 18. The presence of a

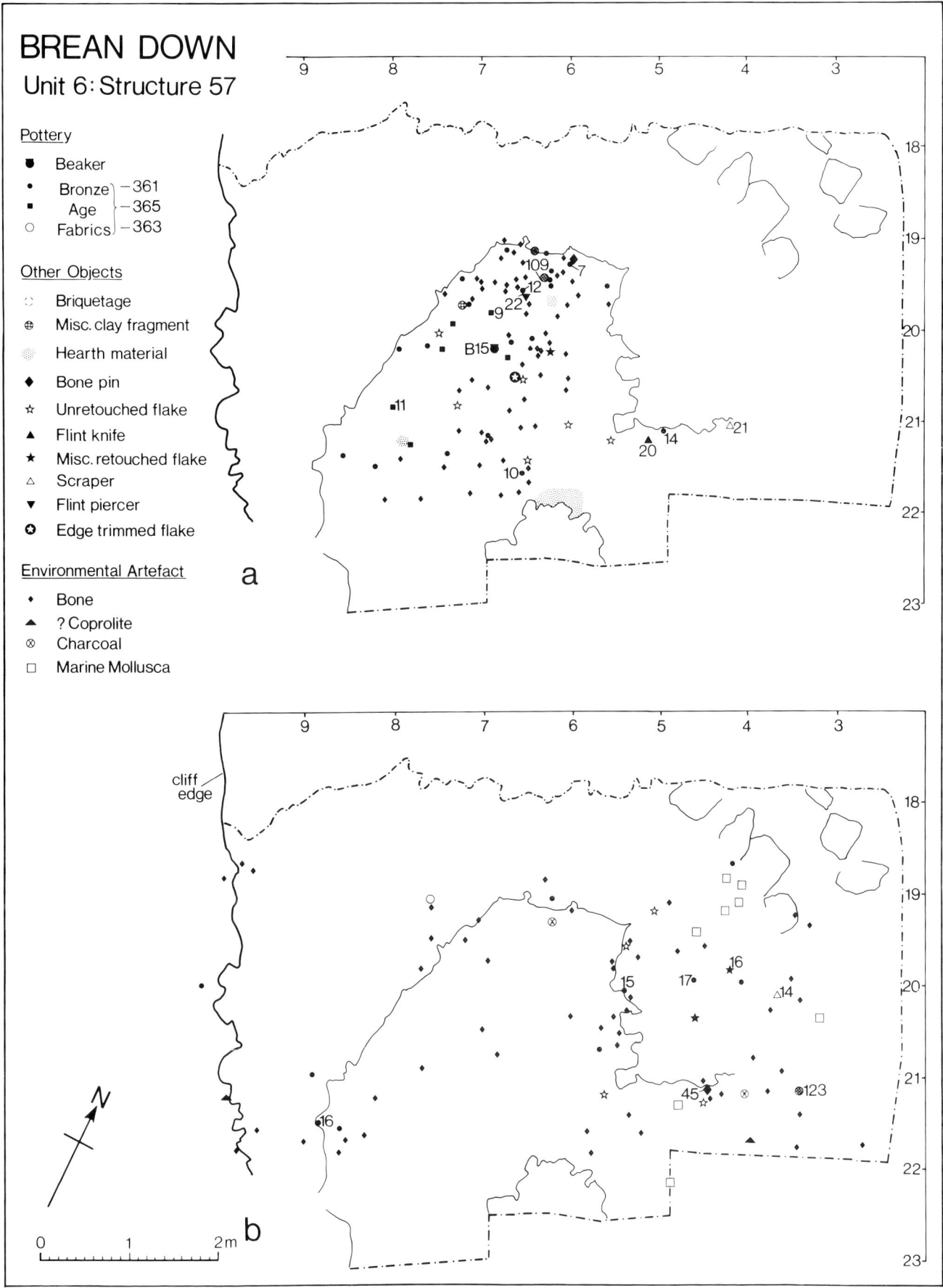

Fig 31 Artefact distributions (a) from the floor level of Structure 57 and (b) from Unit 6 contexts postdating Structure 57; the numbers refer to the illustrated finds of the relevant artefact type

scraper, knife, and piercer in the floor area indicates that activities such as leatherworking associated with the use, rather than production, of flint tools may have been undertaken in the structure, but in view of the tiny number of tools this is only likely if they were curated (Binford 1976; 1979).

Figure 31b plots the distribution of artefacts in Unit 6α contexts which postdate Structure 57. It shows a generally dispersed scatter of bone and pottery sherds with no suggestion of deliberate dumping in the abandoned structure. Much of this material may represent bones scattered by dogs or artefacts which came to rest in a secondary position during structure collapse or robbing.

The evidence of activities associated with Structure 57 is principally negative, the paucity of artefacts, particularly sherds, and ash arguing against normal domestic activities. Other possibilities which suggest themselves are a building for animals, storage, or craft activities. The structure seems very substantial yet small for an animal shelter, and this explanation is considered unlikely in view of the evidence elsewhere within the Brean sequence for staining associated with organo-phosphate accumulation (Chapter 16); there was no pronounced evidence of staining within Structure 57. As regards the other possibilities, some further light is thrown on activities particularly during the latter part of Unit 6 by micromorphological examination (Chapter 16) of Unit 6a 6m north of the structure. The unit consists of silty clay with lenses of ash. The ash is evidently from the burning of peat which the pollen evidence (Chapter 18) suggests could derive from the peats exposed in the intertidal area. This evidence for the use of peat as fuel is a rarity in southern British contexts. There is a later Somerset record from the Huntspill Romano-British briquetage mound (Leech *et al* 1983). The practice of burning peat is, however, well documented on prehistoric sites in the north, for instance in Beaker horizons at Northton (Simpson 1976) or during the Neolithic at Pool, Sandy (Hunter 1987). The presence at Brean of vitrified ash and melted quartz suggests high temperature fires. Another fascinating piece of micromorphological evidence is the presence of a layer of microscopic bone dust which might be the product of *in situ* boneworking on the midden.

The main component of Unit 6a as revealed by micromorphology is grey silty clay, much of which seems to be of estuarine origin and presumably derives from the flats below the site. How and why this reached the site is a puzzle, especially since it is clearly not a localised deposit because Unit 6a appears from descriptions and photographs to have been of essentially the same character in the section studied by ApSimon *et al* (1961). Richard Macphail suggests (Chapter 16) that the clay may have been introduced to the site for cultivation, yet the excavated area of Unit 6a was clearly not cultivated because the many fine laminae of sediment would surely have been disrupted. Another possibility is that the silt derives from flooding, a topic considered more generally in Chapter 8. The Unit 6a deposits occurred up to almost 11m OD so they are most unlikely to have been deposited by flooding *in situ*. Perhaps, however, parts of the settlement lower down the slope were occasionally inundated and during the cleaning up of these areas quantities of silty clay were dumped on the slope behind the structures. Probably the most likely explanation is that the silt was introduced to the site as daub and was subsequently dumped upslope during rebuildings. The Butser experiments (Reynolds 1979) have emphasised the quantity of daub required for building; for instance 3.5 tonnes of clay and the same of earth for the 6m diameter Maiden Castle House. It must, however, be remembered that we have no certain evidence of wattle and daub structures in Unit 6, although one is present in the overlying Unit 5b.

Unit 6a seems to consist of a thin midden which probably partly accumulated against the wall of Structure 57 but was almost certainly, in view of the 1961 observations, much more extensive. What is surprising, in view of the micromorphological evidence for the extent of anthropogenic inputs to this layer, is the tiny quantity of pottery, just 28 sherds, and other artefacts recovered from the excavated area. This suggests that the midden is waste not from a domestic structure but from a part of the site associated perhaps with craft activities which involved the use of peat as fuel, and some hints of bone- and leatherworking. The same area was used for the dumping of silty clay, probably discarded daub. This model would see Structure 57 as possibly associated with these craft and productive activities rather than domestic occupation. Another possibility is that it was a storage structure analogous to the cleitean of St Kilda and elsewhere which, when complete, it would have resembled (Stell and Harman 1988). Other structures almost certainly once existed within the Unit 6 complex. ApSimon *et al* (1961, 81) note within Unit 6a 'large weathered blocks of limestone up to 4ft (1.2m) long. These are presumably the remains of houses or other structures.' This evidence, together with hearths, we can calculate was some 10–15m north-west of Structure 57.

4 Middle Bronze Age structures in Unit 5b

The stratigraphy

Unit 5 as described in 1961 consisted of blown sand; the existence of two loamy bands was noted but no traces of occupation were found. During the section drawing exercise in 1984 (Fig 6) and subsequent excavation in 1985 it became clear that there was a major occupation horizon within Unit 5. This occurred in a part of the section largely obscured by slump at the time of the work reported in 1961. The following stratigraphic sequence is now recognised within Unit 5, beginning at the base.

Unit 5d

Made up of two contexts, 58 and 153 (Fig 15). Context 58 is a blanket of brownish yellow (10YR 6/6) blown sand up to 1.1m thick. Vertical sections of this layer when etched by the wind revealed minute layering and dune bedding. The context was virtually sterile of stones and contained only five sherds. A curious find was a probable mammoth rib perhaps brought by man from the Pleistocene section. There were also a number of bones at the very base of this layer resting on Context 61 (Unit 6a) and possibly let down onto the surface of 6a by a winnowing episode which intervened between Units 6a and 5d. Context 153 is identical to 58; it is a 0.8m thick deposit which infilled oval stone structure 57 in Unit 6α (Fig 27.5); it contained only three sherds of which one (18) is illustrated, and two coprolites (Fig 153.10 and 17). Contexts 58 and 153 can be correlated as part of a single blanket of blown sand.

Unit 5c

This was provisionally recognised in 1984 (Bell and Straker 1984) but is now regarded as part of Unit 5b.

Unit 5b

The main occupation horizon investigated in 1985, which is chiefly notable for the discovery of two structures (59 and 95) partly constructed of stone (Fig 32) and associated with a large artefact assemblage. Within Unit 5b a number of distinct stratigraphic horizons can be recognised (Figs 15, 17, and 18). The base of the unit was marked by a distinctly stained band (106) of olive yellow (5Y 6/2) sand 20mm thick. In places there was a thin greyish brown (7.5YR 6/2) band at its base. Band 106 was cut by a drip gully surrounding Structure 59 (Fig 7) and also appeared to be absent from the area of Structure 95, implying that here it may have been removed by terracing, though this was not demonstrated directly by a section. The green staining itself is the result of post-depositional chemical factors (Chapters 15 and 16) but it appears to have picked out a stabilisation surface predating the structures. Elsewhere in Unit 5b, in and around the structures, similar faint staining of green, brown, and yellow tinges picked out the outlines of features, layer boundaries, and the floors of structures. This proved to be an important factor facilitating the identification of stratigraphic relationships in otherwise rather uniform sand deposits.

In the lower part of the trench below about 11.8m OD were terraces for the two structures partly surrounded by gullies. Both terraces and the gullies cut the sterile sand 5d and the lower green-stained band (106). In the area of the structures and to their south the unit consisted to a large extent of anthropogenically introduced material: stone for building, silty clay for floors and hearths, ash, fired clay, pottery, bone, etc. Here the unit averaged 0.3m in thickness but was up to 0.5m in places.

Upslope of the structures above about 11.8m OD there was a complete contrast, with very little occupation evidence, the unit being characterised mainly by two bands of stained sand together c 0.3m thick. The lower green band (106) has already been described. The upper band (78) was a brown (7YR 7/4) compacted surface crust 0.15m thick which was interpreted in the field as a stabilisation surface. Micromorphological evidence (Chapter 16) suggests that the layer owes its present form partly to post-depositional downwashing of ferruginous organophosphates. Surface 78 covered the whole of the excavated area extending over and therefore postdating the two structures and all their associated contexts. In the excavated area the surface lay between 10.5 and 12.2m OD with a slope of 8° and a direction of dip of north 160° south. Figure 33 is a plan of this surface. By the time it formed there was little trace of the underlying building terraces, although scattered stones represent parts of the structures projecting through the surface. On the compacted surface it was easy to isolate some localised evidence of rabbit activity.

The two bands of staining which represented Unit 5b above about 11.8m OD (Fig 15) can almost certainly be correlated with the two 'loamy bands' recorded in 1961 within Unit 5. The original field drawing which was simplified as ApSimon *et al* 1961, fig 19 (with the bands being omitted) shows that they were between 12.5 and 12.8m OD. In the 1985 section the bands died out upslope at c 14m OD.

Unit 5a

A single context (19) comprising yellow (10YR 7/6) blown sand up to 1.3m thick which totally blanketed Unit 5b (Fig 15). The layer contained no stones but some bones and 36 pottery sherds, of which one (66) is illustrated. Remarkably, the sherds are of seven different fabrics, which strengthens the impression that artefacts in these sand layers are the result of mixing and intrusion from above and below.

Excavation and sieving

The total excavated volume of Unit 5d was 34 cu m; since the unit was sterile it was removed by shovel.

Fig 32   The excavation of Structures 59 (left) and 95 (right) in Unit 5b (photo: A Philpott)

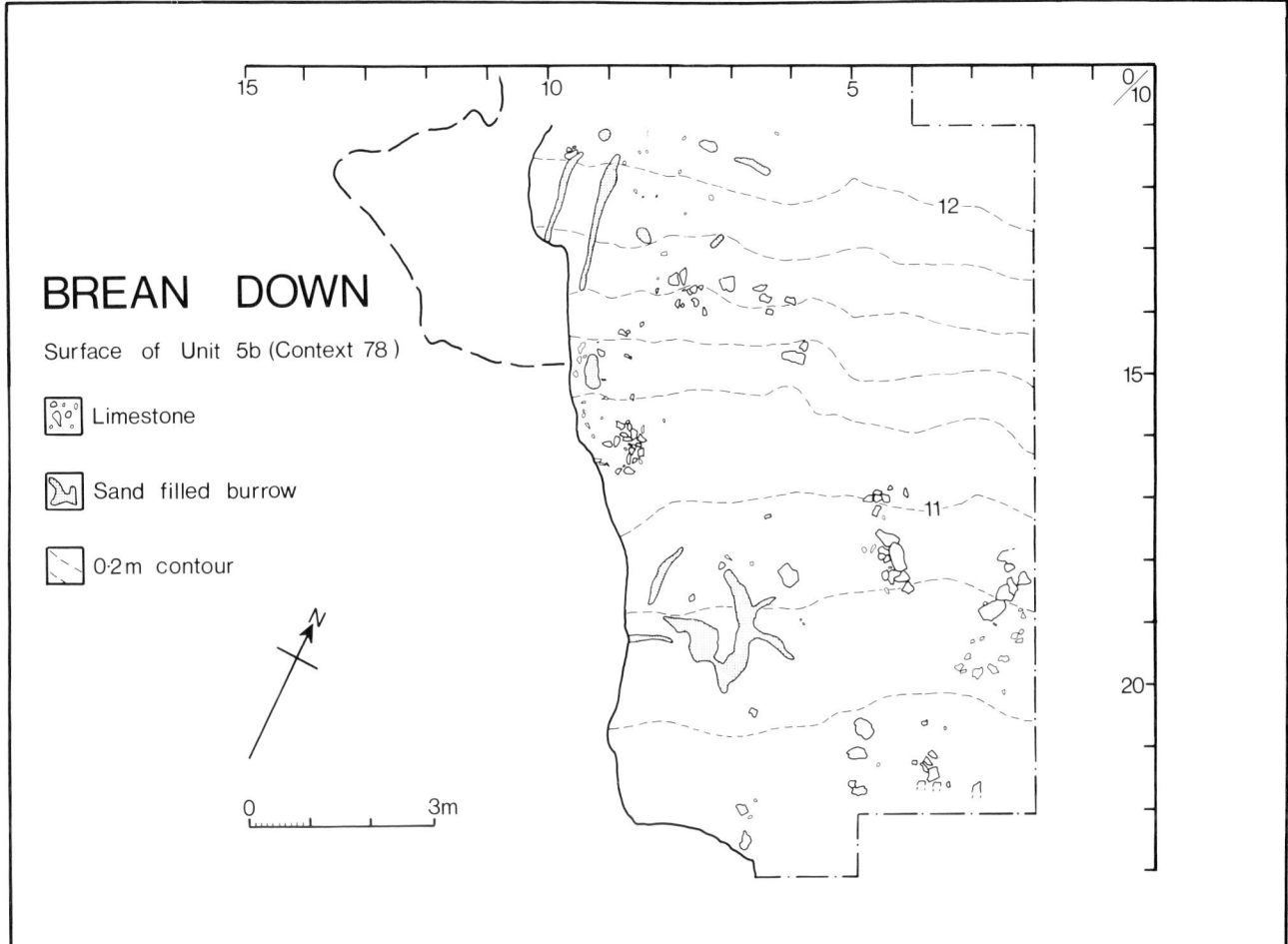

Fig 33 Contoured plan of the surface of Unit 5b

The only exception was the hand-excavated baulk at B = 4–5m and A = 18–22m where 2 cu m were trowelled. Sieving was restricted to sample column I from which 12 buckets of Context 153 were wet sieved and 51 buckets dry sieved.

The total volume of Unit 5b excavated was 30 cu m. In general all finds were three-dimensionally recorded. However an exception had to be made in the case of some restricted features, notably the drip gullies, where for reasons of time some finds had to be recorded by context. For sieving purposes the unit was divided into 1m squares and a sieving programme was carried out in 55 grid squares which made up the floors of the structures and the occupation area south of Structure 95. Logistically it was not possible to sieve north and east of Structure 95 where 49 squares were situated outside the main area of occupation deposits and where there was little macroscopic evidence of activity. An average of five buckets was wet sieved from each square. The total number of sieved buckets was 320: of these 70 were from the floor area of Structure 95, 52 from the floor area of Structure 59, and most of the remainder from occupation surfaces south of Structure 95, including 48 buckets from sample column I. The remainder of the sediment from the sieving squares was dry sieved.

The total excavated volume of Unit 5a was 58 cu m. Since it was sterile sand, this unit was excavated by shovel except for the 1m wide trowelled baulk of which 9 cu m were excavated but produced few finds. Sieving was restricted to sample column I from which 8 buckets were wet sieved and 64 buckets dry sieved.

Structure 59

This structure was first recognised as a terrace with a possible stone structure during the section drawing exercise in 1984 (Figs 6 and 7, Feature F). Being somewhat precariously situated on a little projecting bluff of Unit 5b it was under active erosion by the sea. Excavation in 1985 (Fig 35) showed that about one-third of a roughly circular structure survived, the remainder having already been eroded away. Originally the structure would have had an internal diameter of c 4m.

Features below the floor of Structure 59

Context 104

A pit revealed in the cliff section 1.65m by 0.2m+ and 0.35m deep (Figs 6 and 27, Section 59). The fill (103) consisted of sand with numerous small lenses of fine grey ash and some patches of partly fired clay. It contained an illustrated briquetage pedestal (95) and another unillustrated fragment (5699).

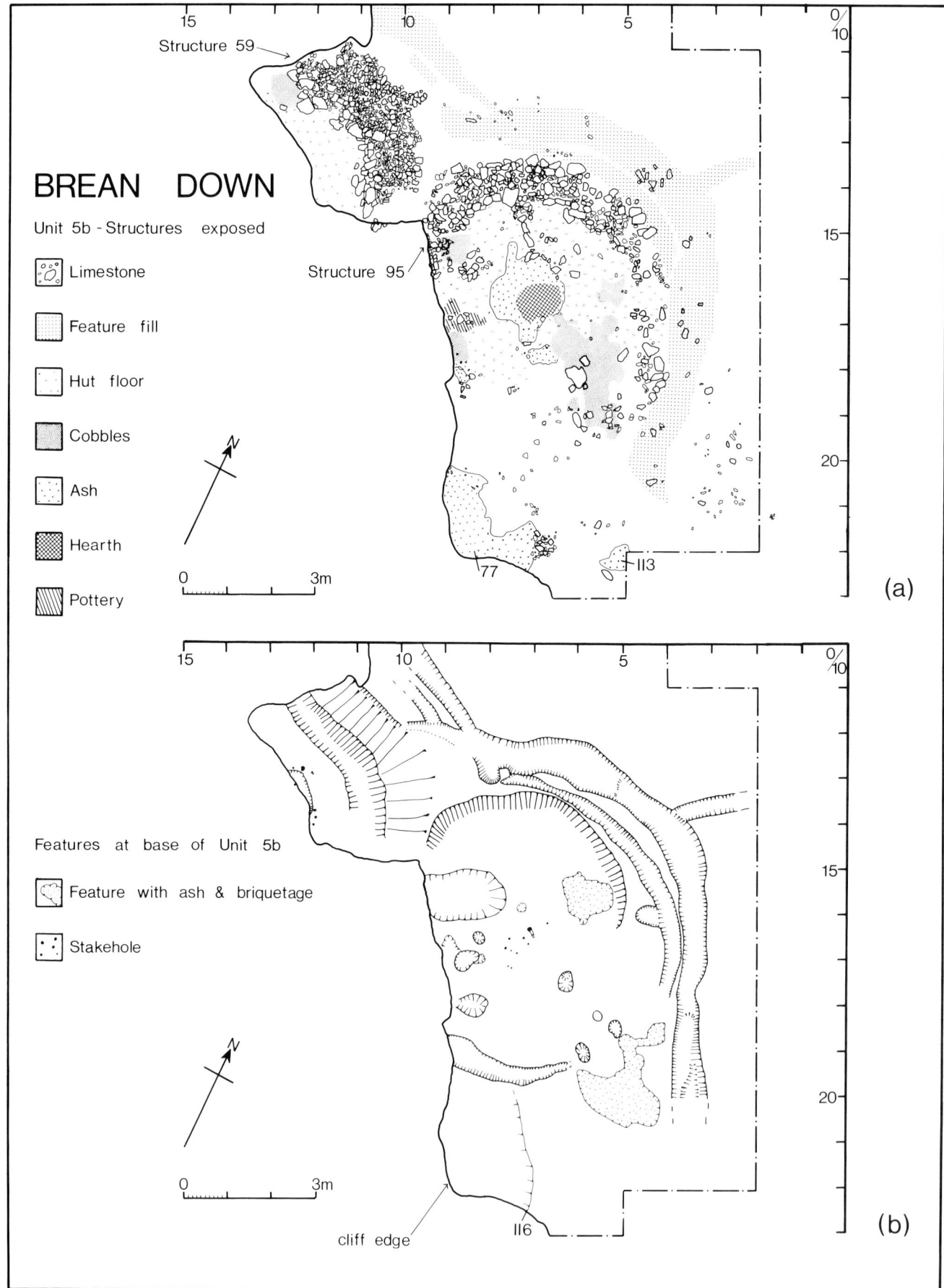

Fig 34 Plan of structures in Unit 5b and cut features at the base of Unit 5b

Fig 35 Structure 59 (photo: M J Allen)

Context 279

A bowl-shaped depression 0.4m in diameter and 0.3m deep (Fig 6). The fill (146) was 20mm of sandy clay overlain by sand with finely divided charcoal.

Contexts relating to Structure 59

The terrace and wall, Contexts 64 and 59

There was no evidence as to whether Contexts 104 and 279 predated the terrace or were cut from the base of the terrace before the floor (60) of Structure 59 was laid. The terrace (64) cut 0.7m into the slope, and round the edge of the level terrace floor was a foundation trench 0.5m wide and 0.25m deep (Fig 34). Set in this were large blocks of limestone forming the inner face of the wall (Fig 36). The blocks were of irregular shape averaging 0.4×0.3×0.2m and in places the wall survived up to three blocks high, c 0.4m. The triangular space between this facing wall and the back of the terrace was filled with small pieces of limestone to make a wall 1.2m wide. A few rather larger blocks lay on the outside of the wall but there was no well-defined outer face. An entrance to the structure faced north-west and here the foundation trench curved north to take the substantial stone blocks flanking the entrance. One of these (0.56m×0.25m×0.2m) was set vertically to form a door frame (Fig 37). The entrance itself was cobbled (97). Within the stones of the wall one virtually complete briquetage pedestal (70) was found and there were two other illustrated pedestal fragments (76 and 96).

Floor, Context 60

A well-defined, compacted, level surface 0.1m thick at 10.9m OD apparently formed from silt and sand. The surface was a distinctive olive yellow (5Y 6/6) and overlay yellowish brown (10YR 6/6), and there were lenses of grey (7.5YR 7/0) ash and patches of poorly fired, yellowish red (5YR 4/8) clay (eg 136 and 137). Between the compressed laminae of sediment comprising the floor were faint impressions of fibrous material, perhaps reeds or straw used as flooring. The presence within the floor of fragments of distinctive fired silty clay and lenses of ash identical to those forming the hearth in neighbouring Structure 95 implies that the eroded portion of Structure 59 may have contained a hearth. One ash lens (114) underlay the entrance cobbling and produced a piece of briquetage pedestal (71). Five stakeholes 40mm in diameter and 100mm deep were found within the floor (Fig 34) and are reminiscent of the stakeholes around the hearth in Structure 95. Within the floor was a sizable fragment of a briquetage vessel (97) and pedestal fragment (80).

Gullies, Contexts 170 and 123

These were concentric with the wall of Structure 59 (Fig 36). Gully 170 (Fig 37) was 0.32m wide and 0.16m

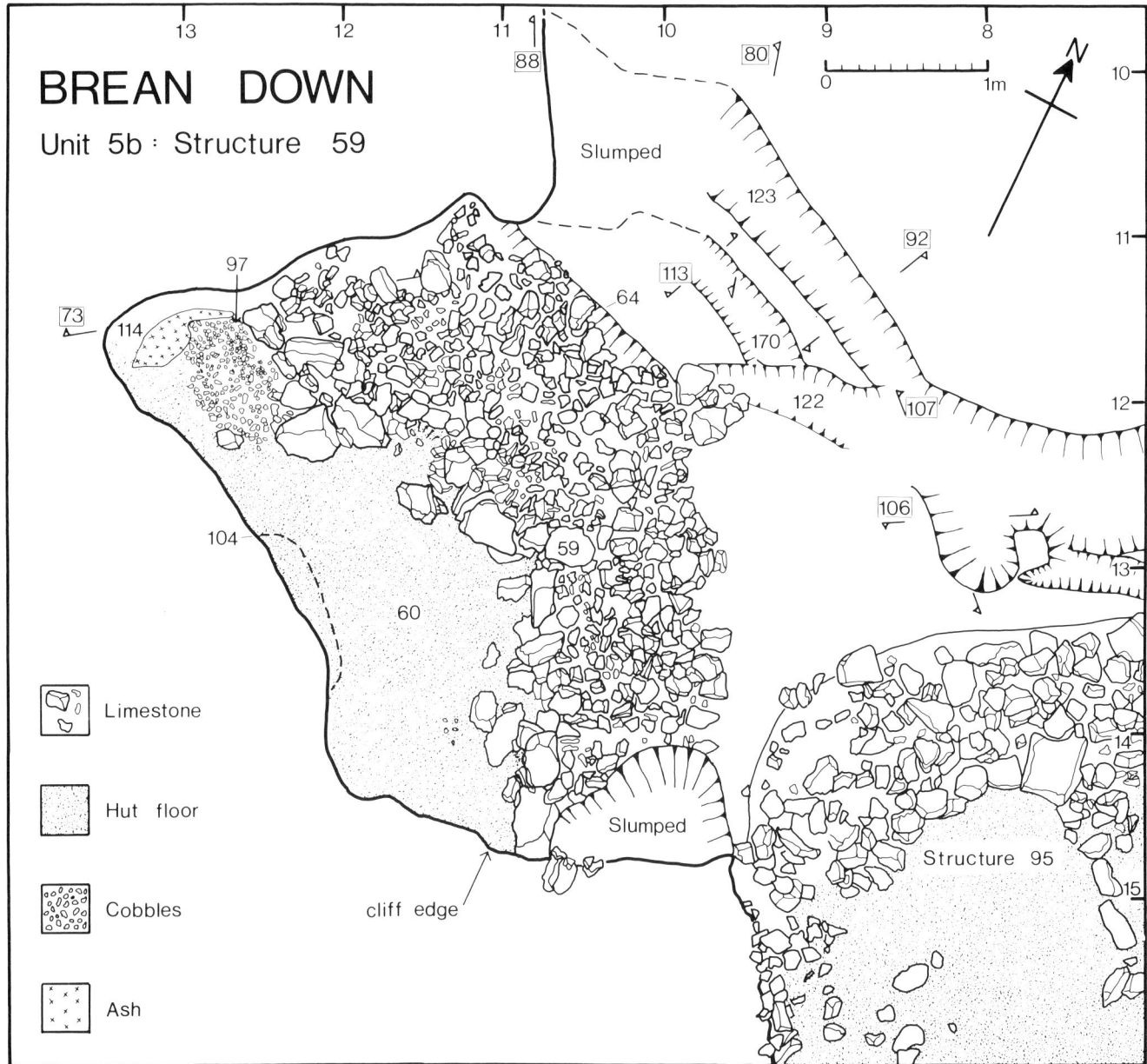

Fig 36 Plan of Structure 59

deep with a basal fill of 40mm of raw clay (169) overlain by 0.12m of sand (168). Gully 123 (Fig 37) was 0.5m wide and 0.45m deep with a sand fill (125) containing lenses of silty clay and an upper fill of ash (124). Figure 37, Section 80 suggests that the gully may well have been recut and a further section drawn in 1984 but not reproduced here shows at least three or four intersecting gully cuts in the position of 170 and 123. Both gullies were cut by the two latest recuts of the drip gully (122) round Structure 95 (Fig 37, Section 107). However, gully 123 came to an end against the wall of Structure 95 and gully 122 appeared to respect the wall (but not the gully) of 59. Presumably, therefore, the two structures are contemporary although it is possible that 95 remained in use longer than 59.

Sediments postdating Structure 59

When the structure went out of use the wall collapsed and blown sand infilled the terrace. Some of these sediments had already been stripped out by erosion before the excavation. The stabilisation surface (78) covered the terrace infill.

Structure 95

This structure was roughly circular with an internal diameter of between 5.6 and 6m. It consisted of a terrace with crescent-shaped stone wall and a level floor in the centre of which was a hearth. Round the periphery of the floor was a feature interpreted as a wall trench. There was a cobbled entrance facing south-east. Running round the back of the structure was a gully interpreted as a stormwater drain. The structure was well preserved apart from the erosion of a chord 1m wide on the west side. A 1984 drawing (Fig 6) shows the section revealed by this erosion. With hindsight it is evident that the section shows the terrace, floor, stone wall, and wall trench but in fact the structure was not recognised as such until its excavation in plan during 1985.

In all probability the earliest feature in the area of

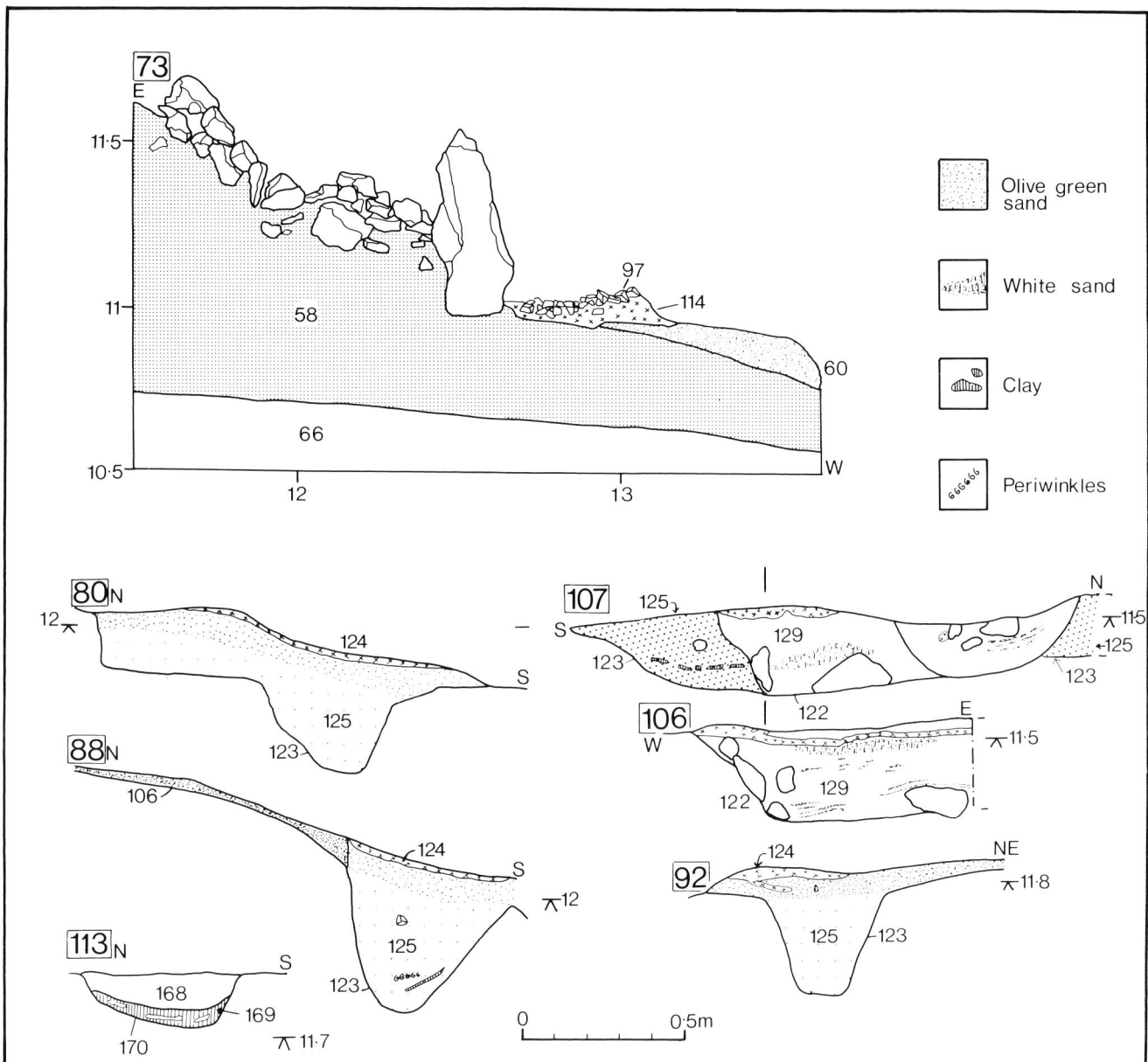

Fig 37 Sections relating to Structure 59

Structure 95 is the terrace (98) itself; this was cut up to 0.7m into the dune. Theoretically some of the features sealed by the floor could have been truncated by the terrace but, as explained below, this is unlikely to be true of all except perhaps 179, 175, and 149.

Features below the floor of Structure 95

These are shown by broken lines on Figure 38 and in section on Figure 39.

Context 179

A shallow pit or gully 0.9m long by 0.3m deep filled with various lenses of stained sand (180) and cut by wall trench 138 (Section 119).

Context 175

Shallow pit 0.5m by 0.4m and 0.23m deep with some grey silty clay in fill (176) and cut by wall trench 138.

Context 280

Irregular, poorly defined hollow 2m by 0.5m and 0.3m deep filled by 'dirty' yellow sand (165) with charcoal and limestone blocks and cut by Context 161. Contained illustrated sherds 20 and 21.

Context 161

Pit 1m by 0.38m and 0.38m deep. Fill (155) of sand with charcoal flecks. As Section 110 shows, compaction of the feature fill has caused ash and floor layers to settle into the feature; the resulting hollow has then been filled with limestone pieces and cobbles (154), which overlie the floor layers. Contained illustrated sherds 56 and 57, fired clay objects 119 and 120, and two bone pins, 42 and 43.

Context 158

Small pit or posthole 0.3m in diameter by 0.1m deep, fill (159) of laminated ash (Section 108).

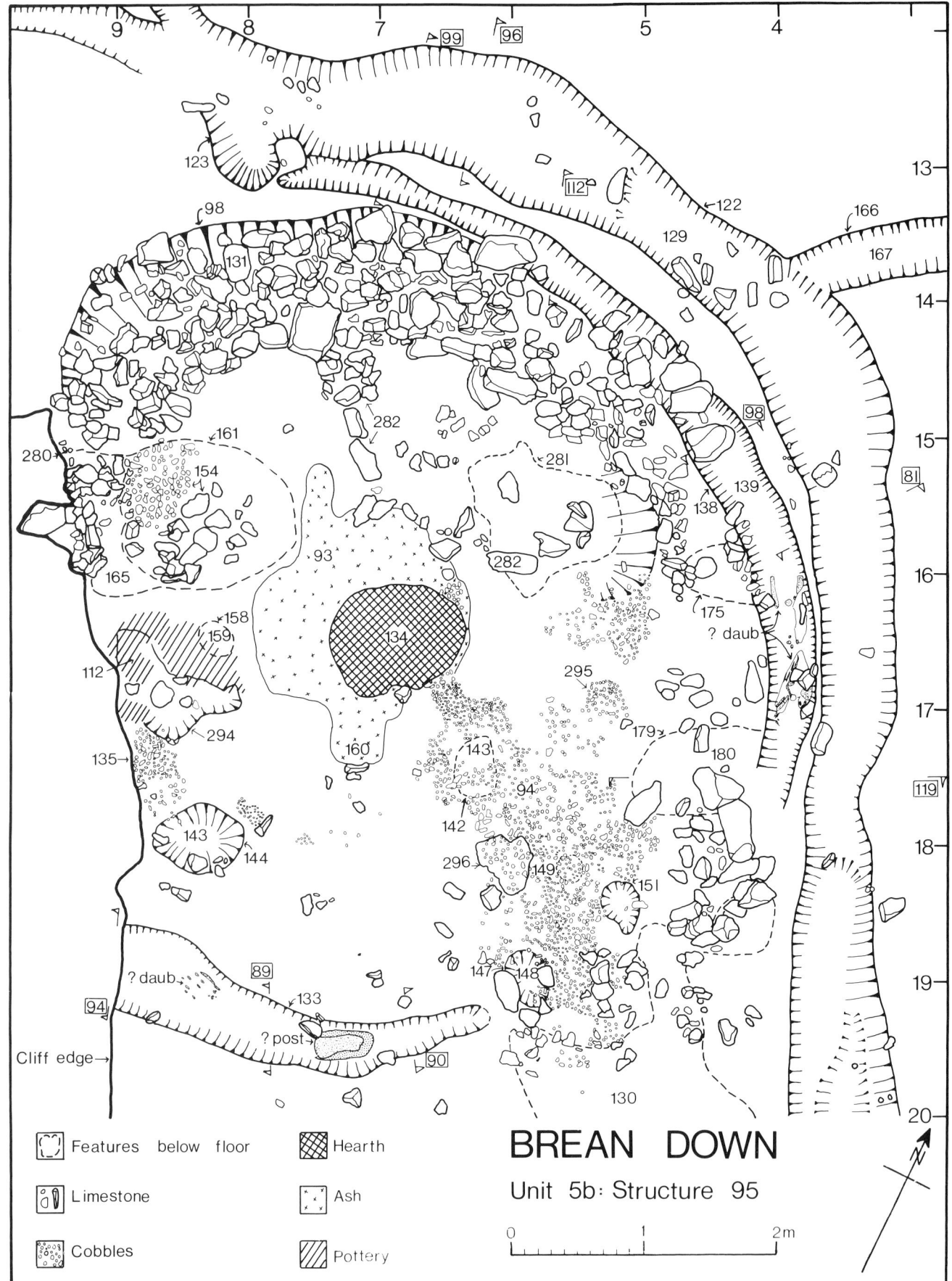

Fig 38　Plan of Structure 95

Context 142

Hollow 0.32m wide and 0.5m deep (Section 97) containing laminated ash (143) with a piece of repoussé-decorated bronze (5).

Context 149

Possible shallow posthole, diameter 0.18m, depth 0.2m, sealed by entrance cobbles (Section 103). Fill (148) contained a bone awl (47).

Context 130

An irregular area 2.4m by 1.4m and 0.15m deep outside structure entrance but partly sealed by entrance cobbles (Fig 15). Contained much hearth clay and ash which had clearly been used to fill up a hollow worn by passage.

Contexts 263, 264, 266, 267, and 265 (Fig 39)

Localised shallow intersecting scoops of depth c 0.1m filled with sand and ash. Some stratified below hearth, 134, others adjacent but below the floor.

Contexts 258, 259, 261, and 262 (Fig 39)

Stakeholes, diameter c 40mm, sealed below hearth but filled with hearth material. They clearly represent stakes driven through earlier hearths to support pots or other objects over the fire. A mass of stakeholes of similar description were found around a hearth at Nornour (Butcher 1978, 53).

Comment on features below the floor

Though the above features were all sealed by the floor or hearth of Structure 95 it is unlikely that they all predate the life of the structure. In fact, this is probably only the case with Contexts 179 and 175, which were cut by the wall trench; these two contexts, together with 149, are also set apart because they did not contain the distinctive hearth clay and ash which were found in the other features and in later Structure 95 contexts. The other features are thought to relate to early stages in the structure's life. What seems to have happened is that replacement of the hearth and perhaps floor was associated with the use of old hearth clay and briquetage to fill hollows which had worn in the floor, which were then sealed by a new floor.

Contexts contemporary with the floor (Sections on Fig 39)

Stone wall, Context 131

This was a crescent-shaped stone structure against the back face of the terrace (Fig 40). It was 4m long and 0.9m wide narrowing virtually to a point on the east side; the west side was eroded. An inner facing wall survived to an average height of two stones. There were a few large limestone blocks in the bottom course but on the whole the facing wall was noticeably less substantial than in Structure 59 and it was not set in a foundation trench. The triangular space between the inner face and the back of the terrace was filled with smaller limestone pieces and a rough outer face was formed by some rather larger pieces of limestone. A careful search was made for any possible continuation of the stone wall to the south, or evidence that it had been robbed in this area and had once completely surrounded Structure 95. Occasional stone blocks did occur round the periphery of the floor (Fig 40) but no evidence was found to suggest that the wall ever continued beyond the back face of the terrace. Illustrated artefacts from the stone wall are sherds 58 and 64, and briquetage pedestals 76 and 85.

Floor, Contexts 93 and 281

This was a compact, clearly defined, and generally level surface at 10.9m OD. It was a very dark greyish brown (10YR 3/2) made up of multiple localised laminae of sediment some of which were olive green (5G 7/2) stained. The total thickness averaged 0.1m. Generally speaking the floor surface was relatively clean of finds, most of which occurred in lenses and hollows within or at the base of the floor laminae. Context 281 was a particular concentration of ashy material and much briquetage in the lower part of the floor and below the floor just north of the hearth. Illustrated artefacts from the floor are briquetage pedestals 72, 73, 82, 84, 86, 88, 90, and 92, possible loomweights 117 and 115, a clay slab 121, and a fragment of repoussé decorated bronze 5. Forming part of the floor itself were a number of smaller contexts, as follows:

Hearth, Context 134

A well-made, roughly circular, silty clay platform 1m by 0.8m and 0.1 to 0.05m thick of distinctive reddish brown (10YR 4/3) colour. Within the laminated make-up of the hearth were occasional pale reddish orange (2.5YR 7/4) patches. A dome of laminated ash (Fig 39, Section 78) 90mm thick covered the hearth and its surround over an area 1.7 by 1.4m. Individual ash laminae were interbedded with the silty clay of the floor. The ash contained little macroscopically visible wood charcoal, which may suggest that, as elsewhere on the site (Chapter 16), some of it derived from the burning of peat. Within the ash dome was a lens of sand possibly representing an interruption in the hearth's use. On the south edge the ash extended into a shallow rectangular feature (160), 0.3 by 0.2m, on the south side of which was a stone set on edge. One is inclined to see this as a deliberate feature, perhaps an ash box or a position in which something like a pot could be set next to the hearth.

Pottery concentration, Context 112

A hollow within the floor 0.75 by 0.5m in diameter and up to 0.3m deep. It contained light yellowish brown sandy silt with large numbers of pottery

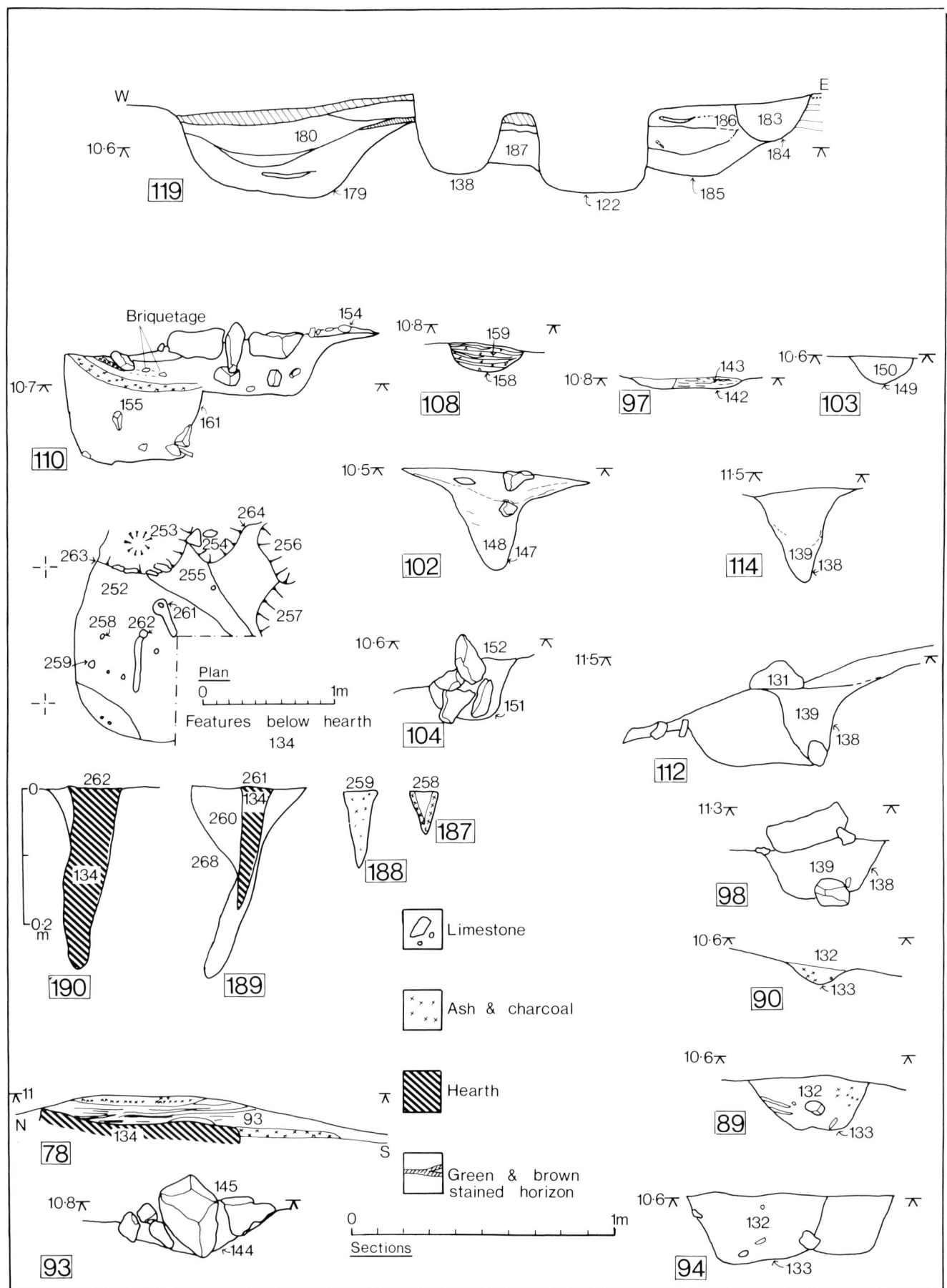

Fig 39 Sections relating to Structure 95

Fig 40 Structure 95 from the south-east during the early stages of excavation (photo: M J Allen)

sherds (as shown on Fig 38). Some lay in a hollow at the base of the floor but others were within individual laminae of the floor, so the feature and the pottery are clearly contemporary with the floor. Part of Context 112 had been cut away by a shallow scoop to the south (294) which may account for the incomplete vessels. Illustrated artefacts include pottery nos 22–34, 53, 54, and 65, three pieces of briquetage pedestal (72, 83, and 88–90) and joining fragments of a briquetage tray (98–101), and a slate tool (35).

Context 144

Hollow within the floor 0.64 by 0.58m and 0.2m deep, containing yellowish brown (10YR 5/4) sand and large and medium limestone blocks (Fig 39, Section 93).

Context 282

In the north-east quadrant of the structure some limestone blocks were set in the floor (Fig 38). Four of these formed a rough radial line but the others were not in a clear alignment; however, they roughly delimited an arc with straight sides of 2m and 1.3m. This, together with the rather more uneven nature of the floor in this area, may imply that it was divided off from the rest of the floor.

Context 154

A hollow in the floor 0.8m in diameter had been formed by compaction of the fill of Context 161 (Fig 39, Section 110) and was filled with large stones which projected through the floor. Adjacent was a patch of cobbles 0.7m in diameter.

Cobbles, Contexts 135 and 94

Figure 38 shows a number of other localised cobble patches. The main concentration was in a very irregular strip 3m long by 1m wide from just outside the entrance to the hearth. Several distinct patches of cobbling testified to successive attempts to consolidate a worn and probably sometimes muddy entrance.

Wall trench, Contexts 133 and 138

At the edge of the circular floor was a trench (Fig 41) which was dimly perceived in places but could not be delimited clearly until the floor was largely excavated. On the south side the trench was up to 0.4m wide and 0.2m deep. Figure 39, Section 94 implies that the feature had been recut. It became shallower approaching the entrance and there may have been some erosion of the floor and wall trench at its south edge. The slot was interrupted by the south-east facing entrance, from where it ran upslope, becoming more V-shaped, and was 0.25m wide by 0.34m deep, its deeper profile here supporting the idea of some

Fig 41   Structure 95 showing wall trench, stormwater gully, hearth, and terrace wall (photo: M J Allen)

truncation on the south side. The slot ran *outside* the main terrace wall (131) and appeared to terminate on the north side of the structure. This may be illusory, as the area between Structures 59 and 95 had an intersecting palimpsest of gullies relating to the two structures. This area was especially difficult to resolve because sand had filtered into the vacuous interstices of the two walls, blurring the features. Furthermore, there had been some recent erosion of the area between the two structures. Some limestone blocks partly or wholly overlay the slot (Figs 38 and 39, Sections 112 and 98). These blocks (north-west of Section 98) were, however, slightly separate from the stone wall (131) so there is uncertainty as to whether they are *in situ*.

When about 0.1m of sandy trench fill (132 and 139) had been removed, linear patches of silty clay appeared in two areas (Figs 42 and 43). In places these patches were parallel to the sides of the trench but one ran diagonally across the axis of the trench. These patches are suggestive of daub cladding on a wattlework wall. Within the trench fill west of the entrance was an oval patch of stained sand 0.4 by 0.2m (Fig 42). This might represent the shadow of a vertical element such as a plank or post, but no other evidence of such elements was found suggesting that, apart from the entrance posts, the walls were of wattle and daub. Illustrated artefacts are sherds of briquetage vessels (103, 104, and 108), two coprolites (Fig 153.8 and 9), and a shale pebble (36).

Entrance postholes, Contexts 151 and 147

There was a 0.6m wide entrance facing south-east and flanked by two postholes (Fig 39, Sections 102, 104). Posthole 147 was 0.23 by 0.28m and 0.37m deep. Posthole 151 was 0.3 by 0.4m and 0.24m deep. Both postholes had stone packing round the top. The entrance and a strip up to the hearth was cobbled (94) and in places the irregular cobbling extended up to 0.7m outside the entrance, but there was certainly no evidence of a porch. Just outside the entrance was the already noted hollow worn by passage (131) which had been filled with ash and hearth clay and was overlain on one edge by cobbles.

Gullies

Context 122

This ran concentrically with the back wall of Structure 95 and between 0.3 and 0.05m outside the wall trench 138. Its interpretation as a stormwater gully is supported by the fact that it did not enclose the southern side but ran off downslope. It was U-shaped, between 0.7 and 0.4m wide and varying in depth between 0.27 and 0.5m. Sections through the gully (Fig 44) show a varying number of recuts, three in Section 99, two in Section 96, and one in Section 81.

The gully fill (129) was largely yellow (10YR 8/6) sand with distinctive staining of brownish yellow (10YR 6/6) and reddish yellow (7.5YR 8/6) and bands of fine ash. Such characteristics picked out individual edges and layers within features which were otherwise sometimes virtually invisible. As Section 107 (Fig 37) shows, the last two recuts of 122 cut the gully (123) round Structure 59. Gullies of the two structures did, however, respect one another; they each terminated against the other's stone walls and the latest recut of 122 became shallower and was deflected to the north as it approached Structure 59, presumably so that water did not drain into that structure. Illustrated artefacts are briquetage pedestals 75 and 93.

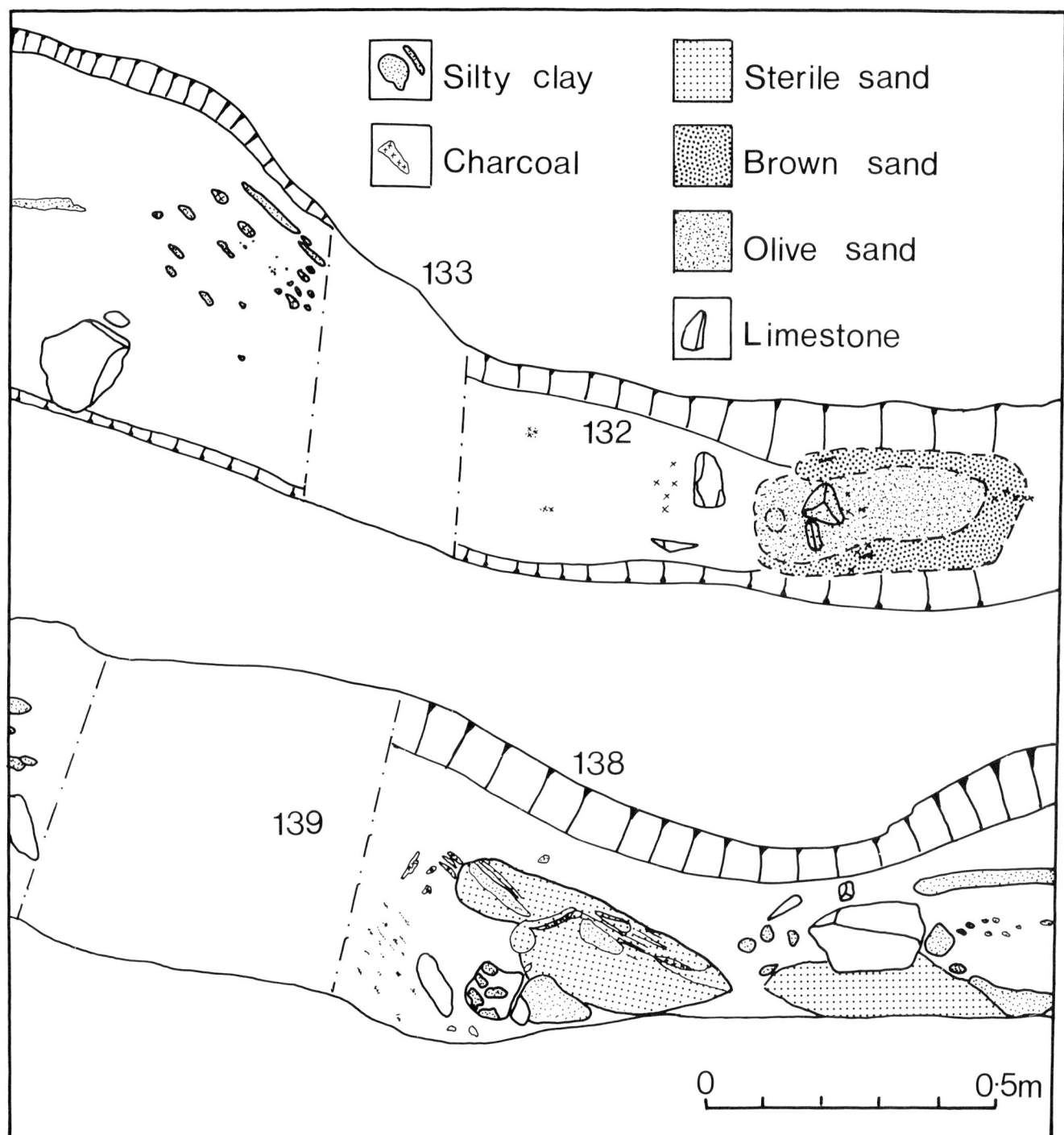

Fig 42   Plan of the wall trench of Structure 95

Fig 43   Wall trench (139) of Structure 95 showing silty clay patches (photo: M J Allen)

Contexts 184, 185, and 187

Section 119 (Fig 39) revealed the existence on the east side of a somewhat bewildering series of gully cuts which are thought likely to be predecessors of Context 122. It was impossible to resolve these in plan.

Context 166

A gully east of Structure 95 (Fig 38) to which it is probably not related. It was U-shaped, 0.43m wide, and 0.22m deep with a fill (167) of yellow brown (10YR 5/4) sand. It was cut by gully 122. Bearing in mind the intersecting gully arcs of Structures 59 and 95 it is just possible that a third structure lay to the east of the excavated area, and there are further hints of this in the form of hearth debris revealed at this horizon to the east by the auger survey (Chapter 8).

Contexts south of Structure 95

Context 116

Hollow at the base of Unit 5b, diameter 2.3m, but truncated to the west by the cliff, depth 0.2m. Fill (115) of sand with some occupation material including a distinct patch of charcoal (128). The existence of much hearth debris in this feature suggests that, although it is at the very base of Unit 5b, it may well be contemporary with the early phases of Structure 95. Illustrated artefacts are sherd 61, one coprolite (Fig 153.13), and two sherds of briquetage vessels (106 and 114).

Contexts 77 and 113

Overlying Context 116 was an irregular spread of ash and sand (77) up to 0.1m thick. The ash was similar to that forming a dome over the hearth (134) and, together with the presence of hearth clay, suggests that this represents hearth detritus probably removed from Structure 95. Illustrated artefacts are sherd 55 and a fragment of copper alloy wire (6); another tiny (unillustrated) fragment of copper alloy (177) was found in 1984. 1.6m to the east was a smaller patch 0.8 by 0.55m of similar material (113).

Sediments postdating Structure 95

Figure 44, Section 60 shows the sediments infilling the terrace of Structure 95; these are described from the bottom upwards.

Context 91

Green (10YR 7/6) stained pure sand which formed a layer 30–40mm thick over the floor and a crescent-shaped small dune against the north-west side of the terrace. This gave the impression that sand may have blown in through the door after abandonment but while the walls were still standing.

Context 105

This is not shown on the section; it was silty sand abutting tumbled limestone from the terrace wall. The silt component *might* suggest that this layer was partly derived from collapsed daub walls. Contained a bone awl (50).

Context 79

Triangle of sand infilling the back of the terrace, containing illustrated sherd 63.

Context 92

Burnt sand and stone collapsed from the stone wall.

Additional finds

In the early stages of defining Structure 95 a few artefacts were simply assigned to this number; they are thought to derive from sand and limestone wall collapse in the terrace. They include the following illustrated pieces: pottery sherds 59, 60, and 62, and a flint scraper 23.

Context 53

In addition to the closely defined contexts recorded above, 53 was a general number assigned to the

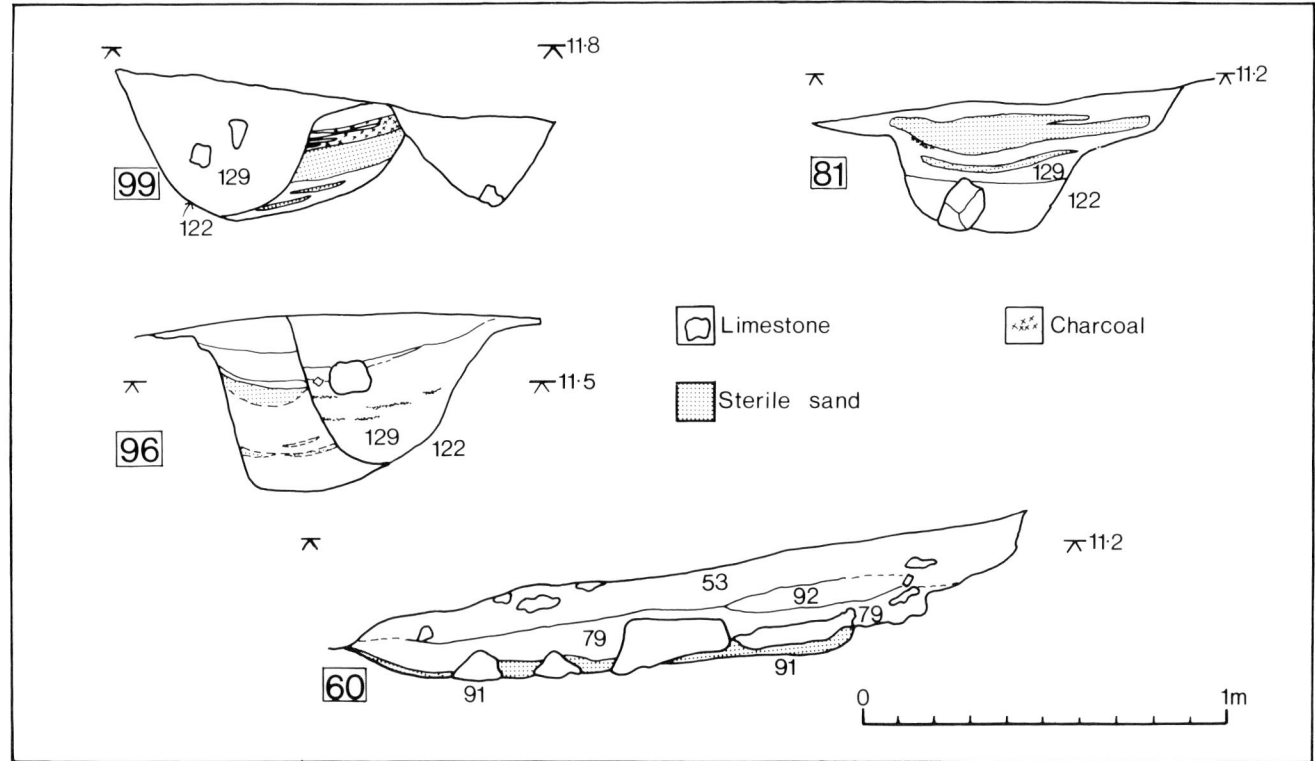

Fig 44 Sections of the stormwater gully and terrace fill of Structure 95

spread of occupation evidence making up Unit 5b. The following illustrated finds were assigned to this context: sherds 35–52; briquetage pedestal fragments 74, 75, 77, 79, 81, 87, 91, and 94; fragments of briquetage vessels 102, 105, and 107; clay ball 124; possible loom weight 116; flint scraper 24; bone objects 48, 54, and 68; copper alloy wire 6; and illustrated coprolites, Figure 153.2–7, 12, and 15–16.

Context 78

As already noted, this was a hard crust apparently representing a stabilisation surface which overlay and postdated Structures 95 and 59 and all the other contexts in Unit 5b.

Discussion and interpretation of the structures in Unit 5b

Structure 95

The critical question is whether we are dealing with a timber building represented by the wall trench, which was replaced by a stone building represented by the stone wall (Context 131). Certainly there are parallels for such a sequence at Holne Moor where a middle Bronze Age wooden structure was replaced in stone (Fleming 1988, 82). Such an interpretation finds a measure of support in that some possibly *in situ* stones of the wall overlay the wall trench. Assignment of the wall trench to an early phase in the life of the structure could also be suggested by the difficulty in delimiting parts of it until the floor had been largely excavated. Even so, the floor would probably have been laid, and certainly repaired, after construction of the walls, thus completely covering the inner edge of the wall trench. Furthermore, the floor and walls both incorporated silty clay introduced to the site for building purposes, so wall collapse may have further obscured the wall's position. The floor of a timber phase building preceding construction of the terrace would have sloped at c 10° which would be unusual among Bronze Age structures, which generally have a level terrace floor. Most importantly, a careful search produced no evidence that the stone wall had ever continued completely round the structure; it also appeared too insubstantial to have been carried to any height and thus to have represented the main wall. It seems more likely that its basic function was to retain the unstable sand face at the back of the terrace; consequently it seems that the stone wall and the wall trench are of a single structural phase.

Perhaps it will be considered curious that the terrace retaining wall is internal rather than external to the structure and perhaps more curious still that the structure itself was built on a slope and only the floor was terraced in. In fact the base of the wall trench runs upslope, from 10.30m OD on the south side to 11.34m OD on the north side. Though initially curious, these arrangements find an interesting parallel in many of the middle Bronze Age so-called Deverel-Rimbury houses on the Wessex and Sussex chalk. Originally it was assumed that the structures at Itford Hill (Burstow and Holleyman 1957) and Shearplace Hill (Rahtz and ApSimon 1962) were small circular buildings with their walls represented by a ring of postholes. This interpretation was challenged independently by Avery and Close Brooks (1969) and by Musson (1970), who showed that the post-ring represented internal supports within a larger structure, the outer wall of which was represented at Shearplace Hill by a wall slot. Guilbert (1981) has subsequently demonstrated the widespread nature of such double ring structures in Bronze Age and Iron Age Britain. The key point as far as the Brean structure is concerned is Musson's (1970) argument that at Itford Hill and Amberley Mount the floor included the whole of the terraced area with a wall, now lost by erosion, on the back of the terrace. Subsequent excavations at Black Patch have confirmed that the entire terraced area was roofed, although in this case Drewett (1982a) argued that the rafters rested directly on the back of the terrace rather than on a low wall. Perhaps Brean Structure 95 should be seen as a translation of the constructional technique inferred by Musson to an unstable sand site where a retaining wall for the back of the terrace was essential.

The Brean building is not, however, a carbon copy of a chalkland Deverel-Rimbury house since it lacks convincing evidence for their most conspicuous structural feature, the ring of posts now interpreted as internal roof supports. Double ring structures with internal roof supports are widespread in the middle Bronze Age, as for instance in the waterlogged roundhouse foundations on peat at Chapel Tump Farm, Gwent (A Whittle and S Green, pers comm) and the internal post-rings within the stone houses of the south-west. The only postholes within Brean Structure 95 (eg Figs 38.158, 142, and 149) were slight and below the floor, except for the posts flanking the entrance. One possibility, however, is that internal posts stood directly on the floor or on stone pads, which would be logical in view of the underlying soft sand. A large piece of limestone just inside the entrance (296) could be a post-pad and the positions of others might be marked by the stone-filled feature (144), the stone pier (282) projecting from the terrace wall, and possibly also by some of the cobbled patches (154, 135, and 295). The last in particular is roughly circular and suggests a patch of cobbling protected below a post or stone. These possible post-bases do all lie roughly on a circle 4m in diameter, the centre of which corresponds to the roughly circular area delimited by the wall trench. But this evidence is too insubstantial to allow the conclusive inference of the existence of a post-ring.

Indeed such a ring is not necessary in a building of this size (P Reynolds, pers comm), as is demonstrated by the reconstructions of the Maiden Castle house at Butser (Reynolds 1979) and Iron Age houses at Castell Henllys, Dyfed. The possibilities for the walling of Brean Structure 95 are a ring of close-set posts, or planks, or a wattlework wall. Despite a careful search, no evidence was found to suggest that substantial posts or planks had been set in the trench, with the possible exception of the oval area of sand shown on Figure 42. Instead the distinctive pattern of silty clay patches seems much more likely to derive from daub covering on wattlework walls. The remarkable strength of such basketwork walls (Reynolds 1979; Musson 1970) does not rely very much on the rigidity of the vertical members, which as a consequence do not require deep foundations. Basketwork walls based on stakeholes or posts rather than wall trenches may be inferred at Trevisker (ApSimon and Greenfield 1972) and at Gwithian in the Beaker structure in layer 8 (Megaw 1976) and in the middle/late Bronze Age in layer 3 (Thomas 1958).

Though the wall trench at Brean is notably better preserved than elsewhere it is nonetheless a familiar middle Bronze Age architectural technique, seen for instance in the outer wall at Shearplace Hill (Avery and Close Brookes 1969), Hog Cliff Down (Ellison and Rahtz 1987), and Stackpole Warren, Dyfed (Williams 1986). During the Iron Age wall trench structures, sometimes without evidence of internal roof supports, became widespread, as for instance at Little Waltham (Drury 1978) and Cat's Water (Pryor 1984).

It should be noted that the wall trench does not delimit a precisely circular area, but instead extends slightly uphill in an oval. Such subcircular structures are represented in timber by Trevisker House A (ApSimon and Greenfield 1972) and in stone at Shaugh Moor House 15 (Wainwright and Smith 1980). The juxtaposition between the wall trench and the surrounding gully, interpreted as a stormwater drain, suggests that the eaves projected no more than 0.5 to 0.6m beyond the wall line, possibly rather less in view of the closely adjacent nature of Structures 95 and 59 which appear to have been contemporary. Peter Reynolds suggests (pers comm) that this implies a wall only c 1m high, otherwise the wall base would have been too exposed to the weather.

A hypothetical reconstruction of Structure 95 is shown in cross-section on Figure 45 and as part of a more general reconstruction of life in Unit 5b in Figure 50. In addition to the conclusions reached in the foregoing discussion these reconstructions make the following assumptions which are based in part on the results of experimental reconstructions of Iron Age buildings at Butser (Reynolds 1979; 1982):

i The roof pitch was c 45°.
ii A differing wall height would have been necessary to produce a level wall plate. The wall height above the base of the wall trench is assumed therefore to have been c 1.6m on the south side and c 0.7m on the north side.
iii There was a wall plate on top of the wattlework walls.

Structure 59

Since only one-third of this building remained it presents much greater problems of interpretation. The critical question is whether it represents a similar construction technique to Structure 95 or a basically stone-walled structure. To some extent this hinges on a rather enigmatic small gully (Fig 36.170) the basal fill of which was silty clay somewhat reminiscent of the supposed daub in the wall trench round Structure 95. However, Context 170 was shallower, much less clearly defined, and further from the stone wall. It seems more likely to have been a stormwater gully rather than a wall trench. If so, we must consider whether in this instance the stone wall does represent a structural wall rather than simply a retaining wall for the terrace. Certainly Structure 59 had much more substantial facing blocks set in a foundation trench, like the Stannon Down stone houses (Mercer 1970); also the facing wall survived to a greater height and

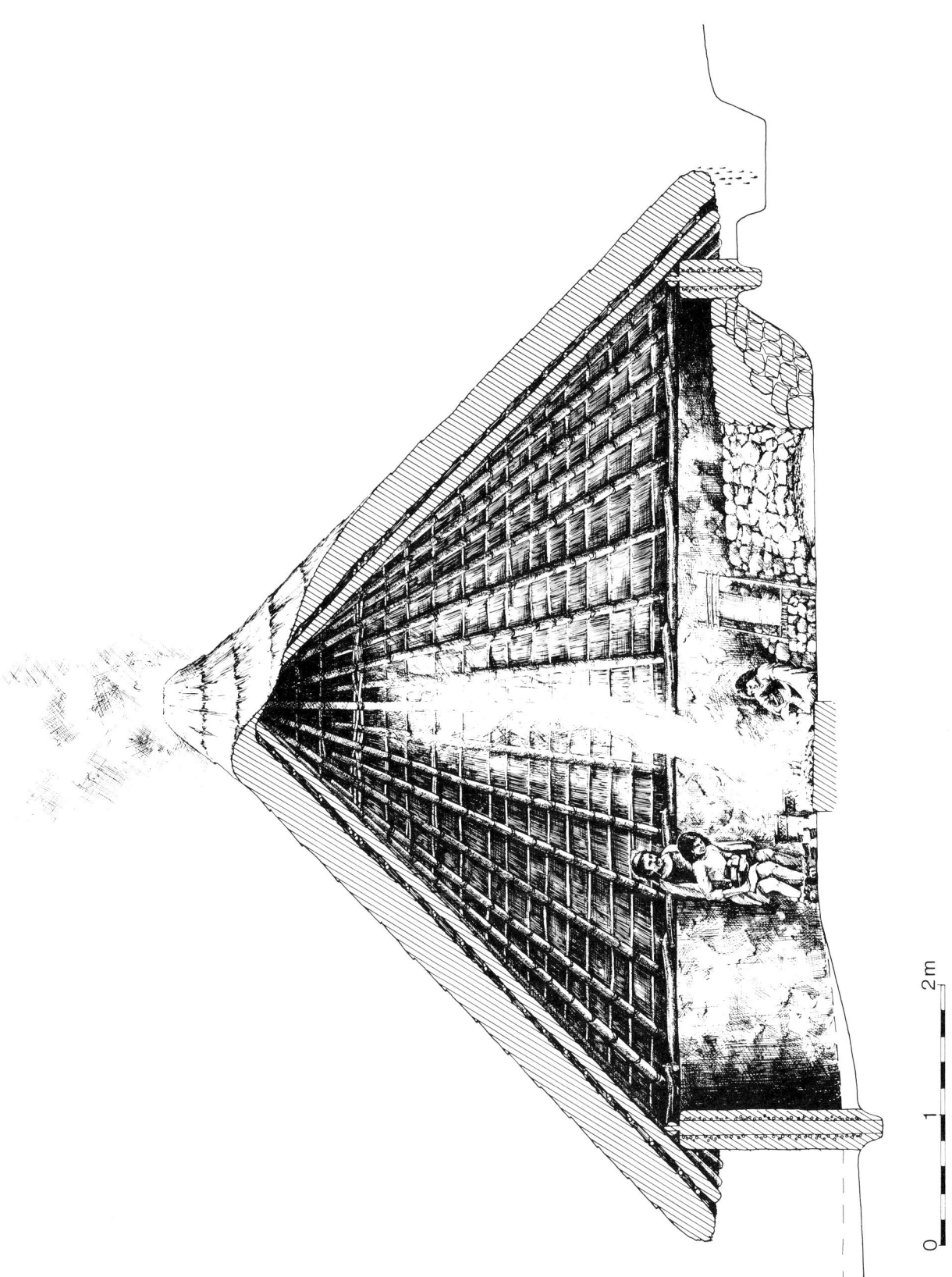

Fig 45 Hypothetical reconstruction of Structure 95 in cross-section

the terrace fill contained a much greater proportion of tumble. Furthermore, unlike Structure 95, the surviving side of the doorway was constructed of stone, including one large block set vertically as a door-post. Because the structure is fragmentary we clearly cannot be absolutely confident that Structure 59 had walls entirely of stone, but this does seem to be the most probable interpretation.

Comparable structures in the south-west are the hut circles of Dartmoor (Wainwright and Smith 1980; Fleming 1988) and Bodmin Moor (Mercer 1970), or the Scilly Isles sites such as Nornour (Butcher 1978) or Halangy Porth (Ashbee 1983). The experimental reconstruction of the Conderton House, a building of similar type though larger and of Iron Age date, has been discussed by Reynolds (1982). The reconstruction drawing of Brean Unit 5b (Fig 50) assumes a basically stone building rather smaller than Structure 95 but with a similar wall height, roof pitch, and conical thatched roof. If our conclusions regarding its stone walls are correct, then it is interesting and puzzling that two apparently contemporary and so closely adjacent structures were constructed in such totally different ways.

The date of Unit 5b

As Ann Woodward shows in Chapter 11, many of the characteristic features of the large pottery assemblages from Unit 5b are matched most clearly in the Trevisker series of the south-west. A relatively late date in the Trevisker spectrum is suggested typologically. Other ceramic traits are matched by Deverel-Rimbury material in Wessex.

Four radiocarbon dates are available for Unit 5b. The earliest, 3420 ± 100 BP (HAR-7016), is from Context 103, a pit below the floor of Structure 59. Charcoal from the overlying floor (Context 60) gave a result of 2730 ± 100 BP (HAR-7017). Two dates are available from Structure 95, one from charcoal within the stone wall (Context 131), 2940 ± 100 BP (HAR-7019), the other from burning (Context 93) associated with the hearth, 2870 ± 80 BP (HAR-7018). The three dates from Structures 59 and 95 are not statistically separable and can be combined to give an uncalibrated date of 2847 ± 65 BP. The date from Context 103 is significantly earlier and it has already been noted that this feature could relate to a phase of activity predating Structure 59. On balance, however, this is not considered likely. Context 103 contained ash which is thought likely to relate to activities within the structure itself at an early stage in its life. If that is so, then it is probable that Structure 59, which is believed to have been of stone, was originally constructed much earlier than the largely wooden Structure 95. This perhaps helps to explain the differing constructional styles of the two buildings. The fact that the gullies of both structures appear to respect one another shows that at one stage they were in contemporary use, and the radiocarbon evidence confirms that this was the case during the ninth century BC uncalibrated.

Though the hypothesis of an earlier origin for Structure 59 is attractive it raises other problems. The stabilisation surfaces upslope of the structures in Unit 5b were poorly developed as Richard Macphail's contribution (Chapter 16) shows, and it would perhaps be surprising if they marked an occupation surface with a life of five or six hundred years. This might, however, be explained if some erosion had occurred of the Unit 5b surface in that area.

Artefact distributions and activity areas in Unit 5b

Recent research has demonstrated that several middle Bronze Age settlements in southern England show a high degree of patterning in artefacts and structure types which has proved the basis for inferences about function and social structure (Ellison 1981; 1987; Drewett 1982a; Tomalin 1982). In evaluating the Unit 5b evidence in the context of the various hypotheses put forward by these authors, we must have due regard to the nature and problems of the archaeological record. Bonnichsen's (1973) study of Millie's Camp highlighted the imperfections of the record in reconstructing activity patterns, and Simms' recent (1988) ethnoarchaeological study of a Bedouin camp showed that certain areas were kept very clean and many activities left no archaeologically recoverable trace. Particular attention also needs to be paid to the role of taphonomic factors, eg dogs, trampling, aeolian activity, etc in the formation of the record. In what may seem, by comparison with the southern English middle Bronze Age evidence, to be a somewhat pessimistic discussion Whittle *et al* (1986, 135) recently highlighted the effect of pre-depositional, depositional, and post-depositional factors affecting artefact distributions on hut floors. In reconstructing activity areas the critical question is the origin of the artefacts themselves: to use Schiffer's (1976; 1987) definitions, whether they are primary (deposited at the location of use), secondary (dumped away from the location of use), or *de facto* (abandoned within an activity area). These concepts have been percipiently discussed in a British context by both Drewett (1982a; 1982b) and Pryor (1980a). Brean offers particular potential for the further archaeological investigation of these questions, firstly because the evidence is more securely stratified than on the average chalkland Deverel-Rimbury site, secondly because virtually all the artefacts were three-dimensionally recorded, and thirdly because we can compare the artefactual evidence with environmental evidence including sediment chemistry and magnetic susceptibility.

The distribution of artefacts in Unit 5b is shown in Figures 46–49, augmented by some more detailed distributions in the chapters below on the artefactual and environmental evidence. Figure 50 represents a hypothetical reconstruction of life in Unit 5b based on evidence outlined in this chapter.

Structure 95

A general point to make about the distributions as a whole is the absence of material in the central area of the floor which was clearly kept very clean up to the

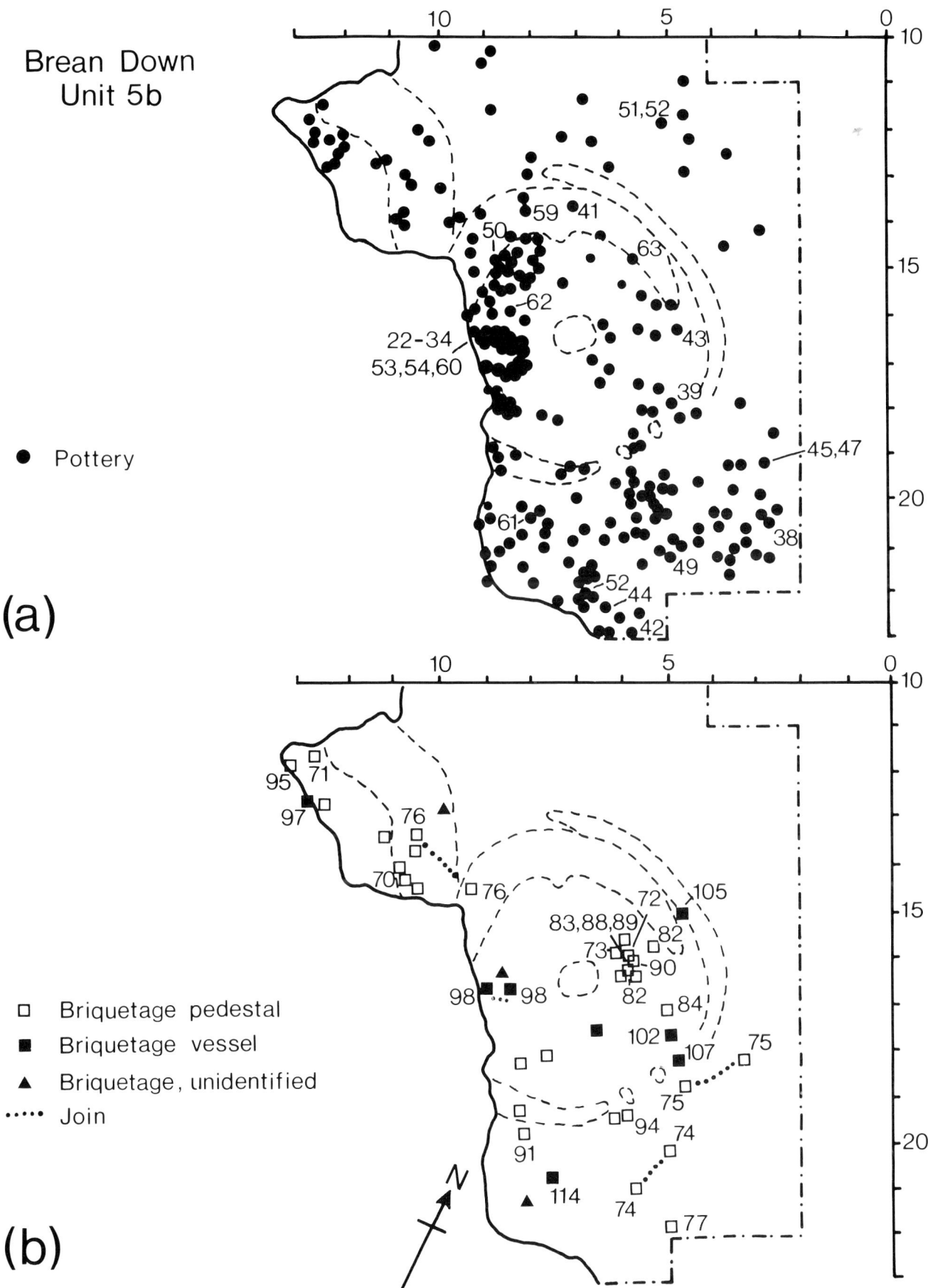

Fig 46 Unit 5b structures: distribution of (a) pottery (for the distribution of different fabrics see Fig 102b) and (b) briquetage; the numbers show the position of illustrated finds of the relevant artefact type

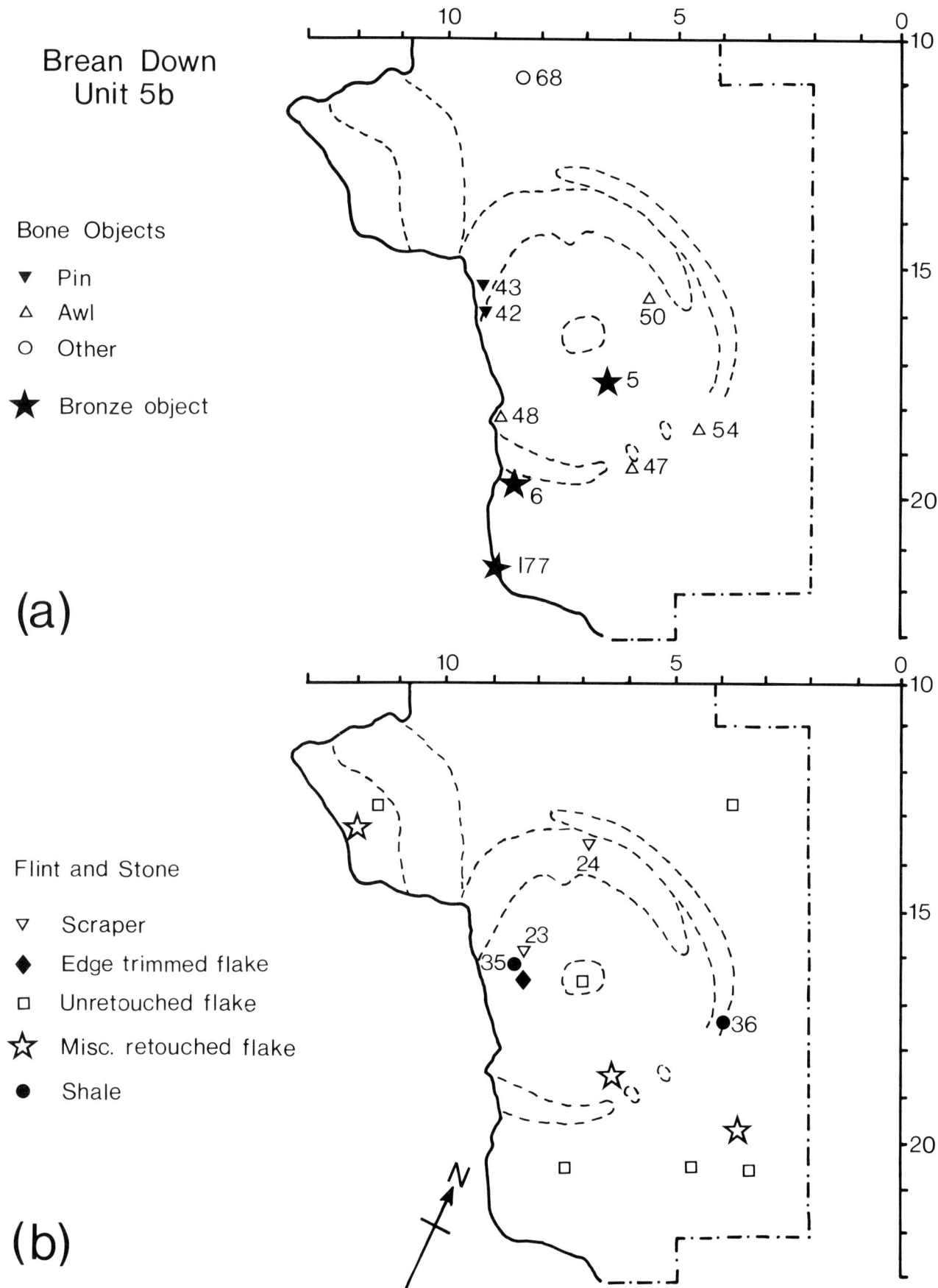

Fig 47 Unit 5b structures: distribution of (a) bone and metal artefacts and (b) flint and stone artefacts; the numbers show the position of illustrated finds of the relevant artefact type

time when the structure was abandoned. Artefacts were concentrated round the periphery, as is shown particularly by the distributions of bones (Fig 48b) and pottery (Fig 46a); something similar, though less pronounced, is seen in Black Patch, Hut 3 (Drewett 1982a, fig 10). Schiffer (1987, 299) notes that such a fringe of small abraded artefacts round the walls characterises structures without secondary (post-abandonment) refuse deposits.

The pottery from Structure 95 was concentrated in the area west of the hearth, with the major concentration in Context 112. Much of this pottery came from just four exuberantly decorated pots (22–25). The question is whether this pottery was dumped as secondary rubbish to fill an inconvenient hole in the floor or whether it is primary rubbish relating to activities which took place more or less at this point. The latter interpretation is favoured because the four pots, though not complete, were represented by many pieces, and parts of the vessels must have been removed by a later feature (294) which cut into 112. It was evident from the relationship between the sherds and the individual laminae of floor sediment that successive episodes of pot deposition had taken place here and nowhere else on the hut floor. Furthermore, the pottery concentration west of the hearth is associated with a lesser concentration of bone (Fig 48b) and hearth fragments (Fig 49b). It may be significant that the dome of ash (93) above the hearth spreads well beyond it to west and north but is confined to its edge on the east side. All this suggests that the area west of the hearth was used for cooking activities and food preparation. Perhaps pots were stored in the shallow hollow (112), or rested there to cool when they had been taken from the hearth. Occasional breakages may perhaps simply have been trampled into the base of the hollow.

In direct contrast to the pottery distribution was that of briquetage pedestals (Fig 46b) which were concentrated north-east of the hearth in an ash-filled hollow within the floor. This situation, together with their broken nature, shows they were not *de facto* rubbish. Yet the fact that briquetage occurs with ash both here and just outside the entrance clearly suggests that the briquetage relates to activities which took place within Structure 95 itself. Other briquetage fragments were found elsewhere within the floor area. It may be significant that there were no briquetage vessel sherds in the hollow which contained most of the pedestals. Briquetage vessels were as a whole less well represented than pedestals so perhaps, together with their contained cake of salt, they were mostly taken elsewhere for consumption or exchange, as was certainly the case with the more substantial salt containers of the Iron Age (Morris 1985). In Chapter 14 it is considered probable that ordinary domestic pottery was used to carry and store the saline liquor from the estuary, and perhaps even to carry out some form of pre-evaporation, as van den Broeke (1986) has argued for Iron Age sites in the Netherlands. Nonetheless it does not seem to us likely that the main concentration of pottery in Structure 95 relates in any direct way to the salt extraction process because within the structure the pottery and briquetage have such different distributions.

The Brean evidence suggests, therefore, that the final stages of salt extraction took place within the same structure as cooking and food preparation, though perhaps on a different segment of the floor area. The association of these two hearth-based activities seems logical in view of the necessity in salt extraction to keep a constant watch in order to maintain the fire, prevent boiling, and top up the gradually evaporating liquor. This association between salt extraction and a wider range of other activities in Structure 95, and probably also in Structure 59, is the basis for our contention that at Bronze Age Brean salt extraction was a cottage industry. In this respect it may contrast with 'Red Hill' sites which emerged in the later Iron Age and Romano-British periods, both on the Somerset Levels (Leech 1981b) and in Essex (de Brisay 1978).

Flint was neither being worked nor apparently used to any great extent in the excavated area of Unit 5b (Fig 47b). The assemblage is impoverished and in direct contrast to the many flints within the broadly contemporary Black Patch settlement (Drewett 1982a) which is admittedly on chalk. In Structure 95 there were only two typologically distinct tools, both scrapers (23 and 24), and the condition of 23 is such that Alan Saville argues (Chapter 13) that it may be residual. There was also a rather fine shale scraper (35) from the structure. The paucity of lithic evidence seems unlikely to result purely from curation (Binford 1976); this implies that metal was used to a greater extent than on the chalk sites, which would be logical in view of the site's position on the border of the Highland Zone. Certainly many of the bones in Unit 5b had exceptionally delicate cut marks which it is thought were made with metal tools. If so metal objects were being very carefully curated; the only metalwork finds were tiny fragments of repoussé-decorated bronze strip (5) and bronze wire (6). The size and findspot of these pieces are consistent with their being fragments of broken objects which became trapped in hollows or cracks in the floor, thus presumably primary rubbish.

The paucity of scrapers supports Bruce Levitan's contention (Chapter 20), based on the paucity of horncores and phalanges, that hides were being prepared elsewhere. Subsequent stages of leather-working may, however, have taken place in Structure 95 because there were several bone awls, pins, and points (Chapter 14) around the periphery of the floor (Fig 47a).

Dog coprolites were very few within Structure 95 by comparison with the area outside (Fig 48a), as one might predict. There was, however, one coprolite from the floor, one from the terrace wall, and three from the wall trench. Thus, despite obvious attempts at cleanliness, it is clear from the evidence for human intestinal parasites within dog coprolites, and from a possible human coprolite (5681, Context 53, exact findspot not recorded) that this faecal material in and around the domestic structures played a part in perpetuating the cycle of parasite infestation.

Phosphate values are higher within Structure 95 than outside (Fig 124), in complete contrast to the distribution of coprolites. This makes it unlikely that high values reflect the use of Structure 95 as a latrine

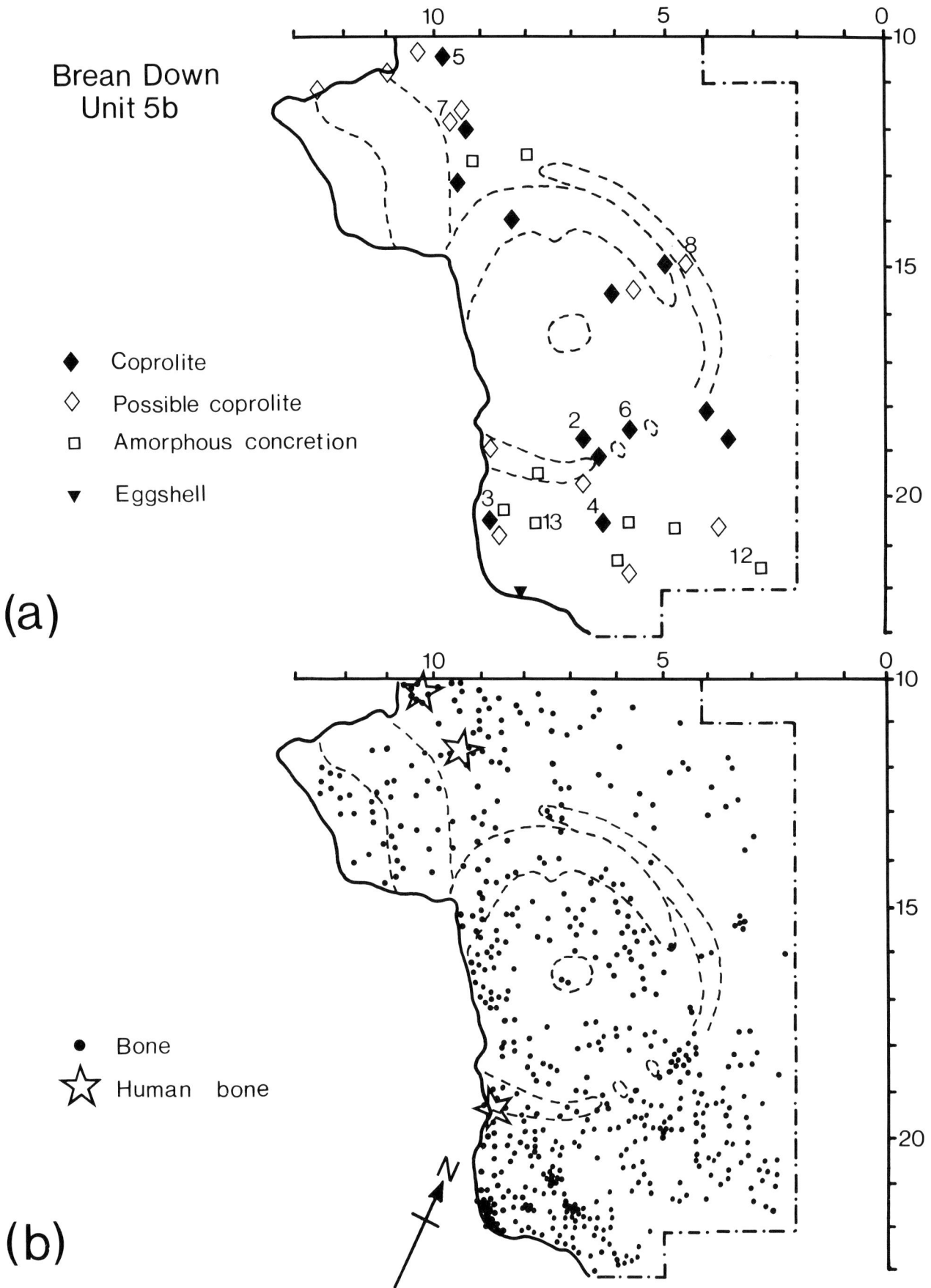

Fig 48 Unit 5b structures: distribution of (a) coprolites (the numbers show the positions of illustrated coprolites) and (b) bones

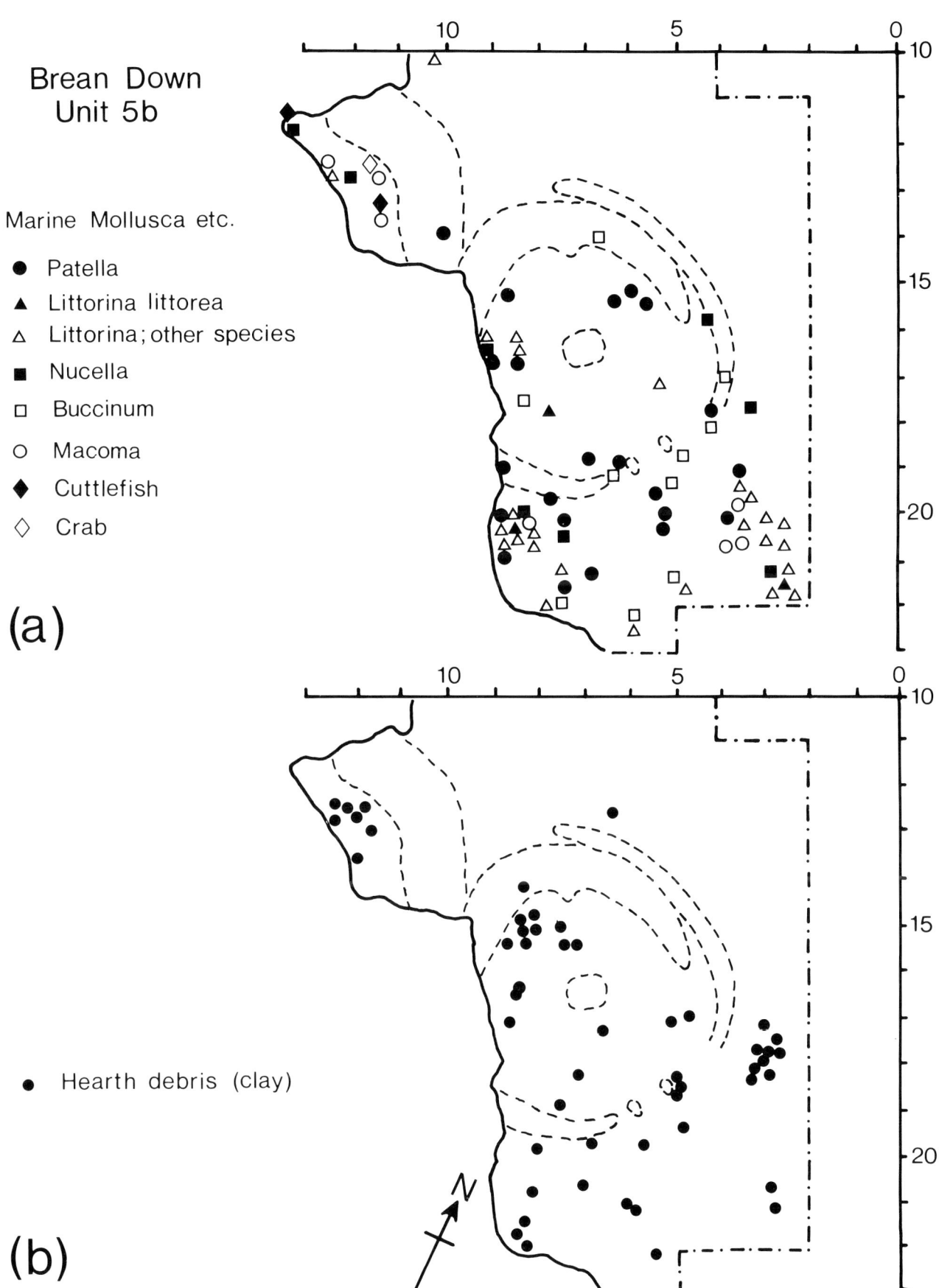

Fig 49 Unit 5b structures: distribution of (a) marine Mollusca and (b) hearth debris

after its abandonment. Furthermore, if the high values are due to the use of dung or other phosphate-rich material in the making of the floor or to the structure's temporary use as a byre, uniformly high values would be expected throughout the floor area, whereas the values are lower just within the entrance and high values are concentrated at the back of the hut opposite the entrance. The likelihood is that phosphate enhancement relates to activities during the life of the structure, perhaps from ash and other residues of food preparation which the bone and pottery evidence suggests occurred in the same general area.

Magnetic susceptibility values (Fig 132), which probably relate to the incorporation of burnt material, were highest at the hearth and the area to its north and west where cooking activities seem to have been concentrated. The eastern part of the interior just inside the entrance gave consistently low values similar to background levels north and west of the structure, despite the fact that briquetage was concentrated within this area of the floor. It may be significant that high magnetic susceptibility values occur in the south-west segment of the floor where phosphate values are not particularly high, suggesting that enhancement of these two parameters may not be purely the result of ash and burning-related processes.

The presence of a good hearth makes it likely that people slept in Structure 95 but there is no conclusive evidence as to where. If the interpretation which has been advanced for the terrace wall is accepted, then the stone bench envisaged, some 0.8m high, 1m wide, and 6m long might, if suitably covered, have provided sleeping accommodation for up to three adults. However, the presence of significant numbers of artefacts in the interstices of the terrace wall might imply that the platform was used for other activities or for storage. What is in question is whether these artefacts are primary rubbish or the result of post-depositional factors such as, for example, the collapse of the external daub wall which, as Schiffer (1987, 300) notes, may have incorporated some artefacts. Indeed this might be a partial explanation for the tendency of artefacts to be concentrated round the periphery of the floor. If so those artefacts would be secondary rubbish.

An alternative or additional sleeping area is suggested by the presence of a crude line of stones running south from the middle of the terrace wall. This is somewhat reminiscent of the radial piers of the Nornour stone houses (Butcher 1978) though much less clearly defined. These stones, together with a few at right angles, possibly delimited a segment of the floor which was rather more uneven than elsewhere, had few artefacts, and was c 2m by 1.3m, possibly room for two sleeping adults.

Another activity which may be attested in Structure 95 is weaving, because three loom weight fragments (115–117) were found, two of them in ash above the hearth (Context 93).

Structure 95 has produced evidence for a much wider range of activities than we would expect within one small hut or would infer from contemporary chalkland sites. This must be partly due to better preservation and a wider range of data sets at Brean. Presumably not all activities took place simultaneously, but the resulting artefact scatter is not so much of a palimpsest as to obscure clear patterning which implies the deliberate zoning of activities within the structure.

The area outside the structures

Outside the entrance to Structure 95 was a spread of pottery, bone, briquetage, and hearth debris. Bones, pottery, and marine Mollusca were more abundant here than within the structure except for the area west of the hearth. For reasons of light one might suppose that certain activities were best performed just outside the structure. Indeed, an activity area outside hut I at Thorney Down was interpreted in this way (Ellison 1987). However, the artefact distributions south of Structure 95 do not show evidence of the patterning which was such an obvious feature of the distributions within the structure. Furthermore, much of the material was associated with dumped ash and hearth debris which, it can reasonably be assumed, was secondary rubbish derived from Structure 95. The activities attested are those already evidenced from more primary contexts within the structure. It may be that activity patterns outside have to some extent been blurred and homogenised by a greater exposure to taphonomic factors. Tomalin (1982, 233) has noted the effects of trampling and muddiness outside entrances, and coprolites show that dogs were very much in evidence here. It is especially noteworthy that, with just a few exceptions, the coprolites were outside the structures.

A second concentration of dog coprolites occurs in the angle between Structures 95 and 59, an area which has a minor concentration of bones but little pottery or other artefacts. This encourages the belief that the bones, including a couple of human bones (Fig 48), had been taken to this shady area behind the two structures by dogs. If so, their activity was not sufficiently intensive to give rise to higher phosphate values (Fig 124). In fact the whole area upslope of the structures and to a lesser extent west of Structure 95 had very little evidence of human activity in terms of artefacts, phosphate, or magnetic susceptibility (Fig 132). The contrast between this area and that south of Structure 95 is highlighted by comparison of micromorphological sample N from that area, with its very high anthropogenic inputs, with sample K from the area upslope of the huts which consisted of 99% pure sand.

Structure 59

Since only one-third of this structure survived we naturally do not have such a good idea of the activities performed there. The floor was remarkably clean of finds, though there was a scatter of pottery, bone, and hearth debris just inside the entrance. It is considered that this evidence, together with the presence of ash within and below the floor, indicated the existence of a hearth in the now lost part of the

Fig 50   Reconstruction drawing of the structures and activities in Unit 5b

structure. The highest magnetic susceptibility values are indeed in the area of the main artefact scatter, but the values are low by comparison with Structure 95 so there remains some doubt as to whether Structure 59 contained a hearth. There was a cluster of briquetage from Structure 59, including the two most complete pieces: a sizeable piece of vessel (97) found within the floor and a virtually complete pedestal (70) from the interstices of the wall. The pedestal may be a *de facto* rubbish item stored in a crevice within the wall, though the tips of its tines were broken. Other fragmentary briquetage was also found in the wall together with 17 sherds of pottery and 32 bones, but the status of these items in terms of types of rubbish is uncertain. Flints were restricted to a single flake and one retouched piece and there were no bone or metal artefacts. Two probable coprolites were found within the interstices of the wall but none elsewhere in the structure. Phosphate values were generally similar to those in Structure 95, the highest values being just inside the entrance where most of the finds were concentrated.

Comparison of the structures and conclusions

Ellison (1981) has shown that many middle Bronze Age settlements in southern England comprised modular units of a major residential house, ancillary structures, animal shelters, and open air activity areas. In terms of size Structure 95, with a diameter of 6m, is at the very bottom end of the range of major residential structures as shown by Ellison (1981, fig 15.1). However, the range of activities represented, together with the concentration of decorated pottery, possible textile production, and the fragments of metalwork, strongly suggests that, in terms of previously adopted definitions, we should class this as a major residential structure. If our estimates of the original size of Structure 59 (*c* 4m in diameter) are correct then it is smaller than all the major residential structures and near the bottom of the range for ancillary structures. Though the range of activities indicated in Structure 59 is more limited than for Structure 95 and the proportions of mammal bone (Chapter 20) and sediment chemistry (Chapter 15) suggest subtle differences, the artefacts imply essentially similar activities concerned with food preparation and salt extraction. There was no evidence that the smaller structure was ancillary, as is suggested for paired structures elsewhere (Tomalin 1982). The problem in considering function is that we have no idea what additional structures lay outside the excavated area, although there are hints of others inland, both from the existence of gully 166 and the discovery of hearth material in the auger survey.

The two closely adjacent structures which have been excavated are very reminiscent of the groups of structures familiar from Deverel-Rimbury settlements and often interpreted as the residences of extended families. At Black Patch, Drewett (1982a, 341) argued that the proximity of huts suggested a close relationship between occupants. What is curious at Brean is that the doorways face in diametrically opposite directions. Also arguably symbolic of the relationship between the users of the two structures are their stormwater gullies; these are basically independent and were separately recut, but respect one another in that the gully of Structure 95 was so cut as to prevent water draining into Structure 59. It is surely significant that the temptation to put a single more effective stormwater gully round the two structures was resisted.

5 Late Bronze Age occupation, Unit 4

The stratigraphy

This part in the sequence is extremely simple stratigraphically compared to the area reported in 1961 when nine subdivisions of Unit 4 were recognised (Table 1). The sequence as revealed in 1983–7 comprised a thick sterile sand deposit (Unit 5a) sealed, on the northern part of the site, by an occupation horizon, Unit 4, which is regarded as being roughly equivalent to the group of Units 4b–c and f–h previously identified. Unit 4 is sealed by a stony colluvial deposit, Unit 4a, which is discussed in Chapter 6.

The occupation horizon is a fairly homogeneous deposit consisting of a single layer (Context 16) which, with various associated features, some of them filled by Context 16 material, comprises Unit 4. It was a greyish, yellow brown (10YR 4/2) sandy loam, and stones were common (c 5%) throughout but locally abundant (c 50%). At the northern part of the site the layer was up to 0.6m thick but it thinned downslope and ended in an extremely irregular edge in the southern half of the excavation (Fig 51). This ragged edge is believed to be the result of an erosion episode during the post-medieval period. South of Context 16 post-medieval pottery was present down to this level (Fig 70b). Furthermore the filling of the post-medieval erosion feature contained a considerable quantity of prehistoric pottery, the fabric composition of which showed that it was derived from the eroded portion of Context 16. On the northern part of the site, however, where the Bronze Age stratigraphy had not been cut into, there was very little prehistoric pottery in later layers (Fig 70a). The post-medieval erosion feature is considered to be basically a dune blowout modified by some rainwater gullying. Animal burrowing at the interface between Unit 4 and the later sediments gave rise to the vertical migration of artefacts within the post-medieval sediments.

Excavation and sieving

Since Unit 4 was an essentially homogeneous layer (Context 16) it was divided into 1m grid squares for excavation which took place in spits of 0.1m which were modified to respect any stratigraphy where it occurred. Context 16 was present over 60 sq m of the trench and the total volume of sediment excavated was 19.5 cu m. Sieving arrangements differed north and south of the 10m line on the A axis. To the south one bucket per metre square per spit was water sieved and the remaining sediment was dry sieved. This proved to be extremely time-consuming with the result that, when it came to excavate the area north of the 10m line where Context 16 was thicker, the strategy had unfortunately to be modified. In this area a chequerboard arrangement was followed with wet sieving of three buckets and dry sieving of the remainder in alternate grid squares. Even this strategy had perforce to be modified in the lower part of Context 16, with the result that it proved possible to sieve only about 25% of the grid squares/spits in this northern part of the site. From Context 16 as a whole the total number of buckets wet sieved was 149 and the total dry sieved was 555.

Features at the base of Context 16 (Fig 51)

Context 26

A shallow bowl-shaped depression c 1.3 by 1m and up to 0.25m deep. The fill was sand with humic patches. In addition to bones, with evidence of gnawing, there were five sherds of late Bronze Age pottery, two post-medieval sherds, and part of an iron nail.

Context 55

A bowl-shaped depression 2m by 2.5m by 0.3m deep containing sand with humic patches and detached blocks of Context 16 material (Figs 15, 52, Section 36). Context 55 cut Contexts 51 and 71. In addition to a high proportion of rabbit bones (30%) it contained 30 bones of other species, some with evidence of gnawing; among the bones were articulated bones of cattle. Other finds were 12 prehistoric sherds and one piece of post-medieval pottery.

Context 276

Bowl-shaped depression of diameter 1.5m and depth 0.5m, with a fill of sterile sand with a lens of dark brown sand at the base. The section (Fig 18.13) suggests that the overlying Context 16 has subsided into this feature.

Interpretation of Contexts 26, 55, and 276

These enigmatic, rather poorly defined features are believed to relate to animal burrowing. The size of the bowl-shaped depressions suggests that they are part of a badger's sett which Bruce Levitan suggests, on the basis of the gnawed bones, may have been reused by foxes. Such an explanation would account for the humic, rather disturbed nature of the fill, the presence of a few sherds of post-medieval pottery and an iron nail, and the indication from Figure 18.13 that Context 16 had subsided into one of these features. The animals seem to have burrowed into the loose sand of Context 19 using the much more consolidated sediment of Context 16 as a 'ceiling' which subsequently collapsed into the feature. Thus the archaeological record on this part of the site has been significantly modified and a quantity of animal bone introduced as a result of post-depositional factors operating during the post-medieval period. This process of chamber collapse is one of the factors which, with erosion, has helped to form the ragged southern edge of Context 16.

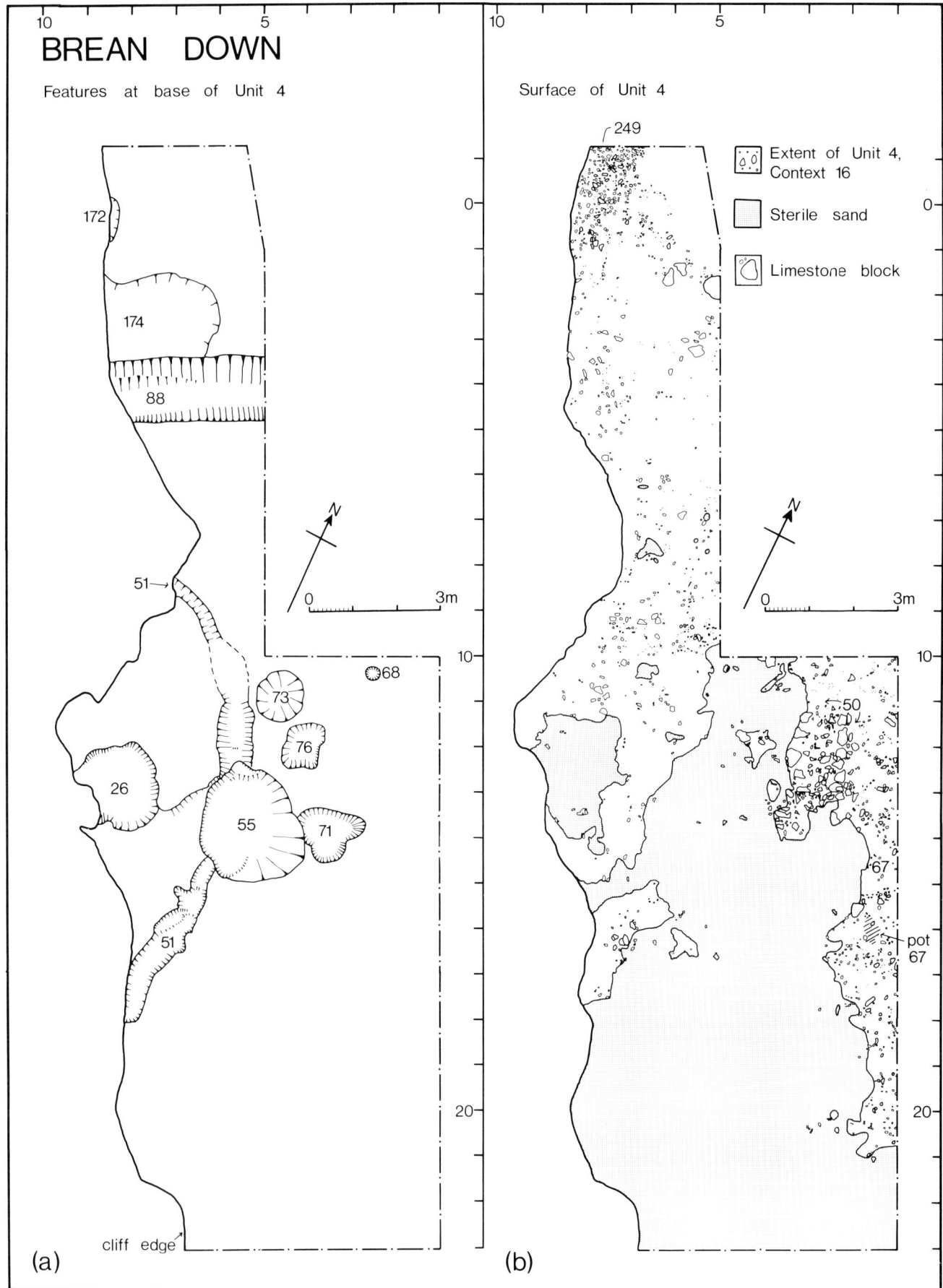

Fig 51 Plan of Unit 4: (a) features at the base of Unit 4; (b) the surface of Unit 4

Context 51

A curving gully of very irregular plan (Fig 51) and profile varying between V-shaped and U-shaped and between 0.4 and 0.7m wide and 0.1 and 0.3m deep (Fig 52). It was filled by sandy loam (52) identical to Context 16 and similarly rich in pottery and other artefacts. In view of the evidence for animal activity at the 16/19 interface the possibility was considered that this was a burrow. However, this idea was rejected because the edges were too clearly defined and there was no indication that the fill had accumulated by collapse from above, although in Sections 24 and 25 (Fig 52) the fills had been affected by rabbit burrows. If this gully originally surrounded a circular area then that would have been c 10m in diameter. No evidence was found in the surviving part of its interior for a structural terrace.

Context 71

This was 1.3m by 0.4m by 0.27m deep with fairly vertical sides and a fill of brown sandy loam, Context 70 (Figs 51 and 52, Section 49), containing several large stones and two sherds of Bronze Age fabric 481 including illustrated sherd 103.

Context 72

Irregular pit, continuing east of the excavated area, 2.6m by at least 1m by 1.2m deep (Fig 51). Fill of sand

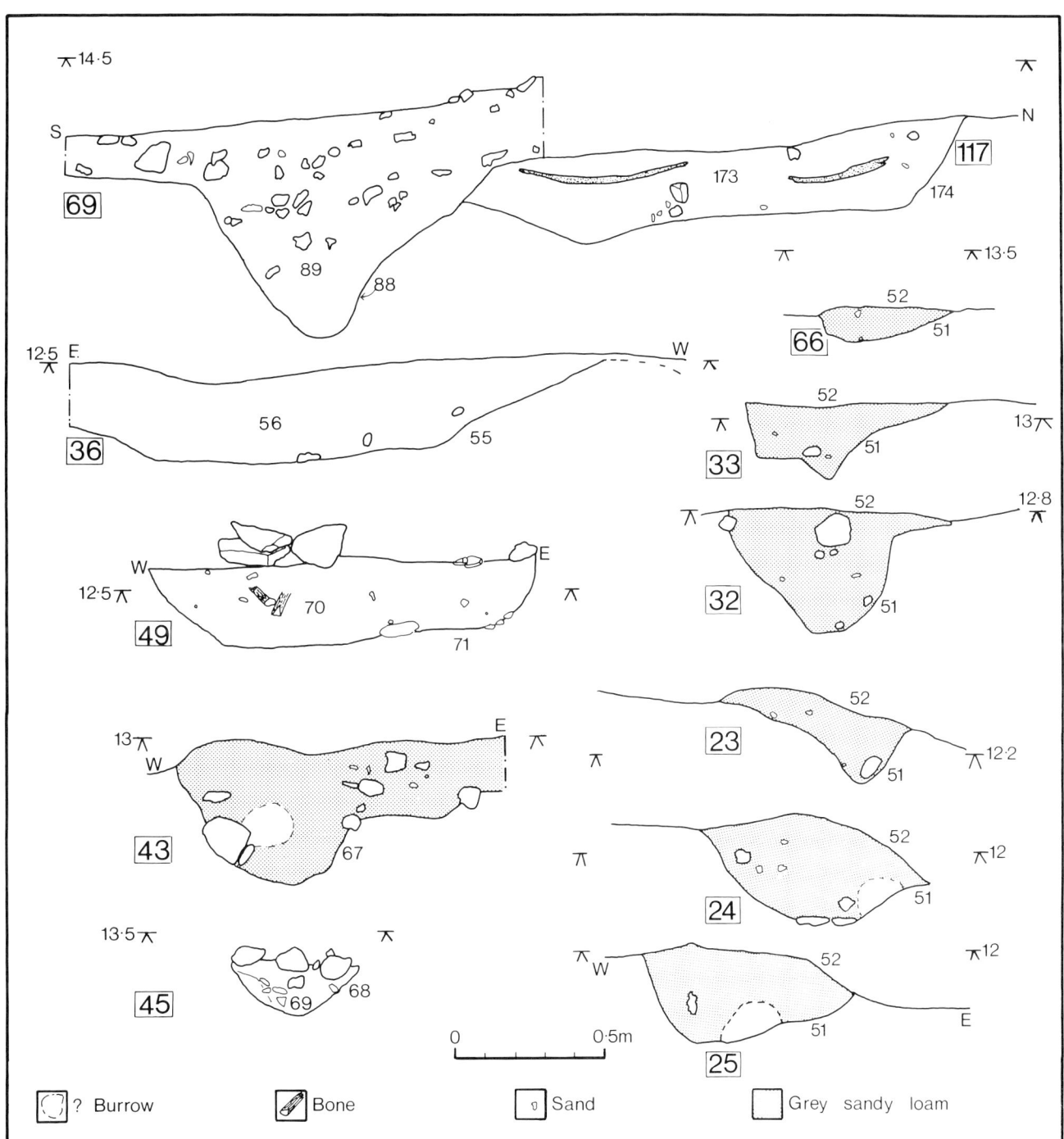

Fig 52   Sections of features in Unit 4

with a little charcoal, containing five sherds of Bronze Age pottery including illustrated sherd 102.

Context 76

Hollow 0.9m by 1m by 0.23m deep (Fig 51), containing one Bronze Age sherd.

Context 73

Circular depression of diameter 1.05m and depth 0.2m (Fig 51), containing seven bones and three marine molluscs.

Context 68

Posthole, diameter 0.3m, depth 0.16m with a packing of limestone.

Context 174

Bowl-shaped depression 2.5m by 1.8m by 0.25m deep. The only finds were two bones but it was not an animal burrow as it was clearly cut by ditch 88 (Fig 52, Section 117).

Features within Context 16

Context 111

On the northern part of the site and 0.2m from the base of Context 16 was a somewhat irregular surface made up of limestone of varying sizes (Fig 53). This limestone spread had a clearly defined southern edge and, irregular though it was, must presumably have been roughly laid to create a hard surface.

Context 88, ditch

A feature which was first recognised and recorded in the weathering cliff face in May 1983. On the 1984 section drawing (Fig 6) it is shown as Feature B. Subsequent excavation showed the ditch to be cut

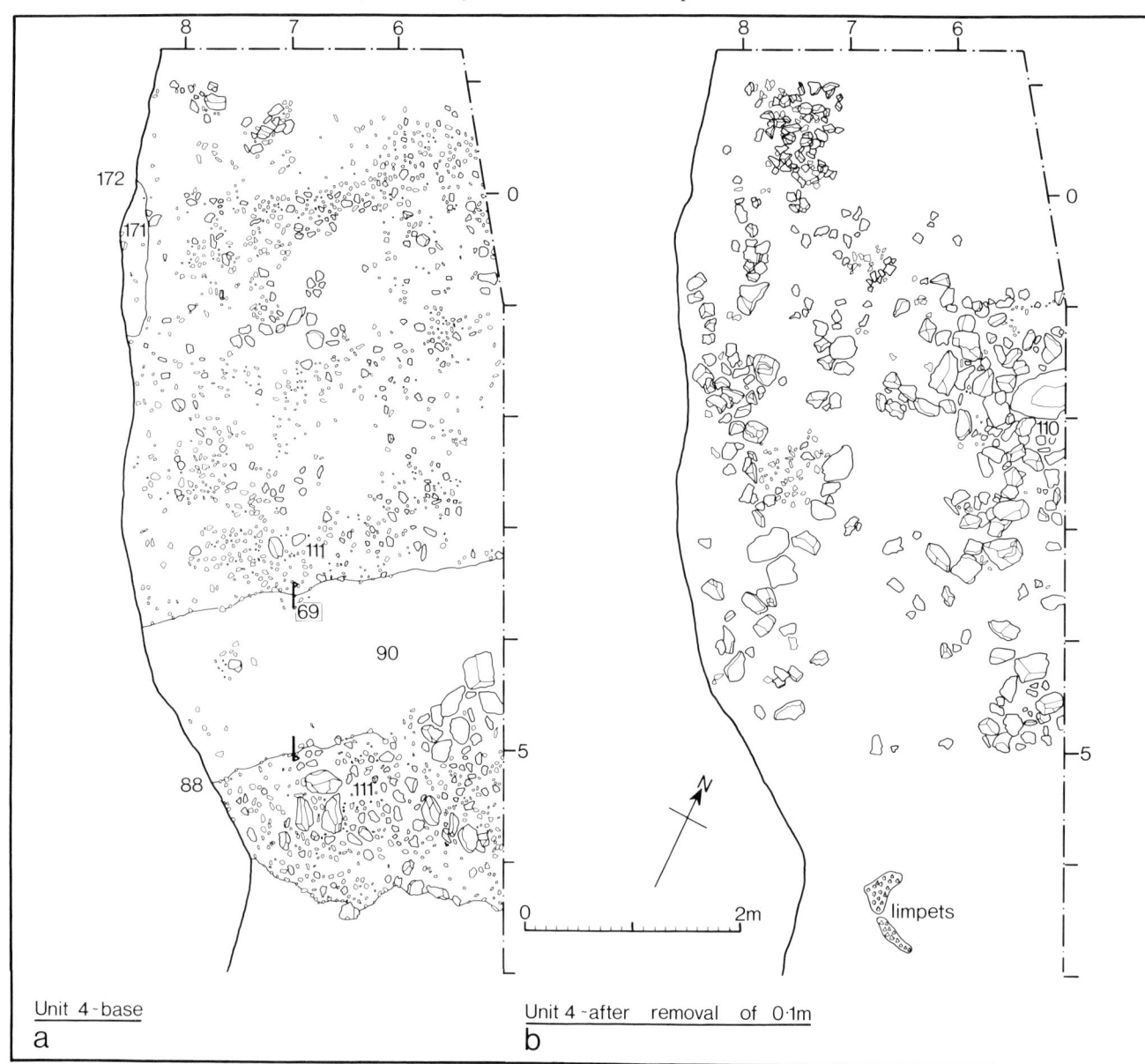

Fig 53 Plans of the northern part of Unit 4: (a) the base of the unit; (b) surface of the unit after the removal of 0.1m

Fig 54 Ditch (88) section from west (photo: M J Allen)

from the lower part of Context 16 through the limestone surface (111). The ditch was 1.4m wide and 0.7m deep (Figs 15, 54, and 52, Section 69). The fill consisted of two layers: a greyish brown (10YR 5/2) sandy loam with common stones (89) and artefacts including 14 sherds of prehistoric pottery, among which were illustrated vessels 105–107, and a coprolite (Fig 153.1); and, in the section as originally exposed, a lens of overlying sterile sand (90).

The main section (Fig 15) shows that 0.5m north of the ditch and on the surface from which it was cut was a lens of sand (278) 0.5m thick and 1.6m wide. The significance of this feature was not appreciated during its excavation, but the section suggests that it is a bank associated with the ditch, in which case the limestone blocks (110) on its surface may represent tumbled revetting. The spread of limestone blocks at this level (Fig 53) extended well beyond the hypothetical bank on either side and was without obvious alignments.

1984 Features C and D

Section drawing in 1983 and 1984 revealed that 2m north of the ditch were two horizontal lenses of sandy silt; the lower lens (Fig 6.D) was 0.2m thick and 3m long, with above it a 0.15m layer of sterile sand which separated it from the upper lens (Fig 6.C) which was 0.4m thick and 3.7m long. Both lenses had evidence of green/grey staining which seems to be comparable to that found on the floors of structures and in areas of intensive occupation activity in Units 5b and 6. Both lenses contained pottery, including vessel 110 which was from the lower lens. When this area was excavated in 1985, it became clear that the earlier section drawing had recorded almost the last vestiges of a feature. Only a tiny remnant (Fig 53, Context 172) remained to show that the feature containing the lenses cut the stone surface 111 and was therefore dug from the same stratigraphic horizon as the ditch (88). It is obviously not possible to advance a confident interpretation of such a vestigial feature, but there seem to be two main possibilities. The first is suggested by the fact that the lenses were horizontal indicating perhaps a terrace for a building; the green staining might support this idea. Any structure must certainly have been of wood or wattle because there was little stone in close association. The second possibility is suggested by a section drawn on 10 May 1983 when the ditch section and the sequence of lenses showed very similar stratigraphies. This could suggest that the ditch turned a right angle to the north, or that it was met by another ditch from this direction, both cross and longitudinal profiles being exposed in the highly irregular sandcliff face. Some measure of support for the idea of a ditch corner or junction here derives from the rather L-shaped plan of the limestone spread (110, Fig 53) which has been interpreted as possible collapsed bank revetment.

Relationship to the bracelet find

Though erosion has now ruled out complete resolution of the above problems they have been rehearsed

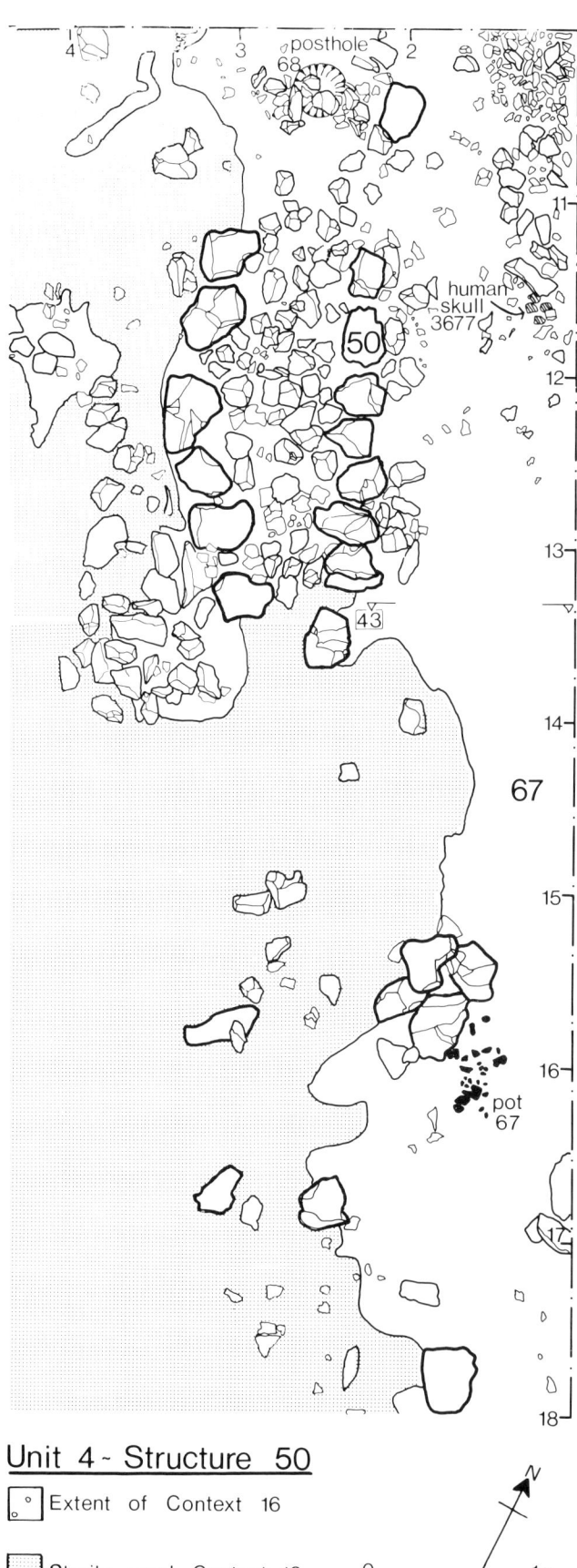

Fig 55 Unit 4, Structure 50

Fig 56 Structure 50 at an early stage of excavation (photo: M J Allen)

in some detail because of their relationship to the gold bracelets found by Keith Crabtree in the weathered section on 6 May 1983. The slumped block in which the bracelets were found (Fig 5) is marked on Figure 6. Most of the block comprised humic sand, but 50mm below the bracelets was a transition to sterile sand. The block must therefore derive from the base of Unit 4, perhaps from the ditch or a collapsed part of the C/D feature just to its north.

Stone Structure 50

This was formed of two parallel rows of large limestone blocks roughly 0.2 by 0.3m (Fig 55). One row comprised six blocks and was 2.3m long, while the other comprised eight blocks and was 2.5m long. The rows had outer faces 1.2m apart and between them was an infill of smaller limestone pieces (Figs 56 and 57). At some stage a fire had been lit against the east side of the wall because two large stones and several small ones were reddened by heat. To the south Structure 50 was cut by the post-medieval erosion feature, but the existence of a few large limestone blocks within surviving areas of Context 16 and in Context 13 indicates that it may originally have continued and been robbed where it was exposed during the post-medieval period. To the north the rows end 1.2m from the baulk although a single aligned stone block could suggest its former continuation. Alternatively, the presence of a posthole (68) between the two rows suggests that they may have been interrupted by an entrance. The most probable interpretation of Context 50 is a boundary wall of large facing stones and an infill of smaller stones.

Parallel with Structure 50 to its east was a shallow, poorly defined gully feature (Fig 55, Context 67 and Fig 52, Section 43). This was 0.2–0.4m deep; it was filled by Context 16 material and contained a particularly dense concentration of artefacts, including the greater part of a reconstructable pot (67) and illustrated rim 104, half a spindle whorl (34), and fragments of human skull (3677). The shallow gully seems likely to be associated with Context 50 as a component of the same boundary.

Context 249

When the surface of Context 16 was cleaned at the north end of the site it revealed the edge of a cobbled surface of limestone pieces (Figs 51 and 58). A 1m width survived, to the west cut by the cliff, to the north disappearing below the section. Removal of the limestone surface showed that it was not a feature fill. Presumably it represents a hard surface laid down during the final stages of the Unit 4 occupation episode.

Fig 57 Structure 50 after removal of smaller stones (photo: M J Allen)

Finds and their distribution in Unit 4

The distributions of pottery (Fig 104), bone (Figs 149 and 150), and other artefacts (MF1:A5) emphasise clearly the areas where Context 16 remained and pick out its eroded southern edge. There are concentrations corresponding to features which were filled by Context 16, eg the curving gully (51) and gully 67. Even so the spread of occupation material is uniformally dense and neither the field evidence nor the distributions have pinpointed concentrations relating to particular types of activity. The conclusion is that we have a midden of 'secondary refuse'.

The only exceptions to this are three reconstructable vessels which might have been broken *in situ*. Vessel 67 was found crushed in Context 16 material filling gully 67 (Fig 55), several joining fragments of Vessel 106 were found in the fill (89) of Ditch 88, and Vessel 110 was found in lens D.

The pottery in Unit 4 is quite distinct from that in the underlying Unit 5b; it is, as Ann Woodward shows (Chapter 11), a plain ware late Bronze Age assemblage. The characteristic pottery fabric is 481 containing calcite; also confined to this unit is fabric 521 which contains sand. In addition there is a small proportion of grog-filled fabrics (361–363) which are present in earlier units. The illustrated vessels are nos 67–117. Other finds included 13 pieces of worked bone (44, 52–53, 56, 59–67), four pieces of worked shale (37, 38, 40, and 41), a spindle whorl (34), a copper alloy plate (4), a loom weight (118), two hammerstones of Carboniferous Limestone, and 29 flints of which two are illustrated (25 and 26).

Additionally there was a small intrusive component in Unit 4: 13 sherds of post-medieval pottery including those pieces already noted from Contexts 26 and 55. Rabbit bones accounted for 12% of the faunal assemblage; they were all found between 7 and 17m on the A-axis. There was no disturbance or rabbit activity in the northern part of the trench where Unit 4 was sealed by a significant depth of compacted colluvium, Context 25.

Also noteworthy are 15 human bones from Unit 4 (Fig 150). Some of them may perhaps have been intruded from the overlying sub-Roman cemetery by

Fig 58 The north part of the excavation trench showing the surface of Unit 4 in plan (cobbled surface 249 on left) and Units 4a and above in section (photo: M J Allen)

rabbit activity because most were from the area of the trench where this was concentrated. However, this does not account for all the human bones; in particular, several fragments of human skull (3677) were found in gully 67 (Fig 55) and were certainly contained in Context 16 sediment. Another human bone came from the northern part of the site where Context 16 was well sealed.

Conclusions

In 1961 Unit 4 was dated to the early Iron Age (ApSimon *et al* 1961, 125). The gold bracelets are, however, a late Bronze Age type, as discussed by Stuart Needham (Chapter 12), with parallels elsewhere dated between 1000 and 650 BC. Reassessment of the Unit 4 pottery following the bracelet discovery showed that, in common with much pottery once ascribed to the early Iron Age, this material should more properly be regarded as late Bronze Age. Ann Woodward (Chapter 11) concludes that it belongs to Barrett's (1980) 'post Deverel-Rimbury' group, and is well paralleled among assemblages from the area dating to the first quarter of the first millennium BC, in particular the South Cadbury 4 assemblage (Alcock 1980).

No distinct hearth areas were identified in Unit 4 and there was little charcoal. It was, in any case, considered inadvisable to use concentrated samples of the charcoal which was present for radiocarbon dating because of contamination by rabbit activity in Unit 4. Consequently a number of bones were selected for radiocarbon dating and produced the following results: 3400±90 BP (HAR-9155), 3100±100 BP (HAR-9153), and 2730±70 BP (HAR-9151). Only the last of these dates is in agreement with the date around the first quarter of the first millennium BC suggested by both the pottery and the gold bracelets. HAR-9155 and 9153 seem to be somewhere between 100 and 400 years too early both in terms of the artefacts and in view of the presence of a consistent group of later dates in underlying Unit 5b.

The association of gold bracelets with a pottery assemblage and an occupation horizon is of especial importance. There is a particularly striking comparison with the recent discovery at Potterne, Wiltshire, of a bracelet of exactly the same type, called by Taylor (1984) the 'Potterne type'. That find seems to have come from an occupation horizon dated to c 750 bc which was sealed below an extensive late Bronze Age midden (Gingell and Lawson 1984). Though the Brean bracelets were in slump it has proved possible to pinpoint the position from which they were derived. Some uncertainty remains, however, regarding the nature of the feature in question, the most likely interpretations being a ditch or a terrace for a structure. The Brean find is most unlikely to represent a casual loss and was presumably deliberately concealed. One possibility is that it was some sort of dedicatory deposit associated with the settlement or establishment of boundaries. This is reminiscent of the Ebbesbourne Wake, Wiltshire, hoard found in the bank of a field system (Moore and Rowlands 1972). Alternatively the presence of a gold scrap with the two bracelets hints that this might have been a founder's hoard, which carries with it the possible implication that gold was worked on the site.

Unit 4 seems to have been subdivided by a series of boundaries. The ditch represents an east–west boundary and there is the now untestable possibility that this ditch was joined by another represented by the feature containing lenses C and D. Then there is Structure 50 of which the most plausible interpretation is as a partly robbed north–south boundary wall. Neatly constructed boundaries such as this with large facing stones and an infill of smaller stones are found, for instance, on Dartmoor on Holne Moor (Fleming 1988) and Shaugh Moor (Smith *et al* 1981). The subdivisions in Unit 4, particularly the use of both stone banks and ditches, suggest a similarity to very much better-preserved and rather earlier fields in layer 5 at Gwithian (Megaw *et al* 1961).

Thus the nature of activity represented by Context 16 emerges as a critical problem. Sediment analysis shows that the deposit is basically sand with between 11 and 14% silt. Micromorphology shows that it was rooted throughout the period of its accumulation and was subject to continuous disturbance. Richard Macphail (Chapter 16) suggests that this was the result of trampling or ploughing and favours the latter because Context 16 material is of essentially the same composition 100m inland in Soil Pit V. No conclusive evidence was, however, found for cultivation and Ann Woodward and the writer feel that the pottery assemblage includes sherds which are altogether larger and less abraded than those generally found in cultivated deposits such as lynchets. Cultivation of the northern part of the trench would also seem to be ruled out by its intensely stony nature and the survival of limestone surfaces (111 and 249) within Context 16. Nonetheless, the presence of boundaries within the excavated area leaves open the possibility that this area was on the periphery of tilled land, which might explain limited sherd comminution and means that we cannot totally rule out the possibility of tillage. Either way, the evidence for trampling is absolutely clear. Some of the pottery, including Vessel 67, had been crushed into the surface of the layer. In general, the context resembled the puddled and trampled surfaces which developed during rain on paths and barrow-runs around the excavation.

An important question is the origin of the grey silt which seems to be responsible for much of the distinctive character of Context 16. The most likely source is the flats to the south. An important observation made during the excavation was that artefacts seemed to occur particularly in areas of denser grey Context 16 material, thus suggesting the possibility that sandy silt containing artefacts was dumped from elsewhere. This might represent dumped floor material or daub. Another possibility is that the material was purposely added to help create a man-made soil. Certainly there are prehistoric precedents for the creation of man-made soils in the south-west as Gwithian shows (Megaw *et al* 1961).

All the evidence suggests major anthropogenic inputs to Context 16, which we can regard as a midden-type deposit. Interestingly, it has been argued that middens are a particularly characteristic feature of late Bronze Age and early Iron Age sites, the classic example being the 5ha midden up to 2m thick at Potterne, Wiltshire (Gingell and Lawson 1984; 1985). In discussing a more modest 0.3m thick deposit at Wallingford, Thomas *et al* (1986) list a number of further examples. This raises the question of whether patterns of activity which produced middens were especially characteristic of the late Bronze Age or whether the survival of this type of deposit is more likely in the topographic situations exploited during the late Bronze Age. Some of these deposits, but not Potterne, are certainly in valley situations, yet the contrast at Brean between Unit 4 and the preceding occupation horizons suggests that there may be something in the idea of distinctive late Bronze Age activity patterns.

At Potterne no adjacent settlement has been found from which the midden material may be derived, but at Brean the indications are otherwise. It has been noted that the 1961 Unit 4 stratigraphy was more complex, with nine subdivisions being recognised. The report refers to 'numerous weathered limestones...almost certainly part of ruined structures' (ApSimon *et al* 1961, 85). Indeed the original field drawing, kindly made available by Arthur ApSimon, which he simplified as figure 19 in his report, shows an area between 13.3 and 13.8m OD with multiple lenses of sediment including hearth material. Within 1m of these was a pile of boulders. Given the known OD height of this evidence it would correspond to 8–10m on the A-axis. Bearing in mind the calculated rate of coastal retreat it is possible that a domestic structure represented by these lenses and boulders was contained by gully 51 which, it has been suggested, might have surrounded a circular area 10m in diameter. Such a gully might have been intended to direct stormwater away from a structure. Similar gullies of smaller diameter surrounded the structures in Unit 5b and another curving gully with much pottery was found in Unit 4 in Soil Pit II (Chapter 8).

The basic contention, therefore, is that Unit 4 consists of a shallow midden of domestic refuse which was dumped from elsewhere. This accumulated within rectilinear areas enclosed by stone walls and ditches, the main function of which may have been stock enclosures although the possibility of tillage is not ruled out. No domestic structures occurred within the excavated area but there are hints that these lay nearby.

6 The sub-Roman cemetery and Iron Age to medieval stratigraphy

The stratigraphy

Sediments spanning the period between the Iron Age and the end of the medieval period were only preserved on the northern half of the site. To the south they had been lost by post-medieval erosion. Recognition of this episode is one reason why the 1961 stratigraphic sequence had to be elaborated as outlined in Table 1. Unit 3b was subdivided: 3b2 which is included in this chapter dates broadly to the medieval period, whereas 3b1 is later and is included in the succeeding post-medieval chapter. Unit 3c has also been subdivided to give due emphasis to the fact that a distinct layer of blown sand lies between the cemetery and Unit 4a. The unit sequence described in this chapter is therefore as follows:

3b2 sand with large, medium, and small limestone pieces – main Context 23
3c1 sub-Roman cemetery – many contexts
3c2 blown sand – Context 31
4a   colluvium – Context 25

Unit 4a (Fig 59) is the earliest; it comprises a single context, 25, a reddish brown (5YR 4/4) loamy sand with abundant limestone pieces, clearly derived from Pleistocene breccia deposits and subsoil horizons above the sandcliff on the south side of Brean Down, as micromorphological examination (Chapter 16) confirms. This high energy slopewash deposit covered much of the sandcliff and must have formed at a time when runoff and erosion processes were occurring on a much larger scale than they are today.

Considering the inferred mode of deposition of Context 25 the layer showed a marked lack of any sorting and had a smooth regular surface except where it had been cut by later burials. This might suggest that following its deposition the layer was mixed by tillage, an idea favoured by Richard Macphail (Chapter 16). Manuring from the domestic midden is unlikely because artefacts and charcoal were virtually absent. One fragment of iron is illustrated (Fig 66.6).

Overlying Unit 4a between c 15 and 21m OD in the section (Figs 15 and 16) was a sand layer (Unit 3c2) made up of a single context (31). It was 0.4m thick and comprised sterile, apparently wind-blown, light yellow brown (10YR 6/4) sand with occasional limestone pieces.

The next unit is 3c1, a cemetery of which eight *in situ* burials have been excavated or partly recorded. The grave cuts were very indistinct (see below), but in all probability the burials were originally cut from the top of Context 31 (Unit 3c2). This was overlain by Context 23 which was the principal context forming Unit 3b2. It was a brown sand (10YR 4/3) with common medium and large subangular limestone blocks. Some of these at the base of the layer were grave markers relating to the underlying cemetery.

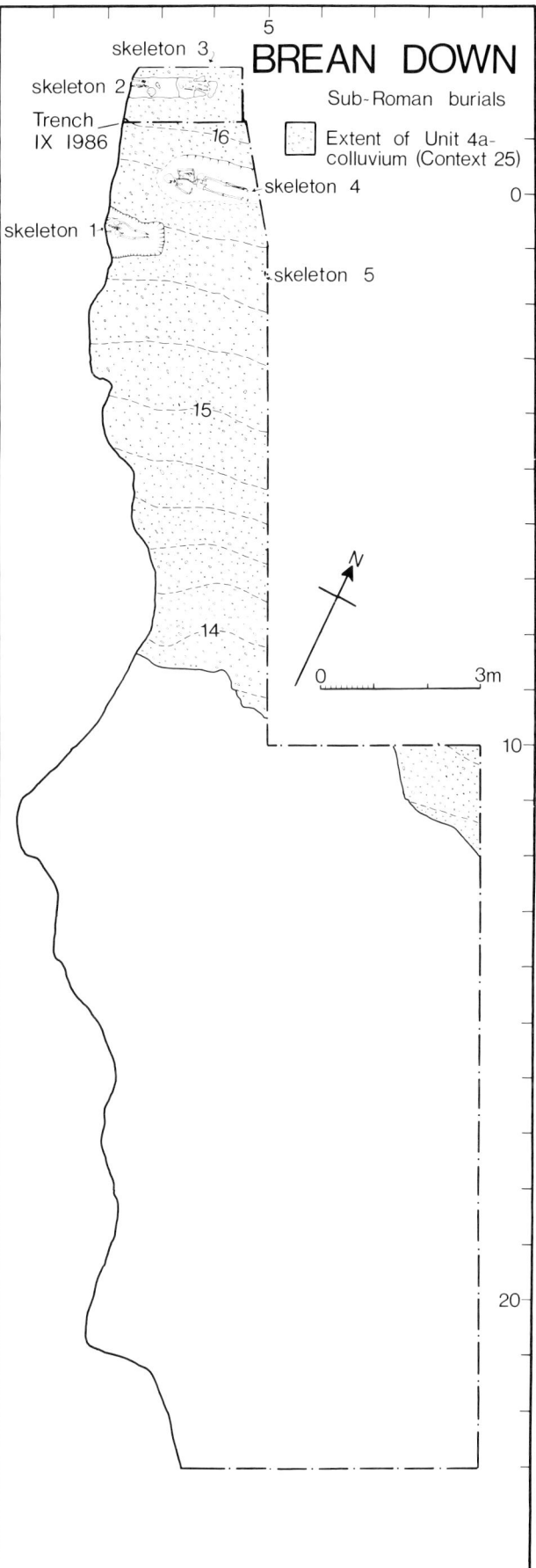

Fig 59 Plan of Unit 4a showing positions of overlying sub-Roman burials in the main (1985) excavation trench and Trench IX (1986)

Context 23 was up to 0.9m thick but there was often no absolutely clear boundary between this horizon and overlying post-medieval deposits.

Excavation of the cemetery and the human bone evidence

by Bruce Levitan

The presence of human bone in the sandcliff was first recorded by Knight (1902). ApSimon *et al* (1961) note various finds of human material made between 1930 and 1959, including ten burials which were revealed in a six-year period in the 1950s.

During the section recording exercise in April 1984 a human pelvis was recorded (Fig 6). In the main 1985 excavation trench human skeletons were confined to the northern 3m of the trench. There was one largely complete burial (32), about half of another (20), the rest of which had already been eroded away, and the skull of a third burial (65) which only just impinged on the trench and lay largely inland. During 1986 the sandcliff north of the main trench was cleaned for drawing (Fig 16); this involved removing loose scree but not cutting into *in situ* sediments. In the process three further skeletons were revealed and small trenches IX–XI were opened up so that these could be excavated. Such small trenches on an exposed cliff face were certainly not ideal excavation conditions but it was considered preferable to allowing continued erosion of the burials. In the event it provided important new information about burial practice on the site.

Preservation of burials varied greatly and appeared to relate to depth of overburden. Those burials with 1m or more of overburden at the southern end of the site were generally well preserved (eg Fig 62) whilst burials to the north which were not so deeply buried were poorly preserved. Parts of several skeletons had also been lost by coastal erosion prior to the excavation. Consequently none of the skeletons is complete, though one (32) is nearly so.

There are too few individuals to form a firm idea of the character of the cemetery. Ageing and determination of sex and stature were hindered by poor preservation. A number of burials were recovered piecemeal on several separate occasions as they weathered from the cliff; this means that sometimes it is not certain to which skeleton some bones should be attributed. These factors have limited analysis and interpretation. All of the eight burials were orientated east–west with their heads to the west. One was a baby, two were juveniles or teenage, and four were adults, one about 30, one about 30–35, and one possibly very aged. Two of the adults provided height estimates of *c* 1.7m. One was a male.

Skeleton 1: Context 20

The identifiable grave cut for this burial was shallow, averaging 170mm. In places it was visible at the very base of Context 31 but it only became clearly defined where it cut the much more consolidated Context 25. The grave fill (28) consisted of yellow sand with reddish brown redeposited Context 25. The 1984 section (Fig 6) shows a depression in the surface of Context 25 1.8m north of feature B, which is probably where the end of the grave cut was clipped by the section. Just outside the grave and up to 1m above its floor within Contexts 23 and 31 was a concentration of large limestone blocks (Fig 60, Context 54), which, in view of what was subsequently found covering skeleton 7, probably represent grave markers. Whether they were originally placed largely outside the area of the grave or have subsequently been disturbed is unclear.

Prior to excavation three separate chance discoveries of bone seem to derive from this burial. On 7th February 1985 Martin Bell found a skull, a few vertebrae, and a scapula, followed on 31 May 1985 by more vertebrae and ribs. In about June 1985 S J Parkhouse recovered more ribs, vertebrae, and parts of a pelvis which he has kindly given us. During the excavation later in 1985 (Fig 60) the bottom half of a juvenile was excavated in the same position; the vertebrae were present from the eleventh thoracic down to the sacrum, together with part of the pelvis, both legs, and the lower parts of both arms. There were five right and five left ribs but all are fragmentary so this count is approximate.

Assuming that these bones are all from a single individual, then they are from a youth aged about 15. The evidence for this is that in the maxilla the permanent teeth were erupting and the third molar was unerupted, in the mandible the fourth premolar was erupting and the third molar was unerupted, and none of the epiphyses on the long bones, vertebrae, and scapula were fused. Sexual features were inconclusive but it was possibly a male. Teeth abnormalities were noted: the right second incisor was rotated in the mandible and both mandibular canines were shifted laterally outside (labial) to incisors.

Skeleton 2: Contexts 21 and 226

In 1985 human bone was noted in the cliff face just beyond the north end of the trench. The upper part of the body of an immature individual (Context 21) was salvaged, but the precarious position meant that the bones could not be planned.

In 1986 the remainder of the skeleton (Context 226) was observed weathering from the cliff face and Trench IX was opened up so that this could be excavated (Fig 60). The trench was 2m by 1m and adjoined the 1985 trench to the north. A grave cut was recognised in the basal part of Context 31 and *c* 0.3m from the base of the grave which was cut 100–150mm into Context 25. A pronounced V-shaped depression on the surface of this context in the 1984 section (Fig 6), 0.6m north of the Unit 4 label, is likely to be where the section clipped the western end of the grave. At the eastern end the grave seemed to be continuous with that of a baby (skeleton 3), though some small limestone blocks round the feet of skeleton 2 might be part of a grave lining.

The bones recovered in 1985 and 1986 seem to come from a single individual, a child aged about 4–5

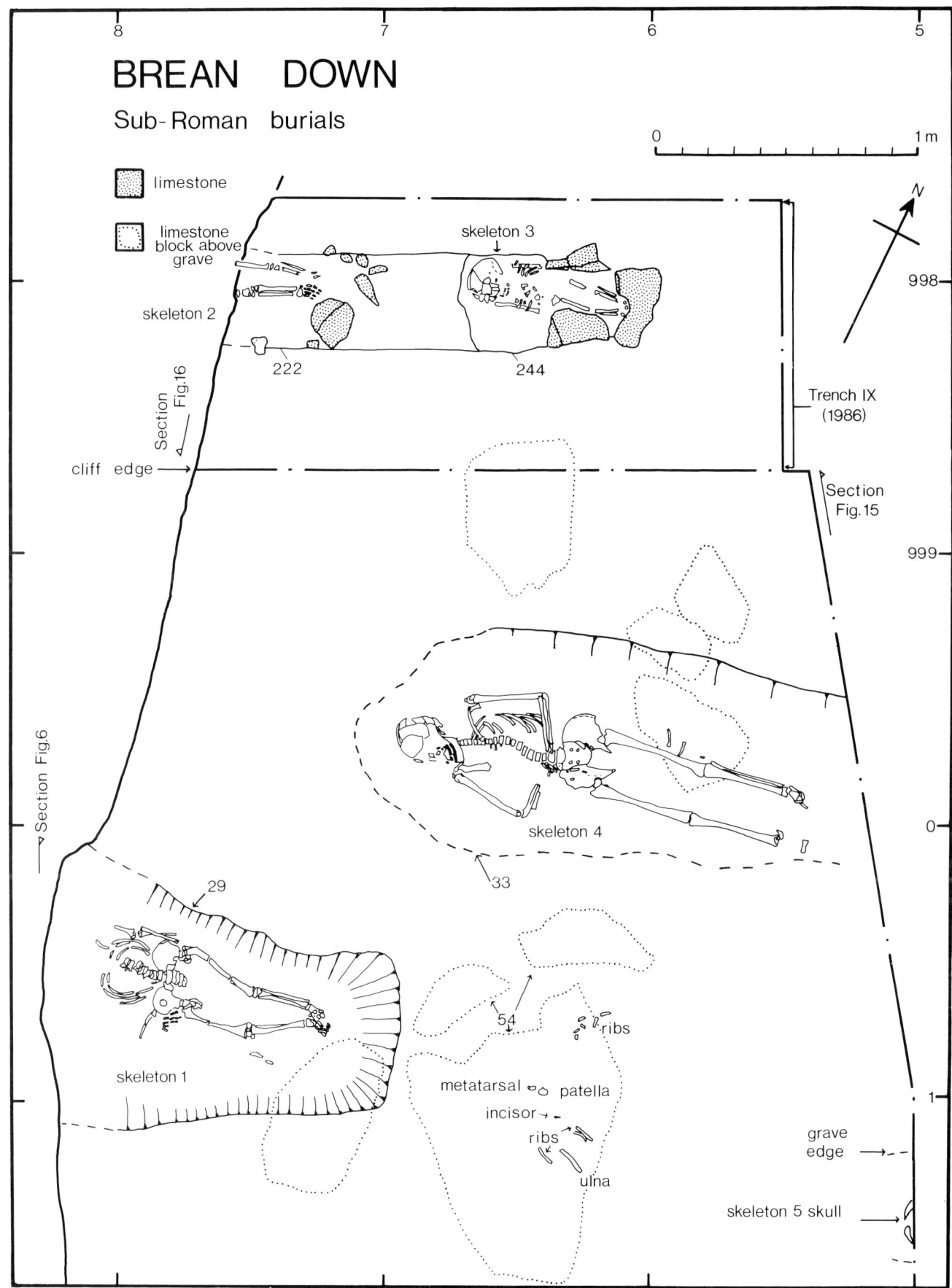

Fig 60 Sub-Roman burials in the northern end of the main excavation trench (1985) and Trench IX (1986)

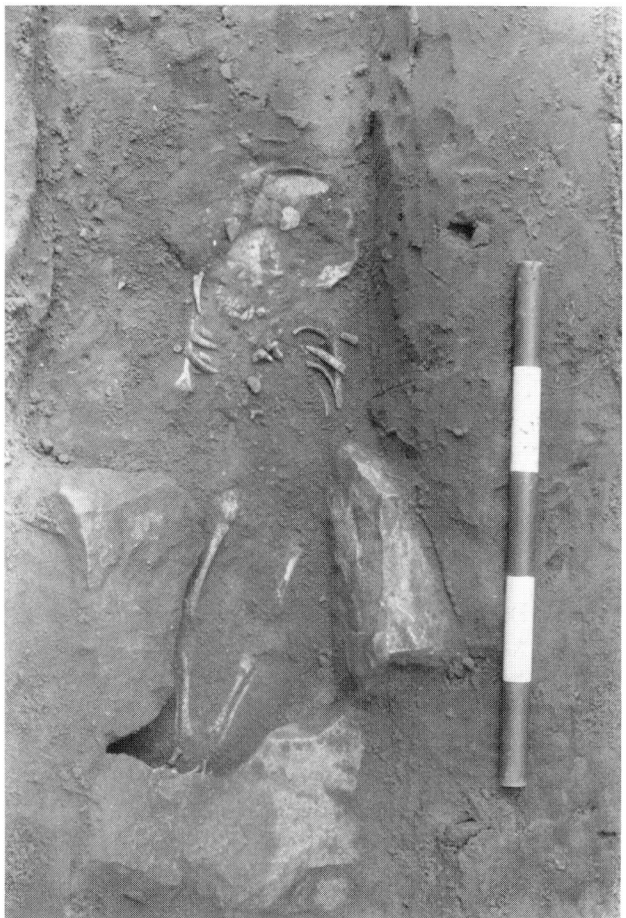

Fig 61 Infant burial 3 with stone grave lining round feet; scale 0.5m (photo: M J Allen)

on the surface of Context 25. Four limestone blocks were found c 0.5m above the burial but it is uncertain whether they were related to it in any way. This was the most complete of the burials excavated (Figs 60 and 62). Some disturbance of the grave by rabbit activity had, however, occurred and this is probably the source of the small group of bones 1–1.5m to the south which included the distal part of a right ulna which undoubtedly derives from skeleton 4. The burial was that of an adult male individual; sex designation is based on the criteria of Genoves (1969) and Brothwell (1963). The adult dentition was complete with all teeth in wear, including third molars, and judging by tooth wear criteria (Brothwell 1963) age was about 30–35; in addition all epiphyses were fused. A dental abnormality was noted: both lower second molars and the left lower canine were rotated. Stature of the individual can be estimated from 1.61m (right femur) to 1.67m (right humerus) with a mean of 1.63m±45mm (95% limits).

Skeleton 5: Context 65

This skeleton was discovered during the 1985 season after a collapse of the section. Only the skull and parts of the upper body most at risk from imminent erosion were removed. The only trace of a grave cut was a shallow depression in the surface of Context 25 (Fig 15). Two limestone blocks on either side of the

years, still with milk dentition, the molars not yet erupted; the mandible contained incisors 1 and 2, canine, premolars 3 and 4, and the first molar was visible in the crypt. None of the epiphyses was fused. Sex could not be determined.

Skeleton 3: Context 225

This infant burial was revealed in Trench IX in the course of uncovering skeleton 2. It occupied a grave 0.76m by 0.35m, the east end of which was clearly demarcated by three limestone blocks forming a cist around the feet (Figs 60 and 61). The grave was definable within Context 31 but only at about the level of the burial itself. The sides of the grave seemed to be continuous with that containing skeleton 2 so they may have been associated, although skeleton 3 was at a slightly higher level. Preservation of skeleton 3 was poor, one reason for which is undoubtedly the young age of the individual, less than six months old (milk teeth not in wear). Many of the bones were preserved too poorly to be recovered and those that were are generally incomplete.

Skeleton 4: Context 32

No grave cut was defined for this burial except in places at the level of the grave itself. The burial rested

Fig 62 Skeleton 4 (photo: M J Allen)

skull might represent part of a grave lining. The bones recovered indicate an adult individual about 30 with adult dentition, including third molar in wear. All present epiphyses were fused. The height of the person was about 1.65m (ulna) to 1.69m (humerus) with a mean of 1.67m±40mm (95% limits).

Skeleton 6: Context 247

During the initial section drawing exercise in April 1984 a female human pelvis and articulated femora were recorded and marked on the section (Fig 6.A). The only indication of a grave cut was a shallow depression in the surface of Context 25. Drawing of the section north of the main trench in 1986 (Fig 16) also revealed a fragment of human bone in a slight depression in the surface of Context 25. This was in the same position as 1984 Feature A relative, for instance, to the late Bronze Age ditch (Fig 6.B) and is almost certainly the same burial. It has not, however, been excavated.

Skeleton 7: Context 212

While the sandcliff face was being cleaned and drawn in 1986 skull fragments were noted and 0.8m above these was a limestone boulder (Figs 16 and 63). Trench X 3m by 2m was opened up to uncover this burial. It showed that the boulder lay within Context 23 and measured 1.15m by 0.6m by 0.5m. It rested on a stony surface near the base of Context 23. The two largest pieces of limestone on this surface proved on further excavation to form part of a wall on the north edge of the grave. The grave lay directly below the massive limestone block. It was an elongated oval 0.7m wide and over 1.8m long since it was eroded at the west end. Only the upslope (north) edge of the grave was revetted, by seven large limestone blocks averaging 0.5 by 0.3m (Fig 64). The grave had been cut into Context 25 in order to produce a flat base. The grave edges could be traced to 0.7m above the floor where they were revetted on the north side, but only 0.3m above the floor on the south side.

The skeleton was essentially complete, but so badly preserved that it was impossible to rescue the bones in one piece, and all were in a friable, highly eroded state. Beyond saying that it is an adult, it is impossible to define age, stature, or sex. All the mandibular teeth had been lost ante-mortem and no upper teeth were recovered; this possibly implies a very old individual.

The skeleton was partly extended, but the legs were drawn up so that the knees bent (Fig 64). The bones of the left hand and lower right arm had a distinct grey staining, but this was not associated with any object. There were a number of finds from the grave but all were within the fill rather than certainly associated with the burial. These included four sherds of prehistoric pottery of which one is Beaker (B19), two are Bronze Age grog-tempered ware (Fabric 361), and one may be Iron Age. There were three sherds of Romano-British pottery (6508 – pottery or tile, 6521 – samian, and 6544 – mortaria), one fragment of a shale bracelet (39), and a hob nail (Fig 66.5). The skeleton produced a radiocarbon date of 1430±70 BP (HAR-8549).

Skeleton 8: Context 213

Here again skull fragments were revealed during section drawing in 1986 and Trench XI 2m by 3m was opened up to excavate the burial (Fig 63). The grave cut was very indistinct except at the base where it cut slightly into the Pleistocene breccia Unit 8b. The grave was rectangular: 0.6m by more than 1.9m long with a number of small pieces of limestone lining it at the head end and with one block near the feet. The grave contained one prehistoric, probably Iron Age, sherd. This was the most northerly burial and the least well preserved. The skeleton was undoubtedly originally a complete extended burial of an adult but preservation was too poor for determination of age, sex, or stature. It provided a radiocarbon date of 1550±80 BP (HAR-8548).

Unarticulated human bone

In addition to the burials noted above 132 other human bones were found in contexts contemporary with or postdating the cemetery (summarised in MF1:G2). Thirty-five of the bones were from Unit 3c1, ie on the horizon of the burials themselves but not actually in articulation. Most, if not all, of these bones may have become disarticulated as a result of animal (mainly rabbit) disturbance, and the group of bones just to the south of burial 32 has already been noted. Seventeen of the bones came from Context 23 (Unit 3b2) which overlay the cemetery. Eighty of the human bones came from Unit 3a, which was an erosion feature of post-medieval date (Chapter 7). Distribution plots of the human bones (Fig 65) show that those in Units 3c1 and 3b2 are mostly close to the known burials from which they are likely to have been derived by rabbit activity (Chapter 20). This is not, however, a likely explanation for the considerable number of bones recorded in Unit 3a, some of which are 21m from the nearest known burial. These probably represent other burials eroded during the post-medieval blowout episode, before which the cemetery must have extended further south.

Some human bones were found in the auger survey: a skull from hole 15/995 (50515) and a piece of proximal tibia and fibula shaft from hole 5/995 (50041); these show that the cemetery extends at least 15m inland from the present cliff.

Dating and conclusions

The finds from this part of the stratigraphy are very few indeed and of little help in dating. They are augmented by one or two artefacts of probable Iron Age to medieval date which were found redeposited in later contexts. The finds are briefly noted later in this section and are considered in detail on MF1:A6 – 10.

The major erosion episode responsible for the deposition of Context 25 dates stratigraphically some-

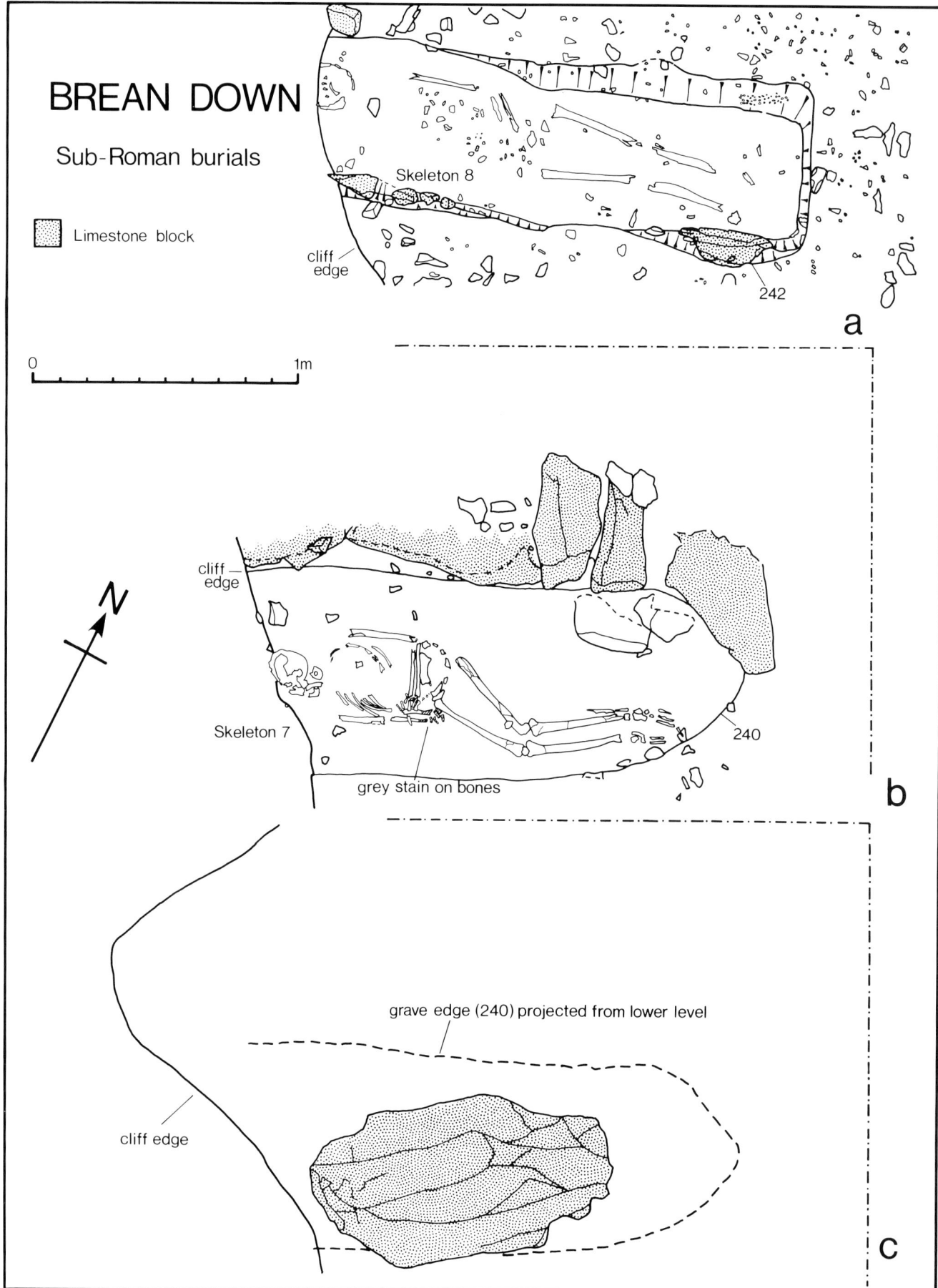

Fig 63 Plan of (a) skeleton 8, (b) skeleton 7 and wall to north, and (c) the large boulder covering skeleton 7

Fig 64   Skeleton 7 (photo: M J Allen)

time between the late Bronze Age and the end of the Roman period. The seven artefacts from the excavated 6.4 cu m of this context are of no help with dating, being mostly bones or probably redeposited. There are a few possible Iron Age sherds from Context 16, which suggests that Unit 4 may have been exposed during part of that period, but most of the possible Iron Age and all the Roman material comes from contexts which are virtually certain to postdate the fourth century AD. It is interesting to speculate as to the possible causes of the erosion episode which led to the deposition of Context 25.

One possibility is that extensive erosion on the south side of the Down was associated with the construction of the hillfort, which Burrow (1976) established as having occurred between 2260±150 BP (Birm-719) and 2050±100 BP (Birm-718). Hillfort construction is perhaps one event in landscape evolution which is inherently likely to have been associated with major clearance and perhaps erosion. Other possibilities are that erosion was caused by the establishment of field systems on the Down, or an episode of exceptionally heavy grazing. Either way an Iron Age date for the episode seems probable.

A particular stratigraphic difficulty was establishing from which horizons the sub-Roman burials were cut. Some were only visible in the consolidated sediment of 25, some in the lower part of Context 31, one (212) was certainly cut from the surface of 31, and several of those reported in 1961 were cut from the same stratigraphic position. No land surface was present in the areas excavated recently but there were hints of an intervening erosion episode. It is considered likely that all of the burials were originally cut from the surface of Context 31 but that the grave cuts have been obscured by bioturbation and perhaps winnowing. Context 31 itself was a blown sand deposit; it contained a single sherd of prehistoric, possibly Iron Age pottery (6538). The layer was a maximum of only 0.4m thick although there are hints that it may originally have been deeper. For instance the huge covering block over skeleton 7 was stratified in Context 23 and there was a concentration of stones, including other large blocks, near the base of 23. Some of these may originally have been grave markers but in its present form the surface is interpreted as a stone pavement created by deflation of sand which once contained the stones.

Dating evidence from the excavated 13 cu m of Context 23 is very limited: two sherds of Bronze Age pottery, two possible Iron Age sherds, and one piece of samian with rivet repairs (2113). Two fragments of post-medieval pottery and one piece of twentieth-century glass show that parts of the layer have been disturbed more recently. We can conclude therefore that Context 23 accumulated sometime between about the eighth and sixteenth centuries AD during which time no artefactual evidence of human activity was deposited in the excavated area.

The burials were all orientated east–west with their heads to the west. With the exception of a single early discovery which was said to have had a iron knife (ApSimon *et al* 1961, 86), they were all without grave goods. Such burials are often believed to be Christian, although Rahtz and Watts (1979) have emphasised that it is seldom possible to prove this conclusively. Three radiocarbon dates are now available for the burials: the earlier find of a skeleton from the cliff face (Rahtz 1977; Burrow 1976) 1300±80 BP (Birm-246), skeleton 7 1430±70 BP (HAR-8549), and skeleton 8 1550±80 BP (HAR-8548). Calibration (Chapter 9) gives HAR-8548 a date of 415–600 Cal AD, HAR-8549 a date of 560–660 AD, and Birm-246 a date of 654–786 AD. The two Harwell dates show that the burials relate to that fascinating three-hundred-year period of Somerset archaeology between the collapse of Roman Britain *c* AD 410 and the eventual Saxon conquest of the area sometime in the second half of the seventh century. The calibrated Birmingham date hints that the cemetery might have continued in use after this. The archaeology of this period has in recent years been comprehensively reviewed (eg Rahtz and Fowler 1972; Rahtz 1974; 1982; 1983; Burrow 1981). The first of these papers lists six cemeteries of probable sub-Roman date in Somerset and South Avon including Brean. Since then a further probable example has been identified at Wembdon (Langdon 1986).

Of particular interest in relation to the sub-Roman cemetery are the stone grave structures. Two of those reported in 1961 (nos 6 and 2) and three of those reported here had stone linings. It also seems possible that some of the blocks of stone reported in 1961 from Unit 3b were grave markers rather than the remains of a building, as originally suggested. Such stone grave structures are widely represented in post-Roman contexts in the west of Britain. Somerset examples include Glastonbury Abbey (Radford 1981), Nettleton Shrub (Wedlake 1982), and Henley Wood and Cannington (Rahtz and Fowler 1972). Examples are also known in what is considered to be a late Roman context in Ilchester's Northover cemetery (Burrow 1984) and Bradley Hill (Leech 1981a). On the Welsh side of the Severn Estuary at Atlantic Trading Estate, Barry Docks, a fine series of stone-lined burials, many with cover slabs, has recently been excavated by the Glamorgan Gwent Archaeological Trust (Newman and Parkin 1986). Further examples in the south-west include Mawgan Porth (Bruce-Mitford 1956), Beacon Hill, Lundy (Gardener nd), and several sites on the Scilly Isles where there are slab-lined and cist burials of both Romano-British and sub-Roman date (Ashbee 1974; Thomas 1985). In view of Iron Age precursors for slab-lined and covered burials at Harlyn Bay and other sites in Cornwall (Whimster 1977) it is tempting to see this as a pre-Roman trait which became widespread in the sub-Roman period which Rahtz (1983) envisages as a return to a pre-Roman social system.

Iron Age and medieval small finds

The present excavation produced 16 sherds of probable Iron Age date, discussed on MF1:A6, and 18 sherds of Romano-British date, discussed by Peter Leach on MF1:A7–8. These include the following sherds: four of second-century samian, three of third- or fourth-century mortaria, nine of grey ware, and one of Black Burnished Ware. The sherds were mostly abraded and from post-Roman contexts, although

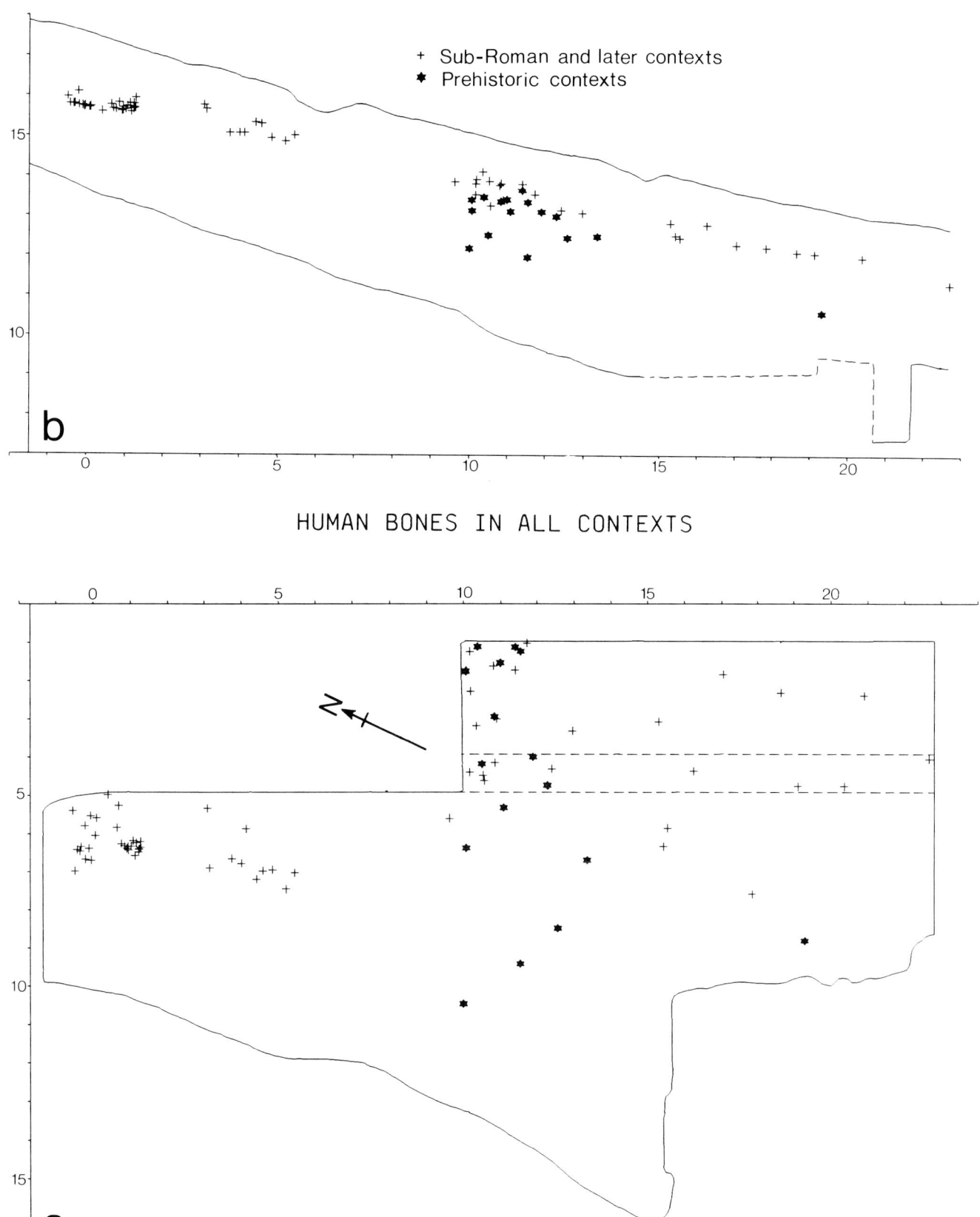

Fig 65 Distribution plots of human bones not associated with specific skeletons: (a) horizontal distribution; (b) vertical distribution

three were found on a possible Romano-British surface in Soil Pit VI (Chapter 8) and three others were from the grave containing skeleton 7. Arthur ApSimon reports (pers comm, 25.9.85) that 30 years' collecting by members of the University of Bristol Spelaeological Society produced just five unstratified Romano-British sherds which are housed in the Society's collection. Metal and glass finds are illustrated on Figure 66 and discussed by Jennifer Foster on MF1:A9–10. They are briefly described as follows:

1 A bronze pin of Romano-British type, Context 13
2 and 3   Brass lace-ends similar to examples from the Brean Romano-Celtic temple (ApSimon 1964–5, 254, no 3) but also with parallels in post-medieval contexts, Context 13
4 Copper sheet, Context 13
5 Iron hob nail, Context 212, the grave containing skeleton 7
6 Flat iron object, Context 25
7 Blue cylinder bead of Roman or post-Roman type, Context 13
8 Yellow biconical bead which X-ray fluorescence analysis shows was a lead-rich glass likely to be post-Roman (Guido 1978, 16), Context 13

Most of these finds are from Context 13, which also contained much post-medieval material. The exceptions are the nondescript piece of iron (Fig 66.6) from Context 25 and the single hob nail (Fig 66.5) from the grave of skeleton 7; this latter may be a residual find, though Leech (1981a) discusses the association of hob nails with Romano-British burials. Only one of the artefacts, the yellow bead, seems likely to be of Dark Age date. Bearing in mind the evidence for the continued currency of Romano-British artefacts, including pottery (Burrow 1981), on sub-Roman sites in Somerset, it is possible that some of the other items reached the sandcliff in this period. However, the quantity is tiny, Mediterranean imported pottery is absent, and there are no identifiable local post-Roman fabrics. Consequently we must conclude that there is no evidence for a sub-Roman, or for that matter Roman, settlement on the sandcliff.

Settlement pattern

This brings us to the origins of the cemetery population. Did it serve a dispersed population, some of whom may have continued to live on the clay lands where there is increasing evidence for Romano-British settlement and drainage (Leech 1981b; McDonnell 1979; 1985; 1986)? Conversely, were there more dramatic, sub-Roman changes, with the cemetery serving a nucleated settlement as inferred at Cannington (Rahtz 1969) and between Henley Wood and Cadbury Congresbury (Rahtz and Fowler 1972)? It is perhaps unlikely that drainage works could have been maintained into the fifth century. There is evidence for Roman and some post-Roman activity on the Down. The Romano-Celtic temple was constructed c AD 340 and demolished c AD 390 when a small building was constructed just to its south and used into the fifth century (ApSimon 1964–5). Leech and Leach (1982) have suggested that this building, and an east–west inhumation in the temple annexe, relate to conversion of the site to Christianity. Burrow's (1976) excavation of the hillfort on the east end

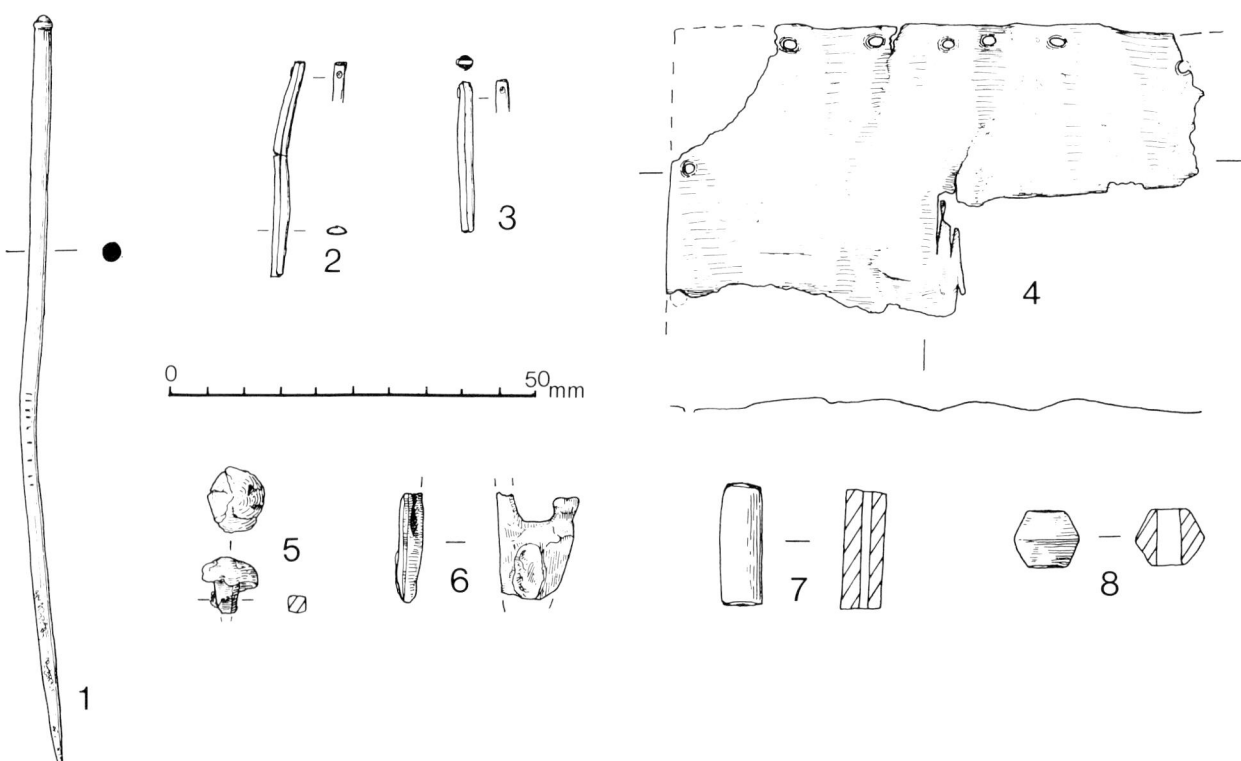

Fig 66   Artefacts of probable Roman to early medieval date: nos 1–4 copper alloy; nos 5–6 iron; nos 7–8 glass; scale 1:1

of the Down was designed to test the hypothesis that this too was post-Roman. In the event it proved to be Iron Age with an overlying scatter of Romano-British sherds.

Abandonment of the cemetery may have resulted from the Saxon conquest or a shift 3km along the sandbar to the present site of St Bridget's church. If so that shift was associated, not as originally suggested by ApSimon *et al* (1961) with initial reclamation of the flats in the tenth and eleventh centuries AD, but with renewed intensification of land-use on flats originally settled and drained in the Romano-British period.

7 The post-medieval period

by Martin Bell and Cathy O'Mahoney

The stratigraphy

This part of the sequence comprised the modern topsoil (Unit 1) and part of Unit 3, which in 1961 was seen as a simple succession of three layers. Artefact distributions from the 1985 excavations revealed a more complex situation because post-medieval dune erosion had removed late Bronze Age to sixteenth-century deposits on the southern half of the site; the erosion feature then filled with sand containing post-medieval pottery. The late Bronze Age to medieval stratigraphy, including the sub-Roman cemetery, survived on the northern part of the site. For these reasons the 1961 unit sequence had to be elaborated as outlined in Table 1. Unit 3 was subdivided: 3b2 was the northern part of the site where medieval stratigraphy survived; 3b1 and 3a were the southern area of post-medieval deposits. Unit 3b1 comprised thin lenses of charcoal, shale, and post-medieval pottery (Context 18) which probably corresponds to the occupation of a building reported by ApSimon *et al* 1961. Unit 3a consists of two layers of blown yellowish brown (10YR 5/6) sand (Contexts 12 and 13) with few stones and much evidence of rabbit disturbance. These layers were distinguished from the earlier Context 23 (Unit 3b1) to the north, not by any clearly defined edge, but by the more stony nature of 23 and the radically different artefact content of the two deposits. Overlying the sequence described were a series of twentieth-century blown sands and stabilisation deposits (Contexts 8–11). The curved bank of a World War II anti-aircraft position encroached slightly on the excavation trench.

The post-medieval stratigraphy was removed in 0.1–0.2m spits by pick and shovel, the artefacts spotted being three-dimensionally recorded. In all 180 cu m were excavated, including 21 cu m in the more carefully trowelled baulk. Sieving was limited to the 1 sq m column 1 which was sampled at 0.1m intervals, 14 samples being dry sieved and 4 wet sieved.

Post-medieval pottery

The post-medieval pottery is illustrated in Figures 67 and 68 and is discussed in detail by Cathy O'Mahoney on MF1:A11–B7. In summary, the assemblage consists of 400 sherds, about half of which were from local Somerset kilns at Nether Stowey and Donyatt. The following vessels are illustrated:

1. A large Donyatt cistern with two bungholes and decoration on the neck of white slip wiped through with a finger; part of the exterior is green glazed
2. A Donyatt jug with white slip decoration marked with a tool
3. A Nether Stowey candlestick decorated with white slip, some copper green in the glaze, and an unusual sgraffito pattern
4 and 5 Nether Stowey bowls with decoration of slip and a series of interlocking S marks in sgraffito
6. A Nether Stowey jar with some glaze, slip, and traces of sgraffito decoration
7. A Nether Stowey pancheon
8. A Nether Stowey pancheon with pouring lip
9. A Nether Stowey pancheon with applied horizontal thumbed strip decoration
10. A Nether Stowey tripod pipkin with internal brownish green glaze
11. A Nether Stowey jar with internal pitted green glaze
12. A Nether Stowey jar with internal dull brownish green glaze
13. A Malvern ware bottle or jug
14 and 15 Cistercian ware cups
16. A Spanish olive jar with internal thin green glaze
17. A Spanish olive jar

Most of the assemblage appears to form a group with a relatively narrow date range. All the Donyatt vessels are hollow-wares of sixteenth-century type and the date range of the Nether Stowey industry is now thought to be 1580–1600, although use of these vessels would have continued into the seventeenth century. None of the pots of this type from Brean Down would look out of place in the assemblage from Narrow Quay, Bristol, which is dated to AD 1580–90 (M Ponsford and V Russett, pers comm). The Malvern and Cistercian wares and some Frechen stoneware also suggest a sixteenth/seventeenth-century date. The absence of recognisable late seventeenth- or eighteenth-century Somerset types of pottery and the absence of parallels between this collection and that from St Nicholas' Almshouses, Bristol (Barton 1964), closely dated to the mid seventeenth century, suggest that the occupation ended before then. There are few sherds of definite late seventeenth- or eighteenth-century pottery, indicating very limited use of the area at this time. The nineteenth and twentieth centuries are much better represented by 95 sherds, most of which are from Context 12.

In the late sixteenth- and early seventeenth-century assemblage the wide range of vessel types, together with the relative completeness of vessels, indicates domestic occupation involving the following activities: cooking, brewing, processing of dairy products, and storage.

Other finds

Metalwork, bone, and ivory objects of probable post-medieval date are illustrated in Figure 69 and described in detail by Jennifer Foster on MF1:B8–9. In summary, the illustrated objects are as follows:

1. Brass book clasp riveted in two places to an iron plate which has traces of leather. Decorated by three concentric circles. The object has sixteenth- and early seventeenth-century parallels. Context 13
2. Brass pin with globular head. Context 18.5
3. Half a circular brass bell. Context 13
4. Lead clasp, probably modern. Context 11

THE POST-MEDIEVAL PERIOD

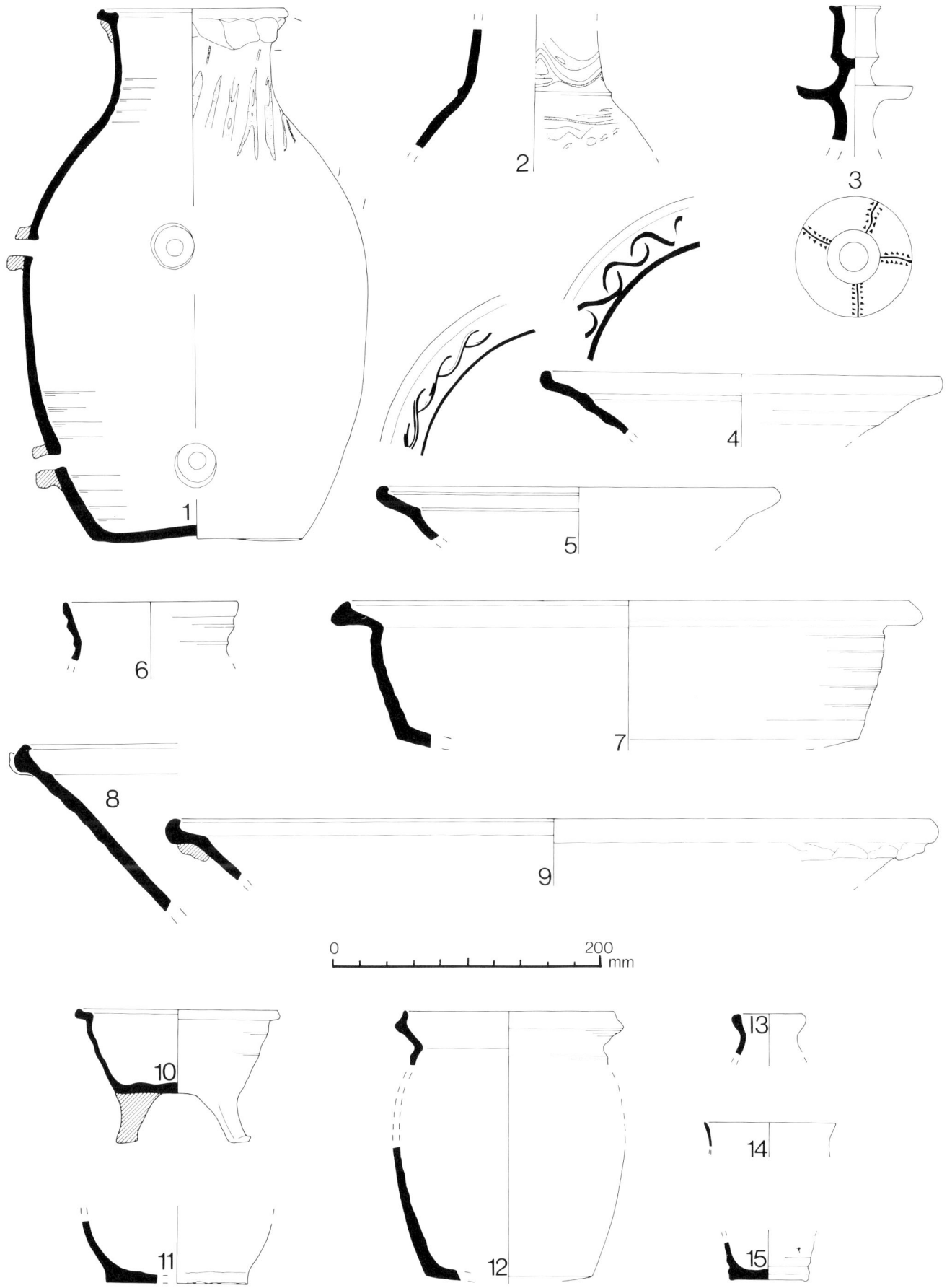

Fig 67   Post-medieval pottery nos 1–15; scale 1:4

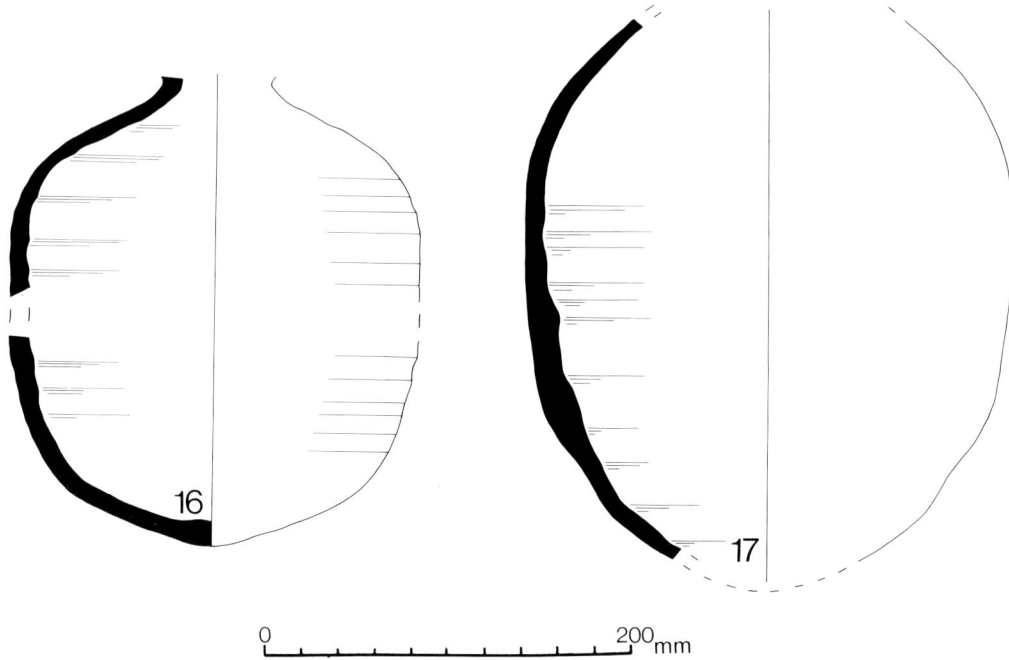

Fig 68   Spanish oil jars 16 and 17; scale 1:4

5   Flat, thin bone strip with tapering bevelled edges. Context 13
6   ?Ivory strip with two straight edges. Context 18

A few clay pipes are discussed by Stephen Minnett on MF1:B9; all the identifiable pieces are nineteenth-century.

Artefact distributions

The dune blowout in the southern part of the trench was first clearly defined by computer plotting of the artefacts during the excavation. Finds were very much concentrated in the upper 1.5m south of A=7m where Bronze Age pottery, clearly derived from the erosion of Unit 4, was abundant in association with post-medieval pottery (Fig 70a); both were absent from the northern part of the trench. There was also the irregular southern edge of Unit 4 (Fig 51) showing it to have been cut by erosion. Elsewhere the blowout did not have sharply defined edges, probably because of constantly changing morphology, slumping, and extensive faunal disturbance.

The distribution of pottery dated to the late sixteenth and earlier seventeenth centuries AD (Fig 70b) is largely confined to Contexts 13 and part of 12. The distribution is denser and more narrowly defined stratigraphically in the centre of the excavation and

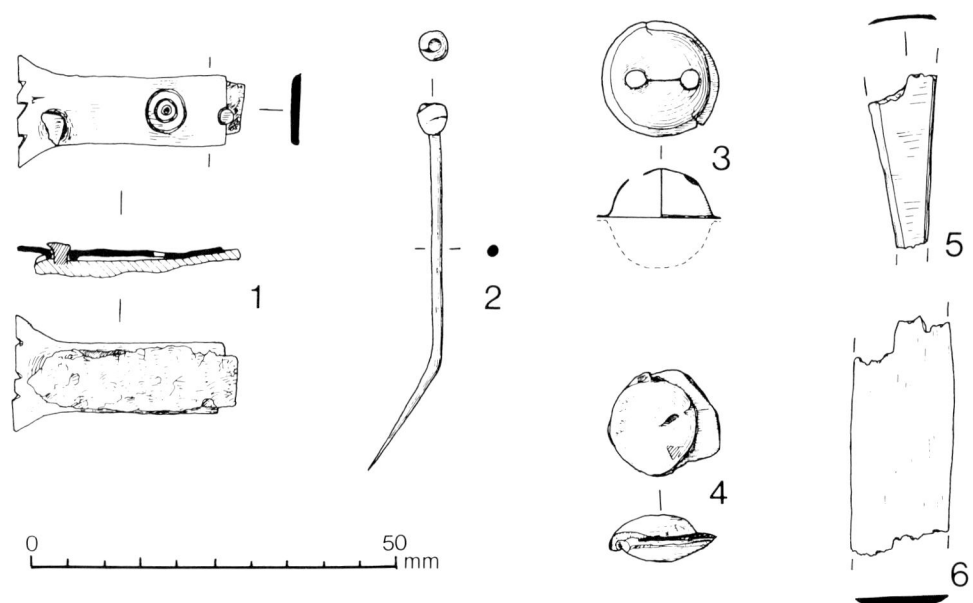

Fig 69   Post-medieval small finds: nos 1–3 copper alloy; no 4 lead; no 5 bone; no 6 ivory; scale 1:1

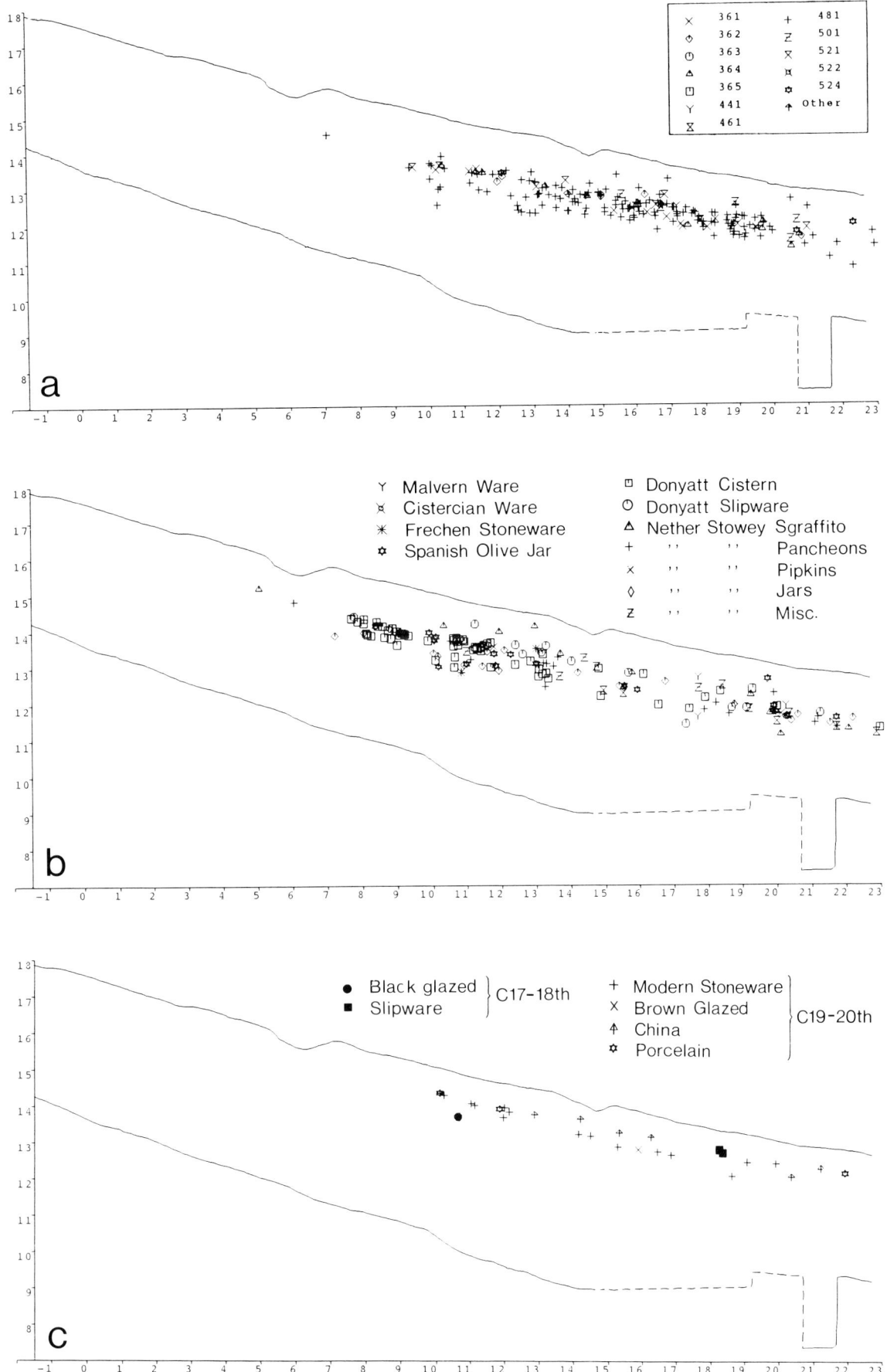

Fig 70 Artefact distributions: (a) prehistoric pottery in Units 1–4a with key to pottery fabrics; (b) sixteenth- and seventeenth-century pottery; (c) later sixteenth- to twentieth-century pottery

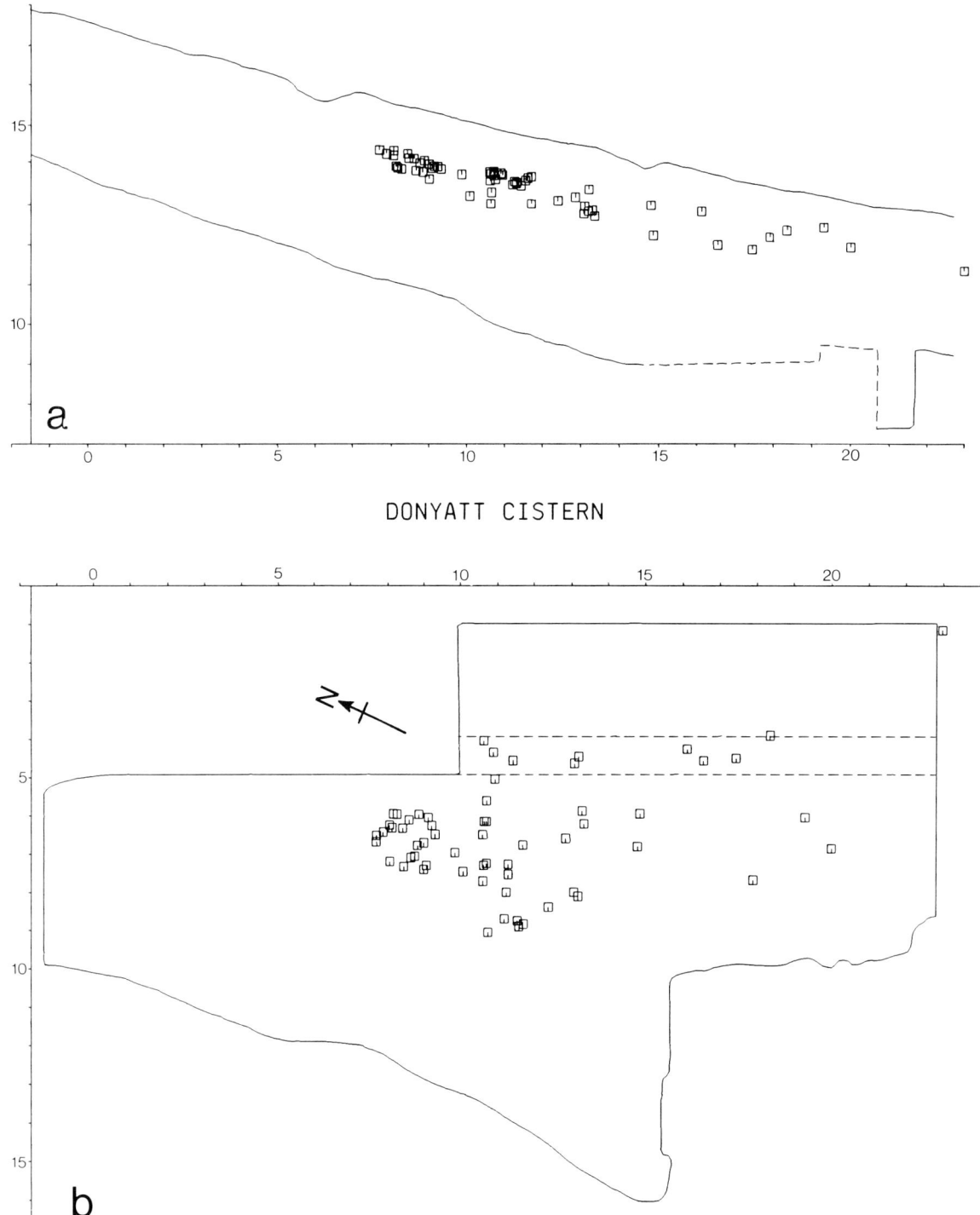

Fig 71 Distribution of sherds of a single Donyatt cistern: (a) horizontal distribution; (b) vertical distribution

this is brought out by the distribution (Fig 71) of sherds of a single Donyatt cistern which were scattered both vertically and horizontally by erosion of the blowout and associated rabbit activity. There was so little later seventeenth- and eighteenth-century pottery that we cannot derive any conclusions from its distribution. Nineteenth- and twentieth-century sherds overlay the earlier post-medieval material and were largely from a band between 0.5 and 1m below the present surface, roughly corresponding to Context 12. Twentieth-century glass and other artefacts were largely confined to Context 11.1 and above. The distribution of a range of other finds such as coke, coal, building materials, and recent metal artefacts is shown on MF1:B10. Their distribution is concentrated in the upper part of the post-medieval sequence, suggesting that most reached the site in the nineteenth and twentieth centuries. Some of these objects in earlier deposits probably derive from faunal disturbance.

Conclusions and historical evidence

ApSimon *et al* (1961) noted traces of buildings exposed in the cliff face in 1936–7 and 1957–9. They also report a sgraffito decorated dish very similar to Figure 67.4 and 5. Comparing their section to ours, the terraced floor of the building they identified lay between *c* 5 and 9m on the A-axis, ie slightly upslope and 6m to seaward of the concentration of sixteenth- and earlier seventeenth-century pottery reported here. Traces of burning and occupation spread (Context 18) probably relate to the life of this structure. In view of the apparent contemporaneity between the blowout and the building it is likely that the cutting of the terraces for the building helped trigger erosion, and artefacts derived from domestic activity in the building then accumulated as the blowout filled with sand. Jane Evans of Woodspring Museum has suggested that this building may relate to historical evidence for a rabbit warren at Brean Down.

The first record of the warren was in AD 1361 (Knight 1902). In *c* AD 1610 a group of men were charged before the Star Chamber with poaching and damaging the warren. The case papers (Baker 1919) refer to two buildings. One is the lodge which 'tyme out of mynde hath been for lodginge of the Keepers'. The other was the home of Thomas Bond of London, Lord of the Manor and owner of the warren. This stood within earshot of the lodge. Since the pottery assemblage is later sixteenth- and early seventeenth-century, the sandcliff site is likely to be that of one of these buildings. The other probably lay at Brean Down Farm 600m to the east. A recent survey of this farm by Commander E Williams (pers comm) suggests that the original building is late medieval, but the structure was replaced in the seventeenth century. This is probably the house described as newly built when it was sold by Bond in 1637 (Knight 1902). It seems probable, therefore, that the sandcliff structure was the warrener's lodge, although the situation is complicated by E Bowen's 1750 Map of Somerset which marks 'lodge' on the site of Brean Down Farm and nothing on the sandcliff. Perhaps the functions of the lodge were transferred here after the abandonment of the sandcliff building in the early seventeenth-century. There is cartographic evidence for a later building on or near the sandcliff on maps by Day and Masters (1782), Crocker (1819-Skinner Ms British Library Add Mss 33,653), and Colt Hoare (1821), and in view of this it is surprising that so little eighteenth-century pottery was found.

8   The auger survey, soil pits, and intertidal archaeology

Introduction

The focus of the archaeological project was, of necessity, the cliff face where the archaeological deposits were undergoing active erosion. Proper understanding of the site demanded, however, that this small area studied in detail be set within a wider context. From the archaeological resource management point of view a decision on whether the sequence warranted protection from the sea rested partly on how far the archaeological horizons extended inland. If, for example, only the last vestiges remained then it might be cheaper to excavate than preserve; conversely, if the occupation extended a long way inland, then preservation might be the only economic option. Linked to this were the following research objectives:

1   What is the inland extent of each occupation horizon?
2   How variable is the sequence inland?
3   What is the stratigraphic relationship between the sandcliff deposits and the silty clay flats which lie just to the south?

These problems were confronted by putting down about 100 auger holes and seven soil pits designed to investigate the sediments up to 100m inland (Fig 72). Additionally there was some very limited investigation of the intertidal area.

The auger survey

by Keith Crabtree

During the two working summers of 1985 and 1986 about 100 auger borings were made on a grid parallel to the exposed face of the southern slope of the cliff at 5 or 10m intervals (Fig 72). The auger borings were made using a simple screw auger, a bucket type Garrett auger with a 0.1m diameter bucket, or an Eylénkamp Riverside auger with a 0.05m diameter bucket. The Garrett was the most used and coped extremely well even with the stony colluvial layers. A power-driven postholer was used experimentally but proved unsatisfactory. Most borings took two persons half a day, owing to the physical effort of boring plus the recording of the material using colour (Munsell), texture, stoniness, and consistence as criteria. The work represented approximately 90 man days and the average depth of auger borings was 2.25m with a maximum depth of 5.93m. Of the auger borings 69 reached the distinctive palaeosol on top of the lower breccia at which point the boring was terminated. A number were stopped by large stones in the upper stony colluvium (Unit 4) and one (20/990) was stopped by metal and remains from the wartime building on the site. A single person (KC) recorded the large majority of the boreholes, making possible a better degree of consistency in the recording.

The profiles are presented on a three-dimensional diagram, Figure 73. Each auger hole is placed on its correct Ordnance Datum line and the coordinates are given for the first hole on each grid line. Auger holes are at 5m intervals downslope except along coordinate 900 where variable intervals are used to accommodate the roadway and the ditch, and along coordinate 990 where no record is available for 20/990 because of the presence of debris from a wartime hut. Three more detailed north–south sections along the lines of the coordinates are presented separately in Figure 74 and all the other north–south sections are on MF1:B11–C4. Finds of pottery are marked by asterisks on Figure 73.

As augering proceeded it became clear that there were a limited number of easily recognised horizons, often with a repeated pattern, which could be related to the stratigraphy exposed in the sandcliff section. The augering ceased when the auger reached the impenetrable stones of the breccia (Unit 8b). Usually within the auger bit one found only a few stone fragments in a dark reddish matrix. This matrix was a part of the palaeosol (Unit 8a) distinguishable by its dark reddish brown colour, its clay texture, and by the inclusion of large charcoal fragments. On the lower slopes the palaeosol was overlain by a colluvium which was sandier in texture than the clay of the palaeosol and slightly lighter in colour.

The palaeosol or the colluvium was in turn overlain by the yellow sands of Unit 5. In places, between coordinates 995 and 970 again on the lower parts of the slopes, the sands had intercalated within them a layer of distinctive grey clay and charcoal. These deposits, which can be correlated with Unit 5b, were similar to those found in the excavation associated with the hearth in Structure 95. In a few borings a thin upper layer of the sands was stained olive green and this was also found to be a distinctive feature of Unit 5b in the main trench.

Overlying the yellow sands was the upper reddish to grey stony colluvial material of Unit 4 and Unit 4a. In about a third of the borings the grey colluvium of Unit 4 with many charcoal fragments was present. In 16 borings fragments of late Bronze Age pottery were recorded in this layer. This very distinctive deposit was recorded in the sandcliff face, in most auger lines up to coordinate 910, and in Soil Pit V on coordinate 900, indicating the large areal extent of the late Bronze Age occupation debris layer. With the exception of some of the footslope borings, and a few where it was replaced by Unit 4, all auger borings contained the stony red colluvium of Unit 4a. In a few auger borings and in Pit V a thin layer of sands was present within (eg 65/910) the upper reddish colluvium or between (eg 05/970, 15/970, 40/945) the colluvium and the greyish occupation layer.

The upper sediments on which the present soil has developed are an orange sand, varying from being relatively stone-free near the surface to quite stony at depth.

Along coordinates 910 and 900 the auger survey included estuarine dark grey to brown silty clays with some sand lenses which underlay the yellow sands

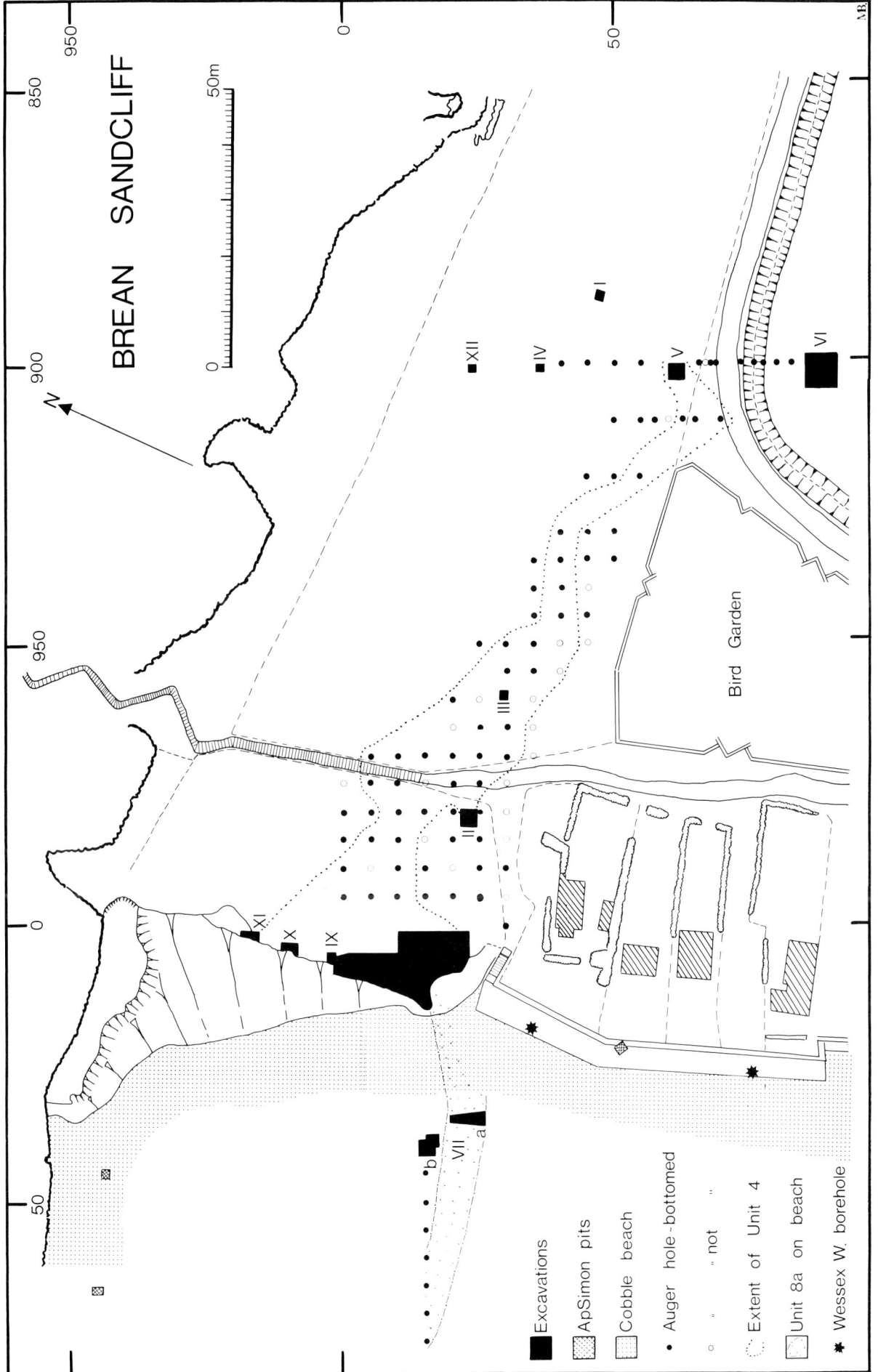

Fig 72 Plan of sandcliff showing the relationship between the main trench and the soil pits and auger holes; also shown is the extent of late Bronze Age Unit 4 and the approximate outcrop of the basal palaeosol Unit 8a on the beach

and overlay the palaeosol and breccia. These silty clays are associated with the rising sea level reaching an elevation close to that of today possibly during the Neolithic period (see Godwin *et al* 1958; Kidson 1977). In our augering they extended to about 5m above OD while we recorded the palaeosol down to just below 0m OD and presumed it to extend lower than that to the south.

Where soil pits were later dug adjacent to the auger holes the pits confirmed the stratigraphy as already determined from the auger borings (Figs 75 and 76). Undoubtedly there is an error factor of ±0.1m in the depth recordings when using the augers. Some of the subtle variations within the lower yellow sands (Unit 5) and in the occupation and hearth debris layers are also lost in the auger borings. Nevertheless it is felt that the auger survey provided very good detail over an extensive area and was able to pick out the main stratigraphic horizons and provide a basis for the siting of the large soil pits. The presence of the Bird Garden restricted borings at the foot of the slope from coordinates 965 to 920. The upslope portion (ie above coordinates 20 to 45) of the sandcliff here contained only fairly shallow profiles, with the orange sands (Unit 3) resting directly on the truncated palaeosol on the lower breccia (Unit 8b). These shallow sites were not augered in detail.

A fuller description of the identified horizons is given below, based upon the field record of the auger borings and tied into the stratigraphic nomenclature of the excavated section wherever possible.

The stratigraphy as evidenced from the auger survey

On the cross-sectional diagrams the deposits as identified by the auger survey are correlated with the units as defined originally by ApSimon *et al* (1961). They are recorded on the sectional diagrams and listed below as seen in the auger borings.

Unit 8b

The breccia was not sampled with the auger. The stones were generally too large for the auger and the matrix extremely tough. Augering was stopped when the auger met the resistance of the breccia.

Unit 8a

The palaeosol developed on the breccia. This was distinctive in both its texture (sandy clay to clay), its colour (2.5YR, dark reddish brown), and by the inclusion of quite large fragments of charcoal. Its thickness as penetrated by the auger varied as to whether the auger hit a stone or not in its upper horizon. There was a tendency for the thickness to increase downslope. In the excavated areas this palaeosol appeared quite stony but in the auger borings it was not easy to separate which stones were effectively within the palaeosol and which within the breccia.

Unit 7

No trace of this unit, the 'Beaker sand', was found either in the auger or soil pit surveys.

Unit 6

Colluvium above the palaeosol. This horizon was difficult to separate in the auger borings. It was usually identified as being a layer of sandy loam to clay loam of yellower hue (5YR) overlying the distinctive reddish clayey palaeosol of Unit 8a. The amount of sand included varied as one might expect if colluviation occurred at the same time as wind-blown sand was beginning to accumulate. Only the lower slope sites had the colluvium at all well developed.

Unit 5d

Yellow sands very similar to those described under 5a below.

Unit 5b

Hearth debris varying from sands to almost pure clays or silty clays in texture, with colour varying from speckled red through to grey clay usually with flecks of charcoal. This disposition varies from massive to laminated. The layer in the excavations was best developed on the hut floors, eg the hearth in Structure 95 and the lens of hearth debris to the south (Context 77), but in the auger survey similar material was located and is regarded as debris periodically thrown out from the huts. Hence it is scattered generally downslope and inland from the huts. Its presence in auger borings away from known and excavated huts may indicate the occurrence of other middle Bronze Age huts still buried in the sandcliff. The deposit extends at least 25m to the east (eg 25/975).

Unit 5a

The yellow sands. These appear very clean, pure, and quite coarse. Their colour varies little and is 7.5YR 5/4 to 10YR 5/6, brown to yellowish brown. On the upper part of the slope they are absent, but lower downslope they appear and thicken to reach a thickness of at least 2.5m. In places they appear almost uniform throughout, but in other borings (eg 20 and 25/995, 15 and 25/990, 25/985, 30/980, and 30/970) there are intercalated deposits (see below).

Unnamed unit within Unit 5a

Olive green sands identical to those of Unit 5a except for their colour which tends to be yellowish brown to olive yellow (10YR 5/6 to 2.5YR 6/6). These are sands stained with a greenish tinge and lie below either the upper colluvium (Unit 4a) or occupation layer (Unit 4). This staining was a characteristic of the Unit 5b occupation horizon in the main trench and its causes in that context are discussed in Chapters 15 and 16. The auger survey, particularly borings 20/980 and 20/995, indicates that further inland similar staining exists within Unit 5a. This might hint at the existence of another occupation horizon within Unit 5a or it might represent iron organo-phosphate staining derived from the overlying Unit 4.

Unit 4

The late Bronze Age occupation layer. This layer is distinguished by its colour (generally 7.5YR 4/4, brown to dark brown), by the presence of a lot of flecks of charcoal, and by the occasional inclusion of fragments of late Bronze Age pottery. It is often quite stony and has a more loamy texture than the underlying sands. In most cases it directly underlies the upper colluvium (Unit 4a) but in some cases it seems to replace it. There may have been a problem in the identification of thin layers of colluvium in the auger samples and the varying degrees of redness and greyness of the debris layer. In a few borings (eg 15/975 and 20/970) Unit 4 interdigitated with 4a while in several (eg 40/945, 05, and 15/970) there was a thin layer of sands similar to Unit 3 between the two stony colluvial layers. One of the main aims of the auger survey was to find the areal extent of the occupation debris and Figure 72 shows the proven extent of Unit 4 in relation to the pattern of auger holes.

Unit 4a

The upper red colluvium. This was distinctive and usually very stony. One auger boring (60/910) failed to penetrate it because of the stones. The stones were angular to subangular. It was distinguishable by its cohesiveness caused by increased silt and clay content, and by its colour (5YR 4/4, reddish brown). In a few borings (eg 25 and 30/965, and 20 and 25/970) this layer appeared to be replaced by Unit 4, the grey occupation debris layer, while in the lower borings along coordinates 995 to 980 it is missing and the orange sands rest directly on Unit 5a, the yellow sands. It is not known whether this is due to downslope wedging out of the colluvium or to later erosion of it. In the excavated face this loss of the red colluvium in the lower slopes was clear (Fig 15). In the auger borings the colluvial layer was devoid of artefacts except in 40/935 where a late Bronze Age pottery fragment occurred. This may be due to failure to recognise, in that boring, the underlying Unit 4 which often contained such artefacts or to reworking of Unit 4 by the colluviation process. It should be noted, however, that no such reworking was evident in the main trench where artefacts were very few in Unit 4a.

Unit 3

The orange sands. In a number of the auger borings these could be separated into two distinct sands. The upper was coarser while the lower was finer and less consolidated. At times this lower unconsolidated sand was difficult to extract with the auger and often the hand and arm had to be extended down the bore hole and the sand removed manually. Where easily distinguishable in the field the two sands are recorded separately, but where not easily distinguished the coarse sand symbol has been used on the diagrams. Stoniness varied, but it is not possible to indicate this on the diagrams as its assessment in the field is very subjective and depends upon chance factors (eg whether a stone is struck with the auger or not). On the whole the stones were more rounded than in the colluvium below. The upslope sites often had more stones, some of which were weathered and quite rounded. The downslope sites were almost stone-free in some borings.

Unit 1

Modern soil developed on underlying deposits, usually Unit 3 (orange sands), but in the area of the clay levels developed on the estuarine or alluvial sands, silts, and clays. The modern soil varies in its development in relation to the amount of truncation by slope processes, in part accentuated by agricultural practices. On part of the sandcliff slope, roughly below a line from coordinate 45/945 to 55/900 and within the fenced-off field, ploughing has caused a much thicker layer definable as part of the modern soil. This ploughing is evidenced from wartime photographs and from the presence well down in the profile of modern artefacts and animal bones. Similarly, sites within the area of the wartime hut included deeper soil profiles with signs of disturbance such as fragments of metal and modern glass.

Estuarine silty clays of the flats

In the auger holes at the base of Soil Pit VI, the colluvium, Unit 6, was originally recorded in the field as lying beneath estuarine silts and clays and overlying the palaeosol. This deposit had the character of the Unit 6 material already recorded in a number of the slope auger holes. However, it was subsequently found to include marine diatoms and it is now thought to be reworked from the underlying palaeosol by marine action. It has been plotted on the cross-section of coordinate 900 as a separate deposit. Genetically it is not the same as Unit 6 although its stratigraphic position and its field appearance are equivalent to Unit 6.

The marine sandy silts and silty clays were not given a unit number by ApSimon *et al* (1961) as they were time transgressive with some of the units. One could readily separate several distinct horizons within the silts. In borings 69/900 to 82.5/900 the upper horizon was a sandy clay or sandy silt with a brown colour (7.5YR 4/2–4/4). This was underlain by massive silty clays, greyer in colour (10YR 5/2, greyish brown to 5Y 5/1, grey), in which occurred occasional bands or lenses of sands. The relatively close sampling interval along line 900 plus Soil Pit VI enabled the relationship of some of these bands and the main silts or clays to be seen. Some of the bands would appear to be lenses only while others are more continuous and in places quite coarse. Plant fragments are recorded towards the bottom of the auger holes in Soil Pit VI but were not seen elsewhere during the auger survey. While preparing the samples from the auger holes at the base of the pit for pollen analysis, it was apparent that the silts and clays varied in the amount of free carbonate. Many of the lower samples effervesced freely when acid was added but the upper clays and silts did not. Similarly, in the process of oxidising with hydrogen peroxide, the amount of organic matter present varied considerably between the samples as evidenced again by the vigour of the reaction. The samples were not routinely tested for carbonate in the field.

The soil pits

The positions of these were determined partly by the results of auger survey and partly by specific objectives. Pit II was 20m inland from the excavation trench and was designed to establish whether occupation extended to the inland limit of National Trust property. Pit III was 40m inland and was designed to establish whether occupation continued into farmland to the east. Pits XII, IV, V, VI, and I were on a transect 100m inland. Along with close interval augering at critical points of the transect these were designed to look at the relationship between the sandcliff and the silty clay flats. Soil Pit VII was designed to examine the basal palaeosol (Unit 8a) on the foreshore where it dipped below the beach. Pits V, VI, and VII were excavated using a JCB, while the remainder were dug by hand. During hand digging and cleaning of the JCB-excavated pits artefacts were three-dimensionally recorded and MF1:C5 provides a full breakdown of the prehistoric pottery fabrics present in each soil pit context.

Soil Pit II

This was 3m square but below 1.8m it was stepped in for safety to 1.5m square; the sides were somewhat battered and the base was 1m square and the overall depth 3.3m. It was largely dug using a shovel but occupation horizons and a 50m wide strip of the sequence were trowelled and finds three-dimensionally recorded. The sequence (Fig 75) was as follows:

Context 117

Reddish brown (5YR 4/4) sandy clay loam, basal palaeosol, Unit 8a.

Context 49

Dark reddish grey (5YR 4/2) silty clay with much charcoal, containing two Bronze Age sherds and an illustrated Beaker sherd (B17), Unit 6b.

Context 118

Reddish grey (10YR 5/1) sandy clay with light olive brown (2.5Y 5/6) staining, Unit 6a. Contained one Bronze Age sherd.

Context 48

Yellow (10YR 7/6) sterile sand, Unit 5d.

Contexts 45, 46, and 47

A series of coloured sand bands, the lowest dark grey (2.5Y 5/6) at the base and olive green (5Y 6/6) on the surface overlain by very pale brown sterile sand (Context 46) and above this a light brown (7.5YR 6/4) sandy loam crust (Context 45). This sequence of bands closely resembles Unit 5b as it was at about 9m on the A coordinate in the main trench. No pottery was found at this horizon in Soil Pit II.

Context 40

Yellow (10YR 7/6) sand, stone-free and sterile, containing three Bronze Age sherds, Unit 5a.

Contexts 38 and 44

Dark greyish brown (10YR 4/2) sandy loam with stones. Unit 4, late Bronze Age occupation horizon. Finds included 81 sherds (50084) probably from a single (unillustrated) vessel of fabric 522. Another particularly significant find was a copper bracelet (3). At the base of Context 38 were a number of related contexts. Context 42 was a V-shaped gully 0.8m wide by 0.5m deep. Its curvature within the soil pit suggests that it may have enclosed a circular area upslope. It was similar to gully Context 51 in the main trench. The fill (Context 41) was a light brownish grey (10YR 6/2) silty loam and it contained 20 Bronze Age sherds. Context 43 was a shallow bowl-shaped depression at the base of Context 38; it was 0.6m in diameter and 0.14m deep and contained a circular fired clay 'counter' (122). The Unit 4 contexts together produced 280 sherds of Bronze Age pottery; this, together with the copper bracelet and the presence of features, establishes unequivocally that this occupation horizon extends at least 20m inland from the main trench.

Context 39

Dark yellowish brown (10YR 5/3) loamy sand with stones confined to north-west corner and not on section. Probably Unit 3b2.

Context 37

Dark yellowish brown (10YR 4/4) sand, Unit 3a.

Context 36

Very dark grey brown (10YR 3/2) topsoil, Unit 1.

Soil Pit III

This was 1.5m square with battered sides and 2.8m deep. The sequence (Fig 76) was as follows:

Context 87

Breccia, Unit 8b.

Context 86

Reddish brown (5YR 4/3) silty loam, Unit 8a. There was no evidence here of overlying Unit 6 deposits.

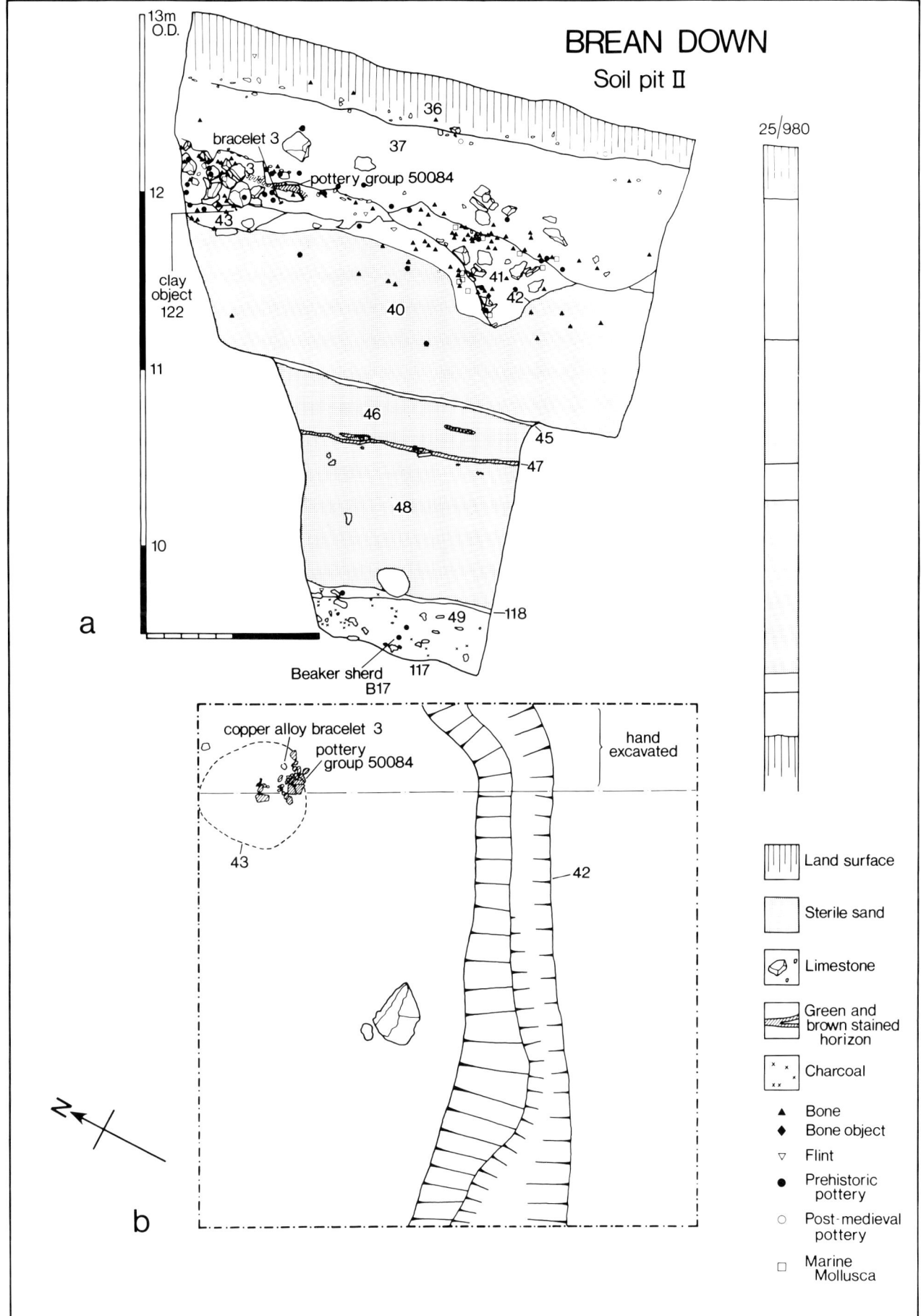

Fig 75 Soil Pit II: (a) section with auger hole 25/980, 0.5m south; (b) plan of Unit 4

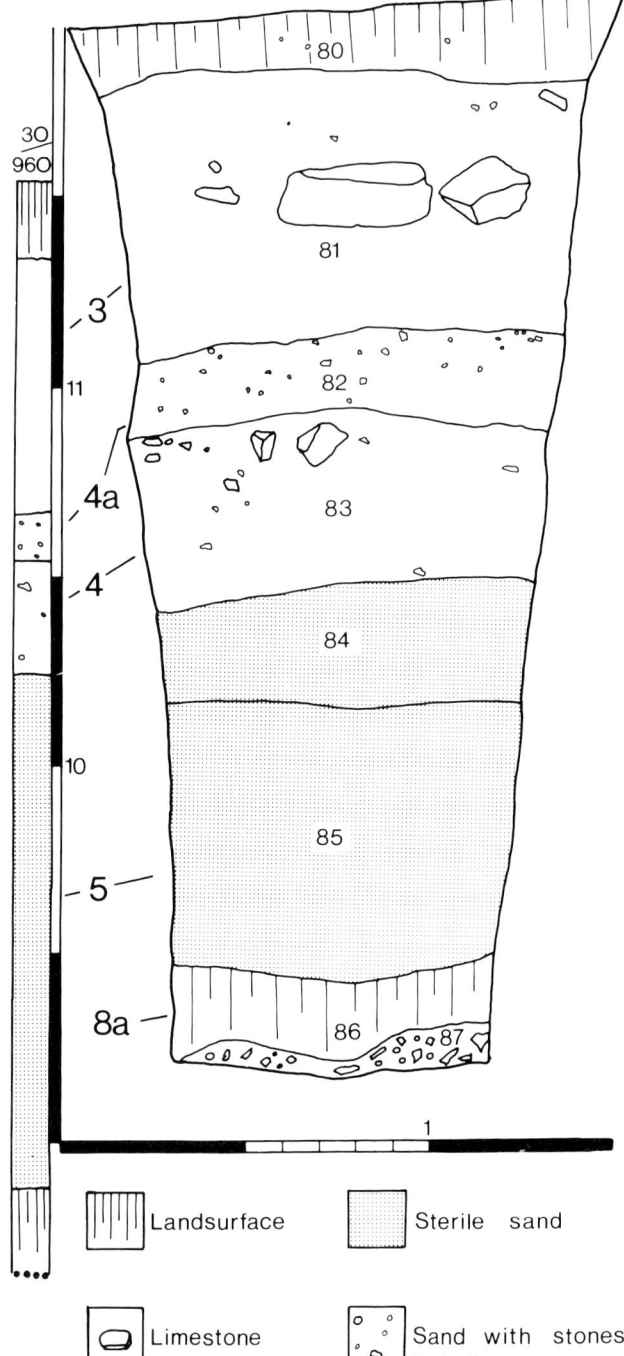

Fig 76   Section of Soil Pit III showing auger hole 30/960, 2m to the south

Context 85

Brownish yellow (10YR 5/6) sterile sand, Unit 5. No clear evidence was found in Soil Pit III for the Unit 5b occupation horizon.

Context 84

Yellow (10YR 7/6) unconsolidated sterile sand, Unit 5.

Context 83

Dark greyish brown (10YR 4/2) sandy loam with occupation material including bone, shell, fired clay, and 28 sherds of pottery. This clearly corresponds to Unit 4 and shows that the occupation extends at least 40m inland from the main trench.

Context 82

Reddish brown (5YR 4/4) sandy loam with small and medium stones, colluvial deposit, Unit 4a.

Context 81

Yellowish brown (10YR 5/4) sandy loam with large stone blocks, Unit 3.

Context 80

Dark brown (10YR 3/3) topsoil, Unit 1.

Soil Pit XII

This was the most northerly pit on the main transect of soil pits (Fig 77) and was well upslope at c 20m OD (Fig 72). It was 1.5m square and 1.2m deep. The stratigraphy (Fig 78) was as follows:

Context 236

Reddish brown (5YR 4/3) silty clay with large limestone blocks, Breccia Unit 8b.

Context 235

Dark reddish brown (5YR 3/6) silty sand with abundant limestone, Breccia Unit 8b.

Context 234

Reddish brown (5YR 4/6) sand with limestone fragments, ?Unit 3.

Context 233

Dark brown (10YR 3/3) topsoil, Unit 1.

The pit showed that there was a maximum depth of c 0.5m of post-glacial stratigraphy and the basal palaeosol had been entirely eroded away.

Soil Pit IV

This was on the transect at 14.5m OD; it was 1.5m square and 2.1m deep. The sequence (Fig 78) was as follows:

Context 211

Reddish yellow (7.5YR 6.6) sand with veins of calcium carbonate deposit. This clearly represents the main Pleistocene sand, Unit 9, which has been reached at a point where the overlying breccia is only 1m thick. The post-glacial deposits at this point on the transect are less than 0.3m thick.

Contexts 209 and 210

Reddish brown (5YR 4/3) silty loam with abundant angular limestone, Breccia Unit 8b/c.

Fig 77 *View from the south along the soil pit transect; from foreground to background Pits VI, V, IV, and XII (photo: M J Allen)*

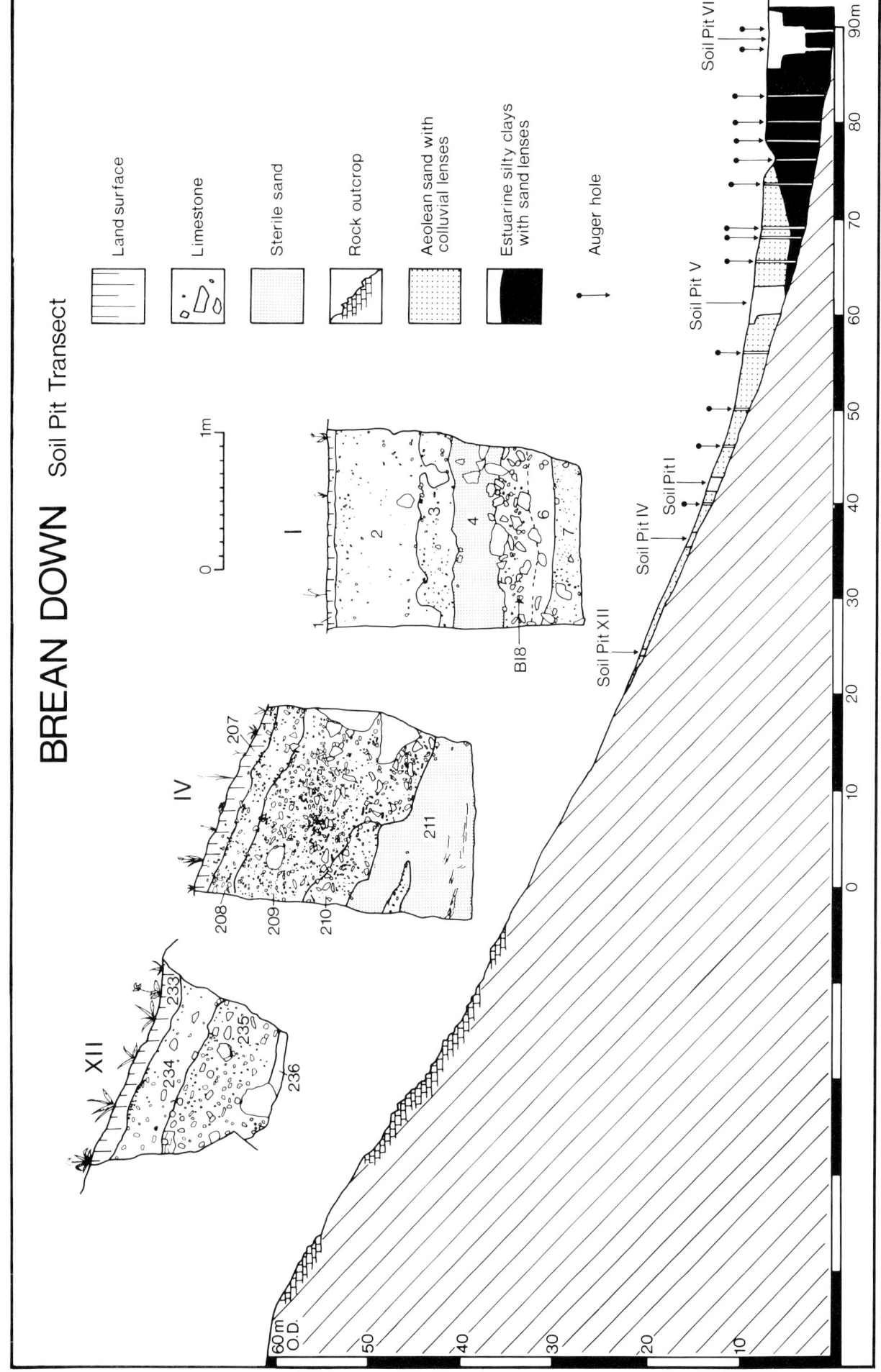

Fig 78 Soil pit and auger transect along the 900m coordinate, from the top of Brean Down (left) to the estuarine flats (right) showing the stratigraphy in Pits XII, I, and IV

Context 208

Reddish brown (5YR 4/4) sandy silt, abundant stones, ?Unit 3. This produced five sherds of Bronze Age pottery and a tiny comb-impressed Beaker sherd (50500, unillustrated).

Context 207

Dark brown (7.5YR 3/3) sandy silt topsoil, Unit 1.

Soil Pit I

This was 11m east of the transect at 16m OD. It was 1.5m square and 1.9m deep. The sequence (Fig 78) was as follows:

Context 7

Yellowish red (5YR 4/6) sandy clay loam, Breccia Unit 8b.

Context 6

Yellowish red (5YR 4/6) clay loam, stone free, Unit 8a.

Context 5

Reddish brown (5YR 4/3) silty clay loam with abundant stone, charcoal present. Three Bronze Age sherds and one Beaker sherd (B18), Unit 6.

Context 4

Yellowish brown (10YR 5/6) sand, Unit 5.

Context 3

Reddish brown (5YR 4/4) sandy clay with common stones, Unit 4a.

Context 2

Reddish brown (5YR 5/4) sand, one Bronze Age sherd, Unit 3.

Context 1

Dark brown (7.5YR 3/3) humic topsoil, Unit 1.

Soil Pit V

This was on the transect at *c* 8.4m; it was 6m north of the road to Brean Down Farm (Figs 72 and 78) which seems roughly to mark the boundary between the slope/dune deposits and the silty clays of the flats. The pit was 4m square. It was largely JCB excavated but the edges were cut back by hand and artefacts recorded in the process. The sequence (Figs 79 and 80) was as follows:

Context 219

Stony Pleistocene breccia.

Context 218

Dull reddish brown (2.5YR 4/4) silty clay forming a basal palaeosol shown by micromorphological sample E to represent a wet colluvial/estuarine interface. Contained bone and charcoal but no pottery. Equates with Unit 8a probably with a thin, though not clearly defined, colluvial surface equating with Unit 6b.

Context 288

Also overlying the basal palaeosol/colluvium was grey silty clay confined to the lowest part of the trench in its south-west corner (Fig 79). The surface of this layer was at 4.87m OD and it was a maximum of 0.17m thick. It is interpreted as the product of estuarine inundation. Micromorphological analysis of sample E 1.4m north of the edge of this layer confirms the input of estuarine sediments at this horizon. The interpretation is further confirmed by the auger survey (Fig 78) which clearly shows this grey silty clay thickening to the south as the basal deposits dip.

Context 220

Large and very large limestone blocks forming a spread resting on Units 6/8a. The spread was 1.5m wide, confined to the east half of the pit and with a rough linear edge running north–south. West of this edge was the basal palaeosol (8a)/colluvium containing a much smaller proportion of stone. Within the spread, stone size tended to decrease towards the periphery suggesting that the feature may have been associated with clearance – perhaps either a clearance cairn or a wall deriving from clearance. There was some associated bone or charcoal but no pottery. If the clearance hypothesis is correct then it can probably be correlated with the well-attested cultivation episode at the time of Unit 6b since it clearly rests on the basal deposits.

Context 217

Bright brown (7.5YR 5/8) sand, stone-free, containing bone in greater concentrations than any of the other blown sand layers (Fig 79), suggesting that some agency responsible for bone dispersal (?dogs) was active in this area whilst the dune was accumulating. Unit 5d. Near the base of this context on the west section (not shown on Fig 79) was a thin (30mm) reddish brown (5YR 4/6) stabilisation horizon underlain by 0.1m of sterile sand and then by the underlying palaeosol.

Contexts 215 and 216

Yellowish brown (10YR 5/4) silty sand with one very large limestone block and about ten medium stones. It produced bone and one Bronze Age sherd of Fabric 361. This can probably be correlated with Unit 5b and, in view of the artefacts and stones, may indicate that this occupation horizon extends much further inland than was suggested by the other soil pits and the auger survey.

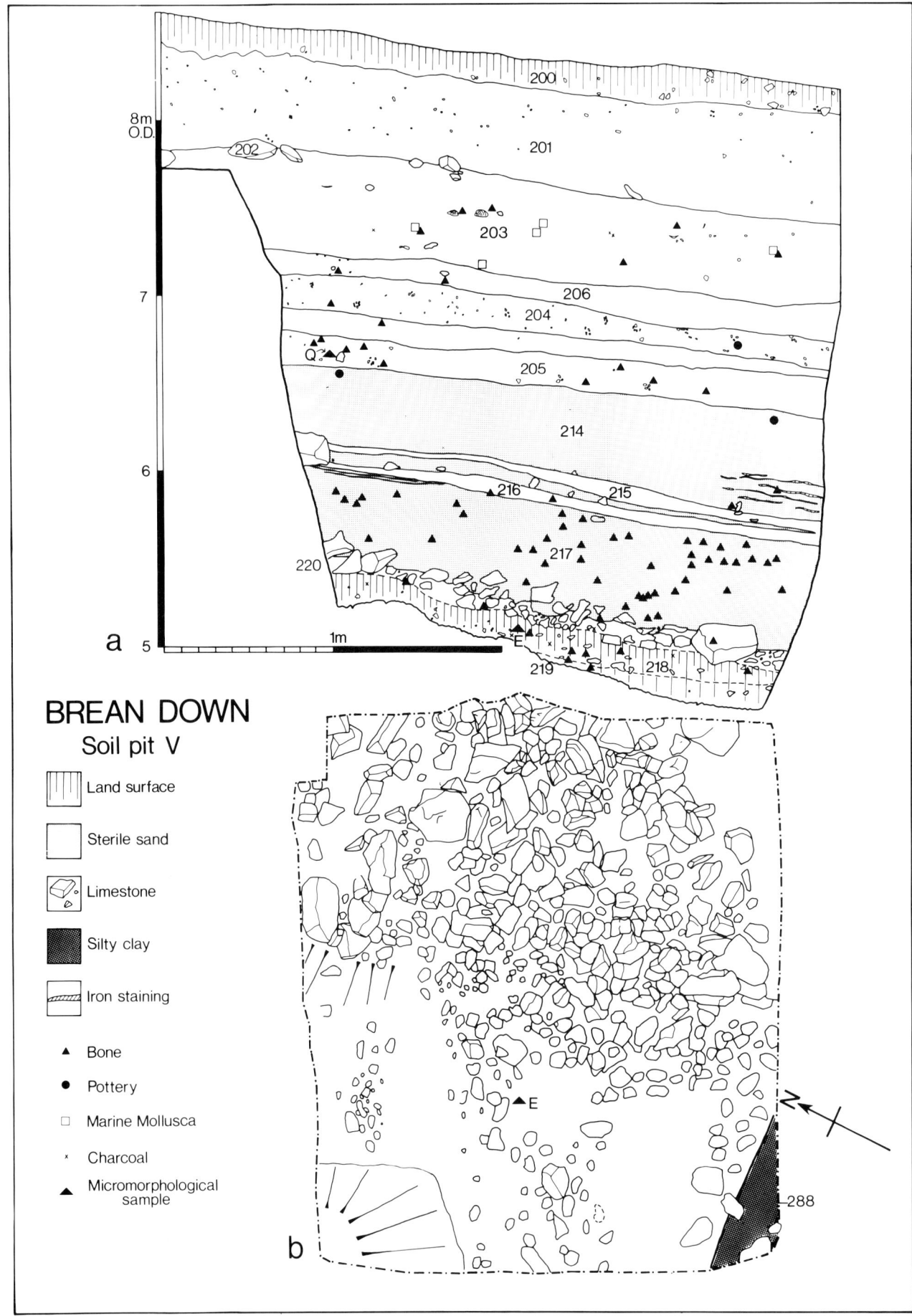

Fig 79 Soil Pit V: (a) section and (b) plan of stone feature (220) on surface of Unit 6

Fig 80   Soil Pit V: section showing stone feature (Context 220) on the surface of Unit 6 (photo: A Philpott)

Context 214

Light yellowish brown (10YR 6/4) sterile sand with localised evidence of iron staining picking out bedding surfaces within the dune. Contained two Bronze Age sherds. Probably Unit 5a.

Context 205

Dull reddish brown (5YR 4/3) silty sand, containing eight Bronze Age sherds. In the field this context was of almost identical appearance to Unit 4 in the main trench and this very close comparison is confirmed by micromorphological sample Q (Chapter 16). Thus Unit 4 extends at least 100m inland and still contains pottery and bone. To explain the extensive nature of this unit Richard Macphail suggests cultivation (Chapter 16), yet the archaeological evidence from the main trench (Chapter 5) argued against cultivation and led to the suggestion that trample by stock might have been responsible.

Context 204

Dark reddish brown (5YR 3/6) sandy clay with small and medium limestone pieces, colluvial deposit, Unit 4a.

Context 206

Yellowish brown (10YR 5/6) sand, stone-free, Unit 3.

Context 203

Dull reddish brown (5YR 4/4) sand with some oyster shells, bone, daub, and charcoal, Unit 3.

Context 202

About 19 large limestone blocks forming a rough spread in the north-east corner of Soil Pit V, associated with oysters, daub, coke, and two sherds of Romano-British pottery (both 50529 unillustrated). It seems probable that this stone represents spread from a structure but its date is unclear. Unit 3.

Context 201

Dull reddish brown (5YR 4/4) sand, three post-medieval sherds, one clay pipe fragment, Unit 3.

Context 200

Brownish black (5YR 3/1) sandy topsoil, one post-medieval sherd, one clay pipe fragment, Unit 1.

Soil Pit VI

This was located 22m south of Soil Pit V on the silty clay flats which are here at c 6.5m OD (Fig 77). The pit was 6m square but was stepped in at a depth of 1.3m to 3m square. It was dug by JCB and then cleaned by hand, which produced a few artefacts. Its depth was 3.5m, and deposits below this were investigated by means of four auger holes close to the four corners of the pit. The stratigraphy of these auger holes is shown on Figure 81. The sequence was far deeper than, and radically different from, that revealed by Soil Pit V, in that it consisted predominantly of waterlain silty clays in contrast to the basically aeolian sands of Soil Pit V. Because of this contrast, correlation between Pit VI and the unit sequence from the sandcliff is a particular problem, the partial resolution of which depends on data derived from several sources. Consequently the basic sequence will be outlined here and correlation questions are largely deferred until the concluding section of this chapter.

Context 238

The base of the sequence as revealed by augering was at c 0m OD where stony breccia was overlain by dark brown (10YR 3/3) sandy silt which clearly corresponds to the basal palaeosol (Unit 8a) of the sandcliff sequence as auger survey between Pits V and VI confirmed (Fig 78).

Context 232

Above the basal palaeosol the auger holes showed a complete change to grey (5Y 5/1) silt near the base of

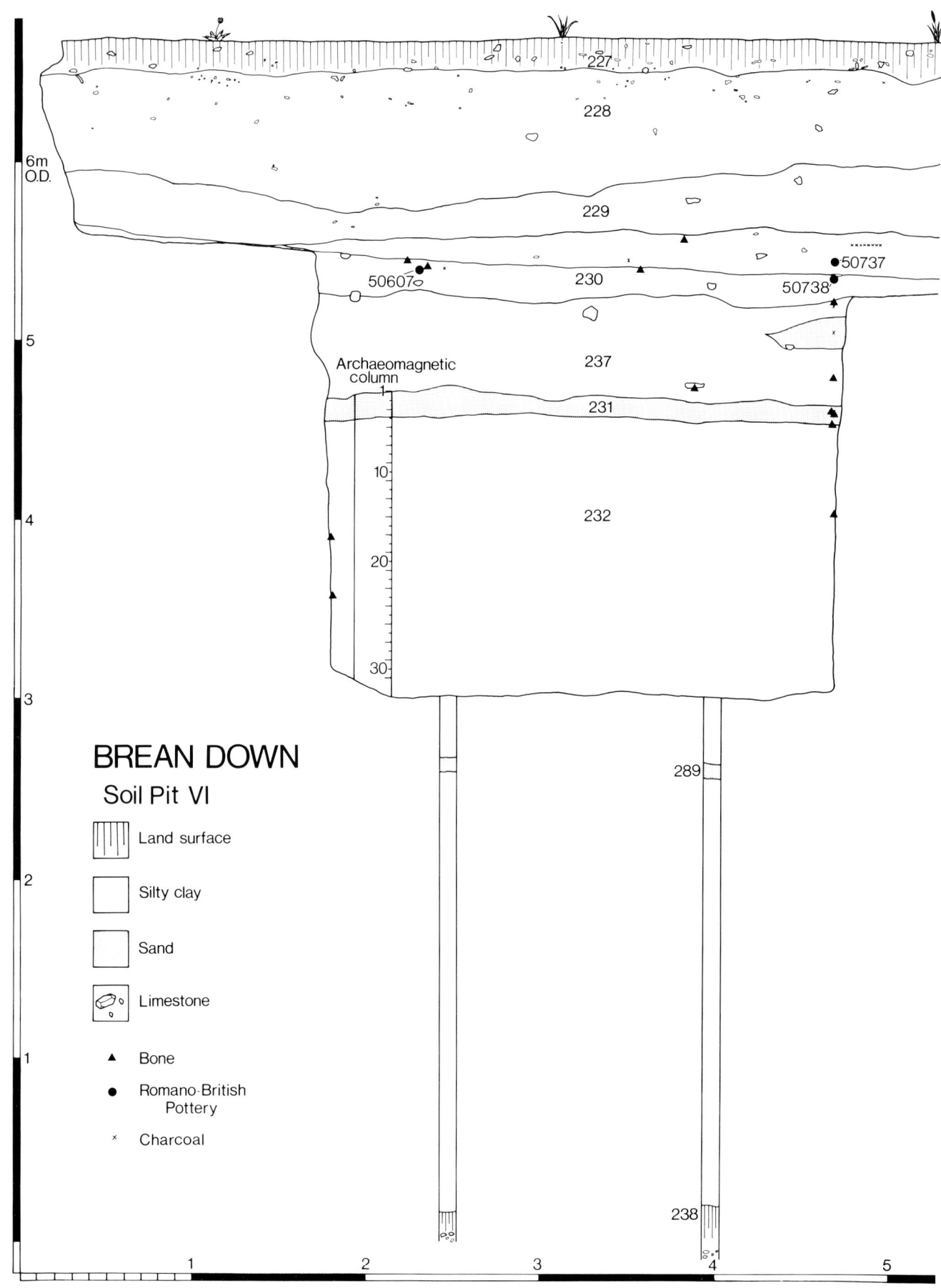

Fig 81 Soil Pit VI: section showing archaeomagnetic dating column

which were occasional traces of waterlogged plant macrofossils and shell fragments. A sand lens (Context 289) was encountered at 2.6m OD in the two holes on the north side of the pit and at 2m OD in the two holes on the south side. Above this was greyish brown (10YR 4/2) highly mottled silt, the upper part of which was exposed in the base of the pit and produced three bones.

Context 231

Greyish yellow brown (10YR 5/2) sand band 0.2m thick, containing three bones. The top of this layer marks the top of the 1.6m long archaeomagnetic dating column, the implications of which are more fully discussed in the conclusions to this chapter.

Context 237

Grey (10YR 5/1) silt, containing a lens of burnt clay and charcoal, as well as two bones.

Context 230

Greyish brown (7.5YR 5/2) silt containing more sand than the deposits above and below and greenish grey (10YR 5/1) mottles. There were charcoal flakes, four bones, small patches of burnt purple clay, and one Romano-British sherd (50607, unillustrated). This more sandy horizon which averaged 0.3m thick was interpreted as a weakly developed old land surface.

Context 229

Grey (5Y 4/1) silt with grey brown mottles and some manganese staining. Two Romano-British sherds (50737 and 50738, both unillustrated) came from the base of this layer.

Context 228

Dull brown (7.5YR 5/3) silt.

Context 227

Brownish black (7.5YR 3/2) silty loam topsoil, with one clay pipe fragment.

Intertidal archaeology

The discovery in 1936 of two Beakers in a pit cut into the palaeosol on the foreshore (Taylor and Taylor 1949) was the first indication of the archaeological potential of the intertidal area. This was further emphasised by ApSimon *et al*'s (1961, fig 15) demonstration that the basal palaeosol (8a), together with some of the underlying Pleistocene deposits, most notably the breccia (8b/c), outcrop on the beach. The Severn Estuary has one of the highest tidal ranges in the world (11m at Brean Down) exposing a very gently sloping coastal flat which at Brean is 1.5km wide from mean low water to the sea wall. The upper part of the zone is covered by sand, the lower part by a variable, highly mobile, and treacherous cover of mud which makes fieldwork difficult. Growing public and commercial interest in plans for a tidal barrage across the Severn Estuary led to feasibility studies which suggested that the most suitable place for a southern barrage terminal was within 1km south of Brean Down (Gavaghan 1986). Consequently a very limited investigation of the intertidal area was carried out in 1986 and it is hoped that in due course this will be followed by a more detailed programme of work.

Soil Pit VII

This was located on the beach in the intertidal area some 25m south-west of the main excavation trench (Fig 72) at a point where the beach surface was at 5.3m OD. This is slightly below the high water spring tide level of 5.77m OD and well below the Highest Astronomical Tide Level of 7.16m OD. Two adjoining areas were opened up on the foreshore. Pit VIIa was machine-cut 2m by 7m to a maximum depth of 1.5m. At the north end the basal palaeosol (Unit 8a) overlying breccia was present 0.2m below the present beach. It was exactly as represented in the cliff face and contained much scattered charcoal. This surface dipped steeply to the south (Fig 25); it was followed by the trench down to *c* 4m OD. It was impossible to go deeper and impossible also to enter the pit for sampling and recording purposes because the sides were very unstable running sand. Nonetheless it was observed that at about 4m OD the palaeosol was overlain by grey silty clay similar to the sediments revealed in Soil Pit VI. Micromorphological sample F was obtained from the JCB scoop and on analysis proved to be a mixture of colluvium and estuarine/marine silts. Above the basal palaeosol and silty clay was an undifferentiated sand deposit. It was not established whether this was marine sand or whether some of it was *in situ* sandcliff deposit such as possibly the 'Beaker sand', Unit 7.

A second area (Fig 72, VIIb) nearby was opened up with the objective of examining the palaeosol surface in the approximate area where the pit containing two Beakers was found on the foreshore in 1936 (Taylor and Taylor 1949). Some 12 sq m were cleaned but it was found that the palaeosol had been entirely eroded away in this area, exposing the underlying breccia which was partly disturbed and reworked incorporating later beach deposits. Finally a line of auger holes was put down on the beach along the A 15m grid line at 5m intervals west of Soil Pit VII (Fig 72). Those between 35 and 55m on the A-axis encountered only breccia. However, the holes at 60–75m encountered the palaeosol dipping to the west and it was traced down to 3.75m OD. It is clear from this very limited work in the intertidal area that the basal palaeosol is present in places only perhaps 0.2 to 0.4m below the present beach. Clearly it maintains the southerly dip seen in the main trench. These observations together with the 1936 find make desirable further archaeological examination of the beach palaeosol and its associated contexts.

Intertidal peat

ApSimon *et al* (1961, 94) recorded the presence of foreshore peats south of Brean Down. These deposits are not a conspicuous feature of the intertidal area, being a long way from the sea wall and covered by a variable thickness of glutinous mud. Peat was, however, exposed and briefly examined during February 1987. The area investigated was at grid reference ST 29145846 (Fig 3), 527m west of the sea wall and 400m south of the limestone cliff of Brean Down. Here, over an irregular and gullied exposure perhaps 100m north–south, was a compressed and laminated *Phragmites* peat 0.18m thick. Its base was at 0.15m OD and it overlay blue silty clay which was proved by augering to a depth of 2.5m or c −2.3m OD. A block including the peat and the top of the underlying silty clay (Fig 133) was removed for laboratory dissection and analysis. A sample from the very base of the peat gave a radiocarbon date of 5620±100 BP (HAR-8546); pollen and macrofossil evidence from the peat are described in Chapter 18.

Other aspects of the intertidal zone

During September 1987 the Severn Tidal Power Group conducted a programme of coring and seismic survey in the area 1.5km south of Brean Down and we are grateful to them for discussing some aspects of their preliminary results. These demonstrated the existence of peats sporadically over a wide area of the intertidal zone and at a range of OD heights. The seismic survey also produced possible indications of a substantial linear east–west feature which might relate to a buried channel of the River Axe. Such a channel is to be anticipated because this river, which now flows north into Weston Bay (Fig 1), has a shallow rock cut channel at its mouth between Brean Down and Uphill (A Heyworth, pers comm) rather than the deeply cut channels of most Flandrian river mouths in southern Britain. Clearly the Axe once flowed south of Brean Down but its former course and the date at which it changed course to the north remain to be established.

Other features in the intertidal zone may have some archaeological significance, although at present they are of absolutely unknown date and uncertain character. Steers (1960, pl 72) has published an air photograph which seems to show a hitherto unremarked-on large circular feature, not unlike an embanked enclosure, on the foreshore between Black Point and the sandcliff. The oblique angle from which this feature is photographed makes its size and exact position rather difficult to establish and only parts of the feature show on later air photographs taken at times of more extensive mud cover. Arthur ApSimon (pers comm) remembers noticing linear arrangements of stones in the intertidal area when he was working at Brean. Air photographs (eg Steers 1960) and observation on the ground show a linear stony feature running south-west from Black Point, which Richard McDonnell (pers comm) interprets as a fish trip, and Jane Evans and Christopher Richards (pers comm) have photographed rough lines of stones and a row of very closely set wooden stakes in this area. At present there is no evidence for the date of any of these features; they require detailed survey and investigation.

The archaeological potential of intertidal zones is clearly revealed on the opposite side of the estuary by the recent discovery of prehistoric footprints, trackways, huts, and activity areas (A Whittle, S Green, and S Parry, pers comm) and Romano-British drainage systems (J Allen and Fulford 1986) in the intertidal Gwent Levels. Lower down the Bristol Channel there have been recent investigations of Mesolithic, Neolithic, and Romano-British intertidal deposits at Westward Ho!, Devon (Balaam *et al* 1987) and on the Essex coast recent surveys have also demonstrated the potential for integrated environmental and cultural studies of the intertidal zone (Wilkinson and Murphy 1986). Thus the potential exists at Brean for extending the detailed sedimentary and archaeological survey already undertaken on the sandcliff to the intertidal zone. It is only as a result of such work that it will be possible to resolve many of the uncertainties noted in this section.

Correlation and conclusions

The soil pit and auger survey showed that the evidence of occupation extended well inland. Wherever it was examined the basal palaeosol (Unit 8a) was characterised by charcoal, and fragments of Beaker pottery were found up to 130m inland. In Unit 5b hearth debris extended up to 25m east of the cliff face, suggesting the existence of further structures in that area. Most extensive of the occupation deposits was Unit 4 which extended 100m inland in a band between 35 and 5m wide. In the excavation trench the downslope edge of this unit was an artefact of subsequent erosion by a post-medieval blowout.

Not only did some occupation horizons extend well inland but between them was essentially the same series of blown sands and colluvial deposits. Evidently the main stratigraphic units are not the result of very localised factors but of major changes in the depositional regime affecting the whole of the sandcliff. The implications of this in terms of causative factors will be pursued in the concluding Chapter 23.

A third objective of the survey was to look at the relationship between the sandcliff deposits and the estuarine flats to the south. This was clearly of crucial importance if the well-dated sandcliff sequence was to be correlated with the wider sedimentary picture for the Somerset Levels to the south (Kidson and Heyworth 1976) and the Severn Estuary to the north (J Allen 1987; J Allen and Rae 1987; J Allen and Fulford 1986; 1987). These relationships were investigated chiefly by means of a transect along the 900m line and are summarised in Figure 78 and presented in rather more detail in Figure 74a. At the base of the whole sequence is the basal palaeosol (Unit 8a) formed on underlying Pleistocene breccia. At the southern end of the transect the palaeosol was overlain by silty clays, which upslope were overlapped by, and partly interleaved with, the sandcliff sequence. Apart from the basal palaeosol, the diachronous (time transgressive) nature of which has already been emphasised (Chapter 2), the earliest post-glacial sediments to be examined were those associated with the intertidal peat which was underlain by 2m+ of grey silty clay.

This *Phragmites* peat (Chapter 18) formed essentially under fresh water conditions but probably with some occasional marine inundation. The peat is at 0m OD and represents a regression episode which is represented by peat formation at this height over much of the Somerset Levels (Kidson and Heyworth 1976, 233). The radiocarbon date of the Brean peat was 5620±100 BP (HAR-8546) and this can be compared with dates between *c* 5300 and 5600 BP for the OD peat elsewhere in the Levels (Kidson and Heyworth 1976, table 1). The auger holes at the base of Soil Pit VI encountered fragmentary plant macrofossils just above the basal palaeosol at OD and it seems probable that these correlate with the OD peat.

In the 7m silty clay sequence of Soil Pit VI biological evidence was only well preserved in the lowest part. Here diatoms and ostracods between them make it clear that the deposits are marine, though laid down in a brackish environment which seems to have been separated from the open sea by a precursor of the existing dune barrier (Fig 1). Neither diatoms nor ostracods are present in closely comparable deposits above 2m OD. Their absence is regarded as due to subsequent diagenesis which may have had an increasingly important effect as the rate of sea level rise and thus sediment accumulation declined. More resistant marine forms were, however, present above 2m OD, suggesting that the entire silty clay sequence between OD and at least 4.6m OD is likely to have been laid down under essentially similar environmental conditions. This deposit can be correlated with the Wentlooge Formation which J Allen (1987) has shown to be the main post-glacial sedimentary unit in the Severn Estuary attaining a thickness of up to 15m in places. Its base is diachronous and relates to the time of Flandrian marine encroachment. The deposit ceased to form at about the Romano-British period. At Brean Anthony Clark's archaeomagnetic dating sequence (Chapter 9) provides a chronology for part of the Wentlooge Formation and helps to correlate it with the sandcliff sequence. The lowest archaeomagnetic sample was at 3.06m OD. The result was 5580 BP (corrected to 6410 Cal BP). This is very close to the radiocarbon date for the intertidal peat which is 3m lower. That implies either that these basal clays built up very rapidly indeed or, more probably, that the turbulence, which Anthony Clark notes as affecting the bottom ten archaeomagnetic samples, has given rise to imprecise dates in the lowest samples. The turbulence may reflect a greater marine influence until *c* 4700 BP (corrected to 5450 Cal BP) after which perhaps the coastal barrier extended further to the south. Within the silts dating to the Neolithic were two peaks of magnetic intensity and susceptibility at 4560 BP (corrected to 5290 Cal BP) and 4220 BP (corrected to 4840 Cal BP).

These small-scale peaks may reflect phases of Neolithic burning or erosion on the sandcliff. They are followed by a pronounced peak of magnetic intensity at 4.37m OD dated 3830 BP (corrected to 4250 Cal BP). Anthony Clark suggests that this may correlate with a major activity episode on the sandcliff and indeed the date is very similar to one of those for charcoal in the basal palaeosol, 3810±90 BP (HAR-8990) (corrected to 4085–4410 Cal BP, Chapter 9).

The archaeomagnetic dating column ended at 4.73m OD, dated 3360 BP (corrected to 3630 Cal BP). This sample was at the top of a 0.15m wide sandy lens which may correlate with Unit 5d of the sandcliff sequence. Above the archaeomagnetic column was a further 0.6m of estuarine grey silts underlying an horizon of apparent Romano-British date. 0.6m of sedimentation between 3360 BP and the Romano-British period seems very little. There is evidence elsewhere for a regression phase during part of this period represented by a thick peat band in the upper part of the Wentlooge Formation. This peat was swamped by marine incursion *c* 2450 BC (J Allen and Rae 1987). On the south side of the estuary there is also evidence for a marine incursion into the Glastonbury area from the Axe valley between 2850 and 2500 BC (Housley 1988). Regrettably the Brean archaeomagnetic sequence did not extend up into deposits of appropriate date but at the moment there does not seem to be clear evidence for this distinct incursion in the third millennium BP which registers so very clearly up to 30km inland. It is of course possible that there was some sort of hiatus in deposition or even an erosion episode between 3450 and the Romano-British period, but there was no clear evidence for this in the field.

This brings us to the critical question of whether Brean Down was an island at the time of its Bronze Age occupation. Kidson and Heyworth (1976) published a series of reconstruction maps showing the changing extent of marine influence in the Somerset Levels between 9000 and 4000 BP. These show the Down as an island during the period of maximum marine influence between 6000 and 5000 BP but suggest the existence of a dryland connection to Mendip via Uphill by 4000 BP. The inferred connection does, however, assume that by this date the River Axe had not broken through to debouch into Weston Bay. To the south of the sandcliff the existing evidence suggests a slowly accreting saltmarsh surface during the Bronze Age. Analogy with recent saltmarshes in the estuary suggests that accretion may well have taken place to above Mean High Water Spring Tide, in which case the flats would only have been inundated by occasional spring tides. The hypothesis of only occasional inundation is all the more likely in view of the evidence for a regression phase represented by peat growth during the Bronze Age elsewhere in the estuary. Thus, in the absence of evidence for peat growth around the Down during the Bronze Age and in view of the evidence for continual but slow sedimentation, it seems that the Down was technically an island. In all probability, however, it was only surrounded by the sea at certain high tides for a small proportion of the year, particularly during the winter months.

Overlying the grey clays in Soil Pit VI was a stabilisation horizon with three unabraded Romano-British sherds. The date and sandy nature of this horizon suggest a correlation with Context 31, Unit 3c2, which was the only post Bronze Age episode of sterile sand deposition on the sandcliff and was cut by the sub-Roman burials. The Romano-British horizon in Soil Pit VI probably correlates with J Allen and Fulford's (1986) Wentlooge surface which, in the type area on the other side of the estuary, was embanked and extensively drained during the Romano-British period. Elsewhere, similar Romano-British works may be inferred from the distribution of sites and artefacts, notably on the south side between Clevedon and Sand Point where it was long ago realised that the siting of the Wemberham villa implied contemporary sea defences (Boon 1980). In Somerset there is also evidence of extensive Romano-British activity and almost certainly drainage in the Axe valley upstream of Cheddar (McDonnell 1979) and on the inland fringes of the Somerset Clay Levels (McDonnell 1985; 1986).

The Romano-British surface at Brean was sealed by 1m of grey and brown silt, the interpretation of which is problematical. The question is whether we should also regard this as part of the Wentlooge Formation. On some sites the published descriptions also imply the occurrence of Romano-British material within the Wentlooge Formation, eg at Crooks Marsh Farm, Avonmouth (J Allen and Rae 1987, 303). Generally, however, the Wentlooge surface was not the subject of post-Roman inundation and corresponds to present-day ground level. In these areas subsequent estuary sedimentary formations, the Rumney, Awre, and Northwick Formations, are confined to the area seaward of the sea wall. The two last are of nineteenth- and twentieth-century date and are clearly not relevant to the upper part of the Brean stratigraphy. It is, however, possible that the top metre relates to the Rumney Formation. The idea of post-Roman inundation of this area is highly speculative and needs to be tested by further work; it might, however, be one possible explanation for the apparent absence of Romano-British sites and drainage features in the seaward part of the Somerset Clay Levels (McDonnell 1985; 1986) and in the Axe valley below Cheddar (McDonnell 1979). An alternative explanation for their absence is, of course, that this area was not settled and drained during Romano-British times yet the Brean sherds do suggest the possibility of Romano-British activity on the flats. Whether or not there was any post-Roman inundation there is good evidence that the flats at Brean had been reclaimed and drained by the time of Domesday (ApSimon et al 1961). Even so, we should not completely rule out the possibility of subsequent inundation events of a minor nature in sedimentary terms. One such is suggested by ApSimon et al's (1961, fig 21) sounding south of the sandcliff where they found a sixteenth- or seventeenth-century buckle below storm beach deposits within which were lenses of estuarine clay. It is tempting to interpret this as the product of a storm inundation event and to correlate it with evidence for the development of a blowout in the sandcliff during the sixteenth- and early seventeenth-century occupation. One possible context for these events was the major storm surge in 1606–7 noted by J Allen and Fulford (1986).

B The Bronze Age cultural evidence

9 Scientific dating

Radiocarbon dating

by Jill Walker

Twenty-two samples from Brean Down have been dated by radiocarbon and of these 21 were submitted to Harwell between 1986 and 1988; the remaining one was dated by Birmingham and reported by Shotton and Williams (1973). The complete list of results in order of stratigraphic unit and with details of the material dated and context is given in Table 3.

Measurement technique

The samples measured included 5 bones, 1 peat, and 16 charcoal, and all underwent the standard processes of the laboratory which include pretreatment and combustion to CO_2 followed either by conversion to benzene and liquid scintillation counting or gas proportional counting, depending upon the size of the sample.

Pretreatment

For charcoal and peat the AAA method was used, ie a first 30 minute hot acid wash (3M HCl) to remove carbonate contamination, followed by an alkali wash (hot, 30 minutes, 1M NaOH for charcoal; cold, 10 minutes, 0.25% NaOH for peat) to remove humic contamination, followed by a further cold acid wash (3M HCl), rinsing until neutral with demineralised water, and finally oven-drying at approximately 100°C.

Bone was completely demineralised in acid (1M HCl), given an alkali wash (1% NaOH) and a further acid 1M HCl wash, and finally rinsed to neutral in demineralised water and oven-dried.

Chemical processing

After pretreatment all samples were combusted to CO_2 in a vacuum rig. At this stage an aliquot of the gas was removed for measurement of the stable isotope ratio $^{13}C/^{12}C$.

For samples large enough to be measured by the liquid scintillation counting method, ie containing 0.5g or more elemental carbon, the next process was the synthesis of benzene from the carbon dioxide through the stages of lithium carbide and acetylene. The acetylene was converted to benzene using a vanadium pentoxide catalyst, then dispensed ready for counting with a proprietary benzene-based scintillant (NE 231A).

For samples containing less than 0.5g elemental carbon the CO_2 was counted directly using gas proportional counting and the only remaining step was a rigorous purification over copper and silver/platinum.

Counting

Liquid scintillation counting

The samples were batch counted in liquid scintillation counters optimised for low-level counting following the procedures laid out in Otlet and Warchal (1978). Samples were counted in association with background and 'modern' (NBS oxalic) standards produced through the laboratory processing rigs, in a ratio of 3 to 4 samples to each background and modern pair. Each sample was counted to achieve either 40,000 total counts or 2000 minutes total time.

Miniature gas proportional counting

After purification the CO_2 was compressed into a Harwell 30cc gas proportional counter (Otlet *et al* 1983). This was then placed in the heavily shielded counting system and counted for period between 4 and 6 weeks aiming to collect a total of 20,000 counts.

Estimation of errors

The ± error term (1 sigma) quoted with the result by the Harwell laboratory is an estimate of the replicate sample reproducibility and is based on an estimate of all sources of error, not just counting statistics alone (Otlet 1979). For the liquid scintillation system the usual error term is ±1%, ie ±70 to 80 years for samples of optimum size (5g carbon); where samples fall short of this optimum the error term is increased. Unfortunately most of the Brean Down samples were below the optimum size and hence the error terms range from ±80 to ±140 years.

Calibration

The results were calibrated using the calibration program of Stuiver and Reimer (1986). The Stuiver and Reimer program uses two different methods to produce calibrated dates. The first gives simple age ranges which are generated by taking the end-points of the ±1σ and ±2σ ranges of the radiocarbon age distribution and finding where they intercept with the calibration curve. The second calculates the probability distribution of the radiocarbon age, ie it takes the Gaussian distribution of the radiocarbon age and creates a transformed distribution of calibrated age by taking all intercepts of the Gaussian with the calibration curve and weighting them according to their probability. Stuiver and Reimer then quote the ranges which represent 68.3% (1σ) and 95.4% (2σ) of the area of the transformed distribution. Because of the peaks and troughs observed in the transformed distribution there may be a number of ranges in the 1σ and 2σ areas and the relative area provides an estimate of the importance of each range. The full calibration data are shown in Table 4, though the following discussion and Figure 82 are based purely on the intercept method.

Table 3 Radiocarbon dates listed by stratigraphic unit

Harwell ref	Sample ref	Age BP	Calibrated date (Cal BC) 1σ	2σ	Material dated (charcoal identifications by Vanessa Straker)	Context and method of collection
Unit 8a (Neolithic-Beaker palaeosol)						
HAR-7023	BD 6171–8	4720±140	3680–3350	3790–3045	Charcoal: Fraxinus excelsior Pomoidae Corylus avellana Prunus cf avium Quercus Ulmus + unident	Context 63 – hand collection
HAR-8547	BD UBSS6	3460±80	1890–1685	2020–1540	Charcoal: Quercus – mature and twig Prunus cf spinosa Pomoidae	Collected by H Taylor 1936
HAR-8990	BD 60531	3810±90	2460–2135	2560–1985	Charcoal: Ulmus + unident	Context 63 Dry sieving of Grid Sq 8/12
HAR-8993	BD 60521	3390±90	1870–1545	1930–1510	Charcoal: Ulmus, Pomoidae + unident	Context 63 Dry sieving of Grid Sq 12/13
Unit 7 (Beaker sand layer)						
HAR-9156	BD 6192	3560±90	2035–1770	2185–1680	Charcoal: Euonymus europaeus Pomoidae Prunus cf spinosa + unident	Context 188 Hand collected from distinct thin charcoal band in sand (Figs 15 and 27)
Unit 6b (early Bronze Age colluvium)						
HAR-7022	BD 6062–7	3890±130	2575–2145	2865–1985	Charcoal: unident	Context 66 – hand collection
Unit 6a (early to middle Bronze Age occupation)						
HAR-7021	BD 5886–6	2600±90	835–765	920–420	Charcoal: Pomoidae Corylus avellana	Context 61 Sieve collected from distinct charcoal band (Fig 27) at depth 50–100mm – clay above and below
HAR-8992	BD 5886B	2770±90	1020–830	1210–800	Charcoal: Pomoidae Corylus avellana	Same sample as HAR-7021
HAR-8991	BD 6020	3120±90	1510–1310	1610–1135	Charcoal: Corylus avellana Ulmus sp Acer campestre + unident	Context 61 – sieve collected
Unit 6α (early to middle Bronze Age structure)						
HAR-7020	BD 6153–5	3310±80	1730–1515	1870–1430	Charcoal: unident	Context 63 – sieve collected from 50–100mm depth
Unit 5b (middle to late Bronze Age occupation)						
HAR-7016	BD 5801–1	3420±100	1880–1620	2020–1510	Charcoal: unident	Context 103 – sieve collected
HAR-7019	BD 6013–4	2940±100	1310–1000	1420–900	Charcoal: unident	Context 131 – sieve collected
HAR-7018	BD 5803–3	2870±80	1210–925	1310–840	Charcoal: unident	Context 93 – distinct charcoal patch associated with final use of hearth in Structure 95 (Figs 38 and 39)
HAR-7017	BD 5749–2	2730±100	1000–810	1155–780	Charcoal: unident	Context 60 – sieve collected
Unit 4 (late Bronze Age occupation)						
HAR-9155	BD 2056	3400±90	1875–1615	1940–1510	Animal bone	Context 16
HAR-9151	BD 4716	2730±70	975–820	1040–800	Animal bone	Context 16
HAR-9153	BD 1352	3100±100	1505–1260	1610–1090	Animal bone	Context 16
			(Cal AD)			
Unit 3c (sub-Roman cemetery)						
Birm-246	BD —	1300±80	654–786	600–890	Human bone	Collected by A ApSimon, submitted by P Rahtz
HAR-8549	BD 6543	1430±70	560–660	450–690	Human bone – femora, tibia, and fibulae	Context 212 – Skeleton 7
HAR-8548	BD 6530	1550±80	415–600	270–650	Human bone – all that remained of skeleton	Context 213 – Skeleton 8
Foreshore peat			(Cal BC)			
HAR-8546	BD PT385	5620±100	4655–4360	4720–4250	Peat – for macrofossils see Chapter 18	Removed as block (Fig 133) sampled in lab

Table 4 Radiocarbon dates – full calibration data

Harwell ref	Sample ref	Age BP	Intercepts 1σ	Intercepts 2σ	Calibrated date (Cal BC) 1σ	Probabilities	2σ	
Foreshore peat								
HAR-8546	BD PT385	5620±100	4655–4360	4720–4250	4580–4360	100%	4730–4330	98%
							4280–4245	2%
Unit 8a (Neolithic–Beaker Palaeosol)								
HAR-7023	BD 6171–8	4720±140	3680–3350	3790–3045	3690–3350	1		
HAR-8547	BD UBSS6	3460±80	1890–1685	2020–1540	1885–1730	82%	2020–2000	2%
					1730–1690	18%	1985–1605	97%
					1560–1540	1%		
HAR-8990	BD 60531	3810±90	2460–2135	2560–1985	2455–2425	10%		
					2395–2185	82%		
					2165–2145	8%		
HAR-8993	BD 60521	3390±90	1870–1545	1930–1510	1875–1840	12%	1935–1505	100%
					1815–1805	4%		
					1780–1605	78%		
					1555–1540	6%		
Unit 7 ('Beaker sand' layer)								
HAR-9156	BD 6192	3560±90	2035–1770	2185–1680	2035–1865	73%	2140–1685	99%
					1845–1770	27%		
Unit 6b (early Bronze Age colluvium)								
HAR-7022	BD 6062–7	3890±130	2575–2145	2865–1985	2575–2535	9%	2865–2810	4%
					2510–2190	88%	2770–2725	2%
					2160–2145	3%	2700–2670	1%
							2670–2030	93%
Unit 6a (early to middle Bronze Age occupation)								
HAR-7021	BD 5886–6	2600±90	835–765	920–420	895–875	7%	925–460	98%
					855–760	49%	450–415	2%
					685–655	12%		
					645–545	32%		
HAR-8992	BD 5886B	2770±90	1020–830	1210–800	1020–830	100%	1210–1180	2%
							1165–800	98%
HAR-8991	BD 6020	3120±90	1510–1310	1610–1135	1515–1305	99%	1615–1155	99%
Unit 6α (early to middle Bronze Age structure)								
HAR-7020	BD 6153–5	3310±80	1730–1515	1870–1430	1690–1515	99%	1865–1845	2%
							1770–1430	98%
Unit 5b (middle to late Bronze Age occupation)								
HAR-7016	BD 5801–1	3420±100	1880–1620	2020–1510	1880–1630	100%	1980–1510	99%
HAR-7019	BD 6013–4	2940±100	1310–1000	1420–900	1300–1270	9%	1410–920	100%
					1270–1020	93%		
HAR-7018	BD 5803–3	2870±80	1210–925	1310–840	1195–1185	4%	1300–1275	2%
					1160–970	82%	1270–890	95%
					970–930	14%	885–845	3%
HAR-7017	BD 5749–2	2730±100	1000–810	1155–780	1000–810	100%		
Unit 4 (late Bronze Age occupation)								
HAR-9155	BD 2056	3400±90	1875–1615	1940–1510	1875–1835	15%	1945–1510	100%
					1820–1795	8%		
					1785–1610	77%		
HAR-9151	BD 4716	2730±70	975–820	1040–800	975–965	7%	1040–800	100%
					935–820	93%		
HAR-9153	BD 1352	3100±100	1505–1260	1610–1090	1510–1470	13%	1610–1550	4%
					1470–1260	87%	1550–1090	95%
Unit 3c (sub-Roman cemetery)					*(Cal AD)*			
HAR-8549	BD 6543	1430±70	560–660	450–690	555–665	100%	440–710	100%
HAR-8548	BD 6530	1550±80	415–600	270–650	425–570	91%	340–650	100%
					575–590	9%		

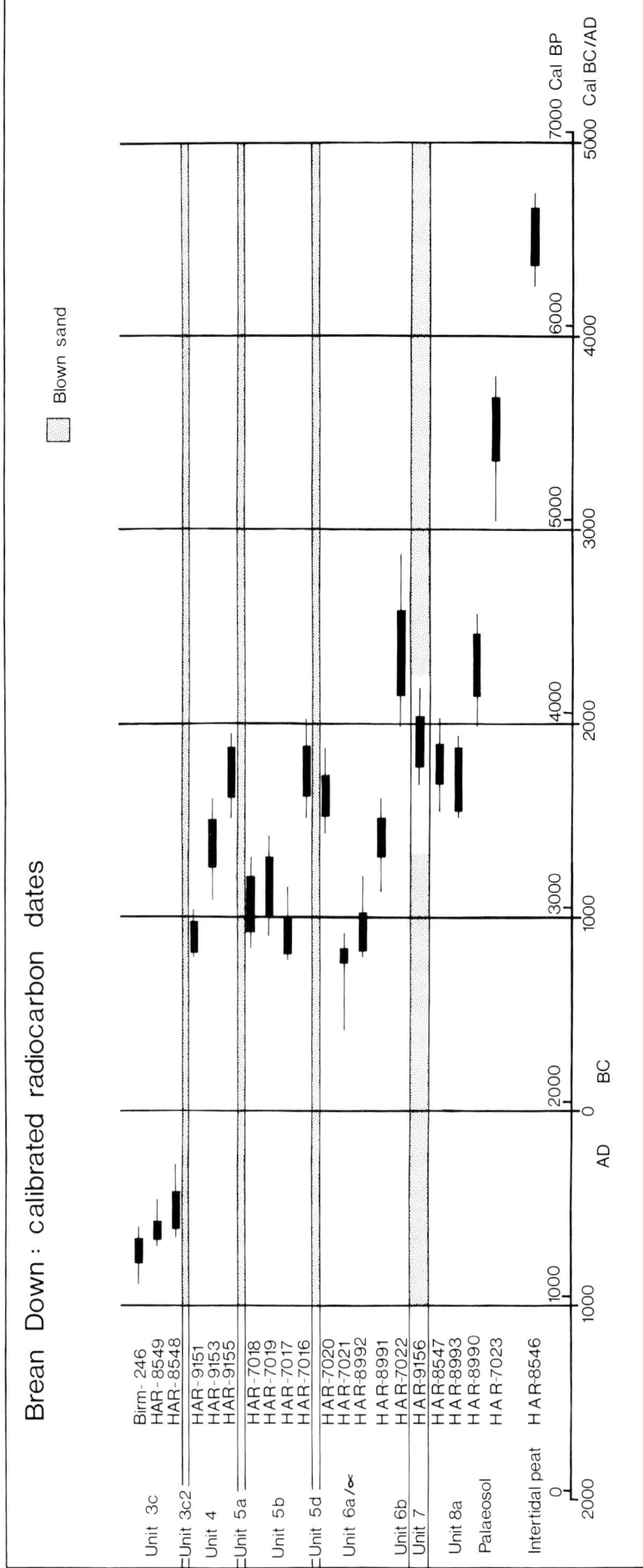

Fig 82 *Calibrated radiocarbon dates at one and two standard deviations*

Interpretation of the data

The calibrated results, showing both 1σ and 2σ ranges are plotted in Figure 82 according to their stratigraphic units. It is seen that most of the results fall in a 1200 year period between c 850 Cal BC and 2000 Cal BC and that there is considerable overlapping between the units; a rather less clear chronological picture has emerged than was hoped for at the outset of the programme.

The units and their relation with each other are discussed briefly below and the archaeological significance is discussed more fully by Martin Bell in the following section.

In Unit 8a HAR-7023 is clearly considerably earlier than the other three results and must be considered to belong to a different phase of activity. HAR-8547, 8993, and 8990 form a separate group but, although the results overlap in the 2σ ranges, the Ward and Wilson (1978) test would not accept them as forming a single distribution but would reject HAR-8990. The possibility of three phases being represented within this unit must, therefore, be considered.

Unit 7 contains only one result, HAR-9156, which is statistically indistinguishable from HAR-8547 and 8993 in Unit 8a and, similarly, HAR-7022, the only result from Unit 6b, cannot be distinguished from HAR-8990 in Unit 8a.

Within Units 6a and 6α two groups appear. HAR-7021 and HAR-8892 are replicate check measurements which agree closely; the weighted mean of the two results is 2685±65 BP (calibrated age ranges 905–805 Cal BC 1σ and 990–790 Cal BC 2σ). This is clearly different from HAR-8991. However, HAR-8991 does agree with HAR-7020, the only result from Structure 57. Although the relationship of this structure to Unit 6a was not clearly defined (see Martin Bell's comments below), the possibility of a link to one of the 6a phases was considered and this is confirmed by the dating.

Unit 5b contains results from samples related to Structures 59 and 95; HAR-7017, 7018, and 7019 form a statistically indistinguishable group. HAR-7016 is considerably earlier and statistically indistinguishable from HAR-7020 from Structure 57, Unit 6α. In addition HAR-7017, 7018, and 7019 form a statistically acceptable group with HAR-7021 and 8992, the late results from Unit 6a, although the grouping is not as close as for HAR-7017, 7018, and 7019 on their own and the T value of 8.08 from the Ward and Wilson test is acceptable at 5% but not 10% confidence levels. HAR-7016, 7020, and 8991 form a similar statistical grouping acceptable at the 5% level.

Unit 4 produced a series of results with a wide spread of ages which cannot be combined. HAR-9151 fits with one group of results from Unit 5b and HAR-9155 with HAR-7016 from Unit 5b and all fall in the general range from the site.

Unit 3c is the sub-Roman cemetery and here there are two Harwell dates plus a determination made earlier by Birmingham. For the latter we have used the result given by Shotton and Williams (1973) in *Radiocarbon*. Rahtz (1977), however, notes that this date needs to be corrected, apparently (see Rahtz 1977, 59, note 4) because of a revised $^{13}C/^{12}C$ ratio. Without quoting a specific revised determination he says that this gives a date centering on the sixth (rather than the seventh) century. If no correction was made for the stable isotope ratio $^{13}C/^{12}C$ this could indeed make the result up to 100 years older. In the preface to the list Shotton and Williams state that the 1σ error quoted refers only to a statistical analysis of sample, background, and standard count rates; it must, therefore, be an underestimate of the true error term since all other sources are ignored. Even if no correction is made for these factors, however, the three results do form a group.

Conclusions

If we look simply at the way the radiocarbon dates group together and ignore for the moment the fact that some of those forming groups are from separate stratigraphic units, the distinct groups set out in Table 5 may be suggested.

It should be noted that the results from Unit 4 have not been included in this analysis but overlap with groups D to G. The Birmingham date was not included in Group H because of queries on the error term and $\delta^{13}C$.

The analysis suggests 5 to 7 phase of activity with groups B and C separated by at least 500 years,

Table 5 Groupings of radiocarbon dates (some from separate stratigraphic units)

Group	Unit	Harwell refs	Weighted mean Age BP	Calibrated dates Ranges (Cal BC)	
				1σ	2σ
A	Peat	8546	5620±100	4655–4360	4720–4250
B	8a	7023	4720±140	3680–3350	3790–3045
C	8a+6b	8990, 7022	3835±75	2460–2145	2555–2045
D	8a+7	8547, 8993, 9156	3470±50	1885–1740	1930–1680
E	6a+6α +5b	7016, 7020, 8991	3275±50	1625–1515	1680–1440
F	5b	7017, 7018, 7019	2850±50	1095–930	1210–900
G	6a	7021, 8992	2685±65	910–805	990–790
				(Cal AD)	
H	3c	8548, 8549	1480±50	545–635	440–660

groups C and D separated by *c* 100 years, D and E being continuous, and a gap of 200 years to groups F and G which themselves overlap. Finally there is a 1000 year gap to group H, the sub-Roman cemetery. Although this analysis does not agree with the original plan of obtaining results for each unit because of sample problems (possible residuality, combinations, etc, described in more detail by Martin Bell below), it does provide a framework against which to compare the other archaeological evidence.

Comments on the radiocarbon dates

by Martin Bell

Brean's well-stratified sequence of Bronze Age occupation phases characterised by contrasting pottery assemblages seemed an ideal site for an attempt to refine Bronze Age chronology. So it was decided, in consultation with the project's archaeological advisers, to try to obtain four radiocarbon dates from each of the main horizons.

The quality of the material dated was somewhat variable; information on this is included in Table 3. Where available, discrete charcoal lenses were selected as more likely to relate to a single burning episode. These better quality samples were HAR-9156 (Context 188), HAR-7021 and HAR-8992 (from the same sample in Context 61), and HAR-7018 (Context 93). In some other cases dating had perforce to be conducted on an amalgamation of several pieces of charcoal from part of a horizon. Sometimes, as is indicated on Table 3, this was derived from hand sieving of the sediment. Charcoal was scarce in Unit 4 and was also considered unreliable for radiocarbon dating because of the evidence for significant faunal (largely rabbit) intrusion in that unit. Thus dating of Unit 4 was based on bone which, being larger, was thought unlikely to be intruded and did not involve amalgamation of many small samples.

The results discussed above by Jill Walker refine some aspects of the site's chronology. However, if all the dates are accepted, each of the main occupation units covers a long range and they overlap in time to a considerable extent. Indeed, some of the groups of dates (A to H) identified in Jill Walker's conclusions as statistically indistinguishable include material from more than one stratigraphic unit. Thus the dating programme is of limited value in its original objective of helping to pinpoint more accurately the dating of the pottery and artefact sequence. The dates in the following discussion are uncalibrated unless otherwise stated.

Unit 8a The radiocarbon dates show that there was activity on this surface for a long period from the early fifth millennium to the mid fourth millennium BP, which extends to more than 2000 years when the dates are calibrated. Jill Walker's statistical examination of the dates suggests three possibly independent phases of activity as follows: (1) an otherwise unattested earlier Neolithic phase represented by 4720 ± 140 BP (HAR-7023); (2) 3810 ± 90 BP (HAR-8990); (3) 3460 ± 80 BP (HAR-8547) and 3390 ± 90 BP (HAR-8993). Phases 2 and 3 are within the range of determinations elsewhere for contexts with Beakers (Gibson 1982, fig 2), but Phase 3 is late in that range and HAR-8547 is particularly noteworthy because it was apparently associated with a Maritime Beaker, a type generally thought to be early (p 26). There is, however, no reason to reject the date itself which corresponds very closely to HAR-8993. The latter was from below Unit 7 sand and, together with HAR-9156, shows that the unit accumulated in the mid fourth millennium BP. Taylor and Taylor (1949) show that the putative burial with which HAR-8547 was associated occurred after some sand deposition had begun, thus confirming a late date.

Unit 7 The one date 3560 ± 90 BP (HAR-9156) is a little earlier than the two latest dates in Unit 8a, but Ward and Wilson (1978) tests by Jill Walker show that there is no significant difference between the three dates (t = 1.8 for Chi square of 5.99 at 5%). There is no likelihood of reworked charcoal in this context (188); it was a discrete thin charcoal band without any colluvial component.

Unit 6b One date 3890 ± 130 BP (HAR-7022) has a very large error term increased still more by calibration. It is, however, significantly earlier than the Unit 7 date (t = 4.36 for Chi square of 3.84 at 5%) and, presumably therefore, than the two latest dates in Unit 8a. It is not significantly different from HAR-8990 in Unit 8a (t = 0.26 for Chi square of 3.84 at 5%) and probably in view of the micromorphologically confirmed colluvial origin of 6b the charcoal is redeposited from 8a.

Unit 6a Three dates were obtained: 2600 ± 90 BP (HAR-7021), 2770 ± 90 BP (HAR-8992), and 3120 ± 90 BP (HAR-8991). The single sample which produced HAR-7021 and 8992 seemed to be archaeologically one of the best quality samples since it was a lens of charcoal between two clay bands. Yet this sample is 400 to 600 years more recent than the dating bracket suggested for the Unit 6 pottery (Chapter 11).

Unit 6α Because Structure 57 was not fully excavated its relationship to Unit 6a was never totally resolved. In the field the impression was that Structure 57 probably related to a late stage in Unit 6a. However, the date of 3310 ± 80 BP (HAR-7020) is earlier than the three dates from Unit 6a, which suggests that the structure may relate to a late phase of Unit 6b or an early stage of Unit 6a. Unlike the three Unit 6a dates, HAR-7020 is in line with that suggested for pottery from Units 6a and 6α.

Unit 5b The earliest date stratigraphically and chronologically is 3420 ± 100 BP (HAR-7016) from a pit below Structure 59. Ward and Wilson (1978) tests by Jill Walker show that it is not statistically separable from HAR-7020 in underlying Unit 6α (t = 0.74 for Chi square of 3.84 at 5%). The structures produced the following consistent group of dates: 2730 ± 100 BP (HAR-7017) from the floor of Structure 59; 2940 ± 100

BP (HAR-7019) from the wall of Structure 95; and 2870±80 BP (HAR-7018). The last was from a particularly good quality sample, a discrete charcoal spread associated with a late phase of the hearth in Structure 95. HAR-7017–9 are in agreement with the pottery dating evidence from Unit 5b.

It should be noted that the dates from Unit 5b show considerable overlap with those of 6a. Ann Woodward (pers comm) has considered this question and writes as follows:

'A possible explanation is that the biconical and Trevisker traditions overlap chronologically in the south-west, as the dates quoted in Chapter 11 show. The two occupations could be very close in time, that is if the blown sand Unit 5d built up very quickly. If so, the contrasts in pottery type would suggest that they were effected by different populations or the same population served by different potters.'

Unit 4 The dates were 3400±90 BP (HAR-9155), 3100±100 BP (HAR-9153), and 2730±70 BP (HAR-9151). The first two are earlier than the dating suggested by parallels for the gold bracelets, c 3000–2600 BP (1000-650 BC), or the suggested pottery dating in the first quarter of the third millennium BP. HAR-9151 is in good agreement with the cultural evidence. Even more worrying is that the two early dates are themselves earlier than the apparently consistent group of dates from the underlying Unit 5b.

Unit 3c The burials produced three dates: 1300±80 BP (Birm-246), 1430±70 BP (HAR-8549), and 1550±80 BP (HAR-8548). These dates are in line with archaeological expectation (p 80) and confirm a broadly sub-Roman date for the cemetery. Calibration indicates that two of the burials are likely to relate to the period before the Saxon conquest of this area, probably about the second half of the seventh century. The published date Birm-246 could imply that the cemetery continued in use later but, as Jill Walker notes, there is some evidence that the true date should be earlier.

Conclusions

The main puzzle is the very wide and overlapping date ranges for a well-stratified sequence of occupation horizons which produced quite different pottery assemblages. These large date ranges are further increased by the effects of calibration (Fig 82) which, for instance, adds 580 years to the possible one sigma range of Unit 8a. Wide date ranges with some anomalous results (in terms of the artefact evidence) were obtained from both bone in Unit 4 and charcoal in the underlying units. Bone dates earlier than expected could be caused by the reworking of old bones by colluvial processes or dogs. Charcoal dates earlier than expected would have been produced by heartwood from old trees; in no case do we have any information about the age of the trees which produced the charcoal. A further possibility on this coastal site is that the results could have been affected by the burning of driftwood which, as Schiffer (1987, 311) demonstrates, could be of some age. Another factor could be the use of peat as fuel, for which there is micromorphological evidence, but that would be likely to produce very much older dates than the apparent discrepancies represented here, unless the proportion of contaminating peat charcoal was small. The earlier than expected date of HAR-7022 can be explained reasonably confidently in terms of charcoal eroded from Unit 8a. With hindsight it was an unsuitable sample to date but it was all that was available in Unit 6b.

Some of the most puzzling of the Brean dates, particularly the three from Unit 6a, are younger rather than older than expected. Intrusion of later charcoal must be considered but seems unlikely in view of the good quality context which produced HAR-7021 and HAR-8992 and of the fact that Unit 6 was sealed by c 1m of sterile blown sand.

The question is, has there been much more reworking, intrusion, and disturbance than was originally inferred? The artefactual evidence helps to quantify this problem. Let us assume a worst possible scenario, that the main pottery fabrics which are very abundant in one unit and rare in another are intrusive or reworked in the unit where they are rare. Sometimes this is a reasonable assumption. Beaker sherds make up 4.4% of the Unit 6 assemblage and are all thought to be reworked. In the later horizons it is questionable, because pottery fabrics are quite likely to have continued in use from one unit to another. Even so, if all the pottery of Fabric 481 in Unit 5b was intrusive from Unit 4, that would indicate 0.3% intrusion. If in Unit 4 the occurrence of Fabrics 361, 363, and 364 is entirely the result of reworking from Unit 5b, then that implies reworked proportions between 0.2 and 8.8%. The faunal evidence in Unit 4 consisted of 12% rabbit bones, but rabbits are unlikely to have introduced the much larger bones dated, especially not from earlier underlying horizons at least 1m below. The relatively low level of mixing implied by the artefactual evidence could explain the odd anomalous date, but it does not offer a convincing explanation for the broad and overlapping ranges of the sequence as a whole.

With hindsight it would have been preferable to have concentrated only on samples of unquestionable quality (but note the puzzling dates from Unit 6a samples which were considered of high quality), and perhaps where possible to have obtained charcoal by dissection of sediment blocks in the laboratory rather than by hand-picking and sieving in the field.

Archaeomagnetic measurements

by Anthony Clark

These measurements were made on behalf of the Ancient Monuments Laboratory by the Clark Consultancy at Guildford. The samples were measured for directional remanence with a Molspin archaeomagnetic magnetometer. Details of the methods and terms used are given in Clark *et al* 1988.

Hearth (Context 134) in Structure 95, Unit 5b (AJC-18)

Sixteen samples of this were taken by the disc method and orientated by magnetic compass. Initial analysis gave a mean result too far west for the late Bronze Age date expected, and plotting the individual measurements showed a linear spread of readings suggesting that there had been variable settlement across the hearth. Partial AF demagnetisation tests were made on two pilot samples to ascertain whether the problem might be due to excessive post-heating viscous magnetisation of some samples; but these samples showed good magnetic stability (median destructive field about 25 mT in both cases) and only modest directional changes. The result after demagnetising all samples to 25 mT was:

Dec = 2.1°E; Inc = 68.6°; alpha-95 = 2.5°

This suggests a second–third century BC date, which is unacceptable. Removal of the more obviously scattered readings brought little improvement. The direction of dispersal of the readings indicates increasing subsidence in an easterly direction, which is consistent with visible cracking on this side. The blown sand underlying the hearth was clearly insufficiently stable.

Sediment column from Soil Pit VI, north section (Fig 81) (AJC-19)

A vertical series of 31 samples was taken from the lower part of this sondage. The samples were collected by pushing 50mm uPVC tubes vertically into the sediment to produce an almost continuous 1.66m column from 3.06m to 4.72m OD. Most of the material was firm silt, but the three uppermost samples were from the band of sand: this was very wet and seemed semi-fluidised, yet produced sensible results only slightly more scattered than the firmer material. The samples were orientated by a theodolite-mounted magnetic compass clear of the influence of the steel props supporting the shuttering of the trench. The preparation of the samples was completed in the laboratory by slight trimming back into the tubes and sealing with plaster of Paris.

Initial measurements showed that the samples retained a quite strong natural remanent magnetisation (NRM) with coherent trends that could be matched to the geomagnetic curves established by Turner and Thompson (1982) from their study of British lake sediments. A pilot sample (10 from top) was subjected to AF demagnetisation tests, and showed good stability, with median destructive field of 20 mT, and only small changes of declination and inclination values up to this level. However, it was felt that viscous components should be more gently removed from the remaining samples by storage in zero field. Remeasurement after four months in zero field showed a substantial improvement in smoothness of the declination and inclination curves traced out by the samples, except as noted below.

The final results are summarised in Figure 83. This shows the declination and inclination curves of Turner and Thompson compared with the curves obtained from Brean: first the raw data (A and C) and then a two-point running mean (B and D) in both cases. The matches were obtained by visual inspection, and then tested statistically. The matching process is similar to that of dendrochronology, except that there are more variables: there are no definite year markers in the data, and much depends on distinctive turning points in the curve (marked in roman lower case and Greek letters). The rate of deposition is not known, nor whether it is variable; thus the data have to be stretched or compressed, not necessarily uniformly, to fit the reference curve. A suitably sophisticated development of computerised dendrochronology matching programs would be of great value for this work.

The lowest ten samples produced a much more erratic plot than those above, presumably due to disturbed conditions of deposition, and the following analysis is based only on the upper 21 samples. Correlation coefficients (r) between the Brean curves and the reference curves for the raw data were: declination 0.78 (t = 5.43); inclination 0.72 (t = 4.50). Shifting the declination curve down by one reading reduced r to 0.77, and by two readings to 0.61. Shifting it upward by one reading reduced r to 0.57. Shifting the inclination curve down by one reading reduced r to 0.67, and upward by one reading to 0.66. Using the two-point running mean values for the test gave r = 0.74 for declination and 0.82 for inclination. A perfect match gives r = 1. These results satisfactorily confirm the visual fit.

This analysis shows that the period of deposition in tranquil conditions ran from about 4700 BP (5480, 5450 Cal BP) to 3360 BP (3670, 3630 Cal BP). Assuming a uniform deposition rate, the lower samples affected by turbulence would go back to about 5630 BP (6420, 6410 Cal BP). The first calibration figure in each case is derived from the curve of Clark (1975), which was used by Turner and Thompson (1982), and equates with their calibration of the lake sediment curve reproduced here. The second is the modern calibration of Pearson *et al* (1986) and Pearson and Stuiver (1986), using the statistically most likely value where alternatives exist. The small differences between these figures are a tribute to the quality of Clark's early curve. Error terms are difficult to establish with real objectivity, but ±90 at the 68% confidence level may be suggested for all dates except the last, which is dependent upon the uncertain validity of the assumption of uniform deposition.

Magnetic intensity and volume susceptibility (measured with a Bartington MS1 laboratory system) are also plotted. Both show modest maxima about 4560 BP (5330, 5290 Cal BP) and 4220 BP (4880, 4840 Cal BP), while a distinctive peak at about 3830 BP (4300, 4250 Cal BP) is most clearly shown by intensity, and should coincide with the period of maximum human activity on the slope above. The low intensity and magnetic susceptibility of the three uppermost samples are due to the sandy layer, and the low values of intensity on either side of the last intensity peak are probably caused by dilution of the normal sediment by increased input of such material. The weakness of

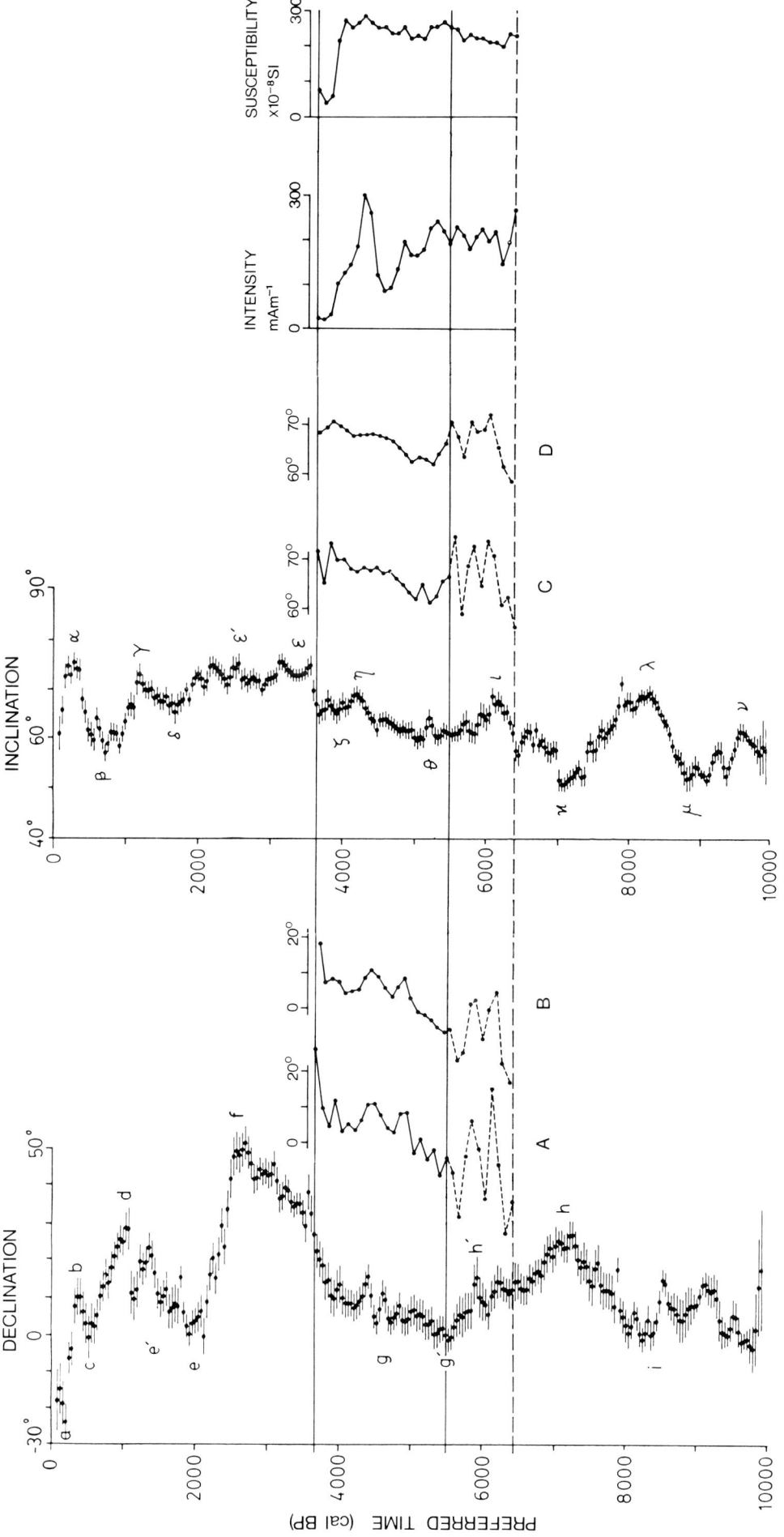

Fig 83 Magnetic measurements on the Brean Down sediment column compared with the declination and inclination curves of Turner and Thompson (1982): A and B, and C and D are respectively the raw data and two-point running means of the Brean declinations and inclinations; the poorer quality lower data points are joined by broken lines

these variations in the susceptibility plot is difficult to explain, but it does show an overall background increase with time, presumably reflecting man's exploitation of the landscape.

Some points can be made about the broader relevance of the Brean measurements to the reference curve. This was built up from cores taken from Loch Lomond, Windermere, and Llyn Geirionydd. The data were of variable quality, and a major problem was to determine azimuth and inclination references, which could not be marked on the cores. Now that the essential first stage of establishing the basic form of the reference curve has been achieved, it may well be possible to refine it by the accumulation of good quality 'onshore' data such as were provided by the 21 upper samples from Brean, directly levelled and orientated and covering a period of nearly 2000 years.

The lake sediment curve is made up of points separated by about 40 calendar years, each being the centre of a three-point running mean forming an 80-year 'window'. Each of the 21 best Brean samples represents about 86 years, so that the two-point running mean forms a 172-year window. The 86-year window of the raw data is also of quite good quality, so that the overall resolution is not greatly inferior to that of the reference curve. After correction for the geographical separation of the lakes from Brean, the mean declination for Brean is 3.3° east of that estimated by Turner and Thompson for the reference curve, while the mean Brean inclination is 5.4° the steeper. Comparison with archaeomagnetic data suggested an easterly declination discrepancy of 6.8° for more recent times (Clark *et al* 1988).

Acknowledgements

I am most grateful to Gillian Turner and Roy Thompson for permission to reproduce their reference curves.

10 Bell Beaker pottery

by Richard Harrison

Bell Beaker material occurs in twelve stratified contexts: Unit 8a (Context 63); Unit 7 (62); Unit 6b (66); Unit 6a (61); Unit 6α (157, 162, and 163); Unit 6 (5, Soil Pit I, 49, Soil Pit II); Unit 3a (13, 212); and Unit 3b (208, Soil Pit IV). Of these, only the material from 8a, the palaeosol, and Context 62, a thin occupation layer stratified within the wind-blown sand of Unit 7, can be accepted as from primary contexts. Finds of Beaker pottery in Unit 3 are clearly derived; those from Unit 6 may be derived from older Beaker occupations originally located upon the palaeosol.

Catalogue of sherds

Only decorated sherds are included individually. The amorphous plain body sherds are counted. The catalogue is arranged stratigraphically. Numbers refer to published illustrations with site find number in brackets.

Primary contexts (Fig 84)

Unit 8a, Context 63, the palaeosol

(Distribution of sherds shown on Fig 20b)

B1 (6440) Minute body sherd with impression of two small teeth
B2 (6468) Body sherd decorated with parallel lines of coarse horizontal comb impressions
B3 (6492) Body sherd decorated with a band of light comb impressions in a lattice design; above them are one or two light horizontal lines of comb impressions
B4 (60509) Body sherd with a single horizontal line of faint comb decoration
B5 (60522) Minute body sherd with two parallel lines of coarse comb decoration
B6 (6444) Body sherd with light finger-nail impressions
B7 (6414) Minute plain rim sherd, probably Beaker

There are another 19 minute plain body sherds, all of them probably from Bell Beakers, judging by the fine and well-levigated clays used.

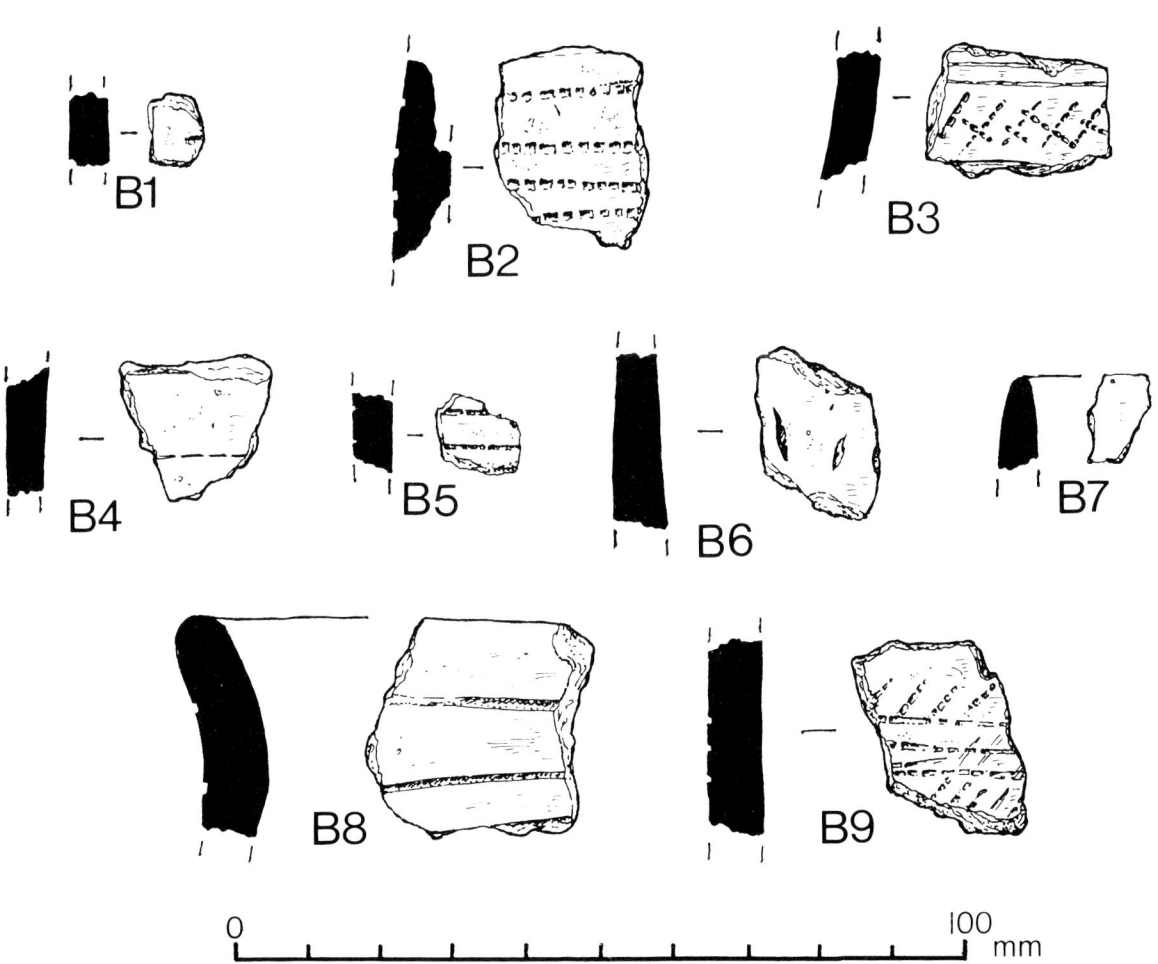

Fig 84 Bell Beaker pottery from primary contexts; scale 1:1

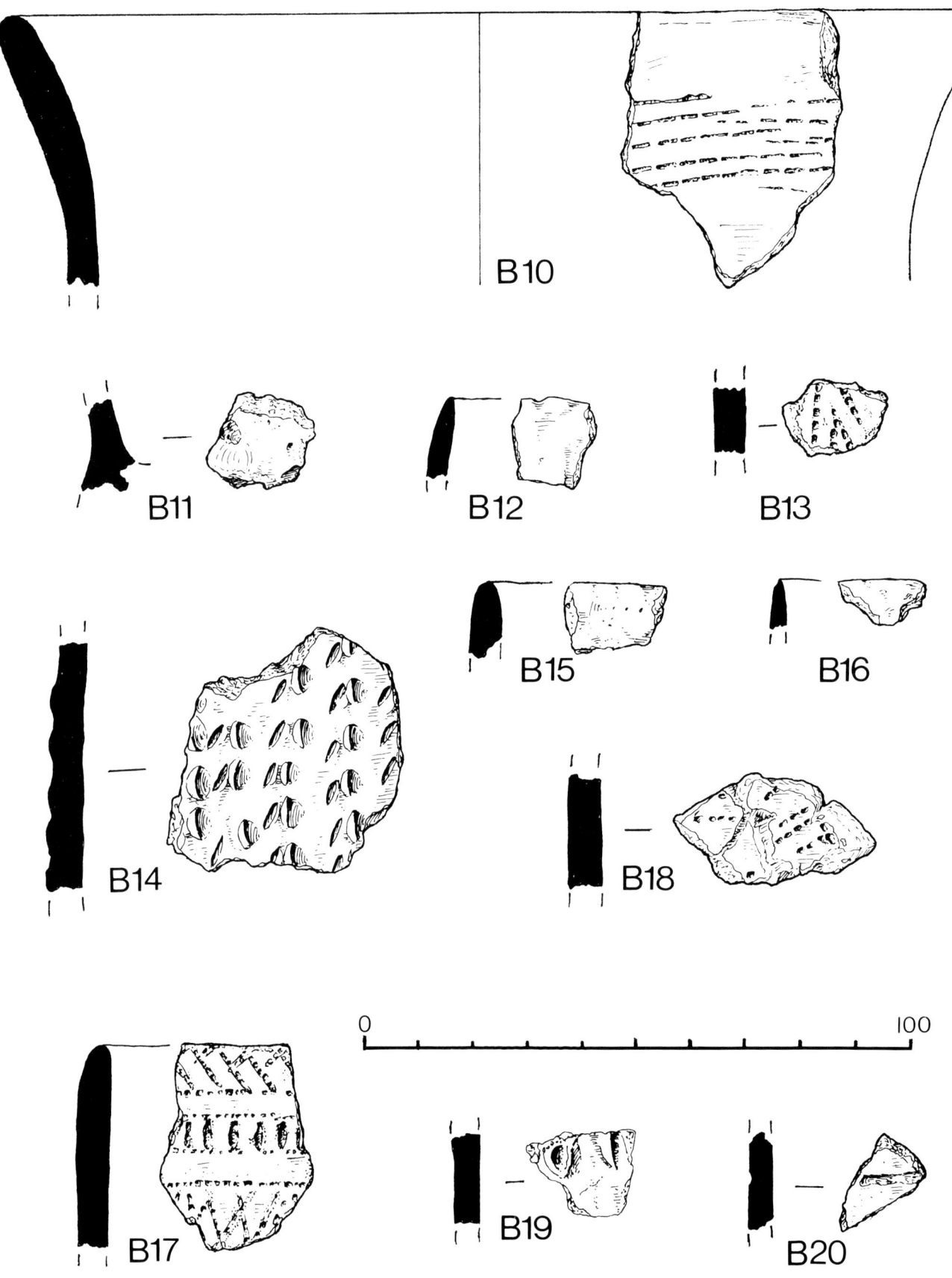

Fig 85   Bell Beaker pottery from secondary contexts; scale 1:1

Unit 7, Context 62

B8 (60492) Everted rim sherd, decorated with shallow, lightly incised lines, widely spaced
B9 (6265) Body sherd with coarse comb decoration using a broad band filled with horizontal and diagonal elements
Not illustrated (6265) Plain body sherd of Beaker fabric

Secondary contexts (Fig 85)

Unit 6

B10 (6110) Everted rim from a Bell Beaker with comb decoration confined to a band below the rim. Context 66, Unit 6b
Not illustrated (5991) A tiny sherd, perhaps Beaker. Context 61, Unit 6a
B11 (5903) Small body sherd from near the base of a vessel decorated with finger-nail impressions. Context 157, Unit 6α
B12 (5926) Plain rim sherd, probably Beaker. Context 162, Unit 6α
B13 (60448) Body sherd decorated with coarse comb impressions arranged in a triangular motif. Context 163, Unit 6α
B14 (60827) Body sherd with paired finger-nail impressions. Context 163, Unit 6α
B15 (6097) Small, plain rim sherd, probably Beaker. Context 163, Unit 6α
B16 (6134) Another. Context 163, Unit 6α
Not illustrated (6145) Body sherd of Beaker fabric. Context 163, Unit 6α
B17 (50219) Rim sherd from a straight-necked Bell Beaker, with deep comb stamping in a lattice pattern, arranged in wide zones. Context 49, Soil Pit II, Unit 6
B18 (50017) Small reconstructed body sherd decorated with a toothed comb impression, arranged in a triangular motif. Context 5, Soil Pit I, Unit 6

Unit 3

Not illustrated (50500) Small sherd decorated with a toothed comb impression. Context 208, Soil Pit IV, Unit 3b2
B19 (6526) Small body sherd with finger-tip decoration. Context 212, Unit 3a
B20 (587) Small sherd with a horizontal incision. Context 13, Unit 3a

Conclusions

The varied styles and techniques of decoration from at least 18 ornamented vessels dispersed through 12 stratigraphic contexts probably represent more than one episode of pottery manufacture, although precise types cannot be assigned to the sherds.

The collection includes 4 rusticated and 18 comb or incised sherds; this compared with the 18 sherds and

Table 6 Number of decorated Beaker sherds by stratigraphic unit

Stratigraphic unit	1985–7 excavations	ApSimon et al 1961
Unstratified	0	5 (nos 17–21)
Secondary contexts	9	0
Unit 7 'Beaker sand'	2	6 (nos 11–16)
Grave cut into Unit 8a	0	2 (restorable vessels nos 7–8)
Unit 8a (palaeosol)	7	7 (nos 1–5)
Totals	**18**	**20**

2 restorable Beakers that ApSimon published in 1961, from material that had been retrieved from the cliff face when it was prepared for recording, or found on the beach below.

Table 6 is interesting in several ways. First, the deposits examined by ApSimon *et al* were relatively richer in Bell Beakers than those excavated recently, which agrees with the view that the stratigraphic units containing Bell Beakers are thinning out and not appearing in the area being studied now. Secondly, the lack of Beakers in secondary deposits in ApSimon's collection is almost certainly due to his small sample, and the fact that the 1985–7 excavations moved a large volume of soil. Statistically, the frequency of Beakers in secondary contexts is so low as to be insignificant, except in Unit 6. Thirdly, there is nothing to contradict ApSimon's perceptive remarks on the two phases of Beaker occupation which he identified: an older one represented by the grave with its Cord-Zoned Maritime and Rusticated Bell Beakers, cut into the palaeosol (Unit 8a), and a later one within Unit 7 (the 'Beaker sand'). In the top of the palaeosol ApSimon records the only All-Over Comb (AOC) Beaker sherd from the site; the type is diagnostic, and always early in the Beaker series in southern Britain. The early Beaker occupation may once have belonged to an activity horizon of which all trace has now gone, and which only survived minimally even when ApSimon *et al* first recorded the sequence correctly. Today no trace remains of this early stage, although it must be said it is a short-lived phenomenon. The Beaker sherds from the palaeosol (Unit 8a), from both collections, do not have a preponderance of typologically early decoration, and their motifs can be matched among the later group of Beakers from the henge at Gorsey Bigbury, on the Mendips (Grimes 1938).

The 1985–7 collection of Beaker pottery does not show a clear seriation, but it has proved that there was an occupation within Unit 7, even though this was a transitory one. ApSimon *et al* noted that fishing in the marshes nearby may have been one attraction, and mentioned a pike jawbone from the base of Unit 6b – in contact with Unit 7.

Judging from the grave, and the two stratified collections in primary contexts, it is quite possible that the Bell Beaker occupation took place as isolated, short visits, spread over many centuries; certainly there is nothing suggesting intensive or long-lived activity.

A note on the petrology of two Beaker sherds

by David Williams

The following sherds were submitted for detailed examination in thin section under the petrological microscope: B9 (6265) and B17 (50219). Both examples were characterised by containing scattered angular inclusions of grog. The fabric is quite fine-textured with only a small amount of quartz grains and fairly frequent pieces of grog. It is difficult to suggest likely geographical source areas; they fit into the general 'grog' fabric group established for pottery examined from Brean Down.

11 The Bronze Age pottery

by Ann Woodward

Introduction

The recent excavations at Brean Down have produced a large collection of Bronze Age pottery which in terms of both its size and variety contributes most significantly to our understanding of the Bronze Age sequence in Somerset. The three distinct assemblages, which were separated stratigraphically by layers of sterile sand and were associated with specific structures and features, have been dated independently by the radiocarbon method. They provide insights into the domestic organisation of three periods within the Bronze Age and may be compared with ceramic developments elsewhere in the county and beyond into the south-west peninsula, south Wales, and Wessex. Taken together with the results of analysis of the middle and late Bronze Age ceramic assemblages from Norton Fitzwarren (Woodward forthcoming), the transitional, but highly innovative, aspects of the Somerset assemblages may now be appreciated more clearly.

The total stratified assemblage comprised 4425 sherds weighing 34.392 kilos, while a further 540 sherds recovered from less secure contexts (ie Units 1-4a, the auger holes, and unstratified) were not weighed. The pottery was counted and weighed by context and all feature sherds were recorded by pro forma; in general the sherds had been three-dimensionally recorded on site and computer-generated plots of fabrics and selected form categories have been prepared. Where possible, joining sherds were located and vessels reconstructed; most of this work was accomplished by Jennifer Foster who also drew the sherds selected for publication. The overall distribution of pottery is well demonstrated in Figure 86, a vertical plot of all sherds by fabric. This shows the relatively small later early Bronze Age biconical urn assemblage at the base, associated with Structure 57 in Unit 6, and separated by sand from the substantial middle Bronze Age Trevisker-related assemblage found in and around Structures 95 and 59 of Unit 5b. Above a further sterile layer of sand lies the dense concentration of late Bronze Age pottery within Unit 4.

Fabrics

by David Williams and Ann Woodward

Twelve type fabrics were defined macroscopically by Ann Woodward and these categories were used throughout the analysis and quantification of the material. Twenty-five samples, belonging to the nine more common type fabrics, were submitted to David Williams who was able to verify the identifications and to classify them into six major fabric groups.

Macroscopic descriptions

Fabric 361 Grog fragments of varying size, sub-rounded, ill-sorted, densely distributed, soft. Often a pink-buff outer surface; otherwise grey

Fabric 362 Grog, as 361, with rare, angular calcite inclusions, ill-sorted

Fabric 363 Sparse grog fragments of varying size with

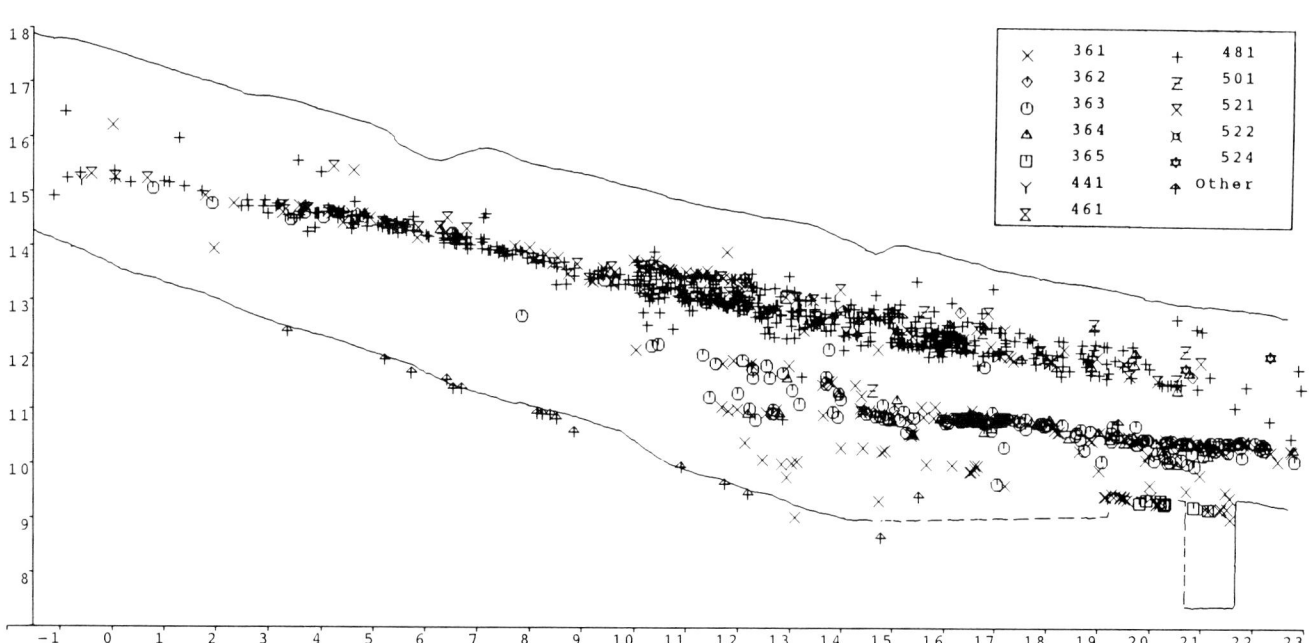

Fig 86 Vertical distribution of all sherds by fabric

medium density of small to medium-sized limestone inclusions. Soft, grey-black, partly vesicular

Fabric 364 Grog, as 361, but a much harder fabric with a smoothed surface; usually grey-black

Fabric 365 Grog, sand, and some sparse limestone inclusions

Fabric 441 Sparse platy shell

Fabric 461 Fossil shell

Fabric 481 Dense calcite inclusions, all sizes, angular, ill-sorted

Fabric 501 Sparse rounded limestone inclusions, varying sizes

Fabric 521 Dense quartz sand

Fabric 522 Sand and sparse rounded limestone inclusions

Fabric 524 Sand and sparse calcite and vegetative inclusions; black exterior surface, red interior

Microscopic descriptions

The full report by David Williams is housed in the archive.

Group 1:   Limonite (Fabric 365)

Thin sectioning reveals subangular grains of quartz and small pieces of limestone, both with what appears to be a brown coating of limonite, together with light brown grains of ?limonite. Limonite has been identified in an examination of the soil samples at Brean Down (Cornwall 1961), and if correctly identified here, suggests a local source for this vessel.

Group 2:   Grog (Fabrics 361 and 363)

The sherds contain scattered angular inclusions of grog (crushed pottery). Also present in some of the samples are grains of quartz, chert, a little sandstone, and limestone. Owing to the widespread use of grog tempering in late Neolithic and Bronze Age pottery, it is difficult to suggest an origin for these sherds, other than a local one.

Group 3:   Quartz/limestone (Fabric 521)

The sherds are coarse in texture and have frequent grains of quartz ranging up to 0.80mm in size and fragments of cryptocrystalline limestone, together with flecks of mica and some sandstone, chert, and argillaceous material.

Group 4:   Quartz (Fabric 521)

Frequent grains of sub-rounded to subangular quartz ranging up to 1mm across in size, with flecks of mica and a little chert and iron ore. One sample also contains some quartzite.

Group 5:   Calcite (Fabrics 364, 481, 521, and 524)

All sherds contain large twinned angular fragments of calcite scattered throughout the fabric, the frequency varying between some of the sherds. The Fabric 521 sample is basically a fairly sandy fabric but does also contain a number of pieces of calcite. Apart from calcite, also present in this group are inclusions of cryptocrystalline limestone, quartz grains, and occasional chert, iron ore, quartzite, and sandstone. In most cases the large size, comparatively fresh condition, and angularity of the calcite strongly suggest that it was deliberately crushed and added to the clay as a tempering agent. Calcite can be obtained from the local Carboniferous Limestone deposits of Brean Down and several pieces were found during the excavation, particularly in Unit 4 (see p 175). It may also be worthwhile noting that one of Peacock's (1969b) fabric groups for Iron Age Glastonbury ware was calcite-tempered, and an origin in the Mendips suggested.

Group 6:   Limestone (Fabrics 364 and 501)

The most prominent inclusions seen in thin section are fragments of limestone scattered throughout the fabric; some of the pieces are fairly well-rounded; also present are some quartz grains, chert, calcite, and sandstone. It is difficult to be precise about the derivation of the limestone given its undiagnostic nature. However, in the absence of further information a local source seems most likely.

David Williams had also studied petrologically a series of samples from the previous excavations directed by ApSimon, including many of the sherds published in 1961 (ApSimon *et al* 1961). This material included examples from all the groups defined above except Group 6: limestone. Sectioned sherds included the following items illustrated in ApSimon *et al* 1961: fig 25:4, fig 27:22, 23, 27, 29, and 41, fig 28:43 and 44 (grog-tempered Group 2), and fig 27:31-33 (limonite-tempered Group 1). In addition, two further groups not represented in the more recently excavated assemblage were defined.

These were flint-tempered (one sample only) and a series of sherds tempered with felspathic tuff; the latter included the sherd illustrated in ApSimon *et al* 1961, fig 29:14. Thin sectioning shows frequent discrete grains of plagioclase felspar (oligoclase-andesine composition), together with a little mica, quartz, chert, limestone, and sandstone. Some of the felspar has partially altered to sericite. A very similar fabric has been noted by Peacock (1969b) in a few sherds of Glastonbury ware from Somerset, and attention was drawn to the Silurian volcanic rocks of Beacon Hill near Shepton Mallet, which are largely composed of andesitic and felspathic tuffs (Green and Welch 1965). A similar origin for the Brean Down pottery would agree well with the petrology of the fabric.

The distribution of fabric occurrences in the recent excavations is summarised in Table 7 and, for the more common type fabrics, in Figure 87. These show quite dramatically that the early and middle Bronze Age assemblages of Units 6 and 5b are characterised by the grogged fabrics, while the Unit 4 late Bronze Age pottery is predominantly tempered with calcite (Fabric 481). The sandy fabrics (521) are also confined to Unit 4, but grogged Fabrics 361, 362, and 363 occur

THE BRONZE AGE POTTERY

Table 7 The occurrence of Bronze Age pottery by phase unit

	Fabric	361	362	363	364	365	441	461	481	501	521	522	524	Totals
		Grog	Grog/calcite	Grog, hard	Grog/limestone	Grog/sand/limestone	Shell	Fossil shell	Calcite	Limestone	Sand	Sand/limestone	Sand/veg/calcite	
	Unit													
No of sherds	4	178	20	31	4	-	4	1	1770	-	54	1	8	2071 sherds
Wt (g)		997	170	298	60	-	85	50	12161	-	302	5	160	14288 g
	4 (soil pits)	25	3	-	-	-	-	-	123	-	2	82	-	235 sherds
		158	25	-	-	-	-	-	914	-	6	695	-	1788 g
	5a	3	4	3	3	-	-	-	21	-	1	-	1	36 sherds
		65	100	70	25	-	-	-	311	-	40	-	50	661 g
	5a (soil pits)	-	-	-	-	-	-	-	5	-	-	-	-	5 sherds
		-	-	-	-	-	-	-	28	-	-	-	-	28 g
	5b (59)	11	-	16	3	-	-	-	-	-	-	-	-	30 sherds
		198	-	193	50	-	-	-	-	-	-	-	-	441 g
	5b (95)	399	3	400	355	-	-	-	-	2	1	-	-	1160 sherds
		4515	58	2278	2515	-	-	-	-	10	15	-	-	9391 g
	5b (other)	202	5	334	104	-	-	-	5	18	3	-	-	671 sherds
		2475	30	2030	945	-	-	-	85	165	45	-	-	5775 g
	5b (soil pits)	1	-	-	-	-	-	-	-	-	-	-	-	1 sherd
		2	-	-	-	-	-	-	-	-	-	-	-	2 g
	5d	3	-	6	2	-	-	-	-	-	-	-	-	11 sherds
		70	-	130	50	-	-	-	-	-	-	-	-	250 g
	6α (57)	43	-	2	4	43	-	-	-	-	-	-	-	92 sherds
		470	-	30	25	250	-	-	-	-	-	-	-	775 g
	6α (other)	17	-	3	1	-	-	-	-	-	2	-	-	23 sherds
		335	-	55	10	-	-	-	-	-	15	-	-	415 g
	6a	19	-	9	-	-	-	-	-	-	-	-	-	28 sherds
		53	-	45	-	-	-	-	-	-	-	-	-	98 g
	6b	16	-	15	-	26	-	-	-	-	1	-	-	58 sherds
		240	-	50	-	100	-	-	-	-	15	-	-	405 g
	6 (soil pits)	6	-	-	-	-	-	-	-	-	-	-	-	6 sherds
		25	-	-	-	-	-	-	-	-	-	-	-	25 g
	7	1	-	-	-	-	-	-	-	-	-	-	-	1 sherd
		25	-	-	-	-	-	-	-	-	-	-	-	25 g
Total sherds														4425
Total kilos														34367
Sherd counts only														
	1–4a	20	12	-	23	-	1	-	196	5	7	2	3	269
	1–3	5	-	-	-	-	-	-	12	-	2	-	-	19
	(soil pits)	-	-	-	-	-	-	-	-	-	-	-	-	-
	auger holes	13	-	-	2	-	-	-	95	-	-	-	-	110
	unstrat	39	1	8	27	-	-	1	139	-	1	-	-	216
	unstrat/unclass	-	-	20	-	-	-	-	-	-	-	-	-	20
Total														634
Total sherds														5059

in percentages which suggest rather more than residuality from the underlying or nearby earlier deposits. Amongst the grogged fabrics there is some internal chronological differentiation. Thus Unit 6 contexts produced all the sherds of Fabric 365 (grog plus sand and limestone) whilst Fabrics 363 (grog plus more dense limestone) and, more particularly, Fabric 364 (reduced fabric with hard surface) are more common in the middle Bronze Age Unit 5b.

Biconical vessels largely from Unit 6 (Fig 88)

1. Rounded shoulder with raised plain cordon. Fabric 361. Find 5975, Context 66, below Structure 57
2. Body sherd from shoulder with slight offset ridge. Fabric 361. Find 5930, Context 66, colluvium below Structure 57
3. Rounded shoulder with a row of irregular fingernail impressions at carination. Fabric 361. Find 5931, Context 61, gleyed colluvium adjacent to Structure 57
4. Plain square rim. Fabric 361. Find 6049, Context 61, gleyed colluvium adjacent to 57
5. Plain beaded rim with squared profile, possibly from a bowl. Fabric 363. Find 4896, Context 61, gleyed colluvium adjacent to 57
6. Rim and upper portion of vessel with inturned flattened rim, decorated with finger-tip impressions arranged in a very irregular spaced row some distance below the rim. Fabric 363. Finds 5952, Context 61, gleyed colluvium adjacent to 57 (Unit 6a) and 4273, Context 58, sterile sand below Unit 5b

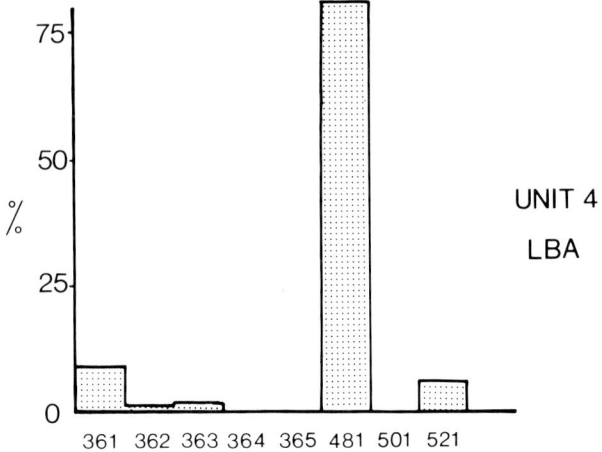

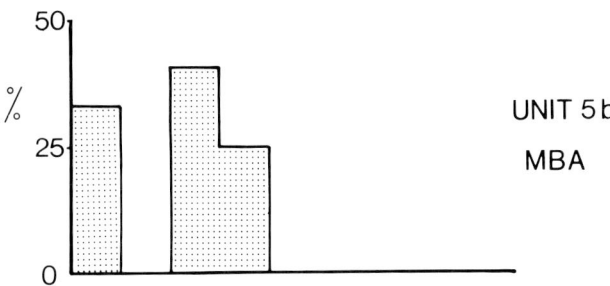

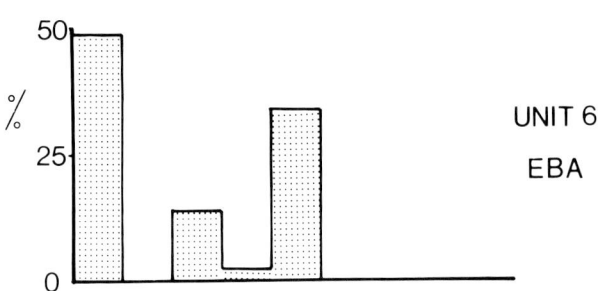

Fig 87 The occurrence of stratified prehistoric pottery fabrics by major unit

7 Plain, slightly tapering rim. Fabric 361. Find 5936, Context 163, within Structure 57
8 Plain, tapering rim, almost hooked. Fabric 365. Find 6051, Context 163, within Structure 57
9 Plain, sub-square rim. Fabric 365. Find 6175, Context 163, within Structure 57
10 Body sherd pierced with circular perforations arranged in rough rows. Fabric 361. Find 6228 (and another, not illustrated, find 6178), Context 163, within Structure 57
11 Plain angled shoulder. Fabric 365. Find 6151, Context 163, within Structure 57
12 Plain rounded shoulder. Fabric 361. Find 6173, Context 163, within Structure 57
13 Simple base angle with traces of circular perforations above the base. Fabric 361. Find 6167, Context 163, within Structure 57
14 Simple base angle. Fabric 361. Find 6198, Context 177, floor of Structure 57
15 Body sherd from curved body of a jar, bearing a plain horizontal applied ovoid lug and traces of incised decoration. Fabric 361. Find 5919, Context 157, wall collapse of Structure 57
16 Simple base angle, outer surface damaged. Fabric 361. Find 5909, Context 157, wall collapse of Structure 57
17 Rim, incurved and with slight internal bevel, decorated with a regular row of finger-tip impressions just below the rim. Fabric 361. Find 6001, Context 156, Structure 57
18 Plain flattened rim with slight internal bevel. Fabric 361. Find 6037, Context 153, sterile sand, Unit 5d
19 Sub-square rim with slight internal bevel and a random arrangement of finger-nail impressions below the rim. Fabric 361. Unstratified sherd in Woodspring Museum, 1983
20 Body sherd from vessel with curved profile and bearing traces of an irregular row of finger-tip impressions at the belly. Fabric 363. Find 6138, Context 165, a basal context in Unit 5b
21 Plain sharply angled shoulder, outer surface damaged. Fabric 361. Find 6017, Context 165, a basal context in Unit 5b

Assemblage characteristics

The main formal and decorative characteristics of the assemblage may be summarised as follows:

Rim forms: simple – 7 instances, including nos 7, 8; flattened – 6 instances, including nos 9, 4, 5; hooked, with slight internal bevel – 6 instances, including nos 6, 17, 18
Shoulders: sharp – 8 instances, including nos 11, 1, 2, 21; rounded – 8 instances, including nos 12, 3, 112, 113
Base angles: simple, from out-flaring vessels – 7 instances, including nos 13, 14, 16
Decoration: row of finger-nail impressions – 8 instances, including nos 3, 17, 112, 113; irregular row of finger-tip impressions – 4 instances, including nos 6, 20; all-over perforations – 2 instances, including no 10; random finger-nail impressions – 3 instances, including no 19; incised lines – 2 instances, including no 15
Lugs/handles: plain oval horizontal lug – 2 instances, including no 15; horseshoe cordon – 4 instances, including nos 59, 60

All these traits occurred in the Unit 6 assemblage (nos 1–17), except for the illustrated horseshoe cordons which were found as residual items in Unit 5b. Two of the round-shouldered wall sherds with rows of finger-nail impressions were found in Unit 4 (nos 112 and 113) but are ascribed to the early Bronze Age assemblage on the grounds of surface colour and fabric, as well as form. A selection of traits was found on sherds residual in the sand of Unit 5d (13), or unstratified (19), or the base of Unit 5b (20 and 21). In detail, various traits may be matched with those on sherds from ApSimon's Units 6c 'Limpet Hearth' and 6b and the Unit 6 assemblage appears to amplify the biconical vessel series defined by him. One type illustrated by ApSimon is not replicated in the new

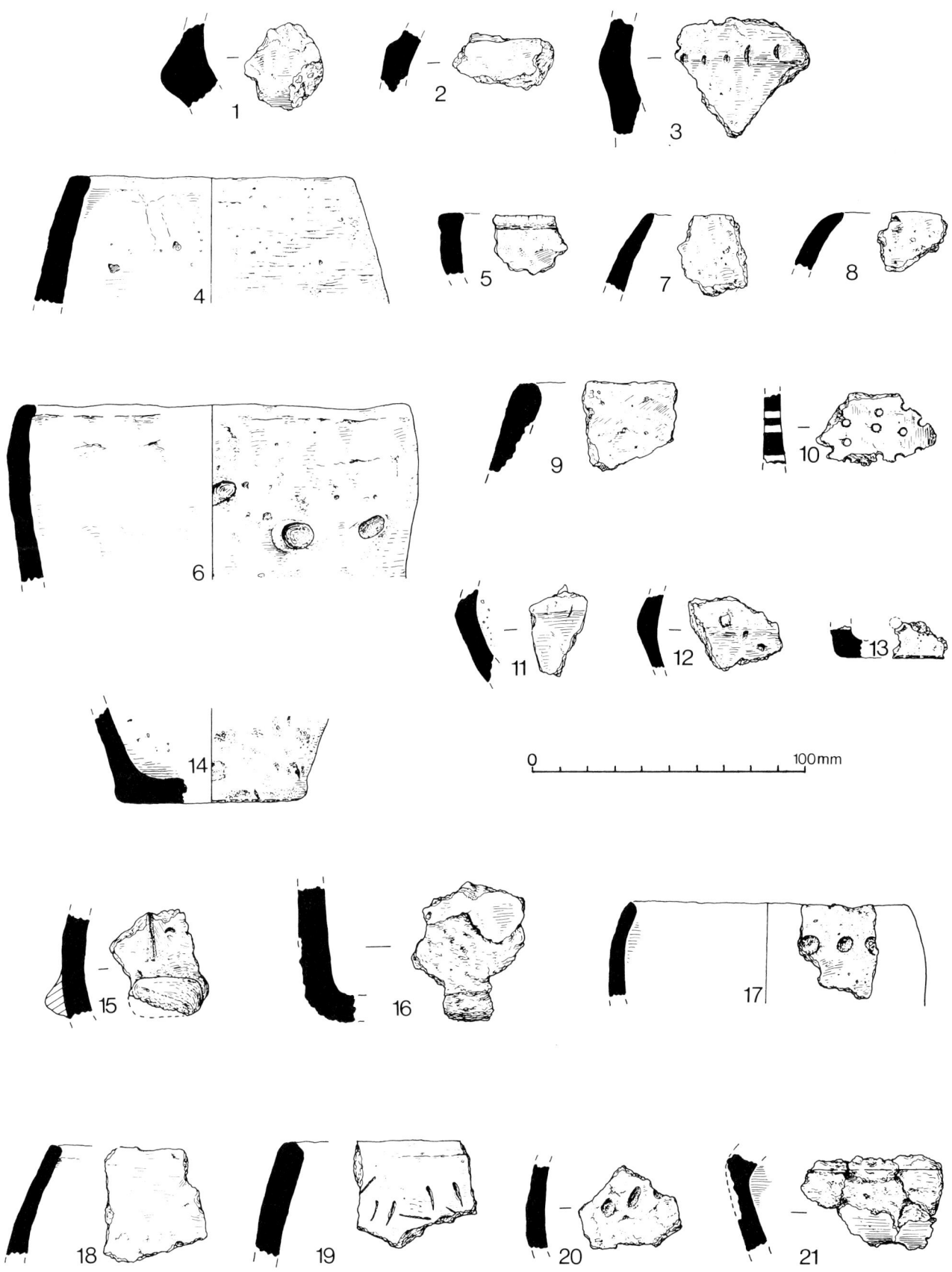

Fig 88 Pottery largely from Unit 6; scale 1:2

assemblage and that is the rim sherd with a concave internal bevel and decorated on the bevel and on the exterior in impressed cord technique (ApSimon *et al* 1961, fig 27:22).

The simple and flattened rim forms are found on biconical vessels from the earlier excavation (ApSimon *et al* 1961, fig 27:34 and 35, from the Unit 6c 'Limpet Hearth') and Shaugh Moor, Devon (Wainwright and Smith 1980, fig 19, P12). Sharp shoulder angles were also found at Shaugh Moor (ibid, fig 18, P4 and fig 19, P13) and more rounded ones in the ApSimon assemblage (1961, fig 27:23 and 29 from Unit 6b). The simple bases are also matched at Shaugh Moor (Wainwright and Smith 1980, fig 18, P5) and in ApSimon *et al*'s report (fig 27:26 to 28 from 6b and 38 from 6c). Rows of finger-tip or nail impressions are of course a common characteristic of the biconical urn series as a whole and nearby may be found on the less well-known burial urns from Tynings Farm, Cheddar: North Barrow, Pits 1 and 2 (Taylor 1933; 1951; ApSimon 1969, 45). The vessel form with slightly hooked and bevelled rim and a row of irregular impressions below (eg nos 6 and 17) is matched by fig 27:41 in the ApSimon assemblage. The plain oval lug is another common motif of the biconical series and occurs at Shaugh Moor (Wainwright and Smith 1980, fig 18, P1) and at Cannington (A ApSimon, pers comm).

Thus the biconical assemblage belongs to a well-defined series of later early Bronze Age pottery, defined recently by Tomalin as a domestic development linked to the floruit of his Form 3 urns derived from the stone-tempered vessels of his 'Inception Series' (Tomalin 1983). Locally, similar assemblages occur at Shearplace Hill, Dorset (Rahtz and ApSimon 1962; Tomalin 1983) as well as at Shaugh Moor in Devon, and these are well paralleled by a series of domestic assemblages recently studied in East Anglia (Mildenhall and Hockwold: Tomalin 1983; Grimes Graves: Longworth and Ellison 1988). Similar vessels are also known now from a series of sites in south Wales, including those from a disturbed domestic cave deposit at Lesser Garth Cave, Radyr, Glamorgan (Savory 1980, fig 72, 505:1–6).

The predominantly grog-tempered fabrics of the Brean assemblage are matched at Shearplace Hill, where they soon give way to the flint-tempered recipes of the Dorset Downs Deverel-Rimbury ceramic group, but the Shaugh Moor assemblage is characterised by volcanic inclusions (95%) and a few vessels tempered with quartz sandstone (Tomalin 1982, 239–40). All, however, appear to have been locally manufactured.

The radiocarbon date from Structure 57 of Unit 6, 3310±80 BP (HAR-7020), matches in well with the date range of *c* 3300–2950 BP argued for the Shaugh Moor assemblage by Tomalin (1982, 229–30), while the date of 3130±180 BP (NPL-19) from a combined sample at Shearplace Hill may date early Bronze Age and middle Bronze Age levels. Thus it can be taken to provide a *terminus ante quem* for the biconical assemblage found there. The date of 3890±130 BP (HAR-7022) relates to Context 66 which underlies and predates the structure in Unit 6 and contained sherds of biconical vessels (nos 1 and 2). Finally it should be mentioned that two sherds from ApSimon's Unit 6c (ApSimon *et al* 1961, fig 27:31 and 33), tentatively identified as Grooved Ware by Gibson (1982, 115–16), are now felt by Arthur ApSimon and Elaine Morris (pers comm) to be fragments of briquetage. Of the three radiocarbon dates from Unit 6a, 2600±90 BP (HAR-7021), 2770±90 BP (HAR-8992), and 3120±90 BP (HAR-8991), the last corresponds to the other Unit 6 dates but the other two imply that activity on Unit 6a may have continued later (Chapter 9).

Trevisker-related vessels from Unit 5b

Context 112, within Structure 95 (Figs 89 and 90)

22 Vessel 1. Jar of conical profile with flattened, slightly expanded rim. Below the rim a zone of roughly incised decorations comprising hatched zones, opposed filled triangles, and some cross-hatching, all confined between two finger grooves. Two repair holes, drilled after firing. Simple plain base angle. Fabric 361. Finds 5368: 10, 17, 26, 30, 35, 43, 44, 47, 64, 79, and 88

23 Vessel 2. Rim to shoulder of almost straight-sided jar with flattened, externally expanded rim and slight internal bevel. A zone of roughly incised decoration approximating to alternately hatched triangles arranged between a finger groove located just below the rim and an applied plain cordon at the shoulder. Fabric 361. Finds 5368: 10, 34, and 91, and 5124

24 Vessel 5. Rim to shoulder of a straight-sided jar with flattened, externally expanded rim. Incised opposed filled triangle decoration between two shoulder grooves. Fabric 361. Finds 5368: 70 and 75

25 Vessel 4. Rim to shoulder of a jar with slightly curved profile and flattened rim with slight external expansion. Below the rim a zone of very irregular horizontal double chevrons bounded by two horizontal incised lines above and one below. Fabric 364. Finds 5368: 4, 7, 51, 72, 74, 90, and 91

26 Body sherd decorated with a finger groove above opposed incised hatched triangles. Fabric 364. Find 5177

27 Flattened rim with slight internal bevel; two horizontal incised lines below the rim. Fabric 361. Find 5368: 56

28 Simple rim with slight internal bevel; traces of incised chevron below a horizontal line. Fabric 363. Find 5742

29 Body sherd from a straight-sided jar decorated with an incised filled triangle or chevron standing on a horizontal line. Fabric 361. Find 5368: 95

30 Vessel 8. Body sherds from straight-sided jar with incised diagonal lines below a horizontal line towards upper part of vessel. Fabric 363. Find 5641

31 Body sherd from straight-walled jar with an applied horizontally perforated lug and a row of finger-tip impressions. Fabric 361. Find 5368: 55

THE BRONZE AGE POTTERY

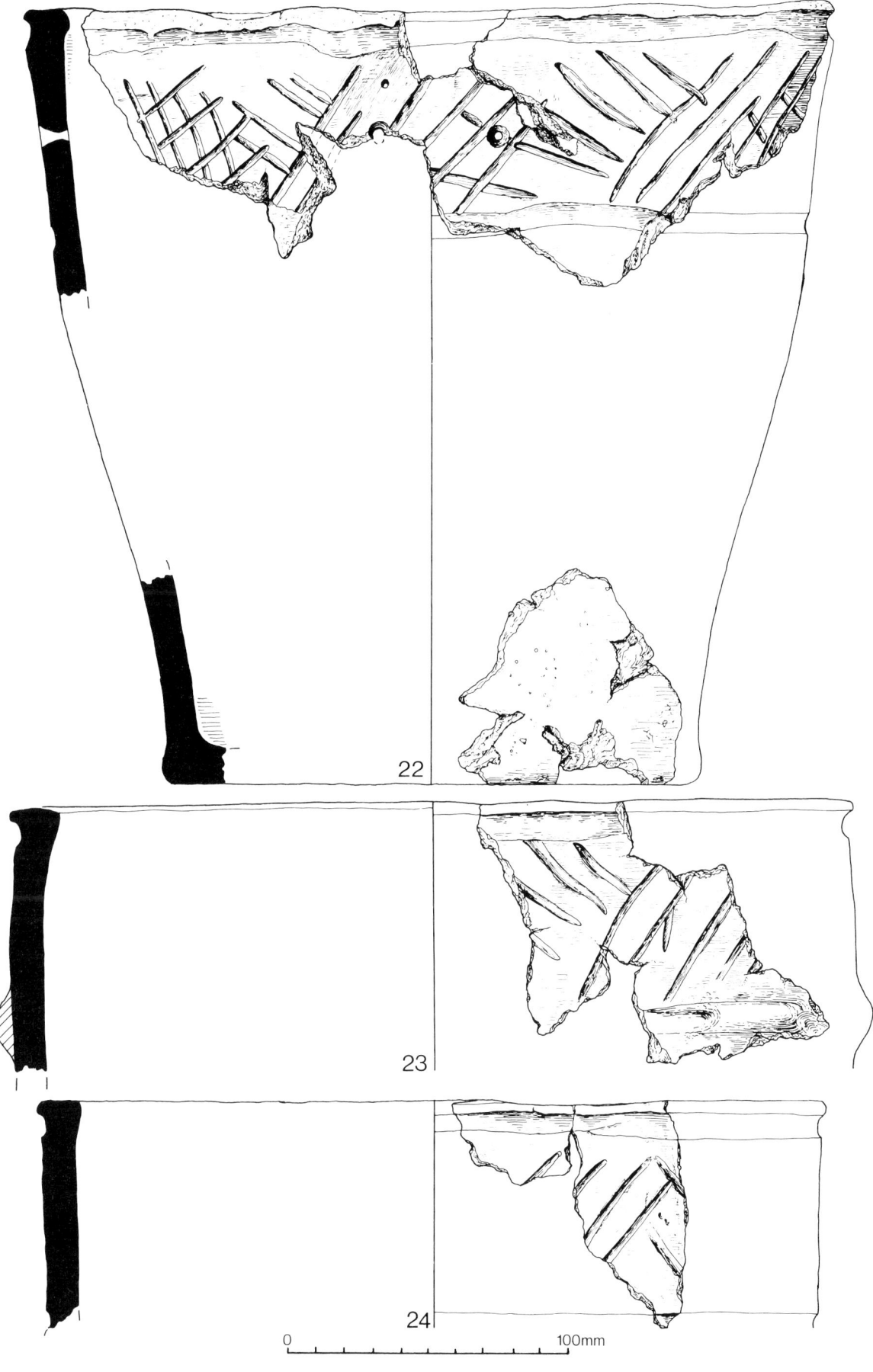

Fig 89 Trevisker-related vessels from Unit 5b, Context 112; scale 1:2

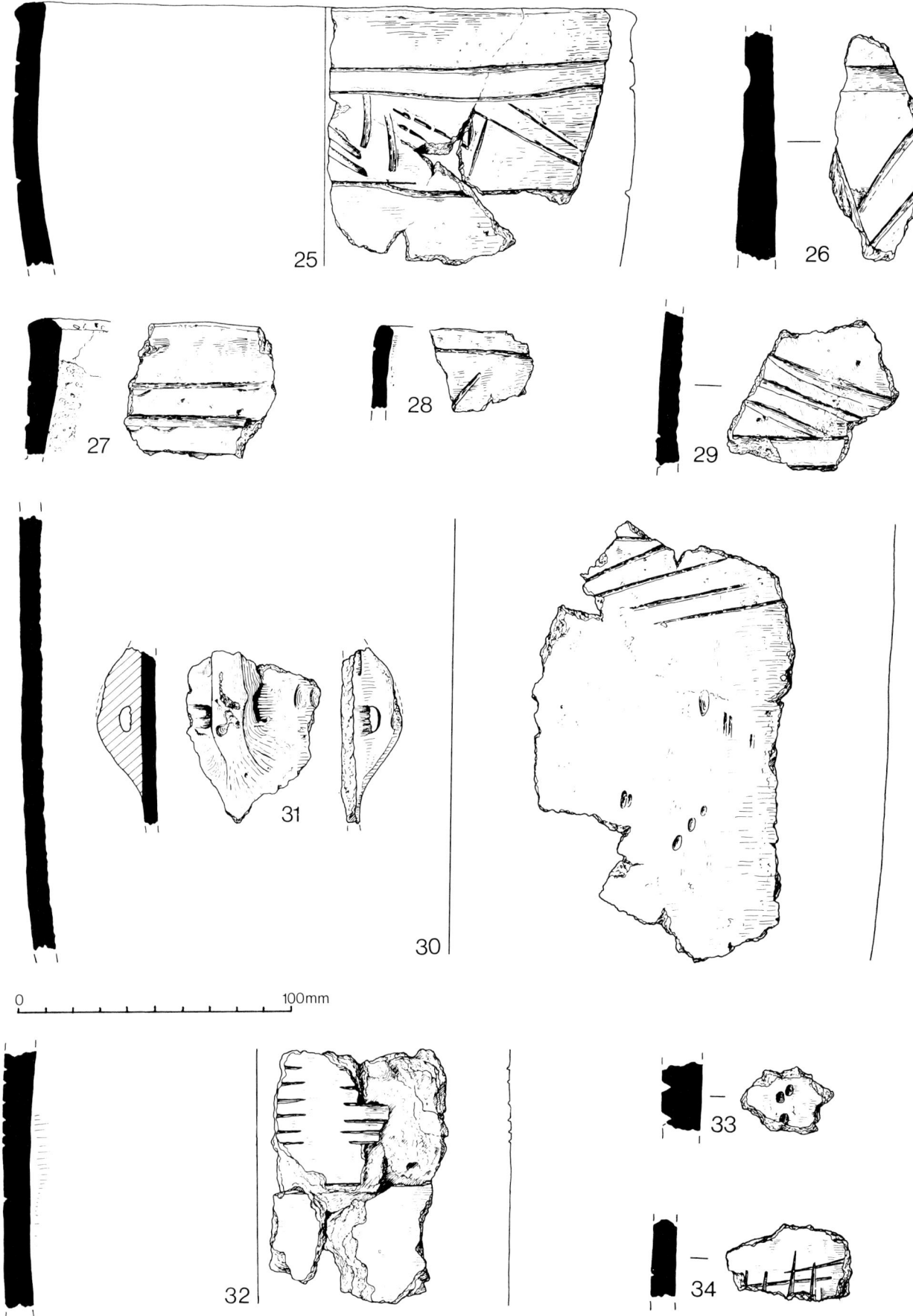

Fig 90   Trevisker-related vessels from Unit 5b, Context 112; scale 1:2

32 Vessel 3. Wall sherd from straight-sided jar with traces of groups of incised horizontal lines above a single continuous horizontal line. Fabric 361. Finds 5368: 13, 55, and 92
33 Wall sherd decorated with punched circular impressions; design indeterminate. Fabric 361. Find 5274
34 Wall sherd decorated with incised irregular cross-hatching. Fabric 361. Find 5368: 87

Context 53, above Structure 95 (Fig 91)

35 Simple rim, slightly everted with a row of slight finger-tip impressions and incised rough horizontal chevron decoration below the rim. Fabric 361. Find 6033a
36 Simple flattened rim of globular jar. Below the rim part of a zone of alternately hatched triangles below two horizontal lines, all incised. Fabric 361. Find 6033b
37 Slightly beaded flat rim from a small jar. Below the rim closely spaced vertical incised lines. Fabric 361. Find 5261
38 Simple rounded rim of globular jar decorated with groups of diagonal incised lines below a pair of horizontal incised lines. Fabric 364. Find 5374
39 Flattened and externally expanded rim with two irregular incised lines below. Fabric 364. Find 5592
40 Straight wall sherd with rough incised double chevron. Fabric 364. Find 4830
41 Wall sherd from globular jar decorated with incised linear swag motif. Fabric 363. Find 3654
42 Vessel 7. Rim and shoulder of globular jar with out-curved rim with external bevel. Immediately below the rim, decoration of opposed filled triangles executed in single impressed cord technique. Fabric 364. Finds 4450 and 70005
43 Wall sherd from globular or shouldered jar decorated with unevenly spaced incised lines. Fabric 361. Find 4781
44 Rim sherds from a round-bodied jar with simple flat rim and horizontal line decoration immediately below, executed in impressed double cord technique. Fabric 364. Finds 4472, 5206, and 60320
45 Flat rim from globular or shouldered jar. Traces of vertical incised lines below the rim. Fabric 361. Find 4991
46 Simple flat rim and upper zone of straight-sided jar. Filled incised chevron above a horizontal incised line. Fabric 364. Find 5198
47 Wall sherd from slightly globular vessel with a plain applied cordon and interior decoration executed in very fine and cord-impressed technique. Fabric 363. Find 4991
48 Flat rim with punched circular impression below. Fabric 361. Find 5188, cf no 33 above
49 Wall sherd with part of a perforation, bored prior to firing. Fabric 361. Find 4971
50 Wall sherd from slightly globular vessel with vertical handle of semicircular section and two uneven rows of finger-tip impressions. Fabric 363. Find 5884
51 Simple base angle. Fabric 361. Find 4838
52 Vessel 6. Base angle with slight external expansion. Fabric 361. Finds 4838 and 5203/5204

Context 112, within Structure 95 (Fig 92)

53 Vessel 9. Shoulder zone from slightly biconical vessel with an applied square-sectioned cordon decorated with closely-spaced small finger-tip impressions, ?residual biconical urn. Fabric 364. Finds 5166, 5822, and 5368: 78 and 85
54 Raised shoulder cordon decorated with a row of finger-nail impressions, ?residual biconical urn. Fabric 361. Find 5776

Other contexts (Fig 92)

55 Thin wall sherd decorated with incised individual horizontal chevrons above a zone of broken vertical chevrons. Fabric 361. Find 5029, Context 77, ash spread south of Structure 95
56 Wall sherd, sharply grooved to provide a ribbed effect. Fabric 363. Find 5967a, Context 155, pit below the floor of Structure 95
57 Flat rim, damaged, with rusticated finger-tip and finger-nail decoration below. Fabric 361. Find 5967b, Context 155, pit below the floor of Structure 95
58 Wall sherd from globular jar with incised opposed filled triangle decoration. Fabric 363. Find 5984, Context 131, terrace wall of Structure 95
59 Wall sherd bearing part of an applied plain curved cordon, probably part of an arc handle. Fabric 361. Find 5448, Context 95, stone structure terrace fill
60 Shoulder sherd bearing part of a plain applied horseshoe handle. Fabric 361. Find 5124, Context 95, stone structure terrace fill
61 Slightly out-turned simple rim with part of a perforation surviving below. Fabric 363. Find 5412, Context 115, hollow at the base of Unit 5b
62 Base angle. Fabric 361. Find 5163, Context 95, stone structure terrace fill
63 Flattened, externally expanded rim with a row of finger-nail impressions along the outer edge and a further row below. Fabric 363. Find 4904, Context 79, blown sand overlying Structure 95
64 Wall sherd with a raised square-sectioned cordon decorated with a row of finger-tip impressions. Fabric 364. Find 211 (1983–4). Probably from Context 131
65 Flattened rim and straight wall sherd. An incised horizontal line below the rim and a raised square-sectioned cordon decorated with finger-nail impressions. Fabric 364. Find 149 (1983–4). Probably from Context 112

Note: Nos 56, 57, 59, and 60 may be residual fragments from biconical urns.

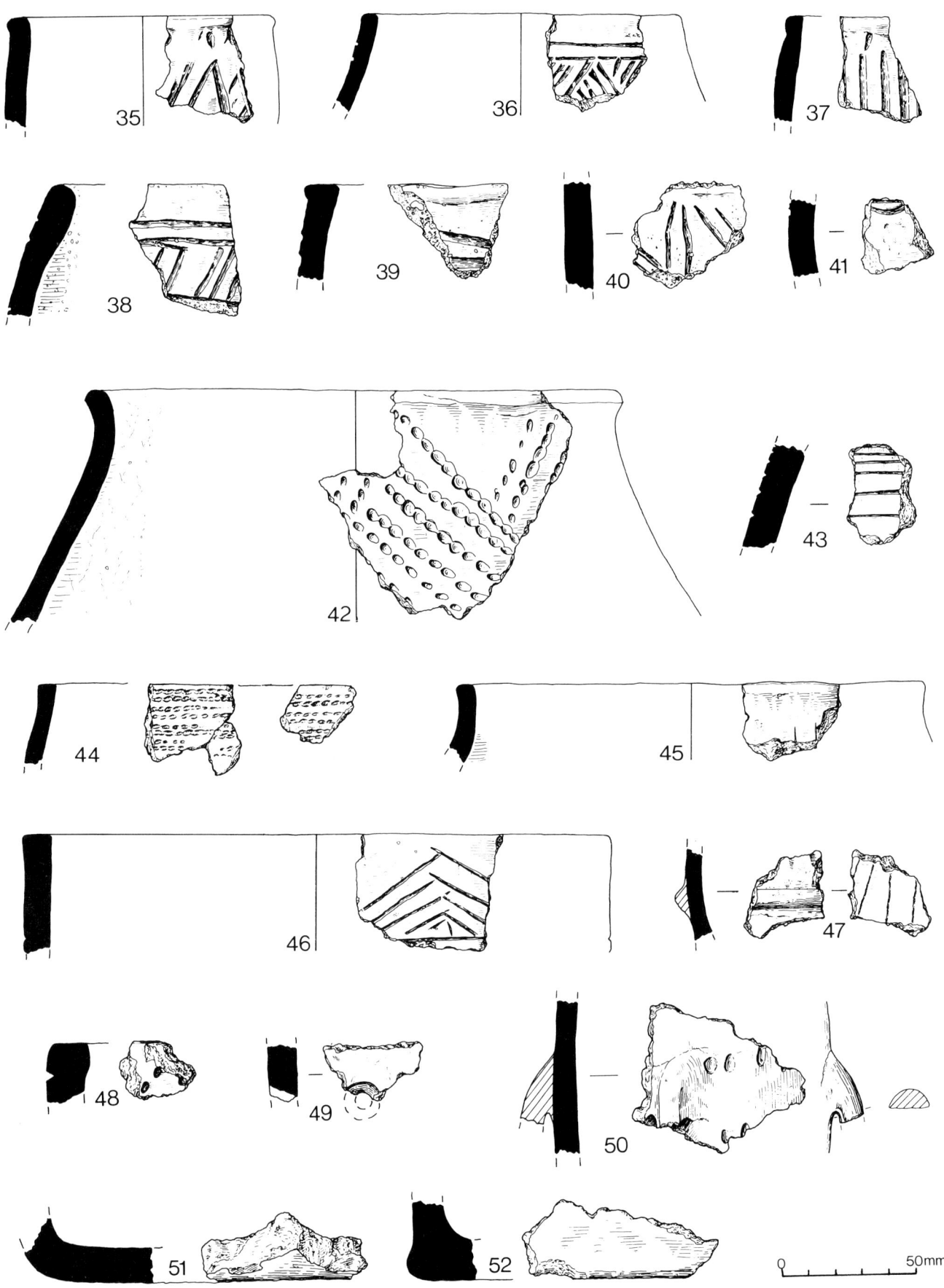

Fig 91   Trevisker-related vessels from Unit 5b, Context 53; scale 1:2

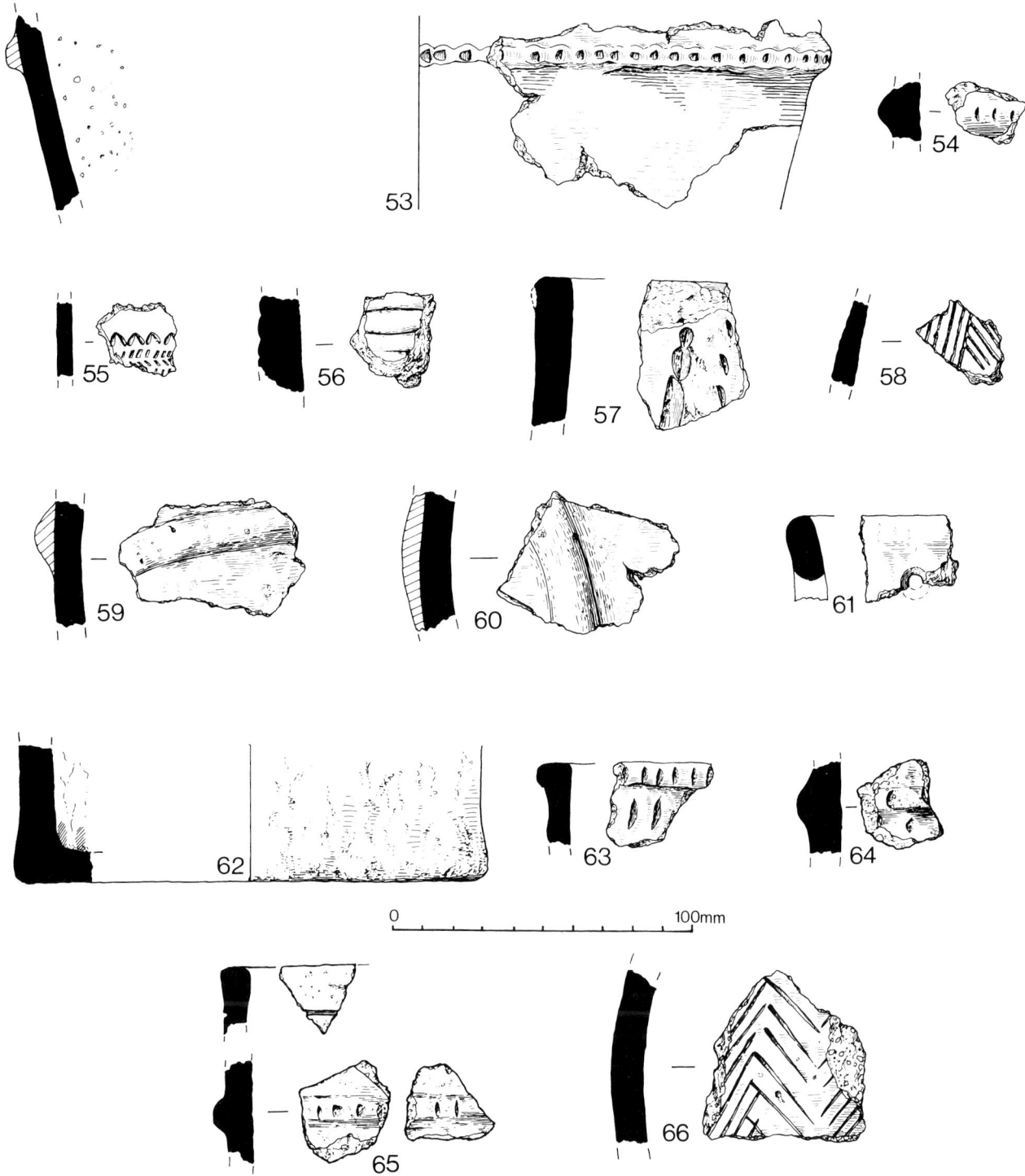

Fig 92 *Trevisker-related vessels from Unit 5b: nos 53–54, Context 112 (residual); nos 55–56 other contexts; no 66 from Unit 5a; scale 1:2*

Unit 5a (Fig 92)

66 Wall sherd from globular jar decorated with sharply-incised multiple horizontal chevrons. Fabric 481. Find 4491, Context 19, sterile sand

Assemblage characteristics

The main formal and decorative characteristics of the middle Bronze Age assemblage may be summarised as follows:

Rim forms: flattened – 30 instances, including nos 36, 37, 44, 46, 48, 57, 65; flattened and expanded – 9 instances, including nos 22, 23, 24, 25, 39, 63; out-turned – 5 instances, including nos 35, 42, 45, 61; slight internal bevel – 5 instances, including nos 27, 28, 38

Shoulders: plain cordon – 4 instances, including no 47; finger-tip decorated cordon – 5 instances, including nos 53, 54, 64, 65; slashed cordon – 1 instance (not illustrated)

Base angles: simple – 14 instances, including nos 51, 62; externally expanded – 1 instance, no 52

Decoration: finger-groove – 13 instances, including nos 22, 23, 24, 26; finger-tip or nail impressions – 9 instances, including nos 31, 50, 63; finger-tip impressions on top of rim – 1 instance (and note no 63); row of perforations – 3 instances, nos 49, 61;

circular impressions – 3 instances, including nos 33, 48; incised diagonal lines – 6 instances, nos 26, 28, 29, 30, 38, 39; incised horizontal lines – 29 instances, including nos 27, 28, 32, 36, 38, 43, 65; incised horizontal chevron – 14 instances, including nos 25, 35, 40; incised opposed filled triangles – 5 instances, nos 22, 23, 24, 36, 38; incised vertical lines – 2 instances, nos 37, 45; incised vertical chevron – 1 instance, no 55; incised curved 'swag' motif – 2 instances, including no 41; incised cross-hatching – 2 instances, nos 22, 34; cord-impressed horizontal lines – 1 instance, no 44; cord-impressed opposed filled triangles – 1 instance, no 42; tooth-comb impressions – 1 instance (not illustrated)

Lugs/handles: vertical perforated lug – 4 instances, including no 31; vertical strap handle of semicircular section – 1 instance, no 50

It is immediately apparent that many characteristics of this middle Bronze Age assemblage can be matched on pottery belonging to the Trevisker Series of south-western Britain. Although the preliminary classification and chronological development proposed for the Trevisker Series by ApSimon (in ApSimon and Greenfield 1972) can be faulted in detail and would benefit from some updating in the light of some more recent discoveries it remains a penetrating and thorough analysis of the characteristics of this class of pottery. The traits recognised at Brean will be matched with those found in the Trevisker Series where possible and subsequently parallels for the remaining features and motifs will be sought elsewhere.

The Brean rim forms are all found in the Trevisker assemblage and especially in vessels belonging to ApSimon's Styles 3 and 4. However, while most of the Trevisker rims exhibit an internal bevel, the commonest form at Brean is the simple flattened rim. Amongst the decorative motifs, rows of finger-nail or tip impressions, often used for marginal definition, are also found at Trevisker (ApSimon and Greenfield 1972, fig 17, 40; fig 18, 49, and fig 19, 68; all Style 4), as are circular impressions (ibid, fig 19, 70; Style 3/4). Within the repertoire of incised motifs represented at Brean, the following were found also at Trevisker: horizontal lines, often used as borders to decorative zones, horizontal chevron (particularly common at Trevisker, eg ibid, fig 18, 48 and 50; fig 19, 56 and 63), vertical chevron (ibid, fig 17, 36 and 37), and cross-hatching (ibid, fig 17, 38). Cord-impressed decoration, more characteristic of the earlier styles at Trevisker, is rather rare at Brean; the bands of horizontal lines may be paralleled in ibid, fig 16, 31 and fig 19, 59, 69, and 71. The simple base angles also occur on Trevisker vessels. The flattened rim form and horizontal incised lines are found on Trevisker style sherds from Cannington (A ApSimon, pers comm), while the unusual globular form of vessel 42 can be compared to that of the urn from Gwallon Down, Cornwall (Patchett 1944, fig 12, G5). Shoulder cordons of any kind are rare on Trevisker vessels, although an unusual flat plain cordon was found on one of the vessels from Tredarvah, Cornwall (Pearce and Padley 1977, fig 13, 15–18). A group of unstratified sherds found by ApSimon (ApSimon et al 1961, fig 28:43–51) display many of the characteristics listed above, notably the flattened rim form, incised horizontal grooving, chevrons, and a finger-nail impressed border. They probably belong to the same assemblage, although no layers equivalent to Unit 5b were located in ApSimon's area of examination.

Trevisker traits not represented or occurring rarely at Brean include the very diagnostic plaited, double, and single cord-impressed geometric motifs characteristic of Trevisker Styles 1 and 2. This might suggest that the Brean assemblage lies late in the overall Trevisker spectrum. The other main trait not represented is the paired finger dimple form of lug. However, these do occur elsewhere in the county, for instance on the vessels from Elworthy (Abercromby 1912, pl 94.464) and Bridgwater (unpublished, Taunton Museum, but described by ApSimon in ApSimon and Greenfield 1972, 338). The other major group of Somerset Trevisker-related pottery, that from Norton Fitzwarren (Woodward forthcoming), displays a similar range of traits to the Brean assemblage, although it is a rather smaller collection and the variety of motifs is not as great. In particular, plain cordons, finger-grooves, rows of perforations, strap handles, and incised swag and opposed filled triangle motifs are not represented at Norton Fitzwarren. As in the case of the biconical assemblage described above, glimpses of connections across the Severn to south Wales are afforded by some recent finds: a collection of pottery and flints from Chapel Tump Farm, near Newport, includes sherds displaying simple and flattened rims and rough incised chevron decoration very similar to that found at Brean (S Green, pers comm).

The main traits found amongst the Brean middle Bronze Age assemblage that cannot be related to the Trevisker Series are finger-impressed decoration on top of the rim, shoulder cordons, finger-grooves, rows of perforations, and the cord-impressed or incised motifs involving groups of vertical lines, swags, or opposed filled triangles. As we have seen, several of these are represented at Norton Fitzwarren and indeed rough cordons and grooving do occur occasionally on Trevisker-related vessels from Dartmoor (eg Dewerstone and Raddick Hill, Meavy: Fox 1964, pls 38 and 41). However, the major occurrences of this group of traits lie with the Deverel-Rimbury regional groups to the east and south-east. Thus, the finger-grooving is a particular characteristic of the Dorset Downs group where it occurs on Type IIb globular urns and on a specialised class of bucket urn. The incised swag and opposed filled triangle motifs, on the other hand, are strong members of the motif repertoire relating to the Type IA globular urns of Central Wessex (see Ellison 1975 for discussion and definition of these groups). Finally, the rows of perforations and impressed rim tops are traits more commonly found in East Anglia and the south-east, though they do occur sporadically but significantly across southern England. These distributions have recently been discussed in relation to the assemblages of middle Bronze Age pottery from Grimes Graves, Norfolk (Longworth and Ellison 1988).

The potters at Brean Down, therefore, seem to have been in contact with a wide range of other groups, although the mechanics of these contacts cannot be detailed. The fabric analysis indicates that all the vessels were locally manufactured and there is no doubt that, however diverse the sources of inspiration, the resulting style was both internally consistent and startlingly innovative (see especially the vessels depicted in Fig 89), even though the technique was rather crude in comparison with the globular urns being produced further to the east.

The fabrics of the middle Bronze Age assemblage, as David Williams has argued, indicate nothing more than local manufacture apart from the sherds tempered with felspathic tuff from the ApSimon collection. At Norton Fitzwarren most of the Trevisker-related pottery was again tempered with grog, although significant quantities contained inclusions of quartzite or felspathic tuff (Williams and Woodward forthcoming). The sherds with volcanic inclusions were similar to those from Brean and, in both cases, the inclusions probably derive from Beacon Hill, Shepton Mallet. At Norton Fitzwarren, the volcanic-tempered sherds include jars with incised chevron decoration and it may be that certain classes of ware were imported to the site. However, no pottery of this group was recognised amongst the recent assemblage from Brean. The domestic Trevisker pottery from the type site in Cornwall was characterised by very diagnostic fabrics incorporating gabbroic inclusions derived from weathering clays in the Lizard peninsula (ApSimon and Greenfield 1972, 333). Although these clays were exploited for pottery which reached Somerset in the Neolithic and Iron Age periods (Peacock 1969a; 1969b), gabbroic pottery does not appear to have been used in the county during the Bronze Age, although specific funerary 'imports' have been identified further south.

The three radiocarbon dates from Structures 59 and 95, 2940±100 BP (HAR-7019), 2870±80 BP (HAR-7018), and 2730±100 BP (HAR-7017), belong quite fittingly to a late stage of the middle Bronze Age. Dates from classic Trevisker domestic sites in Cornwall such as those of 3070±103 BP (NPL-21) from Gwithian, layer 5, and 3060±95 BP (NPL-134) from Trevisker, hut A, are rather earlier, but, as argued above, the Brean assemblage on typological grounds would lie relatively late in the series. The earlier date of 3420±100 BP (HAR-7016), obtained from a sample of the pit fill below the floor of Structure 59, would predate the series quite considerably.

The plain ware assemblage from Unit 4

Vessels in Fabric 481 from Context 16 (Figs 93–95)

67 Restored plain jar with high rounded shoulder and inturned rim which is flattened and externally expanded to provide a beaded effect; slightly expanded base angle. Rim type 2. Find 1700
68 Plain inwardly hooked rim. Rim type 1. Find 1071
69 Plain inwardly turned rim with flattened top. Rim type 2. Find 4890
70 Plain inwardly hooked rim and upper wall of straight-sided jar. Rim type 1. Find 3337
71 Rim and upper body of straight-walled jar with internal rim bevel. Finger-smoothed surface. Rim type 3. Find 350a
72 Rim with internal bevel from round-shouldered jar. Rim type 3. Find 350b
73 Rim with internal bevel from a round-shouldered vessel. Finger-smoothed surface. Rim type 3. Find 4704
74 Rim with internal bevel from straight-sided vessel. Rim type 3. Find 3156
75 Rim with internal bevel from globular or shouldered vessel. Rim type 3. Find 4701
76 Slightly out-turned rim with internal bevel and straight upper wall. Rim type 3. Find 2521
77 Rim with deep curved internal bevel from a round-bodied jar with a row of incompletely perforated circular holes below the rim. Rim type 3. 1984: unstratified, probably from Context 16
78 Flared rim and shoulder of sharply-carinated plain bowl. Rim type 4. Find 4173
79 Flared rim of plain jar or bowl. Rim type 4. Find 3360
80 Flared rim of plain jar or bowl. Rim type 4. Find 2909
81 Expanded rim of necked and sharp-shouldered jar. Rim type 5. Finds 3442 and 3433
82 Flattened rim of slightly-necked shouldered jar or bowl. Rim type 5. Find 4812
83 Sharp shoulder from a jar, decorated with a row of finger-tip impressions. Find 4216
84 Everted, deeply bevelled rim from shouldered, straight-sided jar. A row of circular impressions (not finger-tip) below rim. Rim type 5. Find 2092
85 Short flared rim with external expansion from a round-shouldered jar. Rim type 4. Find 3722
86 Flared base angle, externally expanded. Find 2358
87 Base angle with very marked external protrusion. Find 2923
88 Unusual flat sherd with edge-groove, possibly a lid. Find 60136
89 Body sherd with an applied strip smoothed on to form a grooved decorative effect. Find 60027
90 Base angle with smoothly expanded exterior. Find 2790
91 Flared, thin-walled base angle with marked external protrusion. Find 4768
92 Simple rim from plain cup. Rim type 6. Find 4575
93 Simple plain rim. Rim type 6. Find 2565
94 Simple plain rim. Rim type 6. Find 4058
95 Simple plain rim with very slight internal bevel. Rim type 6. Find 4882
96 Flattened rim from jar, decorated on the top with inclined finger-nail impressions. Rim type 7. Find 4671
97 Flattened, slightly expanded rim, decorated on the top with inclined diagonal incised lines. Rim type 7. Find 4584
98 Flat rim with incised diagonal lines on body below. Rim type 7. Find 2627
99 Flattened, slightly incurved plain rim. Rim type 1. Find 3656
100 Flat, slightly expanded plain rim. Rim type 7. Find 2309

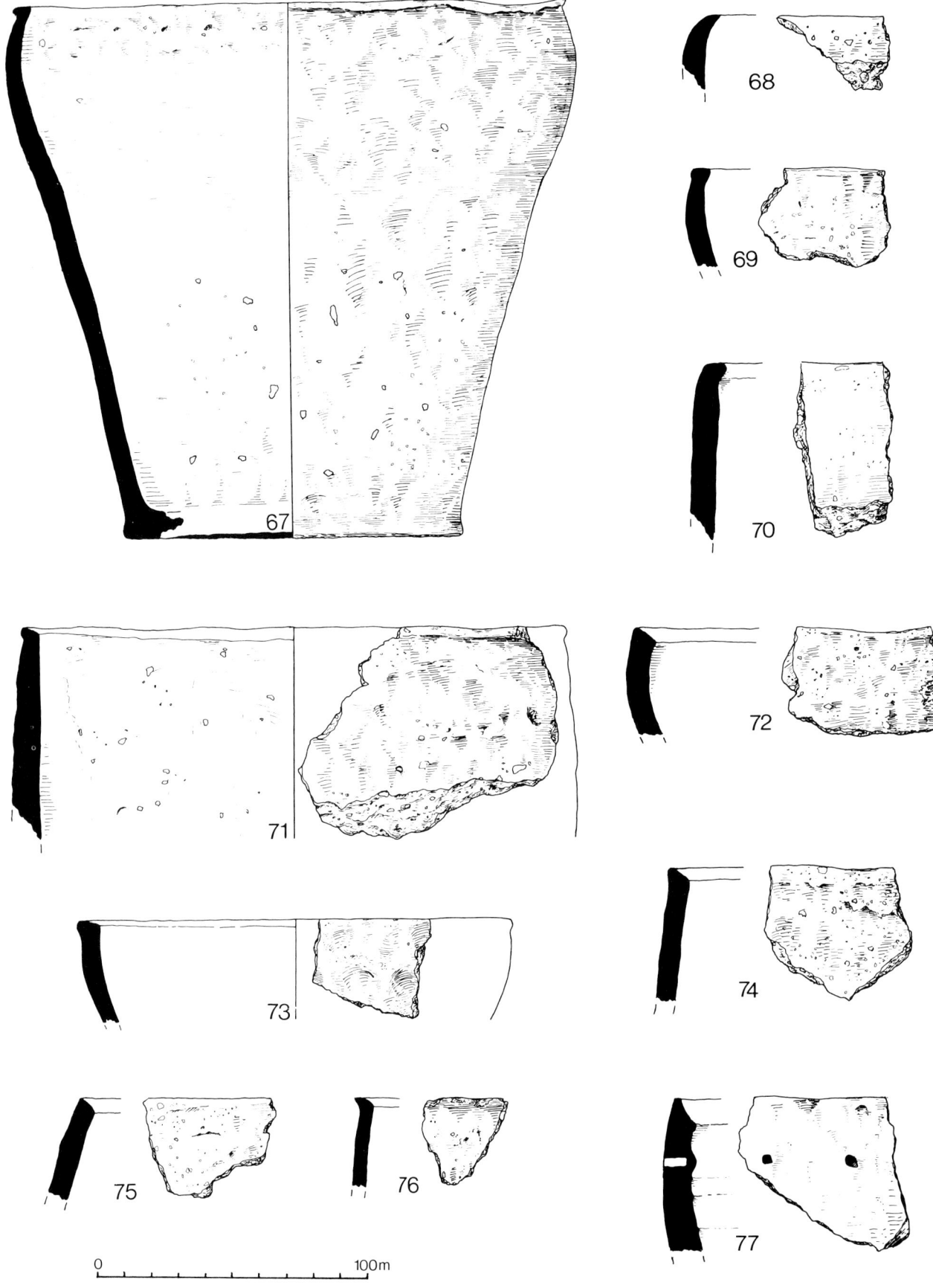

Fig 93 Vessels in Fabric 481 from Context 16; scale 1:2

THE BRONZE AGE POTTERY

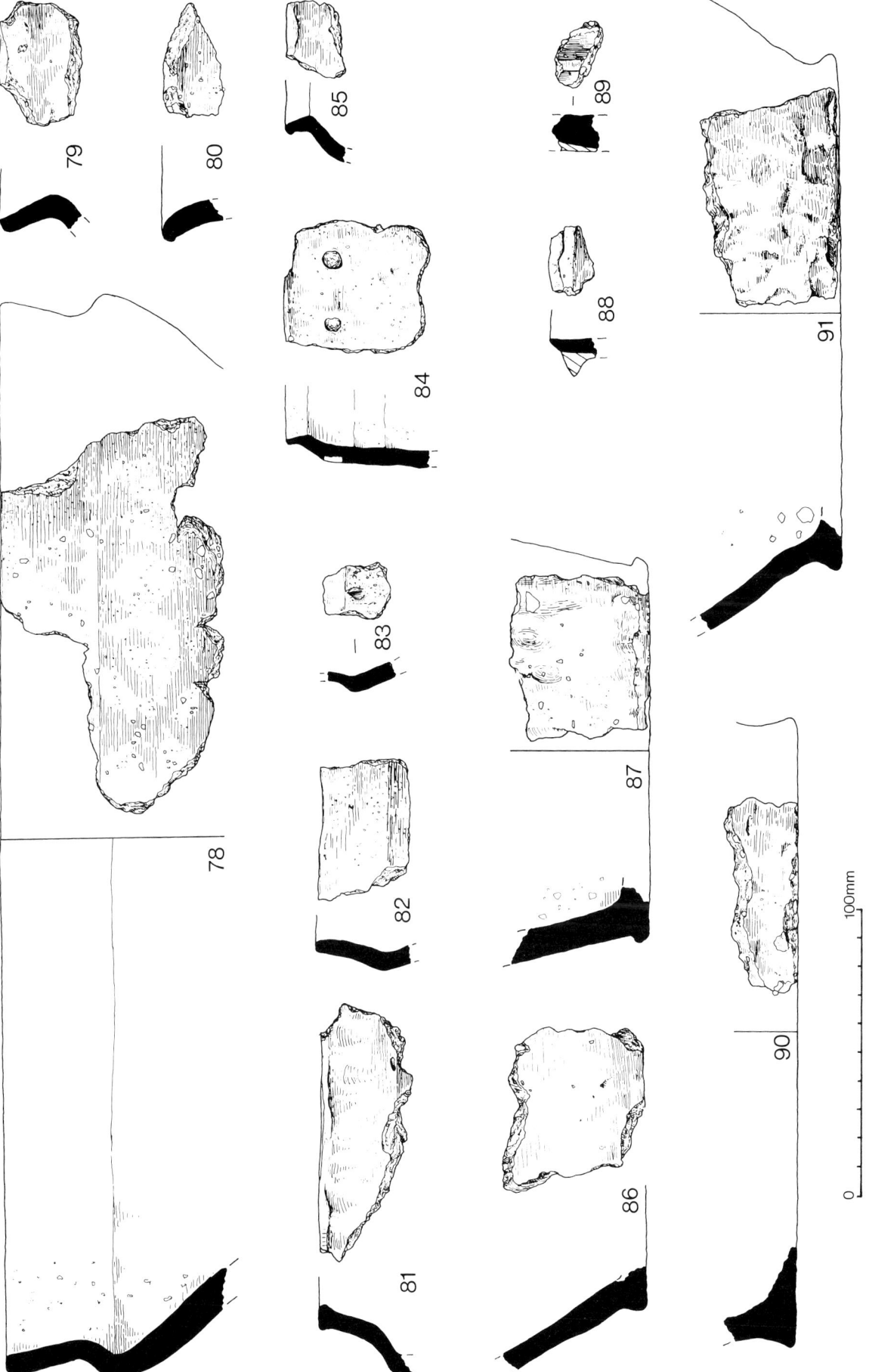

Fig 94 Vessels in Fabric 481 from Context 16; scale 1:2

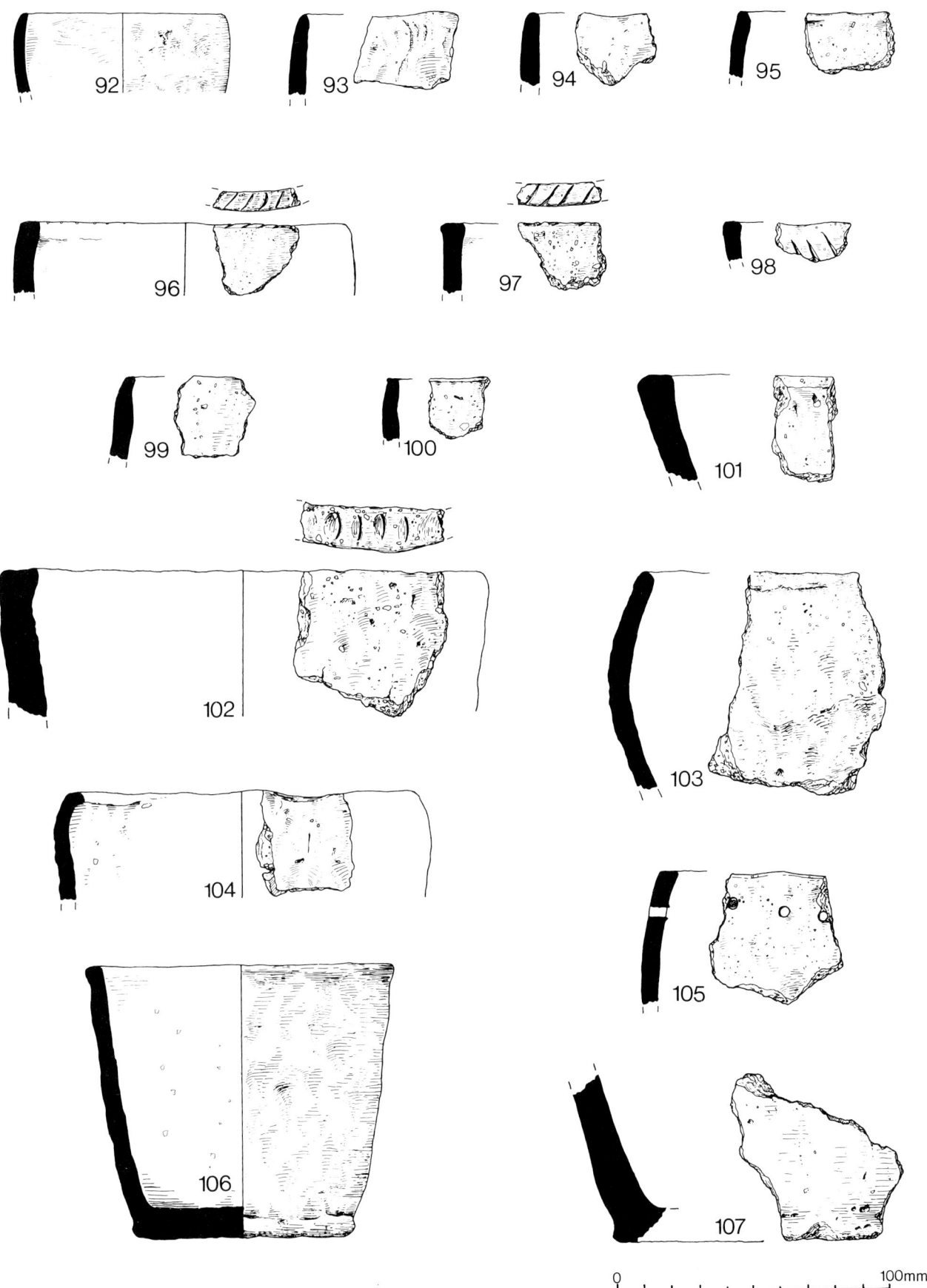

Fig 95 Vessels in Fabric 481 from Context 16 (nos 92–103) and from features within Context 16 (nos 104–7); scale 1:2

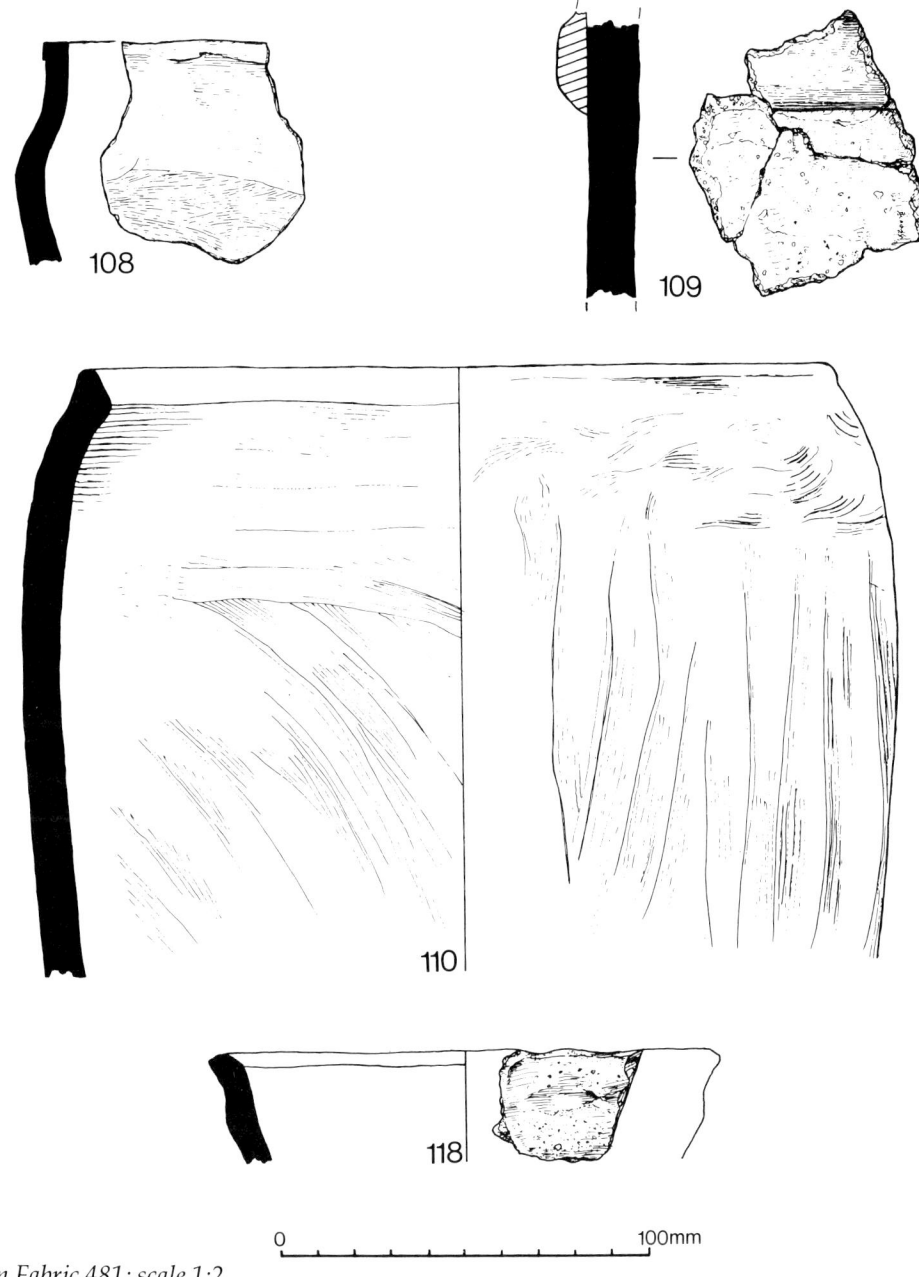

Fig 96   1983 finds in Fabric 481; scale 1:2

101 Flat rim from plain bowl. Rim type 8. Find 4771

Vessels in Fabric 481 from features at the base of Context 16 (Fig 95)

102 Flat, slightly expanded rim, decorated on the top with a row of finger-nail impressions. Rim type 7. Find 4715. Context 72
103 Round-bodied plain jar with simple rim. Rim type 6. Find 4209. Context 70

Vessels in Fabric 481 from features within Context 16 (Fig 95)

104 Inturned rim from plain jar. Rim type 1. Find 3812. Gully 67

105 Flattened rim with a row of circular perforations below. Rim type 6. Find 5386. Ditch fill 89
106 Complete small plain jar with simple, slightly out-turned rim and slightly expanded base. Rim type 6. Find 5484. Ditch fill 89
107 Slightly expanded base angle. Find 5279. Fabric 524. Ditch fill 89

1983 finds of Fabric 481 (Fig 96)

108 Flat rim, slightly expanded, and shoulder from plain jar. Rim type 7. Find 11. Found 0.2m above top of ditch 88, probably within Context 16
109 Straight wall sherd with part of an applied flattened wide cordon. Find 1. Found on the base of Context 16
110 Plain shouldered jar with internal rim bevel and vertical finger-smearing on lower body. Rim type

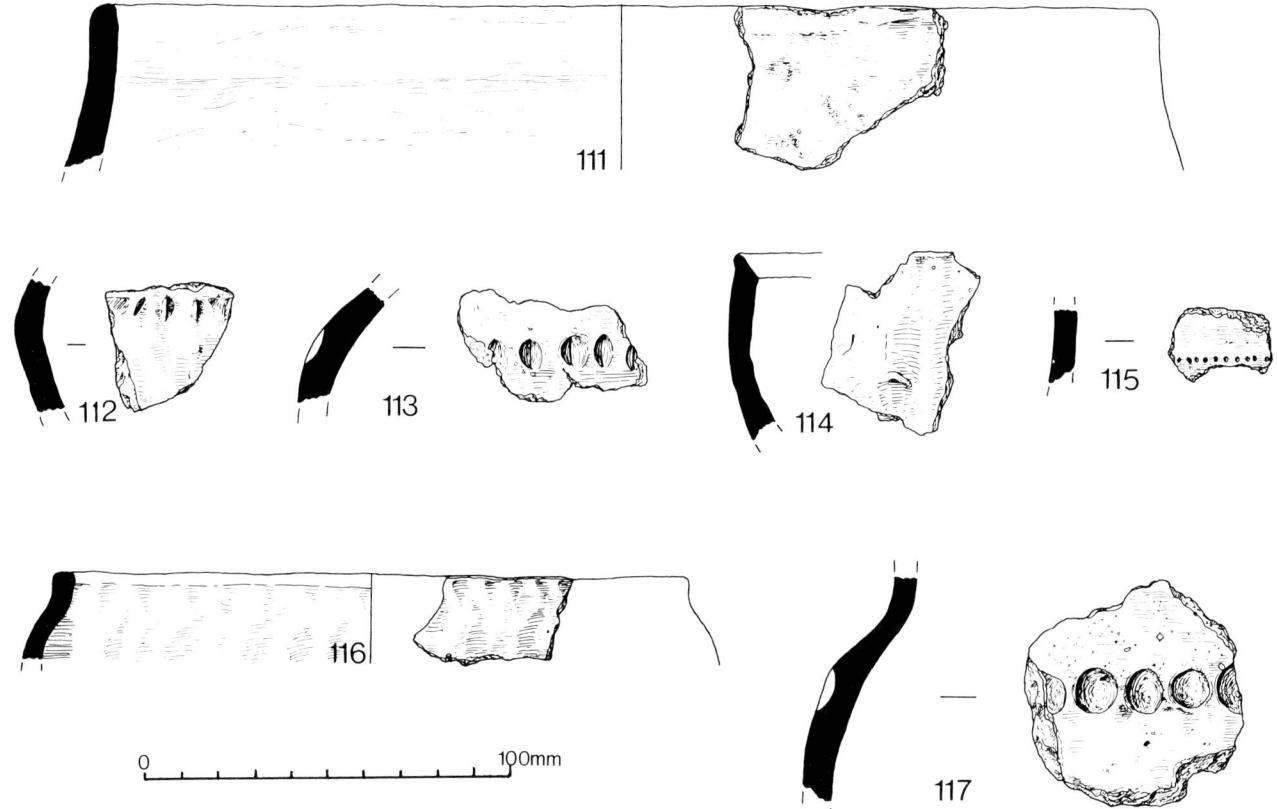

Fig 97 Vessels in fabrics other than 481 from Context 16; scale 1:2

3. Find 26. From feature D (Fig 6)
118 Rim with internal bevel and straight neck. Finger-smeared exterior surface. Rim type 3. Find 349. From vicinity of gold bracelets, 1983

Vessels in fabrics other than 481 from Context 16 (Fig 97)

111 Simple flattened rim from plain shouldered jar. Fabric 441. Rim type 6. Find 4778
112 Shoulder fragment decorated with a row of irregular finger-tip impressions. Fabric 361. Find 3544
113 Shoulder sherd decorated with a row of closely-spaced finger-tip impressions. Fabric 361. Find 3640
114 Plain rim with internal bevel. Rim type 3. Fabric 521. Find 3210
115 Wall sherd, probably from neck, decorated with a row of tooth-comb point impressions. Fabric 521. Find 4061
116 Flat rim from plain shouldered jar. Rim type 6. Fabric 521. Find 3995
117 Sharp shoulder fragment, probably Iron Age with a row of large closely-spaced finger-tip impressions. Fabric 461. Find 4091

Assemblage characteristics

The main formal and decorative characteristics of the late Bronze Age assemblage may be summarised as follows:

Rim forms: (1) simple incurved hook-rim – 8 instances, including nos 68, 70, 99, 104; (2) flat expanded – 2 instances, nos 67, 69; (3) internal rim bevel – 28 instances, including 71–77, 110, 114; (4) out-flaring – 11 instances, including 78–80, 85; (5) straight or everted – 7 instances, including 81, 82, 84; (6) simple – 34 instances, including 92–95, 103, 105, 106, 111, 116; (7) flattened – 35 instances, including 96–98, 100, 102, 108; (8) flat (bowl) – 2 instances, including 101

Shoulders: weak – 3 instances, nos 67, 84, 110; sharp – 8 instances, including nos 78, 81–83, 108; flat cordon – 2 instances, including no 109; plain rounded cordon – 1 instance (not illustrated)

Base angles: simple – 10 instances, including no 106; externally expanded – 20 instances, including nos 86, 87, 90, 91, 107

Decoration: row of perforations – 2 instances, nos 77, 105; row of finger-tip impressions – 2 instances, including no 83; row of circular impressions – 1 instance, no 84; point-tooth comb – 1 instance, no 115; diagonal slashes – 3 instances, including no 98; diagonal incised lines on top of rim – 1 instance, no 97; finger-nail impressions on top of rim – 2 instances, nos 96, 102

Surface treatment: finger-smearing – very common, including nos 71, 73, 110

The first observation to be made concerning the Unit 4 assemblage is that decoration of any kind is extremely rare. Indeed, it forms a group of plain wares similar to those recently defined by Barrett for an early stage of the late Bronze Age (Barrett 1980) and termed by him 'post Deverel-Rimbury'. The closest

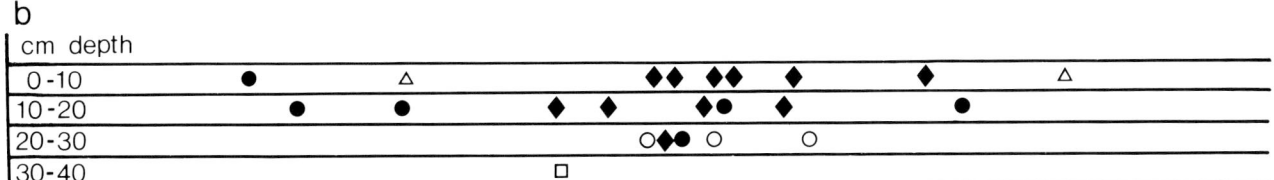
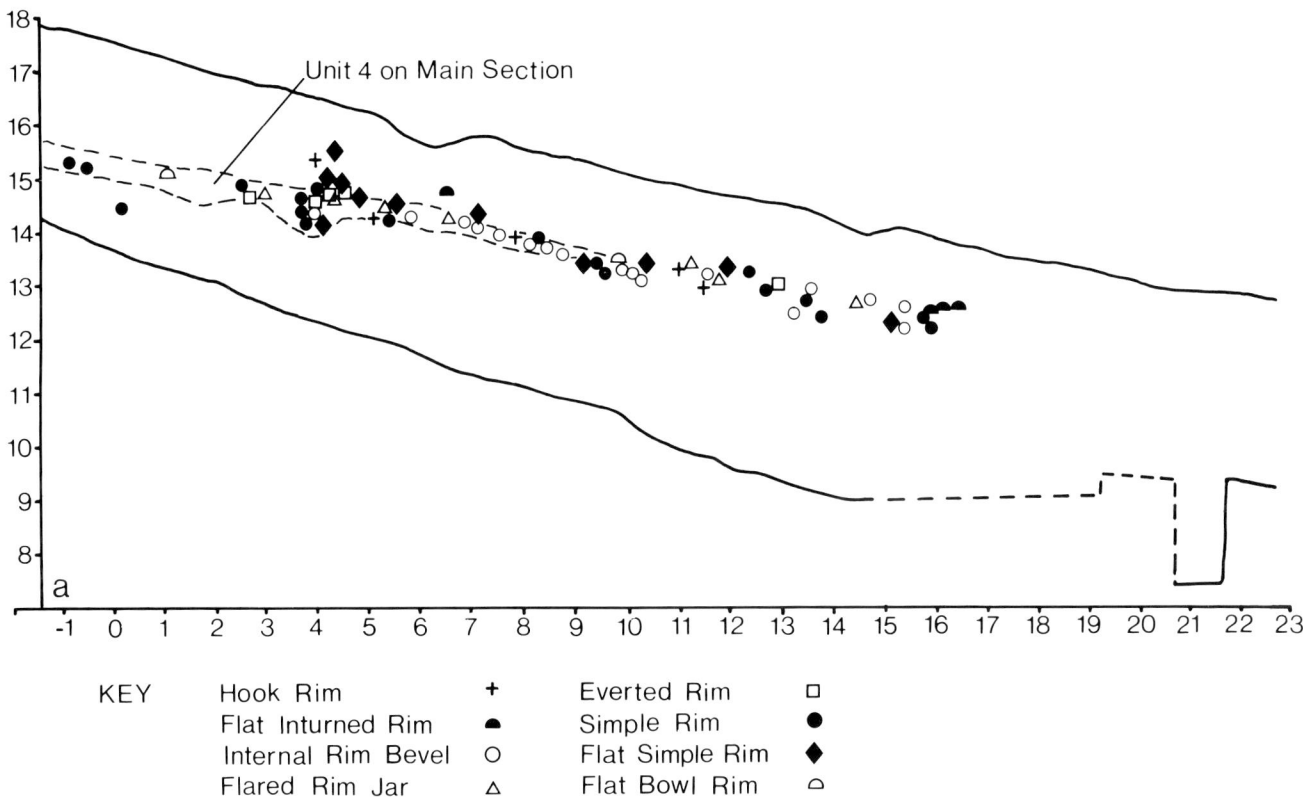

Fig 98 Distribution of rim types in Unit 4: (a) shows the three-dimensionally recorded rims and (b) shows the depth at which rims recorded by grid square were found

sites which have produced such assemblages in Somerset/Avon are Combe Hay, Bath (Price and Watts 1980) and South Cadbury (Alcock 1980: the 'South Cadbury 4' assemblage). An important but small group has also been identified in the excavated pottery sequence from Norton Fitzwarren (Woodward forthcoming) and reference will also be made to some Thames Valley groups. The simple hook-rim jars (rim type 1) equate to Form II defined by Barrett at Rams Hill (in Bradley and Ellison 1975, fig 3:5, 9) and are found at South Cadbury (Alcock 1980, fig 12.5), Combe Hay (Price and Watts 1980, fig 24, 6, 7, and 17), Norton Fitzwarren, and Cannington (A ApSimon, pers comm). The type with internal rim bevel (rim type 3) occurs at South Cadbury (Alcock 1980, fig 12.1) and Combe Hay (Price and Watts 1980, fig 24, 20); the flattened types (7 and 8) also occur at Combe Hay (Price and Watts 1980, fig 12, 2) and South Cadbury (Alcock 1980, fig 12.2 and, for a bowl, fig 12.4). The common simple rim, type 6, equates with Barrett's Form I at Rams Hill and there are many examples at Combe Hay. Amongst the assemblage originally regarded as Iron Age recovered from Brean by ApSimon, examples of rims with internal bevel are notable (ApSimon et al 1961, fig 28:1 and 6). Of the shoulder types, the weak variety conform to Form III at Rams Hill (Barrett in Bradley and Ellison 1975, fig 3:5, 14), weak shoulder and plain cordon occur at Combe Hay (Price and Watts 1980, fig 24, 20 and 16), and a sharp shoulder comes from South Cadbury (Alcock 1980, fig 12.1). The externally expanded base angles are a type trait for the 'post Deverel-Rimbury' group and occur at South Cadbury and Rams Hill. The finger-smeared or fluted surface treatment is also a very common characteristic of all these assemblages.

Of the rare decorative techniques and motifs listed for the Brean assemblage, three of them – rows of perforations, rows of finger-tip impressions, and diagonal incised lines on top of the rim – can be paralleled at South Cadbury (Alcock 1980, fig 12.5 and 1; fig 14.5 and 6 respectively), while the diagonal slashes and finger-nail impressions on top of the rim are evidenced on sherds of probable late Bronze Age date from Cannington (A ApSimon, pers comm).

The two vessel forms that are not found in the other known Somerset assemblages of late Bronze Age date are the angular or rounded bowls with

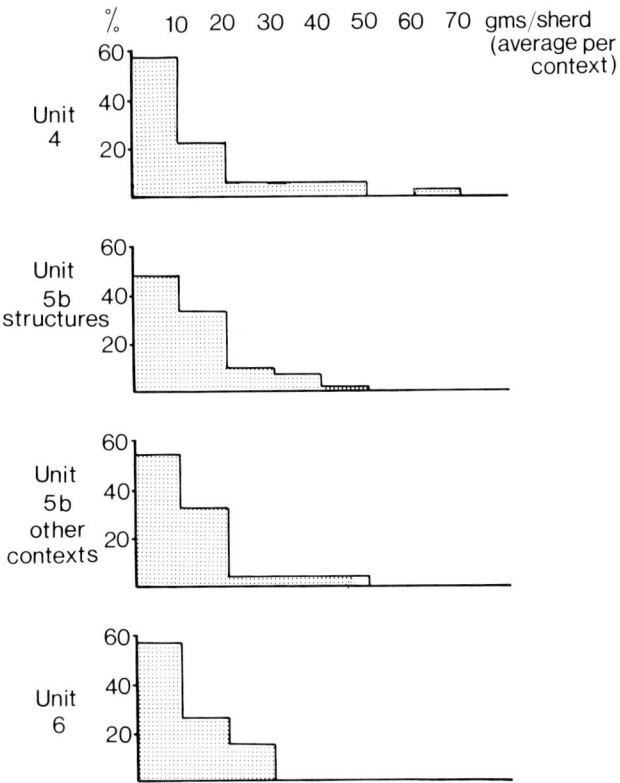

Fig 99 Sherd weight categories showing distribution of sherd weight

straight inclined or out-flaring rims (nos 78–80 and 81–83 respectively). However, these types form a significant component of the contemporary plainware assemblages of the middle Thames Valley, as exemplified by Forms 2 and 3 at Aldermaston, Berkshire (Bradley et al 1980, 233, fig 11), where they date probably from c 2750–2950 BP (the tenth or ninth century BC) (ibid, 235 and 248). The sharp shoulder of our no 78 is also matched at the same site (ibid, fig 13, 33F). These vessels are tempered with dense but small inclusions of crushed flint – Aldermaston fabric F. A fine series of such small angular or rounded bowls has also been defined at Wallingford, Berkshire, again within a predominantly plain-ware assemblage (Thomas et al 1986). Here the angular to rounded bowls were characterised by small flint inclusions (ibid, 186, fig 4, 28–31, site fabric 4), while an example of a bowl with wide flaring rim (ibid, fig 4, 32) was in a fine sandy fabric with only a few flint grits.

In order to investigate the possibility that the wide range of formal traits might represent a long sequence of cultural change, it was decided to plot vertically the positions of sherds possessing the eight distinct rim types defined above. In particular, it was hoped to define any temporal separation between potentially earlier types, eg the internal rim bevel, which might relate to the preceding earlier Bronze Age assemblages, and possible later developments such as the inception of the flared-rim bowls and jars. However, the resulting distribution, shown in Figure 98, displays no clear typological separations and it appears therefore that the assemblage may be regarded as a uniform one. This accords with micromorphological evidence (Chapter 16) for the homogeneous nature of Unit 4.

The predominance of calcite-gritted fabrics at Brean, mixed with some vessels displaying grogged or sand-tempered composition, may be compared with the distinctive calcite-dominated fabrics of the South Cadbury 4 assemblage. However, there the calcite was often combined with large plate-like fragments of fossil shell. The Combe Hay late Bronze Age sherds were tempered with shelly and oolitic limestone, whilst the Thames Valley assemblages have fabrics containing varying amounts of flint. Yet again, local manufacture is indicated although the ubiquity of heavy stone tempering may be a general characteristic of the plain ware traditions.

Two of the radiocarbon determinations from Unit 4, 3400±90 BP (HAR-9155) and 3100±100 BP (HAR-9153), appear to be rather early, although the date of 2730±70 BP (HAR-9151) compares well with the sequences of dates between c 3050 and 2750 BP (the eleventh to ninth centuries BC) from Rams Hill (Bradley and Ellison 1975, 35–8), South Cadbury 4 (Alcock 1980), and Aldermaston Wharf, Berkshire (Bradley et al 1980, 248), and with the date of 2650±120 BP (Birm-445) obtained from Combe Hay (Price and Watts 1980, 25 and 32).

Fragmentation

As the site provided data from a dramatic sequence of Bronze Age domestic deposits, and the potential locations of primary and secondary refuse deposits of varying date and function were defined, it was decided to study any variability in vessel fragmentation by analysing the occurrence of the range of sherd weights amongst the different contexts. Thus the percentages of sherd weight categories from less than 10 to 70g per sherd were plotted for the Unit 6 structural deposits, the in situ domestic layers and the other deposits in Unit 5b, and the more generalised deposit of Unit 4 (Fig 99). The histograms show that the distribution of sherd sizes was fairly uniform throughout the site. It was suspected that the Unit 5b structures might have produced larger fragments of vessel as there is other evidence to suggest that a series of vessels had become smashed in situ. However, the very highest ratios were obtained in fact from Unit 4. This may indicate that the pottery in the Unit 4 deposits derived directly from domestic structures very close by. Alternatively, the high ratios may have been a reflection of the harder fabrics, and a related lower breakage rate, represented in Unit 4. However, an investigation of the sherd size range for a single hard fabric type (481) demonstrated that this was not the case.

Form and function

In recent years it has become customary to seek evidence for the varying functions of ceramic vessels by considerations of their forms and, in particular,

THE BRONZE AGE POTTERY

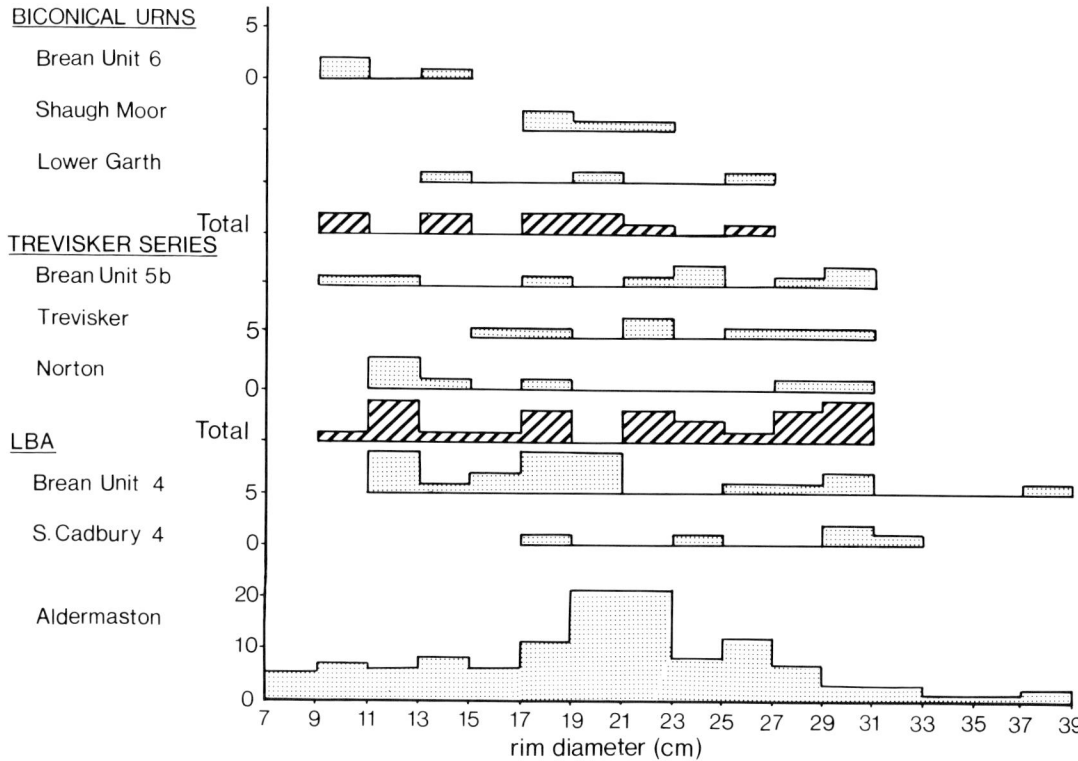

Fig 100   The occurrence of rim diameters in selected south-western Bronze Age pottery assemblages (sources of data as follows: Shaugh Moor – Wainwright and Smith 1980, fig 19; Lower Garth – Savory 1980, fig 72; Trevisker – ApSimon and Greenfield 1972; Norton Fitzwarren – Woodward forthcoming; South Cadbury – Alcock 1980; Aldermaston – Bradley et al 1980)

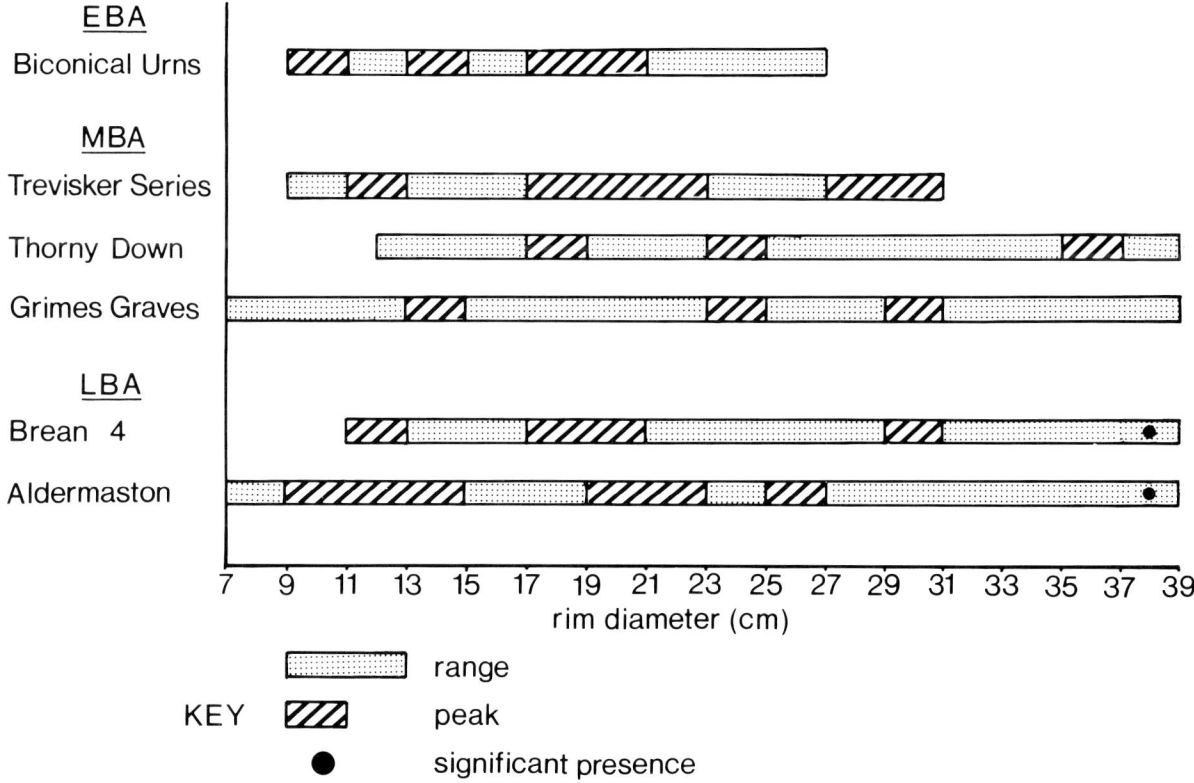

Fig 101   Rim size ranges for selected Bronze Age assemblages and assemblage groups (sources of data as follows: Trevisker – ApSimon and Greenfield 1972; Thorny Down – unpublished study by author (material in Salisbury Museum); Grimes Graves – Longworth and Ellison 1988; Aldermaston – Bradley et al 1980)

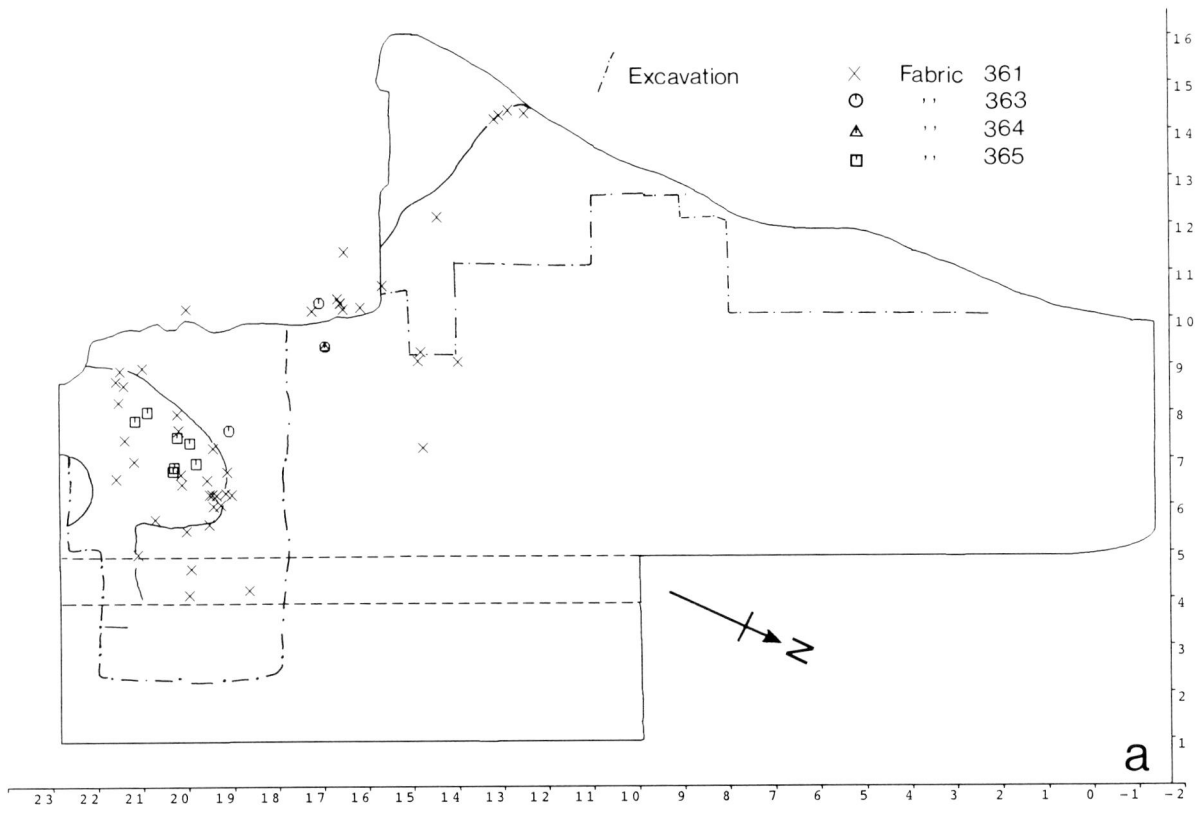

PREHISTORIC POTTERY IN UNIT 6

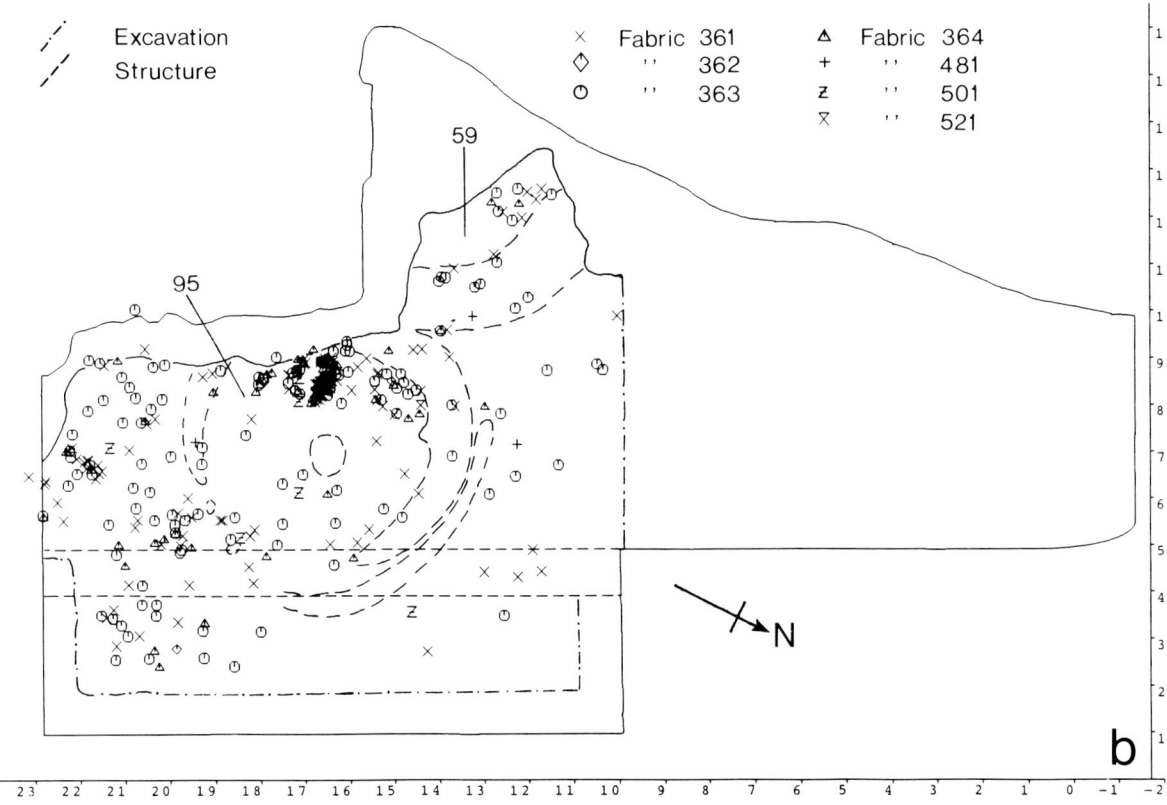

PREHISTORIC POTTERY IN UNIT 5b

Fig 102 Distribution of prehistoric pottery fabrics (a) in Unit 6 in relation to Structure 57 (for the find spots of illustrated sherds see Fig 31) and (b) in Unit 5b in relation to Structures 59 and 95 (for the find spots of illustrated sherds see Fig 46a)

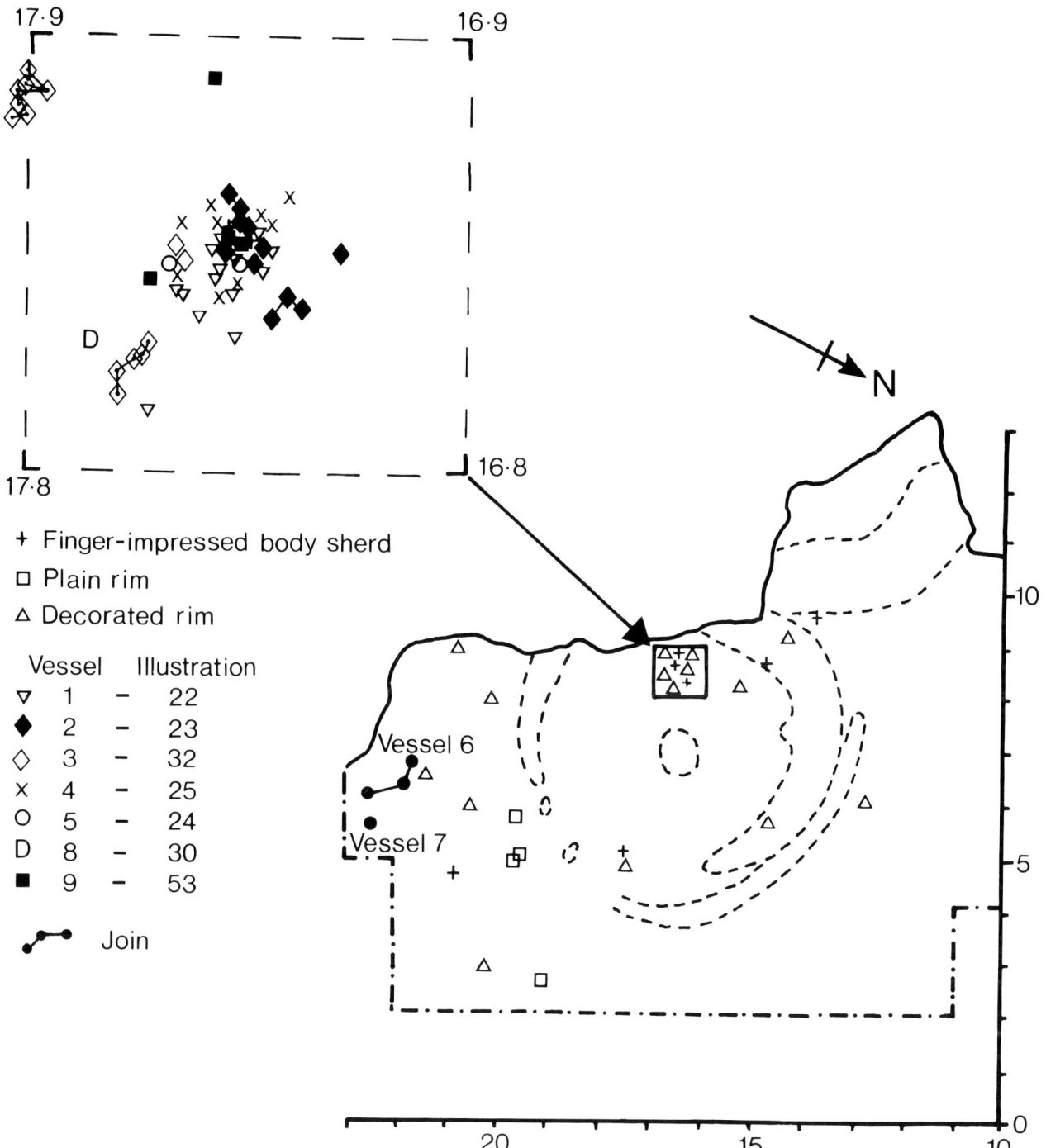

Fig 103 Distribution in Unit 5b: (a) of reconstructed vessels and selected ceramic traits; (b) detailed distribution of reconstructed vessels in grid square 16/8

their sizes (Barrett 1980; Ellison 1981). A recent analysis of early and middle Bronze Age pottery from East Anglia has attempted to extend these methods to domestic assemblages which consist largely of small sherds, by comparative measurements of rim diameters, varying sherd thickness, and base diameters (Longworth and Ellison 1988). The assemblage from Brean Down provides a unique opportunity to study the size ranges of vessels from three different periods of the Bronze Age. The data are given in Figure 100, alongside comparanda from other sites mainly located in the south-west. The histograms show various peaks which may be consolidated in diagrammatic form (Fig 101) and are compared with two further domestic middle Bronze Age assemblages from elsewhere in the country.

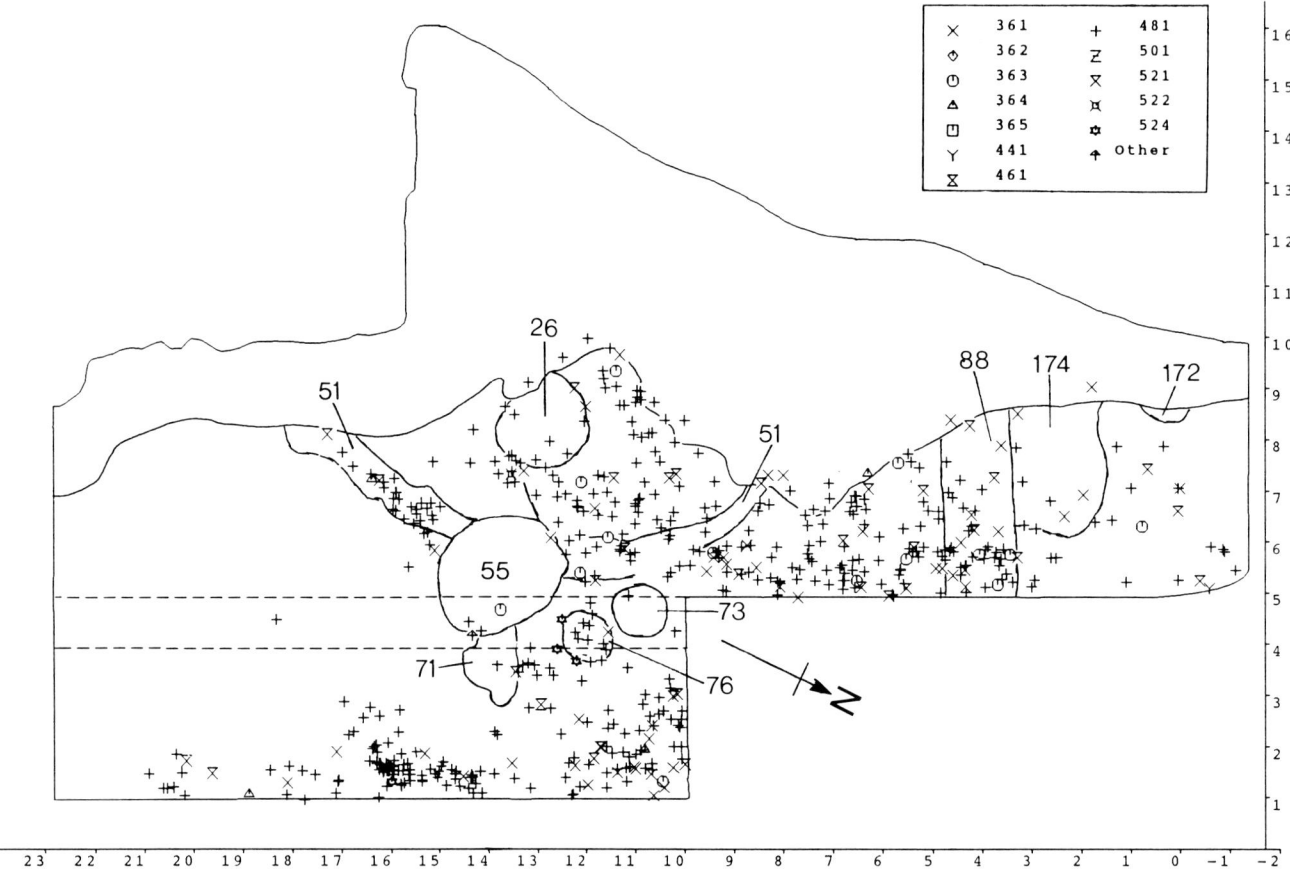

Fig 104 *Distribution of prehistoric pottery fabrics in Unit 4 in relation to features*

One of the more obvious conclusions that may be drawn from these figures is that there is a general increase in the overall range of vessel sizes through time from the early to the late Bronze Age. However, it should be noted that the very restricted size range plotted for the biconical urns applies to the domestic assemblages only. Larger vessels were being produced but they occur only in burial contexts. In Somerset the best-known examples of sepulchral biconical urns are those from Tynings Farm, referred to above. For the early and middle Bronze Age groups, the three main size peaks in each range represent the three functional groups defined for middle Bronze Age assemblages further east (Ellison 1981). The heavy duty storage jars and everyday cooking pots of medium size can readily be separated from the smaller, more carefully executed, and often decorated jars and cups which were probably employed at table. Within the Trevisker assemblages the same three categories may be proposed, but complex decoration is much more widespread, extending to the everyday and heavy duty wares which are more often plain in southern and eastern England. For the late Bronze Age assemblages the development of a wider form repertoire, as discussed by Barrett (1980), is evidenced by the emergence of four peaks per assemblage. In the case of the Brean assemblage this phenomenon is caused mainly by the introduction of very large thin-walled bowls.

Distribution in relation to structures and features

The recording of the coordinates for all stratified pottery finds by computer has allowed the plotting of various distributions in relation to their contemporary structures and associated features. In Unit 6 (Fig 102a), a plot of all fabric types shows that the ceramic finds were concentrated mainly within the confines of the tumbled spread walls of Structure 57, although a fairly substantial scatter of sherds was also located to the north-west of the hut. With most of the pottery belonging to a single fabric type (361), little patterning of types may be observed.

For Unit 5b the overall distribution of pottery fabrics is shown in Figure 102b, where the patterning of ceramic finds in relation to Structures 59 and 95 may be viewed. The patterning relative to 59 is difficult to deduce as such a small portion of the structure survived, but the patterns in and around Structure 95 are more informative. The concentrations within and in front of the house are roughly similar in degree, but that outside is more generalised than the interior distribution which is characterised by two distinct groupings towards the back of the floor area (located in Contexts 112 and 154 respectively). Outside the building, the uniform concentration of sherds around and on either side of the entrance contrasts significantly with the sparse scatter of sherds to the east and north of the house walls. Figures 103a and b show the distributions of selected decorative traits, the reconstructable decorated vessels, and of plain rim sherds. Most of the vessels occurred in a single grid square, within Context 112 (see Fig 103b), but further decorated vessels were represented by sherds scattered across the house floor and outside its entrance. It may prove significant that plain rims occurred only outside the building, but the sample numbers are very small. Further observations concerning these distributions are made in Chapter 4 where they are compared with other artefact types in Unit 5b.

The dense distribution of pot sherds in Unit 4 forms a fairly uniform spread (Fig 104). The only apparent patterning is a negative one in relation to many of the features. This is particularly noticeable in the case of Contexts 174, 51 (north segment), 73, 26, 55, and 71. These stand in marked contrast to the ditches/gullies 88 and 51 (south segment) and pit 76, which contained substantial quantities of pottery. The relevance of these observations in relation to the distributions of other artefact types is considered in Chapter 5.

12 Bronze Age metalwork

The gold bracelets and Class B1 bracelets in Britain

by Stuart Needham

The finding of the two gold bracelets, an associated gold fragment (Fig 105), and a rim sherd has been described in Chapter 1 (p 6). They derived from a slumped block of Unit 4, the origin of which is discussed in Chapter 5 (p 69).

The two bracelets are in a good state of preservation, though both show signs of minor crushing (Fig 106.1–2). They are very similar in overall weight (Table 8). The lengths, breadths, and widths as tabulated also indicate that the two have very similar forms and indeed in cross-section they are both essentially flat. The edges of Bracelet 2 are very slightly flanged, or lipped, on the outer face. This is probably due to forging as hammermarks are discernible on the narrow sides. Bracelet 1 has much smoother angles in section with a slightly dished outer face. This form can be explained as a polished up version of the more irregular Bracelet 2. Towards the terminals the flat band is forged into a circular section as it narrows to a constriction just before expanding to a 'buffer' end. The transition between flat and circular sections is effected by neat U-shaped facets which terminate the flat inner and outer faces of the band. The circular terminals bear numerous longitudinal facets which were presumably created in the forging. The traces of these facets are rather diffuse on Bracelet 1 when compared with Bracelet 2, where they remain crisp, and this again points to the former having received a higher degree of finish. This also shows itself in the shaping of the terminal 'buffers', which are fairly neat and oval on Bracelet 1 and rather more irregular on Bracelet 2. It is possible therefore that Bracelet 2 had yet to receive its final finishing at the time of deposition. It had clearly, however, been brought to its intended form and we should not exclude the possibility that it may have been used.

A small fragment of gold strip (2a) was found with the bracelets. It is 8.3mm long, 6.2mm wide, and 1.3mm thick and could therefore have belonged to a similar ribbon bracelet. It weighs 0.522g. Three edges are broken and contorted, while the fourth is intact and flattened.

Table 8 Dimensions and weight of the gold bracelets

	Bracelet 1	Bracelet 2
Maximum diameter (as found)	54mm	54.5mm
External length	170mm	180mm
Maximum width	8.2mm	9.2mm
Minimum width of terminals	3.5, 3.6mm	3.2, 3.6mm
Diameter of terminals	4.5–5.3mm	4.3–5.0mm
Length of terminals	4.5mm	6.5mm
Thickness at point of maximum width	1.6mm	1.5mm
Weight	25.461g	25.382g

Also found in association with the bracelets was a rim sherd (Fig 96.118).

Penannular gold bracelets are well known in the middle and late Bronze Ages of Britain and Ireland (Taylor 1980, 66–8). They show great diversity, however, making use of many different terminal and cross-sectional forms, which have yet to be fully elucidated. Flat 'ribbon' bands, as found at Brean Down, form a minor group amongst which certain terminal forms are recurrent, for example coil-ended (Hawkes and Clarke 1963, 231–3). The buffer terminals of Brean Down type are now known on several British ribbon bracelets (Hook and Needham forthcoming). The bands have neatly flattened sides, usually accompanied by vestigial flanging as seen at Brean Down. Such bracelets have recently been identified as a specific type, termed the Potterne type by Taylor (1984) or class B1 in the writer's scheme (Hook and Needham forthcoming). These would fall within Taylor's general 'expanded terminal' class (1980, 66–8). Some B1 bracelets are old finds: single finds from Lincolnshire Fens (British Museum WG 7) and Fore Abbey, Co Westmeath (Armstrong 1920, no 420), one in the Caister-on-Sea hoard, Norfolk (Hawkes and Clarke 1963, pl VII.2; Elvère 1988, 31, fig 5), and two in the Bexley Heath 2 hoard, Kent (Taylor 1980, 83 Kt 34 + 36). A comparable terminal fragment made of bronze, not gold, was associated with a hoard from Tŷ Mawr, Anglesey (Lynch 1970, 211, fig 69.7). One gold bracelet in the Tisbury hoard, Wiltshire (Hawkes and Clarke 1963, pl XI.6), is closely related, but is more lightweight and has thickened terminals of subrectangular section. Another, in the Morvah hoard, Cornwall, is similar but much heavier (Hawkes and Clarke 1963, 231, fig 53.1).

Five recent finds in addition to the Brean Down hoard, however, prove to include B1 type bracelets; some have important associations. At Craig-yr-Wolf, Clwyd, one of two gold bracelets is of the relevant type (Green 1983, fig 13, no 2). Both were found tightly coiled inside the socket of a bronze axe which is datable to the Ewart Park phase, c 900–700 BC. This date also applied to the above mentioned bronze hoard from Tŷ Mawr, Anglesey. Another B1 bracelet was turned up at Potterne in Wiltshire on a site now demonstrated to have been a rich settlement in late Bronze Age and early Iron Age times (Gingell and Lawson 1984; 1985; Taylor 1984). Most recent of all were the discoveries of a hoard of three gold bracelets at Rosemorran, Cornwall, one of which was of B1 type (unpublished), and a single B1 bracelet from St Martins, Isles of Scilly (unpublished). A range of loosely related penannular bracelets are associated in the Rosemorran, Tisbury, and Bexley Heath 2 hoards. The forms are generally ascribed to the late Bronze Age (c 1000–650 BC), but the general isolation of gold metalwork from other material goods has precluded any refinement in its chronology.

In total 17 B1 bracelets have been identified in Britain and Ireland, with four related pieces on the continent (Elvère 1988). Their distribution is shown in Figure 107 and they are listed fully in Hook and Needham forthcoming. Some interesting points may be made. The great majority, 15 examples, come from southern Britain and they therefore join the related

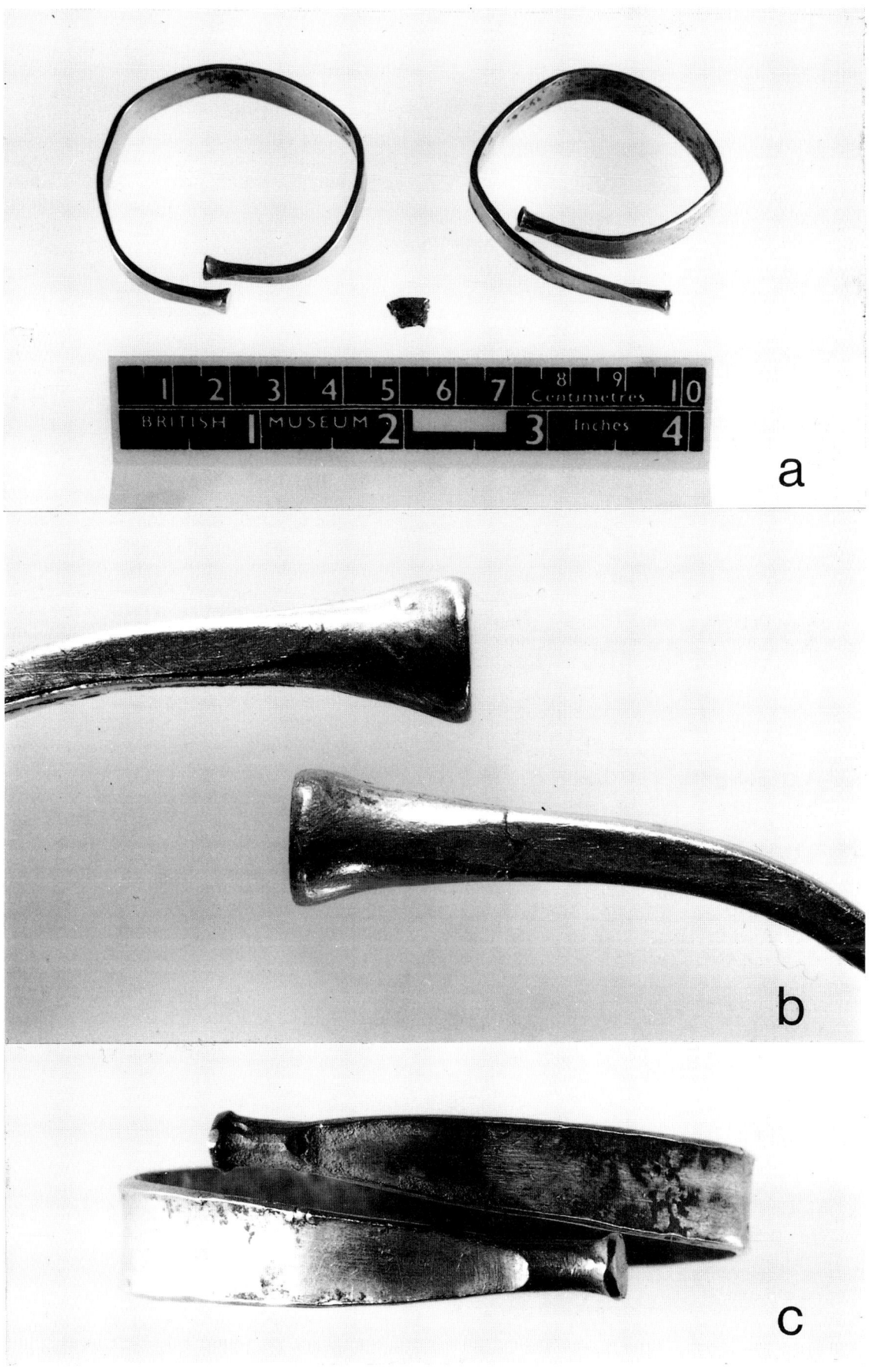

Fig 105   Gold bracelets from Unit 4: (a) bracelets 1 and 2 and gold scrap 2a; (b) bracelet 1 showing terminals; (c) bracelet 2 showing terminals (photos: British Museum)

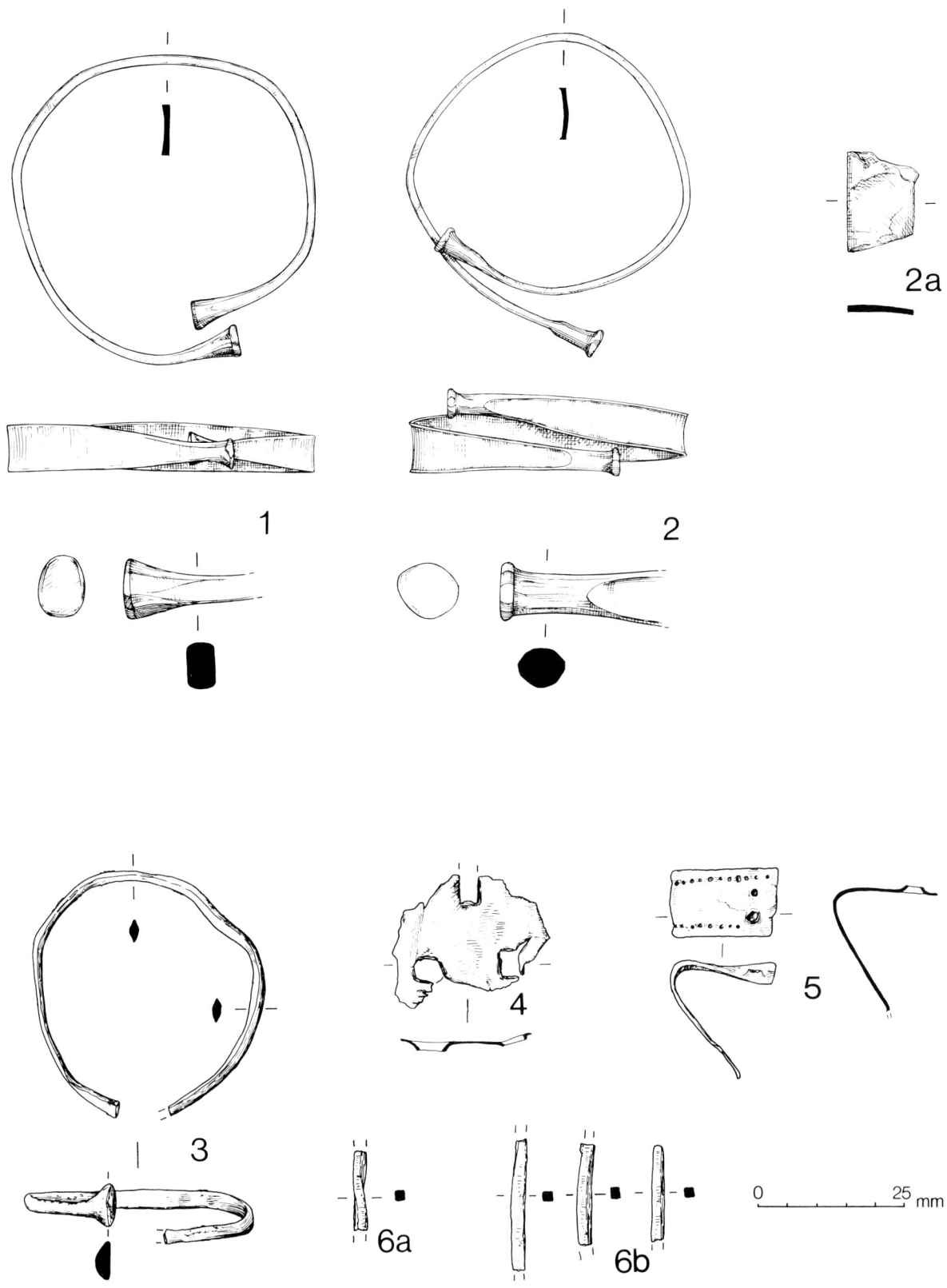

Fig 106   Bronze Age metalwork: nos 1–2a gold (British Musuem drawings), 3 copper, 4–6b copper alloy; scales 1–5 1:1, 2a and 6 2:1

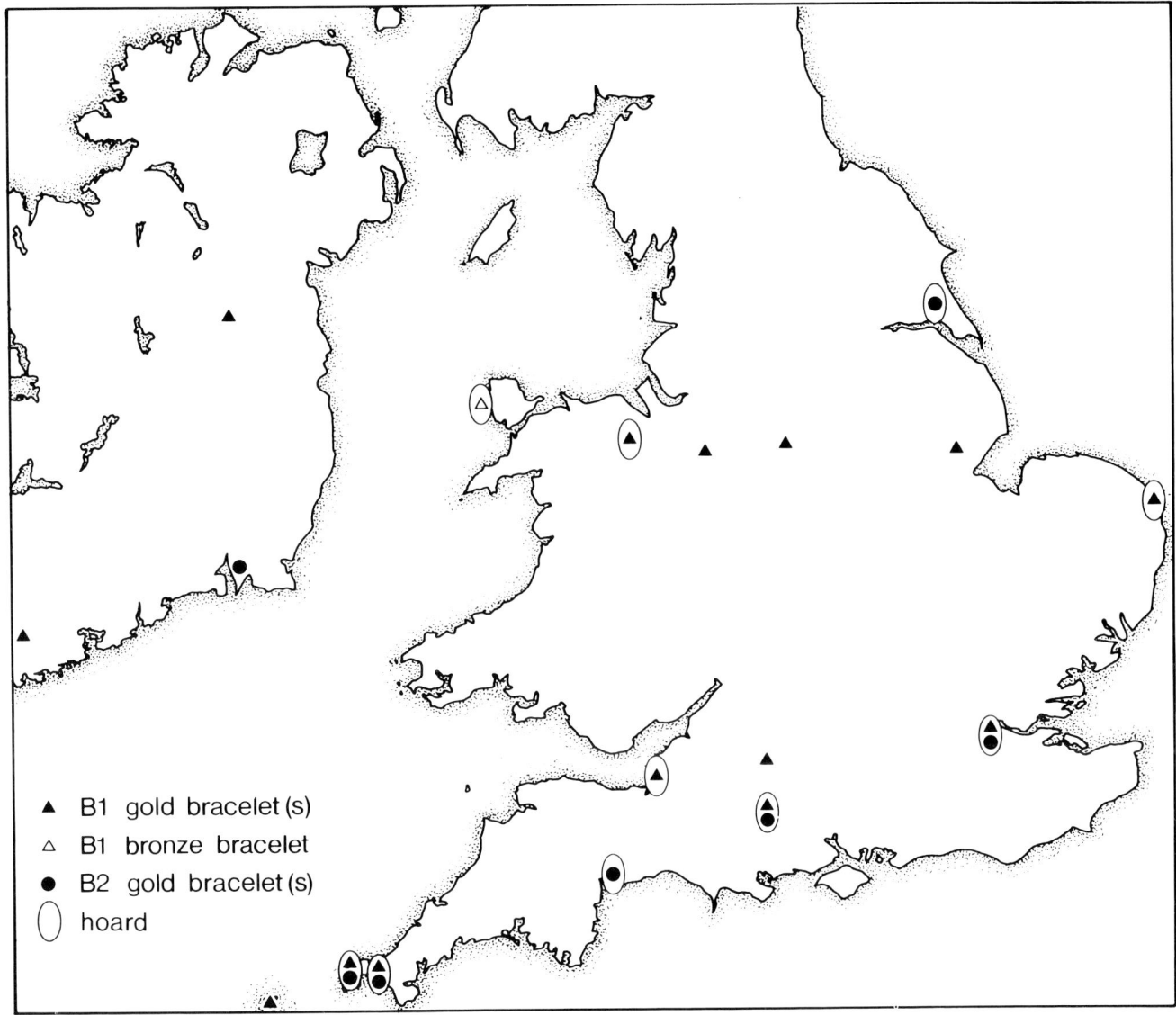

Fig 107 The distribution of Class B late Bronze Age bracelets (Hook and Needham forthcoming): B1 – buffer terminals; B2 – coiled terminals

coil-ended ribbon bracelets (Hawkes and Clarke 1963, 232, fig 54) in representing specifically British rather than Irish forms.

The unity of the B1 type may also be emphasised by consideration of weights; at least ten examples fall within the limits 23.5 to 28g. This suggests relative standardisation achieved perhaps through the manufacture of the bracelets from a bar-blank cast to a consistent size. It is conceivable that the bar ingot from Craig-yr-Wolf is just such a blank since it weighs 28.5g (Green 1983). The full significance of this finding will only emerge from the comprehensive weighing and plotting of Bronze Age goldwork. The lack of a high degree of finish on one of the Brean Down bracelets (no 2) is not in itself particularly convincing evidence for a local manufactury, but the small fragment could be a piece of scrap.

Although the B1 type appears essentially to belong to a goldworking tradition, the Tŷ Mawr find raises the possibility at least of a parallel bronze series. Bronze bracelets, unlike their gold counterparts, seem mainly to have been excluded from hoard deposits and are thus scarce in many parts of the country. They are, however, increasingly turning up on late Bronze Age settlement sites as these are subjected to more excavation. Indeed a copper example comes from the same stratigraphic unit at Brean Down itself (Fig 106.3 – see below). None as yet compares closely to B1 gold bracelets.

Very few similar objects of probable late Bronze Age date are recorded from Somerset. At Hope Wood, near Wookey Hole, a similar sized bracelet to the Brean examples is recorded by Haldane (1969). The cross-sectional area was semicircular. The weight was 23.7g, thickness 2.3mm, hoop width 4.8mm, and the external length 155mm. The expanded terminals with a flat, D-shaped end match those on the Brean copper example (below) rather than those on the gold bracelets.

A fragment of a gold bracelet was recovered from the South Cadbury excavations (Alcock 1971). This had a C-shaped cross-section and outwardly flattened terminal, and compares with many class C gold bracelets elsewhere.

A penannular gold ornament or 'tress-ring' of Bronze Age date was reported by Gray (1925) as having been found near Castle Cary in the early nineteenth century. This was a hollow ring of triangular cross-section and a ribbed surface, weighing approximately 3.25g.

Acknowledgements

Drawings of the gold (Fig 106.1–2a) are by Philip Compton of the British Museum.

Copper alloy objects

by Jennifer Foster

Some metalwork was present in Bronze Age Units 5b and 4 (Fig 106). In all there were eight copper alloy objects. The copper bracelet (no 3) from Unit 4 is probably datable to the Ewart Park phase, comparable in date with the gold bracelets (nos 1 and 2); a scrap of bronze sheet (no 4) also came from this late Bronze Age unit. From Unit 5b came a piece of decorated sheet bronze (no 5), some twisted bronze wire (6a and b), and a tiny fragment (177).

3 (50150) Copper bracelet. Unit 4, Context 38, Soil Pit 2. Hoop thickness varies 1–2mm; hoop width varies 2–3mm. Terminal width 6mm. Diameter now 40mm, probably much distorted (the Hope Wood bracelet, for example, had a wide gap between terminals and a diameter of 58mm). X-ray fluorescence analysis: virtually pure copper

Simple beaten copper penannular bracelet with no decoration. There is one remaining elliptical terminal, abruptly expanded with a flattened end; the other terminal was lost in antiquity. The bracelet is buckled and bent, but with only slight corrosion. The hoop of the bracelet is thin with a section varying from ovoid to plano-convex; the flattened end of the terminal is also plano-convex. The width and thickness are not uniform. X-ray fluorescence analysis showed it to be of fairly pure copper; this is very unusual indeed for a late Bronze Age bracelet (S Needham, pers comm).

Simple bracelets have been discussed by Needham (in Longley 1980, 21). The Brean example is one of a group with expanded terminals, which have been included in the rather general category of 'Covesea bracelets' after the assemblage found at the Sculptor's Cave, Covesea (Benton 1930–1); there were three distinctive bracelets in this hoard with 'terminals beaten up from inside outwards to form irregular knobs' (ibid, 182). Bracelets which have been assigned to this group include a series from Scotland (Coles 1959–60) and the bracelets from the Heathery Burn assemblage (Britton and Longworth 1968). The Brean bracelet differs from the Covesea bracelets in some details: the section is plano-convex (as the Heathery Burn bracelets, but unlike those from Covesea which were rectangular in section), the terminals are also plano-convex, rather than ovoid (see, for example, the bracelet from Ivinghoe Beacon; Cotton and Frere 1968, 209), and the terminals are expanded only in the side view (see Fig 106.3), not outwardly turning when viewed from above (eg see Ivinghoe Beacon, fig 11, no 1; Heathery Burn, fig 10:1, no 3). A closer parallel is the gold bracelet from Hope Wood, Wookey Hole (Haldane 1969). As Needham notes above, the expanded terminals with flat, D-shaped ends match the copper bracelet rather than the gold examples. It is also D-shaped in section, unlike the gold bracelets (Fig 106.1–2) which are flat-sectioned.

Hoards containing similar bracelets, eg the Heathery Burn cave deposit, are dated on typological grounds within the Ewart Park phase of the late Bronze Age, from 900–700 Cal BC (Megaw and Simpson 1981, 312ff). For example, at Ivinghoe Beacon the bracelet was dated c 850–600 BC (Cotton and Frere 1968, 209) and the Minnis Bay hoard contained swords, spears, and axes of the Carp's Tongue sword tradition c eighth–seventh centuries BC (Worsfold 1943, pl XII, nos 39, 40, 43, and 44). Some of these hoards also contain twisted wire and bronze sheet, as at Brean, although in the latter case the twisted wire and decorated sheet came from the underlying Unit 5b.

4 (4066) Sheet bronze. Unit 4, Context 16. Length 27mm. X-ray fluorescence analysis: bronze with some zinc

Small fragment of sheet bronze (thickness approximately 0.2mm) with three rectangular holes punched in it. Distorted, buckled, and cracked. One edge is torn. This may be a fragment of scrap bronze.

5 (60386/5747) Sheet bronze. Unit 5b: 60386 Context 93, Structure 95; 5747 Context 143. Width 11mm, thickness 0.5mm. X-ray fluorescence analysis: bronze, slight trace of lead

Two joining fragments of sheet bronze now bent almost in half, with the underside now outermost; probably originally flat. The sides are parallel and there is one square-ended terminal; the other end is broken. There are two rivet holes at the squared end. Two rows of repoussé dots are clear on what was the underside (shown uppermost in Fig 106); there is no longer any trace of the decoration on the face of the bronze, presumably as a result of corrosion and wear.

This was presumably a decorative strip on a wooden object, attached with copper alloy tacks. A similar fragment from the Minnis Bay hoard (Worsfold 1943, pl XII, no 59) was decorated with a line of small dots parallel to the main axis; it was suggested that this and other fragments decorated leather. It is possible that this was a strip strengthening for a leather bucket (Briggs 1987, 168).

6 (60818, 5108) Bronze wire. Unit 5b: 60818 Context 53; 5108 Context 77. Lengths: 60818 7mm; 5108 11mm, 8mm, 7.5mm. Thickness 1mm. X-ray fluorescence analysis: 60818 bronze; 5108 bronze with some zinc

Four fragments of rectangular-section wire, slightly twisted. They may possibly have been intended for a twisted wire bracelet (eg like that from Monkswood; Smith 1959, fig 2:2) or ring (like that from the Minnis Bay hoard; Worsfold 1943, 35). However, there is no evidence of curvature now.

Not illustrated (177) Tiny fragment of copper alloy (no analysis possible). Unit 5b, Context 77

Acknowledgements

X-ray fluorescence analysis was undertaken in the Ancient Monuments Laboratory, Fortress House, by Jerry McDonnell and Justine Bayley. I am grateful to Stuart Needham for his advice.

Gold-coloured metal spheres

During water-sieving for plant macrofossils at Bristol University some tiny gold-coloured metal spheres were found in samples from Unit 6, Context 163 and Unit 8a, Context 127. Examples were analysed by Duncan Hook of the British Museum Research Laboratory whose report below makes it likely that the spheres are contamination by solder from the sieves or drying oven, etc, rather than ancient metal-working residues.

Analysis

by Duncan Hook

Five samples were subjected to analysis using X-ray fluorescence spectrometry. The following quantitative results were obtained:

Sample no	Elements detected	Comments
Context 163, 60846	Cu, *Pb*, Sb, Sn	Solder?
Context 163, 60823	Fe, Ni, *Cu*, Zn	Brass (65:35)
Context 163, 12809	Fe, Ni, *Cu*, Zn, trPb, trSn	Brass (60:30)
Context 163, 60838	Cu, Zn	Brass (60:40)
Context 127, 60600	Fe, Zn	Modern?

No gold was detected in any of the samples analysed and it therefore seems unlikely that they are connected to the bracelets from Brean Down.

13 The flint and chert artefacts

by Alan Saville

A collection of 198 items from the recent series of excavations was submitted for examination. Nine of these were regarded as unmodified and of entirely natural origin, leaving a total of 189 humanly modified pieces. The overall typological composition of the collection is given in Table 9 and MF1:C6 provides an inventory and concordance with the original find numbers.

Raw material

All the pieces in the collection are of flint except in two instances: an edge-trimmed flake of dark grey/black smooth chert (30) and a miscellaneous retouched piece of brown coarse greensand chert (29). Both these pieces came from superficial contexts, which also produced post-medieval remains, so their relationship to the prehistoric phasing of the site is unknown, though typologically they are undoubtedly of prehistoric manufacture.

The flint artefacts are generally, except when burnt, in an uncorticated condition with a predominantly medium grey colouration, with pieces of darker and lighter grey flint also present. To judge from the evidence provided by those artefacts which retain sizable areas of cortex or thermal exteriors, there are basically two kinds of flint raw material represented. Firstly, there is a 'chalk-type' flint with a relatively thick and relatively unabraded, but coarse, cortex. Such flint was presumably imported to the site in nodule form from flint-bearing regions to the east. Secondly, there is a flint with a thin, smooth, waterworn cortex (or waterworn and densely stained exterior produced by thermal or natural mechanical exposure of the internal flint), sometimes with numerous chatter-marks. This type of flint undoubtedly derives from local beach pebbles. In neither case was the internal flint sufficiently distinct from macroscopic examination to permit separation of the beach and the imported types when there was no, or too small an area of, cortex present. Thus the small numbers of flint artefacts which could be assigned to either flint type form so small a proportion of the collection that it is only feasible to give a very general indication of the overall importance of the different sources through time (see below).

In terms of size, all the instances of identifiable beach-pebble flint artefacts are small, whereas the imported flint was large enough for the production of implements like no 33. Nevertheless, as can be appreciated from the accompanying illustrations (Figs 108–110), the general size of artefacts, irrespective of the raw material, was small.

Technology

The six cores are all in residual form, with a mean maximum dimension of 31mm (max 38, min 24) and a mean weight of 8.9g (max 17.4, min 3.4), but include examples of standard multiplatform flaking (12) as well as écaillé technology (26, 31, and 32). The latter is a flaking technique generally assumed to involve the use of an anvil and to be particularly suited to the exploitation of small, thin pebbles (Norman 1977).

Of the 47 complete unretouched flakes, only 22 are 20mm or more in length or breadth, and of these only one example is of blade proportions. Blades are occasionally represented among the implements (13), but in general the technology in this collection is a flake one.

Refitting pieces were searched for throughout this collection but none was found, either within or between contexts.

Context and typology

In Table 10 the artefacts are subdivided according to their typology and with regard to the major stratigraphic units outlined elsewhere in this report. This table excludes seven pieces which were without any stratigraphic designation, 43 pieces from the superficial layers forming Units 4a, 3, and 1, and a single piece from Unit 5a, an out-of-context intrusion.

The totals from each unit are regrettably small, and do not permit any meaningful comparison of 'assemblages' between units or with assemblages from other sites. Nor is there much to be gained from a consideration of the spatial distribution of these flints within their contexts, since with a maximum of 54 items in any one unit, there is little potential for isolating meaningful concentrations. Nevertheless, the existence of a stratigraphic sequence, with precise ceramic associations and radiocarbon dating, offers an opportunity to evaluate the stratigraphic subdivisions of the flint collection in terms of its typologically distinctive pieces.

Table 9 Typological analysis of all struck flint and chert artefacts

type	number	weight in grams
unretouched flakes, complete	47	98.4
unretouched flakes, broken	77	129.0
unclassified burnt fragments	8	19.2
cores	6	53.3
core fragments	4	51.5
edge-trimmed flakes	10	42.0
scrapers	10	119.5
knives	2	28.0
leaf-shaped arrowheads	2	2.1
piercer	1	1.2
'fabricator'	1	12.9
rod	1	14.8
unretouched flake with edge gloss	1	1.0
gunflint	1	7.4
miscellaneous retouched pieces	18	133.5
Totals	189	713.8

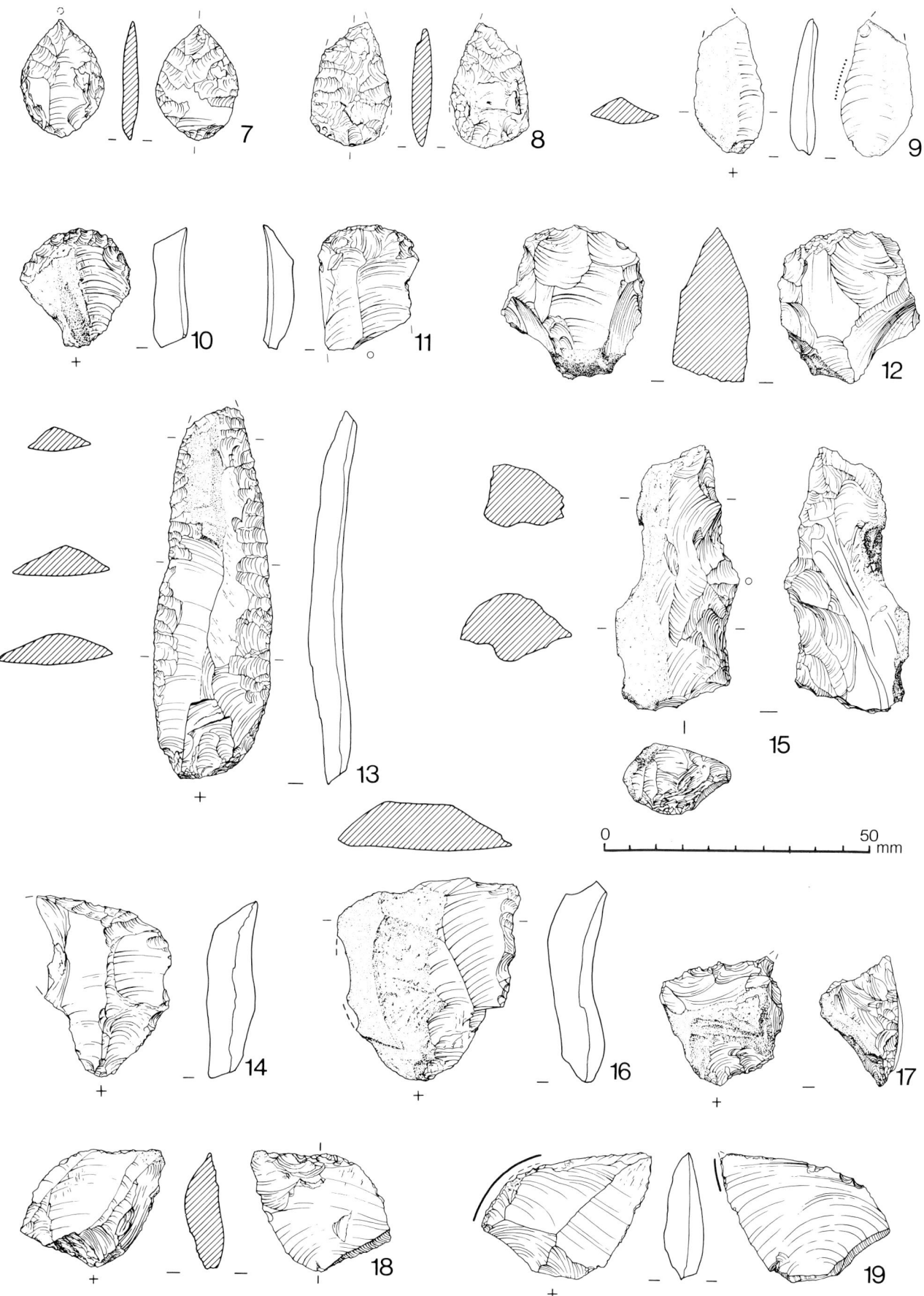

Fig 108 Flints from Units 8a (nos 7–9), 7 (10–12), and 6 (13–19); scale 1:1

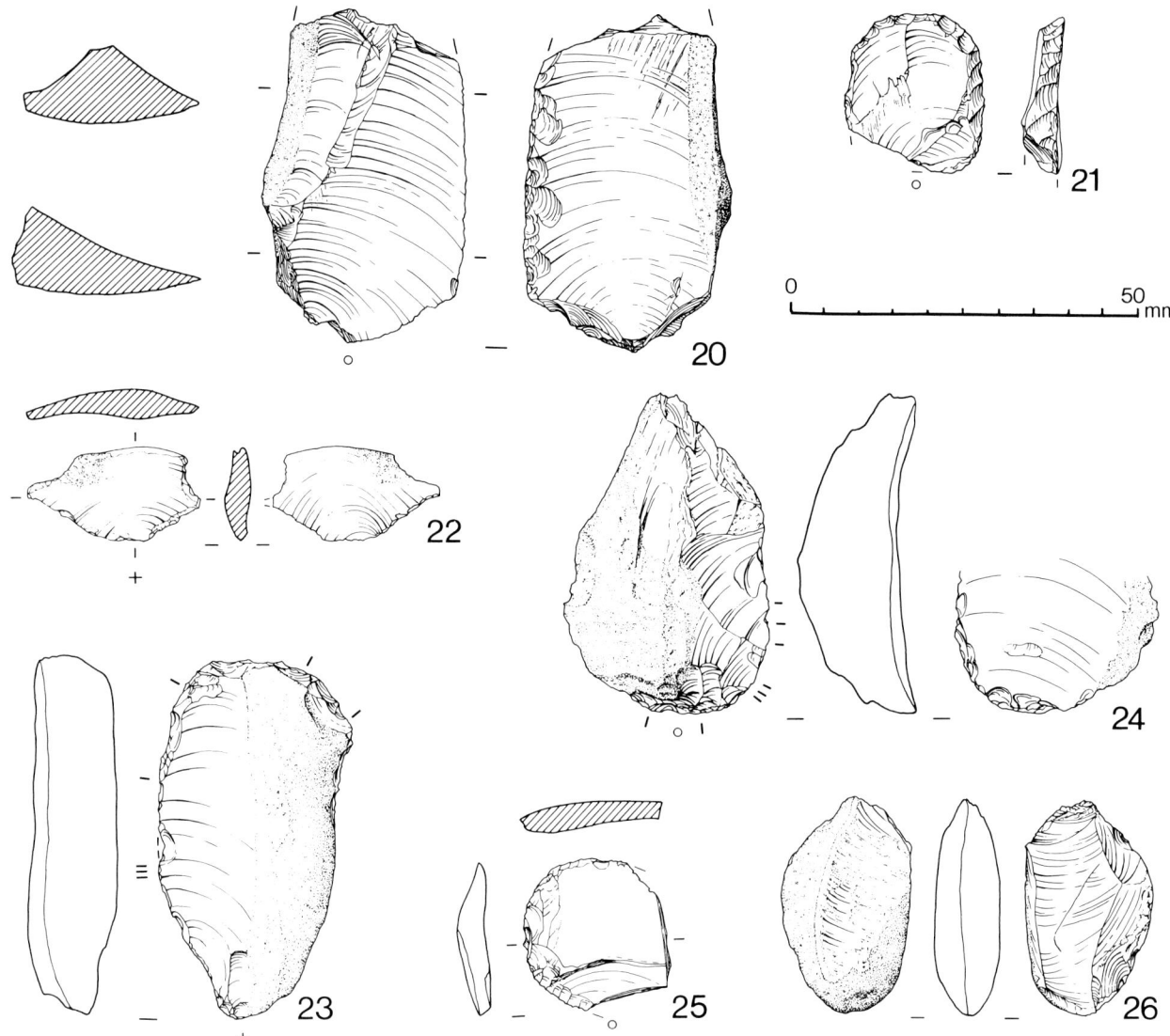

Fig 109   Flints from Units 6 (20–22), 5b (23–24), and 4 (25–26); scale 1:1

Unit 8a

The most distinctive and diagnostic prehistoric forms present are the two leaf-shaped arrowheads. The complete example (7) is small and squat with an attenuated point, clearly made on a flake blank with the tip of the arrowhead at the bulbar end of the original flake. This arrowhead is a type 4A (Green 1984, 21), a type commonly found in Somerset and the south-west (Green 1980, 215). The other arrowhead (8), broken as a result of burning, is also small, though less squat, and when complete would probably also have been classifiable as a type 4A.

Although Green (1980, 94–7) accepted the continuity of leaf-shaped arrowheads into the early Bronze Age, largely on the basis of an association with a collared urn burial in Derbyshire, there are no direct associations with Beaker burials, and the overwhelming majority of associations are with early/middle Neolithic contexts and artefacts. At Brean Down the burnt arrowhead (8) is from Context 63, which has an associated radiocarbon date of 4720±140 BP (HAR-7023). The complete arrowhead (7) from Context 127 is in a fresh condition and there is no reason to regard it as a residual or derived find, with the implication that an earlier third millennium bc date would be appropriate for this as well.

The only other diagnostic item from Unit 8a is the unretouched flake with edge polish (9: the dots against the ventral edge show the position of the polish), a type which is increasingly being recognised from Neolithic sites in particular (Saville 1981, 126). One of the Unit 8a miscellaneous retouched pieces is an unclassifiable but complete and extensively retouched piece with écaillé-type removals across the bulbar surface.

Only three pieces from Unit 8a retain any assessable amount of cortex, and all appear to be of imported flint.

Unit 7

The two scrapers from this horizon, which are both from Context 62, are of distinctive forms. One is complete (10) and is a 'thumbnail' end scraper, while the other (11) is the distal segment of an end-of-blade scraper with quite minimal and very shallow retouch. The former has visible wear abrasion on the leading

THE FLINT AND CHERT ARTEFACTS

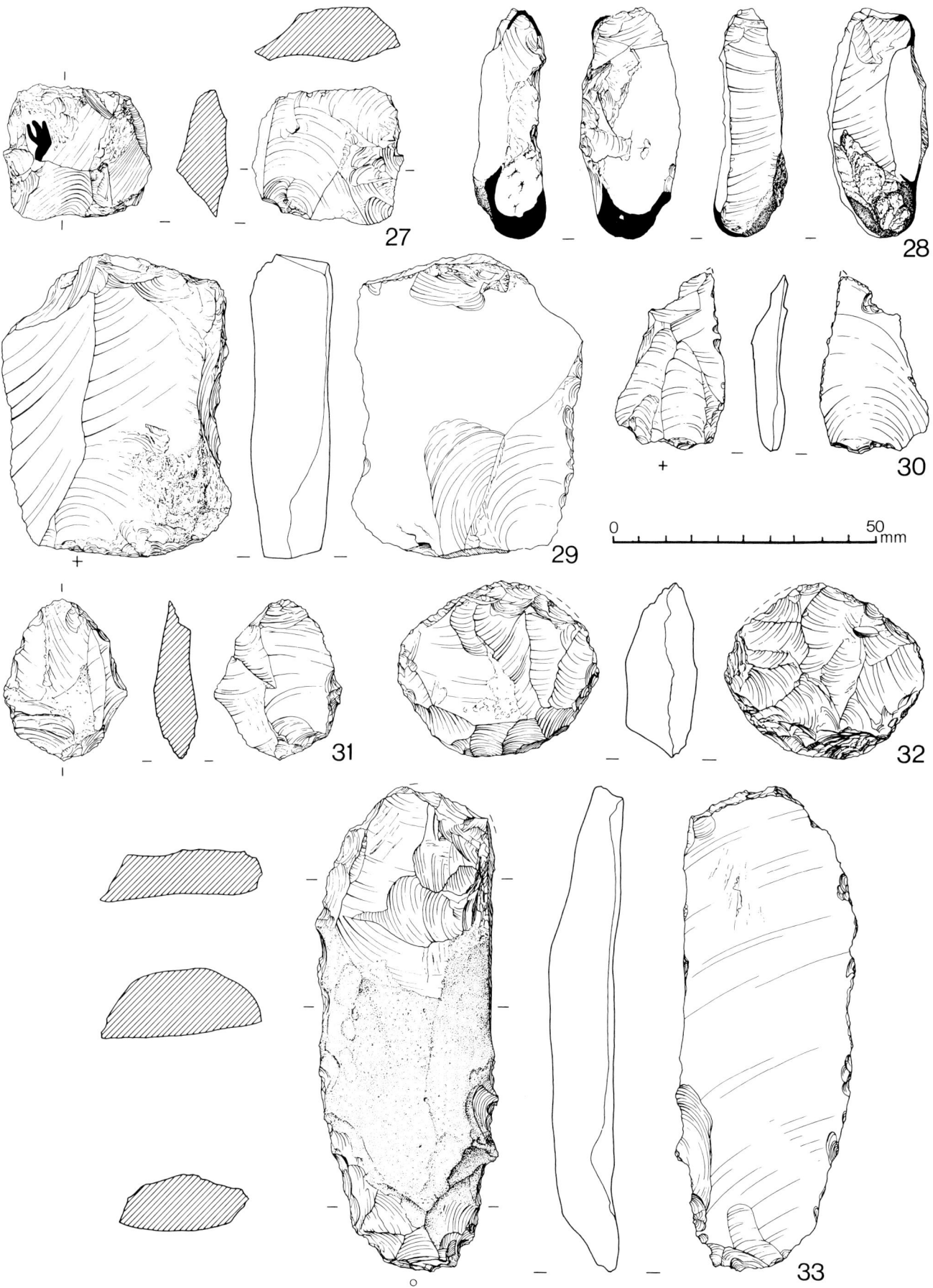

Fig 110 Flints from modern, residual, and unstratified contexts (nos 27–33); scale 1:1

Table 10 Typological analysis of flint artefacts from stratified contexts

	Major stratigraphic units					
type	8a	7	6	5b	4	Totals
unretouched flakes, complete	6	5	13	3	8	35
unretouched flakes, fragmentary	14	2	21	4	12	53
unclassified burnt fragments	1	2	3	-	1	7
cores	-	1	-	-	1	2
core fragments	-	-	-	1	3	4
edge-trimmed flakes	-	1	3	1	2	7
scrapers	-	2	3	2	1	8
knives	-	-	2	-	-	2
leaf-shaped arrowheads	2	-	-	-	-	2
piercer	-	-	1	-	-	1
rod	-	-	1	-	-	1
unretouched flake with edge gloss	1	-	-	-	-	1
miscellaneous retouched pieces	3	-	7	4	1	15
Totals	27	13	54	15	29	138

Key to flint-bearing contexts in each unit (no of flints in brackets):

Unit 8a: 6 (1); 63 (21); 127 (3); 218 (2)
Unit 7: 62 (8); 188 (5)
Unit 6: 57 (1); 61 (11); 66 (8); 118 (2); 156 (5); 157 (2); 163 (23); 163/57 (1); 177 (1)
Unit 5b: 53 (10); 59 (1); 60 (1); 95 (1); 159 (1); 251 (1)
Unit 4: 16 (26); 41 (1); 52 (2)

---

scraping edge. Both scrapers are of Beaker/early Bronze Age form.

The core from Context 62 is a residual multiplatform example (12), worked on imported flint. A very small chip from Unit 7 is struck from a beach pebble, but otherwise the flint is unsourceable.

The presence of a fine unretouched thinning flake with a faceted butt from Context 188 can be noted.

Unit 6

The blade knife (13) from Context 61 has shallow invasive retouch along both lateral edges. It is broken at the tip, but appears from the scar patterns at the break to have continued being used in its present form. Such knives are classic Bronze Age artefacts. The other knife from this unit is broken and of a somewhat unusual form (20), in that the retouch is effected inversely on a flake, the platform of which has been removed by inverse retouch. The piercer (22) is even less characteristic, being an *ad hoc* form on a short, broad flake with the lateral projections on both edges being trimmed as points, in one case unifacially, in the other bifacially.

Two of the scapers are also Bronze Age forms. One, which is damaged by heat, is a thick extended-end scraper with steep scalar retouch (cf Clark 1933, fig 3); the other is broken on the left side, but is an end scraper, again with scale-flaking (14). The third scraper is a broken discoidal type (21).

The rod (15) is a short prismatic tool, fashioned transversely on a segment of a broad flake. This implement has a scraper-like edge at its base and a burin-like facet at its tip. There is no polish or abrasion at either pole.

The miscellaneous retouched pieces include a flake with knife-like retouch and a rounded point (16), a small, stubby flake with peripheral scraper-like denticulate retouch and a possible piercer-point, now broken (17), and a small flake with a 'splintered' inverse distal edge like that of a pièce esquillé (18).

One of the edge-trimmed flakes from this unit is illustrated (19).

None of the artefacts in this unit appears to be fashioned on beach-pebble flint.

Unit 5b

The two scrapers from this unit are both end scrapers, one with the working edge on the bulbar end of a flake (24). The more conventional example (23) is in a slightly 'rolled' condition with a faint bloom of cortication, and is probably residual in this context. The retouched edge has become smooth in patches from extensive wear (indicated on the illustration by transverse lines against the edge of the tool), and the same applies to the other end scraper (24).

There is little evidence for the exploitation of beach pebble flint among the pieces from this unit.

Unit 4

The scraper (25) is a fragmentary side scraper and has very shallow invasive retouch. The dense cortication of this piece, compared with the other flints from this context, suggests that it is residual.

The core (26) is an écaillé type, in this case definitely made on a beach pebble. Apart from the core, nine of the flakes are certainly manufactured from beach pebble flint.

Modern, residual, and unstratified material

Another 39 pieces were found in Contexts 12, 13, and 18, part of Unit 3 which is associated with post-medieval pottery. The gunflint (27) is from this unit, and must be seventeenth century or later in date. The 'fabricator'/strike-a-light (28) is perhaps more likely to be as modern as the gunflint than to be a residual prehistoric implement. The rest of the items from this horizon, including the two chert flakes (29 and 30), would appear to be prehistoric, but this is a miscellaneous batch of artefacts with no other typologically distinctive items. The presence of a core from Context 12 is worth noting, however, since this piece, which is in a fresh and uncorticated condition, is an écaillé type (31). Another écaillé core, this time a more elaborate discoidal version (32), was found in Unit 4a (Context 25), a stony colluvial soil, which presumably explains the dense surface cortication of this piece.

The other unstratified material in the collection does not merit any comment, except for an exceptional piece collected from the beach below the site. This is a large and extensively retouched flake (33) with attributes of both scraper and knife type. It has been classified as an atypical scraper, because it is probable that the distal terminal was formerly a convex scraping edge, which at some stage broke, though the implement continued in use with the broken edge showing signs of use for a scraper-like purpose. The left-hand side edge also shows considerable signs of use, and slight polishing has occurred on the most prominent ripples on the ventral surface. The good condition of this piece suggests that it has only recently eroded out of the sandcliff, and typologically a Bronze Age date would seem most probable.

Conclusions

The importance and very great interest of this collection lie in the fact that it presents a very rare opportunity to look at a potentially stratified sequence of flint 'assemblages' from the Neolithic into the later Bronze Age. All the more unfortunate, then, that the recovered collection is so small, and does not allow the investigation of technological questions which necessitate much larger samples than these. Nevertheless, by examining the typology within the various stratigraphic units, some points of interest have emerged.

The only distinctively Neolithic items, the two leaf-shaped arrowheads, were stratigraphically at the base of the excavated sequence (Unit 8b). The flake with edge gloss was associated with them, while the most typologically Neolithic of the scrapers (23) was probably residual within its Unit 5b context. The ceramic associations of Unit 8b itself were exclusively Beaker, and it is probable that all these Neolithic items were residual from some earlier activity at the site, perhaps to be linked with the c 4720 BP radiocarbon date.

Those pieces which typologically would be classed as Beaker period or later, such as the knives and many of the scrapers, were from Unit 7 or higher in the sequence, in correct stratigraphic association with Beaker and later pottery.

There is little evidence for the exploitation of beach pebble flint in this collection until Unit 4, the very late Bronze Age in terms of the ceramic associations. This is also true of the écaillé technology, which one would expect to be preferentially applied to beach pebbles. The écaillé technology has been observed as a common phenomenon of western coastal sites from Cornwall to south Wales (Johnson and David 1982, 85), but with an uncertain, though probably post-Mesolithic, chronology. The Brean Down evidence would suggest a very late date within the sequence of Bronze Age flint use.

The small number of artefacts from the basal palaeosol, despite the extent excavated, is likely to indicate either that this area of the site was peripheral to any knapping or occupation zones or that Neolithic activity as a whole at Brean Down was minimal, since the level of flint discard known from other Neolithic sites is so much greater.

On the other hand, the number of artefacts from Unit 6, given the limited spatial extent of this unit, is quite impressive. None of the 54 artefacts appeared to be obviously residual, and this collection suggests the employment by the middle Bronze Age occupants of a fully flint-using technology. By the late Bronze Age of Unit 5b, the horizon of the main Bronze Age structures, the presence of flint artefacts is again low, and the collection also includes some pieces which do appear residual. In this case, since Unit 5b was clearly a zone of intensive occupation, the low level of flint discard must be a reflection of minimal flint use. This is almost certainly an echo of the known decline in the amount and range of flint and stone tool use during the Bronze Age period (Ford *et al* 1984), and carries the implication that by the late Bronze Age the inhabitants at Brean had alternative metal implements to replace their previous reliance on flint tools.

It should be noted, however, that no obvious 'decline' in technological standards is apparent through the Neolithic and Bronze Age levels until Unit 4, and even here the technological contrast produced by the écaillé method is obviously related to an increased exploitation of beach pebbles (ie the technology is conditioned by the raw material). This changeover from imported to beach pebble flint can presumably be seen as another indication of the relative unimportance attached to flint tool use during the later Bronze Age with locally available raw material sufficing for *ad hoc* and intermittent requirements, and long distance flint acquisition a thing of the past.

14 Other Bronze Age artefacts

by Jennifer Foster

Introduction

The range of non-metallic artefacts in Bronze Age contexts at Brean is wide and illuminating in terms of the activities carried out in the settlement. Of particular interest is the well-preserved briquetage which is considered at some length. There are also worked bone objects, other fired clay items, and shale armlets, nearly all from well-stratified contexts with good groups of pottery.

It would have been impractical to divide the artefacts into unit groups; they are therefore discussed together and contexts given for each entry. Included in this chapter are objects from later contexts which are obviously Bronze Age in date. It has been necessary to give publication numbers for illustrated finds in a consecutive sequence beginning with the metalwork (Chapter 12). Finds numbers are given in the catalogue in brackets following the publication number: eg 34 (1776). Where more than one number is given for an artefact, it comprises several joining pieces. Distributions of these artefacts are shown for Unit 6 (Fig 31), Unit 5b (Figs 46-49), and Unit 4 (MF1:A5). I should like to thank the following people: Peter van den Broeke for his helpful suggestions on the briquetage; Arthur MacGregor for his comments on the bone objects; Chris Green, Beth Richardson, and members of staff at the Department of Urban Archaeology, Museum of London, for discussing the post-medieval finds; and Justine Bayley and Michael Heyworth for their prompt analysis of a variety of objects.

Pottery spindle whorl (Fig 111)

34 (1776) Half of a flat spindle whorl, originally thought to be stone and latterly reidentified as pottery (see below, geological specimens by Reg Bradshaw), broken across the perforation. Well-made, but not completely symmetrical. Slightly hour-glass shaped hole due to the method of drilling. Spindle whorls of this shape are common on Bronze Age sites (eg see O'Connell 1986, 60). Diam 38mm. Unit 4, Context 16

Stone object (Fig 111)

35 (5624) Broken shale tool (see report below by Reg Bradshaw). It has one edge which has been chipped into a curving shape; the other edges are breaks. This edge is now very smooth and has obviously been subjected to considerable wear, resulting in many fine scratched lines in parallel groups on the flat surface, showing the direction of use. Stone tools are notoriously difficult to classify (Rees 1986, 75ff), but the very clear use wear on this artefact shows that it was used for

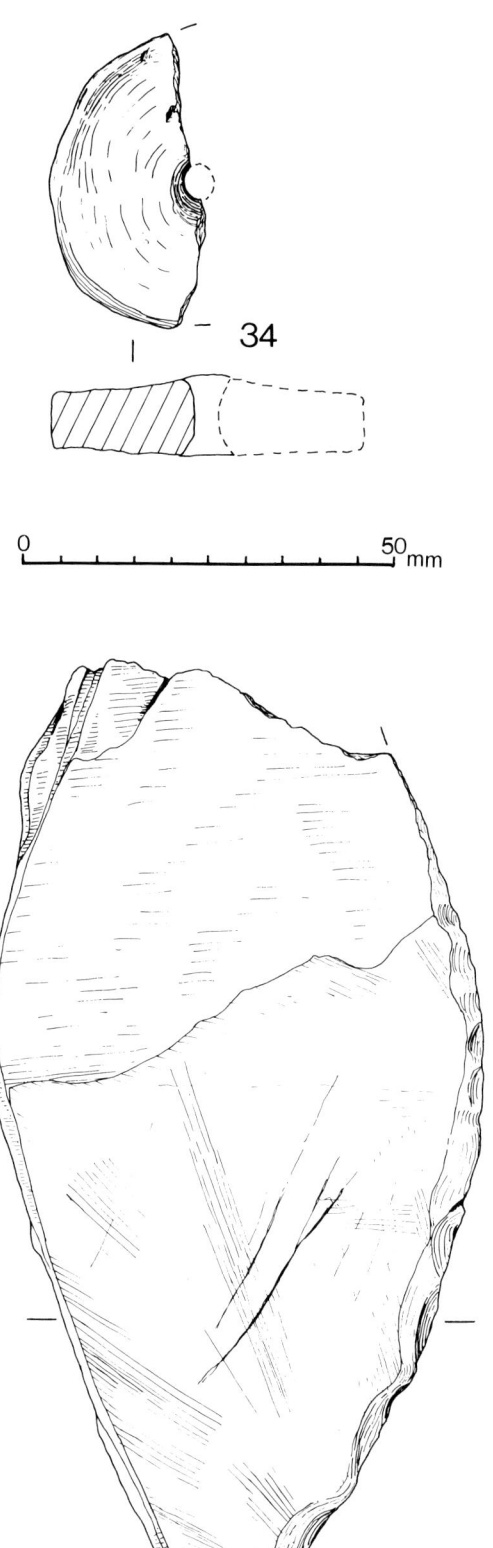

Fig 111 Pottery spindle whorl no 34 and stone object no 35; scale 1:1

scraping and suggests contact with gritty particles. In view of its association with Structure 95 it is tempting though unproven to suggest a link with the salt production process. Length 128mm. Unit 5b, Context 112. Associated with Vessel 8 (Fig 90.30: 5641) inside Structure 95

Not illustrated There were also two rounded hammerstones from the late Bronze Age Unit 4, Context 16, of limestone (no 3537) and sandstone (no 1710); see report below by Reg Bradshaw.

Shale objects (Fig 112)

The Bronze Age shale objects from Brean consist of an unworked pebble (no 36) from 5b, probably picked up from the beach, two armlet fragments, and two blanks from Unit 4. A further fragment of armlet (no 39) was found in the fill of sub-Roman grave 212. Visually there is no difference in the armlets, although the X-ray fluorescence analysis (see below) does distinguish no 39 from those of Bronze Age date. It has not been possible to identify the shale source(s), but the objects are all shale, rather than jet. I have followed Calkin's usage of 'armlet' rather than bracelet in this report, avoiding any implication as to whether they were worn on the wrist or above the elbow (Calkin 1953, 46).

Shale was used widely in the Bronze Age for beads, buttons, pendants, and armlets; this is no doubt due to the versatility of shale, which is tough but relatively soft, can be easily worked with stone tools, and gives a high polish (Calkin 1953, 46). Armlets are known from the early Bronze Age, eg at Swine Sty, Derbyshire (Mackin 1971a), where there was a shale industry associated with flint cutting tools within a circular stone house, and the late Bronze Age at Petters Sports Field (Longley 1980, 31). The size of the finished armlets from Brean (40–45mm internal diameter) is within the range for Bronze Age armlets in general, eg three bracelets from Swine Sty (Mackin 1971a) which were 40, 52, and 60mm; on the other hand those from Runneymede were 82 and 76mm internal diameter (Longley 1980, 31).

All Bronze Age armlets were produced by boring the inner hole and chipping, then grinding the outer circumference; lathe turning was a late Iron Age innovation (Calkin 1953). At Swine Sty, 60 pieces of shale armlet were found and a great deal more waste shale. Starting with blocks, the centre and edges were removed by flaking, gouging, pecking, cutting, and

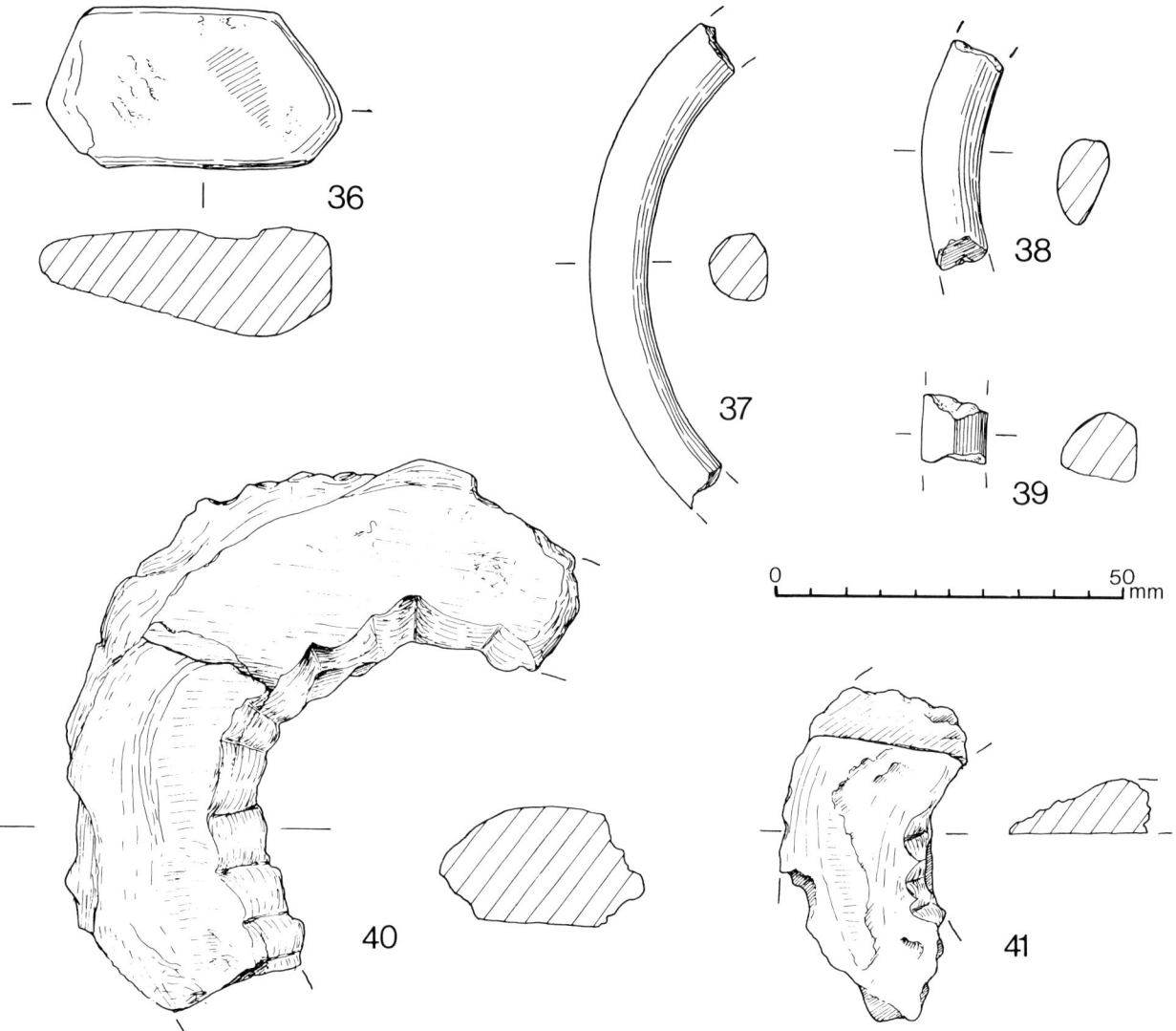

Fig 112   Shale objects, nos 36–41; scale 1:1

abrasion. These processes can be clearly seen on the blank from Brean, no 40 (Fig 112). At Swine Sty only stone and flint tools were used, no metal ones (Mackin 1971b). This was the case, even during the Iron Age, eg at Eldon's Seat (Cunliffe and Phillipson 1968). Roughouts have been found on a number of sites (eg Potterne, C Gingell, pers comm; and Shearplace Hill, Rahtz and ApSimon 1962). During the Bronze Age the raw material was apparently traded as roughouts rather than finished items; presumably the armlet blanks from Brean Down broke as they were being finished. At Iron Age Kimmeridge breakages were common as the slab was perforated (Calkin 1948, 40). Compared to sites like Swine Sty and, later, Kimmeridge and Eldon's Seat, all of which are close to the shale source, it is evident that there was no shale industry at Brean as such; the inhabitants were just finishing ornaments for personal use.

36 (5718) Shale pebble, with rounded edges, possibly sea-weathered. Presumably intended for manufacture into a small object such as a bead or pendant; it was too small for an armlet. 41×21mm. Unit 5b, Context 139
37 (4794) Armlet segment with D-shaped section, very well-made. Original diam: outer 45mm, inner 40mm. Unit 4, Context 16
38 (3926) Armlet segment of oval section. Well-finished. Original diam: outer 40mm, inner 30mm. Thickness 11mm. Unit 4, Context 16
39 (6531) Armlet fragment, D-shaped section. Max thickness 10mm. Unit 3d, Context 212 (fill of grave)
40 (4163) At least half of an armlet blank, roughly chipped into a circular shape. The intended item would have been about 40mm external diameter (as no 38). Outer diam 45mm, inner 25mm. Unit 4, Context 16
41 (4054) Fragment of an armlet blank, possibly part of no 40 (4163). Outer diam 40mm, inner 25mm. Unit 4, Context 16

X-ray fluorescence analysis of the shale objects

by Michael Heyworth

The six shale objects were submitted to qualitative X-ray fluorescence analysis to confirm their identification as shale rather than jet. It has been shown that jet and shale can be distinguished by elemental analysis (Pollard *et al* 1981). The main discriminating element is iron which was found to be at much lower levels in jet than in non-jet material, such as shale. A number of other elements were also suggested as discriminators between the two.

For comparison a fragment of jet was also analysed. The fragments from Brean Down had consistently higher iron levels than the jet fragment, and they can therefore be confirmed as shale. However, there were some interesting variations in the composition of the Brean Down fragments which relate to the context of the finds. Four of the armlet fragments (37, 38, 40, and 41) came from the same context (16). These fragments all had low levels of zinc and strontium. Another armlet fragment (39) came from a later context (212) and had no traces of zinc or strontium. The shale pebble (36) contained no zinc but did contain lead which distinguished it from the armlet fragments. These variations in composition may relate to different sources of shale, though they may also be due to differences in burial conditions between the contexts. It is not possible to pinpoint the source of the shale.

Bone objects

(Bone identifications by Bruce Levitan)

The range of bone objects from Brean Down is typical of that from other Bronze Age sites, eg Heathery Burn hoard (Britton and Longworth 1968) and Runnymede Bridge (Longley 1980, 27): the usual metapodial awls and dress pins, and less common gouges and smoothers; in other words, mainly practical items. A limited range of bones was chosen from which to make these artefacts: sheep metapodia and tibiae, and cattle tibiae, with occasional other bones.

Pins (Fig 113)

42 (6032) Beautifully made and polished pin, probably of deer antler; flattened at both ends, circular-section in the middle with a fine point. Probably a dress or hair pin. Similar to an example from Runnymede Bridge (Longley 1980, 27). Length 88mm. Unit 5b, Context 155 (Structure 95). ?Deer ?antler
43 (6048) Pin probably of deer antler, very similar to no 42, and from the same context. Flat at one end, circular-section at the other. Length 77mm. Unit 5b, Context 155 (Structure 95). ?Deer ?antler
44 (60152) Tip of a pin, circular-section. Length 25mm. Unit 4, Context 16
45 (6038) Broken bone pin, beautifully made and finished with a flattened section. Length 48mm. Unit 6, Structure 57. ?Sheep-size ?long bone

Awls (Fig 113)

There is one unusual awl from Brean Down (no 46: 263) for which there are few parallels. Apart from this there are nine of more usual type manufactured from sheep metapodia and tibiae (see similar examples from Heathery Burn (Britton and Longworth 1968) and Runnymede Bridge (Longley 1980, 27)). The most likely use for the Brean Down awls was in leatherworking, but they could have had many other functions; for example they could have been used to execute the deeply incised decoration which is a feature of the pottery in Unit 5b.

46 (263) Beautifully made and polished awl with very sharp but asymmetrical point. Flat rectangular section throughout its length. A tool for a specific purpose, presumably an awl. A very similar example came from Skara Brae, again with an asymmetrical tip, although this one is pierced through the plate (Clarke 1976, 241), and

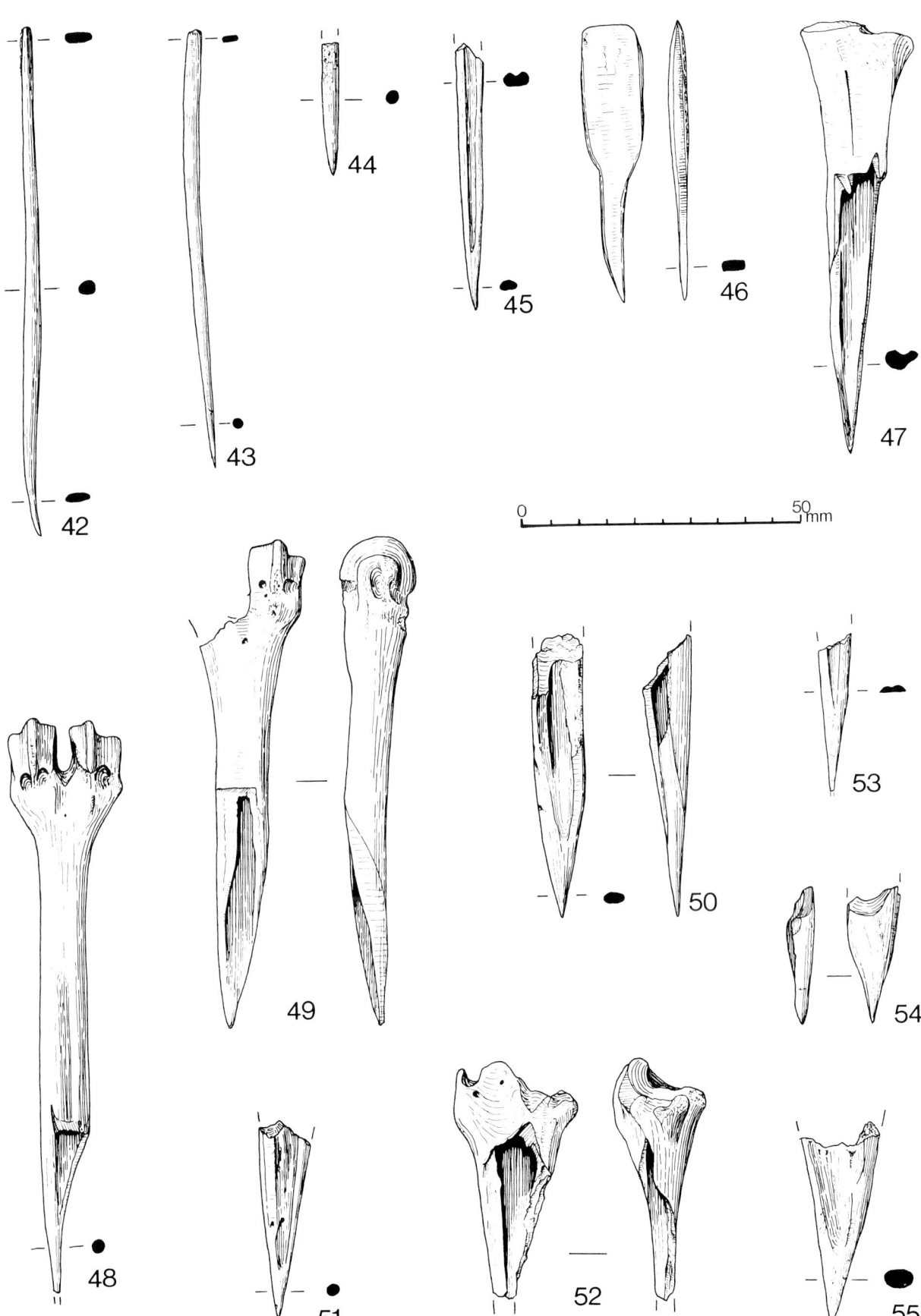

Fig 113 Bone pins and awls, nos 42–55; scale 1:1

is Neolithic in date. Length 48mm. Unstratified. Cattle rib/scapula

47 (5905) Very fine sharp point with wear traces on the tip. Burnt. Length 75mm. Unit 5b, Context 148 (Structure 95). Sheep metacarpal (left proximal)
48 (4576) Very well-made, well-worn awl with shiny surface. Asymmetrically cut point with tip missing. Length 100mm (incomplete). Unit 5b, Context 53. Sheep metatarsal (left distal)
49 (5480) Broken awl, either worn or deliberately made asymmetrical. Note the post-medieval context, but probable Bronze Age type. Length 86mm. Unit 3a, Context 13. Sheep metatarsal (right distal)
50 (4920) Broken point of an awl. Very finely made and well-worn. Length 50mm (incomplete). Unit 5b, Context 105. Sheep/goat metatarsal
51 (305) Point of an awl, well-worn tip. Length 34mm (incomplete). Unstratified, but probably deriving from Structure 59. Unit 5b. Sheep/goat metatarsal
52 (6040) Top of an awl, point missing. Length 43mm (incomplete). Unit 4, Context 16. Sheep/goat tibia (right distal)
53 (4868) Point from an awl, broken tip. Length 28mm. Unit 4, Context 16. ?Sheep-size ?long bone
54 (60391) Point, possibly from a metapodial awl. Very sharp tip. Length 24mm. Unit 5b, Context 53. Sheep/goat tibia/metatarsal
55 (303) Bone point, broken. Worn tip. Length 35mm. 1984, unstratified. Cattle tibia/metapodial

Four other examples of similar metapodial awls from Brean Down sandcliff have been found, three by ApSimon *et al* (1961, 119) and one, since destroyed, by Dobson (1935, 265).

Gouges and 'chisels' (Fig 114)

These are less common tools, although they usually form part of the larger Bronze Age bone assemblages; for example there were three gouges from the Heathery Burn hoard (Britton and Longworth 1968, nos 142–4), made of sheep metapodia and tibiae. Unlike modern metal tools they were presumably too delicate for woodworking; some might have been used for leatherworking, or with clay. Wooden and bone tools were used in shoemaking as late as 1898 (Salaman 1986, 93–5) for smoothing, flattening, and polishing.

56 (2891) Gouge, carefully worked at the lower (proximal) end, although the tip is missing. Chewed by a canid at upper end. Length 124mm. Unit 4, Context 17 (slumped 16). Sheep/goat tibia
57 (70061) Large gouge, now broken at side and top. Polished surface and tip which is well-worn. Length 110mm. Unstratified in backfill. Cattle tibia
58 (5941) Gouge with well-made tip, now worn and polished. Polished shaft. Broken proximal end. Length 96mm. Unit 6a, Context 61. Sheep/goat tibia
59 (3717) Gouge, polished shaft and slight wear at tip (distal end). Length 129mm. Unit 4, Context 16
60 (3388) Chisel-shaped tool, with very carefully shaped and smoothed working end, which is polished and chipped with wear. Other end broken. A very similar artefact made from a sheep tibia came from the Heathery Burn hoard (Britton and Longworth 1968, no 141). Length 63mm. Unit 4, Context 16. Sheep/goat tibia

Smoothers (Figs 114 and 115)

Tools with smoothed ends, possibly with multiple uses, eg for the preparation of leather or fabric, as a spoon in cooking, or in the manufacture of pottery. Smoothers are usually explained as leatherworking tools. The characteristic Bronze Age implements are generally longer than those from Brean and with both ends rounded (eg from the Heathery Burn hoard; Britton and Longworth 1968). Antler and slate smoothers found in a Beaker grave at Overton Hill (Smith and Simpson 1966, 134) were interpreted as leather-processing tools. They were associated with a related set of tools: flint knife and flake, a strike-a-light and piece of marcasite for lighting a fire, and a bronze awl for piercing. Note that all the smoothers from Brean Down came from Unit 4 (late Bronze Age in date).

61 (3976) Smoother, rounded at lower end due to use, shaft polished. Length 87mm. Unit 4, Context 16. Cattle tibia
62 (1939) Edge of a broken smoother, more carefully made than no 61, with smoothed end and side. Highly polished and burnt. Length 35mm. Unit 4, Context 16. ?Cattle size
63 (4852) Well-used smoother, with polished shaft. Length 130mm. Unit 4, Context 16. Cattle radius (left proximal)
64 (1879) Scraper or smoother. A complete object of distinctive shape possibly used in weaving, the preparation of skins, or in pottery manufacture. A very close parallel for this object from Northton, Isle of Harris (Simpson 1976, fig 12:7, bottom left) is of Beaker date; no identification is given by Simpson. Length 152mm. Unit 4, Context 16. Cattle-size scapula/pelvis

Miscellaneous bone objects (Fig 115)

65 (4751) Object made of red-deer antler broken on both sides. Probably originally used complete, possibly as a handle (?). Length 200mm. Unit 4, Context 16
66 (60024) Flat piece of bone with cut notch and one cut circle. Broken. Length 39mm. Unit 4, Context 16. ?Cattle rib
67 (1140) A well-worn object cut from a tibia shaft with very worn rounded ends. If it is a toggle it is unlike the usual Bronze Age examples which are

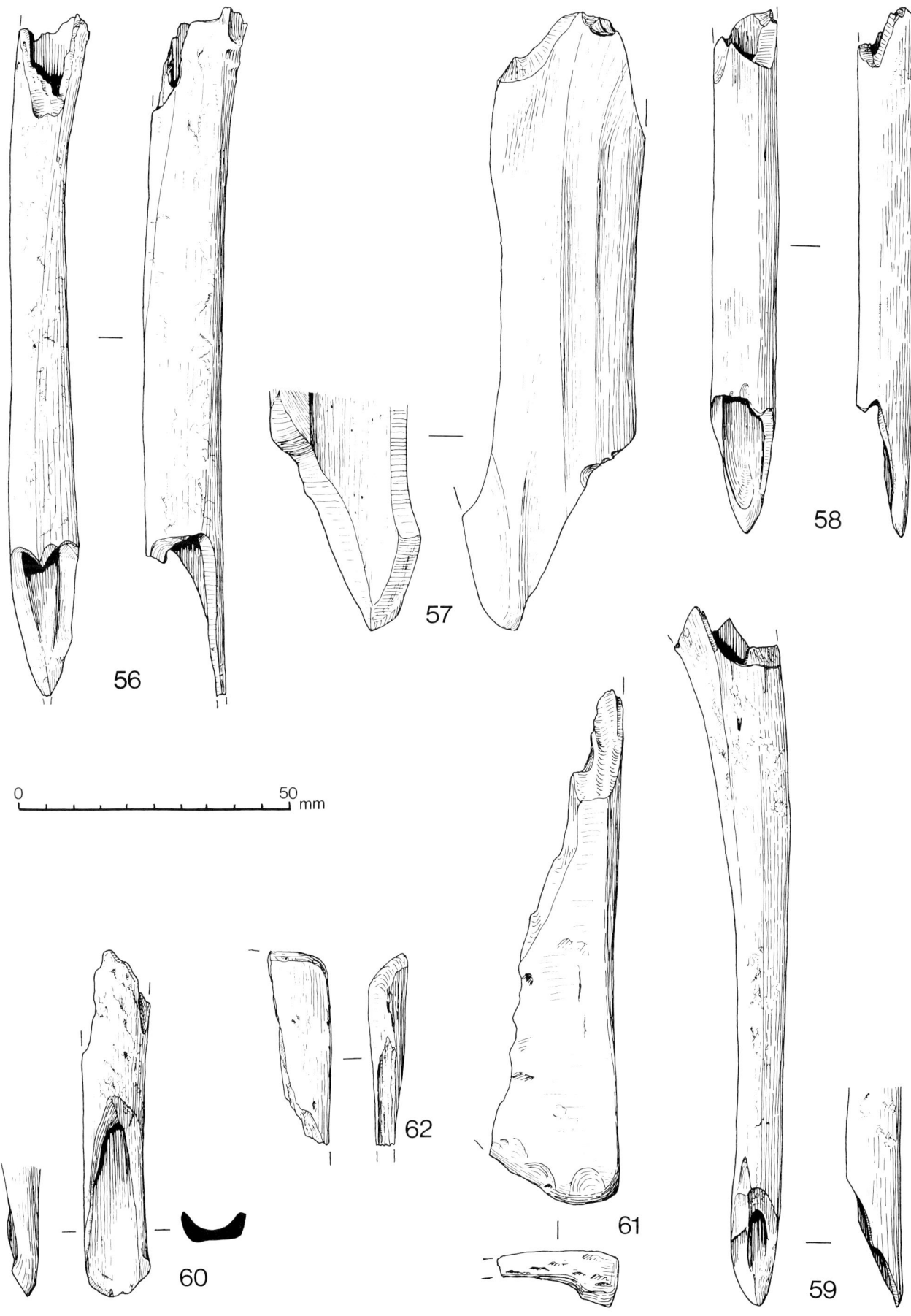

Fig 114   Bone gouges, 'chisel', and smoothers, nos 56–62; scale 1:1

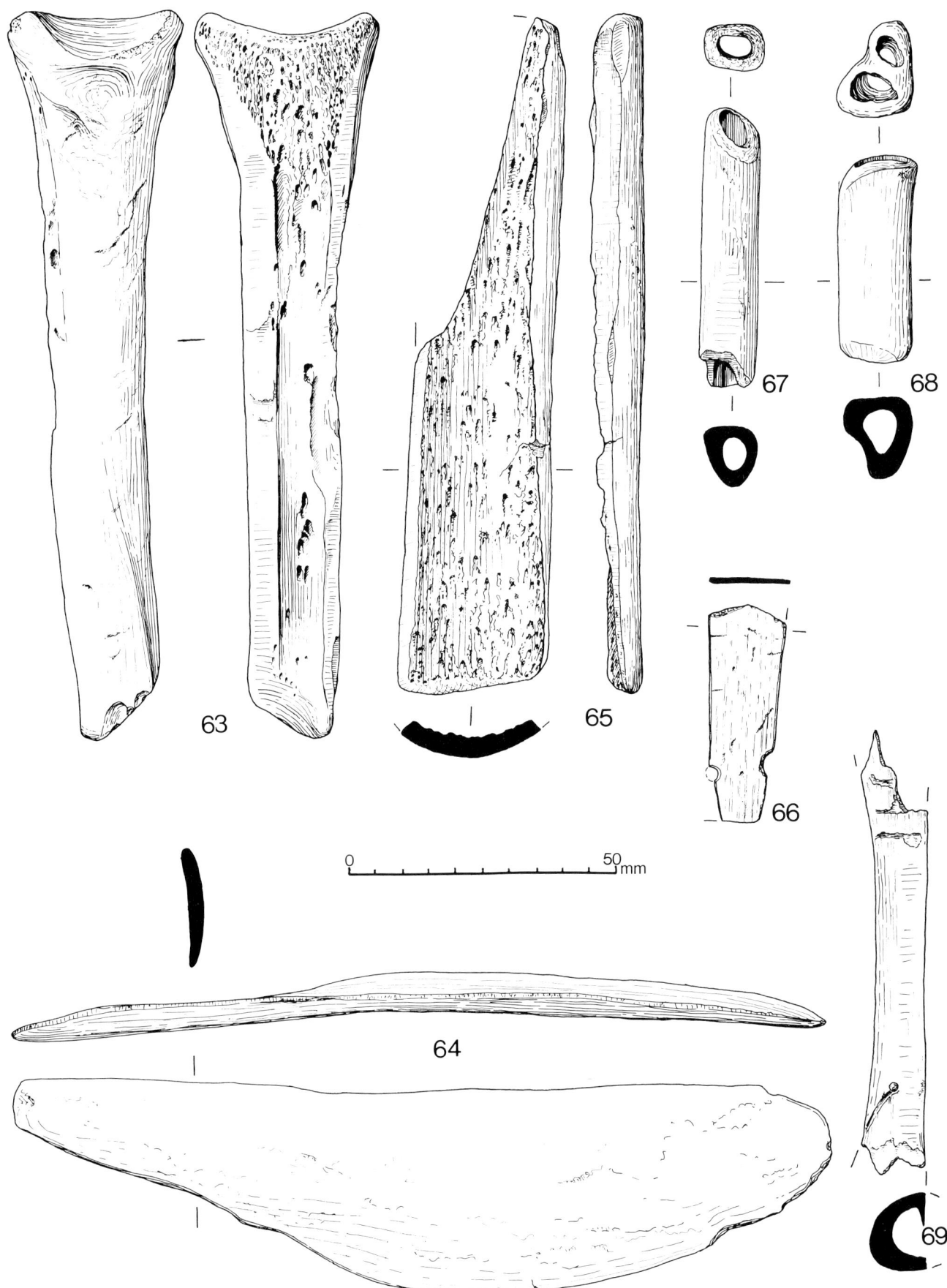

Fig 115 Miscellaneous bone objects, nos 63–69; scale 1:1

pierced through the centre (eg Runnymede Bridge; Longley 1980, 27) and usually of antler. Length 49mm. Unit 4, Context 16. Sheep/goat tibia
68 (4958) Similar object to 67 but cut from a metapodial shaft. Only partly hollow. Very worn with polish over entire surface. Length 32mm. Unit 5b, Context 53. Sheep/goat metacarpal (left proximal)
69 (3309) Bone of Beaker date, a split metapodial with cut marks on the distal end. Length 80mm. Unit 7, Context 62. Sheep/goat metapodial
Not illustrated (1697) Piece of worked bone of trapezoidal shape with two cut and two broken edges. Probably a waste piece. Length 32mm. Unit 4, Context 16. Cattle size bone

Briquetage objects (Figs 116–120)

The salt-making equipment from Brean was confined to the middle Bronze Age contexts, Units 6 and 5b; MF1:C7 outlines the quantities of briquetage and other clay objects found in each of the contexts. The identifiable briquetage consists of two types, three-tined pedestals and brine trays. The catalogue is followed by a detailed discussion.

Pedestals

70 (5520) Almost complete pedestal. The circular pinched out base is slightly rounded underneath with a concave centre. The pedestal shank is circular in section, slightly twisted; the finger-marks of its making can be clearly seen. It flares at the top into three tines, the tips of which are now lost. These are set (as are the tines for all the pedestals) in a T-shaped formation with one opposing the other two. The area between the tines forms a flattened platform. The surface of the entire pedestal is very roughly finished with finger-marks, cracking, and numerous vegetable impressions (probably of chaff with a few indistinct grain impressions). Medium-fired fabric, with vegetable inclusions and sand grains. Surface colour light grey (5YR 8/1), core red (7.5R 4/6). An almost complete pedestal of very similar shape was reported by ApSimon *et al* (1961, fig 30:8), but was unstratified. Height of pedestal 90mm. Diam of base 70mm. Unit 5b, Context 59, Structure 59. Found in the interstices of the stone wall. Fig 119
71 (5463) Top of pedestal with very flat platform. Stumps of two broken tines; the other side is missing. Well made with few finger impressions, like no 70 with circular shank. A few vegetable impressions on surface, including one large chaff fragment. No other visible inclusions. Very pale, light grey surface colour (10YR 8/2). Unit 5b, Context 114, Structure 59
72 (5777, 5783, 5766, 5862) Almost complete pedestal, reconstructed from 20 fragments, smaller than nos 70 and 71. Rounded base with a pronounced concavity in the centre. The shank is carefully smoothed. There are two complete tines (both with rounded ends and approximately 35mm long); the other tine is missing. Vegetable impressions evident on the surface, numerous on the broken inside edges. Surface colour varies from pale orange (5YR 8/4) to light grey (7.5Y 8/1). Unit 5b: 5777 Context 112; 5783, 5766, 5862 Context 93, Structure 95
73 (5740) Top of a pedestal with two remaining tines, both with very rounded ends (approximately 35mm long). The tines are clearly drawn out from the main clay body, not added. A few vegetable impressions on the surface, numerous on the broken edges. Soft, poorly-fired fabric with vegetable inclusions, tiny black flecks, and very occasional small limestone grits. Surface colour light yellow orange (7.5YR 8/4). Unit 5b, Context 93, Structure 95
74 (5691, 5351, 5190, 5172a, 5301, 5765) Pedestal with two remaining tines, lacking the base. Roughly-made shank with deep finger impressions and several finger-prints. The complete tines are much narrower and more pointed than those of the other pedestals and have obviously been drawn out during manufacture, as no 73. Very few vegetable impressions on the surface, although they are evident on the broken edges. Many limestone grits, some 7mm in length, others tiny. Very highly-fired and hard, orange (2.5YR 6/6) fabric. Unit 5b, Context 53
75 (60348, 5049, 5639a – pedestal; 5639b and c – base) Two fragments of a pedestal base and body. Reddish orange (10R 6/6) body with reddish grey (2.5YR 6/1) surface, as no 74. Roughly finished surface with finger-impressions. Base irregular underneath, probably with concave centre. Very rough pedestal shank slightly tapering towards the top, which is much narrower than the other pedestals. The fabric is very hard and highly fired. Vegetable inclusions (locally very common on the surface) and limestone grits up to 7mm in length. Where the pedestal is broken it can clearly be seen that the fabric is twisted and stretched, presumably during manufacture. It is not possible to reconstruct the original height of the pedestal. Diam of base approx 68mm. Unit 5b. Pedestal: 60348 Context 53 (18/4); 5049 Context 53; 5639a Context 129; base: 5639b and c Context 129
76 (6027, 4846) Top of a pedestal in the same fabric as no 75 and originally thought to be the top of this pedestal; if it is then they were broken and widely separated in antiquity (see distribution of briquetage, Fig 46b). This piece is fragmentary, flaring at one side to the base of a tine, which appears to have been drawn out from the body of the clay, not attached. The two joined fragments come from separate structures. Interior 10R 6/6, surface 2.5YR 7/1. Unit 5b: 6027 Context 131, Structure 95; 4846 Context 59, Structure 59
77 (5816) Part of a pedestal with the base of one thin tine and trace of another. Hard fired reddish orange (10R 6/6) body with light grey (2.5Y 7/1)

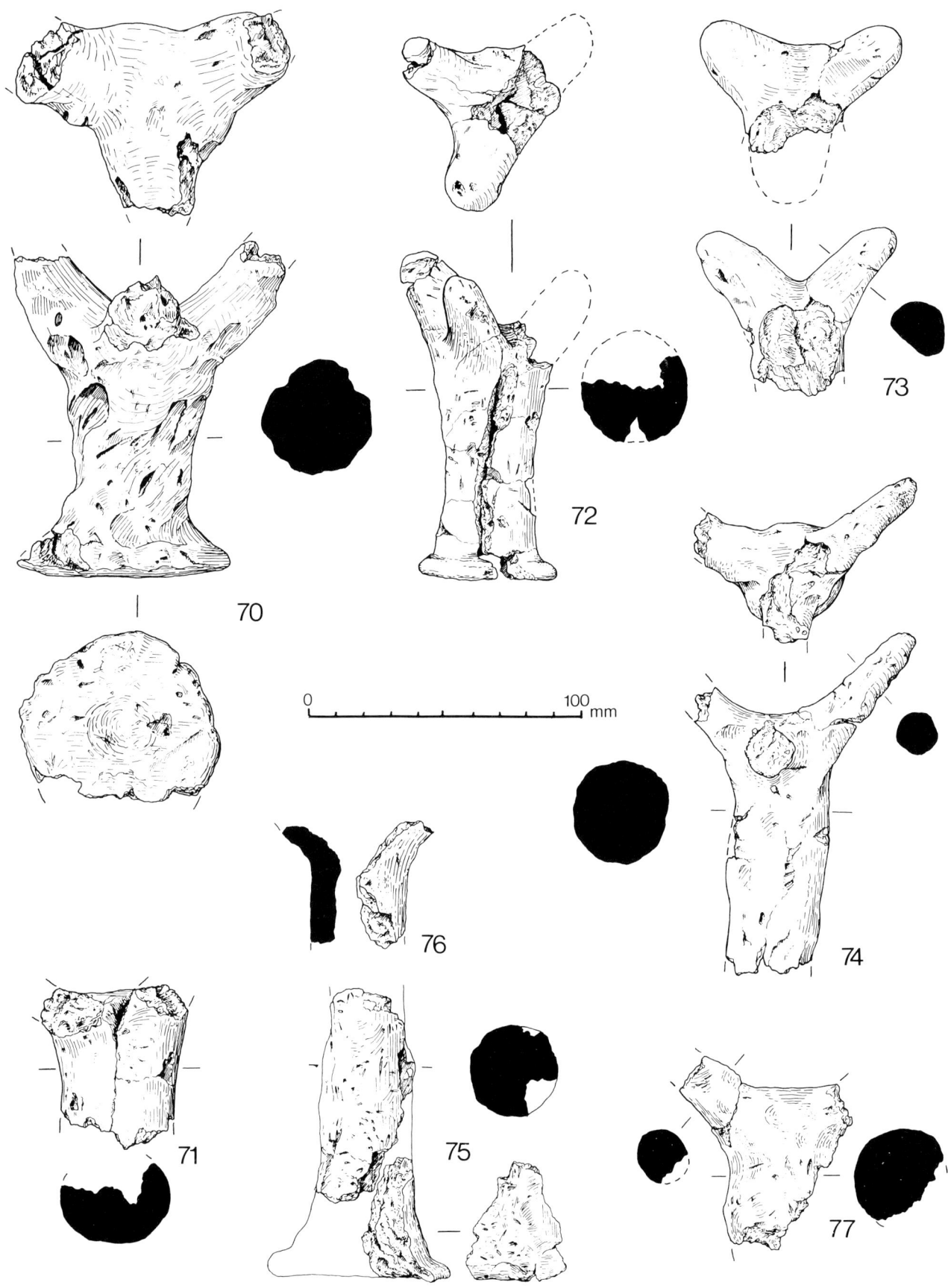

Fig 116   Briquetage pedestals, nos 70–77; scale 1:2

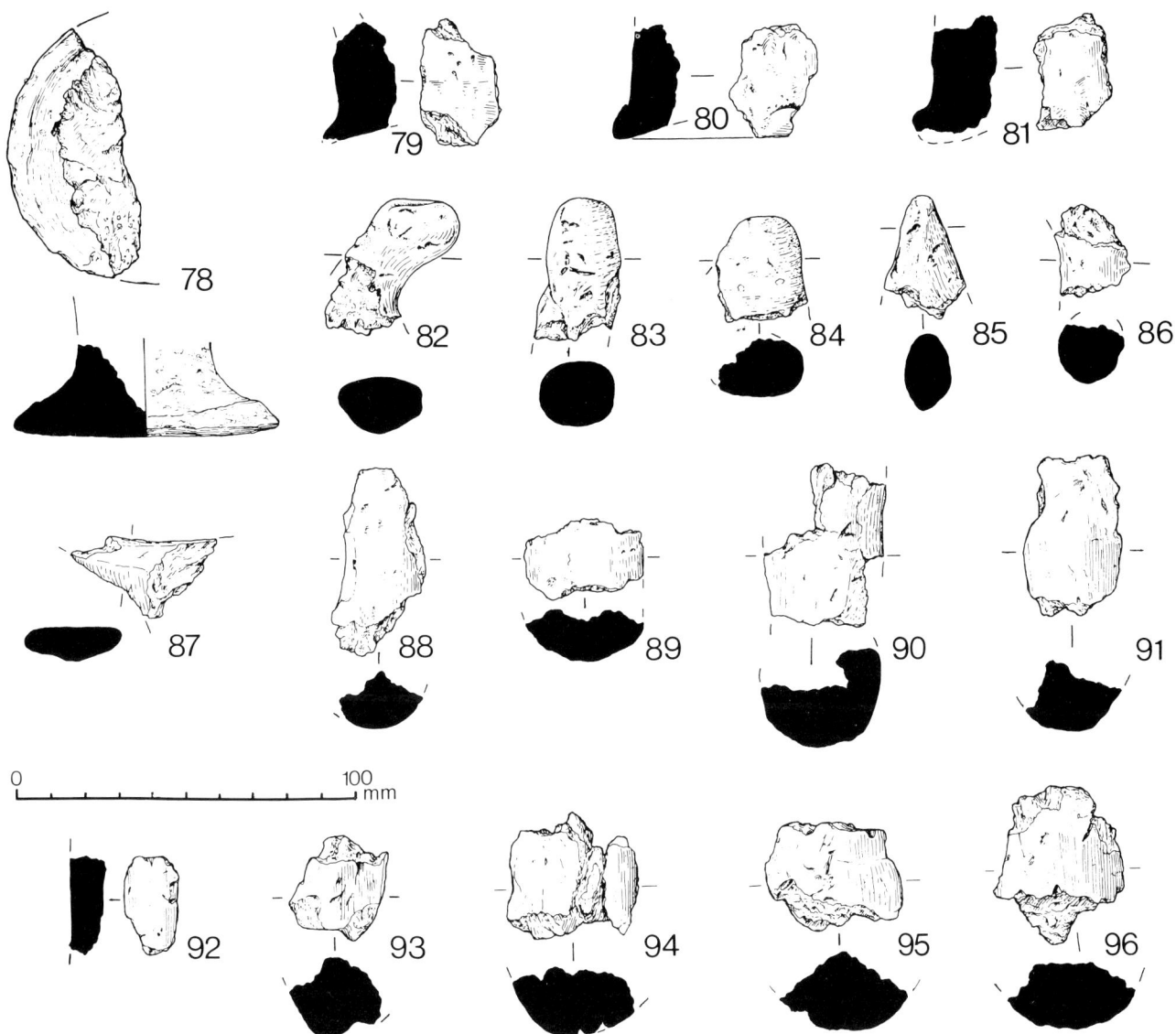

Fig 117 Briquetage pedestals, nos 78–96; scale 1:2

surface. A few surface traces of vegetable material, including cereal grain. Surface smooth with finger impressions, particularly good fingerprints. A few small limestone grits, grog, and small white flecks. Unit 5b, Context 53

78 (247) Part of pedestal base, now very fragile. Larger in diameter than all the other bases but it tapers to a pedestal shank of somewhat similar proportions. The underside of the base is gently curving, not flat, a feature common to the other bases. The flange has been crudely pinched out; the base is not completely circular. A few vegetable impressions on the underside. Dull orange (7.5YR 7/3) exterior, orange (2.5YR 6/6) interior fabric. Vegetable inclusions and limestone grits up to 5mm in length. Diam of base 75mm. Unit 5b, unstratified

79 (4310) Fragment of pedestal base, very highly fired orange (2.5YR 6/6) fabric as nos 74–77. Gritty inclusions (up to 4mm in length) and mica. Unit 5b, Context 53

80 (6039b) Fragment of pedestal base with outturned foot. A few vegetable inclusions and tiny black flecks. Dull yellow orange (10YR 7/4). Unit 5b, Context 60, Structure 59

81 (5675) Very small fragment from a pedestal base with roughly turned-up flange. Vegetable filler and many tiny black flecks. Pale orange (5YR 8/3). Unit 5b, Context 53

82 (5791) Tine from a pedestal, very bulbous in shape with top flattened by a thumb-print. Vegetable impressions on outer surface, numerous tiny black specks and some mica as inclusions. Light yellow orange (7.5YR 8/4). Unit 5b, Context 93, Structure 95

83 (5777) Tine with vegetable impressions found with no 72 but not part of that pedestal. Light yellow orange (10YR 8/3). Unit 5b, Context 112, Structure 95

84 (5717) End of a tine, slightly flattened in section. Surface pale orange (5YR 8/3). Smooth with some vegetable impressions (including an unidentifiable cereal grain). Black flecks and mica. Unit 5b, Context 93, Structure 95

85 (6136) Tine, very flattened with ovoid section. A very short tine (25mm long). Many vegetable

impressions on surface; other inclusions: mica. Light yellow orange (7.5YR 8/3). Unit 5b, Context 131, Structure 95

86 (5864) Part of a tine. Vegetable inclusions on broken surface. Poorly fired soft fabric. Pale orange (5YR 8/3). Unit 5b, Context 93, Structure 95

87 (6310) Possible tine fragment. Very flattened. Highly-fired, almost brittle fabric. No vegetable impressions, minute black specks in fabric. Pale reddish orange (2.5YR 7/4). Unit 5b, Context 53

88 (5777, 5766) Pedestal shank fragment. Vegetable inclusions and tiny black fragments. Found with no 72 but not part of that pedestal. Dull orange (7.5YR 7/3). Unit 5b: 5777 Context 112; 5766 Context 93. Both Structure 95

89 (5777) Another fragment of pedestal shank, possibly from the same pedestal as no 88. Vegetable inclusions on breaks. Light reddish grey (2.5YR 7/2). Unit 5b, Context 112, Structure 95

90 (5777, 5766, 5862) Pedestal shank, vegetable inclusions and tiny black flecks. Diam small (35mm). Possibly from the same pedestal as no 88. Light yellow orange (10YR 8/3). Unit 5b: 5777 Context 112; 5766, 5862 Context 93. All Structure 95

91 (5522) Another fragment of pedestal shank. Pale orange (5YR 8/4). Unit 5b, Context 53

92 (5782) Another fragment. Pale orange (5YR 8/4). Unit 5b, Context 93, Structure 95

93 (5780) Pedestal fragment, very irregular surface. Highly-fired hard fabric. No vegetable inclusions; tiny black flecks only. Pale orange (5YR 8/3). Unit 5b, Context 129

94 (5352) Pedestal fragment. Well-fired fragment with light grey (10YR 8/2) surface; inclusions: tiny black flecks. Unit 5b, Context 53

95 (5820) Fragment of pedestal, with smooth worn surface, pale orange (5YR 8/3) in colour. Some vegetable impressions and finger-print smoothing. Inclusions: vegetable fragments, black flecks, and mica. Unit 5b, Context 103, Structure 59

96 (5425) Fragment from a large pedestal with badly finished exterior. Light grey (10YR 8/2) exterior, pale reddish orange (2.5YR 7/3) interior. A few

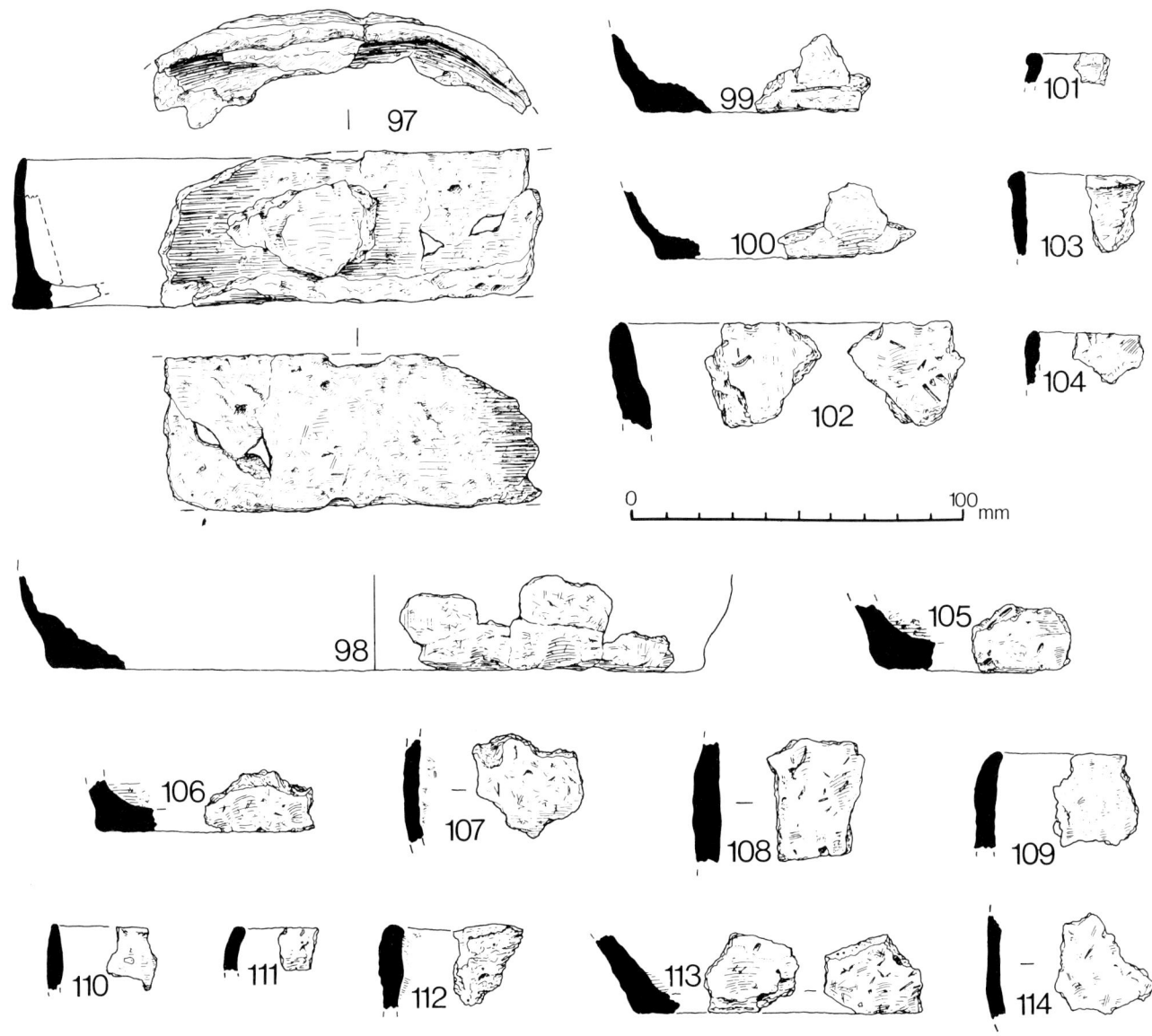

Fig 118   Briquetage trays, nos 97–114; scale 1:2

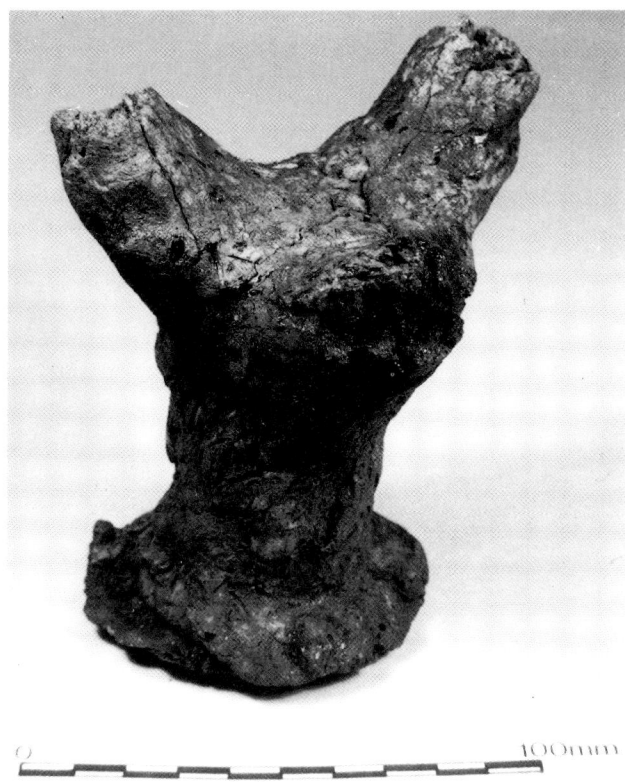

Fig 119 Briquetage pedestal (photo: W Davies)

vegetable impressions on surface, very numerous on broken surface. No other inclusions. Unit 5b, Context 59, Structure 59

Not illustrated
5841 Context 93, Structure 95. Pedestal shank
5699 Context 103, Structure 59. Pedestal shank
5709 Context 53. Pedestal shank
60279 Context 53. Pedestal shank
66   Context 53. Fragment of tine
4019 Context 53. Fragment with a very large unidentifiable seed impression

Evaporation trays

97 (5308) Complete profile of a briquetage evaporation tray. A straight-sided vessel with simple, roughly-made rim and slightly protruding base, the underside of which is very concave (probably distorted). It appears to be a trough with straight sides and curving ends (see discussion below and Fig 120). Another piece of fired clay is attached to the interior of the vessel. The fabric is heavily tempered with vegetable inclusions. It is poorly fired, soft, and was very friable when found. This tray was exposed in the cliff face, etched out and dried by the wind. Such a fragile object might never have been recovered in recognisable form during normal excavation. Dull yellow orange (10YR 7/4). Max depth of tray 40mm, thickness of wall at base 6mm, at rim 4mm. Tapers gradually towards rim which is very thin for the size of the vessel. Unit 5b, Context 60, Structure 59

98 (5822, 5167, 60397a) Base of an evaporation tray, one long curving edge with a diameter of 200mm. There are several circular dimples on the outside of the base, presumably made by fingers pinching the flange together. The underside of the base is flat. The thickness of the wall is unknown as the interior surface has laminated, but it appears markedly thicker towards the base. The tray was at least 25mm deep. Coarsely made with numerous impressions of vegetable remains on the outer surface (including the base) and broken surfaces. Dull orange (7.5YR 7/3) interior. Other inclusions: a few limestone fragments, many tiny black flecks, and mica. Very soft fabric. Unit 5b: 5822, 5167 Context 112; 60397a 16/18. All Structure 95

99 (60397c, 5822) Fragment of tray base, possibly part of no 98. Very laminated inner surface. Vegetable impressions on outer surface, also tiny black flecks. Flat base. Light yellow orange (7.5YR 8/3). Unit 5b, Context 112, Structure 95

100 (60397b) Fragment of tray base, possibly part of no 98, although the fragments do not join. Vegetable inclusions clear on dull orange (7.5YR 7/3) surface. The interior surface is missing. Unit 5b, Context 112, Structure 95

101 (5822) Tiny rim sherd of briquetage evaporation tray, probably part of no 98. Simple bead rim. Vegetable impressions on broken surface, also tiny black specks. Dull orange (7.5YR 7/3). Unit 5b, Context 112, Structure 95

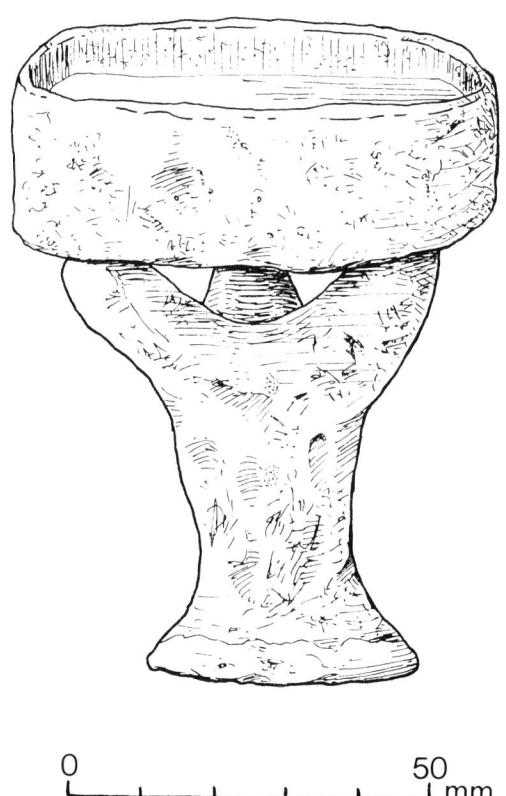

Fig 120 Reconstruction of tray 97 and pedestal 70

Not illustrated

5167 Wall sherd of briquetage tray, probably part of no 98. Unit 5b, Context 112, Structure 95

102 (4719) Rim sherd of tray, very irregular with some thinly pinched areas along top of rim. Reddish grey (2.5YR 5/1) to dark grey (2.5YR 6/3) surface. Soft fabric with vegetable inclusions visible on surface inside and out (including grain impression). Other inclusions: small black flecks and mica. Unit 5b, Context 53

103 (5832a) Nine fragments of tray with one (illustrated) tiny rim sherd. Exactly the same fabric as no 98, very simple bead rim, very friable and crumbly, vegetable impressions on outer surface. Thin walled vessel (c 4mm thick). Pale orange (5YR 8/4) fabric burnt black on external surface. Vegetable inclusions and mica. Unit 5b, Context 139

104 (5832b) Tray rim sherd, possibly part of no 103, same fabric and condition. Pale orange (5YR 8/4) laminated inner surface. Vegetable inclusions and mica. Unit 5b, Context 139

105 (5751) Tray base sherd with unlaminated inner surface, very irregular and pitted. Brownish grey (5YR 6/1) core. Flat base, slightly curved wall in plan. Many vegetable inclusions, including grain, tiny limestone fragments, and mica. Unit 5b, Context 53

106 (5468) Fragment of base, as no 105. Very rough underside. Around outer edges of base are dimples, probably made with a finger-tip, like the edge of a pastry pie. Very numerous vegetable impressions on internal and external surfaces. Pale orange (5YR 8/4) surface. Mica and a few tiny limestone grits and grog. Unit 5b, Context 115 (an early feature of the unit)

107 (5814) Body sherd, vegetable impressions on inner and outer faces. Thin-walled vessel (5mm thick). Unit 5b, Context 53

108 (5974) Nine fragments of tray of which the largest is illustrated. Tray body sherd. 8mm thick, probably from the base of the vessel. Surface pale orange (5YR 8/4). Numerous vegetable impressions. Very soft fabric, very rough outer surface. A few fragments of shell inclusions. Unit 5b, Context 139

109 (5935) Tray rim sherd, rather more substantial than some fragments (max thickness 8mm). Hard orange (2.5YR 6/6) fabric with grits up to 2mm long, black flecks but no vegetable filler. Unit 6α, Context 163

110 (6053) Simple rim sherd, as no 109, red (10R 5/6) highly fired hard fabric, grits up to 5mm long. Blackened interior surface (2.5YR 6/1 reddish grey). Max thickness 4mm. Unit 6α, Context 163

111 (6054) Tray rim sherd as no 109, reddish orange (10R 6/6) fabric. Cream outer surface, inner surface laminated. Black flecks and some grits (up to 1mm). Found with three body sherds. Unit 6α, Context 163

112 (6163) Tray rim sherd as no 109, hard reddish orange (10R 6/6) fabric. Laminated outer surface, flat top, slightly hook rim. Grits up to 4mm long. Unit 6α, Context 163

113 (70010) Tray base sherd, similar in shape to nos 98–101 with flat base and vegetable impressions on outer surface, but reddish orange (10YR 6/6), highly fired and hard fabric, blackened inner surface, and pale dull orange (5YR 7/3) outer surface. Large grits up to 4mm long. Unstratified

114 (60337a) Tray body sherd, hard orange (2.5YR 7/6) fabric, laminating at edges, a few small grits 1mm long and vegetable inclusions. Thin-walled – 5mm thick. Unit 5b, Context 115 (an early feature of the Unit)

Conclusions

The briquetage from Brean Down is of two kinds: pedestals and evaporation trays. There are substantial remains of nine pedestals, which have circular stubby bases, round stems, and three tines protruding from the top. The tines on the pedestals are not set at equal intervals around the pedestals but in a T-shaped formation with one tine opposing the other two. The tines may be stubby with rounded ends, or long and pointed. All of the pedestals have a flattened surface between the tines. In none of the pedestals are the tines applied; they are all drawn out from the body of the clay. The pedestals are roughly made with numerous unsmoothed fingermarks and they vary in size, as is shown in Table 11. Included here is the almost complete pedestal reported by ApSimon *et al* (1961, 120, no 8), obviously part of the same group, although it was unstratified. The three complete pedestals are 90, 90, and 85mm high respectively, but the bases vary from 52–80mm in diameter and the stems 32–40mm.

The evaporation trays are much more fragmentary and scarcer than the pedestals. The most complete example (97) suggests that they were flat based, parallel-sided vessels with curved ends (Fig 120), at least 40mm deep and 120mm long, and probably 60mm wide. They all had very thin walls (most were 4mm thick, although some were 7–8mm), simple roughly-made rims, and pinched bases. In addition to the illustrated pedestals and trays there were also numerous unidentifiable fragments of briquetage (see MF1:C7).

Petrological analysis (see below, report by David Williams) shows that the briquetage could have been, and probably was, made from the local estuarine clay immediately adjacent to the site. The visible fillers in the briquetage were either quartz grits (up to 11mm

Table 11 Variation between briquetage pedestals (measurements in mm)

No	Height	Diam base	Diam stem	Length tine	Distance between tines
70	90	70	40	c 80	c 100
71	-	-	40	-	-
72	85	50	38	c 70	60–80
73	-	-	38	60	60
74	-	-	30	70	100
75	-	70	32	-	-
78	-	80	40	-	-
8*	96	72	36	52	90

*from ApSimon *et al* 1961

in length), eg pedestals 74–77 and trays 109–114, or more commonly chopped vegetable matter, consisting mainly of chaff fragments, eg pedestals 70–73 and the remaining trays. There are several grain impressions, none unfortunately identifiable. The artefacts containing grits are visually distinguishable from those containing vegetable matter in that they are reddish orange in colour, sometimes with a grey surface, and highly fired. Those with a vegetable filler are softer – some indeed can be scraped with a finger-nail – and pale orange in colour. Morris (1985) suggested that firing temperatures for briquetage are low (less than 850°C), which could easily be achieved in a bonfire firing. This certainly appears to be the case at Brean.

The episode of salt-making at Brean Down coincides mainly with the occupation of the two buildings in Unit 5b, Structures 95 and 59 (Fig 46b). Fragments are widely scattered. Significantly, pedestal no 76 consists of two joined fragments, one (4846) from Structure 59, the other (6027) from Structure 95. Several other joined pieces were found over 2m apart (eg nos 6027 and 4846, Fig 116.76). Most of the briquetage came from within the buildings. There was a very large group from Context 112 (including pedestal 72) adjoining the hearth. A few tray fragments were associated with pedestals (eg pedestals 89–90 and trays 98–101 from 112) but on the whole trays came from contexts without pedestal fragments. Presumably this dichotomy is the result of their differing uses (see below). A few fragments of trays came from earlier contexts: one group from 163 (107–112) is from Unit 6α within the floor of Structure 57; another two (106 and 114) are from an early phase of Unit 5b (Context 115). There are no joins between layers and no briquetage from Unit 4. Radiocarbon dates suggest that salt was made here during a period between c 3500 and 2600 BP, as the following dates show: Unit 6α: 3310±80 BP (HAR-7020); Unit 5b (103): 3420±100 BP (HAR-7016); Unit 5b: 2940±100 BP (HAR-7019), 2870±80 BP (HAR-7018), 2730±100 BP (HAR-7017).

The processes involved in prehistoric salt production are still somewhat problematical. Gouletquer (1974, 2) gives a clear and concise analysis of the essential stages; briquetage could be used firstly to evaporate brine and secondly to dry the wet salt. Riehm (1961, 183) experimented with replicas of sand-tempered containers from Halle, dated c 1000 BC, and found that because the containers were porous the brine was sucked up by the clay and split the containers when it was heated. He concluded that it was not possible to produce salt from the stemmed goblets, that they were only for drying the wet salt into standardised salt cakes, and that the brine was first evaporated in large open containers. Many prehistoric sites have produced evidence for this two-stage process. The initial phase could take place in two ways. The first is by solar evaporation, eg in tanks beside the saline springs or on the beach as in Neolithic Poland (Jodlowski 1975, 85) and Roman Essex (de Brisay 1978). The second possibility is to use thick-walled salt-boiling containers as in the Netherlands (van den Broeke 1986), where large vessels were used to produce the wet salt. These have the same form as domestic vessels, but have a fabric like briquetage, porous, soft, and with a vegetable temper. A reconstruction drawing suggests the simple process used (ibid, fig 11) with these vessels; afterwards small open-ended half cylinders were used for drying the salt. Many other sites have produced large briquetage vessels used for evaporating the brine (eg in Lincolnshire: May 1976, 149).

There is no evidence that solar evaporation was used on the beach at Brean, although it may be significant that the tidal range in the Severn Estuary is the second largest in the world. Because particularly high tides only occur every two weeks for a few days, it would have been possible to concentrate sea water by solar evaporation on the upper foreshore between particularly high tides. Bradley suggests June to August as the optimum time for this activity (Bradley 1975, 22); this is also the time of highest salinity in the Bristol Channel (Bassindale 1943, 14–20). Records show that salinity at Weston-super-Mare is 27.3 pp thousand in summer (approximately 80% of sea water) and only 22.1 in winter, owing to dilution by floods from the Severn. Further up the estuary at Aust, salinity is only 50% of sea water. It must be emphasised that no structures have been found on the beach at Brean, nor is there any evidence for other ways of concentrating the brine, such as washing ashes or salt-impregnated clay (Nenquin 1961, 122; Gouletquer 1974, 3). No large briquetage vessels have been found either, unless the clay slabs from 5b represent such a vessel (see nos 119–121). It is possible that ordinary domestic pottery was used as a first stage (P van den Broeke, pers comm), but it seems more likely, in the dearth of any other evidence, that the trays were used for the entire process. Experiments by Matthias (quoted in Kleinmann 1975, 45) showed that replicas of early Halle vessels (c 1800 BC) could have been used directly over heat for evaporating the brine. The difference between these and the containers used by Riehm is that they were thin-walled and straw-tempered.

The brine could easily have been transported from the beach to the Brean settlement in portable containers. We then envisage that it was poured into the evaporation trays, each set on a pedestal and placed around the hearths in Structures 59 and 95 (see reconstructions, Figs 45 and 50). It has been suggested (A Saville, pers comm) that the pedestals would be more stable with the tines pointing downwards. However, the almost complete pedestal (70) is remarkably stable on its 70mm wide base, despite broken edges; also the three tips lie on a circle with a diameter of 110mm, ample for the small trays from Brean, and similar to the support given by modern primus stoves.

Supported on its pedestal the tray would have air circulating beneath, aiding evaporation from the porous sides of the vessel. It is probable that the trays were rectangular with rounded corners (Fig 120), like the Hallstatt containers from Nalliers (de Fleury 1888; Riehm 1961), or the Iron Age vessels from Quiberon (Wilmer 1908, fig 25). Incidentally those latter have very thin walls but incurving sides; they could not have been used as moulds for salt cakes, but must have been directly involved in drying the brine. Tray no 97, the largest fragment, has one straight edge with curving corners at either end; this edge is approximately the same length as the distance between tines. It is just possible that the trays were triangular to match the three-pronged pedestals.

Kay de Brisay has emphasised the fact that brine need not be boiled to produce salt crystals and this is borne out by the fact that none of the briquetage has sooting on the surface. Kleinmann (1975, 45) suggested a temperature of 60–70°C, and by experiment has found that the optimum heat is obtained 200–300mm above the fire. The hearth in Structure 95 was substantial enough to give plenty of gentle heat for evaporation. The fuel used was probably peat which gives a steady heat without flames or much stoking. It is envisaged that the brine was topped up as the salt crystals formed until the entire tray was full of crystalline salt. That the trays were, indeed, used for brine processing is confirmed by analysis by John Evans (see below, p 173). A fascinating account of industrial salt-making in Niger (Gouletquer 1975) indicates that evaporation would take some hours. Here the containers were left overnight, balanced over a fire on three-pronged supports, and the salt cakes were ready by the morning. Nothing was salvaged; all the briquetage was broken up to get the salt cakes out.

There is some evidence that salt cakes were traded in their clay containers. At Son en Breugel, Netherlands, a site with origins in the sixth century BC has produced semi-cylindrical open-ended briquetage vessels. The fabric is typical of briquetage (Van den Broeke forthcoming, 2) and contains coastal diatoms, but the site is 100km from the sea. Van den Broeke suggests that the half cylinders probably travelled in pairs, possibly tied together with string (ibid, 4), and sherds have been found at least 200km from the coast. The earliest British evidence for salt trading comes from Iron Age Kimmeridge (Riehm 1961) and Droitwich (Morris 1985). Morris's distribution maps of briquetage produced at Droitwich are convincing; at the period of maximum production the products extended over an area of a radius 100km from Droitwich. Some of the trays from Brean are very fragile, unlike those from the Netherlands and Droitwich, and are probably under-represented in the archaeological record. There was no reason, of course, to move the pédestals from the point of manufacture, and they were probably reused a number of times.

There remains only to discuss the production of salt elsewhere in Europe at this period and to trace the antecedents of the briquetage from Brean. Gouletquer's wide-ranging survey of salt-making in prehistoric Europe (1974) exemplifies the variety of briquetage used. All sources were utilised from salt springs to salt mines and the sea. Sometimes brine was concentrated in open pools by evaporation, sometimes in large open containers over hearths. There is growing evidence for salt manufacture using briquetage during the Neolithic. Salt springs were definitely being exploited in Poland during the Neolithic (Jodlowski 1975); here brine was evaporated in large pots, then the salt was dried in small cups. Production continued until the Roman period. Recent excavations (1978) have also produced Neolithic briquetage from Halle-Dölauer Heide, in the Saale area in Central Germany (Müller 1987), where small stemmed cups were used from the period of the Körös culture. There is direct evidence about production methods here from about c 1800 BC. The salt-making was around hearths in ordinary occupation structures, some way from the brine source (Matthias 1976; Kleinmann 1975). The rectangular flat-bottomed and chaff-tempered vessels, each supported on two flat-topped pedestals, were remarkably similar to those from Brean Down. By 1000 BC, however, the industry had expanded and a typological series of briquetage can be distinguished with large pans for heating the brine and chalice-like vessels in which to dry the salt into equal-sized salt cakes.

Most other European examples of salt-working are concentrated around the coast, and variations in typology abound. Other sites in Germany begin c 800 BC; eg from Rüssen (River Elster) came three-horned briquetage pedestals for the production of inland salt, very similar to those from Brean (von Simon 1988, Abb 2). Hallstatt sites clustered around the Gironde estuary in France used cylindrical pots resting on trumpet-ended pedestals (Gouletquer 1974, 7), gradually by the La Tène period to be replaced with T-shaped pedestals and rectangular vessels. In the Pays de Retz, Loire Estuary (Tessier 1975), a group of sites have been dated by radiocarbon from 2700±200 BP (no lab number given) to the Roman period (AD 160). The earliest briquetage again is pedestals with cup-shaped ends on which rested cylindrical vessels ('augets'), 50mm in diameter. Later, rectangular vessels were used, as in the Gironde. In the La Tène period rectangular vessels with three-pronged and T-shaped supports were used in the Vendée at Nalliers (de Fleury 1888). In Brittany there is a contrast between the north coast, where cylindrical thick-walled vessels were balanced on fire bars, and the south coast, where rectangular thin-walled vessels were used (Gouletquer 1974, 8). The earliest briquetage in the Netherlands dates from c the sixth century BC: large vessels with the same form as domestic pottery but made of briquetage fabric (van den Broeke 1986), with half cylinders for drying.

Darvill has posed the question why salt production increased in the early first millennium BC and postulates that the increase in ranching and the need to salt meat may provide an answer (1987a, 130). The earliest salt-producing sites in Britain are c 1400 BC, slightly later than the Halle sites, but earlier than the earliest French and Belgian coastal sites. Production at Brean began c 3400–3300 BP, while from the Hullbridge Basin (River Crouch, Essex) charcoal associated with a salt-production hearth has a radiocarbon date of 3020±90 BP (HAR-5733; Wilkinson and Murphy 1986, 187). Late Bronze Age pottery was associated with straw-tempered briquetage vessels, very similar to those from Brean, with simple rims, thin walls (6mm), and pinched bases. The trays were supported on T-shaped pedestals like those from the Gironde. Slight evidence from Fengate, in the form of a few pedestal fragments, a snapped sherd, and a shell-gritted bowl (Pryor 1980b, 18), date between 1280 and 935 BC (Gurney 1980, 7). Nearby at Northey, near Peterborough, a site dated to c 1200–

900 BC, there were 83 fragments of briquetage (Gurney 1980) with a few flared pedestal bases and fragments of vessels. These had shell inclusions and were thicker-walled than the Brean vessels (10–19mm): the largest vessel had a diameter, if round, of 200mm. Slightly later, in the sixth century BC (2490±80 BP (HAR-3092)), there are triangular fire bars and briquetage fragments from Hogsthorpe, Lincs (Kirkham 1981), and pedestals from Mucking with one end cupped and the other spatulate (Jones 1977, 317). Like Halle (Kleinmann 1975, 46), Mucking is at least 2km from the nearest salt water source, so some transportation of brine must have been involved.

There is a great increase of sites with briquetage in the late first millennium around the coast of southern Britain, eg at Kimmeridge (Riehm 1961, 185), in Essex (eg de Brisay 1975), and in Lincolnshire (Swinnerton 1932; May 1976); there is also the first good evidence for commercial exploitation of rock salt at Droitwich (Morris 1985). In the Somerset Levels south of Brean Down briquetage mounds are numerous and very similar to the Red Hills of Essex (de Brisay 1975), with heaps of ash, hearths, broken briquetage, and pottery (Leech 1981b). Few have been excavated, but fieldwork suggests a range of sites from the first century BC to c AD 300. Recently a mound dated to c AD 200 was excavated at East Huntspill (Leech et al 1983). The briquetage was totally different from that from the Bronze Age levels at Brean Down, with a complex system of notched tiles (hearth wall) supporting fire bars and long pedestals (ibid, 75; Leech 1981b, 34). It is interesting that, as at Brean, peat was again used as a fuel (Leech et al 1983, 78).

By the late Iron Age salt production in Britain was far more complex than it appears to have been in the Bronze Age, when salt crystallisation and drying took place in domestic buildings on a small scale. In the late first millennium salt-making was on an industrial scale with the appropriate industrial waste in the form of mounds which are still visible today.

Petrological examination of Bronze Age briquetage

by David Williams

The following pieces were examined: 5777 pedestal tine (Fig 117.83); 5522 pedestal fragment (Fig 117.91); 5814 fragment of tray (Fig 118.107).

Frequent subangular quartz grains, average size 0.30–0.60mm, with some flecks of mica, chert, quartzite, limestone, sandstone, calcite, and a few very dark brown grains which may be limonite. Limonite has been identified in an examination of the soil samples at Brean Down (Cornwall 1961). A local origin seems highly likely. It is interesting to see in thin section that the non-plastic inclusions are not generally spread evenly throughout the clay matrix, but often appear as lenses in the fabric. This suggests that the clay received the minimum of attention before being fired.

Analysis of briquetage fragments

by John Evans

Briquetage from a series of contexts was submitted for analysis – five pedestals and three tray fragments. Two representative samples were removed from each. The samples were crushed, passed through a 125μm mesh sieve and 0.5g of the fine material used for the analysis. Initially the material was extracted with hot water (distilled), and subsequently with a mixture of hot concentrated nitric and perchloric acids (in the ratio 10:2 v/v). The resulting solutions, suitably diluted, were examined for sodium, potassium, calcium, and magnesium ions. The former two ions were determined by flame photometry, the latter two by atomic absorption spectroscopy.

The details of the samples submitted and the results obtained are given in Table 12. The data obtained for the water extracts show a relatively even distribution of each element across the various contexts and structures. Such data can be considered to reflect the 'natural' background levels. The acid extractions, however, show two distinct groups which correspond with the types of briquetage. The marked increases in the levels of all four elements, especially the magnesium values, suggest that the tray material was associated directly with brine processing, magnesium concentrations being higher than those of calcium in sea water. The relatively low values for magnesium for the pedestal group may well reflect the water used for mixing the clay, as opposed to brine. In conclusion, it seems that the trays were associated more or less directly with brine processing, whilst the pedestals fulfilled a supporting role.

Table 12 Chemical analysis of briquetage

Pub no	Find and context no		Water extraction (ppm)				Acid extraction (ppm)			
			Na^+	K^+	Ca^{2+}	Mg^{2+}	Na^+	K^+	Ca^{2+}	Mg^{2+}
84	5717 (93)	Pedestal tine	8–9	1–2	3–4	2–3	12–14	7–8	50–52	20–21
70	5520 (59)	Pedestal body	6–8	1–2	3–4	2–3	12–14	7–8	40–42	23–25
95	5820 (103)	Pedestal body	7–8	1–2	4–5	1–2	14–16	7–8	44–46	21–23
–	4406 (53)	Fragments of pedestal	8–9	3–4	3–4	1–2	12–14	8–9	43–45	25–27
77	5816 (53)	Pedestal top	6–8	1–2	2–3	2–3	10–12	7–8	48–50	30–32
106	5468 (115)	Base of tray (int)	5–7	3–4	3–5	1–2	33–35	15–17	150–155	200–220
108	5974 (139)	Tray	7–8	1–2	4–6	2–3	28–30	14–16	160–165	250–260
103	5832 (139)	Tray rim	8–9	3–4	5–7	2–3	30–32	12–14	180–185	240–245

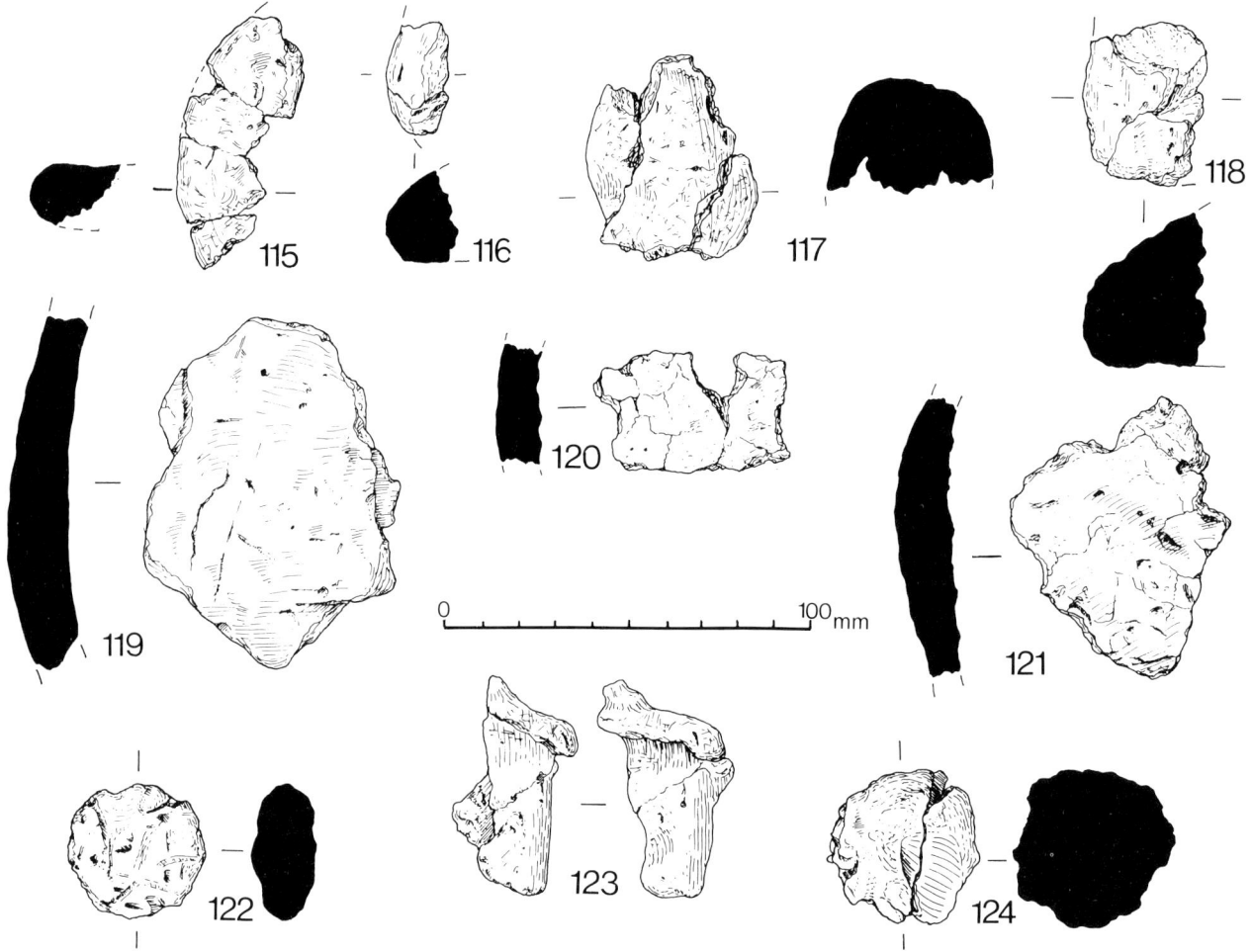

Fig 121   Fired clay artefacts, nos 115–124; scale 1:2

Fired clay objects (Fig 121)

Possible loomweight fragments

115 (60416a) Fragmentary fired-clay object, flat with a curving side. Possibly part of a loomweight of unusual type. Vegetable impressions numerous. Black reduced core, grey surface. There were three other fragments (60416), either part of this object or part of no 117. Probably Unit 5b, Context 93

116 (66) Small fragment of fired clay object similar in shape to no 114 (60416a) but visually different: smooth surface, very few vegetable inclusions, pale orange-pink colour throughout. Possibly part of a loomweight, but a different one from no 115. Unit 5b, Context 53.

117 (60416/5966) Piece of fired clay shaped roughly into a sausage shape similar to the briquetage pedestals. It is possible that it is part of a distorted pedestal, but just as likely that it was part of a bun-shaped loomweight (eg like those from Aldermaston: Bradley *et al* 1980, 243). Many vegetable inclusions. Black reduced core, cream surface. Unit 5b: 5966 Context 93; 60416 probably Context 93

118 (4768) Fired clay object, probably part of a loomweight. Very roughly made. Red surface, black reduced core. Fairly hard fired. No vegetable inclusions, but small grits and mica. Unit 4, Context 16

Not illustrated

4591 Fragment of fired clay possibly from a loomweight. No vegetable inclusions but many small grits. Red oxidised surface, grey core. Unit 4, Context 16

Slabs

119 (5882) Large piece of poorly-fired clay slab, slightly curving in cross-section and very roughly made. Pieces of charcoal adhere to the convex surface. Vegetable impressions obvious on both surfaces. Inclusions: mica and small grits. Grey colour throughout. Thickness 17–12mm. Unit 5b, Context 155. There was another fragment from the same context, thickness 14mm

120 (5967) Another. Vegetable impressions on both faces, other edges all broken. Thickness 12mm. Unit 5b, Context 155

121 (60416d) Another. Grey colour, vegetable inclusions, mica and small grits. Thickness 13–16mm. Probably from Unit 5b, Context 93

These fragments of clay slab (nos 119–121) probably all come from the same object. It is possible that they were part of a very large briquetage vessel (see above, p 171) used in an initial stage for evaporating brine. More likely is that they are fragments from a domed oven.

Miscellaneous fired clay objects

122 (50162) Circular fired-clay 'counter', very rough and crudely made with deep vegetable impressions over the entire surface. Diam 35mm, thickness 14mm. Unit 4, Soil Pit 2, Context 43
123 (6181) Fragmentary piece of highly-fired clay, probably a rejected piece of briquetage. Unit 6α, Context 156
124 (5184) Clay ball. Bright red surface, reduced black core. Unit 5b, Context 53

Geological specimens

by Reg Bradshaw

Seventy-one geological specimens were submitted for identification (MF1:C8–10). Most could have come from Brean Down, which is predominantly Carboniferous Limestone variably dolomitised with thin layers of purplish or reddish dolomitic siltstones, mudstones, or shales. Of particular interest are the pieces of calcite, 9 from Unit 5b and 15 from Unit 4, in view of the fact that the pottery from Unit 4 is calcite gritted. Calcite is locally abundant: (1) in the limestones; (2) in somewhat decomposed granular aggregates (bioclastic limestones); and (3) as pieces of vein calcite.

Some of the specimens are not immediately local but could come from the Mendips or Clevedon/Nailsea area. These include, particularly, some sandstones (two from Unit 4, two from Unit 5b) which are very similar to the Pennant Sandstone. There are also five specimens of dark, somewhat bituminous, polished shales from Units 5a and 4 which could be Coal Measures, and two pieces which might possibly be Triassic sandstones. Another fragment which may have been imported to the site for utilisation is 4356 from Unit 4, a highly calcareous ochreous sand. Two specimens contain copper minerals: one stratified (5344 from Context 59, Unit 5b) contains malachite with a little chalcopyrite, with dark brown rather glassy-looking iron ore; another unstratified (70053 from the beach) is limestone with chalcopyrite, malachite, iron ore, and calcite. It is not suggested that this final specimen from the beach was brought to the site in prehistory by man but it does indicate the local presence of copper minerals. Indeed copper vein has been recorded on Brean, although it is not mentioned in the IGS Weston-super-Mare memoir.

34 (1776) Spindle whorl from Unit 4, Context 16 (Fig 111). Originally thought to be stone, but examination in thin section showed it to be well-tempered pottery. It consists almost entirely of quartz temper (30% of total) which is well sorted with grains up to 0.3mm in diameter in a brown fine-grained anisotropic matrix. In addition to predominantly angular quartz are one or two plagioclase feldspar and one calcite grain, and one or two fine-grained, haematite-stained sandstone pieces. The particles show no preferred orientation.
35 (5624) Shale tool from Unit 5b, Context 112 (Fig 111). Compact, highly calcareous, silty shale

Not illustrated
3537 Unit 4, Context 16. Hammerstone of oolitic limestone
1710 Unit 4, Context 16. Hammerstone of red sandstone

The first two of these stone artefacts are of locally available stone, while the sandstone probably comes from the Mendips or Clevedon/Nailsea area.

C Environmental and economic evidence

15 Physical and chemical characteristics of the stratigraphy

by Sheila M Ross

Introduction

Two series of samples were taken for analysis of particle size and sediment chemistry. In the vertical dimension, the basic stratigraphic sequence was examined by analysis of samples from 12 of the major stratigraphic units. The main trends in these physical and chemical properties are illustrated in Figures 122 and 123, which summarise the numerical data presented for individual samples in MF1:C11 and C12.

In the horizontal dimension, samples were taken on a grid from the main occupation surface, Unit 5b, to investigate the relationship between sediment chemistry and the Bronze Age structures. The results of these analyses are presented diagrammatically in Figures 124 and 125.

The prime objective of physical and chemical analysis was to characterise the main sedimentary units as a basis for further archaeological and palaeoenvironmental interpretations. It was hoped, for instance, that it would help augment and quantify the field evidence for physical events such as soil erosion and wind-blown sand accumulation. Furthermore, it was hoped that chemical analysis, of the Unit 5b surface in particular, would throw light on prehistoric activity patterns and would explain phenomena such as the green, yellow, and brown stained horizons associated with the occupation deposits, particularly Unit 5b. A subsidiary aim of chemical and physical sediment analysis was to complement micromorphological evidence outlined in Chapter 16 and to aid explanation of magnetic susceptibility variations (Chapter 17).

Analytical methods

Sediment samples from 12 contexts were analysed for particle size using the wet sieving and sedimentation procedure described by Avery and Bascomb (1974), after pretreatment with hydrogen peroxide to remove organic matter and cementing substances. Fine fractions in suspension were sampled by pipette. Forms of carbon in the sediment samples were determined using (i) loss on ignition (LOI) at 450°C for 16 hours; (ii) organic carbon was determined using a modified version of the wet oxidation technique described by Walkley and Black (1934), in which the titration end point was determined using 1,10-phenanthroline ferrous sulphate complex solution (0.025M); and (iii) calcium carbonate content was determined using Bascomb calcimeter (Bascomb 1961). Crystalline (immobile) and gel (mobile) forms of iron in sediments were determined in dithionite and pyrophosphate extractions respectively (Bascomb 1968), followed by atomic absorption spectrophotometry using a Pye Unicam SP9. Total phosphorus contents were determined in solution using the colorimetric method of Murphy and Riley (1962) after alkaline oxidation (Dick and Tabatabai 1977). Total nitrogen in the sediments of Unit 5b was determined using a sulphuric acid and hydrogen peroxide microdigestion (Allen *et al* 1974), followed by automated colorimetric detection of ammonium nitrogen in solution using the method of Crooke and Simpson (1972).

Results of stratigraphic analyses

Particle size analysis of the sediments

Sediment samples were divided into the seven different particle size fractions shown on Figure 122, which indicates how the particle size distribution varies through the stratigraphic sequence. The raw data are given in MF1:C11. Working up through the stratigraphy, the main trends are noted below. Cornwall (1961) considers that the palaeosol, Unit 8a, overlying the Upper Breccia, first developed as a *terra fusca*, derived from the *in situ* weathering of Carboniferous Limestones. Soil micromorphological evidence (Chapter 16) indicates that while the basal part of the palaeosol is influenced by relict *terra fusca* the palaeosol is a complex argillic brown earth, with Flandrian weathered additions of aeolian silt and sand. Down-profile, the palaeosol shows decreasing coarse and medium sized sand fractions, with increasing fine silt and clay sized fractions. The clay fraction rises to as much as 40% at the base of the profile, with the fine silt fraction as high as 60%. The high silt fraction provides some supportive evidence for the view that the palaeosol is analogous to the palaeo-argillic brown earth currently forming in loessial deposits over Carboniferous Limestones in several locations in the Mendips, and described by Findlay *et al* (1983) as Nordrach Association.

Moving up the stratigraphic sequence from the palaeosol, textural characteristics of the wind-blown sand sequences, 7 and 5d, are seen as peaks in the medium and coarse sand fractions (up to 20–45% and 40–60% respectively), combined with very low amounts of total silt and clay (10–15% for both fractions). Unit 5a also shows a peak in coarse sand, at about 80%, but a significantly lower (20%) content of medium sand, compared to the other sand layers.

The majority of samples in Units 7, 5d, and 5a are classified as loamy sands, with a few samples classed as sandy loams. All are significantly more coarse in texture than every other unit in the stratigraphic sequence with the exception of Context 25 (colluvial sheet wash) in Unit 4a and Context 31 (early Christian cemetery) in Unit 3c2. These coarse materials represent wind-blown and transported (?eroded) deposits separating three Bronze Age occupation layers in the stratigraphy (Units 6a, 5b, and 4).

For each of the Bronze Age occupation layers, the major stratigraphic elements were analysed to provide background textural information. These were Context 61, representing Unit 6a, Context 53, repre-

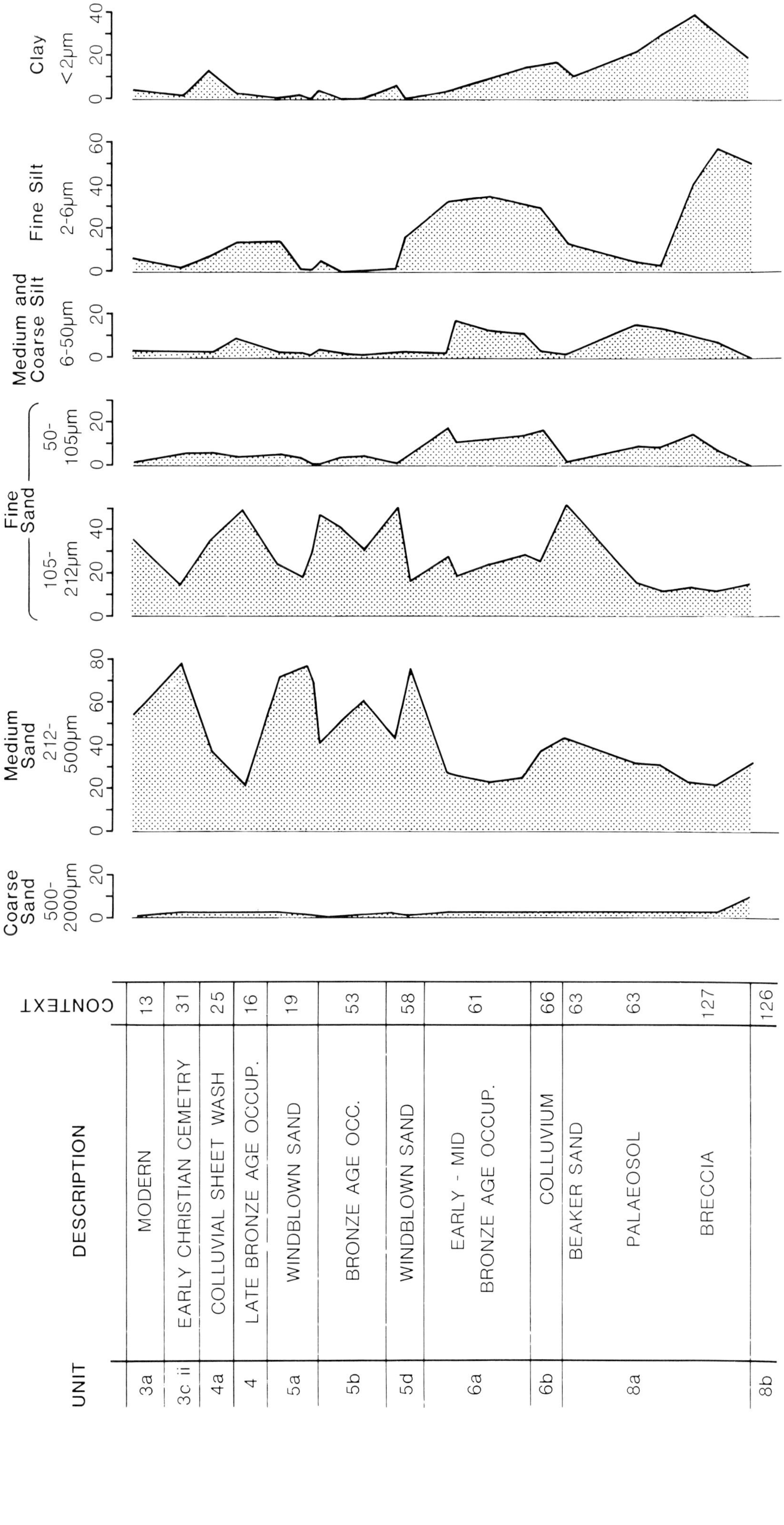

PHYSICAL AND CHEMICAL CHARACTERISTICS

Fig 122 Particle size distribution for sediments of 12 of the major stratigraphic contexts (all values are percentages)

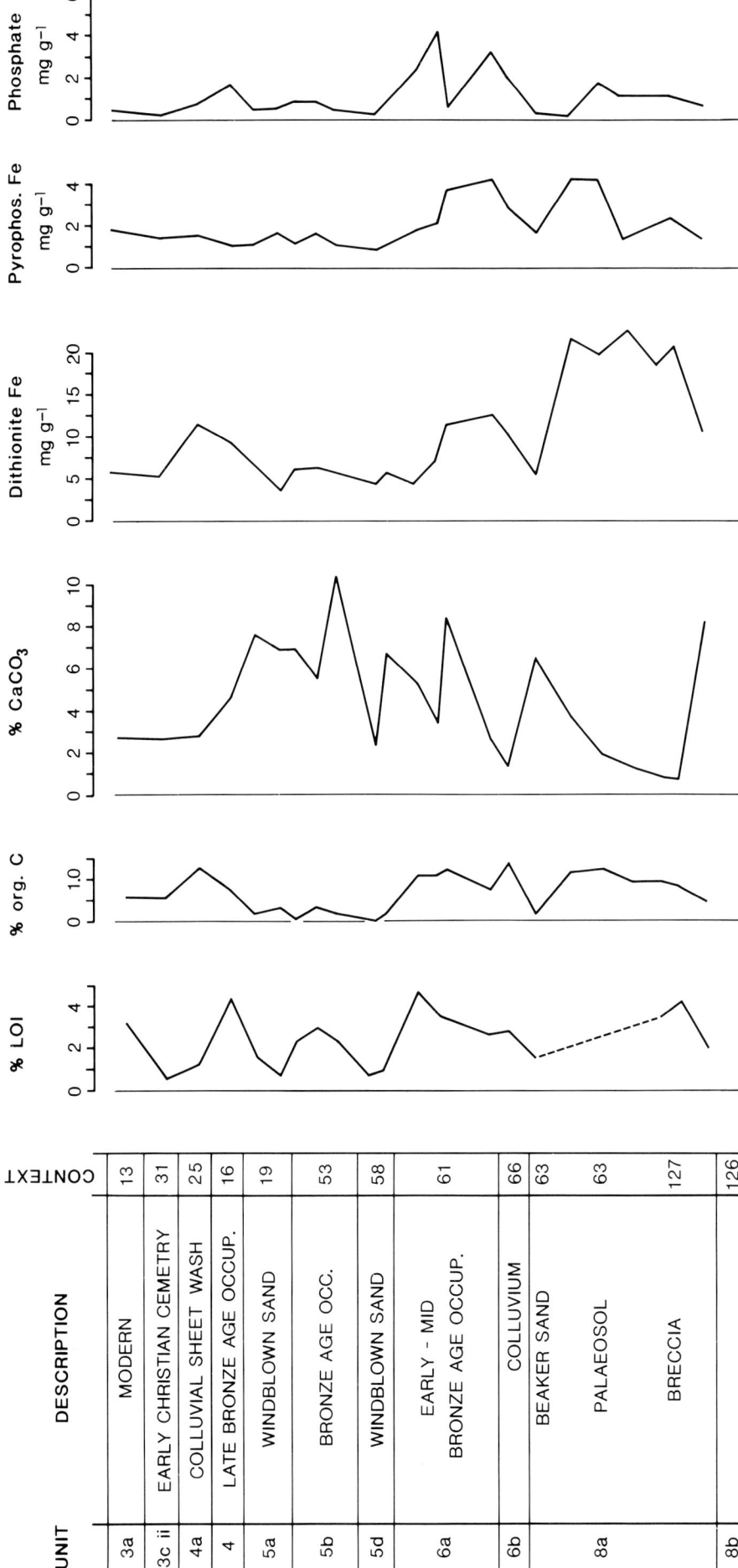

Fig 123 Distribution of loss on ignition, organic carbon, calcium carbonate, crystalline and mobile iron, and phosphate in sediments of 12 of the major stratigraphic contexts

senting Unit 5b, and Context 16, representing Unit 4. All three contexts show distinctive 'dips' in their coarse sand contents, with concurrent increases in the silt and clay fractions particularly in Contexts 61 and 16. In both Contexts 53 and 16, 'dips' in coarse sand content are perfectly paralleled by peaks in medium sand content. Higher contents of fine particles in Units 6a and 4 highlight the colluvial contribution to these layers from erosion of limestone soils on the south side of the Down and also the introduction of silty clay to the site, perhaps for constructional purposes, at the time of Unit 6a, for which there is independent micromorphological evidence. Richard Macphail (Chapter 16) believes that increases in silt and clay content are associated with importation of estuarine/marine silts into the occupation deposits. Context 53 is noticeably sandier in texture than the early and late Bronze Age layers, with total sand content up to 80–85%. Silt and clay fractions in Context 53 amount to only 5–7% and 3–4% respectively. That the main occupation unit, 5b, is not characterised by a peak of fines is noteworthy, since the field evidence showed that there had been no colluvial encroachment on the site at this time. Field evidence indicated some introduction of silty clay material for building purposes, but the sediment samples analysed here came from the area just north of the structures where there was little anthropogenic activity.

Forms of carbon in the sediments

Although the weight loss on ignition (LOI) in a muffle furnace at 450°C for 16 hours was determined for all samples, this figure represents a combination of processes: (i) volatilisation of CO_2 due to the oxidation of organic matter, (ii) volatilisation of CO_2 due to the breakdown of calcium carbonate ($CaCO_3$), and (iii) volatilisation of water, trapped between the crystal layers of silicate clay minerals. Subsequent determinations of organic carbon and calcium carbonate directly were designed to confirm which processes were responsible for losses on ignition.

Forms of carbon in the Brean stratigraphy are given in MF1:C12 and illustrated in Figure 123. LOI at the top of Unit 8a (the palaeosol) rises to almost 7%. Organic carbon values for the top of the palaeosol are relatively low (around 0.3–1.1%), indicating that weight loss on ignition was due either to breakdown of $CaCO_3$ or to loss of interstitial water from clays. $CaCO_3$ content declines quite dramatically from a peak of 7% in Unit 7, overlying the palaeosol, to about 1% at the base of the palaeosol, rising to >10% again in the underlying breccia (Unit 8b). These trends indicate fairly intensive decalcification during soil profile development and explain the very poor preservation of Mollusca and the eroded nature of bone in the basal palaeosol. Two peaks in LOI with depth down the palaeosol profile are mimicked faintly by small peaks in organic carbon (Fig 123), possibly indicating a low organic matter content preserved in the palaeosol. During profile development, iron and aluminium were probably translocated down-profile in an organo-metallic form. The small organic carbon peaks probably indicate the remains of these translocated organo-metallic complexes, which have survived decomposition since the palaesol was buried.

Not surprisingly, all wind-blown sand layers (7, 5d, and 5a) show very low LOI (<1–1.5%), with very low levels of organic carbon (<0.5%). Units 7 and 5d also show extremely sharp drops in $CaCO_3$ content. These 'dips' are due to the fact that the sands are quartzitic and may be the result of some decalcification. Micromorphological evidence indicates some calcitic wind-blown sand in the form of beach shell (R Macphail, pers comm). Three sharp peaks in LOI pick out the three Bronze Age occupation layers, Units 6a, 5b, and 4 (represented by Contexts 61, 53, and 16 respectively). While there are small peaks in organic carbon content in these layers (amounting to 0.5–1.25%), the greatest influence on LOI appears to be their $CaCO_3$ content. Contexts 61 and 53, in particular, show high peak $CaCO_3$ values of 8–10%. These peaks are more likely to be due to the presence of bones, coprolites, or the anthropogenic introduction to the site of shells or other calcareous materials than to naturally occurring precipitation or other deposition processes. Units 6a, 5b, and 4 all contained visible amounts of charcoal. The Walkley Black analysis, used for the determination of easily oxidisable organic carbon, recovers the more active soil organic matter and excludes about 90% of elemental carbon (Hesse 1971). Since 10% of elemental carbon (charcoal) may thus be included in these analyses, this may account for the small peaks in organic carbon in these deposits.

Forms of iron and phosphorus in the sediments

Forms of iron and phosphorus in the Brean stratigraphy are given in MF1:C12 and illustrated in Figure 123. The generally bright red-brown colour of the palaeosol (Unit 8a) can be explained by high contents of crystalline and immobile (dithionite – extracted) iron, up to 20–25mg Fe g^{-1}, which occur throughout the profile (Contexts 63 and 127) (see Fig 123). High levels of mobile (gel) iron oxides are also present at the surface of the palaeosol (Context 63). These trends down the soil profile are fairly typical of a brown earth with some degree of iron movement occurring, but it is impossible from chemical analyses alone to say whether any iron movement has occurred since the soil was buried.

The two major sources of phosphorus in soil are from rock minerals and from organic matter. The results of soil chemical analysis allow explanation of current forms of P in sediments, but do not explain the origin of P. In archaeological deposits, the main interest in the interpretation of soil or sediment phosphorus content is the implication of animal or anthropogenic inputs through dung, urine, food, bedding, middens, or other waste organic materials such as bone, horn, antler, hair, or hoof. There are three major problems in interpreting the actual source of organic phosphorus in sediments: (i) organic matter decomposition occurs continuously, even

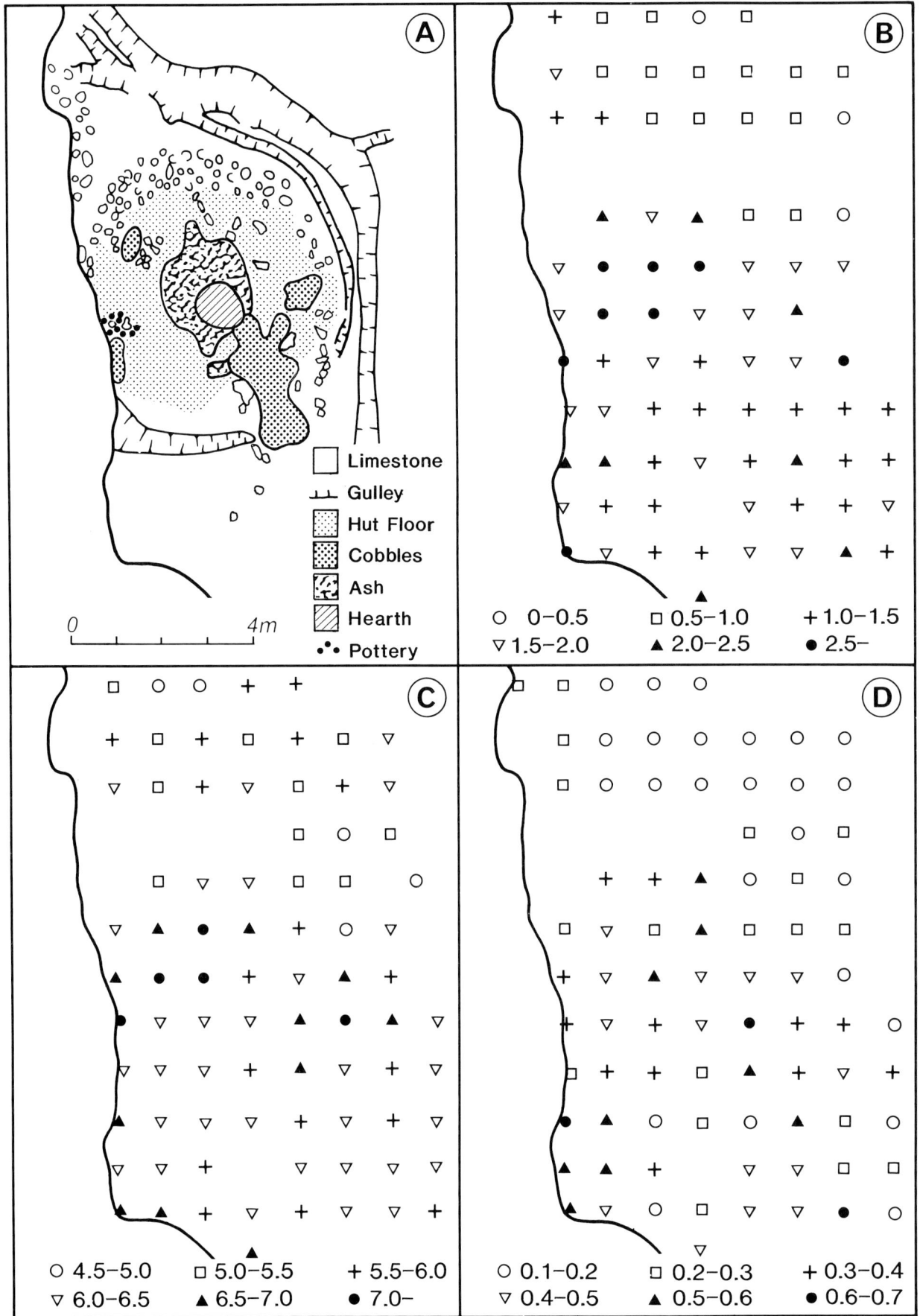

Fig 124a Plan (A) and spatial distribution of (B) phosphorus, (C) crystalline iron, and (D) mobile iron in sediments of Structure 95, Unit 5b (key on Fig 124b)

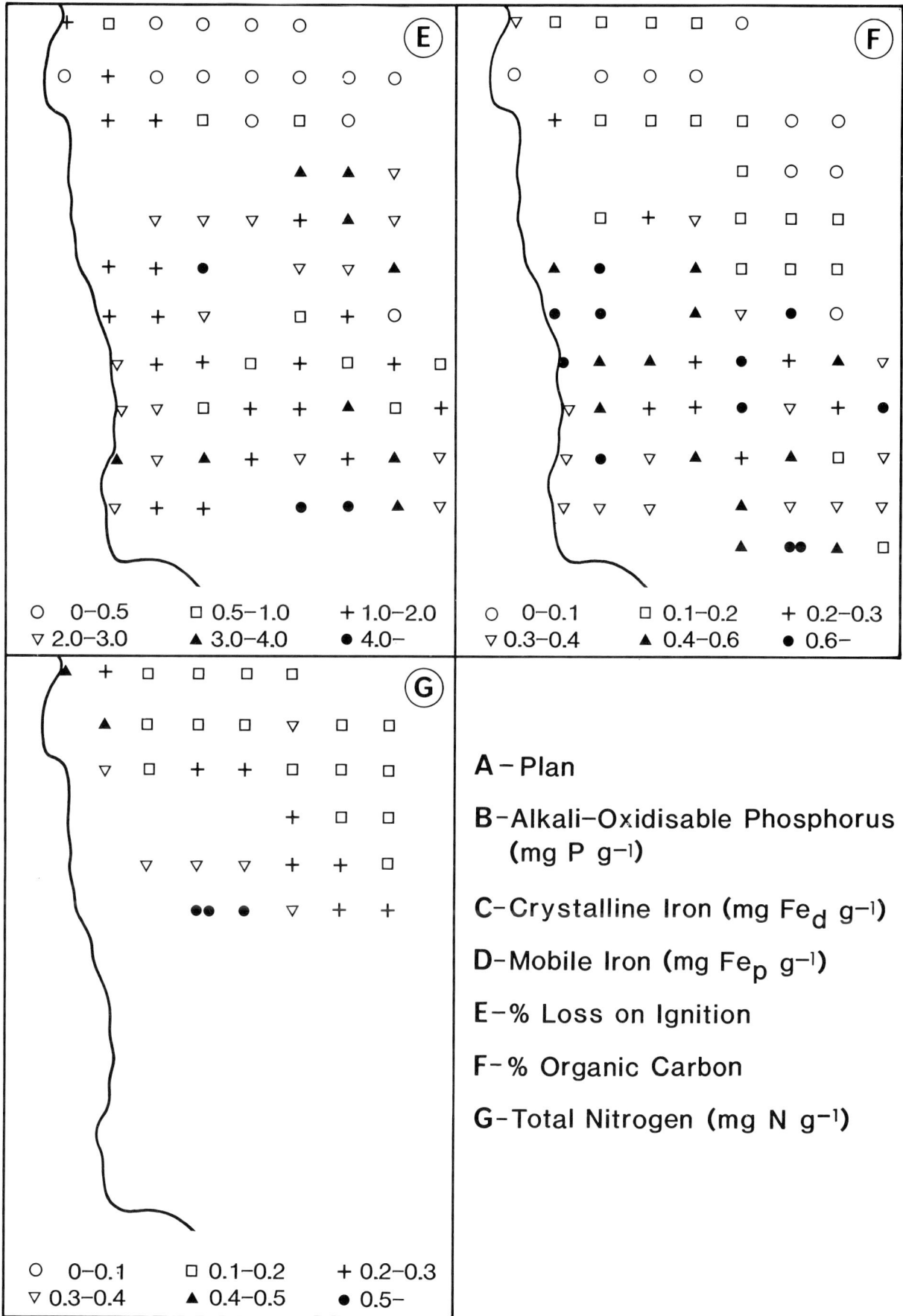

Fig 124b Spatial distribution of (E) loss on ignition, (F) organic carbon, and (G) total nitrogen in sediments of Structure 95, Unit 5b

at slow rates, after the materials are deposited, which means that forms of P are unlikely to occur in the forms in which they were originally laid down; (ii) the mobility of mineralised P, and the form in which it is 'fixed' or precipitated, depend very much on pH and *in situ* iron and calcium concentrations; (iii) the ratio of phosphorus to nitrogen, and to a lesser extent the ratio of phosphorus to other elements such as sulphur, often allow differentiation between different types of organic matter. We would expect, for example, that high P values due to the deposition of faeces and urine would be paralleled by very high nitrogen values and perhaps high amounts of other mineral elements such as sodium and potassium. Since the soluble elemental species present in urine and faeces would very quickly leach away, and the organic nitrogenous compounds would be rapidly decayed, any initial chemical differences would rapidly be lost. For this reason, sediment phosphorus analysis must really be interpreted in connection with other archaeological evidence, such as artefact distributions and sediment micromorphology.

In soil, phosphorus can be immobilised either as iron phosphates or as calcium phosphates. The small but distinct total phosphorus peak in the top of the palaeosol probably indicates phosphate retention in combination with iron oxides, either by adsorption on oxide surfaces, or by precipitation of insoluble iron phosphates such as strengite ($FePO_4 \cdot H_2O$).

Very low levels of both crystalline and mobile iron are found in all the wind-blown sand layers (Units 7, 5d, and 5a). In a few cases, bands of orange-brown iron staining were visible in the field (particularly for Context 19, Unit 5a). These bands were not subsequently found to contain significant quantities of either mobile or crystalline forms of iron. Levels of phosphorus in the same three sand layers are either very low or negligible (<0.05mg P g^{-1}). This may be due to the presence of very little phosphatic material during these episodes, but we must also remember that the very low levels of both Fe and Ca result in very low anion and phosphate adsorption capacities in these layers.

Noticeable peaks in both crystalline and more mobile forms of iron occur in Context 61 of Unit 6a, the Early Bronze Age occupation layer. Only slight peaks in both forms of iron occur in Context 53 (Unit 5b) and Context 16 (Unit 4). In all three Bronze Age occupation layers, small peaks in total phosphorus content mimic those seen for extractable iron content. Middle and lower parts of Context 61 (Unit 6a, the early Bronze Age occupation layer) show by far the most pronounced peaks in total phosphorus content, at about 3.4mg P g^{-1}.

Only in Unit 6a (Context 61) is there a good correlation between organic carbon content and peak total phosphorus content. This is the relationship that we would expect if any quantities of dung had been added to the site. While this relationship may confirm an organic source for phosphorus in the Bronze Age layers, the absence of good correlations in Unit 5b (Context 53) and Unit 4 (Context 16) may simply be due to more complete decomposition of organic phosphates in these layers.

Chemical analysis of Unit 5b

In Unit 5b, a sampling grid was laid down over two round hut structures and their surrounding areas. A grid at 1.0m intervals was laid down over Structure 95, the larger and more complete hut. Upslope, a similar grid was laid down at 0.5m intervals over the less complete Structure 59. Sediment samples were removed for determination of magnetic susceptibility and for a series of chemical analyses: total phosphorus, crystalline and mobile iron, loss on ignition, organic carbon, and total nitrogen. The results are shown in Figures 124 and 125.

Structure 95

This structure is described in Chapter 4.

Alkali oxidisable phosphorus

Background phosphorus values in sediments accumulated upslope of the hut are fairly low, at around 0.5–1.0mg P g^{-1} (Fig 124b). South of the hut and in front of the hut entrance, P values are a little higher (1.0–1.5mg P g^{-1}). The highest P values are inside the hut, in a roughly arc-shaped area surrounding the hearth and opposite the entrance (>2mg P g^{-1}). Had these results been due to the introduction of dung for the making of the hut floor then uniformly high values might have been expected over the whole floor area. As it is, the higher values seem more likely to relate to activities taking place within the huts. Possible sources of this phosphate are introduced organic material, particularly perhaps such phosphate-rich residues from food preparation as bone and blood. The highest levels of phosphate have also been shown by micromorphological studies (Chapter 16) to coincide with the presence of weathered ash. The presence of coprolites (Chapter 21) in and around structures suggests that faeces and urine also contributed to these higher phosphate values. The occurrence of high values in sediments south of the hut confirms the field evidence for the dumping of occupation refuse in that area.

Crystalline and mobile forms of iron

Mobile forms of iron outside the hut walls, in the sands upslope and inland of the hut walls, are very much lower than crystalline or more stable forms of iron. Pyrophosphate (Fe_p, mobile) iron values are typically around 0.1–0.3mg g^{-1}, while dithionite (Fe_d, crystalline) iron values are generally higher, at around 4.5–6.0mg g^{-1}. The pattern is different for the area downslope of the hut, both in the area currently truncated by the sea cliff and in the area immediately downslope of the hut entrance, where both crystalline and mobile forms of iron are high. Both forms of iron, particularly crystalline forms, are high inside the hut, in the central portion of the floor, close to the hearth.

There is a relationship between the distribution of iron and phosphorus in the sediments. Areas of high accumulation, such as the hut floor and immediately outside the hut entrance, may indicate zones where phosphates, mineralised from organic matter such as dung, became 'fixed' in crystalline iron phosphate minerals. This theory is supported by the fact that there is a closer relationship between the distribution of phosphorus and dithionite iron than between phosphorus and pyrophosphate iron.

It is interesting to note that there is also a closer relationship between Fe_d and Magnetic Susceptibility (MS) (Chapter 17) than between Fe_p and MS. This is probably because Fe_d is by far the major component of total iron in these sediments.

Loss on ignition (LOI)

As expected, LOI values in the sand accumulated upslope of the hut are very low indeed (0–0.5%). LOI values within the hut are also lowish, at around 1–3%. Clearly any organic materials originally present on the hut floor have been virtually decomposed. More puzzling are the higher LOI values (up to 4%) corresponding to the stormwater gulley on the east side of the hut.

Organic carbon

The pattern of organic carbon values is fairly similar to that of LOI. There are particularly low background organic carbon values in sand upslope of the hut (0–0.2%). Most of the highest organic C values (0.4–0.5%) lie within the hut, particularly seaward of the hearth. High organic carbon values are also seen just outside the entrance but, like LOI, they are rather variable, with values up to 0.6%.

Total nitrogen

Results are only available for the northern half of the excavated area. Background values in sand upslope of the hut are low, at around 0.1–0.4mg N g^{-1}. Within the part of the hut floor for which we have data, very high values (>1 mg N g^{-1}) are present in the area just north of the hearth, while N values at the outer extremities of the hut floor are lower, at around 0.3–0.4mg N g^{-1}. This is again evidence for the accumulation of high nitrogen organic matter, most probably dung, in the vicinity of the hearth.

High values of LOI, combined with the absence of high organic C and total N values in the stormwater gullies, may indicate the presence of calcareous materials rather than organic material, but this theory should be tested by examining the sediments for Ca and Mg.

Structure 59

This structure, of which only one third remained after coastal erosion, was described in Chapter 4. Horizontal variation of chemical properties in the surviving part of the hut floor is shown as a series of diagrams in Figure 125. Each diagram is also accompanied by a graph showing vertical variation below the hut floor in column 107.

Alkali oxidisable phosphorus

The highest values of P are found in the central section of the hut floor, just inside the entrance (2.0–2.5mg P g^{-1}) with lower values around the peripheries of the floor (1.5–2.0mg P g^{-1}) (Fig 125b). This contrasts with Structure 95 where the highest values are opposite the entrance. Column 107 shows the highest P values on the hut floor itself, with another peak at a depth of 120mm, possibly indicating an earlier floor surface. Below this, P declines to background levels, indicating very little downward movement.

Crystalline and mobile forms of iron

Fe_d (crystalline iron) values are generally lowish (0.5–1.5mg Fe g^{-1}) over the whole of the hut floor with only a couple of high spots up to 2.0–2.5mg Fe g^{-1}. The only pattern to these results is a zone of rather lower Fe_d values to the southern periphery of the hut floor. Column 107 shows little vertical variation in Fe_d. This contrasts with the graph for P.

In contrast to crystalline iron, Fe_p (mobile iron) values are very high throughout the hut floor. Most values are more than twice as high as Fe_d values and more than three times as high as Fe_p values in Structure 95 downslope. Highest Fe_p values in the centre of the hut rise to >7.5mg Fe g^{-1}. These high mobile iron values are the most likely cause of the yellow/green staining which was such a distinctive feature of the floor of Structure 59 in the field. The staining may be an iron phosphate deposit, but it is noteworthy that, although the staining was particularly marked in Structure 59, the overall phosphate levels for the two structures are similar, whereas mobile iron values are dramatically greater in Structure 59. The reasons for these differences are not obvious, although the different slope positions of the two structures could have caused contrasts in leaching or illuviation and hence more transport of mobile forms of iron. Another possibility is that a more compacted hut floor could lead to increased deposition of mobile iron. There is archaeological evidence that Structure 59 may have been in use for considerably longer than Structure 95. None of these explanations seems very convincing and we should also consider the possibility that the much higher mobile iron values on the floor of Structure 59 relate to as yet indefinable chemical contrasts created by activities performed in the two structures. Column 107 shows no clear down-profile pattern.

Loss on ignition

LOI values are low (1–2%) over the whole hut floor apart from one spot in the centre of the floor at 4% LOI which was perhaps near to the original hearth. Column 107 shows that highest values occur on the hut floor.

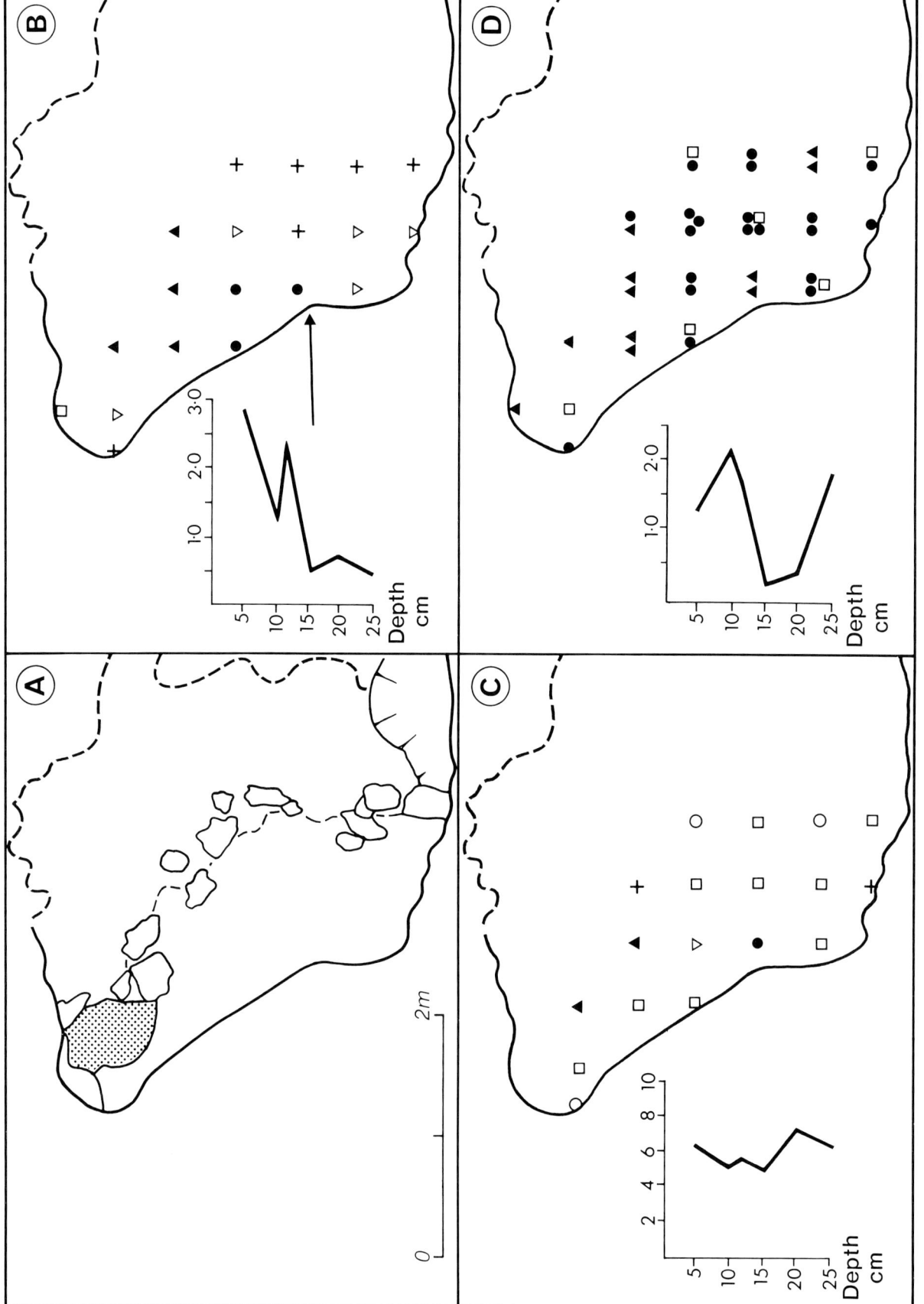

Fig 125a   Plan (A) and spatial distribution of (B) phosphorus, (C) crystalline iron, and (D) mobile iron in sediments of Structure 59, Unit 5b (key to symbols for each property is as on Fig 124; more than one symbol in D represents multiples of those values); graphs B, C, and D show the distribution with depth below Structure 59 (column 107) of P, crystalline Fe, and mobile Fe respectively

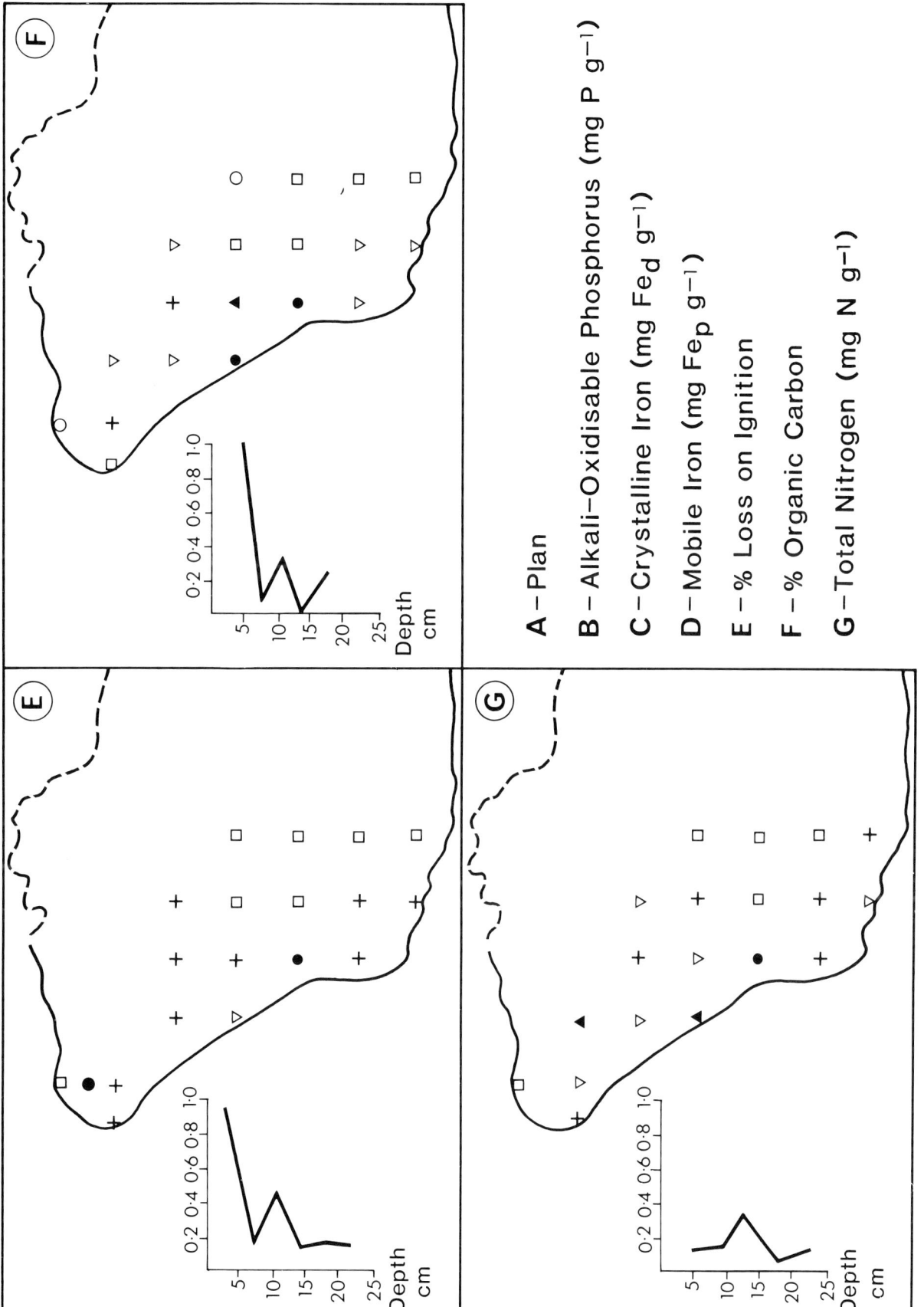

Fig 125b Spatial distribution of (E) loss on ignition, (F) organic carbon, and (G) total nitrogen in sediments of Structure 59, Unit 5b (key to symbols for each property is as on Fig 124); graphs E, F, and G show the distribution with depth below Structure 59 (column 107) of LOI, organic carbon, and total nitrogen respectively

Organic carbon

Organic carbon values show a clearer pattern of the same trends as for LOI, with low values all around the periphery of the hut floor (0.5–1.0%), with much higher values (3–4%) in the centre, possibly around the hearth. Again column 107 shows the highest values on the floor surface.

Total nitrogen

The spatial pattern of total nitrogen in Structure 59 is variable with lowest values around the edges of the hut floor (0.1–0.2mg N g^{-1}) and highest values (0.4–>0.5mg N g^{-1}, in the centre of the hut, along the present cliff edge.

16 Soil history and micromorphology

by Richard I Macphail

Introduction

In 1985–6 a soil micromorphological study was undertaken of the deposits at Brean Down. Of special interest to this present investigation are the 15 soil thin sections of the Pleistocene and Beaker sediments studied by Ian Cornwall and reported in ApSimon et al 1961. His results (both published and archive) and the thin sections themselves, which are housed at the Institute of Archaeology, were studied by the author to assess the potential of the site prior to excavation. These thin sections and Cornwall's data and interpretations were therefore useful at the outset of this present much larger study, where interest has been mainly focused on the Flandrian/prehistoric levels. The Brean Down project is an interdisciplinary study, and of particular importance has been the close collaboration between the author and Sheila Ross regarding the study of chemistry and physical characteristics of the soils and sediments. The magnetic susceptibility of the site, which again can be linked to the nature of the soils and sediments and the effects of occupation upon them, has been assessed by Mike Allen.

Samples and methods

The archaeological soils and sediments were examined and described in the field (Hodgson 1974) from the cliff section (colour MF 1 and 2) and from a number of pits across the site. Seventeen undisturbed box monoliths were taken for thin section (up to 130×50mm in size) description (Bullock et al 1985) and interpretation (Courty et al in press, 1989), using plane polarised light (PPL), crossed polarised light (XPL), oblique incident light (OIL), and ultra violet light (UVL). Soil micromorphology has been established as a technique in soil science since the 1930s (Kubiena 1938) and was applied to archaeological problems from the 1950s (Cornwall 1958) onwards (Macphail 1987a, 357). This technique is acknowledged as the best single method of studying palaeosols (Valentine and Dalrymple 1976) and thus the use of an objective scheme for description and interpretation suggested that the combined investigation of Cornwall's and the recently sampled thin sections would be rewarding.

Soils and sediments around the monoliths were also bulk sampled for grain size, organic carbon, calcium carbonate, sodium dithionite, and potassium pyrophosphate extractable iron analyses using the techniques of Avery and Bascombe (1974). The positions from which the micromorphological samples were taken are marked on the main section drawings by triangular symbols accompanied by a letter.

In summary, semi-continuous thin section samples (colour MF 3 and 4) were taken from a gully at the top of the Breccia (Unit 8a – A), through the Beaker palaeosol (Unit 8a – B, C, D), across the Beaker blown sand (Unit 7 – G), through the colluvium (Unit 6b – H, I), and into Unit 6a (L, M). Single spot samples were also taken (i) of Unit 8a/6b, upslope (J), (ii) on the foreshore (Pit VII) below beach sand (Unit 8a – F), (iii) inland (Pit V) (Unit 6b – E), and (iv) of various Middle Bronze Age occupation and stabilisation levels (Unit 6a – O; Unit 5b – N; Unit 5a/5b – K) (colour MF 5 and 6). Late Bronze Age deposits (Unit 4), both at the cliff face (P) (colour MF 7 and 8) and inland at Pit V (Q) and the overlying colluvial Unit 4 (R), were also sampled.

Cornwall's thin sections of the Pleistocene deposits (Units 13c, 13b, 13a, 12c, 12a, 11b, and 11a) and the post-glacial and Beaker palaeosol (8a) (ApSimon et al 1961) were also examined and characterised but not described in detail. This was done to provide a general reference for the parent materials and early Flandrian pedogenesis on the site, and in the particular case of the Pleistocene deposits to update briefly their micromorphological interpretation, as a record. It was also thought wise to compare the presently excavated palaeosol with the Beaker palaeosol existing in the 1950s in view of the possibility that the actual Beaker occupation was to seaward of this excavation.

Results

Grain size and chemistry are tabulated (MF1:C13 and C14). Soil profile (1–3) descriptions and micromorphological descriptions and preliminary interpretations (thin sections A–R) are given in MF1:D1–E3, while 57 supporting field and micromorphological colour plates are presented on a colour microfiche.*

Discussion

The Pleistocene deposits

A review of Cornwall's thin sections basically supports the original interpretation of these sediments, the characteristics of which are summarised here. Above the Boulder Pile (Unit 13d) (ApSimon et al 1961, fig 16) the Lower Breccia continues as a loosely cemented calcitic deposit mainly characterised by limestone fragments, silt size quartz, and calcite, with aragonite and very fine sand size (50–100μm) or medium to coarse sand size (250–1000μm) soil fragments. Although Unit 13c features small indications of a 'temperate' soil formation phase, such as minor channel development with occasional dusty clay coatings, the major evidence is for a deposit resulting from soil erosion and sediment movement under periglacial conditions. Poorly birefringent rounded brown soil (*braunerde*) fragments occur throughout, and these have the appearance of being soil granules eroded from fine soil lenses (eg link cappings; Bullock et al 1985) found in cryogenic soils (Romans and Robertson 1974; van Vliet-Lanoë 1982; 1985). There are also cracks and lenticular void infills of 'washed'

---

*The colour microfiche is available as an optional extra purchase; see p 18.

silt especially in Unit 13a, again indicative of *in situ* freeze thaw conditions affecting the Lower Breccia. In Unit 13a, which is also the most poorly sorted, there are, in addition to the poorly birefringent soil granules, rather coarse fragments of typical reddish brown beta B clay (*terra fusca*) and orange brown Bt horizon soil (*Braunlehm*) with a striated birefringent fabric (colour MF 9–11).

Unit 13 is strongly heterogeneous. It contains silt size quartz possibly of Tertiary or Triassic origin (Cornwall 1961), as found filling fissures in the Carboniferous Limestone (Cornwall's reference thin section). This material, like the very fine sand size soil fragments, may be of wind-blown origin prior to its deposition in a breccia of small stone size limestone fragments interpreted by ApSimon *et al* (1961, 95) as due to continued limestone comminution by frost action. In Unit 13a deposition was additionally affected by coarse soil colluviation. The occurrence of these eroded soil fragments in Pleistocene deposits is common enough (Bullock and Murphy 1979; Macphail 1985; Catt 1987) and similar mixtures of soil materials are present within the (?Cromerian) breccias and loamy cave sediments of nearby Westbury-sub-Mendip (Goldberg and Macphail in prep) and indicate a comparable source of soil and superficial material from the top of the Mendips.

In a similar way the moderately well-sorted silts and sands of Unit 12 (colour MF 12 and 13), which are interpreted as sediments derived from both the beach area and the Down itself (ApSimon *et al* 1961) – including rare soil fragments – can be compared with the layered silts and sands deposited near sea level at Boxgrove, Sussex, during a Late Temperate/Early Glacial period (Roberts 1986; Goldberg and Macphail in prep).

Unit 11 is made up of material similar to that in Unit 13, but, as suggested by Cornwall (1961), a moderate amount of soil formation took place under short-lived temperate climatic conditions. Unit 9 comprises wind-blown dune deposits (colour MF 14 and 15).

Post-glacial soil formation and Beaker occupation

Origins of the Beta B clay (*terra fusca*)

Both the examination of Cornwall's basal thin section from Unit 8a, termed *terra fusca*, and the study of thin section A (for location see Fig 20) from a gully in the Upper Breccia and thin section B from the base of the 'palaeosol' (Fig 20; colour MF 3; Profile 1, MF1:D1) show that the reddish, slightly rubified (reddened) Beta B clay (Catt 1979, 629) or *terra fusca* (colour MF 16 and 17) is not *in situ*. In all cases it occurs as fine to very coarse (several mm in size) clay fragments surrounded by other soil material (colour MF 18 and 19) as in Cornwall's palaeosol, sometimes as an approximate layer across the slide (thin section B). This reddish Beta B clay has therefore apparently been disturbed and transported.

The origins of this type of Beta B clay relate to the long weathering of limestone and the production of a residual, decarbonated clay, the slight rubification supposedly resulting from having a cooler, more humid climate than the (truly 'Mediterranean') strongly rubified *terra rosa* soils (Duchaufour 1982, 149), although redness can also relate purely to iron content (Dalrymple 1969). Data from the Breccia (Unit 8b) indicate that the Beta B clay is rather low in iron (Chapter 15). Thin accumulations of Beta B clay, as noted in oolitic limestone soils beneath Hazleton Neolithic long cairn (Macphail 1986a) could be considered purely Flandrian in origin, whereas thick deposits probably result from soil formation during several warm stages during the later Quaternary (Catt 1979).

At Brean Down the Upper Breccia (Unit 8b) is believed to occur through the erosion of the rocky slope of the cliff as a result of frost action (ApSimon *et al* 1961, 97–8), and undoubtedly the reddish colour of the deposit is due to the presence of Beta B clay alongside fragments of weathered Carboniferous Limestone, both displaced by cryoturbation. Unit 8a, which was 0.46m in thickness in 1959 (ApSimon *et al* 1961) and 0.23–0.40m at Profile 1 (MF1:D1), is not a homogeneous reddish clay soil, however, and only the basal parts (eg 0.29–0.32m in thin section B; Cornwall's bottom thin section of Unit 8a) contain a significant number of reddish Beta B clay fragments. The question is whether these fragments derive purely from a relict weathered soil (polycyclic brown calcic soil/*terra fusca*; Duchaufour 1982, 233) formed on the Down itself or, as suggested by Cornwall (ApSimon *et al* 1961), developed as a mature *terra fusca* under temperate conditions by the weathering of the underlying breccia in the early post-glacial period (prior to *eutrophic braunerde* formation). Firstly, on this slope none of the Beta B clay appeared to be *in situ* and no Beta B clay/weathering limestone interface was noted. Rather, weathered limestone just occurs as inclusions in the 'Beaker' soil, and Beta B clay occurs as colluvial fragments at its base set in a matrix of brown soil (colour MF 18 and 19) that is regarded as Flandrian in origin. In conclusion, although minor amounts of Beta B clay may have been produced by post-glacial weathering, the majority is considered to be relict of the Upper Breccia, some at least being known to be of pre-Devensian date as Beta B (*terra fusca*) fragments (Unit 13; colour MF 9–11) occur in the deposits which in 1961 (ApSimon *et al*) were described as 'Younger Würm' (Devensian).

Flandrian soil formation, early prehistoric (Neolithic and Beaker) clearance, and primary cultivation (Unit 8a)

Information on this period is derived from Cornwall's thin sections of the Beaker palaeosol and thin sections A, B, C, D, and J (for location see Figs 19 and 20 and colour MF 3). The buried soil (Unit 8a) is both the result of a complicated pedogenic history and an artefact of early prehistoric activity. Firstly, a reconstruction of the pedogenic history spanning some 5000 years, from the deposition of the Upper Breccia considered in 1961 to be in the Pre-Boreal (ApSimon *et al* 1961, 102) to the earliest radiocarbon-dated Neolithic impact around 4720 BP, is attempted.

a) Late Glacial/Early Flandrian

b) Atlantic

c) Neolithic/Beaker Disturbance

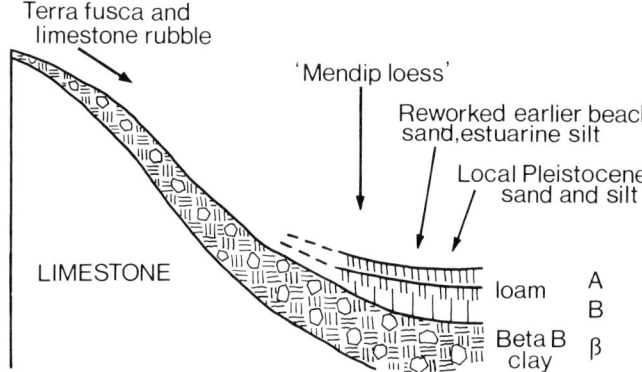
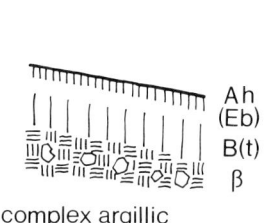
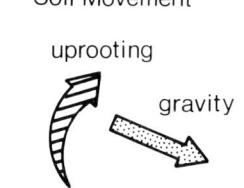

Fig 126 Stages in the soil history of Unit 8a

Micromorphology and grain size characteristics help explain the development of an argillic soil at Brean Down, because *terra fusca* soils formed purely on hard limestone platforms – such as the Down itself – are normally unaffected by this kind of 'brown' soil formation (Duchaufour 1982, 275). The argillic soil of Unit 8a (complex lessived brown soil (Duchaufour 1982, 224) similar to the typical palaeoargillic brown earth, Nordrach Association (Findlay *et al* 1983)) has however formed away from the limestone platform in a 'dry valley' situation, on the unconsolidated Upper Breccia of Beta B clay and limestone talus, with probable aeolian additions of silt and sand. The latter weathered to produce high amounts of crystalline and gel iron (MF1:C14). A strictly layered profile of pure Beta B clay at the base, a mixed middle zone, and a loamy upper soil are absent because of slope related soil erosion and colluviation. The blown sand component, which is rather low at the base of the soil, is readily available either from the dune (Unit 9) or from beach sand, whereas the silt could equally derive from nearby estuarine silts or locally reworked silts from the Pleistocene deposits (see p 188; colour MF 12–15) or from a loessial source affecting the Mendips in general (Catt 1977; Findlay *et al* 1983) (Fig 126a).

Early post-glacial brown soil formation therefore took place as aeolian sands and silts became homogenised with the deep reddish Beta B clay subsoil, through biological activity and weathering processes. These mechanisms acting eventually under a probable broad leaved woodland cover (Chapter 19) produced the reddish brown (Beta B mixed with B(t)), yellowish brown (B(t) and Eb), and darkish brown (Ah) horizon silty soil material of the Flandrian profile, which now only occurs as fragments within the palaeosol (Figs 126b and 127; colour MF 20–24). Brown forest soil formation probably also included the moderate depletion of the upper horizons of clay and iron (Duchaufour 1982, 271ff) (Chapter 15), hence in the latter case the development of yellowish brown fabrics in contrast to the red fabrics of the Beta B clay. This development probably relates to the formation of mainly crystalline iron oxides through the weathering of the aeolian cover up-profile away from the Beta B influenced subsoil (MF1:C14, samples 134–137). Typically the fragments of topsoil are darkly stained by the ferro-manganese replacement of organic matter preserving the Ah microstructure, probably of a moderately acid Mull type (Babel 1975). In short, the Flandrian soil was probably a eutropic, but essentially decalcified, weakly leached brown earth (Fig 126b).

As noted above, the palaeosol is very heterogeneous (at its base) and does not contain actual layered soil horizons. Instead, soil material from the different soil horizons and typically low birefringent and blackish burned soil, sometimes associated with charcoal, are all juxtaposed and only separated by highly birefringent clay infills (Fig 127; colour MF 20–24; Fig 128.iii). This pattern of mixed soil is common to many archaeological buried soils (Macphail 1986b; Macphail *et al* 1987) and is the result of soil disruption probably through either natural tree-throw, natural tree-throw utilised for clearance, or induced tree-throw (Macphail 1987b), combined with colluvial/gravity effects and later disturbance by cultivation (Figs 126c and 128). Present studies of thin sections from the Neolithic buried soil at Maiden Castle, Dorset, show a similar picture (Macphail in prep), whereas large excavated areas of flat prehistoric landscapes buried by alluvium at Drayton Cursus, Oxfordshire, and at Irthlingborough, Northants, show typical tree hollow features with evidence of *in situ* burning of the fallen tree (G Lambrick and M Robinson, pers comm; C Halpin, pers comm). At Brean Down the presence of large (now dated) charcoal in the profile, together with burned soil fragments and associated fine charcoal, could possibly link soil disruption with natural tree-throw utilised for clearance or induced tree-throw itself. No conclusive tree-throw pit features were present at Brean Down, but downslope soil movement or trees only rooting in the loamy soil could account for this. The exact story will never be known, but the interpreted microfabrics and the suggested mechanisms for their

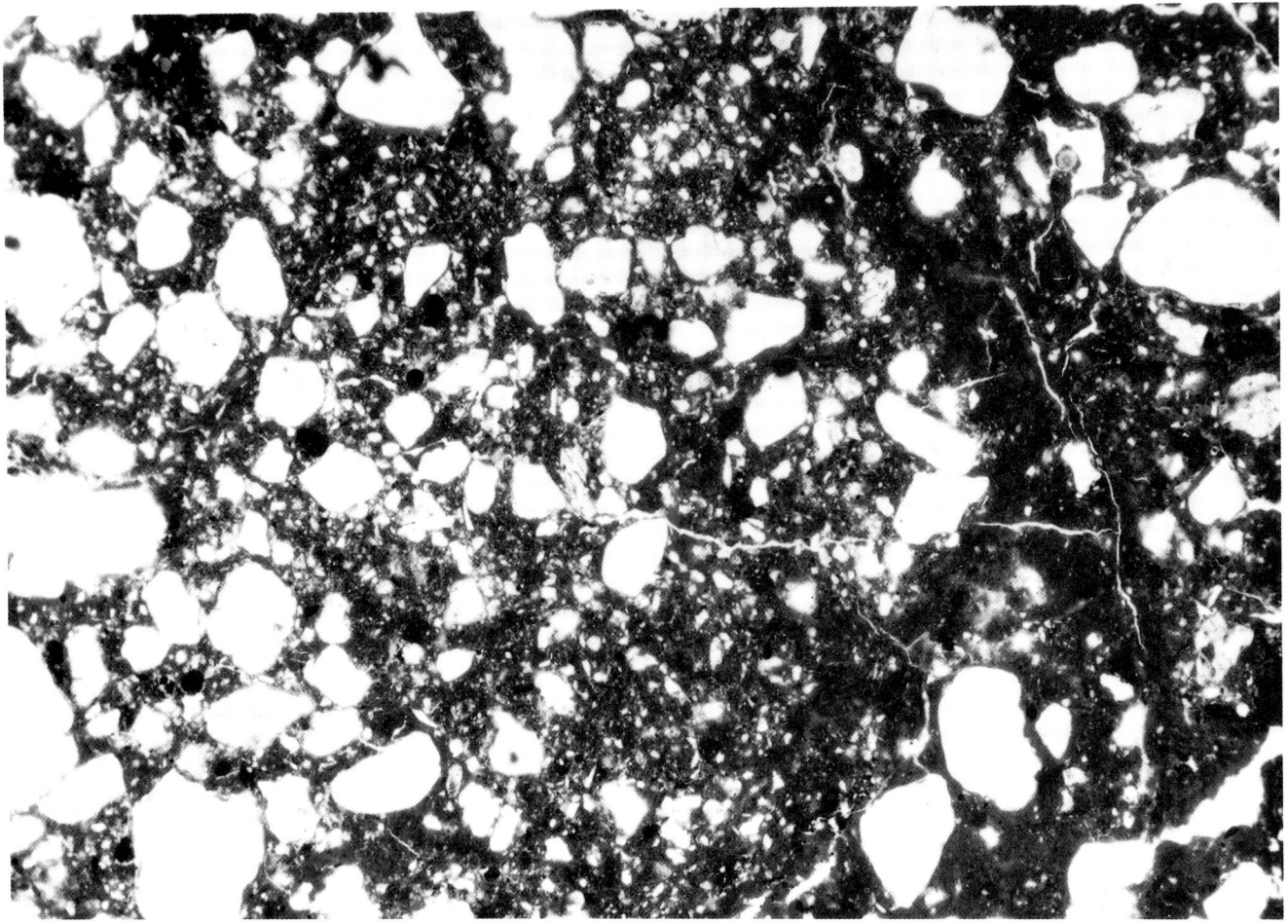

Fig 127 Palaeosol (Unit 8a), thin section B; soil fragments of reddish Beta B clay, yellowish brown silty B(t) horizon, and blackish fine charcoal rich burned soil material, all separated by reddish dusty clay infilling and coating void space; anomalous mixture of various soil horizon material and the infilling of voids by dusty clay to produce a closed vughy porosity indicates soil disruption, probably through woodland clearance; the presence of burned soil possibly also suggests contemporaneous burning, while slight rounding of fragments may be the result of small downslope movement under gravity; plane polarised light; frame length 3.3mm

origin are given in Figures 126c and 128.

The abundant clay infills which give the soil its present argillic character (Soil Survey Staff 1975; Avery 1980), that resulted from the slaking of the forest soil after disruption, are *in situ*, and mainly occur in the basal part (*c* 0.27–0.32m) of the palaeosol. Above, the soil is increasingly homogeneous because of continued post-clearance human activity, combined with more active slope and biological influences.

There appears to be a discontinuity between this basal part of the palaeosol with its clear *in situ* evidence of soil disruption (solid soil aggregates separated by clay infills) and the overlying soil which, while containing fewer soil aggregates (that are themselves rather 'diffuse' in character), more dominantly exhibits a general speckled brown fabric because it is increasingly rich in fine charcoal and organic matter (MF1:C14, samples 136, 137, and 151). Channel porosity is either coated or infilled by very dusty clay that also occurs in the aggregates (Fig 129, colour MF 25 and 26; Fig 128.ii). In the zone approximately between 0.15 and 0.27m (thin section C) there are indications that this brown fabric has resulted from the physical mixing of the various soil horizons listed earlier, with, it is believed (Macphail *et al* 1987), cultivation as a major mechanism producing the coating features and also incorporating some charred organic matter in the process. Mixing by cultivation has been influenced by colluviation (on a 17–20° slope), itself induced by cultivation (Fig 128.iii). Soil movement downslope (reaching below the modern high spring tide level in Pit VII, thin section F, location not on a section) resulted in the 'truncation' of the *in situ* disturbed forest soil profile, although rapid burial by soil from upslope has preserved the features of cultivation from the strong biological (probable earthworm) activity which has almost completely homogenised the rather organic (MF1:C14, samples 137 and 151) top 0.10m of the palaeosol (colour MF 27; Fig 128.i).

The presence of a strongly worked biological fabric characterising the top of the Beaker palaeosol may suggest that cultivation ceased for a period on this part of the site. Experimental (Iron Age) agricultural studies from Butser, Hants (Reynolds 1979), show that in Ap horizons very rich in calcium carbonate and organic matter textural features caused by

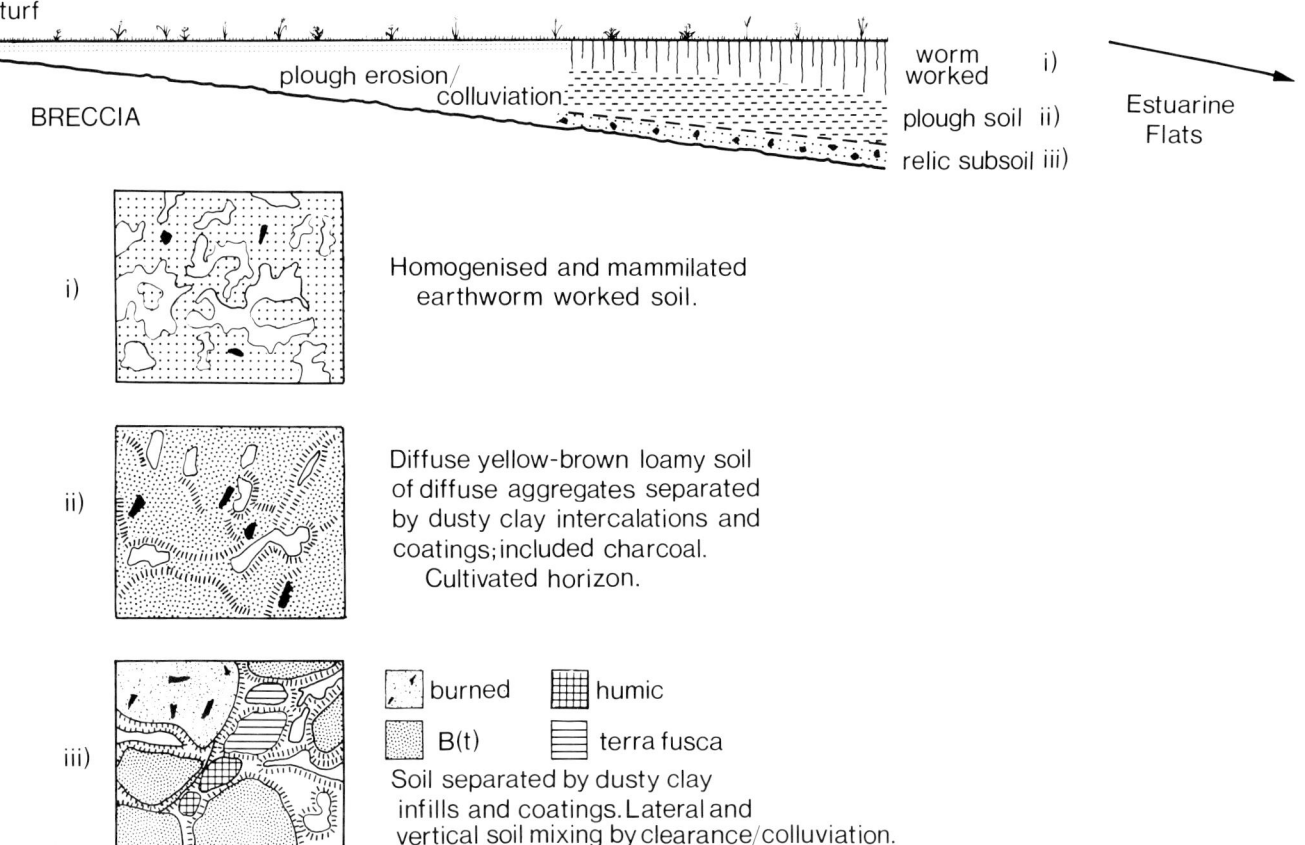

Fig 128 *Schematic section of the basal palaeosol Unit 8a, showing typical microfabrics of the main soil horizons*

ploughing may be obliterated by extremely high biological activity within months (Gebhardt in prep). As the soil at Brean Down was both decalcified and probably far less humose in comparison to the Butser soil (the Brean soil being primarily of subsoil origin – Fig 128.iii) it may be suggested that the soil was uncultivated at least for some seasons and a mull (possible grassland) soil developed.

Upslope, at the base of profile 3, the Beaker palaeosol/colluvium only measures some 0.12m in thickness overall, and examination of the thin section here (J, location on Fig 19) shows the presence of broken up 'turf' (colour MF 28 and 29) at around 0.04–0.06m depth. The shallow nature of the palaeosol here indicates firstly that there was significant soil loss downslope, and secondly that the post-cultivation phase was succeeded by the development of a biologically worked, probably humic topsoil. At profile 1, the biologically worked topsoil was buried by blown sand, whereas at profile 3 it was both sealed by – and incorporated into – a later colluvial deposit (Unit 6b).

Colluvial deposits of Units 8a and 6

Deposits at the loam/silt interface (Units 8a, 6)

Reddish loamy deposits, like the Beaker palaeosol, were further examined 110m inland at Pit V (5m OD) and at Pit VII below the modern beach sand 20m to the west of the main catenary sequence, in thin sections E and F respectively.

At Pit V the sediment which more probably relates to Unit 6 comprises three main fabrics: (i) small amounts of colluvial loam, as previously described; (ii) pale grey silts with amorphous organic matter, phytoliths, and a few diatoms present; and (iii) a mixed loam. The silty material (ii) is identified as a pure estuarine/marine (Chapter 8) silty sediment (colour MF 30–32) that in places is finely mixed (iii) with the more ferruginous colluvium to give an overall clay loam texture for the sediment (MF1:C13, sample 305). In many areas the latter fabric is dominated by intercalations and other textural features of slaking indicating that here was a colluvial/estuarine interface developed under very wet conditions – local hydromorphism leading also to the pseudomorphic ferruginisation of included organic matter in places.

A similar situation seems to have occurred at Pit VII where the reddish colluvium, but here probably contemporary with the Beaker palaeosol, is again apparently enhanced in quantities of silt and phytoliths (?estuarine plant types). It has a fabric further suggesting homogenisation of colluvium with estuarine silts under water saturated soil conditions (colour MF 33). From the evidence of Pits V and VII there therefore seems to have been downslope mixing and interdigitation of the Beaker palaeosol and pre middle Bronze Age loams (Unit 6), which have been shown to be strongly colluvial in character (see below and p 28), with estuarine/marine sediments, clearly demonstrating the close proximity of two coexisting environments.

The 'Beaker sand' (Unit 7) and 'Biconical urn' colluvium (Unit 6)

As described earlier, the 'Beaker sand' (Unit 7) buries the Beaker palaeosol, which after a period of cultivation and colluviation may have been left to develop a stable biologically worked topsoil (Ah). Thin section G (location on Fig 27) spans the junction of Units 8a, 7, and 6c and shows the marked discontinuity between the clays of the basal palaeosol (Unit 8a), the very pure sand of the 'Beaker sand' (Unit 7), and the loamy sand of the overlying colluvium (Unit 6b) (MF1:C13, samples 137, 168, and 152). There is some evidence that earthworms active in the Beaker palaeosol also burrowed into the 'Beaker sand', although there are few features in thin sections G or H to suggest that they were particularly active in the blown sand or actually penetrated the overlying colluvium for very long. The presence of large animal burrows at the top of the deposit (Chapter 2), however, suggests that Unit 7 was not immediately buried. The blown sand itself is made up of mainly medium and fine sand size quartz, with a moderately high calcium carbonate content (MF1:C14, sample 168) because of included shell fragments, although this was not the case for all the blown sand analysed (Chapter 15). Sand size soil fragments, a relic of the Pleistocene deposits (colour MF 9–15), also occur. Although the sand of Unit 7 is rather pure it does contain very dusty clay coatings as a fine fabric, which are believed to have been washed in from the overlying colluvium. The 'Beaker sand' probably had a number of sources, some non-calcareous. It could be a result of the accelerated wind erosion of beach sands, the blowing of which seems to have occurred at a slow rate throughout the early Flandrian, gradually increasing in Beaker times (sand content of B, C, and D: 44%, 52%, and 57%; MF1:C13, samples 135, 136, and 137). There also seems to have been an input from the Pleistocene dune deposits (eg layer 9) perhaps as the brown soil cover (Beaker palaeosol and Upper Breccia) to the seaward side of the excavation was breached, possibly by continued occupation/cultivation induced soil erosion or by progressive marine incursions.

Unit 6b colluvium (thin sections H, I, and J, location on Figs 19 and 27) seems to be well named in that it has features throughout suggesting that it is a ploughsoil colluvium and spread as such over the 'Beaker sand'; as noted above this led to fine soil washing into this lower deposit. The microfeatures are abundant matrix and dusty clay coatings and

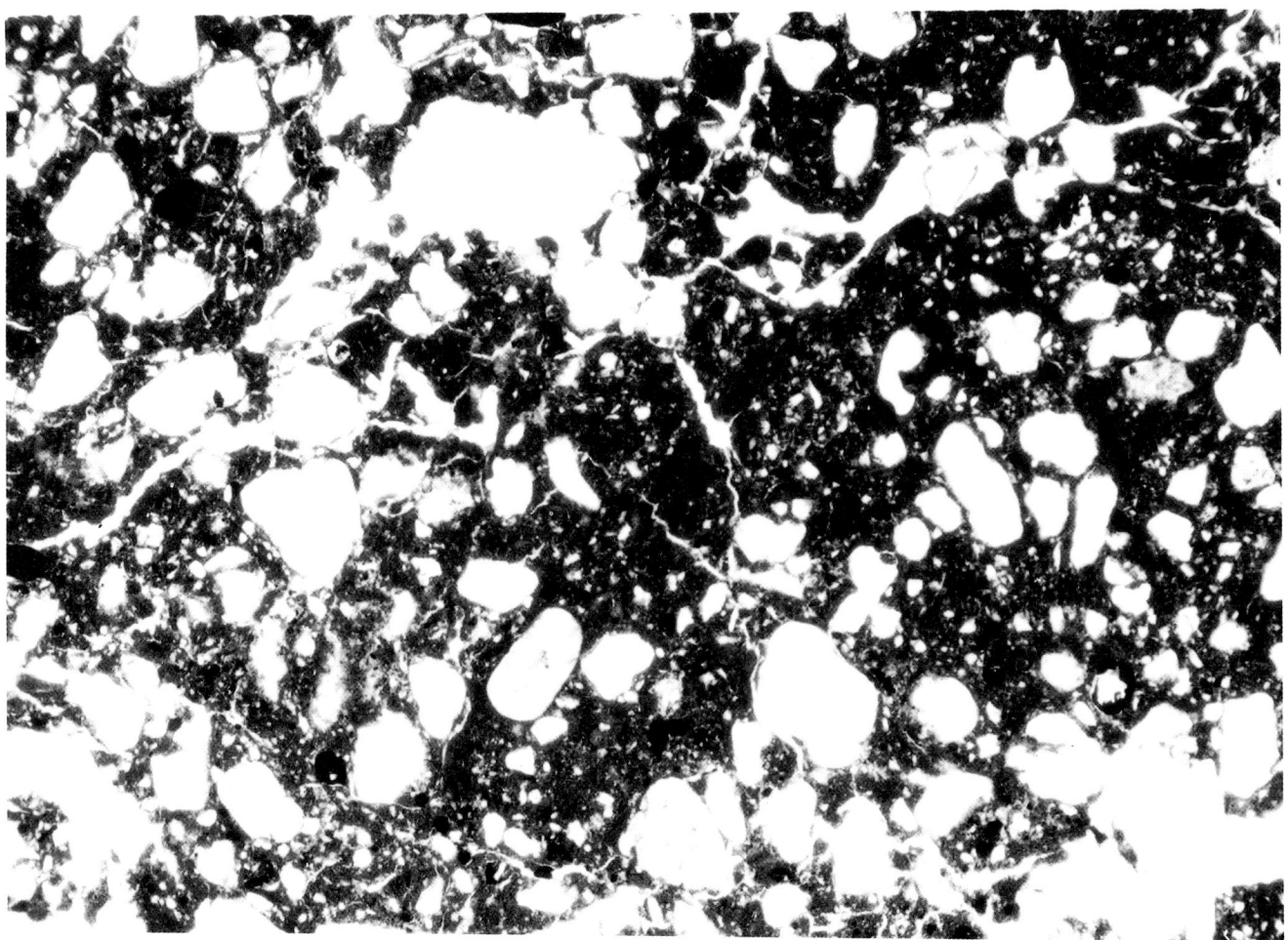

Fig 129 Palaeosol (Unit 8a), thin section C; soil is a homogenised yellowish brown loam containing charcoal; coarse peds with diffuse boundaries and within-ped and between-ped textural features (intercalations and very dusty clay void coatings) all suggest physical mixing and slaking; interpreted as a cultivated fabric; plane polarised light; frame length 3.3mm

intercalations (colour MF 34 and 35), and a sometimes rather dense and vughy fabric resulting from the plough/colluvial mixing of reddish clay fine soil (from Unit 8a) with increased amounts of blown sand (colour MF 36), the latter content rising from 57% at the top of the Beaker palaeosol to 66% (H) and 71% (J) in the Unit 6b colluvium (MF1:C13, samples 172, 152, and 153).

At J in an area of suspected ard marks (Fig 19), there are clear indications of physical mixing of the clay palaeosol and the much more sandy component of the blown sand, which can also be seen to be washed down between peds or clods. Here, at the probable depth limit of the ard, the mechanism for combining the Beaker palaeosol and blowing sand into the sandy loam colluvium (colour MF 36) is apparently illustrated. At J, however, the sand which buries the soil probably relates to the cessation of cultivation because of excess sand blowing.

It was also particularly noteworthy in H and I, which are moderately organic (MF1:C14, samples 152 and 153), that much of the included fine charcoal is 'flakey' and that occasional to many phytoliths are preserved, which possibly indicates an input of burned grass or cereal material into the colluvium to a greater extent than was noted for Unit 8a. Since in the first instance (H) there is a lack of 'anthropogenic fabrics' such as daub or burned soil (Macphail and Courty 1985; M Allen and Macphail 1987), this charcoal material probably does not derive from ploughed-out occupation areas but more likely from stubble burning or from the deliberate (?) spreading of burned organic waste (cereal processing, burned dung)(Macphail 1987c). In addition, some charcoal may be relict of ploughed-out Unit 8a, upslope (thin section J). At H, the absence of occupation soil fabrics could be reflected in a moderate MS value (Chapter 17) whereas in I MS values rise at the same time as some burned soil occurs, in a deposit which also includes a few distinct patches of imported estuarine silts. Here there may be an increase in the intensity of the activity related to the later development of the colluvium including 'manuring'. Silts were, however, used as daub for the walls of structures in the overlying Unit 5b (see p 48), though they may also have arrived in the vicinity, but probably not at this altitude, through natural inundation. Nevertheless, since the fine fabric is reddish, the major component of this colluvium appears to be derived from Unit 8a.

The early Bronze Age occupation deposits, Unit 6a

Deposits from this context were scrutinised consecutively from thin sections L, M, and O (location on Fig 27). The sediments at O are well preserved and retain their original fine (0.2mm) to coarse (3.0mm) layering. In contrast, at L and M, the 0.25m of occupation deposits has been much more strongly homogenised and has also been much more strongly affected by sub-aerial weathering processes. Also it is believed that the deposits differ somewhat in their original character.

At L and M there has been an accretion of sediments made up predominantly of silt and common blown sand with a mainly pale, highly speckled greyish brown fine fabric composed of moderately calcitic ash residue, phytoliths, some fine charcoal, rare diatoms, and patches of amorphous organic matter (colour MF 37, 38, and 39). Pure silty areas rich in phytoliths with few diatoms and amorphous organic matter, which also occur, indicate that much of the sediment derives from imported peaty estuarine silt. The rest of the fabric originates from plant material residues – ash and phytoliths. There are also instances of burned peat and wood and probable *Gramineae* charcoal occurring with rare bone fragments. Textural features such as intercalations and thick infills also indicate slaking and mixing of much of the deposit leading to compaction – a feature typical of ash-rich deposits (Macphail 1987c) – although there is a discontinuity at M between an underlying mixed and weathered sediment and an overlying calcitic ash and sand layer (see below).

In general, the sediments can be regarded as a deposit deriving from occupation, though not necessarily *in situ*. It originated from the deliberate importation of estuarine silts (which were sometimes peaty) for constructional purposes (eg floors) that incorporated blown sand, which is ubiquitous to the site, during their use. This importation also added many probable aquatic plant remains (eg phytoliths) in addition to those possibly from cereal processing and use of 'grass' materials on site, the burning of which, together with local domestic fires, allowed large amounts of calcitic ash to be incorporated. Trampling may be one of the major mechanisms homogenising the deposit (colour MF 42), although the preservation of phytoliths up to 1.5mm in length indicates that the sediments have not been strongly reworked.

Sub-aerial pedogenesis, seemingly during the early Bronze Age (subsequently buried by further occupation ash residue and sand), led to the decalcification of the originally strongly calcitic ashy deposits and the development of restricted areas of amorphous, possibly organo-phosphatic infills that are also rather ferruginous, although only small peaks of Fe and P were picked up in the bulk samples (Chapter 15). These amorphous infills mainly occur as an approximate layer in M (colour MF 40 and 41) and may relate to plants such as lichens colonising the ash (M-A Courty, pers comm). They persist into thin section L, but probably related mobile chemical (organo-Ca, Fe, ?P) complexes have been translocated further down the profile to produce crystalline ferruginous nodules that occur throughout L (colour MF 43, 44, and 45), sometimes in close association with green/blue crystalline material that is petrologically assessed to be the iron-phosphorus mineral vivianite. Although ash is a ready source of phosphate (Wattez and Courty 1987), and a cess input has to be considered on any occupation site, it must be remembered that peats and estuarine silts can also naturally produce vivianite on oxidation. However, the major conclusion is that a combination of weathering and biological activity on exposed ash-rich occupation sediments mobilised phosphorus that in the first instance combined mainly with amorphous organic matter, but also penetrated further down-profile, and probably under localised hydromorphic conditions (poor drainage) produced ferruginous nodules associated with vivianite. Similar features have been noted, for example, from the ash midden at Potterne, Wilts (Macphail 1987c), from a middle Saxon floor, juxtaposed to a hearth, at Jubilee Hall (Macphail 1987d), and 'dark earth' related deposits in general (Macphail and Courty 1985). The chemistry and effect on magnetic susceptibility are discussed further in Chapters 15 and 17 respectively.

The material at O is variable. There are residual ash and sand bands (colour MF 46 and 47), as described from the top of M, which could originate as locally blown material. There are also probable spreads of hearth material (Courty 1984), which differs from the sediments already described by being strongly heterogeneous, containing fragments of burned shell, burned estuarine silt, burned peat, vitrified ash, and melted quartz (melting affecting the grain margins, perhaps needing some 800–1000°C) in addition to sand, a little charcoal (some probably *Gramineae*), and high quantities of ash material, some of which is pseudomorphic of plant cellular material suggesting little disturbance. The presence of high amounts of little-weathered ash in this context (61) also coincides with the highest levels of phosphate measured on the site (Chapter 15). This layer of scattered material, where combustion of fuel has been largely complete in some layers, obviously seems to derive at least in part from fires occasionally reaching higher temperatures than necessary just for cooking purposes (Courty *et al* in press, ch 7.2). Thin section O also features a layer of very coarse charcoal and ash which apparently covers a scatter of burned bone 'dust' possibly derived from local boneworking (Fig 130; colour MF 48 and 49) as worked bone was common in the main occupation areas. The layers at O therefore represent both *in situ* hearths or spreads of material from hearths (eg layered ash over charcoal, typical of *in situ* hearths, Courty 1984) and also trample/wind reworked hearth material (ash) and plant residues (phytoliths), sometimes associated with blown sand or silts. The very high MS levels (MF1:C14, sample 146) also signify the inclusion of hearth material.

Middle Bronze Age, Units 5b and 5a

Both thin sections N (colour MF 6) and K (locations on Figs 17 and 18) are moderately calcitic (MF1:C14, samples 149, 175, and 174), although N differs by being a strongly anthropogenic deposit, whereas K is very much a pure (99%) sand. The division between layers 5a and 5b at K is represented by the 500µm thick amorphous cementation of sand grains presum-

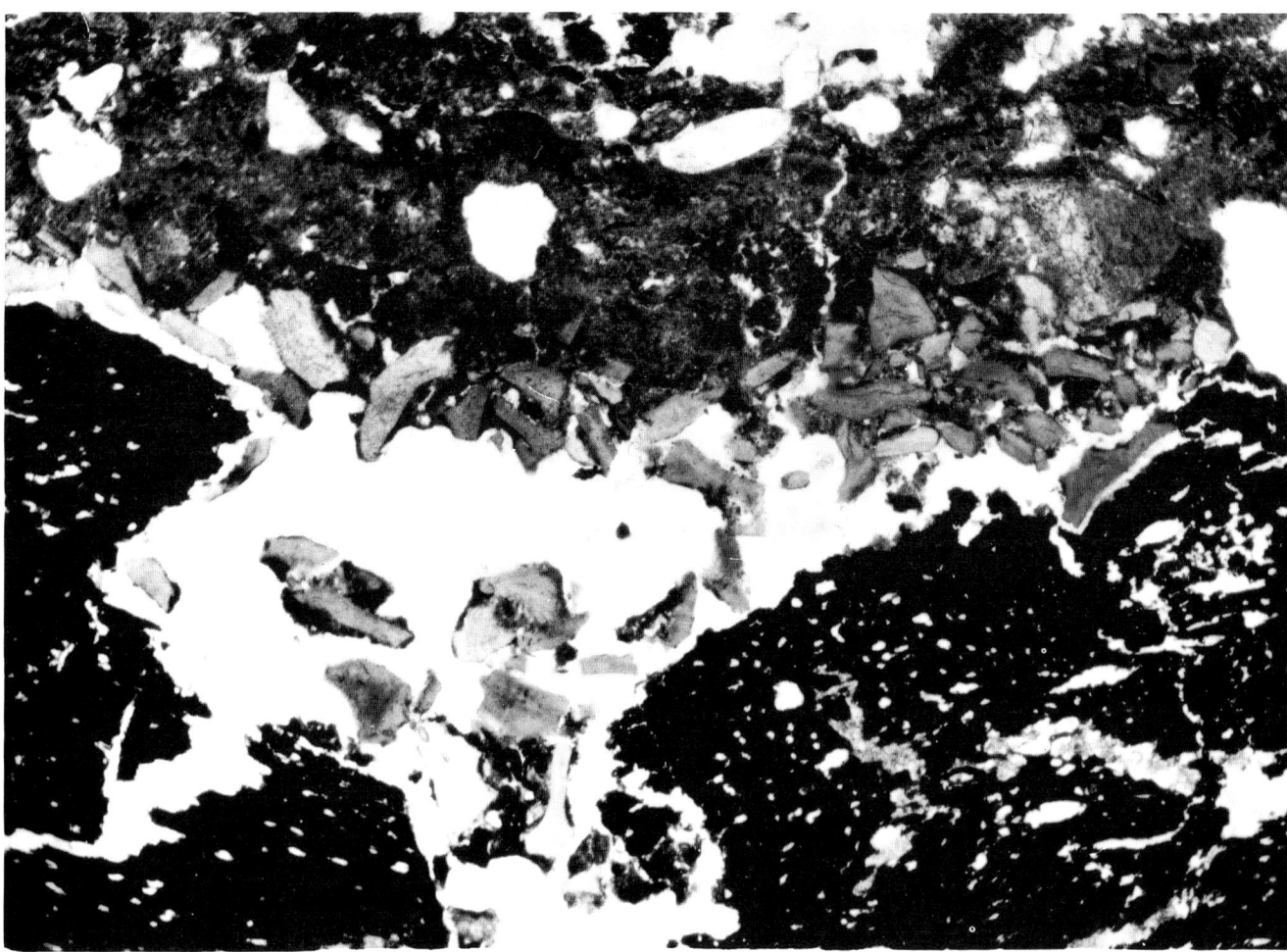

Fig 130   Layered occupation deposit (Unit 6a), thin section O; unweathered (protected) probable low temperature hearth layers comprising coarse wood charcoal, well sorted fine bone fragments, and pure ash of calcium carbonate crystals; plane polarised light; frame length 3.3mm

ably again by possible 'ferruginous organo-phosphate' material, as described for M. It appears that either the junction 5a/5b is an *in situ* stabilisation surface formed by the weathering of an ash layer, or more likely an artefact formed by the downwash of very small quantities of mobile ferruginous 'organo-phosphates' as a wetting front, to form a cemented lamina. Thin amorphous coatings occur throughout, together with rare vivianite. The actual sand is calcareous because of included shell from the beach, whereas there is a notable absence of ash or ash residue (phytoliths). The layer is thus interpreted as blown sand which was affected by the weathering of an overlying ash-rich horizon (as at L, M, and O) acting as a source of mobile 'ferruginous organo-phosphates'. As K is devoid of ash or ash residue material (although calcareous from whatever source elsewhere – Chapter 15), then it seems likely that the ash source was higher up in Unit 5a and that mobilised material was deposited at a hydraulic boundary possibly relating to an old surface formed during the development of these blown sand units (5b, 5a).

The deposit examined in thin section N is rather heterogeneous, any layering being destroyed by faunal working as suggested by the fabric and porosity pattern. As at L, M, and O much of the fine fabric is related to the mixture of imported peaty estuarine silts and phytolith ash residues – some phytoliths, calcite ash crystals, and pollen all being fluorescent under ultra violet light (colour MF 50 and 51). Major characteristics of the layer, however, are the large amounts of strongly burned materials, such as the blackish grey, poorly birefringent material that derives from high temperature fires, that destroyed the calcite ash and fused elemental carbon into vitrified silica originating from the plant opal (phytoliths) (colour MF 52, 53, and 54). The layer also contains weakly burned but reddened heterogeneous non-ceramic material that is unlike hearth material elsewhere (O) and can be possibly interpreted as briquetage which still includes plant temper (colour MF 55). Some of the strongly burned vitrified ash is pseudomorphic of plant material, whereas the suspected briquetage is an apparent mix of estuarine silt with fragments of ferruginous clay, probably from the palaeosol. The strongly burned ash within the deposit which makes these sediments so different from those at L, M, and O seems to suggest a concentration of high temperature burning here (or dumped here); and although the only evidence for 'industry' is briquetage manufacture and salt-making here, which is believed to require only moderately enhanced temperatures (Chapter 14), it may be that there is a connection.

In summary, the middle Bronze Age sediments are predominantly occupation deposits, except for those examined in K (Context 53) where pure blown sand has been weakly cemented by translocated 'occupation residues'. In the main, the sediments comprise imported estuarine deposits (with a leavening of blown sand), anthropogenic inclusions (charcoal, vitrified ash, burned peat, etc), and ash residues. The latter can be divided up into (i) 'solid' residues of calcitic ash and phytoliths, showing peaks in phosphate context, and (ii) weathered remains poor in measurable phosphate that appear to occur as near surface amorphous infills, whereas at greater depth they apparently produce nodules and associated vivianite (Chapter 15). The decalcification process is probably related to the moderately slaked and massive nature of the deposits and their compacted character (colour MF 42) compared with the open unstructured calcitic fabric of little-weathered ash layers (colour MF 48 and 49). The 0.25m of middle Bronze Age occupation deposits, for example, represented by thin sections L and M, is therefore a rather compacted layer, because of weathering (associated with ash breakdown, phosphorus movement, and physical slaking) that seems to have been contemporaneous with the occupation itself.

Late Bronze Age, Unit 4

The late Bronze Age deposits were studied from profile 3, thin section P (location on Fig 15; colour MF 7 and 8) and from Pit V inland, thin section Q (location on Fig 79) respectively. Analyses from both localities show the sediments to be remarkably uniform and homogeneous. They are poorly humic and calcitic (MF1:C14, samples 169 and 307) sandy loams very predominantly composed of blown sand (see Bar Point, Macphail in Evans 1983) with low amounts of silt (11–14%, MF1:C13, samples 169 and 307). They have a darkish brown speckled fine fabric, although the organic carbon content is low, and contain fine charred organic matter, rare bone, rare ash, but many phytoliths. The very abundant textural features (colour MF 56 and 57) and coarse channel porosity suggest that the deposit, while accreting as a (blown sand) colluvium, continued to be perforated by biological activity. As the deposit thickened fine coatings from the slaking of the overlying sediment were translocated down the profile to be superimposed upon earlier coarse coatings.

The sediment has been deposited during continued disturbance, such as trampling or shallow cultivation (?hoeing), rather than *in situ* occupation, because anthropogenic fabrics such as those described from L, M, N, and O are rare. Indeed, cultivation is more likely than trampling because the same fabric seems to extend from the cliff section to Pit V. The moderately high amounts of fine charred organic matter at the cliff section (decreasing inland) and many phytoliths may also support this arable interpretation which is suggested by the combination of biological perforation and soil disturbance. Unfortunately, because the phytoliths are so finely broken up, it is difficult to suggest whether they derive purely from cereal/grass remains or could also originate from additions of estuarine sediments, again either as 'manure' or from the incorporation of previously imported material. This latter is possibly indicated by the amount of silt present and the nature of the fine fabric (colour MF 56 and 57). This interpretation of cultivation, however, can only be applied to the thin, rather stone-free zone at the top of Unit 4 at profile 3, and its more substantial development at Pit V.

Iron Age to Roman colluvium, Unit 4a

A 0.11m long thin section (R) was examined from the Unit 4a sediments in the cliff section (location on Fig 15). The deposit is very homogeneous, but differs from the late Bronze Age sediment by having a reddish brown fine fabric (crystalline iron), a rather calcareous character (MF1:C14, sample 302), and very low clay and silt content (MF1:C13, sample 302) in a strongly stony (limestone) deposit. Here the reddish colour of the fine fabric suggests that soil, similar to the Beaker palaeosol and probably including material from the Upper Breccia or the Down Limestone platform itself (relict *terra fusca*), has been eroded, which in the latter case would also account for the very stony nature of the deposit. As no clay papules were noted, which suggests substantial recycling of the fine material, the exact origins cannot be known. Again, much of the bulk of the sediment is of blown sand origin. Its suspected nature as a colluvium is supported by patchy areas of textural features that predate the major biological working of the deposit, faunal activity probably being enhanced by the calcareous character of the soil. As in the late Bronze Age deposits, the results of long oxidation give no clue to the contemporary organic levels of this horizon. Finally, it is difficult to state categorically whether there was much *in situ* ploughing of the material which appears to have arrived as a moderately high energy (coarse stony) colluvium. The uniform character of the deposit, however, suggests that it was ploughed on site.

Conclusions

A sequence of events can be interpreted from the micromorphology and other data.

(i) The Pleistocene deposits include wind-blown and colluvial silts and soil fragments, the latter of cryogenic soils, temperate soils, and *terra fusca*, all probably originating from the Mendip soil cover. Some of the deposits were variously affected by *in situ* cryoclastic activity and short lived 'temperate' pedogenesis.

(ii) A complex argillic brown earth developed in the Early Flandrian through the pedogenic homogenisation of a lower sequum of beta B clay (*terra fusca*) originating from the breccia (Unit 8b) and an upper sequum of wind-blown silt and sand, variously from the Pleistocene deposits, local beach sand and estuarine silt, and from a general 'Mendip loessial' source (see Fig 126).

(iii) The present palaeosol is a complicated soil, comprising a basal zone of mixed soil relating to clearance, a middle zone giving evidence of cultivation and colluviation, and a topsoil reworked by earthworms. Thus clearance was followed by a significant period of cultivation leading to erosion and downslope colluviation – colluvium mixing at lower altitude with estuarine/marine inundation silts. Cultivation ceased for some seasons allowing biological reworking of the topsoil and the development of a mull horizon.

(iv) The Beaker palaeosol was buried by blown sand, itself perhaps open for some time.

(v) Early middle Bronze Age cultivation continued to erode the palaeosol and the resulting colluvium buried the blown sand and again became mixed with estuarine silts downslope.

(vi) Later during the early Bronze Age occupation, Unit 6a, estuarine silts and peat were imported on to the site mainly for constructional purposes and became intimately mixed with blown sand and domestic debris of ash and charcoal. Preserved layered hearth spreads suggest dominant domestic use of fires. Where ash residues mixed with floor materials of estuarine silt and wind-blown sand were exposed to sub-aerial weathering, partial decalcification, slaking, and compaction took place. Amorphous infills, probably containing organic matter and P, were produced, whereas down-profile nodules and vivianite were deposited probably from translocated P, Fe, and Ca.

(vii) In the middle Bronze Age, domestic occupation also gave rise to ash-rich deposits contemporary with wind-blown sand deposition, but here there are strong indications of higher temperature hearths, possibly for example associated with the briquetage.

(viii) In the late Bronze Age the deposits are primarily characterised by their imported estuarine silt and wind-blown sand content, some areas at least of this 'anthropogenic soil' probably being cultivated.

(ix) A phase of colluviation after the late Bronze Age produced a reddish stony colluvium, probably as erosion of the Head and Pleistocene breccia occurred.

Acknowledgements

The author wishes to thank Stephen Carter for grain size analyses; Dawn Ray and Sheila Ross for chemical analyses; Mike Allen for MS data; the Institut National Agronomique, Paris-Grignon, and Anne Gebhardt for help with thin section manufacture; Marie-Agnès Courty for discussion of the thin sections; and Martin Bell, Sheila Ross, and Mike Allen for discussion of a first draft of this report.

17 Magnetic susceptibility

by Michael J Allen

Introduction

Magnetic susceptibility has been used as a prospecting method in archaeology for nearly 20 years (Tite and Mullins 1970; 1971; Doggart 1985). Now, however, magnetic susceptibility is also being used as a palaeoenvironmental indicator (M Allen 1986; 1988), and thus the aims of the magnetic susceptibility survey at Brean Down were twofold. The first was to explore the potential of magnetic susceptibility as a palaeoenvironmental indicator by examining the chronological/stratigraphic sequence with a view to aiding the interpretation of the site depositional environments. Here, sampling was conducted stratigraphically in conjunction with detailed field descriptions and other chemical and physical analyses (see Chapters 15 and 16). The second aim was to examine the spatial variation over a single temporal unit (phase), in order to aid the identification of activity areas and thus augment the archaeological record.

Magnetic susceptibility (MS) is a parameter which expresses the ratio between the magnetisation induced in a sample and the magnetising field (see Thompson *et al* 1975; Oldfield *et al* 1978; 1985). Strongly magnetic forms of iron oxide (eg maghaemite) have a strongly positively aligned magnetic moment if placed in a magnetic field; moreover they are capable of retaining magnetic remanence when removed from that field. Magnetic susceptibility can be enhanced through pedogenesis (M Allen and Macphail 1987) or through burning (Le Borgne 1960a) which creates strongly ferromagnetic crystalline forms of iron oxide (Longworth and Tite 1977).

Magnetic susceptibility enhancement, ie the conversion of, for instance, haematite to magnetite, provides the basis for interpretation. The levels of susceptibility depend both upon the concentration of iron oxides which are available for conversion from weakly ferri and ferro magnetic forms to strongly ferromagnetic crystalline forms, and the 'intensity/longevity' of the activity and processes inducing enhancement. Le Borgne demonstrated that burning will significantly enhance magnetic susceptibility (1955; 1960a; 1960b) and thus can be used to identify areas of human activity. Further processes associated with occupation (such as trampling) also aid enhancement (see M Allen and Macphail 1985; 1987) and therefore, as can be seen here, it is evident that enhancement need not be totally attributed to 'burning'.

Magnetic susceptibility can also be enhanced by natural pedogenic processes. Topsoils (A horizons) usually display significant enhancement in comparison to subsoils. The pedogenic mechanisms involved in this enhancement are less well understood, though they are certainly a result of complex chemical and biological activity in surface horizons. Further, it has been suggested that magnetic susceptibility variation, when uncomplicated by intensive archaeological activity, seems to reflect vegetational and pedogenic regimes (M Allen 1986; 1988).

An extensive series of magnetic susceptibility readings was recorded from samples taken during the 1985 and 1986 excavations. Magnetic susceptibility was used especially because, although it requires detailed pedological knowledge to provide a comprehensive interpretation (M Allen and Macphail 1985; 1987), sampling on site and recording are rapid, cost-effective, and easy to perform.

Materials and methods

Soil samples taken in the field were air dried and a subsample of 100g <2mm was measured using a Bartington MS2 meter coupled to a 62mm diameter MS2 B coil calibrated for 100g of soil. Where the available soil was less than 100g the known weight recorded was calculated as a percentage of 100g and the magnetic result recalculated using the following formula:

$$100 \div \text{sample wt} \times \text{magnetic susceptibility}$$

The results of analysis are expressed in SI units $\times 10^{-8}$ SI/kg and are presented in MF1:F2–5 and also represented graphically in association with drawings of the appropriate stratigraphy (Fig 131, MF1:E4–7). Magnetic susceptibility measurements from the grid of samples in Unit 5b are presented in MF1:F6–8 and also graphically using a surface calculation programme run on an Amstrad PC1512 + 32Mb hard disk (Fig 132a, MF1:E8–F1).

Two parallel magnetic susceptibility studies were undertaken at Brean Down, involving the preparation and measurement of 246 samples. The first was to examine the susceptible iron content vertically down the cliff profile in order to characterise the deposits and thus provide some basis for aiding determination of the origin and nature of the deposits. The second was a horizontal spatial array of Unit 5b (Context 53) and the structures within it (ie 59 and 95) in order to examine susceptibility variation in relation to anthropogenic activity and thus enhance the archaeological record by attempting to identify activity areas within the unit. The former, stratigraphic examination provides the natural background for the subsequent evaluation of 'anthropogenic' enhancement.

Results and information from the magnetic susceptibility programmes were then discussed and interpreted in the light of data from soil micromorphology, chemical analysis, granulometry, and molluscan analysis.

Sampling

Stratigraphic sequence

Samples from the 5m of stratigraphy (Fig 131) were mainly obtained by removing 100g subsamples from the mollusc columns which were sampled at strategic points in the stratigraphy. These samples were taken

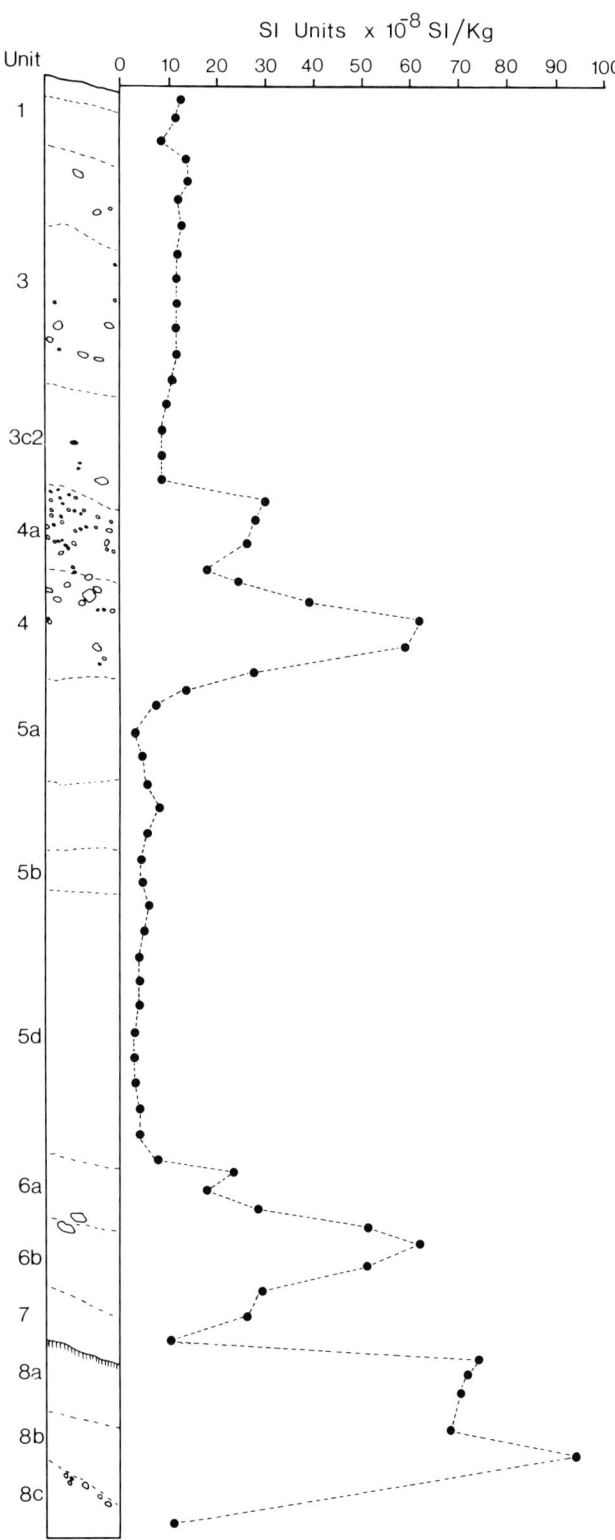

Fig 131 Summary diagram of magnetic susceptibility variation through the stratigraphic sequence at Brean Down

by Martin Bell contiguously at 0.1m intervals, taking care not to cross any obvious physical horizon boundaries. A further sample suite was taken specifically for magnetic susceptibility measurement from the estuarine silts in Soil Pit VI. The main data for the stratigraphic characterisation of the deposits come from 122 samples from the five mollusc columns and Soil Pit VI. Additional samples were also taken in conjunction with soil micromorphological samples taken by Richard Macphail in order to provide strong correlation between the two levels of analysis (see M Allen and Macphail 1987). In total, 138 samples were measured in this programme.

Unit 5b, Context 53

The samples for the programme conducted on a horizontal plane over the structures in Unit 5b were taken on the site grid at 1 or 0.5m intervals as appropriate.

Structure 95

Eighty-three samples were taken from Structure 95 at 1m intervals on the site grid in conjunction with samples for phosphate, dithionite extractable iron, and pyrophosphate extractable iron (Chapter 15). Further, an additional six samples were taken for magnetic susceptibility from individual contexts, eg the storm gully (139), wall fill (131), hearth material (134), and ash spreads (77, 113, and 130) (MF1:F6–7).

Structure 59

Nineteen samples were taken from the small surviving area of this structure at 0.5m intervals and, as with Structure 95, a parallel suite of samples were taken for phosphate and both dithionite and pyrophosphate extractable iron analyses (Chapter 15).

Results

Programme 1: stratigraphy

As stated above, magnetic susceptibility has been used to characterise deposits and also to attempt to evaluate sediment origin. However, the latter theme in this case is made more difficult by the lack of other similar studies in either the locality itself or within similar deposits, ie stratified dune sequences. Nevertheless, with the knowledge of typical magnetic susceptibility results from other sedimentary sequences, these data can augment other physical and chemical attributes, making possible a higher resolution of interpretation and understanding.

Unit 8: Palaeosol

No samples were taken from the lowest portion of Unit 8 (ie 8c), the sandy breccia (ApSimon *et al* 1961). The sampling strategy commenced with 8b (Context 126) in tandem with soil micromorphological samples. The single sample from 8b produced a comparatively low magnetic susceptibility reading of only 10 SI×10⁻⁸ SI/kg. This contrasts dramatically with readings from the overlying deposits of Unit 8a (Contexts 127 and 63), the basal palaeosol. The fill of the gully or ditch (Context 127) cut into the palaeosol was significantly enhanced (68), partly as a result of the high iron content but also because of long-term *in situ* pedogenic weathering of the relict *terra fusca* soil. Samples from the upper horizons of the brown earth (Context 63) also show considerable enhancement (94), again due to the degree of pedogenic activity combined with high crystalline and mobile iron contents. Although here enhancement is probably due to pedogenesis, it is further increased by clearance and limited anthropogenic activity.

Unit 7: 'Beaker sand'

Two columns included three samples from Unit 7. The blown sand horizon produced low magnetic susceptibility readings reflecting the sterile nature of the deposit. It is evident, from the sediments themselves and the lack of archaeological artefacts, that this unit was deposited comparatively rapidly and is probably the result of Flandrian wind erosion of the beach and bar sands. The magnetic susceptibility record supports this and provides no evidence for pedogenic or human activity. However, a thin but discrete burnt activity horizon (Context 188) was observed during excavation, though the sampling strategy was such that this was not evident at the predescribed sample locations. However, samples taken from single contexts specifically to overcome this do indeed show that the basal magnetic susceptibility is low (4) and that the burnt activity horizon is enhanced (16). Furthermore, the sand overlying the burnt horizon also displayed enhancement (12) indicating limited Beaker activity or reworking (MF1:F4).

Unit 6: Beaker/early Bronze Age colluvium

This unit had a complex archaeological history which is reflected in the magnetic susceptibility results. The lower, predominantly colluvial horizon (Unit 6b) is derived from the palaeosol upslope. At its base it displays relatively low magnetic susceptibility (12), which probably represents the initial soil material washed from the fields outside the settlement areas which were not extensively artificially enhanced. However, susceptibility increases significantly through Unit 6b, which indicates increased *in situ* activity on site and a decrease in the 'diluting' hillwash component. This scenario can be paralleled in the chalcolithic hillwash at Uscio (M Allen and Macphail 1987).

The upper component of this unit (6a), although visibly highly anthropogenic, shows a marked decrease in the magnetic susceptibility record. In view of the evidence of intensive human activity it is likely that this decrease is caused by either chemical or physical complications. Although it is possible that iron could be 'locked up' in calcium or iron phosphates and thus be unavailable for magnetic susceptibility enhancement, Sheila Ross's chemical analyses show this not to be the case (Chapter 15). Both phosphate and dithionite iron forms decrease in sympathy with magnetic susceptibility. It is therefore more likely that magnetic susceptibility values have been diluted by the human import of material with low susceptibility. It is plausible that estuarine silts may have been brought to the site and the analyses of such deposits in Soil Pit VI displayed very low susceptibility throughout the *c* 4m sequence (MF1:E7). Indeed this hypothesis is corroborated by Richard Macphail's micromorphological analysis (Chapter 16) which indicated the import of both peaty material and estuarine silts.

Unit 5: Bronze Age blown sand

The 1.5m of blown sand overlying the early Bronze Age colluvium is comprised of Units 5a and 5d. This was sampled upslope of the middle Bronze Age structures discussed below. The 29 magnetic susceptibility readings consistently recorded low values. This indicates the sterile and rapid nature of deposition and also suggests a lack of anthropogenic and pedological activity at the point sampled. However, this unit contained one of the major archaeological phases including two structures and associated activity areas. The results from the stratigraphical analysis indicate that such activity was confined to the downslope areas and this is demonstrated more forcibly below in the spatial analysis of the occupation surface.

Unit 4: late Bronze Age occupation horizons

Sealing the blown sand was a 'grey clay' layer associated with intensive late Bronze Age activity. Indeed this activity is reflected in significant magnetic susceptibility enhancement (up to 62). However, enhancement in the upslope sample column is more subdued (maximum 29). This, like the middle Bronze Age activity in Unit 5, may suggest that the foci of activity were downslope, an area of the late Bronze Age surface which has been much eroded by later natural and human agencies. Enhancement here is primarily a result of human activity such as burning etc, but is also probably due to trampling and puddling. These activities may serve to cause fluctuating wetting and drying enabling oxidisation and reduction within the deposit matrix, resulting in enhancement (M Allen and Macphail 1987; M Allen in prep).

Units 4a–1: Iron Age/Romano-British palaeosol – modern

A distinct rubified soil overlying the late Bronze Age occupation surface, on which and into which the Early Christian graves were cut, also displayed magnetic susceptibility enhancement. The origin of this horizon (Context 25) is probably colluvial, derived from eroded palaeosol and breccia upslope but representing a distinct hiatus or truncation in the sequence. Richard Macphail demonstrates that this horizon contains pedorelics and textural features akin to those identified in Unit 8. These predate the major biological reworking and pedogenesis indicating that

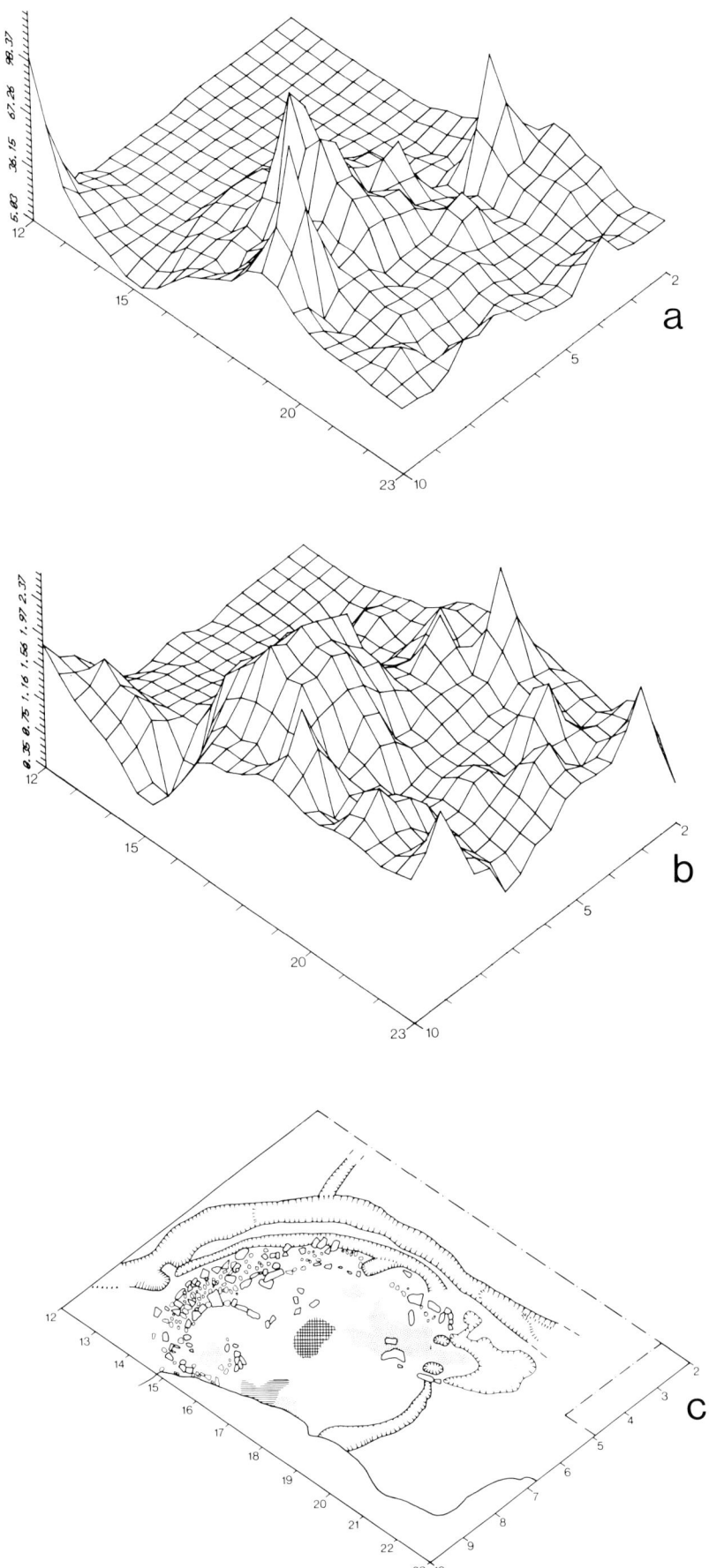

Fig 132 Magnetic and chemical distributions viewed isometrically at 45° over Structure 95, Unit 5b: (a) magnetic susceptibility, (b) phosphate, and (c) isometric plan of Structure 95, Unit 5b

this horizon was a long-term stabilisation horizon. Enhancement here is likely to be a combination of the biological reworking identified by Richard Macphail and the fact that this material originates from deposits with a known high iron content that have been shown to be significantly enhanced.

The upper horizon of colluvium and blown sand deposits, including the modern soil, display low and consistent magnetic susceptibility. Magnetic susceptibility values through the upper deposits average 11.3 SI×10^{-8} SI/kg which is higher than the blown sand sequence in Units 5 and 7. Greater values here are due to a larger colluvial element containing enhanced soil material and the fact that accumulation was gradual, enabling soil processes to occur throughout the development of these deposits.

Summary

The aims of the stratigraphic magnetic susceptibility study, which were to characterise the deposits and aid interpretation of (a) their mode of deposition and (b) the activities occurring within them, have been adequately fulfilled.

Those deposits with significant pedogenesis and human activity were easily isolated. Indeed magnetic susceptibility levels, to a degree, can be seen to reflect the intensity of these activities. Furthermore, detailed examination of the results prompted the hypothesis that material was imported into Unit 6a by human agencies. This hypothesis was corroborated by Richard Macphail's micromorphological analyses.

In conclusion it can be seen that the natural Early Flandrian *terra fusca* soil is iron rich and that the high natural magnetic susceptibility values were enhanced by human action. Blown sand deposits originating from the sand beach and bars produced low susceptibility only by being significantly enhanced by prolonged human activity within them, whilst occupation surfaces (Units 6, 4, and 5b, see below) display not only significant enhancement but also spatial variation which can be used to interpret the nature and patterning of activity rather than to identify its occurrence as this study has done.

Programme 2: Unit 5b

Structure 95 was preserved almost entirely and is described fully in Chapter 4. The magnetic susceptibility values, plotted graphically in Figure 132a, show low background readings in the sand upslope of the building. The values recorded here (MF1:F6–8) compare well with those from the stratigraphic sequence at this point and indicate a lack of human disturbance and activity. Distinct variation of magnetic susceptibility values over the rest of this structure provides a comprehensive picture of activity and refuse patterns.

The stone wall on the upslope side displays slight, and constant, enhancement, enabling it to be detected as a minor ridge in Figure 132a, whilst the area within the building displays considerable and variable enhancement. Values up to 136 were recorded here and the spatial variation of magnetic susceptibility within the hut floor indicates two areas of exceptional enhancement. One area on the seaward side coincides with the occurrence of a large group of Trevisker pottery. Extreme care was taken to ensure that the measured samples contained no pottery and thus enhancement here is associated with anthropogenic activity rather than iron-rich pottery fragments. The second peak in magnetic susceptibility (120) occurred immediately to the east of the hearth. Although the hearth itself produced relatively low magnetic susceptibility values, the burning and ash deposits associated with it were significantly enhanced (175). This pattern is probably due to the low iron content of the imported clay used in the construction of the hearth in contrast to the heating of the relatively iron-rich deposits comprising the hut floor which are highly susceptible.

Downslope of the entrance high magnetic susceptibility values are also recorded, here associated with refuse and hearth-associated material discarded from the hut. The storm gully is clearly depicted by low magnetic susceptibility readings as its fills represent sand and material washed from the upslope areas with low magnetic susceptibility. However, eastwards of the gully high values are recorded indicating the continuation of archaeological activity areas in that direction.

The magnetic susceptibility values compare well with the excavated plan (Fig 132c) and it is clear that the areas upslope of the structure are natural sand deposits with little or no archaeological activity. The centre of occupation and activity is to the south of the structure from where access to the building is gained. The striking contrast between the upslope and downslope areas may indicate that the building was terraced into the sandcliff.

The magnetic susceptibility variation over Structure 59 displays less obvious patterning. This is partly due to the small portion of the structure surviving and also possibly to more severe post-burial chemical taphonomy. Certainly the hut floor and entrances are depicted by high magnetic susceptibility, though the comparisons with other chemical properties are less obvious (MF1:E8–F1).

The contrast in chemical and magnetic susceptibility attributes from the two buildings may allow the suggestion either that they performed specifically different functions or that they were not strictly contemporary and the abandonment of Structure 59 enabled a more complex chemical history to develop before burial by blown sand.

Comparison

A cursory comparison between the chemical analyses described by Sheila Ross (Chapter 15 and MF1:E8–F1) and the magnetic susceptibility results makes possible comment on both interpretation and causation of magnetic susceptibility enhancement. Contrary to many surveys where magnetic susceptibility and phosphate are mutually exclusive, here phosphate provides a very similar overall pattern to that of the magnetic susceptibility (Fig 132b). The building floor and surrounding activity areas display high phosphate values. Both dithionite (Fe_d) and pyrophosphate iron (Fe_p) produced minimal spatial variation as is shown graphically in MF1:E9 and E13 though, as Sheila Ross states, the crystalline iron (Fe_d) is more akin to magnetic susceptibility than pyrophosphate iron (Fe_p) because the former constitutes a major proportion of the total iron. Furthermore, as Sheila Ross states (Chapter 15) the phosphate content depends upon pH and *in situ* iron and calcium contents. Thus it is not surprising here that the magnetic susceptibility seems to reflect the phosphate levels in the sediments. The precise nature of the specific susceptible iron forms and their distribution and chemistry remain unknown, and until further research is directed at the examination of magnetic susceptibility and chemical constituents on a microscopic scale, many of the ambiguities of causation and process must remain unanswered.

Summary

The potential of magnetic susceptibility as an indicator both of palaeoenvironments and of anthropogenic activity episodes is evident from this study. In particular, the variation of magnetic susceptibility over the surface of Structure 95 demonstrated that specific activity areas, rather than just site locations, can be isolated by this technique. It is evident that magnetic susceptibility has great potential for aiding both archaeological and environmental interpretation, though its full potential was not realised here and cannot be realised without further investigative research into pedological and chemical processes of susceptibility enhancement.

18 Pollen analysis, diatoms, ostracods, and the foreshore peat

Pollen analysis of the foreshore peat

by Keith Crabtree

About 0.5km offshore can be found exposures of peat (Fig 3) overlying silts and covered with a thin veneer of present-day mud. At times the veneer is washed off or cut through by drainage channels exposing a thin peat. Coring by the Severn Tidal Power Group has shown this thin peat to occur elsewhere in the intertidal area at or below Ordnance Datum. This work has also demonstrated the existence of other earlier peat bands, the biological evidence from which has not been investigated in the present study. A block of the peat and underlying silty clay was dug out in 1987 (Fig 133) and subsamples from this taken in the laboratory for pollen and diatom analysis. The peat was levelled in relation to Ordnance Datum and was recorded as having its base at minus 0.15m OD.

The stratigraphy of the peat block was as follows:

0–0.005m Veneer of sandy silt grey in colour.
0.005–0.090m Laminated dark brown peat becoming darker on exposure to air. Large *Phragmites* leaves and smaller monocotyledonous leaves and stems mostly horizontal. Becoming compacted with depth. Laminae separated by partings of very fine sand or sandy silts and clays but in total only occupying a small percentage of the bulk. The whole peat is penetrated by small diameter (3–6mm) animal burrows filled with the fine grey silty clay.
0.090–0.150m More massive dark brown peat with many *Phragmites* fragments. Virtually silt free.
0.150–0.240m Grey silty clay with *Phragmites* roots and stems penetrating downwards, but decreasing with depth.
0.240–0.270m Massive grey silty clay with a few fragments of *Phragmites*. Silty clays below the peat have been proved by augering to a depth of −2.3m OD.

Samples from the peat and silt block were taken at 0.015m intervals and prepared for pollen analysis. Some of the peat was virtually free of mineral matter and was treated with warm dilute caustic potash, sieved, oxidised with sodium chlorate and concentrated sulphuric acid in glacial acetic acid, and finally acetolysed with acetic acid. The silts had the oxidation process omitted and hydrofluoric acid treatment in its place. The pollen was finally mounted in glycerine jelly stained with safranine. Counts were made under ×40 objective with ×20 eyepieces swinging on to an oil immersion ×100 objective where a critical examination of the surface sculpturing was necessary.

From 0.06 to 0.12m pollen was quite well preserved, enabling counts in excess of 1000 grains to be made. Above and below this the pollen was sparser and not so well preserved. In these samples counts of only 400–500 grains and spores were possible. The results are presented in Figure 134.

The dominant pollen throughout is grass (Gramineae) pollen with varying amounts of sedge (Cyperaceae) and Chenopodiaceae pollen. The occasionally high Compositae plus up to 40% Chenopodiaceae suggest a saltmarsh peat. The very low arboreal and shrub pollen percentages plus the range of herbs present indicate a very open vegetation community at the site.

The arboreal pollen may give some guide to the woodland vegetation of the Brean Down limestone hill or of the clay levels (if then in existence). The woods would appear to have been deciduous woodland dominated by oak with some lime, elm, and ash. Alder may have been present on the Levels sites. Birch and pine are very poorly represented and yet pine pollen is often concentrated in estuarine deposits. A small amount of hazel was present. Grains of ivy and privet (both of which are insect pollinated shrubs) were both present suggesting relatively local presence of the species.

The lowest two samples in which sufficient countable pollen occurred were 0.135 and 0.15m and these are dominated by the grass and Chenopodiaceae pollen. The presence of *Aster/Bidens* and *Cirsium* types of the Compositae pollen might also support the idea of open saltmarsh or salt flats. Sedge pollen

Fig 133 Block of sediment from the intertidal zone (location on Fig 3); Phragmites peat overlying grey silty clay; scale division 10mm (photo: T Philpott)

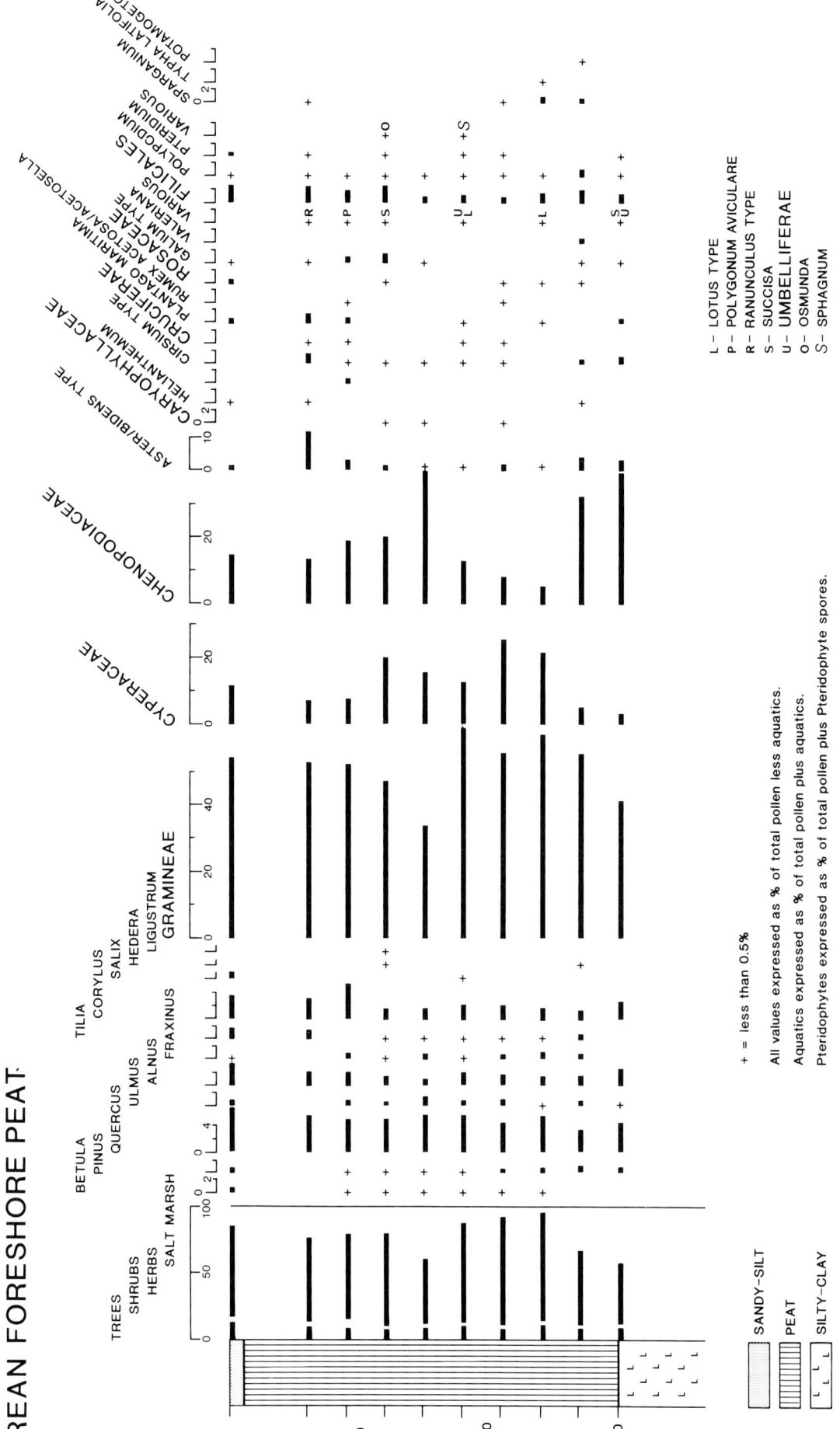

Fig 134 Pollen analysis of the foreshore peat

is low in value. At 0.12m there is a marked fall in Chenopodiaceae pollen and rise in Cyperaceae pollen, and throughout the peats to 0.06m sedge pollen remains fairly high. The Chenopodiaceae values, however, fluctuate, rising again to nearly 40% at 0.075m. At 0.045 and 0.03m Compositae in the form of *Aster/Bidens* type rise to almost equal the Chenopodiaceae at 13.3% while Cyperaceae values have fallen to below 10%. A few grains relatable to *Plantago maritima* occur spasmodically throughout and are not at variance with the saltmarsh interpretation.

Among the herbs occasional grains of *Helianthemum* might be relatable to the presence of *Helianthemum appenninum* on the south-facing crags of the Down today. It is not, however, possible positively to ascribe the *Helianthemum* pollen type to species.

The very low values for Filicales and *Polypodium*, as well as for some of the more resistant arboreal pollen types (eg *Tilia*, *Corylus*), suggest that the pollen record is a real record and has not suffered differential decay or inclusion of reworked material from soils.

A few aquatic species occur in the lower samples, mostly *Sparganium*, which suggests some freshwater swamp development, in keeping with the presence of macroscopic remains of *Phragmites*.

The absence of a number of species associated with agriculture, and the absence of *Fagus* pollen, are in agreement with a view that the peat is pre-Neolithic in date. In general peats of this height relative to OD on the Somerset and north Devon coast have been dated to around 6000–5000 BP (eg Kidson 1977; Balaam *et al* 1987). The silt dating of the marine silty clays in Pit VI at *c* 3m OD is given as *c* 6000 BP by Anthony Clark (Chapter 9). Silts at that site at *c* 0m OD are presumably older. The foreshore peat itself has been radiocarbon dated 5620±100 BP (HAR-8546).

Macroscopic plant remains from the foreshore peat

by Vanessa Straker

The peat and silt block was divided at 0.03m intervals into consecutive 200g (*c* 180ml) samples. The samples were soaked in a solution of 5% sodium hydroxide solution and washed through a stack of sieves with a minimum mesh size of 250μm. They were sorted using a binocular microscope and identified with the help of reference material in the Department of

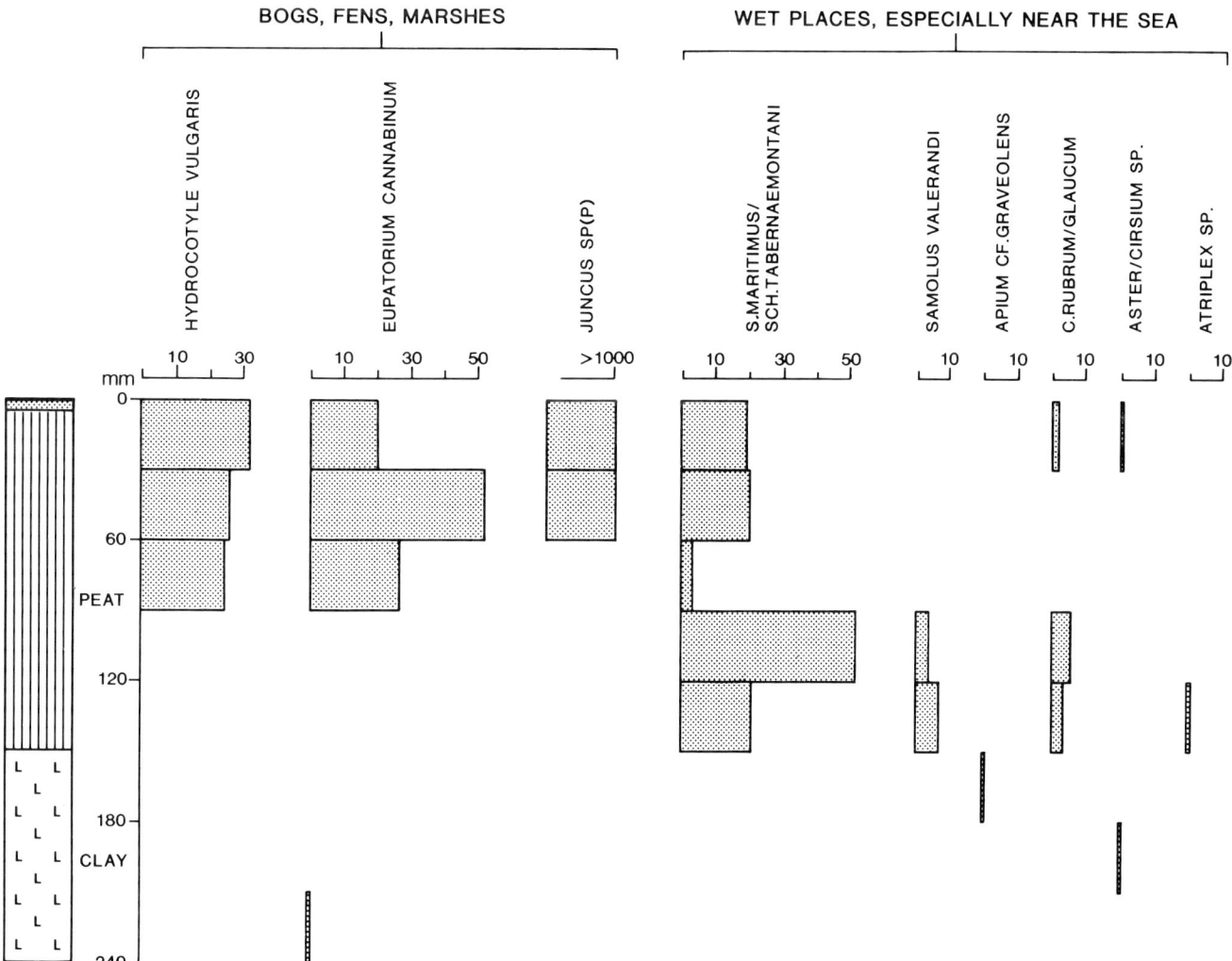

Fig 135 Macroscopic plant remains from the foreshore peat

Geography, University of Bristol. With the exception of the 250μm fraction, where 10% from the top two levels and 50% from the rest of the levels was examined, the samples were sorted completely. Habitat information is taken from Clapham *et al* 1962.

The macroscopic remains of *Phragmites* leaves and rhizomes were noted as described above. As Figure 135 shows the remains of fruits and seeds were more abundant in the peat than in the underlying silty clay and absent completely in the lowest sample between 0.24 and 0.27m depth. The taxa identified are listed below:

Hydrocotyle vulgaris L   Pennywort
Eupatorium cannabinum L   Hemp agrimony
Scirpus maritimus L   Sea club-rush or *Schoenoplectus tabernaemontani* (C C Gmel) Palla   Glaucus bulrush
Juncus sp(p)   Rush(es)
Samolus valerandi L   Brookweed
Chenopodium rubrum L   Red goosefoot or *C glaucum* L   Glaucus goosefoot
Aster/Cirsium sp   Aster/Thistle; owing to poor preservation, the two genera could not be separated
Apium cf *graveolens* L   Fool's watercress
Atriplex sp   Orache

Pennywort and Hemp agrimony are plants of bogs, fens, and marshy freshwater conditions. They were confined to the upper 0.09m, although pollen belonging to the *Aster/Bidens* group which could include Hemp agrimony was recorded in this horizon as well as lower in the profile.

Juncus (rush) was abundant in the upper 0.06m; however, it was not possible to identify it to species level and the *Juncus* could be a saltmarsh species such as *J gerardii* or one of the many freshwater species. Fruits of the Cyperaceae family were abundant in the upper half of the block; the large caryopses are identified as Sea club-rush or Glaucus bulrush. While the former can be found as a saltmarsh plant and will occasionally tolerate freshwater, the Sea club-rush grows in streams, ditches, and bogs, particularly near the sea. Brookweed and Fool's watercress, characteristic of wet places but with a coastal preference, were recorded in low numbers.

Despite the high numbers of Chenopodiaceae pollen, the only members of this family identified in the macroscopic assemblage were the occasional small *Chenopodium* seeds which are most likely to be of Red goosefoot and rarely *Atriplex* sp (orache). Red goosefoot lives on waste places and cultivated ground today, particularly near the sea, but is not a saltmarsh plant. These seeds may have been brought to the site through occasional inundations and relate to communities up or down the estuary.

Acknowledgement

I acknowledge with gratitude the comments of Astrid Caseldine on the plant macrofossils.

Discussion

by Keith Crabtree

The macroscopic evidence supplied by Vanessa Straker throws doubt upon the idea of the peat having been formed under a saltmarsh community. The dominance of *Phragmites* remains may have been in something of a dune slack but the inclusion of a large number of seeds of *Eupatorium* as well as of Carices suggests that the site was wet with standing water but that the water was fresh. Hillman (1981) stresses that *Phragmites* can exist in mesohaline conditions and, according to Ranwell (1972), can even invade *Spartina* saltmarsh beds. The pollen of *Eupatorium* is in the *Bidens* group of the Compositae. Nevertheless the diatoms included in the sample at 0.045m were predominantly marine or saline water diatoms. One therefore envisages that the peat formed from plants growing in a site of predominantly fresh water but that the organic debris accumulation site had at least occasional inundation by the sea, particularly towards the end of the period represented. The sandy silt partings in the upper horizons of the peat support a view of successive inundation or flooding. It is not clear whether the surface veneer of sandy silt is a product of the present regime or contemporaneous with the end of peat accumulation. It is assumed that the worm borings filled with grey silt are probably modern. If that is the case then the marine diatoms recorded in the peat could be modern intrusive diatoms taken down in the worm holes.

Pollen analysis of sandcliff samples and marine silts

by Keith Crabtree

The sandcliff

Samples taken from the excavations to complement the soil samples taken by Richard Macphail and Sheila Ross were prepared for pollen analysis by treatment with dilute hydrochloric acid to remove the carbonate, warm dilute caustic potash to disperse the organic matter, hydrofluoric acid to remove the mineral matter, and then acetolysed prior to mounting in glycerol jelly stained with safranine. All slides were scanned with 10 traverses on each to record what was present. Where a number of grains did occur then counting was continued. Where the number of grains was down to fewer than 2 per traverse, recording ceased after 10 traverses.

In a majority of cases only odd grains occurred, often falling into two distinct categories. The first category was of extremely corroded grains often broken and difficult to identify. The second category was of fairly fresh looking grains. It is probable that the latter were modern grains washed into the deposits or penetrated down the root channels. As a lot of the sediment is sandy and freely drained it seems that downwash of humic matter including pollen is

Table 13 Numbers of grains recorded in two samples from Unit 6a, Context 61

Sample number	159	160
Context	61	61
Unit	6a	6a
Betula		1
Quercus		1
GRAMINEAE	14	2
CYPERACEAE	4	
CHENOPODIACEAE	5	2
COMPOSITAE:		
Aster type	1	
Taraxacum type	1	
Plantago lanceolata	9	2
P maritima	6	
ROSACEAE undiff		1
Galium type		2
FILICALES	4	4
Polypodium	1	
Corroded grains	29	7
CHARCOAL	+	+
Totals:		
pollen recognised	30	13
pollen and spores	35	17

likely to occur. It was anticipated that pollen preservation was likely to be both poor and limited with most of the sediment being so freely aerobic and calcareous, conditions which are usually unsuitable for pollen preservation.

MF1:F9 gives the details of pollen found on a subjective assessment where an asterisk indicates a single grain and two asterisks mean several grains. A cross refers to a very fresh looking (presumed modern) grain. In the case of two samples from Unit 6a, Context 61, grains were present in small numbers and the actual numbers counted are recorded in Table 13.

Although the numbers of grains in these samples are small they are the only samples in the section with counts into double figures and it seems likely that they are grains which are contemporaneous with the deposit. From micromorphological evidence, Richard Macphail suggests that the deposit includes burnt peat. The presence of charcoal and corroded grains would support this and the inclusion of grains of Chenopodiaceae, the high Gramineae, the *Plantago* species, and the *Aster/Bidens* type shows similarity with the pollen recorded from the foreshore peat. It does seem likely that the peat used for burning in Context 61 was derived from the same bed of peat which is now exposed on the foreshore.

For the remainder of the pollen record in the sandcliff deposits it is considered that the pollen includes relatively recent pollen and some older corroded pollen, and little significance can be given to such a record.

The marine silts

Samples from Soil Pit VI were also prepared for pollen analysis but only a few grains were found, mostly in poor condition, and it was not practical to obtain counts from such material. In view of the good preservation of diatoms and ostracods in part of the sequence this is particularly unfortunate, especially as it would have given a guide to the vegetation on the adjacent sandcliff if sufficient pollen had been present.

Diatoms

by Keith Crabtree

Samples from Soil Pit VI and the auger borings at the base of the pit (coordinate 87.6/900.3) were treated with hydrogen peroxide to remove organic matter and at the same time to disperse the fine particles. After washing with distilled water, a few drops of concentrated sediment from the base of the beakers were allowed to evaporate on a round coverslip over a gently heated plate. When the sample was dry a few drops of diatom mountant, hyrax, were added and inverted over a microscope slide. The slide was left for several hours on the heated plate to allow the mountant to dry. Slides were looked at under high power and under oil immersion lens to locate any diatoms amongst the silt and clay particles on the slides. A large number of the samples appeared devoid of any diatoms, a few slides showed traces of fragments of diatoms, while a number did have reasonably well-preserved diatoms present in varying numbers.

After scanning by the author, two slides (from 0.3–0.6m OD) with numerous diatoms on them were inspected by Richard Crawford in the Botany Department, University of Bristol, and he gave a list of the diatoms present as follows:

Paralia marina (Wm Smith) Heiberg (both a large form and a small form)
Thalassiosira decipiens (Grun) Jorg
Arctinoptychus senarius Ehrenburg (Ehrenburg)
Diploneis aestuarii (Hustedt)
Diploneis frag
Campylosira cymbelliformis (A Schmidt) Grun ex van Heurck
Melosira westii (Wm Smith)
Nitzschia spp
Hyalodiscus sp

These are all marine diatoms, many of them being benthic but inshore species. The *Arctinoptychus* and the *Thalassiosira* are probably planktonic.

This ecological tolerance suggests that we are dealing with shallow marine deposits in at least the lower part of the sediments concerned. The evidence from the ostracods (Eric Robinson, below) supports this interpretation.

The following list indicates the levels below the base of the pit at which diatoms were present and also something of their state of preservation:

0.56–0.64m (2.26–2.34m OD) fragmentary ghosts
0.95–1.05m (1.85–1.95m OD) nil
1.30–1.40m (1.50–1.60m OD) ghosts of Centric diatoms
2.00–2.10m (0.80–0.90m OD) a few Centric diatoms
2.30–2.40m (0.50–0.60m OD) rich in diatoms

2.50–2.60m (0.30–0.40m OD) rich in diatoms
2.70–2.80m (0.10–0.20m OD) a few diatoms
2.90–3.00m (0–minus 0.1m OD) a few fragments
3.00–3.10m (minus 0.1–minus 0.2m OD) a few diatoms

Samples taken from higher up in the pit itself were all barren of diatoms, and such samples have not been recorded in the above list.

Samples from the foreshore peat were treated similarly and diatoms were found to be present at a few levels, particularly in the peat but not in the silty clays below. The species concerned seemed very similar to those recorded in the silty clays of Pit VI but also included *Gyrosigma* sp, *Podosira* cf *hormoides*, *Diploneis* cf *bombus*, and *Navicula* sp. It is not clear whether these were diatoms contemporary with the peat accumulation period. It is possible that they were intrusive in later worm channels which contained silty clays. Equally diatoms do migrate into sediment such as mud/peat during certain times of day and surface again when conditions become favourable. Thus we should not attach too much weight to the diatoms in assessing whether the peat accumulated in a saltwater or freshwater marsh.

Ostracods

by Eric Robinson

Samples from two principal types of context were examined for ostracods, firstly from the sandcliff sequence where some larger ostracods had been noted earlier during the microscope sorting of Mollusca, and secondly a series of sediment samples from the estuarine sequence in Soil Pit VI.

Sandcliff sequence

Eight samples were examined from the main excavation trench and one from Soil Pit V.

Unit 6a, Context 61, sample 282

No microfauna

Unit 6, Context 57, sample 127

Cyprideis torosa (Jones) 1v (valve) female

Unit 5d, Context 58, sample 261

Cyprideis torosa (Jones) 1v A-1; 1v female; 1v male

Unit 5d, Context 58, sample 259

Cyprideis torosa (Jones) 3v A-1, 13v female, 7v male
Candona caudata Kaufmann 1v (oligohaline species)
Eucypris heinrichi Diebel and Pietrzeniuk 1v (freshwater species)
Ilyocypris biplicata (Koch) 1v fragment (freshwater species)

This could be an *in situ* fauna from a saltmarsh or creek with perhaps some inwash from landward niches.

Unit 5b, Soil Pit V, Context 215, sample 312, *c* 30g

(The number in brackets at the end of the entry for each species is the total for that species; * = phytal.)

Cyprideis torosa (Jones) 4v A-III, 6v A-II, 40v A-I, 36 female, 13 male valves (99)
Leptocythere castanea Sars 22v female (22)
Leptocythere lacertosa (Hirschmann) 1v (1)
Loxoconcha rhomboidea (Fischer) 2v (2)
Aurila convexa (Baird) 4v A-I (4)
Cythere lutea (O F Müller) 1v A-I, 7v (8)
Cytheropteron nodosum Brady 1v (1)
Eucythere declivis (Norman) 1v female, 2v male (3)
Finmarchinella angulata (Sars) 1v A-I, 3v female 1v male (5)
Finmarchinella finmarchica (Sars) 6v A-II, 12v A-I, 1v (19)
Hemicythere villosa (Sars) 2v A-II, 7v male, 8v female A-I, 10v female (27)
Hemicytherura clathrata (Sars) 3v A-I, 6v (9)
Loxoconcha elliptica Brady 1v A-I, 1v (2)
Pontocythere elongata (Brady) 6v A-I, 6v (12)
Robertsonites tuberculata (Sars) 2v A-II (2)
Sclerocheilus contortus (Norman) 1v (1)

The *Cyprideis* valves total 99; the other valves total 118.

This is a reasonable ostracod fauna of 17 species representing a mixture of two environments. Sixteen species make up what would be a Bristol Channel subtidal offshore fauna. Most of the species are thoroughly marine in their salinity requirements. A limited number are forms which depend on the presence of seaweeds for shelter or food (phytal ostracods); others are bottom dwellers from firm sandy substrates. Missing from the assemblage are elements which make up the fauna of tidal pools and the weed zone of the Bristol Channel as described by Horne (1982). This implies that the fauna derived from an open bay type source. The second element in the assemblage comprises large numbers of *C torosa*, a brackish-water ostracod found in saltmarshes and estuaries often to the exclusion of other species. Both the marine and saltmarsh elements show some evidence of sorting and separation by transport. This is indicated by the incomplete life history record of the assemblage, the missing element being the small immature growth stages. Hydrodynamically very contrasted to their adult stages, these small valves would readily separate from the others in the course of transportation by tides or currents. Most of the *C torosa* valves are left valves of females – more evidence of sorting in transit. The assemblage as a whole with its fully marine element and its single abundant saltmarsh species seems to represent material from a Somerset Levels type environment swept into association with a Bridgwater Bay type marine fauna. At a height of *c* 6m OD it may represent the product of a storm flooding event which encroached on the dune edge.

Unit 5a, Context 19, sample 247

Cyprideis torosa (Jones) 1v A-I, 1v female

Unit 4, Context 16, sample 233

Cyprideis torosa (Jones) 1v female

Unit 4, Context 16, sample 231

Cyprideis torosa (Jones) 1v female

Unit 3c2, Context 31, sample 211

Cyprideis torosa (Jones) 1 v female

These samples, producing just one or two valves, are of little significance except that they show saltmarsh was near to provide *C torosa*.

Summary

The ostracod record from the sandcliff presents problems of interpretation because it is unclear how the ostracods arrived at the point of deposition. The reasonably large assemblage from Unit 5b, Soil Pit V, does possibly represent a marine incursion episode but the small numbers in other samples could also have been introduced by wind-blow or been bird-borne on plumage, carried on seaweed, introduced by man, etc.

Soil Pit VI

The following identifications were made from core (87.6/900.3) samples taken at the stated depths below the base of the pit (Fig 81). The first two samples are from the basal palaeosol (Unit 8a), the remainder are from overlain grey silty clays.

2.80–2.90m (0–0.1m OD)

Red sand, rounded grains, lithic fragments, no microfauna

2.70–2.80m (0.1–0.2m OD)

Red sand, rounded grains, lithic fragments, no microfauna

2.40–2.50m (0.4–0.5m OD)

Cyprideis torosa (Jones) 1v A-V, 7v A-IV, 7v A-III, 12v A-II, 16v A-I, 9v female, 5v male
Loxoconcha elliptica Brady 3v A-IV, 3v A-III, 7v 1c A-II, 5v A-I, 3v female, 5v male
Leptocythere ilyophila (Hirschmann) 1c A-IV, 4v A-III, 4v A-II, 3v A-I, 3v 1c
Ilyocypris bradyi Sars 1v (freshwater sp)
Elphidium gerthi (Van Voorthuysen) 26, *Trochammina inflata* (Montagu) 5

2.30–2.40m (0.5–0.6m OD)

Cyprideis torosa (Jones) 2v A–V, 2v A-IV, 11v A-III, 5v 1c A-II, 4v female, 1v male
Loxoconcha elliptica Brady 1v A-V, 3v A-IV, 3v A-III, 4v A-II, 4v 2c A-I, 3v
Leptocythere ilyophila (Hirschmann) 8v A-III, 14v A-II, 7v A-I, 2v
Elphidium gerthi (Van Voorthuysen) 26, *Trochammina inflata* (Montagu) 3

2.20–2.30m (0.6–0.7m OD)

Cyprideis torosa (Jones) 1v A-IV, 1v A-III, 6v A-II, 9v A-I, 4v 1c female, 3v 1c male
Loxoconcha elliptica Brady 5v A-IV, 7v A-III, 8v A-II, 6v A-I, 4v 2c
Leptocythera ilyophila (Hirschmann) 3v A-III, 8v A-II, 3v A-I, 3v 1c
Elphidium gerthi (Van Voorthuysen), *Trochammina inflata* (Montagu)

2.10–2.20m (0.7–0.8m OD)

Cyprideis torosa (Jones) 1v A-IV, 2v A-III, 3v A-II, 1v female
Loxoconcha elliptica Brady 1c, 5v A-III, 2v A-II, 4v 1c A-I
Leptocythere ilyophila (Hirschmann) 4v A-II, 4v A-I, 1v

1.80–1.90m (1–1.1m OD)

Cyprideis torosa (Jones) A-II 2v
Loxoconcha elliptica Brady A-III 1v
Leptocythere ilyophila (Hirschmann) A-I 1v
Elphidium gerthi Van Voorthuysen, *Quinqueloculina oblonga*, *Trochammina inflata* (Montagu)

1.40–1.50m (1.4–1.5m OD)

Loxoconcha elliptica Brady A-III 1v
Leptocythera ilyophila (Hirschmann) A-I 4v
Elphidium gerthi Van Voorthuysen (brackish/marine)

1–1.10m (1.8–1.9m OD)

Cyprideis torosa (Jones) 2v A-II, 4v A-I 2v. Forams: *Ammonia beccarii* (L), *Elphidium gerthi* Van Voorthuysen (brackish/marine)

0.48–0.56m (2.34–2.42m OD)

No microfauna

Within the pit itself samples were also examined from the following contexts:

Context 232 (3.1–3.3m OD)
Context 232 (3.9–4.1m OD)
Context 237 (4.7–4.9m OD)
Context 229 (5.5–5.7m OD)

None contained ostracods but there were some forams such as *Ammonia* which are associated with saltmarshes.

Summary

Of the assemblage below 2m OD, the following are the salient aspects.

Cyprideis torosa was first described by T R Jones from the tidal creeks of the Thames around Dagenham, which in 1850 was a less polluted habitat. The species thrives, however, in the marshes of the Medway, or in the Blackwater, as well as in the Broads of Suffolk and Norfolk. It has a widespread distribution across Europe, into the marshes of the Mediterranean, the Nile delta, and into the Euphrates-Tigris wetlands in one direction; the other extension is into the East African Rift Valley lakes. All these areas are interconnected by migratory waterfowl who have an active role in the dispersal. *Cyprideis* is highly euryhaline and eurythermal as this dispersal would testify, and survives in waters inhibiting other species of ostracods. It is widely recognised as a prime indicator of 'brackish water' zones in estuaries, especially the tidal waters ranging between 1% and 8–10%, the well-known zone in faunal plots where there is the least faunal species diversity (Remane 1934; Wagner 1957). In some settings of low salinity waters, the species *torosa* develops prominent 'nodes' upon the valve surface in well-defined positions. This is not evident in the Brean Down specimens, but the actual significance is probably not a simple relationship to water salinity but possibly a response to another stress unknown as yet.

Loxoconcha elliptica is a species which is strongly ecologically typed as an indicator of low salinity creeks and saltmarsh, seldom migrating into direct coastal or beach settings. Less eurythermal or euryhaline than *Cyprideis*, its salinity bracket lies between 1% and 10% (Neale 1964). Locally, fossil forms of the species figure in the faunal lists of the less saline levels of the Burtle Beds (Kidson *et al* 1978).

Leptocythere ilyophila shares the low salinity tolerance of the other two species (2–8%, Neale 1964) but, like other species of the genus, represents an ostracod closely associated with seaweeds browsing upon diatoms which in turn cluster upon the fronds of algae.

Environmentally the ostracods in their size range from quite small juvenile moults up to full-grown adults, and in their good preservation suggest that the samples between 0.180m and 0.270m represent living communities *in situ*, without any chance of transport or reworking involved in their make-up.

On this evidence, the interval between 0.4 and 1.5m OD is envisaged as being a period of saltmarsh, possibly barriered from the open estuary by sand banks or dunes. There is none of the character of Bristol Channel foreshore as recently documented by Horne (1982) in studies of seasonal changes at Gore Point, Somerset (Horne 1980). Comparison with Burtle Beds faunas of late Pleistocene age can only be made with limited intervals of the total succession, or localities well inland. Otherwise, the Burtle Bed faunas are markedly more marine in character.

The foraminifera broadly confirm this assessment although the writer cannot speak with authority on the species recorded.

Above 2m OD where ostracods were absent there were some saltmarsh forams and the sediments themselves were of a type which the writer has come to associate with saltmarsh. Such an environment is often not a particularly favourable niche for ostracods and furthermore there seems to be something about the diagenesis of 'warp clays' which attacks the shells and removes them from the subfossil record. Forams seem to be more resistant and can survive. It may therefore be that the essentially similar sediments above 2m OD lack ostracods not because of any major change of depositional regime but because of post-depositional changes.

19 Charred plant macrofossils

by Vanessa Straker

Charcoal from the buried soil (Unit 8a)

Charcoal was abundant in the basal palaeosol (Chapter 2); it was collected both during excavation and as a result of the bulk sieving.

A 20% (approx) random subsample was selected for identification and the results are presented in Table 14. Weight was chosen as the most appropriate means of quantification although it is acknowledged that differential densities of wood species are not taken into account using this method. All the charcoal appeared to come from mature wood rather than twigs or small brushwood. Many of the fragments were very small and contribute largely to the 'unidentified' category. The number of metre squares in which the taxa were present is also recorded and reflects a generally similar picture to the weights.

Ash was the most common species (58%) followed by Pomoidae (6%). This group includes hawthorn, apple, pear, rowan, and whitebeam, but in the present context hawthorn is perhaps the most likely candidate. Hazel, wild or bird cherry, and blackthorn are present in smaller quantities and buckthorn and yew are found only as traces.

It is likely that the presence of the large quantities of charcoal in the buried soil relates to the clearing or burning off of the vegetation before the soil was cultivated and may therefore give us an idea of the vegetation prior to the settlement of the site.

The ash charcoal indicated that the wood was slow grown with very closely spaced annual rings, perhaps implying adverse growing conditions. Ash woods or ash mixed with hazel and other species are characteristic of limestone soils. Rackham (1980) notes that lime-ash woods are characteristic of ancient woods in the Mendips such as Cheddar Wood. Lime charcoal is very soft; it rarely survives in archaeological deposits and is regarded as under-represented in the archaeological record. It is possible then that lime may also have been a component of the vegetation on the Down.

There are two species of hawthorn which cannot be differentiated on the basis of their wood anatomy, but probably *Crataegus monogyna*, which is readily dispersed by seed and is one of the commonest trees to form secondary woodland, is represented at Brean.

The wood of wild and bird cherry is difficult to differentiate. Bird cherry has a longer history in post-glacial Britain, and wild cherry is not known until the fourth millennium BC (Rackham 1980). Wild cherry can grow large and has a patchy distribution in England now, most commonly in the south-east. Bird cherry tends to be an underwood tree and is often regarded as a highland zone species, but its distribution was also probably formerly more widespread and has been identified from leaf buds in a prehistoric deposit from Bideford, Devon (J Jones, pers comm).

Blackthorn or sloe is a small tree which nowadays often forms secondary woodland or scrub. As a common hedgerow species it also tolerates woodland margins.

The large woodland trees (apart from ash) are only represented by traces of oak which can form woodland or secondary woodland on a variety of soil types.

Yew, one of only three native British conifers, can flourish in both woods and scrub and is often associated with limestone soils. Buckthorn is characteristic of scrub.

The presence of sloe, hawthorn, and hazel is confirmed by the finding of a sloe stone, a haw, and a hazelnut in the buried soil.

The National Trust (1982) Biological Survey shows that blackthorn, oak, buckthorn, hazel, and hawthorn grow on the Down today and form woody scrub. Ash, the most common wood in the buried soil, is *not* present.

Assuming that the charcoal does not derive from wood brought to the site from some distance, it would appear that ash woods, possibly mixed with other species such as hazel, were present as well as some scrub characterised by *Prunus* spp, hawthorn, and other taxa such as buckthorn. Though the charcoals alone cannot establish whether this was primary wildwood, pollen from the foreshore peat (Chapter 18) suggests that the latter was oak with a minor component of ash, implying that the ash woodland of the basal palaeosol was secondary.

Other plant macrofossils

During the excavation the sequence of Bronze Age deposits was extensively sampled for a variety of biological remains including plant macrofossils. Most

Table 14 Charcoal from the buried soil (Unit 8a); weight in grams

Taxon		4/11	10/13	11/13	13/13	13/14	60517	6171	Total	% weight	Present in sq
Fraxinus excelsior	Ash	.02	.40	.42	4.98	.26	1.79	2.61	10.48	53.8	7/7
Pomoidae	Hawthorn group		.02	.36	.16	.39	.06	.27	1.26	6.5	6/7
Corylus avellana	Hazel		.33	.17	.07	.14	.01	.02	.74	3.8	6/7
Prunus cf *avium/padus*	Wild/bird cherry		.03		.08		.05	.28	.44	2.3	4/7
Prunus cf *spinosa*	Blackthorn		.09	.12	.13				.34	1.7	3/7
Quercus sp	Oak				.30			.07	.37	1.9	2/7
Rhamnus cathartica	Purging buckthorn	.07				.13			.20	1.00	2/7
Taxus baccata	Yew				.05				.05	.3	1/7
unidentified			1.50	1.57	1.32	.01	.78	.41	5.59	28.70	6/7
Totals		.09	2.37	2.64	7.09	.93	2.69	3.66	19.47	100	

of the bulk samples were processed by flotation on site after soaking in calgon. Samples remaining after the excavation were processed later in Bristol. The floats were poured off into a 250μm sieve and residues collected on a 1mm nylon mesh. Both were sorted completely. The deposits were sampled by context (MF1:F10) which, in the case of some of the thick sand layers, were subdivided into spits. In addition, two sample columns (of single metre squares) were collected which sampled the whole sequence; in some cases 'sterile' sand layers were only sampled as part of these columns. As the aim of the columns was to provide a control throughout the sequence rather than an assemblage for separate consideration, these will not be mentioned further other than to say that no plant remains were recovered from the presumed sterile sand layers (such as Context 62). The assemblage will be discussed by amalgamating the information from the contexts (including those in the sample columns) into the relevant stratigraphic units; individual contexts will only be discussed where the plant remains can add some detail to the interpretation of that context.

The aim of this work was to identify the crop plants and other plant taxa in the archaeological assemblage in order to try to establish:

a What information the assemblages give on the use of plants in the different phases and where they could have come from.
b How important (in general terms) cultivated plants were to the economy.
c The nature of the vegetation on the Down during the Bronze Age. The vegetation on the Down today is largely of limestone grassland with patches of scrub, herb-rich meadow, and coastal cliff communities. The identification of charcoal from the buried soil helps to establish the nature of prehistoric vegetation on the Down (see charcoal report, p 211)

The plant macrofossils extracted from the bulk samples are listed in Table 15. Despite the fact that some mineralised coprolites were found on the site (Chapter 21), no mineralised fruits or seeds were observed; all the plant remains were preserved by means of carbonisation. The concentration of plant remains is generally low, the greatest quantity being recovered from Unit 5b, the main middle Bronze Age occupation horizon. More samples were processed from this unit than the others (1995 litres) which accounts in part for the greater number of macrofossils, but substantial quantities were also processed from Unit 4 (1020 litres), which contained far fewer plant remains. Relatively few samples were collected from Unit 6α relating only to Contexts 156 and 163, but the

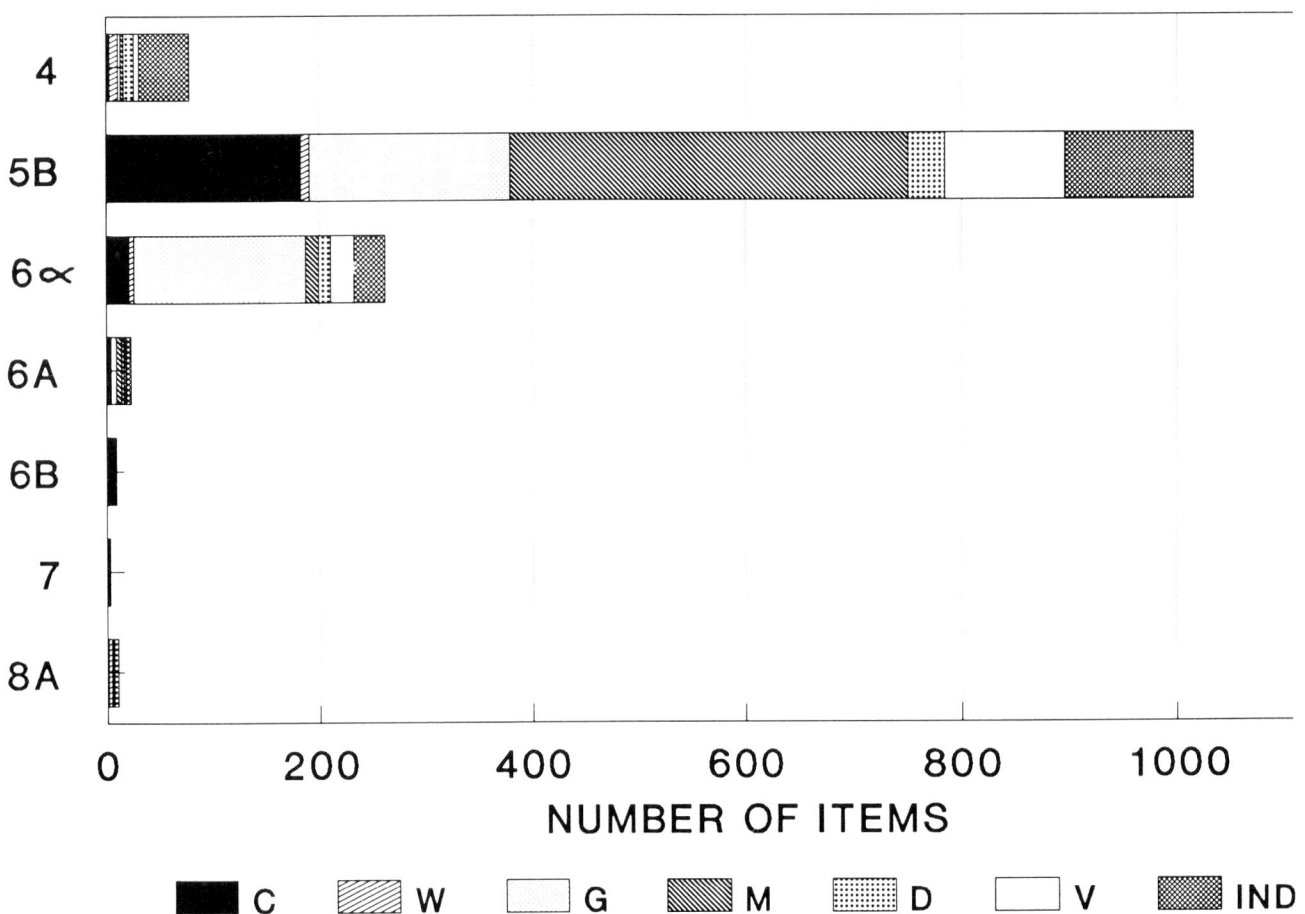

Fig 136 Habitat groups represented by plant macrofossils from the main stratigraphic units: C – cultivated; W – woods, hedges, and scrub; G – grassland; M – marshes; D – disturbed; V – varied; IND – unidentified seeds

concentration was similar to Unit 5b, as is shown at the end of Table 15. Plant remains from units other than 5b and 6α are very sparse (see Fig 136), but this probably relates to the nature of the contexts examined; the relatively rich huts and associated hearths and floors were recovered only within Units 5b and 6α.

Cultivated plants

These consist of wheat (*Triticum* spp), barley (*Hordeum* sp(p)), celtic bean (*Vicia faba*), and possibly oats (*Avena* sp). Figure 136 shows the importance of cultivated plants in the assemblages from the units as a whole and Figure 137 gives a breakdown of the cultivated plants in more detail. From Figure 136 it is clear that cultivated plants do not occur in large numbers and are found in greatest concentration in Units 4, 5b, and 6α.

Wild plants

The wild plants identified are also listed in Table 15. In order to facilitate discussion these taxa have been assigned to habitat groups, wherever possible, to see whether major differences in the nature of the plants reaching the settlement can be distinguished between the different phases. Plants respond to a variety of ecological stimuli and as a result many will grow in more than one strict habitat type. Therefore it was not possible to assign every plant to a group and many have been assigned to the 'V' (various) category. These groups are shown in Figure 136 and the data for Units 6α, 5b, and 4 are expanded in the form of pie diagrams presented in Figure 138. Lists of the plants in each group can be found in Table 16.

The Down at Brean is an SSSI and is owned by the National Trust. Owing to its important flora, certain recent modern biological studies have been carried out. Shimwell mentions the grassland flora on the Down in his paper on the phytogeography and phytosociology of limestone grasslands which have been classified according to the Zürich-Montpellier School of phytosociology and the system of vegetation classification for central and north-west Europe described by Lohmeyer *et al* (1962, quoted in Shimwell 1971). The grassland belongs to the Class Festuco-Brometea Br-Bl and R Tx 1943. This a dry anthropogenic base-rich grassland and includes most of the grasslands on calcareous soils in central and western Europe. The grassland also belongs to the sub-alliance Xerobromion, of which Brean Down is the centre of the Somerset distribution. Narrowing

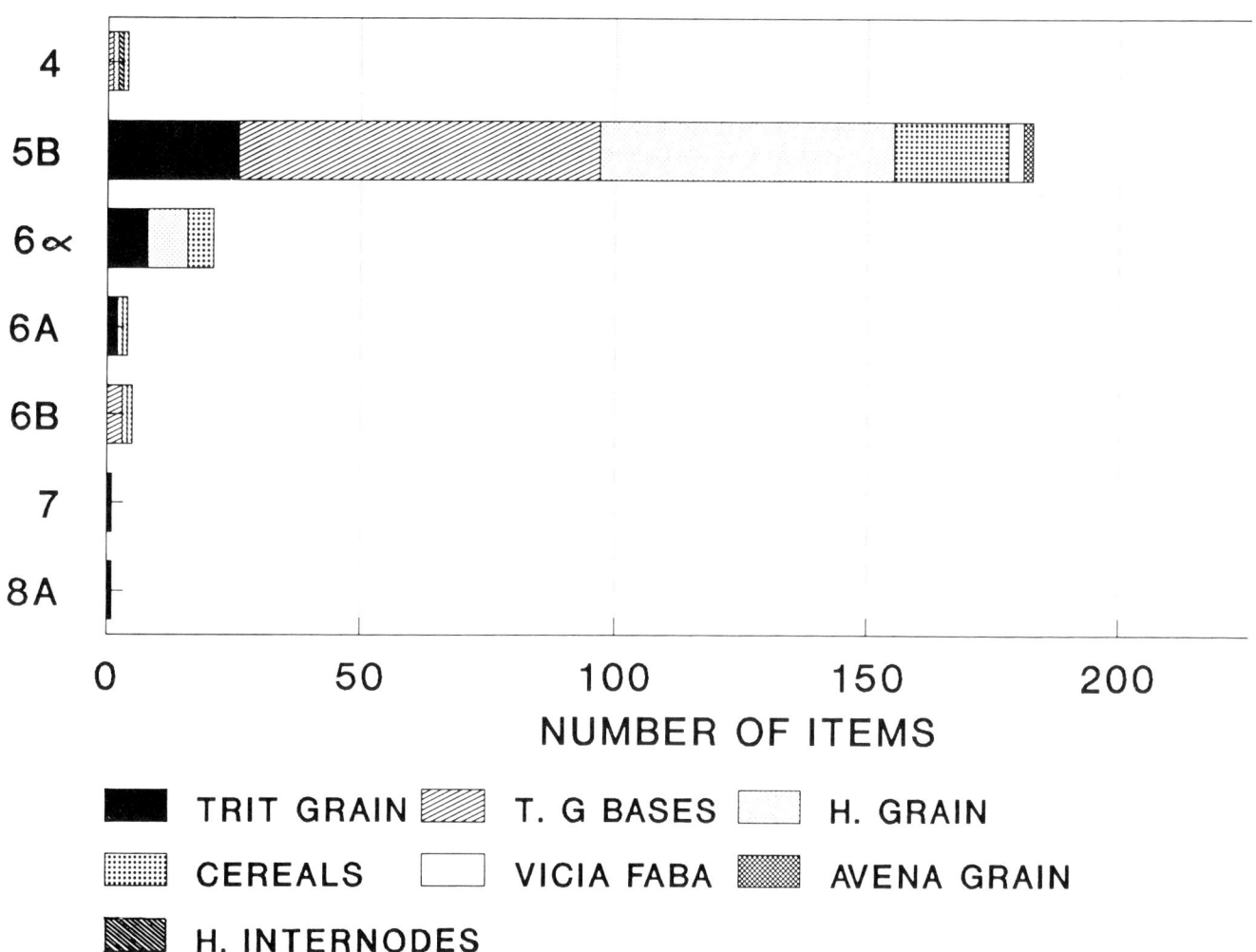

Fig 137 *A breakdown of the types of cultivated plants in the main stratigraphic units*

Table 15 Carbonised plant remains

Taxon	Common name	Habitat pref	Unit 4	Unit 5b	Unit 6α	Unit 6a	Unit 6b	Unit 7	Unit 8a
Avena sp	Oats	c	0	1	0	0	0	0	0
cf *Avena* sp	cf Oats	c	0	1	0	0	0	0	0
Avena/Bromus	Oats/Bromus	c	0	1	0	0	0	0	0
Hordeum sp	Barley	c	1	45	6	1	1	0	0
Hordeum sp hulled			0	5	0	0	0	0	0
Hordeum sp hulled, straight		c	0	4	0	0	0	0	0
Hordeum sp hulled, twisted		c	0	1	0	0	0	0	0
Hordeum sp straight		c	0	2	0	0	0	0	0
Hordeum sp twisted		c	0	1	2	0	0	0	0
Hordeum sp internode		c	1	0	0	0	0	0	0
Triticum monococcum/dicoccum glume base	einkorn/emmer	c	0	1	0	0	0	0	0
T monococcum/dicoccum/ spelta glume bases		c	0	4	0	0	0	0	0
Triticum cf *dicoccum* grain	emmer	c	0	2	1	0	0	0	0
T dicoccum glume bases		c	0	14	0	0	2	0	0
T dicoccum/spelta grain	emmer/spelt	c	0	7	2	0	0	0	0
T dicoccum/spelta glume base		c	0	6	0	0	1	0	0
T cf *spelta* grain	spelt	c	0	1	0	0	0	0	0
?*T spelta* glume base		c	0	1	0	0	0	0	0
T spelta glume base		c	1	1	0	0	0	0	0
Triticum sp grain	wheat	c	0	15	5	2	0	1	1
Triticum sp tail grain		c	0	1	0	0	0	0	0
Triticum sp glume base		c	0	44	0	0	0	0	0
Triticum/Hordeum grain	wheat/barley	c	0	2	0	0	0	0	0
Cereal indet		c	f	21	5	f	1	0	0
Cereal culm node		c	0	0	1	0	0	0	0
Cereal culm base		c	1	0	0	0	0	0	0
CARYOPHYLLACEAE									
cf *Arenaria* sp	cf Sandwort	Da, c, bare ground	0	1	0	0	0	0	0
Caryophyllaceae indet			0	4	3	0	0	0	0
cf *Moehringia trinerva* (L) Clairv	Three-nerved sandwort	W, well drained soils	0	5	1	0	0	0	0
Myosoton aquaticum (L) Moench	Water chickweed	M, damp W	0	2	1	0	0	0	0
Stellaria media agg	Chickweed	Da, V	0	1	0	0	0	0	0
CHENOPODIACEAE									
Chenopodium rubrum L/*glaucum* L	Red/glaucous goosefoot	D, Da, s	1	2	1	0	0	0	0
gen et sp indet			0	48	1	0	0	0	0
Chenopodium cf *album* L	Fat hen	D, Da	0	13	1	1	0	0	0
Chenopodium ficifolium Sm	Fig-leaved goosefoot	D, Da	0	1	0	0	0	0	0
Chenopodium sp(p)	Fat hen etc	v	0	11	8	0	0	0	0
Suaeda maritima (L) Dum	Herbaceous seablite	S, s	0	5	0	0	0	0	0
Chenopodiaceae/Caryophyllaceae			1	11	0	0	0	0	0
COMPOSITAE									
Senecio cf *aquaticus* Hill	Marsh ragwort	M	0	0	1	0	0	0	0
CORYLACEAE									
Corylus avellana L frags	Hazel	W	f	0	f	0	f	0	f
CRUCIFERAE									
Brassica/Sinapis	Rape/turnip mustard etc	V (Brassica esp s, Sinapis esp c)	0	0	1	0	0	0	0
Capsella bursa-pastoris (L) Medic	Shepherds purse	D, Da	0	3	2	0	0	0	0
gen et sp indet (small)			0	9	0	0	0	0	0
CYPERACEAE									
Carex sp(p)	Sedge(s)	V, d	0	22	3	0	0	0	0
Eleocharis palustris/uniglumis	Spikerush	M, pond margins	0	0	1	0	0	0	0
cf *Scirpus maritimus* L	Sea club-rush	shallow water esp s	0	1	0	0	0	0	0
gen et sp indet	Sedges	V, d	1	1	0	0	0	0	0
GRAMINEAE									
Arrhenatherum elatius var *bulbosum* (Willd)	Onion couch	Da, G	1	0	0	0	0	0	0
Bromus sp	Brome	D, Da, G	0	3	0	0	0	0	0
gen et sp indet	Grasses	V, G	1	165	160	2	1	0	1
Gramineae/cereal culm node			0	3	1	0	0	0	0
Gramineae culm node			0	1	0	0	0	0	0
JUNCACEAE									
Juncus sp(p)	Rush(es)	H, M	0	340	4	3	0	0	0
LABIATAE									
Lycopus europaeus L	Gypsywort	M, river banks	2	0	0	0	0	0	0
Mentha sp	Mint	V	0	0	1	0	0	0	0

Taxon	Common name	Habitat pref	Unit 4	Unit 5b	Unit 6α	Unit 6a	Unit 6b	Unit 7	Unit 8a
LEGUMINOSAE									
gen et sp indet		V	2	1	0	0	0	0	0
Trifolium sp	Clover	G	0	14	0	2	0	0	0
Trifolium cf *dubium* Sibth	Lesser yellow trefoil	G	0	1	0	0	0	0	0
Trifolium cf *pratense* L	Red clover	G	0	1	0	0	0	0	0
Vicia faba L var *minor*	Field (celtic) bean	c	0	3	0	0	0	0	0
Vicia/Lathyrus sp	Vetch/tare	D, Da, V	2	3	1	1	0	0	0
MALVACEAE									
cf *Malva sylvestris* L	Common mallow	D	0	0	1	0	0	0	0
ONAGRACEAE									
cf *Epilobium* sp	Willowherb	V	0	1	0	0	0	0	0
PAPAVERACEAE									
Papaver cf *dubium* L	Long-headed poppy	Da	0	1	0	0	0	0	0
PLANTAGINACEAE									
Plantago lanceolata L	Ribwort plantain	G	0	3	0	1	0	0	0
Plantago major L	Great plantain	D, Da	0	1	0	0	0	0	0
POLYGONACEAE									
Bilderdykia convolvulus (L) Dumort	Black bindweed	D, Da	8	0	0	0	1	0	0
Polygonum aviculare agg	Knotgrass	D, Da	0	1	0	0	0	0	0
Polygonum lapathifolium/nodosum	Persicaria	Da, B, D	0	1	0	0	0	0	0
Rumex acetosella agg	Sheep's sorrel	Da, G, H (acid pref)	0	1	0	0	0	0	0
Rumex sp(p)	Sorrel	V	0	7	3	0	0	0	0
gen et sp indet			2	0	1	0	0	0	0
PORTULACACEAE									
cf *Montia* sp	Blinks	D, Da	0	1	3	1	0	0	0
RANUNCULACEAE									
Ranunculus lingua L	Great spearwort	M	0	0	0	1	0	0	0
ROSEACEAE									
Crataegus sp	Hawthorn	W	1	1	1	0	0	1	1
Potentilla cf *reptans* L	Creeping cinquefoil	D, G	0	1	0	0	0	0	0
cf *Prunus* sp (stone fragment)		W	0	0	1	0	0	0	0
Prunus spinosa L	Sloe	W	f	0	f	0	0	0	f
Rosa sp	Rose	W	0	0	1	0	0	0	0
Roseaceae thorn		W	0	0	0	1	0	0	0
RUBIACEAE									
Galium aparine L	Cleavers	D, Da	0	1	0	0	0	0	0
Galium sp	Goosefoot	V	0	3	1	0	0	0	0
cf *Sherardia arvensis* L	Field madder	D, Da, G	0	2	0	0	0	0	0
SCROPHULARIACEAE									
Euphrasia sp/*Odontites verna* Bell (Dum)	Eyebright/red bartsia	Da, G	0	3	1	0	0	0	0
SOLANACEAE									
cf *Atropa belladonna* L	cf Deadly nightshade	W, c	0	1	0	0	0	0	0
Hyoscyamus niger L	Henbane	D, sandy, esp s	0	7	0	2	1	0	0
UMBELLIFERAE									
gen et sp indet			0	0	0	1	0	0	0
URTICACEAE									
cf *Urtica urens* L	Small nettle	D, Da	0	1	1	0	0	0	0
VIOLACEAE									
Viola cf *tricolor* L	Wild pansy	D, Da, G	0	1	0	0	0	0	0
cf *Viola* sp			0	0	0	0	0	0	1
POLYPODIACEAE									
cf *Pteridium aquilinium* (L) Kuhn	Bracken	W, H, acid pref	0	1	0	0	0	0	0
cf Seaweed fragment			0	0	1	0	0	0	0
Unidentified seeds			44	117	28	5	1	1	4
Unidentified A (?Primulaceae)			1	3	1	0	0	0	0
Unidentified stem frags etc			1	1	2	0	0	0	1
Totals			72	1016	259	24	9	3	9
No samples			86	88	22	12	9	1	45
No litres			1020	1995	540	120	90	10	450
seeds/10 litres			.7	5.1	4.79	2	1	3	.2

Key: B – bankside; C – cultivated; D – disturbed; Da – disturbed incl cultivated; G – grassland; H – heathland; M – marshes, fens, ditches; S – saltmarsh; W – woods, hedges, scrub; V – varied; c – prefers calcareous soils; d – damp conditions; s – coastal. f indicates the presence of fragments.

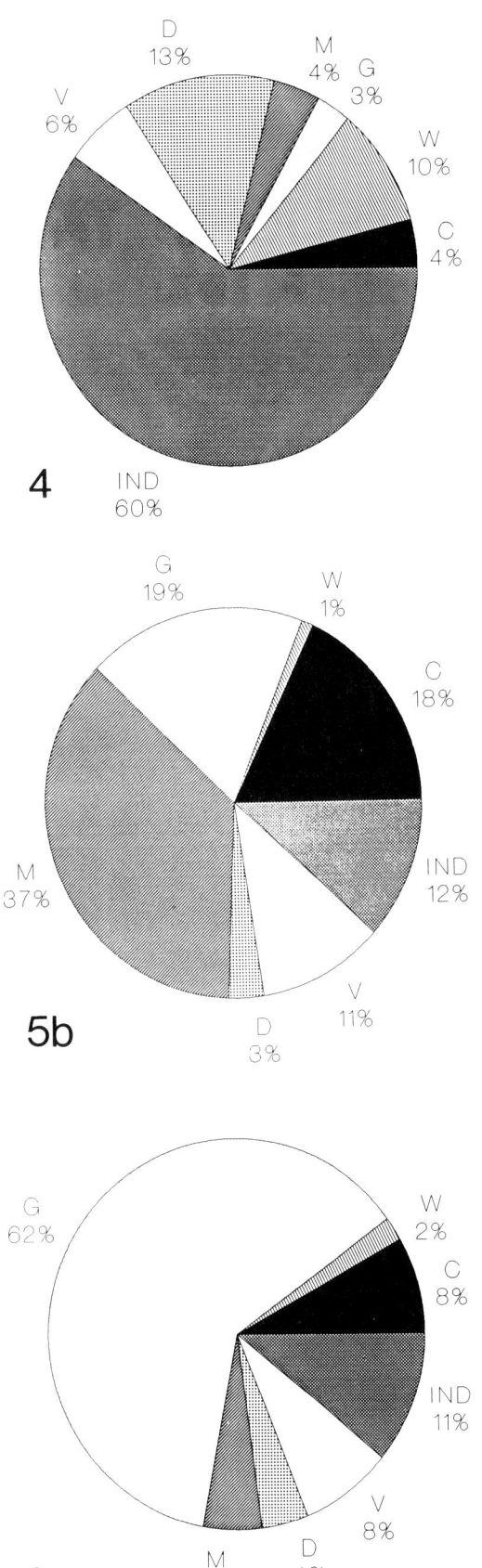

Fig 138 Pie diagrams showing the relative importance of the main plant habitat groups in Units 6α, 5b, and 4: C – cultivated; D – disturbed; G – grassland; M – marshes, fens, and ditches; W – woods, hedges, and scrub; V – varied; IND – unidentified seeds

the description down still further, the Association Poterio-Koeleterium Vallesianae is found at Brean and is now confined to the steeper slopes between 30m and 60m and includes rare species such as *Helianthemum appenninum*, white rockrose (Shimwell 1971). Although this grassland association may have been more widespread in the past, the charred seeds from the Bronze Age deposits do not include species which today would be considered typical of the Association or the sub-alliance Xerobromion. Whether this is the result of differential preservation or because this type of grassland was not well developed during the Bronze Age is open to question.

The National Trust kindly made available the results of its biological survey carried out in 1982.

The survey groups plants generally into scrub communities with bramble and bracken, grassland, and crags and maritime communities, the last primarily on sea cliffs. The nearby saltmarsh was not included in the study but its history has been discussed by Page (1982). Although saltmarsh may well have existed in the vicinity of the Down during the Bronze Age the small area of existing saltmarsh described by Page may not be of very great antiquity.

The taxa identified from the Bronze Age deposits at Brean and also noted in the modern National Trust survey are marked on Table 16. While the National Trust survey found some of these plants in the same habitats as those suggested for the the archaeological material, a few, such as *Malva sylvestris* and *Arrhenatherum elatius*, are found in other habitats, as is indicated on Table 16. This emphasises the importance of looking at communities of plants rather than considering them individually in too much detail. In a modern study, it is much easier to study communities than it is in the archaeological record where the preservation of species is selective and the key species allowing classification into phytosociological groups may not, as could be the case at Brean, be preserved.

Unit 8a

Very few plant remains were recovered from the palaeosol, the earliest deposits investigated in this study. They comprise a single wheat grain and fragments of hazelnut, sloe, and hawthorn which could have been collected locally if scrub vegetation was present on the Down at the time, or could have been derived from clearance by burning. No herbaceous weed taxa were identified.

Unit 7

A single fragment of a haw accompanied by a single wheat grain were the only plant remains from the Beaker occupation horizon.

Unit 6b

This deposit consisted of colluvium eroded in part from the Beaker palaeosol and the few plant remains, consisting of hazelnut fragments, emmer glume

Table 16 Taxa from Table 15 assigned to groups as shown in Figs 136 and 138

C	W	G	M	D	V	IND
Avena sp	cf *Atropa belladonna* *S	*Arrhenatherum elatius* *S	*Carex* sp(p) *GC, M	*Bilderdykia convolvulus*	*Avena/Bromus*	unident seeds
Hordeum sp	*Corylus avellana* *S	*Euphrasia* *S/*Odontites*	cf *Montia* sp	*C ficifolium*	*Brassica/Sinapis* (*B nigra* *GC)	
Triticum spp	*Crataegus* sp *S	Gramineae	Cyperaceae	*C rubrum/glaucum*	*Bromus* sp *GC	
Vicia faba	*Prunus spinosa* *S	*Plantago lanceolata* *GC	*Eleocharis palustris/ uniglumis*	*Capsella bursa-pastoris* *NS	Caryophyllaceae	
	Prunus sp	*Trifolium* cf *pratense* *GC	*Juncus* sp(p)	cf *Arenaria* sp	Chenopodiaceae	
	Rosa sp	*Trifolium* cf *dubium*	*Lycopus europaeus*	*Chenopodium album*	Chenopodiaceae/ Caryophyllaceae	
		Trifolium sp	*Myosoton aquaticum*	*Galium aparine* *NS	*Chenopodium* sp(p)	
			Ranunculus lingua	*Hyoscyamus niger*	Cruciferae	
			Scirpus maritimus	*Malva sylvestris* *GC	*Galium* sp	
			Senecio cf *aquaticus*	*Papaver* cf *dubium*	Leguminosae	
			Suaeda maritima	*Plantago major* *NS	*Mentha* sp	
				Polygonum aviculare agg *NS	*P lapathifolium/nodosum*	
				Urtica urens	Polygonaceae	
					Potentilla cf *reptans* *GC	
					Pteridium aquilinium *S	
					Rumex acetosella agg *GC	
					Rumex sp(p)	
					S arvensis/R peregrina	
					Stellaria media agg	
					Umbelliferae	
					Vicia/Lathyrus *NS	
					Viola sp	

Key: as for Table 15, with the exception that D and Da are here amalgamated as D. C includes all entries of genus *Triticum* and *Hordeum*. National Trust Survey: *GC – grassland and crags; *S – scrub; *M – maritime communities; *NS – not specified

bases, a grain of barley, and a single weed seed, could have derived either from Unit 8a or the cultivation episode responsible for colluviation.

Unit 6a

Plant remains were scarce in Context 61, but a greater range of plants was recorded than in the previous units: barley (a single grain), two grains of wheat, various weed seeds including fat hen (*Chenopodium album*), grasses (Gramineae), henbane (*Hyoscyamus niger*), clover (*Trifolium* sp), and ribwort plantain (*Plantago lanceolata*), and a few seeds characteristic of damp or wet conditions such as rushes (*Juncus* sp(p)) and great spearwort (*Ranunculus lingua*). Most of the weeds are characteristic of disturbed conditions and grassland though fat hen and possibly ribwort plantain may also be arable weeds.

Unit 6α

In Unit 6α two contexts are represented: 156 which relates to the collapse and abandonment of Structure 57, and 163 which is a possible floor layer associated with the same structure.

Context 163 contains a few cereals and a wider range of weed seeds than Context 156; however, the weeds, which include small nettle (*Urtica urens*), sorrel (*Rumex* sp), and clover (*Trifolium* cf *dubium*) could relate more to disturbed ground and grassland than to full arable conditions. A number of scrub or hedgerow taxa such as rose, sloe, and hazel (*Corylus avellana*) are also present, as well as the charred bladder of a species of seaweed. In general the assemblage, although small, is fairly typical of a domestic situation with cultivated and collected edible taxa among the burnt refuse.

In contrast, in Context 156 cereals are very scarce and a number of the weeds are characteristic of wet or damp conditions, notably spikerush (*Eleocharis palustris/uniglumis*), sedges (*Carex* spp), rushes (*Juncus* sp(p)), blinks (*Montia* sp), and water chickweed (*Myosoton aquaticum*). There is also a very large number of charred grass seeds. In this situation the assemblage could reflect the burning of animal dung from animals pastured on damp grassland and stalled in an abandoned hut, or the burning of roofing or flooring material, or a combination of the two. It might reasonably be assumed that originally the roof/floor covering would have consisted mainly of straw and/or the stems of rushes and sedges, with associated arable weeds or plants of damp conditions collected inadvertently. Once the bulk of the material had burnt away, the sort of collection outlined above might remain.

Unit 5b

In Unit 5b, cereals are better represented in the form of grains of wheat and barley, glume bases of wheat, and a few celtic beans (*Vicia faba*). Although the wheat that can be identified to species level, principally on the basis of the morphology of the glume bases, is mostly emmer (*T dicoccum*), spelt is recorded, but only as a single glume base. However, this is of interest as it does not occur in the earlier deposits at Brean where there is the opportunity to look at a series of deposits spanning the whole of the

Bronze Age. In Unit 5b it would appear that barley and wheat are present in roughly equal quantities, if the number of wheat glume bases is taken as roughly indicative of the number of wheat grains originally present and assuming that the chaff was not present only as a source of tinder.

Where preservation was good enough it was possible to identify some of the barley to the hulled form, the type most commonly found in Bronze Age deposits despite the fact that Helbaek (1952) found that the majority of the barley impressions in the pottery he examined were of the naked form. No naked barley was observed.

The only oats (*Avena* sp) present was in Unit 5b and, owing to the lack of the floret base, it was not possible to say whether it was wild or cultivated.

The few celtic beans (*Vicia faba*) that were identified came from Unit 5b. Pulses are not commonly recorded from prehistoric sites and may well be under-represented in the archaeological record as they do not require exposure to heat to facilitate dehusking, which is necessary for hulled cereals such as emmer and spelt. Pulses are therefore less likely to become burnt accidentally. If they were commonly used, pulses could have contributed a valuable source of protein to the diet.

In Context 53, the general occupation horizon comprising Unit 5b, a range of cultivated and wild species is present and is broadly comparable to Context 163 in Unit 6α (above), the weeds primarily coming from grassland and disturbed ground.

A similar though more extensive assemblage comes from the floor of Structure 59 (Context 60), though more plants of wet ground such as rushes and sedges are also present, again possibly relating to burnt roofing or flooring material or even burnt dung. Beneath this layer, a similar range of plants was represented, perhaps relating to an earlier floor layer.

The floor of the other hut (Context 93, Structure 95) was generally similar, containing some wheat chaff and grain, barley, plants of disturbed places, grassland, and a lot of rushes.

Two layers which contained burnt material were interpreted on site as possible hearth clear-out debris (Contexts 77 and 130 outside Structure 95). Some charred plant macrofossils were preserved in both layers though both also contained much fine charcoal. In Context 77, cereal grain, principally barley, was accompanied by a cereal culm node and probable arable weeds such as fat hen and plants of disturbed or waste places such as henbane. This plant, which occurs in several contexts in Unit 5b as well as in Unit 6a, is characteristic of disturbed, sandy conditions but is not found growing on the Down today. The other layer contained only four cereals and comprised mostly rushes and grasses. Neither deposit could be considered as obvious crop processing waste though dry grasses, rushes, and straw (evidenced by the culm node) would have been useful for starting fires.

Bottema (1984) studied the charred seed contents of modern fireplaces in rural parts of northern Syria. He concluded that the charred seeds derived from the local seed rain, food burnt during cooking, gathered vegetable fuel, dung used as fuel, and extant vegetation burned under the fireplace, and of these dung, in this case of sheep, appeared to have been the major source. He connected this directly with the scarcity or absence of wood as fuel. Although the sources suggested above could have supplied the seeds which became charred in the Brean hearth deposits, it is usually thought that the burning of dung was more likely in drier, less wooded climates. Wood charcoal is certainly common in the archaeological deposits and even if the primary woodland had been cleared, scrub regeneration and driftwood available at Brean could presumably have provided fuel for domestic fires and those required for evaporation of salt water.

Bottema's study was on fireplaces in the open and therefore one might expect more from the extant vegetation and local seed rain sources, but at Brean, roofing, flooring, or even the burning of peat for fuel could add to the possible sources of seeds in the hearth. The closest source of peat would have been the accumulation on the present beach (Chapter 18) if it was exposed at the time. This did contain the seeds of rushes (*Juncus* and *Scirpus/Schoenoplectus*) but none of the other taxa identified in the peat appeared on the site and the rush seeds found charred in the occupation deposits could derive from other sources (see above). However the use of peat for fuel is definitely known from a Roman briquetage mound a few miles away at East Huntspill where the charred remains of raised bog species were identified by Caseldine in Leech *et al* 1983.

Unit 4

There are very few cereals in Unit 4. Wheat is represented only by a single glume base of spelt wheat. Barley is similarly scarce, represented only by a grain and an internode, and celtic beans and oats are not recorded at all. Considering the amount of pottery and bone found in Unit 4, the extreme scarcity of the remains of edible plants is surprising. The weed flora is small, though possible weeds of cultivation such as the twining black bindweed (*Bilderdykia convolvulus*) are present with a scatter of edible scrub/woodland resources including hazel, sloe, and hawthorn.

Plant impressions in briquetage

Impressions of plant material were noted in many of the fragments and larger pieces of briquetage; however, for the most part it was not possible to identify these with any precision. The exception was a single fragment (60416, Context 66) which contained charred plant remains rather than impressions of plant material. Among pieces of stem and possible chaff fragments which were not readily identifiable further, there was one glume base. Although it is not completely visible it is tentatively identified as Emmer wheat, *Triticum* cf *dicoccum*, on the basis of the nature of the venation and keels. Emmer is also present in the carbonised assemblage from the Bronze Age units.

Discussion

The results from several recent excavations show that spelt wheat is now known to have been established in the British Bronze Age, though what its status was in relation to emmer is not yet clear. Spelt is recorded at Potterne in Wiltshire (Straker 1987), Black Patch in Sussex (Hinton 1982), Runneymede Bridge (J Greig, pers comm), and West Row, Mildenhall (Murphy 1983; Martin and Murphy 1988) at a similar date to its appearance at Brean. It then becomes very common in Iron Age and Roman deposits.

Emmer, barley (usually but not exclusively the hulled form), and rye (known only from Runneymede) are also known from Bronze Age sites. Pulses are scarce but celtic beans do occur on several East Anglian sites (Fingringhoe; Springfield Lyons, Chelmsford; and Lofts Farm, Heybridge, P Murphy, pers comm) and Rowden in Dorset (W Carruthers, pers comm). They have also been recorded at Black Patch (Hinton 1982), though not at Potterne.

Tubers of the onion couch (*Arrhenatherum elatius*) have been found on Bronze Age and earlier sites (Straker 1987) and could derive from arable, abandoned arable, or ungrazed grassland situations. The tubers were uncommon at Brean (a fragment only in Unit 4) and could have been used to start fires. They are also edible (M Jones 1978).

The question whether the cereals represent crops that were growing locally is difficult to resolve. The 'celtic fields' on the top of the Down have not been dated, and could be of Bronze Age origin despite being traditionally assumed to be of Iron Age date. Other small areas could also have been suitable for small-scale cultivation. Indeed, the southern slope of the Down was used as allotments in the last century (Knight 1902). However, cereal grains and chaff are very scarce in the archaeological deposits. If one takes one aspect of the model proposed by Jones (for Iron Age communities in the Thames Valley), at sites where crops were grown more trace of grains charred by accident might expect to be found in domestic deposits, such as those excavated at Brean, than at sites where they were not produced and were therefore more precious. The arable weed flora is restricted at Brean even in the main middle Bronze Age occupation horizon, and this also makes it difficult to isolate phytosociological groupings and suggest where the crops were grown.

Some of the weeds, such as fat hen, sheep's sorrel, shepherd's purse (*Capsella bursa-pastoris*), chickweed (*Stellaria media*), and cleavers (*Galium aparine*), can be found as arable weeds and are characteristic of the Class Stellarietea, which generally characterises all British arable communities (Silverside 1977). Clover (*Trifolium dubium*), sheep's sorrel, and blinks (*Montia* sp) are more particularly associated with the Alliance Spergulo-Oxalidion, which is characteristic of root crops, spring-sown cereals, and also nitrogenous disturbed land. Although sheep's sorrel, often characteristic of acid arable land, was identified, it can be found at present in pockets of sand accumulated in hollows in the surface of the limestone on the top of the Down.

Unfortunately, recent phytosociological studies are of little help in trying to understand the assemblage of charred seeds, and in the main it is likely that the weeds reflect disturbed, nitrogen-enriched conditions likely in the vicinity of settlements with a wet grassland with stands of sedges and rushes growing in it in the vicinity. There may be small numbers of weeds of cultivated land which arrived at the settlement with cereals. The cereals could either have been grown locally in very small quantities or brought to the site (also in small quantities) from some distance away.

However, despite the evidence for cultivation from the soil micromorphological studies, the charred plant remains do not unequivocally support the suggestion that crops were grown locally.

Other than a few seeds of sea blite (*Suaeda maritima*), there is little evidence for saltmarsh, although it is possible that some of the rushes (*Juncus* sp(p)) could be saltmarsh species such as *J gerardii*. Unfortunately the effect of charring on such fragile seeds means that identification cannot be taken to species level.

Although edible woodland food sources such as hazelnuts and sloes are present, they are in very small amounts, which is surprising since hazel, in particular, is very common on Neolithic and many Bronze Age sites (Moffett *et al* 1989). If hazel had been growing commonly at Brean, far more nut shell fragments would be expected in the occupation deposits.

Generally, the assemblages at Brean support the suggestion that arable intensification did not take place until the late Bronze Age when large areas were exploited to support higher population levels in the Iron Age (Moffett *et al* 1989). This intensification is not seen in the area excavated so far at Brean, but the paucity of crop plants and arable indicators may relate to the nature of activities carried out on the site.

Acknowledgements

I am very grateful to Peter Murphy and Wendy Carruthers for allowing me to quote from unpublished reports.

20 The vertebrate remains

by Bruce Levitan

Introduction

There are few extant bone assemblages in Britain from well-stratified Bronze Age deposits, particularly from domestic sites. Thus, when the rare opportunity to examine such a sequence of vertebrate remains presented itself, this was immediately perceived as one of the main objectives of the excavation project. It is unfortunate that the size of the bone sample recovered is small, but the limitations imposed by the depth of stratigraphy meant that the excavated area was small, particularly in the basal units. Consequently, it was only in Units 4 and 5b that reasonably large samples were available for analysis.

It is essential that an understanding of the stratigraphy be gained before the analysis of the bones is attempted (see Chapters 2–8 for the provenance of the bones and other material).

Bones were recovered from the main stratigraphic units in the following numbers (bracketed figures are numbers of bones identified to species):

Unit 1 – 402 bones (340)
Unit 3a – 2893 bones (2211)
Unit 3b – 144 bones (130)
Unit 3c – 157 bones excluding human burials (54), plus at least 8 human burials
Unit 3c – 14 bones (5)
Unit 4a – 113 bones (35)
Unit 4 – 6095 bones (2604)
Unit 5a – 224 bones (181)
Unit 5b – 3031 bones (1096)
Unit 5d – 729 bones (175)
Unit 6 – 882 bones (538)
Unit 7 – 351 bones (291)
Unit 8a – 62 bones (28)
Unit 6 or 8a – 50 bones (15)

In addition to the 15,127 bones listed above, a further 1482 bones were examined and recorded. Only 29 of these are included in the analysis since they comprise bones from the auger survey and from Soil Pit IV, and unstratified or unlabelled bones. Those from Soil Pit IV are excluded here because they cannot be tied into the main sequence exactly, and the number of bones is too small to warrant separate analysis (43 bones). The auger survey bones are excluded for similar reasons (14 bones). The records for all these bones are held in the site archive (see p 18 for details).

The 29 additional bones are a collection dating from November 1984, picked up by casual visitors to the site. They are from the late Pleistocene part of the section and are worth noting here so that they can be added to the bones described by ApSimon *et al* (1961). They came from Units 11a, 11b, and 12a. They were lent to the author for examination and identification, but were subsequently returned to Woodspring Museum, Weston-super-Mare.

Only the bones from Units 3c–8a are considered here and from Unit 3c1 only the human bones are analysed (see Chapter 6). Analysis of the non-human bones from Units 3c2–8a is limited by sample size; in many cases only a handful of identified bones are present, so that detailed analysis is impossible. Furthermore, the number of bones available for ageing, measurement, and butchery recording is too small for analysis within any single unit. For this reason these three topics are assessed for the Bronze Age in a broad sense, with Units 4a–8a combined (topic v below).

Much of the material recovered from the excavations was recorded using three-dimensional plots which were subsequently loaded into an on-site microcomputer (Chapter 1 and Levitan 1988). As a result it has been possible to produce a number of high precision plots (plans and projected sections) of the bones etc. It should be noted, however, that the number of points plotted on any one plan or section may not correspond exactly to a total given in a table or quoted in the text for the same group. This is because a single point on the plot may represent more than one item, and also a number of bones were not recorded in three dimensions but within a 'general context' (these do not appear on any plot). These factors should be borne in mind when comparing the plots with the quantitative data.

A brief note concerning the methods of representing anatomical frequency is given here, partly in order to avoid repetition in the different sections below, and partly because some of the methods are based on an unpublished source. The results are calculated in two ways. The columns headed NF% in MF1:F12–14 are percentages based upon fragment count totals for each species. The columns headed AI% are percentages based upon anatomical index totals. This index is calculated in such a way as to compensate for the different levels of fragmentation, and also to give a weighting for the different frequency of elements in the skeleton (Levitan unpublished). The AI also have the advantage of being directly comparable between different skeletal elements and also between species. Differences between the results are accountable for partly by the fact that the NF results are not standardised for skeletal element, but the major impact is due to fragmentation. Lower AI results indicate high degree of fragmentation (eg skull) and higher AI a much smaller degree of fragmentation (eg metacarpal). The figures illustrating the anatomical data are presented in two ways: as stacked bar graphs and as cumulative frequencies (Figs 145–148). The latter are used because they give a better visual representation of the data than the bar graphs, though they are not strictly the correct form for this type of data. (Cumulative frequencies imply a direct – usually temporal – relationship between adjacent data.)

The broad aim of the bone analysis is to consider the Bronze Age site economy and to assess the implications of this from a broader perspective (there are also the small Pleistocene collection mentioned above and the sub-Roman cemetery, dealt with in Chapter 6). Thus the bone analysis was divided into the following main topics:

i   The Pleistocene material

ii   The character of the 'Beaker sand' and palaeosol deposits (Units 7–8a)
iii Comparison of the middle and early Bronze Age structures (57, 59, and 95) in Units 5b and 6α
iv   The character of the late Bronze Age deposits (Unit 4)
v   Assessment of ageing, measurement, and butchery data for the Bronze Age assemblage (Units 4–8)
vi   Ecological considerations
vii A small collection of human bones from Bronze Age contexts
viii Analysis of disturbances and intrusions from rabbit activity

i   The Pleistocene material

The bones from this collection are material currently held at the Woodspring Museum, Somerset, recovered in late 1984. There are 29 pieces of bone from horse (scapula, two metacarpals, upper second molar), red deer (tibia), large bovid (three radii, tibia), and large mammal, mostly possibly bovid/cervid (four ribs, 16 small fragments). Many of them are heavily concreted within a brecciated matrix of small pebbles and red sand. One of the horse metacarpals (a right, distal half) has canid-like gnawing marks, and one rib is very large, matching in size and conformation a mammoth rib at Wells Museum. Measurements of the horse and deer bones are given on MF1:G1. The bones derive from Units 12a, 10a, and slump, and the positions in which they were found are detailed on MF1:F11. Whilst this assemblage is too small to be meaningful, it does add to the collection made by ApSimon (ApSimon *et al* 1961), and is useful in this respect.

ii The 'Beaker sand' and basal palaeosol deposits

The 'Beaker sand' (Unit 7) and the basal palaeosol (Unit 8a) represent the earliest activities on the site, but in both cases the bones recovered are very few (Table 17). If small mammals and reptiles (which may be intrusive, but in any case are probably not part of the exploited animals assemblage) are discounted, the identified bones from Unit 7 number 11, and from Unit 8a 18. Clearly these are too few to allow any attempt at detailed analysis. Cattle, sheep, and pig are present in Unit 8a, and cattle and pig in Unit 7. In Unit 7 there are also one bird bone (robin) and three fish bones (eel).

The distribution of bones is illustrated in Figure 139. The apparent difference between the two units is probably of no real significance, and merely reflects areas where the relevant layers were exposed and excavated. In Unit 8a the cattle bones are concentrated at the southern end of the distribution, whilst the sheep and pig bones are concentrated at the northern end. The significance of this is uncertain, but there is the faint possibility that similar patterns of bone deposition occurred here and in later deposits (Unit 5 see topic iii). These will be discussed at greater

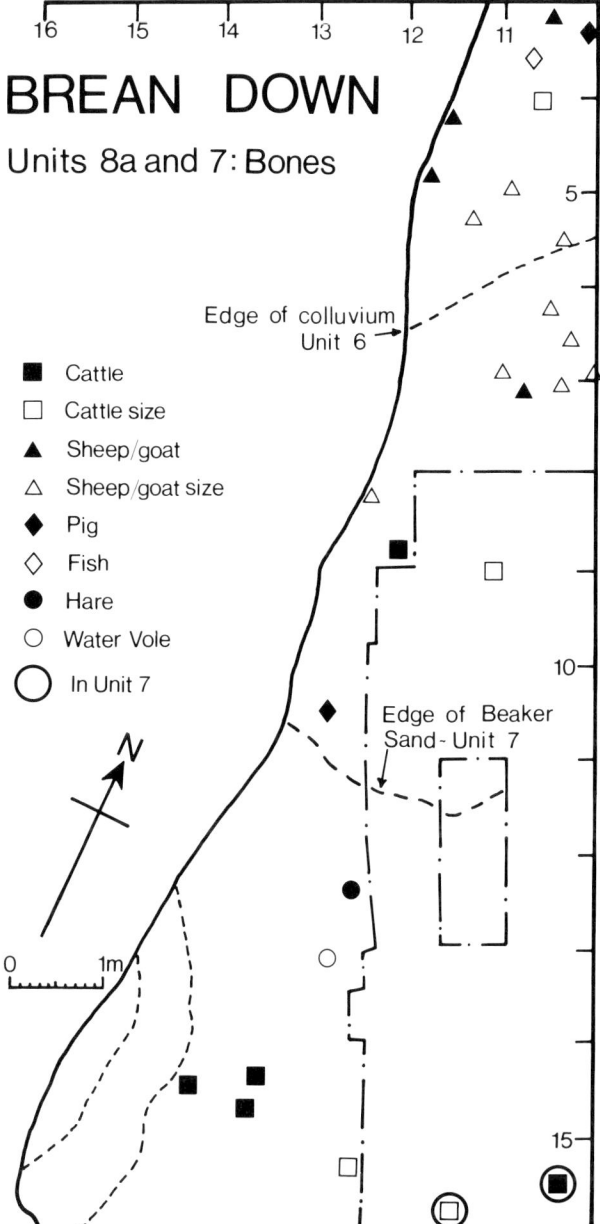

Fig 139   Distribution of animal bone in Units 7 and 8a

length below. Suffice it to note that such patterns do exist here and on other sites (albeit at different periods), and they may be related to activity and to settlement pattern, the smaller bones (ie sheep and pig) being found within or close to the structures and domestic activity areas, and the larger bones (ie cattle) being found at the periphery of the site.

iii   Comparison of the deposits in the middle and early Bronze Age structures

Strictly speaking Units 5a and 5d should be considered here, but the number of identified large mammal bones in these virtually sterile sands is small (Table 17), and the very high frequency of rabbit in Unit 5a throws suspicion upon the usefulness of these results. The bones from Unit 5d have a much

Table 17 Summary of vertebrate fauna

species	Unit 3a no	%	Unit 3b no	%	Unit 3c no	%	Unit 3d+4a no	%	Unit 4b no	%	Unit 5a no	%	Unit 5b no	%	Unit 5d no	%	Unit 6 no	%	Unit 6/8a no	%	Unit 7 no	%	Unit 8a no	%
cattle	253	31.90	17	54.84	0	.00	9	25.71	836	44.92	4	12.50	251	37.86	32	8.23	120	44.61	6	40.00	6	13.95	9	36.00
sheep/goat	424	53.47	13	41.94	6	60.00	17	48.57	853	45.84	3	9.38	339	51.13	18	4.63	93	34.57	6	40.00	0	.00	6	24.00
pig	13	1.64	1	3.23	2	20.00	2	5.71	39	2.10	1	3.13	9	1.36	3	.77	36	13.38	3	20.00	1	2.33	3	12.00
horse	4	.50	0	.00	0	.00	1	2.86	15	.81	1	3.13	2	.30	0	.00	0	.00	0	.00	0	.00	0	.00
dog	66	8.32	0	.00	0	.00	0	.00	11	.59	0	.00	15	2.26	0	.00	5	1.86	0	.00	0	.00	0	.00
deer	1	.13	0	.00	0	.00	0	.00	5	.27	0	.00	3	.45	1	.26	1	.37	0	.00	0	.00	0	.00
cat/etc	0	.00	0	.00	0	.00	0	.00	4	.21	0	.00	4	.60	0	.00	0	.00	0	.00	0	.00	0	.00
small mammal	32	4.04	0	.00	2	20.00	6	17.14	98	5.27	23	71.88	40	6.03	334	85.86	14	5.20	0	.00	36	83.72	7	28.00
Total	793	28.18	31	24.03	10	6.37	35	28.00	1861	30.62	32	14.29	663	22.58	389	60.22	269	35.35	15	30.00	43	12.25	25	40.32
bird	23	40.35	0	.00	0	.00	1	50.00	28	39.44	0	.00	9	60.00	4	12.12	1	.55	0	.00	1	.39	0	.00
fish	11	19.30	0	.00	0	.00	0	.00	24	33.80	1	9.09	2	13.33	21	63.64	107	58.47	1	100.00	3	1.18	0	.00
reptile/amphibian	23	40.35	0	.00	0	.00	1	50.00	19	26.76	10	90.91	4	26.67	8	24.24	75	40.98	0	.00	250	98.43	1	100.00
Total	57	2.03	0	.00	0	.00	2	1.60	71	1.17	11	4.91	15	.51	33	5.11	183	24.05	1	2.00	254	72.36	1	1.61
cattle size	282	43.93	4	28.57	3	3.00	30	37.04	1122	32.98	7	35.00	737	38.73	115	54.50	77	25.25	4	11.76	23	42.59	14	38.89
sheep size	360	56.07	10	71.43	97	97.00	51	62.96	2280	67.02	13	65.00	1166	61.27	96	45.50	228	74.75	30	88.24	31	57.41	22	61.11
Total	642	22.81	14	10.85	100	63.69	81	64.80	3402	55.98	20	8.93	1903	64.82	211	32.66	305	40.08	34	68.00	54	15.38	36	58.06
rabbit	1322	46.98	84	65.12	47	29.94	7	5.60	743	12.23	161	71.88	355	12.09	13	2.01	4	.53	0	.00	0	.00	0	.00
Total	2814		129		157		125		6077		224		2936		646		761		50		351		62	

Unit 1 not included
cat/etc includes mammoth rib (5c) and whale vertebra (5b)

BREAN DOWN
Unit 6: Structure 57

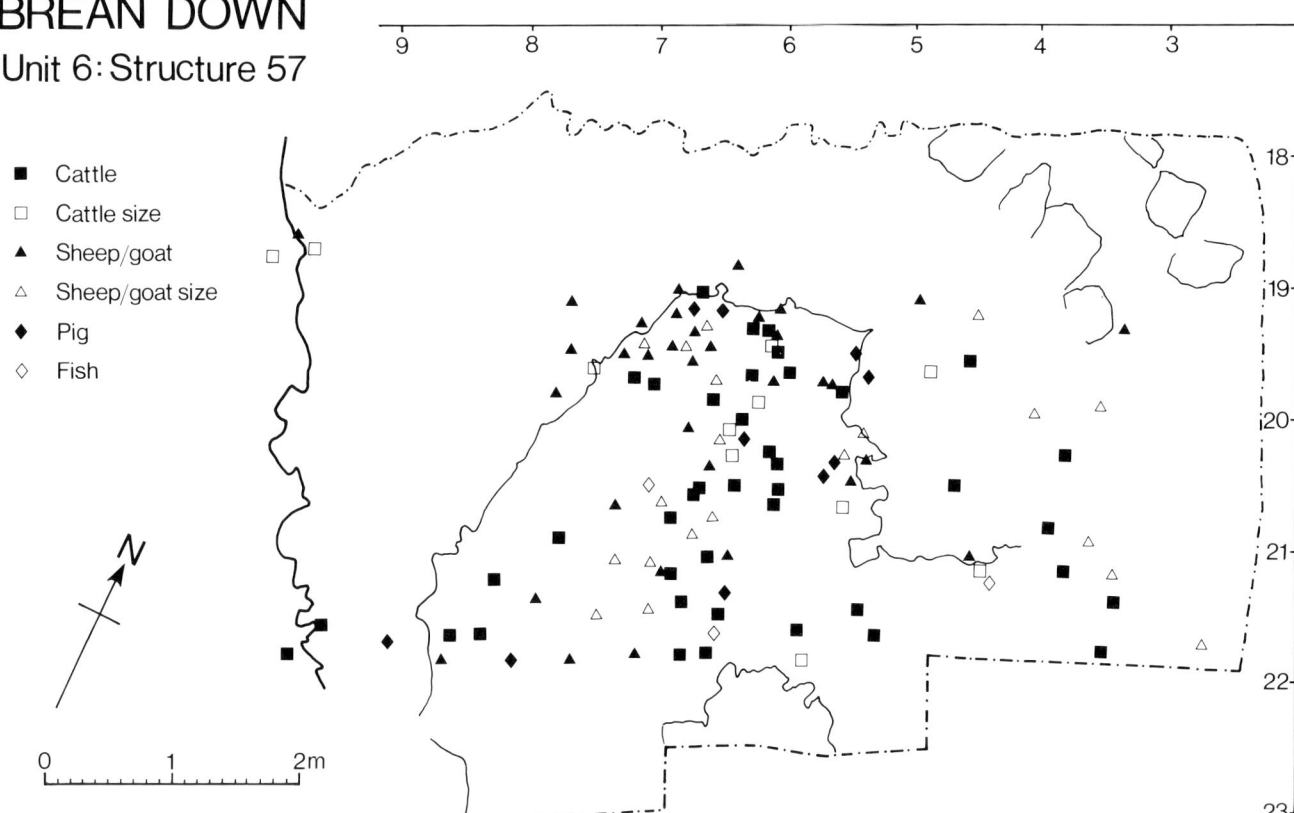

Fig 140 Distribution of animal bone in Structure 57, Unit 6α

smaller proportion of rabbit, but here the sample is dominated by small mammals which are considered in more detail below (topic vi).

Thus only Units 5b and 6 are considered; proportions of species are given in Table 17 and the distributions of bones are shown in Figures 140–142. There are nearly 3000 bones from Unit 5b, yet only 470 of them are from within Structures 59 and 95. Most of the bones come from two contexts: 53 with 1777 bones and 77 with 427 bones. The former was a general occupation spread throughout Unit 5b and the latter a lens of ash and charcoal to the south of the structures. These patterns, which will be shown to have important implications for activities, will be analysed in detail below.

General comparison between the structures

The samples from the three structures (57, 59, and 95) are disappointingly small, with 398, 131, and 339 bones respectively (Table 18). This renders the differences observable in the species representation problematic in interpretation since they could easily result from small sample bias alone. If we put this problem aside for the moment, certain patterns are discernible:

1. There is a greater concentration of bones related to Structure 57 than to Structures 59 or 95.
2. The bones from Structure 57 are clearly concentrated in the northern part of the structure, whilst those in Structure 95 are concentrated in the area to the west of the hearth; a second area of slightly lower concentration in Structure 95 is from the stone wall (Context 181).
3. The proportions of cattle, sheep, and pig differ in the three structures: cattle percentages are 50, 36, and 21 respectively for Structures 95, 57, and 59; sheep are 41, 44, and 68; pig are <1, 14, and 0.
4. There is a large number of fish bones from Structure 57 and few or none from the other structures.
5. There is a large number of grass snake bones and scales from Structure 59 and few or none from the other structures.
6. There are lower percentages of unidentified bones from Structure 57 than from the other structures.
7. There is a fairly even spread of bones throughout

Table 18 Summary of animals from structures

Species	Structure 95		Structure 59		Structure 57	
	no	%	no	%	no	%
cattle	75	49.6	10	21.28	50	35.71
sheep	62	41.06	32	68.09	61	43.57
pig	1	.66	0	.00	20	14.29
horse	0	.00	0	.00	0	.00
dog	9	5.96	1	2.13	1	.71
red deer	2	1.32	0	.00	0	.00
small mammal	2	1.32	4	8.51	8	5.71
Total	151	44.54	47	35.88	140	35.18
bird	5	83.33	0	.00	0	.00
fish	1	16.67	0	.00	107	99.07
reptile	0	.00	2	100.00	1	.93
Total	6	1.77	2	1.53	108	27.14
cattle size	59	34.50	20	24.39	34	23.13
sheep size	112	65.50	62	75.61	113	76.87
Total	171	50.44	82	62.60	147	36.93
rabbit	11	3.24	0	.00	3	.75
Totals	339		131		398	

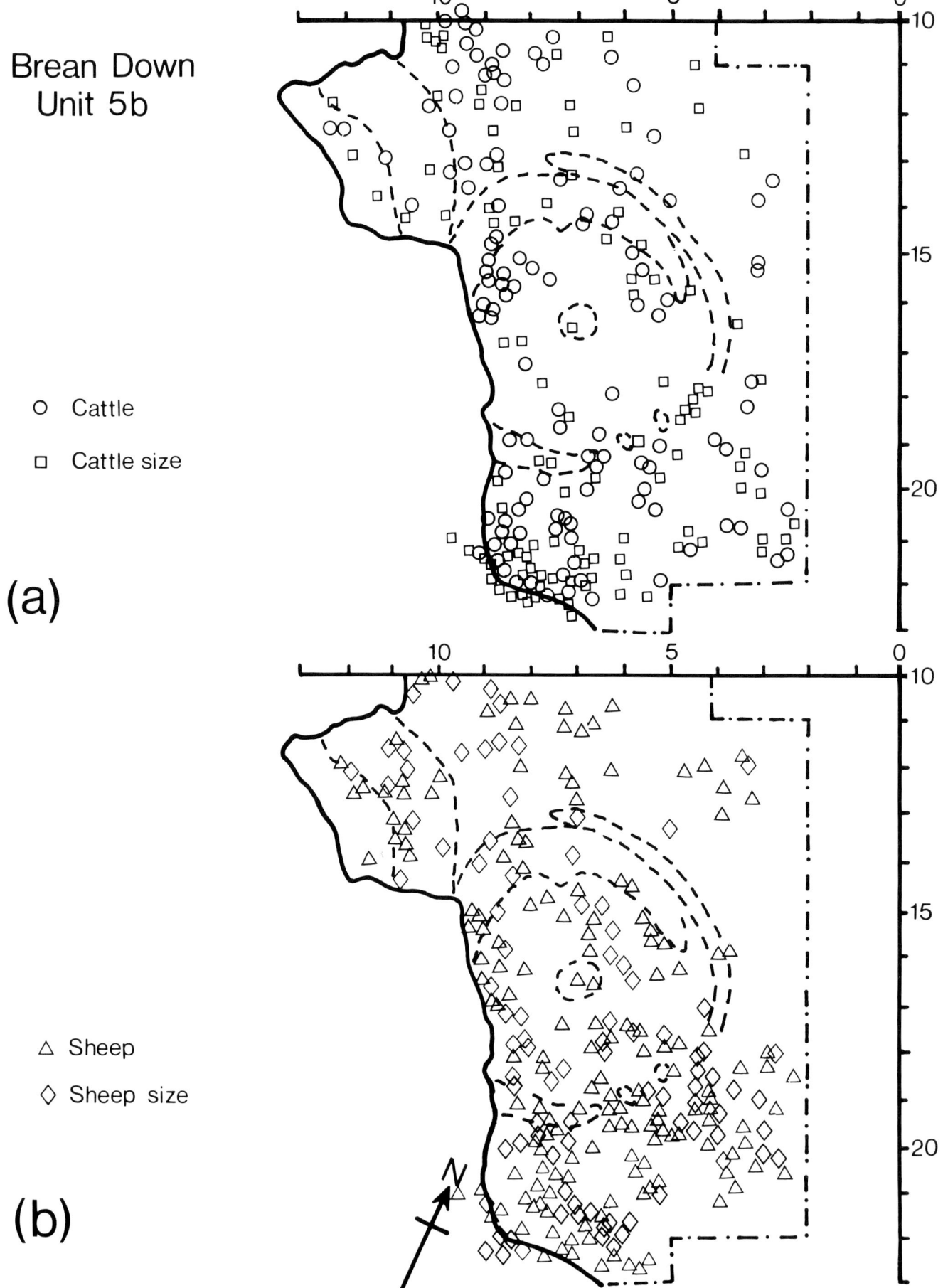

Fig 141 Distribution of animal bone in Unit 5b: (a) cattle and cattle-sized bone; (b) sheep and sheep-sized bone

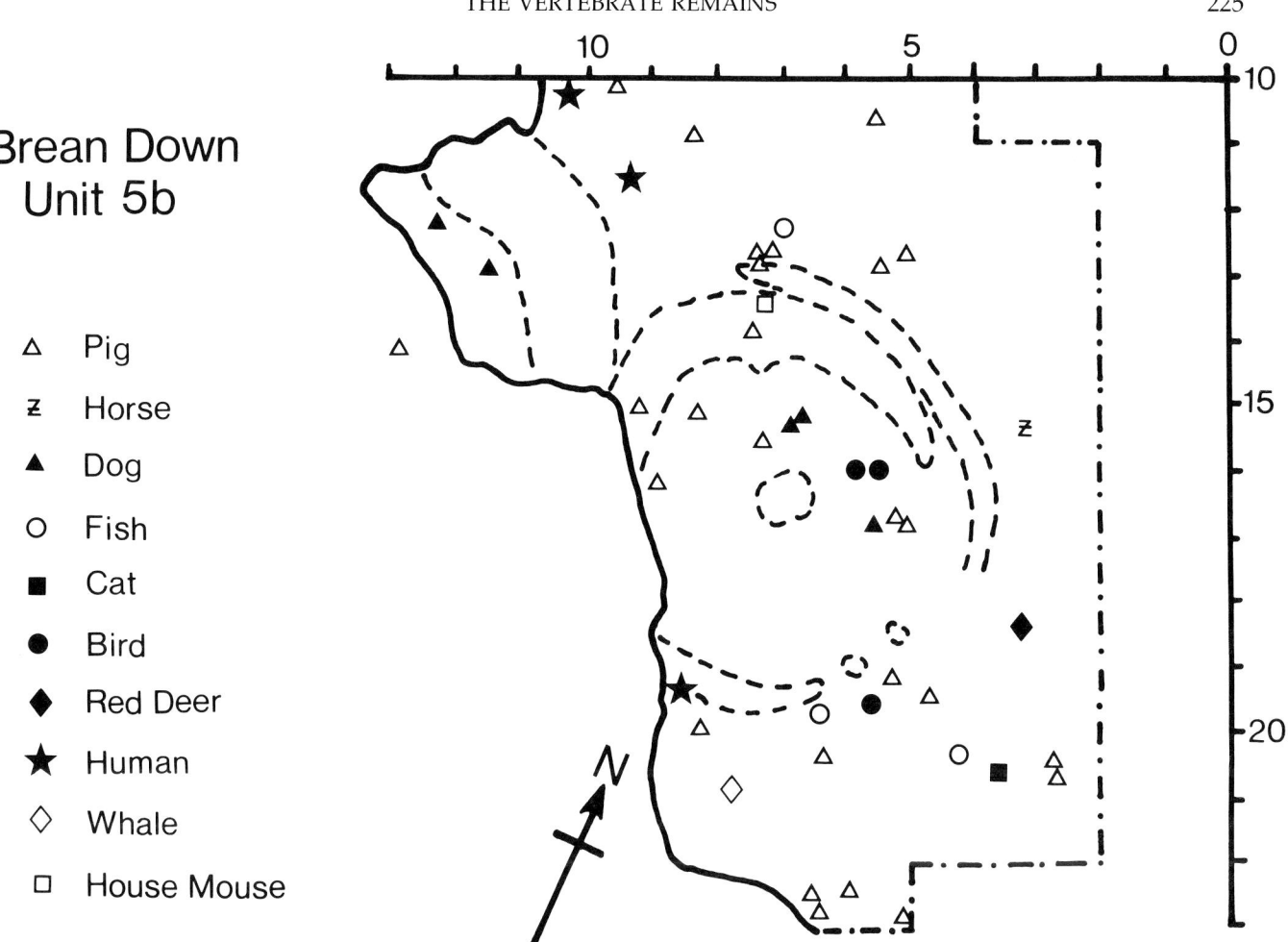

Fig 142 *Animal bone in Unit 5b; species other than cattle and sheep*

the hut floors in Unit 5b, and a very definite concentration fanning out from the entrance of Structure 95, corresponding to dumps of ash and charcoal.

Of Structure 59 only about two-thirds survive. From what is left, however, it appears that Structures 95 and 59 are fairly similar in terms of bone spreads, ie with a sparse concentration within the structures, especially on their eastern sides. However, they are not similar in terms of cattle, sheep, and pig proportions. The proportions of these species are much more similar for Structures 95 and 57, but here there is a difference in bone distribution (noted as point 2 above).

Figure 141 shows that sheep bones are more numerous overall than cattle, but that the cattle and sheep bone distributions are essentially similar (a factor which is backed up by the evidence from 'cattle-size' and 'sheep-size' unidentified fragments). The same can also be said of the bones from Unit 6α (Fig 140), the majority of which relate solely to Structure 57.

Relative frequencies of cattle, sheep, and pig

Table 18 illustrates that the relative frequencies of cattle, sheep, and pig vary between the structures, and there is an apparent contradiction between the percentages from the structures and from the Unit 5b–6 totals. Cattle percentages increase from 38% to 45% in Units 5b–6, yet they decrease from 50% in Structure 95 (Unit 5b) to 36% in Structure 57 (Unit 6). Similarly sheep decrease from 51% to 44% in the two units, but for the two structures quoted above there is an increase from 41% to 44%. These contradictions imply that the bones outside the features are different from those from within, thus backing-up the distribution evidence.

The non-Structure 95 bones from Unit 5b seem to be characterised by higher proportions of sheep and lower proportions of cattle. This is partly influenced by Structure 59 where this pattern pertains, but this accounts for only a small proportion of the non-Structure 95 bones (47 of the 512 identified mammal bones). The relative frequencies of the mammals are illustrated in Figure 143. The result for Unit 6 is the reverse, with cattle bones being relatively more common in the non-structure contexts, and the sheep bones being relatively less common (Table 18 and Fig 144).

Frequencies of pig are consistently low in Unit 5b (Fig 143, Table 18), but they are considerably higher in Unit 6.

The variations described above need not relate to changes in exploitation or disposal patterns from Unit 5b to Unit 6. The area of the settlement that was excavated is very small, so these may be minor variations that form part of a larger, and possibly more regular, pattern.

In summary, there appear to be two major factors at play: the distributions of the bones within and

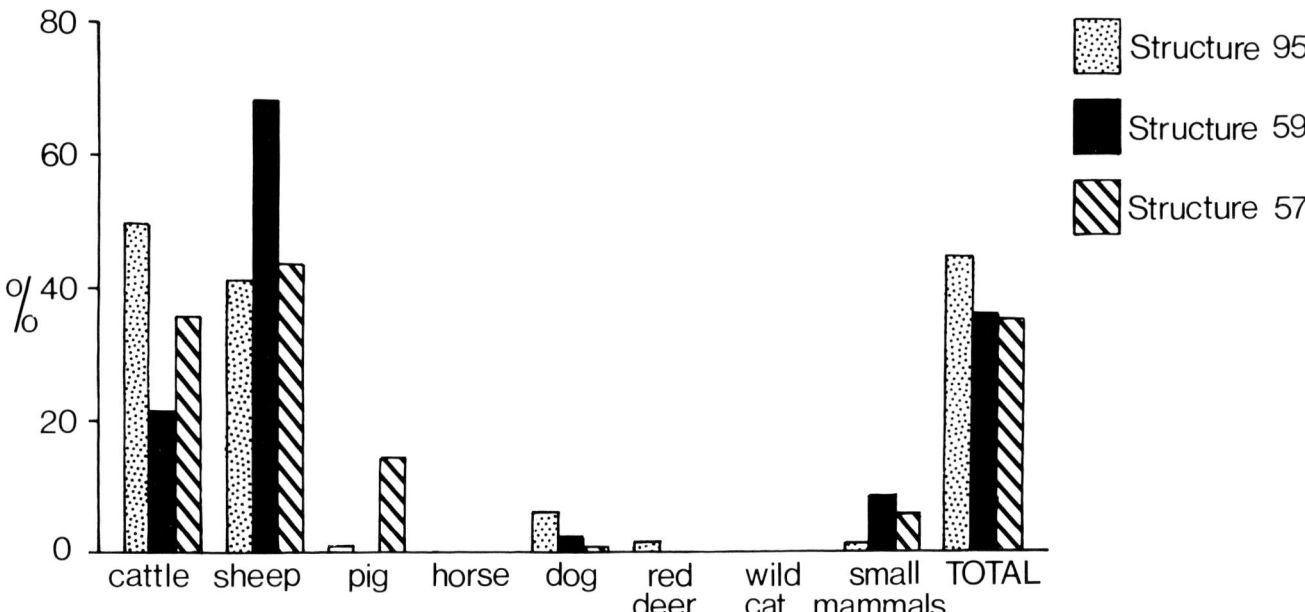

Fig 143 The relative frequencies of mammals in Bronze Age Structures 95, 59, and 57

around the structures, and the proportions of the three main species. The truncated plan of Structure 57 has a very similar bone distribution to that of Structure 95, and perhaps similar functions may be inferred. The sparsity of bones in the centre of the structures is in contrast to the relatively higher concentrations around the edges (particularly the western edge of 95). From this pattern, it may be inferred that the floors of the huts were kept reasonably clean, but that small bones did get left in the peripheries of the hut floor. The fact that there is a concentration to the west of Structure 95 might be significant; the coincidence of pottery (Fig 46a) distribution and contrast with briquetage distribution (Fig 46b) is notable, and surely an activity-related interpretation may be imputed. The idea that material was cleared out of the hut is supported by the fan of material to the south of the hut entrance (Figs 141 and 142). The association of bone, ash, and charcoal implies that the floor sweepings and hearth clear-outs were combined in single 'midden' dumps but need not indicate any further connection.

The scarcity of bones in the gullies of the structure may have resulted from regular recutting which was necessary to keep the gullies free to serve as water conduits.

The much denser concentration of bones in the floor of Structure 57 makes this structure rather different, and it should be noted that there is little other material from this hut (Fig 31). This evidence could be interpreted in terms of hut function, but the actual function of Structure 57 seems obscure. If it was an animal housing structure, the bone concentration seems odd, yet the evidence does not appear to support a domestic function.

The question of bone distributions and concentrations is pursued further in topic iv. The present distributions indicate clear patterning in and around

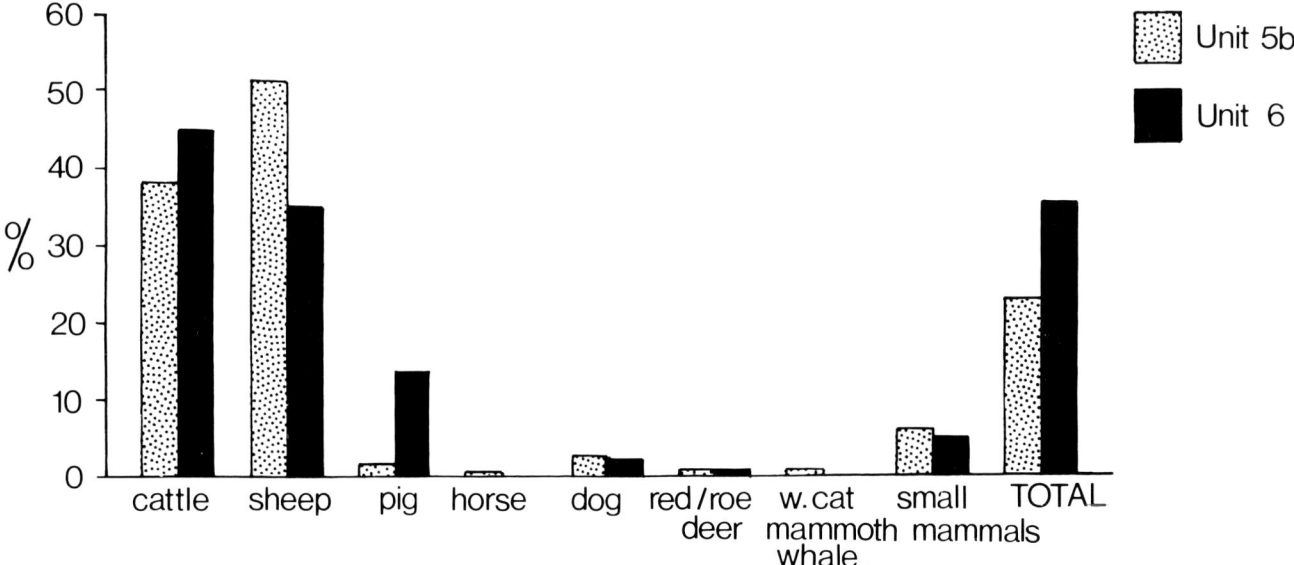

Fig 144 The relative frequencies of mammals in Units 5b and 6

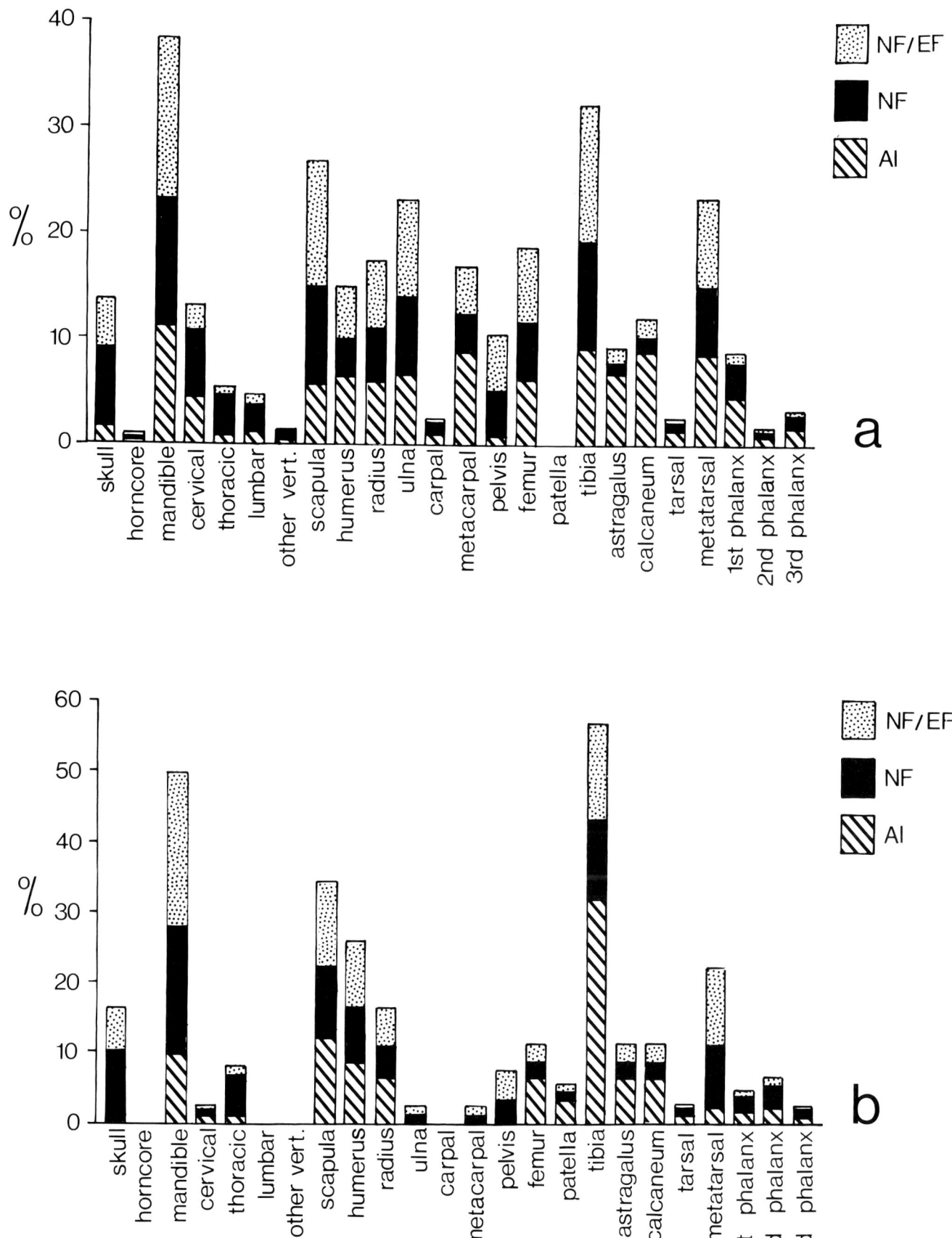

Fig 145 Anatomical representation of cattle bones in (a) Unit 5b and (b) Unit 6: in each case AI is % based on Anatomical Index Method, NF is % of total identified fragments, and NF/EF is % of identified fragments standardised for skeletal frequency

the structures, but there is no evidence for the peripheries of the settlement; the later material (Unit 4) possibly reflects the reverse of this.

Cattle

Anatomical representation of the cattle bones is illustrated in Figure 145 and summarised on MF1:F12–13. The figure illustrates three results, plotted in the form of a stacked bar graph. The %AI is the percentage based upon the anatomical index method; %NF is the percentage of the total count of identified fragments; the %NF/EF is the percentage of the identified fragments standardised for skeletal frequency.

In general all three methods provide a similar picture of anatomical frequency, though there are some obvious differences in results from the different methods of calculation. In general these differences are of three types: (i) the AI results give higher percentages for small, relatively unfragmented elements such as carpals, tarsals, and phalanges (Unit 5b), and astragalus and calcaneum (Units 5 and 6); Unit 6 also has high AI percentages for tibia, but percentages for the carpals, tarsals, and phalanges are low; (ii) the NF results give high percentages for fragile and highly fragmented elements, eg skull, scapula, and pelvis; (iii) the NF/EF results are similar to the AI results for the relatively unfragmented bones, and similar to the NF results for the fragmented elements.

The cumulative frequency graphs (Fig 146) give very different results for Units 5 and 6. Unit 5b has a generally even slope, indicating that all elements are fairly equally represented. Where the slope is steeper, there is a change in the representation pattern, implying that some elements are better represented. This occurs in several places along the slope: between skull/horncore and mandible; between mandible/vertebrae and limb bones; between lower limb bones and upper limb bones. Thus, although the overall trend of the slope is consistent, mandibles and girdles/upper limb bones are better represented than the other elements. Unit 6 is in striking contrast, with extreme changes in slope forming four plateaux and three steep slopes. The plateaux represent groups of anatomies where they are poorly represented, and the steep slopes indicate well-represented elements. The former are skull, horncore, vertebrae, lower forelimb (ulna), and hindlimb excluding tibia, astragalus, and calcaneum. The latter (well-represented) are mandible, upper forelimb (excluding ulna), tibia, astragalus, and calcaneum.

The contrast between the units is difficult to assess because it is not known to what extent the results are representative. At best we can only assume that they represent small areas of the site, so cannot conclude that any differences are due to different types of activity or economy. What can be said is that the areas within and around Structures 59 and 95 (Unit 5b) comprise a general mixture of cattle bones, with poorly represented or absent bones implying that hides were processed elsewhere (horncores and phalanges uncommon – Fig 146). The area relating to Structure 57 (Unit 6) also contains few phalanges (and no horncores), but certain elements are much better represented than any others, implying selectivity in the formation of the rubbish deposit. The form of the selection, however, remains elusive as the elements that are well represented cannot easily be related to particular activities. For example, food waste might include scapula and upper forelimb, but it should also include pelvis and upper hindlimb; butchery waste which includes mandible, tibia, astragalus, and calcaneum ought also to include carpals and radius (Fig 145).

Sheep

The anatomical results for sheep are given in the same way as for cattle (MF1:F12–13, Figs 146 and 147). As with cattle there is a contrast in the results from Units 5b and 6, and the contrast is of a similar nature (Fig 145). In Unit 5b, the representation of elements is much more even than in Unit 6, and the pattern noted for cattle from Unit 6 is repeated, but with much greater extremes, for sheep (Fig 146). The main elements that are well represented are mandible, scapula, humerus, radius, and tibia (as with cattle), but the percentages are higher (MF1:F12–13). The resemblance in patterns between the two species also occurs for Unit 5b, and, as in Unit 6, sheep have better representation of scapula, humerus, and radius (and also of metatarsal, rather than tibia as in Unit 5b) than cattle.

Other mammals

The other mammals present in the deposits fall into three categories: (i) part of the archaeological assemblage; (ii) other contemporary occurrences; (iii) later intrusions. Animals falling into categories (ii) and (iii) will be discussed separately in later sections, though it must be acknowledged that there is a degree of uncertainty about assigning species to these categories (eg some of the small mammals may be contemporary and/or intrusive).

The mammals which fall into category (i) are pig, horse, dog, cat (presumably wild cat), red deer, and roe deer. There are also one bone of a whale and one fragment of rib which is large enough to correspond with that of mammoth. Table 18 shows that all these species are infrequent, with only pig and dog greater than ten bones, and only pig above 10% of identified mammals. The pig bones have been mentioned above and are too few for more detailed analysis.

The very small frequencies with which the other species occur indicate that, if they were exploited, their remains were deposited elsewhere. This cannot be discounted given the small area of the excavation, but on the present evidence it appears as if none was of importance. The occurrence of a possible mammoth rib (in Unit 5d) is of interest since it is almost definitely derived from the Pleistocene layers at the far end of the sandcliff, up against the Down cliffs. The most likely explanation for its presence here is that it was collected by one of the contemporary dwellers and became incorporated in these much later deposits by these means. It is unfortunate that it comes from Unit 5d and not from a location that can be definitely tied in with the Bronze Age occupation.

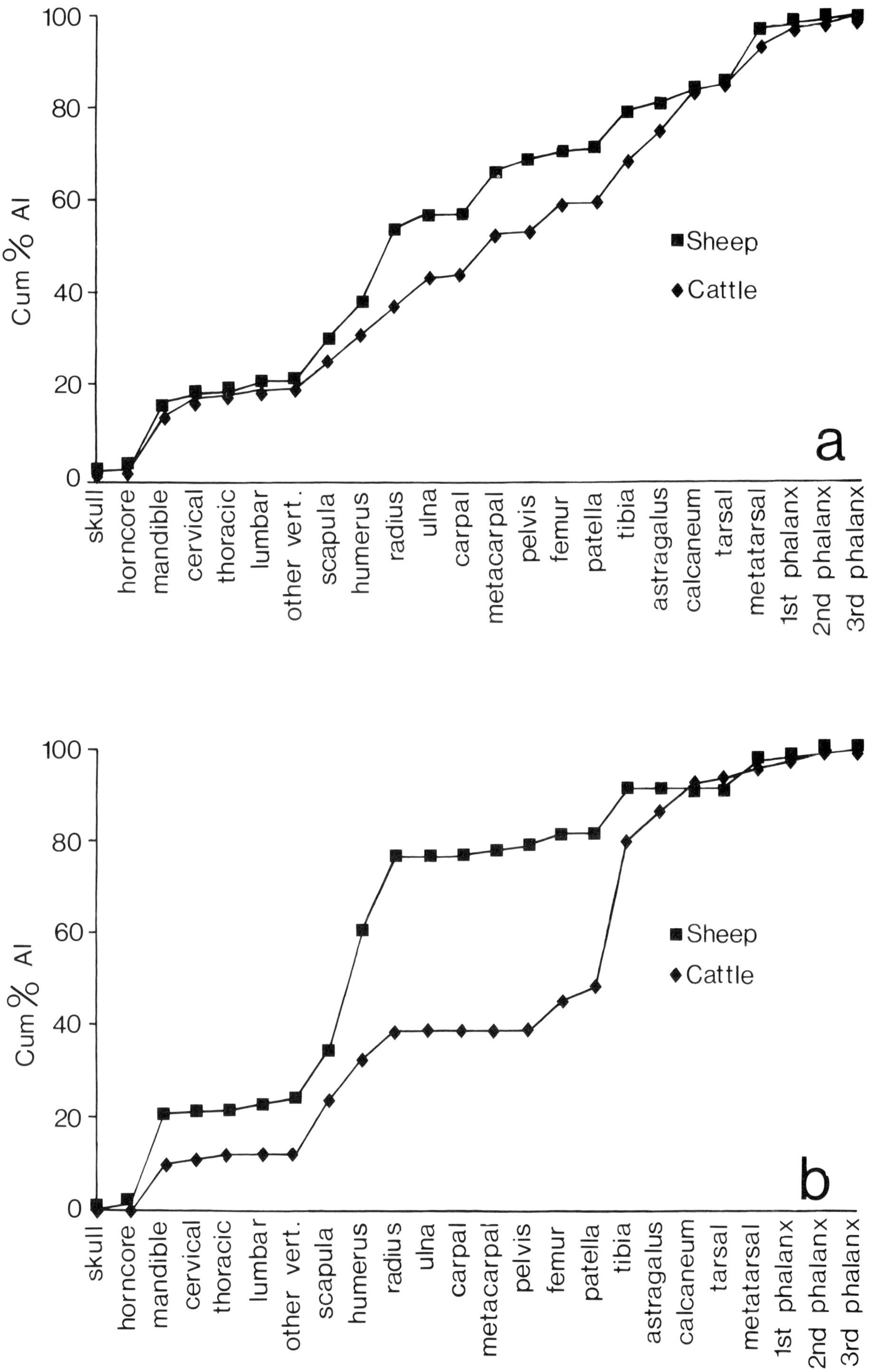

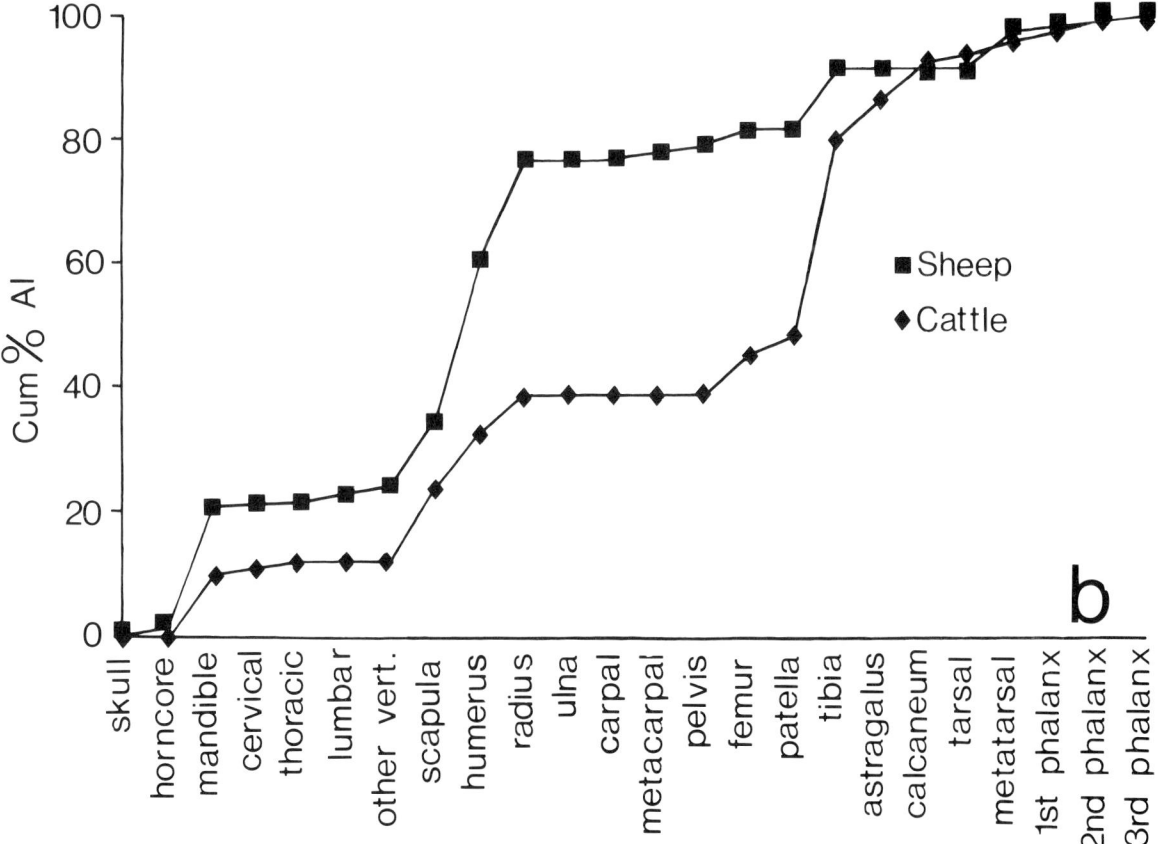

Fig 146 *Cumulative frequency graph showing the anatomical representation of cattle and sheep in (a) Unit 5b and (b) Unit 6*

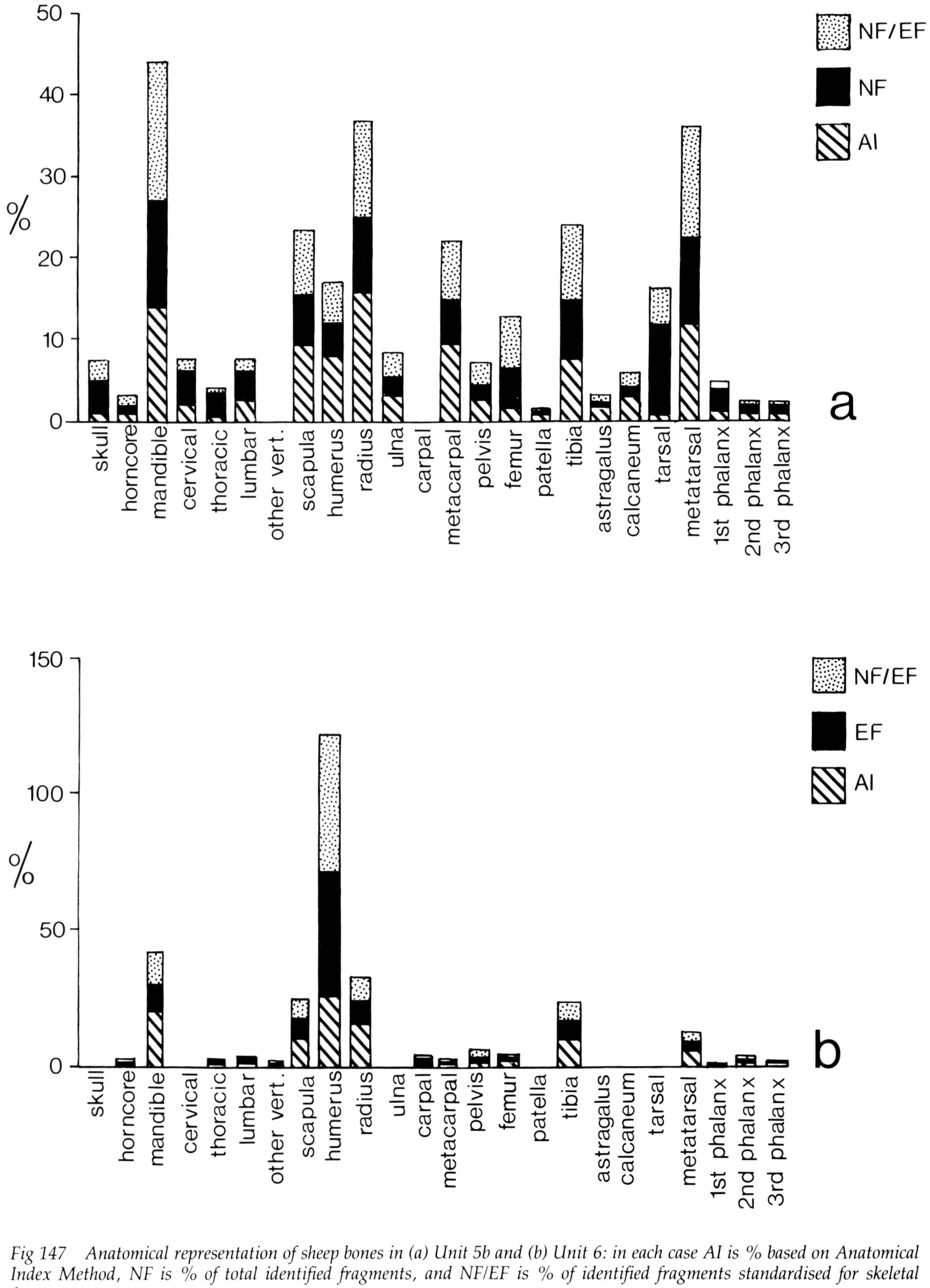

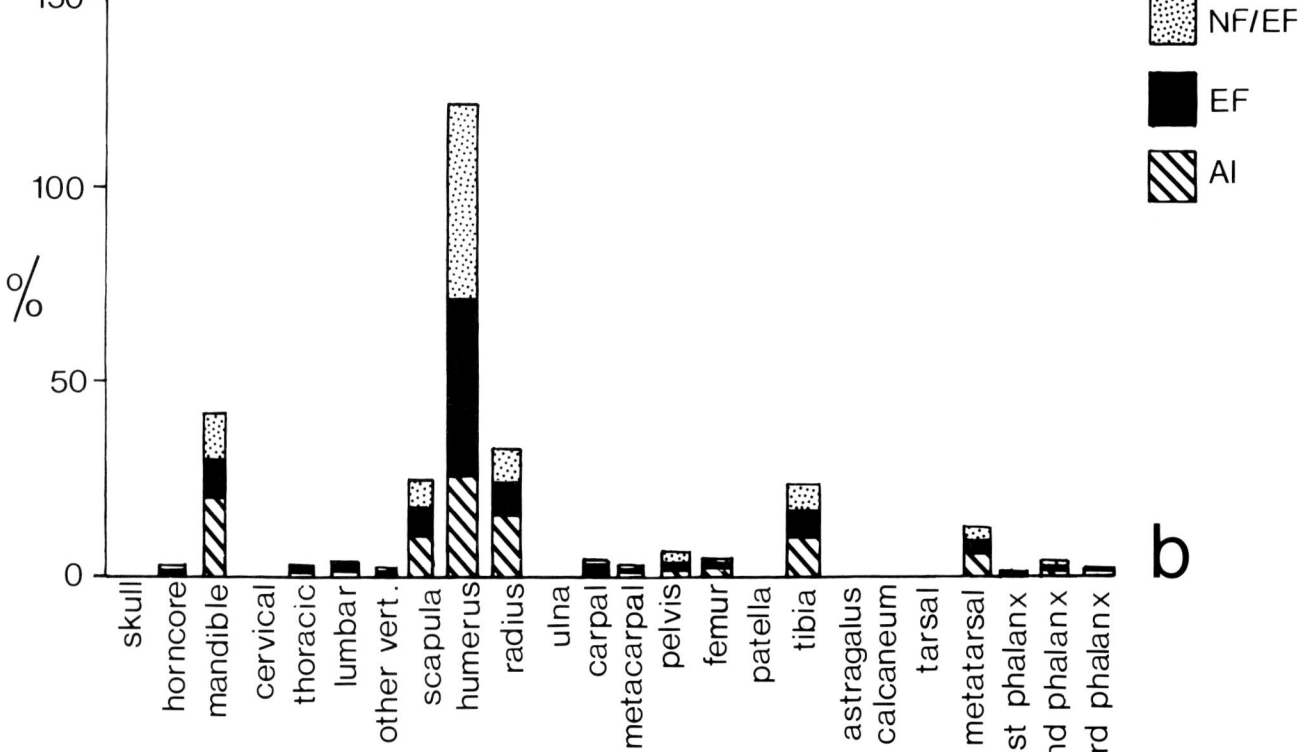

Fig 147 Anatomical representation of sheep bones in (a) Unit 5b and (b) Unit 6: in each case AI is % based on Anatomical Index Method, NF is % of total identified fragments, and NF/EF is % of identified fragments standardised for skeletal frequency

Other vertebrates

Of the other vertebrates, the reptile and amphibian remains almost certainly fall into either or both of categories (ii) and (iii) given above. The birds may also fall into these categories, though this seems a little less likely for category (iii). It will be assumed here, however, that they are actually part of the archaeological assemblage (ie they were exploited by man). The fish may much more confidently be assigned to the archaeological category, though it is just possible that some bones might be food remains of another predator (eg wild cat, fox).

Although sieving was carried out, there is little point in using the quantification of the bones from birds and fish because of the problems discussed above relating to the small area excavated; furthermore, fish are likely to be under-represented as food remains and may be very degraded and unidentifiable if the bones had been eaten (by man or by a scavenger such as a dog). We know that this was happening at Brean because of quantities of comminuted bone present in the dog coprolites (Chapter 21). The numbers of bones, however, are given in Table 19.

Birds

The bird species present are: Unit 5b – woodcock, greylag goose, lapwing, guillemot; Unit 5d – swan, greylag goose; Unit 8 – swan. Notably, all of these species are in some way associated with wetlands or marine environments. The guillemot is the commonest of the auks in north-west Europe and breeds in colonies on cliff faces. It is possible that they bred on the Brean Down cliffs during the Bronze Age, and were exploited for food. The lapwing, commonest of the European plovers, may be found in many environments, including marshland, estuaries, and coastal sandflats, all of which would have been available locally during the Bronze Age so that this species, too, was a probable local wild food source. Both the swan and the goose take advantage of inland or protected coastal waters, so would, again, probably have been locally available. Finally, the woodcock often feeds in marshy and swampy places, so would also have been locally available. In summary, these birds represent local exploitation of wetland and coastal environments.

Fish

The fish present are as follows: Unit 5b – sturgeon, eel, ling; Unit 5d – gadoid: Unit 6 – eel, cod, scad, mullet, ling. Perhaps the most remarkable of these is the single bone of a sturgeon (one of the boney head plates) which must come from an extremely large individual (measurements on MF1:G1). Wheeler (1978, 57) remarks that females up to 317kg in weight and 3.5m in length have been recorded, though such large-sized individuals are today very rare. Alison Locker, who kindly identified this specimen and aided in the identification of the other fish bones, quoted a passage from Houghton 1879, which mentions a sturgeon 8ft (2.4m) in length caught in the Severn near Shrewsbury in 1892. It is a shallow water, bottom living fish in the sea, but spawns in rivers and may be found in the lower reaches of rivers

Table 19 Summary of bird and fish species by stratigraphic unit

Species	Unit 3a	Unit 3d	Unit 4b	Unit 5a	Unit 5b	Unit 5c*	Unit 6	Unit 7	Unit 6/8a
Birds									
Mute swan *Cygnus olor* Gmelin					1	1			
Greylag goose *Anser anser* L					4	1			
Mallard *Anas platyrhynchos* L			2						
Hawks Accipitridae			2						
Domestic fowl *Gallus gallus* domestic	1		1						
Cranes Gruidae			1						
Lapwing *Vanellus vanellus* L					1				
Woodcock *Scolopax rusticola* L					2				
Snipe *Gallinago gallinago* L		1							
Guillemot *Uria aalge* Pontoppidan					1				
Robin *Erithacus rubecula* L								1	
Redwing *Turdus iliacus* L			1						
Songthrush *T philomelos* Brehm			1						
Mistle thrush *T viscivorus* L			1						
Starling *Sturnus vulgaris* L	1		3						
Raven *Corax corax* L			1						
Indet bird	21	15		1	2				
Fish									
Roker *Raja clavata*	3								
Sturgeon *Accipenser sturio*					1				
Eel *Anguilla anguilla*							81	3	
Conger eel *Conger conger*			2						
Salmons Salmonidae			1						
Pike *Esox lucius*			1						
Codfish Gadidae			1				2		
Cod *Gadus morhua*			3			1	9		
Ling *Molva molva*					1		1		
Scad *Trachurus trachurus*							1		
Mullets Mugilidae							2		
Indet fish	8		16	1	20	11			1

* Unit 5c is part of Unit 5b.

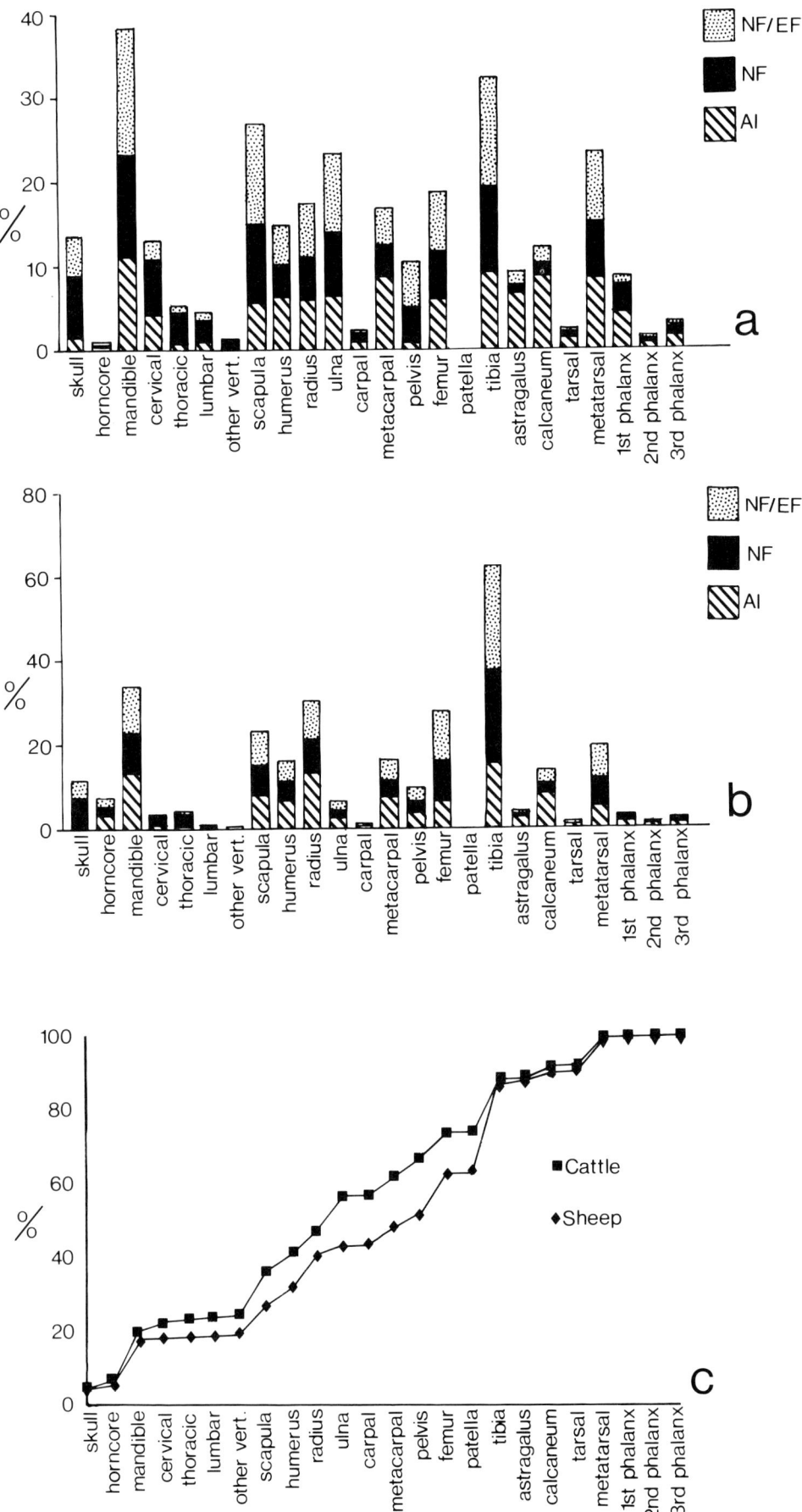

Fig 148 Anatomical representation of (a) cattle and (b) sheep in Unit 4: in (a) and (b) AI is % based on Anatomical Index Method, NF is % of total identified fragments, and NF/EF is % of identified fragments standardised for skeletal frequency; (c) anatomical representation of cattle and sheep using cumulative frequency graph

once it has spawned. The present specimen may have been caught in the Bristol Channel, and is an interesting example of the large size that this fish may reach.

The most abundant fish remains are of eel, with very many vertebrae recovered. They breed in mid-Atlantic, but migrate to Europe where they become elvers in coastal waters before entering rivers. Many stay in estuaries and river mouths so, like the sturgeon, these probably represent local fishing catches. Ling, a cod-like fish, is mainly a deep sea fish, but may also live in shallower waters, on open coasts, and today can be found around the coasts of Cornwall and parts of Devon. It may have been more local in the Bronze Age, but must represent more than just local fishing. The cod, however, may have been caught in local waters. Cod is widely distributed, and may be found in coastal waters right to the shoreline. Today it is generally only young cod which are found inshore. The scad or horse mackerel is not a prime food fish today. Although it may be found close inshore (especially the young), it is mainly a surface swimming, offshore fish. It can be found locally, so may have been caught along with cod and/or ling. Finally, mullet (possibly red mullet) mainly live in shallow inshore waters close to the muddy or sandy sea bed, and so might also have been caught locally. Although most of these fish are poorly represented at Brean Down, it seems safe to assume that fishing in the Bristol Channel, and possibly out into the sea, took place. The ling, perhaps, were not caught locally. The most common fish remains, eel, represent fishing in the Severn estuary, Bristol Channel, and/or local rivers (eg the Axe, which emerges just north of Brean Down, and today flows within 1.5km of the site).

iv The character of the late Bronze Age deposits

The 6077 bones from Unit 4 are dominated by unidentified fragments (Table 17) – 56%. This exemplifies the fact that the bones are generally highly fragmented, including those that were identified to taxon. A second important component of the species list is the high percentage of rabbit bones (12%), and these are undoubtedly intrusive. The effect of rabbit disturbances is discussed in detail in topic viii. The other species may be considered as non-intrusive, with the possible exception of small mammals such as mole. In the following discussion rabbits will be excluded (except in dealing with distribution plots), and percentages of species are based upon the total of identified bones excluding rabbit.

The major mammals

Cattle and sheep/goat are represented in approximately equal proportions (45% and 46% respectively). Of the 66 sheep/goat bones identified to species, 59 (89%) are sheep, and it can be reasonably assumed that sheep were the major of the two species; sheep/goat bones will therefore be referred to as sheep below. Other domestic species represented are horse, pig, dog, and cat (though possibly the cat bones are of wild cat). None are well represented, even pigs being at only 2%.

MF1:F14 summarises information about the body parts of cattle and sheep (loose teeth, indeterminate vertebrae, and metapodia not identified to metacarpal or -tarsal are excluded). Figure 148 illustrates the results using the AI. Both species have in common high proportions of mandibles and lower limb bones, and very low proportions of skull, vertebrae, and phalanges. Differences centre on the degree of representation of certain elements, particularly radius and tibia which are much more common in sheep than in cattle. The sheep bones are generally less fragmented than the cattle bones, and this is reflected in the higher AI total for sheep which is in contrast to the NF totals for the two species (MF1:F14).

Distribution of bones

Figures 149 and 150 illustrate plots of bone distribution for Unit 4. A comparison of the most numerous categories (cattle, sheep, 'cattle-size' and 'sheep-size') shows that there is no difference between these groups, the distributions being nearly identical in each case. Thus it would appear that the bone distribution is independent of species or fragment size.

Although the distribution of bones is fairly even, there are some areas of greater concentration: on the eastern side of the site between about 14 and 19m, and along the eastern side of the northern area of the site (between −1 and 10m). The extent of Unit 4 is also clearly shown by the abrupt change from areas with bone to areas without bone. Unit 4 was considerably thicker in the northern part of the site than the southern, and in the south it tailed off at about 20m. The concentration of bones in the northern part of the site, therefore, may reflect the thickness of the unit there, and this fact emphasises the concentration at the east end since this is at the thinnest part of the unit. The implication is that the bone concentration increases to the east, and perhaps continues to do so to the east of the excavation.

Figure 150 shows the distribution of the bones of the minor animals and rabbits. The former show the same pattern as the major animals. The rabbit bones are present in most of the Unit 4 zone, but interestingly are absent from the northern end, where Unit 4 was sealed by Unit 4a, a hard colluvial deposit, so bones from that end are unlikely to have suffered much disturbance.

Recent studies on Iron Age sites (Wilson 1985; Wilson and Levitan forthcoming) show that distinct patterns in bone distribution occur, with bones of larger animals (cattle and horse) in the peripheries of the site, and smaller bones (sheep, pig, etc) more centrally located. Patterns are evident at Brean Down in Units 5 and 6, as discussed above, although the area excavated is rather too small to take the conclusions about Structure 95 any further. There is also no clear patterning in the bone distributions which might be interpreted in functional terms. However, the increase in concentration of bones to the east might indicate a greater concentration of activity in

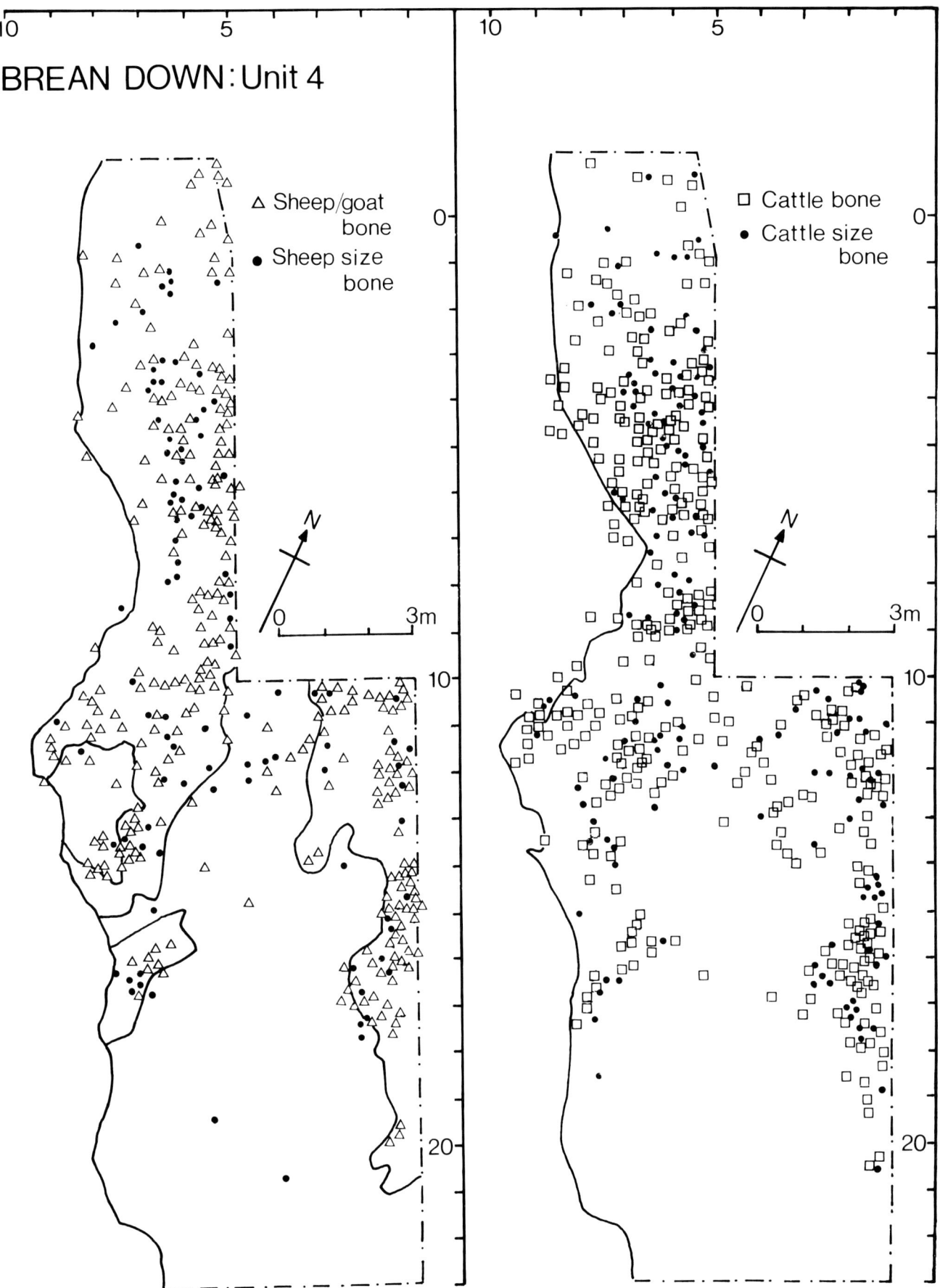

Fig 149 Distribution of cattle and sheep bones in Unit 4

THE VERTEBRATE REMAINS

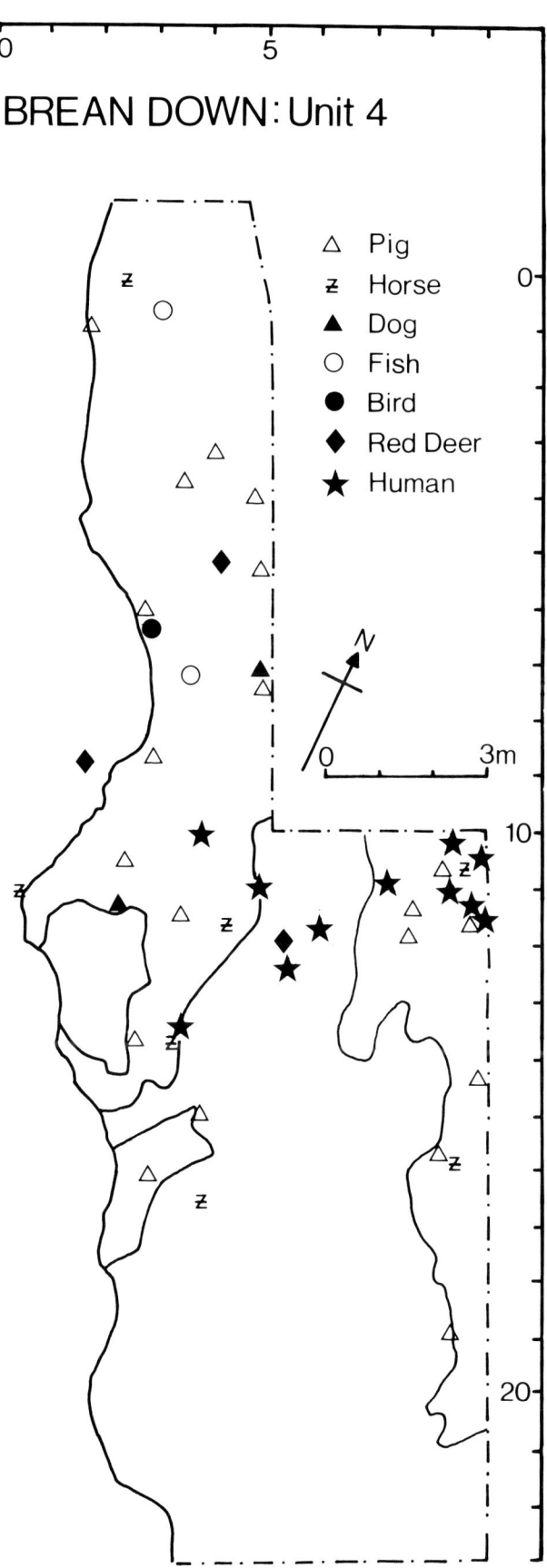

Fig 150 *Distribution of species other than cattle and sheep in Unit 4*

that direction. Furthermore, there is a hint of an increase of bone concentrations in Soil Pit V (Fig 79), well away from the main area of pottery scatter. Similarly, it may be no coincidence that some bones occurred in Neolithic and Bronze Age estuarine silts in Soil Pit VI (Fig 81), also well away from the settlement.

Other mammals

Small mammals which might have been intrusive or just chance occurrences are not considered here (see topic vi).

Horse and dog are the only other domestic mammals present, and in small numbers only. Neither, then, would appear to have been common at this site on the basis of the present assemblage. Similarly the five bones of red deer indicate that this species was exploited, but may have been relatively unimportant. The four bones of cat are possibly all of wild cat which were chance occurrences, or deliberately killed, or possibly kept in captivity (semi-tamed).

Other animals

Numbers of bird and fish bones recovered are given in Table 19, but these are probably under-represented owing to destruction from processing and/or having been eaten, as well as from taphonomic factors. The Bronze Age layers were sieved so it is unlikely that many bones were missed.

Some of the birds may have been chance occurrences, but they are considered to be mainly exploited or exploiters. The fish are most likely to have been part of the archaeological assemblage, as were the other domesticated mammals and larger wild mammals.

Birds

Only one domestic bird is represented – a single bone of domestic fowl. This represents a very early occurrence of domestic fowl, but since the identification is not 100% certain and there is also the possibility of intrusion via rabbit burrows, this occurrence is probably not worth labouring. Both mallard and crane (crane not identified to species) represent wetland environments which would have been readily available locally. Starling and raven are well known today for their association with man, and both were eaten in the past, so it seems likely that these may represent either food remains or/and chance occurrence from living in proximity to the settlement. The redwing is today associated with forests and farmland, and was probably also a local inhabitant, so may represent food remains or chance occurrence.

Fish

Conger eel is a large, marine eel which is common on rocky shores and offshore. Thus they are unlikely to have been caught off the sandy beach zone of the Bristol Channel, but may have been caught from the shoreline around Brean Down, or further south, along the Exmoor coastline. In the latter case, this may be too far away to suggest fishing by the inhabitants of Brean Down, but it may have been traded. Cod may have been locally caught (see above). The salmonid bones may represent either salmon or trout. Salmon spawn in rivers, and may spend up to three years in rivers (as parr) before migrating to the sea. After about three or four years in the sea they return to their original rivers to breed, so may have been caught locally on their outward and/or inward journey. Trout have similar behaviour patterns, though some are non-migratory freshwater living (brown trout). The pike is a freshwater fish, typically inhabiting lowland rivers and lakes, so may have been caught locally in rivers such as the Axe, Yeo, or Brue. Thus there are both marine and freshwater fish represented, indicating that fishing in both environments was taking place, and in both cases locally.

v Ageing, butchery, and measurements: Units 4–8

The small samples of aged, butchered, and measured bones make it impossible to discuss these topics in detail for each unit. The data have, therefore, been combined, and are discussed below.

The ageing results, using the method of Grant (1982), are illustrated in Figure 151. The samples are rather small, especially for cattle. The cattle results indicate three or possibly four peaks in deaths, the earliest and most marked of which is in infant cattle less than a year old, at numerical equivalents 3 and 4. Later peaks are centred on 9–10 (about a year old), 23 (about two years old), 34 (about three years old), and 43 (about four years old). These results, therefore, imply seasonal peaks in slaughter, though in the absence of sex data it is difficult to make any interpretations about economic patterns. The ageing data for sheep are much more evenly distributed, with several minor peaks which occur at approximately equal age stage increments (at 3, 7, 12, 18, 21, 25, 29, 34, 37, and 41). These results imply that sheep were being killed throughout the year with, perhaps, small peaks at approximately three or four monthly intervals. As with cattle, there is a peak in very young individuals (stage 3). In both species these might be infant mortalities.

MF1:G1 lists selected measurements which were taken using the criteria of von den Dreisch (1976). Other measurements are in the site archive, and copies are available from the author. The results are too few to allow any interpretations about the animals in terms of sex separation or of stature and size changes. Few measurements of bones of this period are available, however, and these are a welcome addition to the small corpus that is published. Selected comparisons are made with the recently excavated major Bronze Age site of Potterne, Wiltshire (with the kind permission of Alison Locker), and other Bronze Age sites. These show that the Brean Down cattle and sheep are essentially similar to those from Potterne.

Butchery of the cattle was evidenced mainly by cut marks on the bones (made by a knife or light chop-

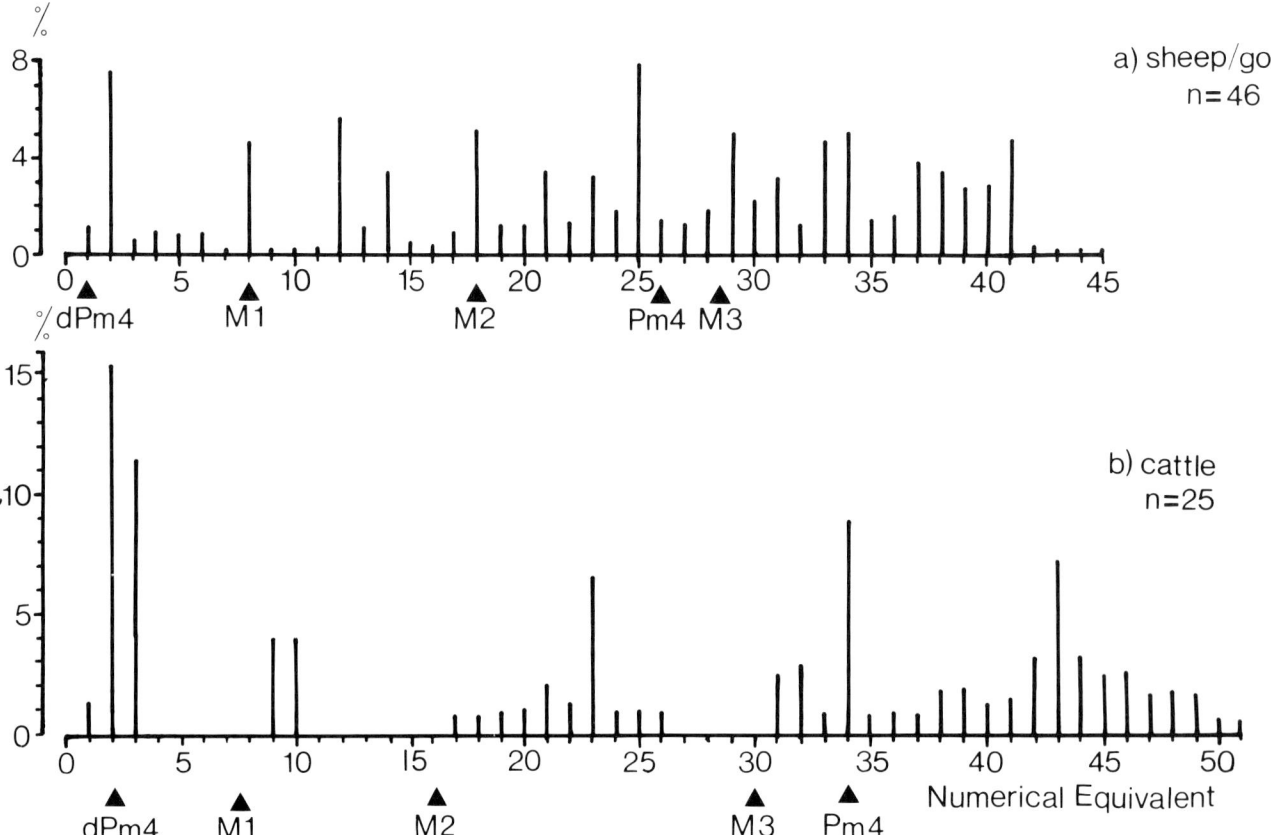

Fig 151 Mandible wear stages for Units 4–8a (adjusted counts) using the methods of Grant (1982): (a) sheep/goat; (b) cattle

per). Chop marks were also evident, but less common, and some bones had obviously been battered or split. The evidence is limited, but in general indicates that the cattle were butchered on the ground, vertebrae having been trimmed laterally and ribs cut through at the caput. For the limbs, the main concentrations of butchery marks are at the shoulder and elbow and at the ankle. Most of the cuts on the scapula indicate filleting, whilst those on the distal humerus and proximal radius and ulna exemplify disjointing. Disjointing also occurred at the ankle. Metapodials were split longitudinally and phalanges had cuts consistent with skinning. Mandibles and maxillae were chopped or battered at the diastema and some mandibles had cut marks on the ascending ramus, beneath the condyle.

Evidence of butchery on sheep bones is even more limited, and almost entirely confined to the hind limb. Butchery was also seen on horncores, ribs, and metacarpals. The relative paucity of butchery may reflect less intensive preparation of the carcase, the smaller size of the animal making it more manageable.

There is no evidence of butchery on pig bones, but one horse metatarsal has been split longitudinally.

Cattle and sheep: summary

Cattle may have been killed at seasonal peaks, once a year, and few were allowed to survive their fourth year. They were relatively small in size, but similar to those from other Bronze Age sites. Butchery evidence indicates division of the carcase into major joints, an activity which probably took place on the ground, with filleting of the meat also evident on some bones. Sheep appear to have been slaughtered more evenly throughout the year, with few surviving beyond about four years. The very limited butchery evidence implies little preparation (eg jointing or filleting).

vi Ecological considerations

In addition to the major mammals discussed above, a number of small mammal remains were recovered, mostly from the sieving. The advantage of these remains is that they provide an insight into the site environment as they are unlikely to have been directly exploited by man but may well have lived as commensals or in proximity. A problem, however, is that they may be intrusive, in their own right (eg mole), or from having exploited other animals' burrows, or as a result of accidental deposition. The following notes on the species represented are made on the basis that they are not intrusive, so this possibility should be borne in mind.

Table 20 lists the species present. The most interesting finds are of beaver and house mouse. The former is an uncertain identification (based on a first phalanx). However, although it is now extinct, it was certainly present in England in the past (eg Coy 1981, 99; Coles and Orme 1988). The earliest certain records for house mouse are Iron Age (eg Harcourt 1979, 155). There have been several finds of house mouse from Bronze Age layers at Potterne (A Locker, pers comm) but the dating of these bones is uncertain. The find from Brean Down is a skeleton from Unit 5b but again the bones have not been directly dated so the possibility that it is intrusive must be considered. If the find is not intrusive, this would represent the earliest find for the species in Britain.

The other species present no surprises, and do not provide very useful environmental indications. Some

Table 20 Summary of small mammals, reptiles, and amphibians

Species	Unit 3a	Unit 3c	Unit 3d	Unit 4a	Unit 4b	Unit 5a	Unit 5b	Unit 5c*	Unit 6	Unit 7	Unit 8a
Mammals											
Mole, *Talpa europaea* L	1	1			4					7	
Pygmy shrew, *Sorex minutus* L					1						
Hare, *Lepus* cf *europaeus* Pallas									1		
Beaver, *Castor fiber* L	4										
Bank vole, *Clethrionomys glareolus* Schreb					1						
Field vole, *Microtus agrestis* (L) Mill					12		5	1	1		
Water vole, *Arvicola terrestris* L					6				2	10	7
Voles, Microtinae	1						1		1		
Wood mouse, *Apodemus* cf *sylvaticus* (L) Hin							1			1	
House mouse, *Mus musculus* L							88				
Mice, Muridae	1				1		1			12	
Rat, *Rattus* sp	1										
Rodent, Rodentia	20		2	4	65	23	23	333	4	6	
Weasel, *Mustela nivalis* L	1				3						
Mustelid, Mustelidae	2										
Cat, *Felis* cf *silvestris* Schreb					4		3				
Small mammal	1	1			5		9		5		
Reptiles and amphibians											
Grass snake, *Natrix natrix* L				1		3	4	8	75	139	
Frog, *Rana* sp	23				19	7				83	1

*Unit 5c is part of Unit 5b.

close cover nearby is implied by the presence of pygmy shrew, water vole, etc, and fresh water by the grass snake, frogs, and water vole (though the last may have been less aquatic in the past). A very similar suite of species was present at Middleton Stoney (albeit in a much later context), and a list of home ranges and habitats is given in that report (Levitan 1984, 138).

vii Human bones from Bronze Age contexts

In addition to the human bones discussed in Chapter 6, 22 bones were found in Bronze Age contexts. Fifteen are from Unit 4, six from Unit 5b, and one from Unit 6 (MF1:G2). The distribution plots of these bones (Fig 65) show that most come from one distinct zone, from c 12m to c 14m OD, and in a zone between 10 and 13.5m on the A (N–S) axis and 1 and 10.5m on the B (E–W) axis. The bones from Units 4 and 5–6 ought to be distinct since there was a thick 'sterile' sand layer (Unit 5b) between them. The coincidence of the bones in the above zone may be no more than chance, and in fact all the Unit 4b bones lie in the eastern part of the zone, and the Unit 5b bones in the western part. The possibility that these bones might have been involved in blowout and associated faunal disturbances (topic viii) must be considered because this zone does represent roughly the northern limit of the hypothesised post-medieval dune blowout (Chapter 7). However, there was no recognisable disturbance related to the blowout as far down as Unit 5b, and even in Unit 4 the clear impression during excavation was that some at least of the human bones (eg the skull fragments 3677 – Fig 55) were certainly embedded in Unit 4 type sediment. Consequently it is considered likely that most of these human bones were associated with Bronze Age layers. In Unit 4 the bones fall into the zone of greatest bone concentration (Fig 150), so need not be seen as more than part of this general pattern.

Generally, the numbers of human bones from the prehistoric layers are too small to postulate the near locality of burials, and certainly the very small numbers from Units 5 and 6 may represent nothing other than chance occurrence. Even the larger number of bones from Unit 4 is less than 1% of the total bones from that unit, so it seems unlikely that these few scattered remains represent anything other than chance occurrences.

The presence of human bone here and on other sites of similar date is, however, itself important. One (highly speculative) scenario which might lead to the incorporation of the odd human bone within domestic rubbish deposits involves the practice of exposure before burial. Immediate burial and/or cremation would seem to preclude the casual incorporation of human bone within settlement debris, but exposure before burial might well have led to this occurrence if the site of exposure was visited by scavenging dogs which could then have brought some bones back to the village (though the human bones present here do not show evidence of canid chewing). It is also possible that a few fragments may have been deliberately brought back to the settlement, possibly by children, or possibly as some kind of talisman. There is no direct evidence of exposure before burial at this site, but there is evidence elsewhere in this region (Levitan et al 1988).

viii Intrusions and disturbances

Analysis of material recovered from Brean Down is hindered by two major problems: disturbance and reworking of material due to sand blow, and intrusions (plus subsequent disturbance/reworking) by rabbits and other animals. The former aspect relates mainly to the sub-Roman cemetery and is discussed in that context (Chapter 6). The evidence is not obtained directly from bones. This section, therefore, is concerned only with bioturbation due (principally) to rabbits.

Before the discussion of the rabbit evidence, it should be noted that in addition to intrusive bones a number of 'disturbance features', which are best interpreted as burrows, were noticed during excavation. These are described below. The bone evidence pertaining to these is, in most cases, inconclusive, and whilst these may well have resulted from the activities of rabbits and even badgers (some of the features were large), the bone evidence cannot be used to help in interpreting them.

A crude, but useful, estimate of rabbit activity can be made by looking at percentages of rabbit bone in the units. This information is given in Table 21. Not surprisingly, the main trend is a fall in rabbit percentages with depth, though this trend is by no means completely consistent. Rabbit frequencies in Units 3a and 3b are above 40%. In the cemetery (Unit 3c1) they have decreased to 24%, and in Unit 4 (late Bronze Age and after) percentages are 12% and below. If Unit 5a is ignored, general proportions of rabbit are similar to Unit 4 for Unit 5 (middle/late Bronze Age), and in Units 6 to 8a there are no rabbit bones at all. Unit 5a is very much an anomaly, with 72% rabbit, but since this unit does not contain archaeological features or deposits, the relative frequency of rabbit is exaggerated (the actual number of rabbit bones is

Table 21 Frequency of rabbit in units from Brean Down

Unit	No	%
1	57	14
3a	1322	46
3b	84	58
3c	47	24
3d	1	7
4a	6	5
4b	743	12
5a	161	72
5b	355	12
Structure 95	11	3
Structure 59	96	13
6	4	<1
Structure 57	3	<1
6/8a	0	0
7	0	0
8a	0	0

smaller than for Units 4b and 5b). In general, therefore, rabbit activity appears to have penetrated to Unit 5, but the amount of disturbance in Units 4 and 5 appears to be relatively small. There is apparently no rabbit disturbance in Units 6, 7, or 8a.

The main impact, therefore, appears to be in the cemetery, and the effects of both wind blow and rabbit activity in the cemetery have been briefly noted above (Chapter 6). In fact, of the 47 rabbit bones recovered from Unit 3c1, 33 are from a single skeleton from Trench IX, relating to skeleton number 2. This leaves only 14 bones, three of which are from Trench X (skeleton 7), one from Trench IX (skeleton 3), one from Trench IX (Context 222), and the rest from the main trench (nine bones). Thus, the apparently high infestation by rabbits in Unit 3c1 is mainly due to one skeleton. It is undoubted, however, that rabbits did cause some disturbances, and it is unfortunate that there were not enough bones recovered to analyse distributions in the hope of identifying the main areas affected.

The rabbit bones in Unit 4 were more diffusely scattered across the site, and Figure 152b illustrates their distribution. This shows that rabbit activity was concentrated mainly in the central part of the site, and the two or three zones of concentration of rabbit bones might indicate collapsed tunnels. Six contexts were noted, during excavation, as possible animal disturbances/burrows. Four of these are from Unit 4: Contexts 22, 56, 72, and 73. Interestingly, none of these contexts appear to be disturbances from the bone evidence alone, since they contain a mixture of species which is similar to Unit 4 in general (not surprising if they are disturbances, but not positive proof). The only context with a particularly high occurrence of rabbit is 56 with 103 rabbit bones, 30% of the bones from that context – a percentage that is much higher than the rabbit for Unit 4 as a whole – and 14% of the rabbit from Unit 4. However, this context also contained the articulated right femur and tibia and the left tibia of the pair of cattle, as well as the articulated third to seventh cervical vertebrae of cattle. These are unlikely to have remained associated in a major animal disturbance, so there is conflicting evidence here.

The distribution of rabbit bones in Unit 5b is illustrated in Figure 152a. This shows one or two concentrations (northern end of Structure 95 and to the south of Structure 95), which might indicate parts of burrows (presumably the bottom-most levels of burrows). This, in fact, corresponds quite well with the areas of burrows noted during excavation and recorded on the surface of Unit 5b (Fig 33). The few other bones, dotted around the area, imply little disturbance. One of the possible animal disturbance contexts noted above comes from Unit 5b. This is Context 107, which contained eight bones from a single infant rabbit. On this basis it appears a very likely candidate for a burrow. The last disturbance context (165) is from Unit 5d and contained only one unidentified fragment, so the evidence from bones is inconclusive.

The overall impression gained from the evidence of rabbit bones is of some localised areas of disturbance, but generally little disturbance below the level of Unit 5b. The only prehistoric level that might be regarded as suspect owing to rabbit activities is Unit 4. In this respect it is interesting to note that most of the suspected animal burrows/disturbances are from Unit 4, and that one of them (Context 56) contained 108 rabbit bones, 14% of the rabbit from the unit. It is also noteworthy that another suspect burrow (Context 107), from Unit 5b, contained part of a rabbit infant skeleton.

Conclusions

The small collection of bones from the Pleistocene layers forms a useful addition to the data published by ApSimon *et al* (1961). The species identified, which include a possible mammoth, are in keeping with the earlier findings.

The earliest post-glacial levels, Units 7 and 8a, rendered samples that are too small for any detailed analysis.

The most fruitful evidence from the prehistoric period comes from Units 5b and 6. The bones from the three Bronze Age structures were compared. The interior of Structure 57 produced a greater concentration of bone than the other structures, especially within the northern part of the floor, but also in the deposits which accumulated with the walls after the structure was abandoned. By contrast, bones were relatively sparse in Structure 95. The central area and hearth were almost devoid of bones, but there was a scatter from the stone wall (Context 131) and a marked concentration west of the hearth corresponding to the main concentration of pottery. Structure 95 had the highest proportion of cattle, whereas Structure 57 had the highest proportion of sheep/goat. Structure 57 also had a relatively large number of fish bones compared with the other structures. In a consideration of the bones from the units as a whole, it was found that most bones from Unit 5b lay outside the structures, with a particular concentration (Context 77) possibly representing a rubbish dump relating to clear-out of a structure (ashy layer, plus unburnt bones). This could explain the relative paucity of bones from Structures 95 and 59. Only a small area of Unit 6 was excavated, so it was not possible to assess the area outside Structure 57 very easily, but the impression here is that the bones outside the structure were more diffusely spread than those inside it – another contrast with the earlier structures. Cattle and sheep were the major species, as in Unit 4.

A number of bird and fish species were also present. Both reflect the surrounding water-oriented environments, with the wetlands of the clay levels inland and to the south, and the Bristol Channel to the west. The extremely large sturgeon has curiosity value, since fish of this size are seldom caught in this locality today, but presumably it would not have been so rare in the Bronze Age. The presence of ling implies some fishing out at sea, though not necessarily by the inhabitants of Brean Down.

The dominance of cattle in all the Bronze Age samples is not particularly surprising, as similar patterns appear on other contemporary sites. Grigson (1982, 308), for example, discusses Beaker and early Bronze Age sites, and of six sites four have cattle

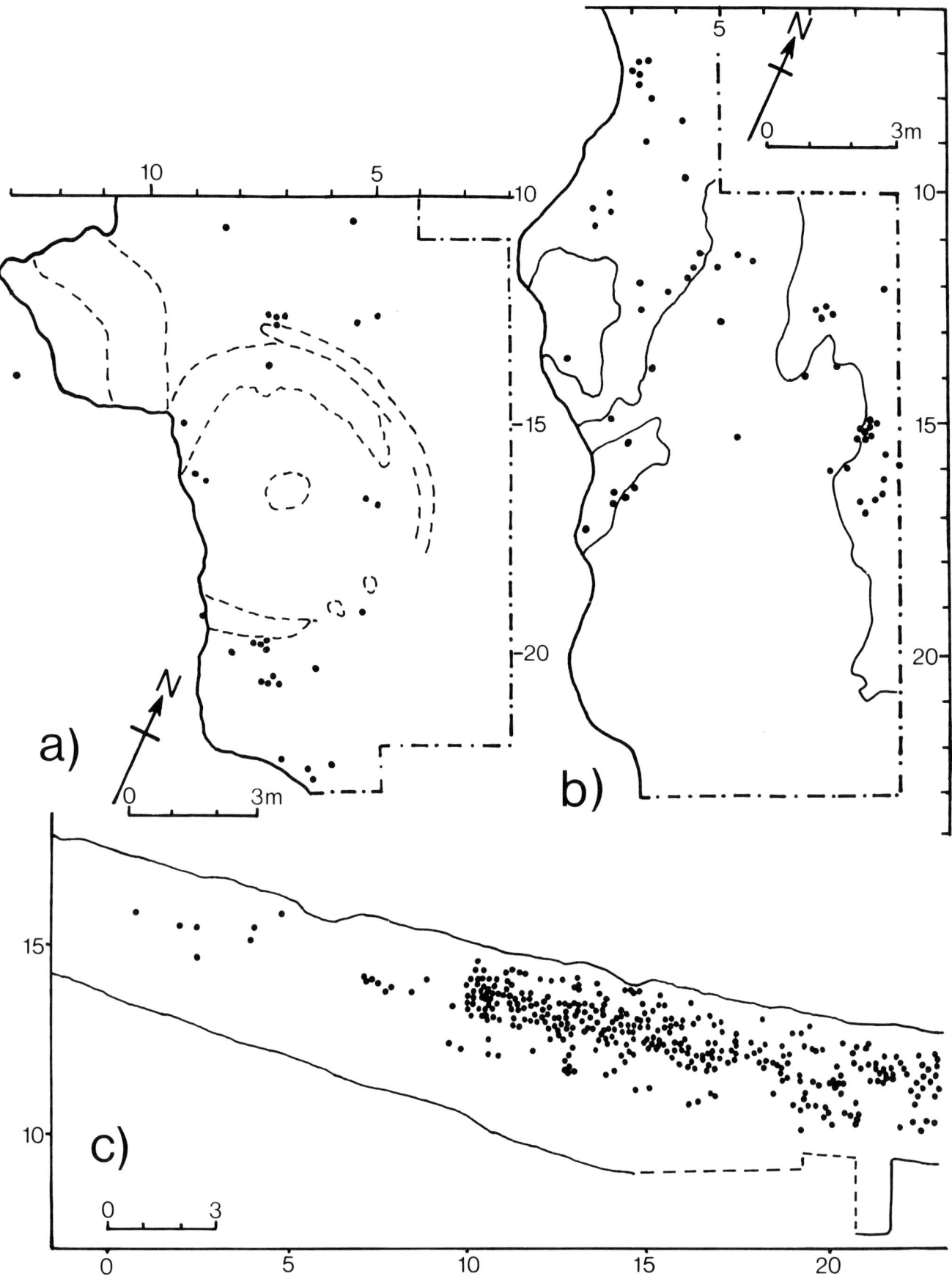

Fig 152   Distribution of rabbit bones: (a) horizontal distribution in Unit 5b; (b) horizontal distribution in Unit 4; (c) vertical distribution in all units

predominant (Windmill Hill, Wiltshire, Poors Heath, Suffolk, Hockwold-cum-Wilton, Norfolk, and Snail Down, Wiltshire). Similarly, cattle are predominant in the earliest layers at Potterne, though by the end of the period represented (*c* 700 BC), sheep are predominant (A Locker, pers comm), and other, later Bronze Age sites also have high proportions of cattle, eg Rams Hill, Berkshire, Itford Hill, Sussex, and Shearplace Hill, Dorset (Burgess 1980, 258). Cattle were also the most common species at Runnymede, Berkshire (Done 1980, 75), though at 57% the percentage is less than at many other Bronze Age sites. Other examples could be quoted, but the sites given above represent a fair cross-section of the Bronze Age bone material from England.

The late Bronze Age deposits are the most problematic to interpret because of the lack of features, except for a small section of ditch and an enigmatic stone spread. Cattle and sheep were the major animals exploited, and cattle, the most important, may have been slaughtered in seasonal peaks. They were small in stature, but similar to other Bronze Age assemblages. The sheep were slaughtered more evenly throughout the year. The bones were fairly evenly distributed across the site, with little indication of the kind of patterning that has been found at rural Iron Age sites in the upper Thames Valley.

The small mammals and the reptile and amphibian remains were briefly reviewed. Some of these may have been intrusive, but in any case the habitats they represented do not give a clear picture of the site environment. The most surprising find is the skeleton of a house mouse from a Unit 5b context. Without a date determination, however, the possibility that it may be intrusive cannot be ruled out. If it is not intrusive it represents the earliest find for this species in Britain.

The question of animal disturbances was discussed, and although rabbits obviously played a large part in the disturbances which did occur, the evidence is reassuring for early levels, with little rabbit present in Unit 5b and none in Units 6–8. Rabbits possibly caused greater disturbances in Unit 4 and in the cemetery, but an investigation of the possible disturbance contexts proved to be inconclusive except in one case, Context 107, which contained a partial infant skeleton of rabbit.

A small number of human bones was also recovered from the prehistoric layers, but these did not represent burials, and cannot be analysed in detail. The presence of odd fragments of human bone at Bronze Age and other prehistoric settlements, however, is of importance as this may point to certain kinds of burial practice, albeit in a rather indirect fashion.

The Brean Down bone assemblage is important, not only because it is one of the largest assemblages of Bronze Age bones, but also because it represents a unique variety of evidence, all of which has unusual or important aspects. Particularly welcome is the opportunity to study bones of the Bronze Age in clear association with well-preserved structures, and to elucidate some information about the nature of this occupation.

21 Coprolites and faecal concretions

by Andrew K G Jones

Introduction

A total of 64 specimens of coprolites and samples of concreted material, collected mainly from Bronze Age occupation deposits, were submitted to the Environmental Archaeology Unit, University of York, for identification and comment. Given the post-excavation timetable of the project and the fact that some material was needed for display, it was impossible to take standard sized samples from the specimens or to examine all samples submitted. The author selected 47 samples for detailed investigation bearing in mind the condition and provenance of the submitted material and the need to survey the material adequately.

During the course of the investigation three main kinds of material were recognised. Some of the submitted samples were clearly coprolites, being of a shape and size consistent with canine faeces and containing small splinters of mammal bone (Figs 153 and 154). The excavator expressed the desire that at least some coprolites were not destroyed during the analysis. Consequently, a number were examined visually and left for posterity.

There was also a group of samples which strongly resembled the coprolites in the nature of their composition and inclusions, but were fragmentary or of an unusual colour. These have been described as 'possible coprolites'.

A third group comprised amorphous concretions of unknown origin. These were variable in colour and form, but several were notable for their glassy appearance when broken.

The samples were examined using a technique based on the procedure outlined by the Ministry of Agriculture, Fisheries and Food (1977, 3) for examining modern faecal samples. A subsample of selected concretions was placed in a 120ml wide-mouthed bottle with measured aliquots of dilute hydrochloric acid in a ratio of 1g sample to 14ml dilute acid. The bottle was allowed to stand for 24 hours and gently shaken by hand to assess if the concretions were thoroughly disaggregated. Once disaggregated the mixture was thoroughly shaken and poured through a freshly flamed sieve of 250μm micron mesh aperture to remove coarse particles. A 0.15ml aliquot of the filtrate was covered by a 22×50mm coverslip and scanned at ×120 using a transmission microscope. Where possible eggs were measured using a eyepiece graticule calibrated to a stage micrometer. Length and width were recorded for all eggs. In addition, length minus polar plugs was recorded for trichurid ova. Recent experiments have shown that, although parasite ova can withstand the rigours of pollen analysis, the size of the eggs can be modified by the process (Hall *et al* 1983). Accurate identification is therefore only possible if samples are carefully prepared using reagents which do not affect egg size.

Results

Visual descriptions of all the individual coprolites belonging to the three groups are given in MF1:G3–6. Table 22 summarises the occurrence of the three types of material in the main stratigraphic units. For the distributions of coprolites in Unit 6α see Figure 31 and for Unit 5b see Figure 48a.

Only three of the coprolite samples produced para-

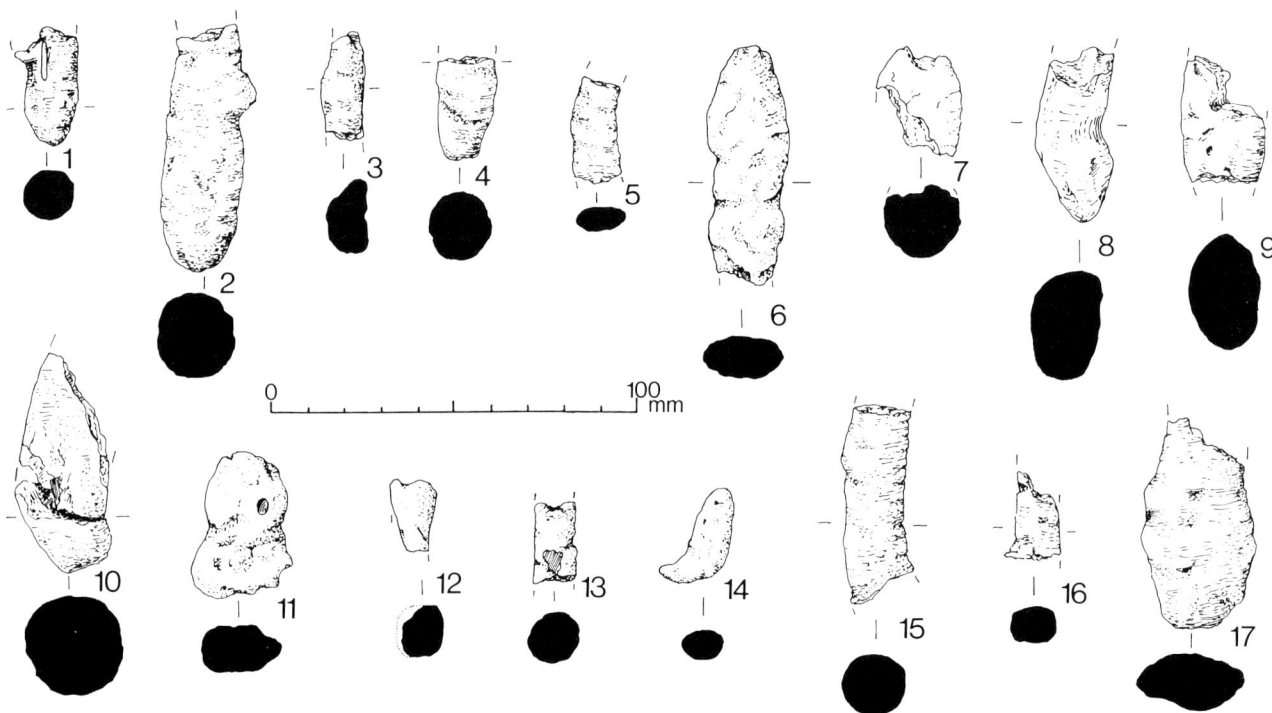

Fig 153 Coprolites (scale 1:2)

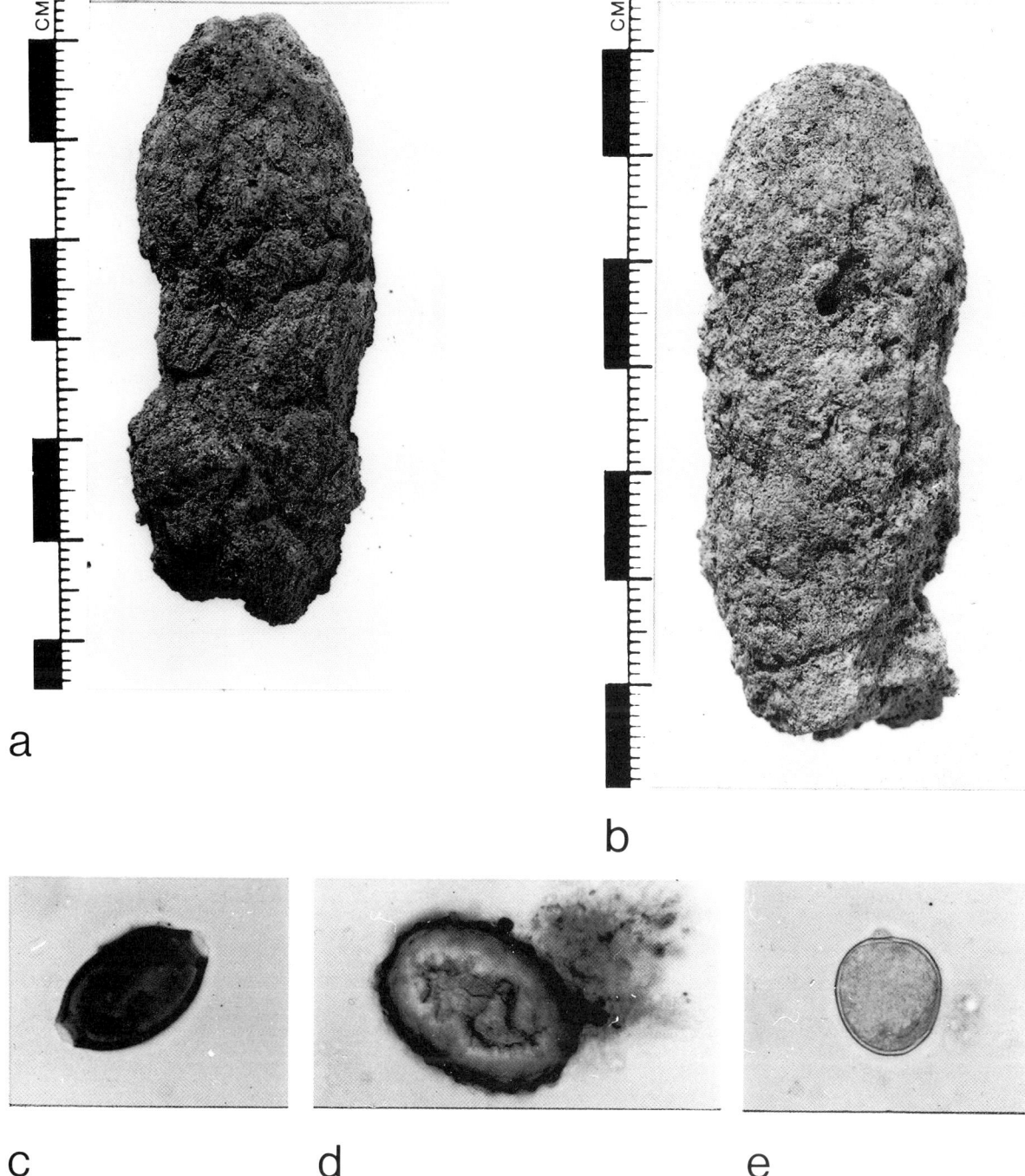

Fig 154 Coprolites: (a) coprolite 60398 (Fig 153.6); (b) coprolite 3895 (Fig 153.2); (c) Trichuris ovum 48.6×32.4μm from amorphous concretion 60335 (Fig 153.12); (d) Ascaris ovum 64.8×50.4μm from possible coprolite 5819c; (e) Isospora or Eimeria oocyst 36×31.5μm from amorphous concretion 4985 (photos: EAU, York)

site ova or cysts while four of the possible coprolite samples gave a positive result. The amorphous concretions rarely contained parasite ova or cysts but samples from Contexts 53 (5618) and 156 (5880) gave the highest counts.

It is apparent from Table 23 that many coprolites and concretions did not contain parasite ova while those that did give positive results yielded low concentrations of ova.

Two kinds of ova were observed. The first, a barrel-shaped structure sometimes possessing two polar plugs, was typical of whipworms – the genus Trichuris (Fig 154c) – and was present at a maximum concentration of 500 ova per gram concretion. Whipworms are parasitic nematodes which infest the lower intestine and caecum of many mammals throughout the world. Eggs are produced in large numbers and shed into the gut lumen and passed with faeces. Light infestations usually cause little harm to the host, while heavy worm burden can cause prolapse of the rectum, diarrhoea, and blood in the faeces.

The condition of the Trichuris ova was assessed by considering the numbers which fall into the following categories:

1   complete, ie possessing two polar plugs

Table 22 The stratigraphic occurrence of coprolites, possible coprolites, and amorphous concretions

	Coprolites	Possible coprolites	Amorphous concretions
Unit 3a	-	1	-
Unit 4	5	-	-
Unit 5b	14	15	19
Unit 5d	1	1	-
Unit 6	-	2	6

2   damaged, ie the shell is complete but the condition of either one or both plugs suggests that the ova are beginning to disintegrate
3   shell complete lacking any trace of a polar plug
4   shell broken or crumpled

All but one of the *Trichuris* ova lacked polar plugs and two fragmentary ova were observed. Many of the eggs were thin-walled. Thus, the preservation of the ova can be described as generally poor.

Because such small numbers of parasite ova were seen in the samples, the egg measurements from all samples were analysed as a single group. Table 24 gives the dimensions of the *Trichuris* ova from Brean Down.

From these measurements and statistics it is clear that the *Trichuris* ova are not from *Trichuris vulpis*, the whipworm of dogs, but that they are of a size consistent with *T trichiura*, the human whipworm. It is possible that individual eggs are from other species, eg *T muris*, but taken as an assemblage this small sample strongly suggests the presence of human whipworms.

The comparison of egg size was based on modern measurements of whipworm eggs gleaned from several sources including parasitological textbooks, data given by Beer (1976) for the whipworms of man and pig, the size of whipworm eggs from Lindow Man (A Jones 1986), and egg measurements of *Trichuris* ova from the coprolite from 6–8 Pavement, York (A Jones 1983).

The second kind of egg present possessed a mammillated outer shell characteristic of the large roundworm – genus *Ascaris* (Fig 154d), a common parasite of pigs and man. *Ascaris* can grow to 300mm and, like the whipworm, produces large numbers of eggs which are passed with faeces. The larvae, which hatch from ingested embryonated eggs, migrate through the host tissues and can cause considerable damage. Nevertheless, many people harbouring small numbers of worms do not suffer severe symptoms. *Ascaris* ova were present in very small numbers. All were fertilised and two were broken.

Unfortunately, the ova of *A lumbricoides* and *A suum*, the large roundworms of man and pigs respectively, produce ova of identical size. However, because they were associated with large numbers of *Trichuris trichiura* ova, the *Ascaris* ova are assumed to be *A lumbricoides*.

Both *Ascaris* and *Trichuris* eggs have been widely reported from archaeological deposits in Britain and mainland Europe including the Danish bog burials (A Jones 1982) and Lindow Man (A Jones 1986). The results from these samples from Brean Down compare closely with those obtained from faecal concre-

Table 23 Results of parasitological investigation

Fig	Unit	Context	Sample	Finds on microscopical examination
Coprolites				
	4	52	60095	1 oocyst, *Isospora* or *Eimeria*
153.1	4	89	5773	No parasite remains, A, F
153.2 & 154b	5b	53	3895	No parasite remains, A, P
	5b	53	4123	No parasite remains, A, F
153.3	5b	53	4514	No parasite remains, A
	5b	53	4989	1 ovum *Trichuris*, P
153.4	5b	53	5268	No parasite remains, F
153.5	5b	53	5393	1 ovum *Trichuris*, 1 ovum *Ascaris*, F
153.6 & 154a	5b	53	60398	No parasite remains, F
Possible coprolites				
	3a	13	705	No parasite remains, F
	5b	?59	227	No parasite remains, A, F
	5b	?59	230	No parasite remains, A, F
153.7	5b	53	4609	1 ovum *Trichuris*, 1 ovum *Ascaris*, F, P
	5b	53	5769	2 cysts of testate amoebae, A
	5b	53	60311	1 fragmentary ovum *Trichuris*, C, F, P
	5b	53	60340	No parasite remains, A, F
	5b	53	60342	1 ovum *Trichuris*, A, F
	5b	53	60364	No parasite remains, A, C, P
	5b	53	60820	No parasite remains, A, F
	5b	125	5764	No parasite remains
	5b	132	5774	No parasite remains
	5b	139	5819/C	1 ovum *Ascaris*, F
	5b	139	5832	No parasite remains, F
	5b	139	6019	No parasite remains, A, F
	5b	168	6021	No parasite remains, F, P
153.10	5d	153	5890	No parasite remains, A, F
153.11	6a	163	60829/A	No parasite remains
	6a	61	6205	No parasite remains, A, F
Amorphous concretions				
	5b	53	4120	No parasite remains, A, F
	5b	53	5141	No parasite remains
	5b	53	5618/A	5 ova *Trichuris*, A, F
			5618/B	3 ova *Trichuris*, F
			5618/C	4 ova *Trichuris*
			5618/D	3 ova *Trichuris*, 1 ovum *Ascaris*
			5618/E	1 ovum *Trichuris*
			5618/F	3 ova *Trichuris*, F
	5b	53	5696	No parasite remains, C, F
	5b	53	60313	No parasite remains, C
153.12	5b	53	60335	1 ovum *Trichuris*, A, F
	5b	53	60338	No parasite remains
	5b	53	60341	1 ovum *Trichuris*, 1 ovum *Ascaris*, F
	5b	79	60260	No parasite remains, A
	5b	107	4985	1 ?oocyst (Fig 154e)
	5b	115	60319	No parasite remains, A, F, PM
	5b	115	60337/A	1 ovum *Trichuris*, A, P
153.13	5b	115	60337/B	No parasite remains, F
	6a	156	5880/A	No parasite remains, A, F, PM
	6a	156	5880/B	3 ova *Trichuris*, A, F, PM
	6a	157	6044	No parasite remains, PM, grass fragments
	6a	162	5926	No parasite remains, A, F
	6a	163	60829/A	1 oocyst, *Isospora* or *Eimeria*
153.14	6a	163	60829/B	No parasite remains, D, F

NB Coprolites illustrated in Fig 153.8, 9, 15–17 have not been subject to parasitological investigation; they are described in MF1:G6.

Key: A – Arthropod cuticle fragments; C – Charcoal; D – Diatom; F – Fungal spores; P – Pollen grains; PM – Plant microfossils, usually pieces of plant tissue or isolated cells

Table 24 Dimensions of *Trichuris* ova

Dimension		St dev	SEM	n
Total length	55.8			1
Mean length −pp	50.0	1.6	0.4	13
Min length −pp	46.8			
Max length −pp	54.0			
Mean width	26.7	1.9	0.5	13
Min width	25.2			
Max width	32.4			

Abbreviations: −pp − minus polar plugs; Min − minimum; Max − maximum; St dev − Standard deviation; SEM −Standard error of the mean; n − number of observations

All measurements in microns

tion samples in Anglo-Scandinavian deposits at 16–22 Coppergate (A Jones 1985).

Discussion

Coprolites

No human coprolites were recognised. The coprolites were clearly passed by a medium sized carnivore judging from their size and inclusions. Many contained splinters and other fragments of broken mammal or bird bone typical of those found in carnivore faeces. They are most likely to be canine in origin despite the disappointing lack of parasite ova and cysts specific to dogs.

The small numbers of parasite ova and cysts in the three coprolites with positive results are not specific to dogs. The oocysts could not be assigned to species, but the size of the *Trichuris* eggs indicates that eggs of the human whipworm, *Trichuris trichiura*, were present. These must have been inadvertently ingested by dogs.

Evidence both from parasite ova and bone fragments clearly testifies to the role as waste disposal agents played by dogs at Brean. This result will have serious implications for the analysis of the bone assemblage (Chapter 20), for experiments by Payne and Munson (1985), Walters (1984), and others have shown that scavenging dogs destroy a very high percentage of the bone they ingest.

Possible coprolites

The nature of these samples, their inclusions, and the concentrations of parasite cysts and ova are broadly similar to those of the coprolites from this site. Thus, it is reasonable to conclude that they are most likely to be dog droppings which have been squashed and deformed.

Amorphous concretions

Most of the concretion samples also gave negative results or low counts of parasite ova and it is not clear if they are flattened canine droppings, perhaps chemically altered, human faeces, or some other form of organic deposit.

One sample (5618) is particularly interesting for it gave counts of up to 500 *Trichuris* ova per gram. It is not possible to estimate accurately the egg concentrations per gram of fresh faeces because the process of mineralisation which has preserved the concretions and coprolites has changed the specific gravity of the fresh faeces. Mineralisation, and the aggregation of non-faecal material in the concretions, means that the observed egg counts are likely to be very different from egg counts on fresh material. Work on a coprolite from 6–8 Pavement, York (Jones 1983) and the specific gravity of the concretions (2.0–2.2) suggest that egg counts should be doubled to give an approximate egg concentration for the fresh deposit.

This is relevant for sample 5618 which gave egg counts of 100–500 poorly preserved ova per gram. This sample certainly contained eggs of the human parasites *T trichiura* and *Ascaris*. Although caution must be exercised when considering the egg concentration data, it is likely that the concentration of eggs per gram of fresh deposits was in the region of 1000. While such a concentration may be found in the faeces of a dog that has recently ingested human excrement containing many thousands of parasite ova, it seems more likely that this sample is poorly preserved human faeces.

A sample (6044) of amorphous concretion from Context 157 failed to contain parasite ova but was unusual as it was composed of plant material, mainly grass fragments. These were of a shape and size consistent with those found in recent herbivore dung. Although there is not sufficient evidence to prove that this sample was dung, it is clearly an organic residue rich in small fragments of grass.

Conclusions

The majority of samples submitted for parasitological investigation appear to be dog droppings. One sample contained relatively high numbers of *Trichuris* ova and may be of human origin. It is clear that some dogs were ingesting human parasite ova. Dog coprolites have preserved small numbers of human parasite ova and bear witness to the fact that the Bronze Age inhabitants of the site haboured intestinal parasites.

Whilst the number of samples producing parasite ova is small, it is most significant that any trace of human parasites can be detected in such ancient material excavated from a site which was not waterlogged and where survival of organic materials other than bone and shell was poor. It is hoped that this study will inspire others to follow the example set at Brean Down and that in future more archaeologists will explore the possibilities afforded by the study of such unsavoury material.

Acknowledgements

The practical work for this report was carried out by Colin Nicholson (sponsored by the Manpower Services Commission to work in the EAU). Philippa Tomlinson kindly examined the grass fragments from sample 6044. Laboratory facilities were provided by the University of York for the Historic Buildings and Monuments Commission for England who also funded the report.

22 Mollusca and other zoological evidence

Non-marine Mollusca

by Martin Bell and Su Johnson

Introduction and aims

The first investigation of post-glacial Mollusca on the sandcliff was by two Cardiff undergraduates working under the supervision of John Evans. Penny Spencer (1974) found shells in the upper horizons, Unit 4 and above, but not in the underlying Bronze Age stratigraphy. Vaughan (1976) examined the whole sequence but only found very low numbers of shells below Unit 3. Both projects involved the investigation of other sand dunes, the overall picture from which was reviewed by Spencer (1975) and J G Evans (1979) but without much discussion of the limited evidence from Brean Down. The current project provided the opportunity to investigate further the molluscan potential of the site and relate it more precisely to the archaeological sequence. This work aimed to provide evidence of the site's environmental history, to try to resolve the introduction dates of certain species, and to investigate the extent to which the sequence had been subject to biogenic disturbance.

Methods

Five columns of samples were taken in the field from the main excavation trench. The locations of these columns are all shown on Figure 155 and in more detail as follows: Column 1 (Fig 15), Columns 2–4 (Fig 18), and Column 5 (Fig 27). Column samples were mostly taken at intervals of 0.1m. The column samples were supplemented by 12 spot samples, three from Soil Pit V and the others from the main trench. A further column of samples from the silty clay sequence in Soil Pit VI is separately described at the end of this part of the report (p 249). A standard sample size of 3kg was used and the methods of

Fig 155 General view of the excavation showing mollusc sampling columns

mollusc analysis were those described by J G Evans (1972). Nomenclature follows Waldèn (1976) for land molluscs and Kerney (1976a) for fresh and brackish water species.

The molluscan sequence on the sandcliff

The results of mollusc analysis are presented in numerical form on MF1:G7 and as a mollusc diagram, Figure 156. Because the stratigraphy consists of a series of superimposed blankets of sediment it has proved possible to link the five columns and the spot samples into a single stratigraphic sequence as one diagram. This is a percentage diagram but the burrowing species *Cecilioides acicula* and the small numbers of fresh and brackish water species are plotted as percentages over and above the remainder of the assemblage and are shown as open histograms on the right of Figure 156. In order to accommodate all samples on one diagram they are shown as of equal thickness. On the left hand side of the diagram is a table which correlates the following sample details: stratigraphic unit, context, column or spot sample number (the latter in a box), sample depth (for column samples), and the numbers of shells. The latter was unfortunately highly variable; 32 of the 58 samples produced fewer than 50 shells and for these samples percentages have not been calculated, but instead species presence is indicated by a black dot. In those samples with more than 50 shells crosses represent non-apical fragments and species comprising less than 1.5%. Mollusc occurrence is particularly patchy in the Bronze Age units partly because the basal palaeosol (Unit 8a) and the colluvium derived from it (Unit 6b) were decalcified, and partly also because much of the sand was probably derived directly from the foreshore. Shells were continuously present in Units 1 to 3 which may have been laid down under conditions of greater stability.

Shell occurrence is not simply a matter of preservation because, as Figure 123 shows, the calcium carbonate content of the more recent sands is lower than some Bronze Age deposits. It should also be noted that there was no clear correlation between the archaeologically attested stabilisation horizons and mollusc numbers. For instance, some of the samples in the main occupation horizons of Unit 5b contained shells, but others very few. Furthermore, within the sterile sands such as Units 5a and 5d, which generally contained few shells, there were individual samples with reasonable numbers. These might represent brief stabilisations, hollows in which shells collected, or accumulations resulting from winnowing.

The results of mollusc analysis are described by stratigraphic unit from bottom to top.

Unit 8a

The basal palaeosol was decalcified and contained only a few partly decomposed shells. Fortunately we know from the other environmental evidence, particularly soil micromorphology (Chapter 16), that the soil supported woodland, was cleared by burning originally in the Neolithic, was cultivated, and then given over to grass before being buried by blown sand (Unit 7) in the mid fourth millennium BP.

Unit 7

The lower part of this blown sand horizon contained only a few shells but the stabilisation horizon (Context 188) in its upper part produced the most diverse assemblage in the sequence. Most abundant were Vallonias, implying open conditions which on the surface of the dune were probably very dry grass sward, as is suggested by the presence of *Helicella itala* and the rare zerophile species *Truncatellina cylindrica*. These species are, however, accompanied by three clausiliids (*Clausilia bidentata*, *Macrogastra rolphii*, and *Balea perversa*) and *Carychium tridentatum*, *Acanthinula aculeata*, and *Aegopinella nitidula*, all of which might point to the existence of damper, more shady conditions. Some of these, such as *Clausilia* and *Aegopinella*, are found on quite dry, south-facing slopes on Gower (J G Evans, pers comm). The sampling point was c 4.5m downslope from the junction of the sand with the underlying palaeosol where damper conditions and longer grass are likely to have obtained. It also seems possible that there was some limited tree or scrub invasion downslope from the rocky crags at this time.

Unit 6

Samples from Units 6b and 6a produced virtually no shells, but they were present in a spot sample (127) from the collapse of Structure 57, Unit 6α, though the assemblage is overwhelmingly dominated by *Lauria cylindracea*. This is a rupestral species which must reflect the specialised microenvironment of the collapsed structure which probably also explains the presence of *Ena obscura*, *Helicigona lapicida*, and *Oxychilus cellarius*, the latter being an important component of rock rubble faunas (Evans and Jones 1973). The presence of Vallonias and *Helicella itala* may reflect more general open conditions.

Unit 5d

Virtually sterile blown sand, only one sample of which contained plottable numbers of molluscs and these predominantly of one species, *Helicella itala*, accompanied by smaller numbers of Vallonias and *Pupilla muscorum*. A similar picture is reflected by the smaller numbers of shells in the other samples and confirms the dry unfavourable environment suggested by the blown sands themselves.

Unit 5b

A stabilisation horizon associated with the main middle Bronze Age occupation. Two samples produced reasonable numbers of molluscs: spot sample 130 from the wall trench of Structure 95 and sample 312, a spot sample from Soil Pit V. Despite the fact that they were 100m apart, both samples produced similar very restricted faunas consisting largely of *Helicella itala* and characterised also by a small proportion of *Vallonia excentrica* and the presence of the zerophile species *Truncatellina cylindrica*. This Unit 5b evidence does not suggest a fully stabilised or densely vegetated surface and that is in line with the micromorphological evidence for rather limited pedogenesis (Chapter 16). This palaeoenvironmental impression of a somewhat brief and insubstantial stabilisation horizon is, however, difficult to reconcile with the substantial archaeological evidence it produced or the lengthy time span suggested by radiocarbon dating (Chapter 9). A possible explanation is that some deflation of the Unit 5b surface occurred and that might account for the large numbers of *Helicella itala* in sample 312.

Unit 5a

Sterile sand of which one sample near the base contained more than 50 shells. All the samples contrast dramatically with those below because the predominant species is *Cernuella virgata* accompanied by another new species, *Cochlicella acuta*, which is particularly characteristic of dunes and coastal grassland (Kerney and Cameron 1979). With these species is *Helicella itala* which is of less proportionate importance than in underlying horizons. A contrast exists, however, between the bleached white appearance of *Helicella itala* and fresher looking *Cernuella virgata*, possibly suggesting an assemblage of more than one date or origin. Further doubts are created by examples of *Helix aspersa*, a Roman introduction in this late Bronze Age horizon. These problems will be returned to in the discussion.

Unit 4

The late Bronze Age occupation horizon had a similar assemblage to Unit 5a, although no sample produced 50 shells. The assemblage is curiously limited in view of the fact that this was a major occupation horizon with, as micromorphology suggests (Chapter 16), reasonably high levels of biological activity. In addition to the samples taken from the main excavation trench in 1985 a further sample had been collected on 10 May 1983 from a point bearing the impression of the gold bracelets found by Keith Crabtree four days previously. It was in the course of sieving this sample that Nick Watson found a further scrap of gold (Fig 106.2a). The sample also produced the following small assemblage closely comparable to the other Unit 4 samples: *Cochlicopa* spp 1; *Vallonia excentrica* 1; *Discus rotundatus* 1; Limacidae 1; *Cecilioides acicula* 3; *Cernuella virgata* 4; *Helicella itala* 2; *Cochlicella acuta* 2; *Trichia hispida* 1; *Cepaea/Arianta* frag; *Pisidium* 4 valves; *Patella vulgata* 1. It should be noted that this assemblage does not include *Candidula intersecta* as has previously been tentatively suggested (Bell 1987a, 6).

Units 4a to 1

In the upper post Bronze Age part of the stratigraphy molluscs were virtually continuously preserved. The assemblages in the colluvium of Unit 4a and the blown sand of Unit 3 were closely similar despite the contrasting types of sediment. *Cernuella virgata* predominated with smaller proportions of *Helicella itala* and *Cochlicella acuta*. The impression is of a stable but somewhat sparsely vegetated dune system. At a depth of about 1m in column 1 and 0.74m in column 2 *Candidula intersecta* appears and increases at the expense of *Cernuella virgata*. Its occurrence in column 2 is above the horizon with sixteenth/seventeenth-century pottery (Fig 70b), suggesting that it is quite a recent introduction. *Cochlicella acuta* declines from Unit 4a upwards and is not present in the topmost sample. This accords with Swanton's (1912, 19) observation that shells of this species (which he called *Helicella barbara*) were common on the sandcliff but he had not found it living. A similar though later decline is shown by *Cernuella virgata*. *Helicella itala* also declines in the upper part of the sequence but this seems to be part of a general trend seen elsewhere in Britain (Preece 1980). These recent twentieth-century ecological changes are also marked by peaks of *Trichia hispida* and *Vallonia costata*, together with higher values of *Punctum pygmaeum*, *Vertigo pygmaea*, and *Vitrina pellucida*. The more diverse twentieth-century assemblage suggests greater vegetation cover, albeit with areas of minor erosion and sand deposition as indicated by the sediments themselves.

Unusual species

Of particular interest is the presence of *Truncatellina cylindrica* in Bronze Age units and Unit 3b2. Today this species is restricted to just three small areas on the eastern side of Britain but there is a 1910 record at Kewstoke only *c* 6km to the north-east of Brean (Kerney 1976b, map 65; Swanton 1912, 40 – called *Vertigo minutissima*).

Pyramidula rupestris has a curious history, being common on rocks and walls today but very rarely found sub-fossil even in apparently ideal situations where it is today abundant (Bell 1983b). A single example was present at Brean in Unit 5d and it is abundant in probable Iron Age contexts at Worlebury hillfort 4km to the north-east (Houghton 1989) and present earlier at Tornewton, Devon (Kerney 1976c).

Testacella maugei has a largely Atlantic south-western distribution in Britain (Kerney 1976b, map 142). It is generally associated with gardens and well-manured places (Kerney and Cameron 1979) and has sometimes been regarded as a nineteenth-century nursery introduction (Swanton 1912). Its occurrence here in Unit 3c2 implies introduction before the sub-Roman period, although it is possibly intrusive because the species is known to be partly subterranean (Kerney and Cameron 1979, 173).

Hand-picked and site-sieved shells

These are of very limited ecological value as Sparks (1961) has demonstrated, because the sample will be biased towards larger species, but comparison with the column samples reveals some significant points. MF1:G8 summarises the occurrence of *Cochlicella acuta*, *Cernuella virgata*, *Candidula intersecta*, and *Helix aspersa* in the hand-picked and site-sieved samples by stratigraphic unit. This confirms that large numbers of *Cernuella virgata* and *Helix aspersa* occur in Units 4 and 5a but also shows both species in Unit 5b before they appear in the mollusc columns. Small numbers of all four species also occur below Unit 5b but in several cases these shells are fresher and clearly recent. During the excavation small caches of *Helix aspersa* and *Cernuella virgata* were found in Unit 5b. It seems possible that these entered rabbit burrows for hibernation or aestivation or were perhaps hoarded by some faunal agency.

Discussion of the sequence

Previous work on sand dunes (J G Evans 1979) has shown that certain key species occur in the following regular sequence: *Helicella itala*, *Cochlicella acuta*, *Cernuella virgata*, and *Candidula intersecta*. There were hints of this sequence in Vaughan's (1976) earlier work at Brean with the first two species in Bronze Age contexts and the second two appearing in Unit 3. The present project has shown that *Helicella itala* is present from the basal palaeosol and that *Cochlicella acuta* and *Cernuella virgata* both appear at the base of Bronze Age Unit 5a although both species are present in the hand-picked and site-sieved material in lower units. Elsewhere *Cochlicella acuta* is present c 3100 BP at Gwithian (Spencer 1975) and more widely by about the Iron Age (J G Evans 1979). It was certainly present at Bantham, Devon, in a hearth dated 1690±80 BP (HAR-5775) and 1440±80 BP (HAR-5776), because one of the apices was burnt (Bell 1987a). *Cernuella virgata*, on the other hand, seems not to have arrived on other sites until the medieval period (Kerney 1966; Spencer 1975), although there is evidence for it in the Iron Age at Maiden Castle (J G Evans, pers comm). A further worrying element is the occurrence of some shells of *Helix aspersa* in the sample columns from the base of Unit 5a. This species seems on all other evidence to be a Romano-British introduction (J G Evans 1972, 175). Finally, much later in the sequence during the post-medieval period, *Candidula intersecta* appears, in line with dating evidence elsewhere (Kerney 1966). We should, however, note that there is an isolated record of this, or a related species, in an early Bronze Age context at Gwithian (Spencer 1975; J G Evans 1979) and it also occurs in the Dark Ages at Gunwalloe (J G Evans, pers comm).

It is difficult to resist the conclusion that the relatively small number of *Helix aspersa* shells in Bronze Age horizons are intrusive. If so, we should also question whether the larger numbers of *Cernuella virgata* and other species are also genuinely associated with Units 5a and 4. Rabbit bones were present in both units (Chapter 20 and MF1:G8) and it is conceivable that the shells were intruded by rabbit activity, but it is important to stress that this must have happened before the post-medieval introduction of *Candidula intersecta*. It should be added that these anomalies do not seem to be the result of a simple misinterpretation of the stratigraphy, which was clear in the area of the sampling column and without macroscopically visible intrusions. Furthermore, the relatively modest numbers of intrusive artefacts do not suggest large-scale biogenic disturbance.

The unresolved question therefore is whether *Cernuella virgata* and *Cochlicella acuta* were genuinely present in the late Bronze Age or whether their occurrence is due to macroscopically invisible intrusions. If the latter, it may have implications for some of the other rather puzzling occurrences of molluscs in dunes, such as the appearance of *Candidula intersecta* and *Cernuella virgata* at different times on individual sites (J G Evans 1979). Such problems may not be easily resolved, for instance by accelerator dating of the shells themselves, because an earlier attempt by Preece (1980) to establish the introduction date of *Cernuella virgata* produced anomalously early dates for both modern and sub-fossil examples, suggesting that this species incorporates dead carbon. A further attempt to clarify the extent of intrusion will be made during a proposed excavation of the sub-Roman cemetery in 1989 in an area where perhaps the earlier deposits may be better sealed.

A more minor observation concerning the formation processes of the molluscan assemblage was that many shells, particularly in the upper part of Unit 1, showed a characteristic pattern of damage. They were eaten away round the whorl, perhaps by a predator, leaving irregular edges and a weakened shell.

Reference should be made to the presence of small numbers of fresh, brackish, and marine molluscs in the samples. The estuarine species *Hydrobia ventrosa* and *Hydrobia ulvae* were the most frequent. Some, eg sample 130 from the wall trench of Structure 95, probably derive from clay imported to the site by man. Others, particularly the tiny unidentified marine molluscs, are likely to be natural constituents of the sand; they are almost equally frequent in sterile layers with no evidence of settlement, particularly in Units 3 and 1.

Mollusca from Soil Pit VI

Samples were taken through the sediment sequence in Soil Pit VI down to 3m OD (Fig 81). Eleven of these were analysed for Mollusca and the results are presented in MF1:G9. Molluscs were disappointingly few and it has already been suggested in Chapters 8 and 18 that the paucity of biota in these deposits relates to diagenesis. Those molluscs present do, however, present a little additional information about how the sediments formed. In the lower part of the sequence below the Romano-British surface (Context 230) both land and brackish water elements were present. The assemblage consists of *Hydrobia ventrosa* with *Leucophytia bidentata* and *Hydrobia ulvae* and *Pupilla muscorum*. The presence of both *Hydrobia* and *Leucophytia* in the sand lens (231) may imply that this was a waterlain sediment rather than a hiatus in estuarine sedimentation marked by aeolian activity. The Romano-British surface (230) did not unfortunately contain molluscs but the immediately overlying horizon (229) may represent conditions of reduced marine influence since it produced the freshwater species *Lymnaea truncatula* in addition to a few Hydrobias, *Vallonia excentrica*, and *Vertigo pygmaea*. The lower part of the overlying context (228) had more *Hydrobia ventrosa* and few land molluscs possibly relating to the sedimentary evidence of renewed estuarine deposition after Roman activity. Samples from the upper part of Context 228 and the present topsoil contain only land species chiefly the Vallonias, Limacidae, *Hellicella itala*, *Trichia hispida*, and *Vertigo pygmaea* which imply open grassland.

The occurrence of a few shells of fully marine species in the lower part of Context 228 and below confirms the evidence from brackish water species for marine influence. The general impression, however, is of a reduced salinity site separated from the sea. Marine influence seems to have ceased in recent times presumably when the sea wall was built.

Acknowledgements

We are grateful to John Evans and Annie Milles for checking identifications of some of the individual helicellids, for discussion of their own work on dune assemblages, and for comments on an earlier draft.

Marine Mollusca

by Su Johnson

Introduction

The results of marine mollusc analysis are summarised in Figure 157, showing the numbers of shells of each species by stratigraphic unit. A more detailed breakdown by context is given on MF1:G10 which also summarises the proportion of shells derived from the three recovery methods, ie hand excavation, dry sieving using a 5mm mesh, and wet sieving using a 0.5mm mesh. This shows that sieving contributed 33% of the shells but does not make a great deal of difference to the relative abundance of the main species which were presumably large enough to be spotted during excavation. Sieving did, however, account for the majority of shells of the infrequent species *Macoma balthica* (Baltic tellin) and the brackish water Hydrobias. On Figure 157 and MF1:G10 the numbers of bivalve shells have been divided by two (hence the presence of ½s). The Littorinas presented problems because what used to be a single species, *Littorina saxatalis*, has now been divided into four, not all of which are identifiable from sub-fossil material. Consequently, following advice from Dr D Reid of the British Museum (Natural History), London, who looked at the Littorinas, these have been grouped as *Littorina* 'saxatalis group'. The total number of shells (943) is surprisingly small considering the site's coastal location.

The mollusc analysis described by statigraphic unit is as follows:

Unit 8a

An assemblage of 15 *Patella vulgata* (limpets) and 1 *Hydrobia*.

Unit 7

There were 83 shells in the Beaker sand, 34 of them from the stabilisation horizon (Context 188) and the remainder from the sand. Both groups were almost entirely *Patella vulgata* with a few *Macoma balthica*.

Unit 6b

There were only 33 shells, nearly all *Patella vulgata*, with a few *Littorina* 'saxatalis group' (rough periwinkles).

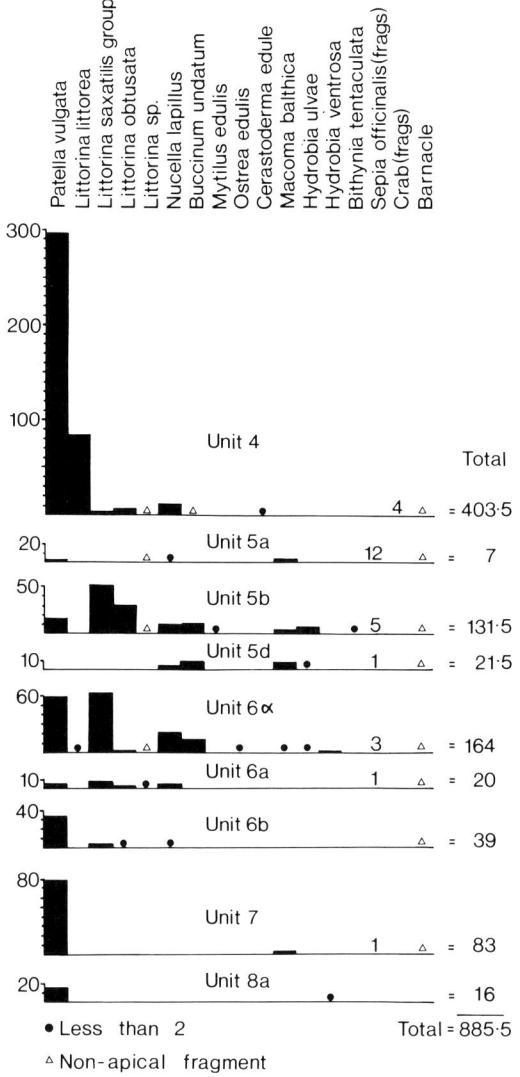

Fig 157 Marine mollusc diagram showing the number of shells per unit; the number of individual bivalve shells has been divided by 2

Unit 6a

Considering that this seems to have been dumped material, the number of shells (20) was very small, mostly *Littorina* 'saxatalis group' and *Patella vulgata*.

Unit 6α

This unit comprising Structure 57 was only excavated to a very limited extent, but it produced the second largest group of shells (164). Curiously, the tiny shells of the *Littorina* 'saxatalis group' were slightly more abundant than *Patella vulgata*. There were a few *Littorina littorea* (common periwinkle), *Littorina obtusa-*

ta (flat periwinkle), *Nucella lapillus* (common dog whelk), *Buccinum undatum* (common whelk), and a solitary valve fragment of *Ostrea edulis* (oyster).

Unit 5d

This 'sterile' sand produced just 20.5 shells, mostly *Buccinum undatum* and *Macoma balthica*.

Unit 5b

Though this unit produced the most extensive evidence of domestic activity, including Structures 59 and 95, and was extensively excavated, the number of shells (131.5) was lower than the Unit 6α assemblage. It is furthermore noteworthy in being dominated by tiny species, the *Littorina* 'saxatilis group' and *Littorina obtusata*. The stormwater gully of Structure 59 (Fig 37, Section 88) produced a group of shells comprising 22 *Littorina* 'saxatilis group' and 7 *Littorina obtusata*. The larger species such as *Patella vulgata*, *Nucella lapillus*, and *Buccinum undatum* are only present in small numbers.

Unit 5a

Sterile sand with just seven shells, mostly *Macoma balthica*.

Unit 4

This produced the largest assemblages of 403 shells and, in contrast to Units 6α and 5b, overwhelmingly comprised *Patella vulgata* (73%) and *Littorina littorea* (21%), the latter having been represented in earlier units only by a single shell from 6α. Shells of the previously predominant *Littorina* 'saxatilis group' and *Littorina obtusata* are very few. Also present were a few *Nucella lapillus*, a single valve of *Cerastoderma edule* (cockle), and a few crab claws.

Units 1 and 3

There were very few shells from these units (MF1:G10); the only significant number came from Unit 3a, consisted of *Patella vulgata* and *Littorina littorea*, and may be associated with the post-medieval occupation.

Variation in the shell shape of Nucella lapillus

In the process of identification of the molluscan assemblage from Brean, it was observed that the shells of *Nucella lapillus* showed considerable variation in shape and size which in a few cases led to doubt as to their identification. However, a review of the literature, and in particular the work of Crothers (1974a; 1974b; 1985), revealed that this species varies in size and shape in relation to the degree of exposure of its habitat. This relationship can be predicted with some accuracy in Cornwall, Devon, and Pembrokeshire, but this is not the case at the eastern end of the Bristol Channel, particularly in Somerset, where an elongated form (often 40mm or more long) also occurs.

With this in mind it was decided to measure the shells and compare them with Crothers' (1974b) modern sample from Brean. Unfortunately the Brean archaeological data present the following problems:

1. The total number of shells complete enough to be included in the analysis was very small (35) and some had damage to the apex.
2. The 35 shells are not all of the same date; some are quite recent, others several thousand years old.
3. The exposure grade of the ancient coastline cannot be estimated with certainty but it does seem reasonable to compare the sample with Crothers' modern sample assuming the same exposure grade, ie 6–7, sheltered–very sheltered, on Ballantine's (1961) scale.
4. It has been assumed that the *Nucella* found at the site were collected from the immediate area and not from further afield.
5. Depending on the purpose for which they were collected, the sample may be biased towards larger shells

The measurement used to describe the variations in shell shape is the ratio between the length of the shell (L) and the height of the aperature (Ap); the higher the value of the ratio, the more sheltered the coastline from which the shell came.

Complete or very nearly complete shells were measured and the results plotted on a graph (MF1:G11). This shows the range and average L/Ap ratios for the sample as well as Crothers' (1974b) predicted and observed values, and shows that the average for the archaeological sample is slightly higher than that found by Crothers.

The archaeological sample from Brean is small but it does suggest that the elongated form with high L/Ap ratios, which characterises the area today, has been present since at least the Bronze Age. This provides some time depth for future discussion of the factors giving rise to this distinctive form.

Discussion

The most striking aspect of the assemblage is its small size given the coastal setting, the length of occupation, and the quantities of sediment excavated and sieved. Bearing in mind the low calorific yield per shell and the number of shells which would be produced by a single meal, shellfish seem to have made a fairly minimal contribution to the diet, particularly in the main occupation Unit 5b. We should not, however, ignore the possibility that shells may have been disposed of in other activity areas or used on fields as soil improvers. Indeed the largest number of shells was from Unit 4 which was basically a midden deposit rather than related to *in situ* domestic activity.

The assemblage changed through time. Units 8a, 7, 6b, and 4 all consisted overwhelmingly of *Patella vulgata*. In Units 6α and 5b *Littorina* 'saxatilis group' and *Littorina obtusata* predominated. These Littorinas are tiny species which makes it doubtful whether they were collected for food. Similarly the Cirripedia (barnacles), which are present in most units, are likely to have found their way to the site in some other way. Elsewhere there is evidence that such small species were brought to sites with seaweed (Bell 1981). Seaweed was indeed being brought to the site at the time of Unit 6α because we have a carbonised seaweed bladder (Chapter 19). Another quite plausible way in which these shells could have been introduced is with saline sediment from the solar evaporation of seawater in the intertidal area. Briquetage resulting from subsequent stages in the salt extraction process was common in Units 6α and particularly 5b (Chapter 14), and such stages are likely to have involved the removal of molluscan impurities. Still other possibilities are that they were brought with introduced sediment or driftwood. Such factors may also account for the presence of *Nucella lapillus* which is regarded as unpalatable (Crothers 1985, 301) but makes up 13% of the Unit 6α assemblage. It is described as plentiful at Brean Down today (Boyden *et al* 1977).

Not all of the other species necessarily relate to human behaviour or diet. The presence of a few shells in the 'sterile' sand layers (eg 5a and 5d) reminds us that some may be natural constituents of the sand. Observation today shows that seabirds drop shells on the sandcliff so we should not attach significance to species represented just by the occasional shell. *Sepia officianalis* (cuttlefish) was found in most units but the largest numbers (MF1:G10) are from layers without occupation (5a and 3a), so these could relate to bird activity; the species can be caught in the Severn Estuary (Boyden *et al* 1977). Of species which are known to have been commonly eaten, only *Patella vulgata*, *Littorina littorea*, and *Buccinum undatum* occur in significant numbers. Even these may have had other uses; for instance Coy (1987) notes the use of *Patella vulgata* as bait and pig food.

The species which are common, *Patella vulgata*, the Littorinas, and *Nucella lapillus*, are all characteristic of rocky shores between tide lines. *Buccinum undatum* is found in the lower shore and below low water on sand and mud, forms occurring in the intertidal zone being smaller than those from deeper water. At Brean smaller forms seem to predominate but some larger specimens may have implications for the exploitation of deeper water, that is if they were not collected as dead shells. Species of sandy shores, estuaries, and muds are poorly represented. *Macoma balthica* is present but in small numbers considering its very great density (up to 880 per sq m; Boyden and Little 1973) at Brean today. This deposit feeder is virtually the only bivalve on the southern shore of the estuary. The filter feeders *Mytilus edulis* and *Cerastoderma edule*, which were extensively exploited elsewhere in the south-west in prehistory (Coy 1987; Bell 1987b), are represented here only by a few shells, but this reflects their virtual absence today in the Severn Estuary owing to the high sediment content of the water (Boyden and Little 1973, 212). This is one reason for the increasing impoverishment of the Severn Estuary fauna upstream, as is demonstrated by a number of studies (eg NERC 1972). Other important factors are reduced salinity up the estuary and the enormous tidal range. Between them these factors would seem to account for the very restricted nature of the Brean assemblage; the present-day fauna of nearby Steep Holm is similarly restricted (Crothers 1981).

There is no certain evidence from the assemblage of ecological change either during the Bronze Age or compared to the present day faunas at Brean. *Macoma balthica* is much less abundant than on the soft sands and muds to the south of Brean Down today, but it is not an edible species. As already noted, the obvious changes between units seem more likely to relate to contrasting activity areas or human behaviour rather than to ecology. Later marine mollusc assemblages from Brean Down hillfort (Burrow 1976) and temple (ApSimon 1964–5) were essentially similar though even more restricted, being overwhelmingly dominated by *Patella vulgata*, although the absence of smaller species might relate to a lack of sieving. Both sites on the Down produced a few *Ostrea edulis* which was only represented on the sandcliff by a fragment from Unit 6α, but this is in line with the general rarity of this species both in pre-Roman contexts (Coy 1987) and in the Severn Estuary today (Boyden *et al* 1977).

Notes on other zoological evidence

by Martin Bell

Barnacles

Plates of barnacles were commonly found during on-site wet sieving (Fig 157 and MF1:G10) and in some of the samples taken for laboratory analysis of land Mollusca (MF1:G7). It is suggested above that they may have been accidentally introduced to the site by human activities which were also responsible for the arrival of small periwinkles.

Crabs

The few examples of crabs (MF1:G10) came from Units 5b and above.

Birds' eggs

Fragments of two eggs were found:

Find 3934, Context 53, Unit 5b. Location on Figure 48a. Large pieces of an egg about the size of a chicken or duck egg, ie *c* 50 by 35mm and shell thickness *c* 0.25mm, matt porcelainous creamy white surface

Find 6029, Context 19, Unit 5a. Small fragments of an egg apparently similar to above

The finds are unusual in a prehistoric context and the eggs are of sufficient size to suggest that they were eaten. The shells are very similar in appearance to modern duck eggs. Mallard and domestic fowl bones (Chapter 20) are both present in Unit 4 but not in Unit 5b. Unfortunately despite Keepax's (1981) demonstration that scanning electron microscopy can be useful in the identification of eggs, it has not proved possible to find a specialist to report on these examples.

D 23 Conclusions

Post-depositional processes

Dune sands are ideal for the preservation of archaeological sequences but, being poorly consolidated, they are also subject to a range of post-depositional processes the investigation of which was one of the project's aims. Since consideration of post-depositional factors is a necessary prerequisite for the analysis of cultural patterns (Schiffer 1987) they are appropriately considered at this stage. Most dramatic was the sixteenth- or early seventeenth-century AD dune blowout which removed parts of the late Bronze Age Unit 4 and the sub-Roman cemetery. This feature's limits were only resolved and its nature appreciated as a result of three-dimensional artefact recording. Difficulties in its delineation result from the fact that a blowout feature in loose sand would have constantly changed its morphology. Slumping would also have played a part. Before excavation the sandcliff face was affected by slumping (Fig 6), but this proved to be a localised problem and the edges of the slumped blocks were easily identified.

Winnowing was foreseen as a potentially significant problem because deflation of sand might have caused heavier artefacts from several episodes to occupy the same surface. Butzer (1982) and Schiffer (1987) drew attention to these processes and Shepherd (1976) recorded the enrichment of horizons by winnowing at Rosinish. At Brean this caused the association of prehistoric and post-medieval artefacts in the blowout, and deflation is also the most likely explanation for 'pavements' of limestone blocks overlying the sub-Roman cemetery. The Bronze Age stratigraphy showed little evidence of otherwise inexplicable horizons of artefacts and stones which might have been caused by winnowing. A probable exception is the presence of several large bones at the base of Unit 5d resting on (but not in) the underlying Unit 6a. It seems likely that these were deposited at an early stage in sand deposition, after which deflation occurred, lowering them to the underlying surface before they were again reburied by further sand deposition.

The degree of rabbit disturbance decreased with depth; it was extensive in Unit 3, where some of the sub-Roman burials were affected, significant in Units 4 and 5a, localised and more easily identifiable in the main occupation Unit 5b, and completely absent in Units 6, 7, and 8a. Larger bowl-shaped disturbances (Contexts 25, 55, and 276) at the base of Unit 4 were more problematic. They contained bones and a few post-medieval artefacts and, though the faunal evidence is inconclusive, are most likely to be badger setts possibly reused by foxes. Faunal disturbance undoubtedly accounts for the presence of occasional post-medieval artefacts in earlier layers and probably also for some apparently intrusive molluscs. If intrusion is responsible for the occurrence of *Cernuella virgata* earlier than on other sites (Chapter 22), and if it also explains some curiously young radiocarbon dates, eg in Unit 6a (Chapter 9), then this implies a degree of intrusion more significant than that suggested by the rabbit bone evidence or the small amount of intrusive pottery alone. The implication is that the extent of intrusion varies according to the class of evidence and further work should address this aspect.

The cultural sequence and its dating

Notwithstanding the post-depositional factors the sandcliff has revealed a well-preserved succession of occupation episodes separated by sand and colluvium. Each occupation has its own distinctive pottery assemblage, as is summarised in Figure 158. The basic sequence can be summarised as follows:

Unit 8a The basal palaeosol which was the land surface for the entire post-glacial period before sand accumulation commenced. It produced some Neolithic flintwork and Beaker sherds. Radiocarbon dates are as follows: 4720±140 BP (HAR-7023), 3460±80 BP (HAR-8547), 3810±90 BP (HAR-8990), and 3390±90 BP (HAR-8993).

Unit 7 Blown sand with evidence for a second Beaker occupation horizon in its upper part, with a radiocarbon date of 3560±90 BP (HAR-9156).

Unit 6b A colluvial deposit derived from erosion of the basal palaeosol upslope. Charcoal (possibly also derived) produced a radiocarbon date of 3890±130 BP (HAR-7022).

Unit 6a An anthropogenic deposit of imported silt and ash with biconical urn pottery. There are three radiocarbon dates: 2600±90 BP (HAR-7021), 2770±90 BP (HAR-8992), and 3120±90 BP (HAR-8991). These dates seem inexplicably late in terms of the overall sequence (Chapter 9).

Unit 6α Oval stone structure, 57, broadly contemporary with Unit 6a and associated with biconical urn pottery and a radiocarbon date of 3310±80 BP (HAR-7020) which fits in well with current views on the pottery dating.

Unit 5d Sterile sand.

Unit 5b The main excavated occupation horizon with two circular structures, 59 and 95, and a good assemblage of pottery of Trevisker type with incised decoration. Radiocarbon dates are: 3420±100 BP (HAR-7016), 2940±100 BP (HAR-7019), 2870±80 BP (HAR-7018), and 2730±100 BP (HAR-7017). The first date is from a context below the floor of Structure 59, while the others form a close group relating to activity within the structures and consistent with the late middle Bronze Age date implied by the pottery.

Unit 5a Sterile sand.

Unit 4 Occupation horizon with a midden-like anthropogenic accumulation, a ditch, and a stone wall, but no domestic structures. It produced a plain ware pottery assemblage of post-Deverel-Rimbury type with radiocarbon dates of 2730±70 BP (HAR-9151), 3100±100 BP (HAR-9153), and 3400±90 BP (HAR-9155); these overlap with the date range of the underlying Unit 5b with its quite different pottery assemblage. HAR-9155 and HAR-9153 suggest a date earlier than that indicated by

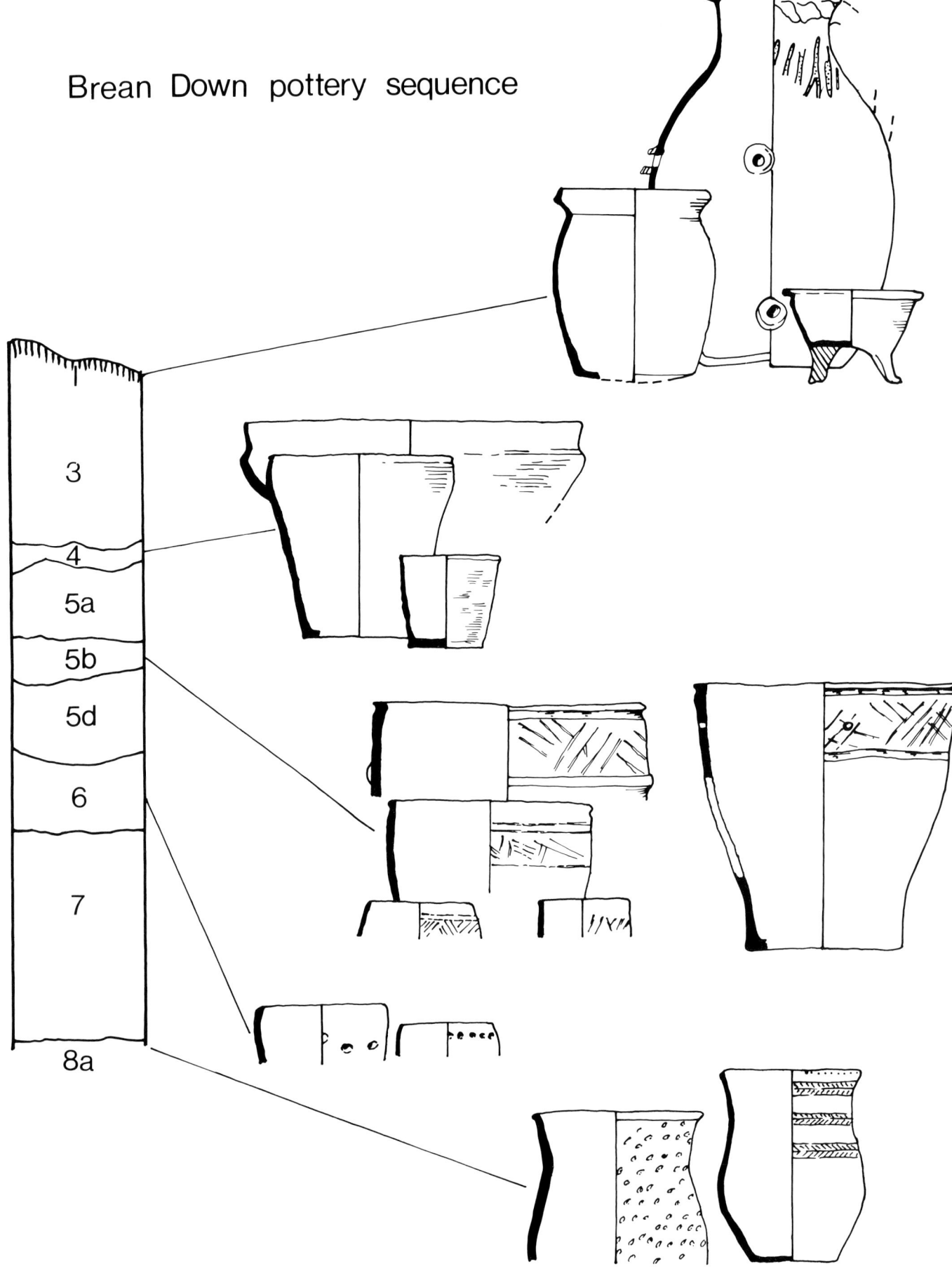

Fig 158 *Summary of the Brean pottery sequence*

the pottery and gold bracelets, which is c 2700–3000 BP (the first quarter of the first millennium BC). This discrepancy is further increased by calibration (Chapter 9). HAR-9151, on the other hand, agrees well with the other dating evidence, even when calibrated.

Unit 4a   Colluvial deposit.

Unit 3c2   Cemetery. Three radiocarbon dates of 1300±80 BP (Birm-246), 1430±70 BP (HAR-8549), and 1550±80 BP (HAR-8548) confirm its dating to the sub-Roman period, probably between the fifth and seventh centuries AD. Birm-246 could imply that the cemetery continued in use longer, but it has already been noted (Chapter 9) that the true date may be significantly earlier than the date published by Shotton and Williams (1973) which has been followed here.

Unit 3b2   Blown sand and limestone, c medieval in date.

Unit 3b1   Blown sand and limestone, post-medieval.

Unit 3a   Blown sand, post-medieval.

Unit 2   Not present in excavated area.

Unit 1   Topsoil, twentieth century.

Particular interest attaches to the Bronze Age sequence which includes the main phases of the period in Somerset and the south-west. Dunes are ideal environments of deposition for sequence preservation, as was shown also at Gwithian (Megaw 1976; Megaw *et al* 1961), Northton (Simpson 1976), and on many sites in the older dunes of the Netherlands (Jelgersma *et al* 1970; Louwe Kooijmans 1985). At Brean it is clear that the occupation is not continuous. The blown sands 5d and 5a represent continuous blankets across the sandcliff. Whilst they were being deposited people moved away for a sufficiently long period to change the fabric, form, and decorative motifs on their pottery. From this we may infer that the abandonments are more likely to have been of 100 years or more rather than tens of years. The radiocarbon dates do not clarify the lengths of these gaps because the date ranges of successive Bronze Age occupations overlap (Chapter 9).

The site formation processes and prehistoric activities represented by successive occupation phases are quite different. In Units 8a and 6b there was evidence for arable. Some of the artefacts may represent secondary rubbish spread with manure. In Units 6a and 6α there were dumps of silt and ash and a structure with few associated artefacts which may have been used for storage or craft activities. The two structures in Unit 5b were characterised by the presence of primary rubbish indicating a range of domestic and craft activities. Unit 4 was a midden-like deposit of secondary rubbish which may have been dumped in an area of animal enclosures. To some extent these contrasts may relate to the fact that only a small part of each settlement horizon was excavated, rather than to true differences in the nature of activities carried out during successive occupations.

Settlement pattern

Somerset, though rich in Bronze Age metalwork finds, has so far produced limited evidence of contemporary settlements (Ellison 1982). In the peatlands we have much environmental and trackway evidence but we can only infer the locations of settlements from the convergence points of trackways (Coles and Coles 1986, fig 35). Some areas of relict landscape survive on the limestone upland of Mendip, where there are barrows and some undated field systems (Fowler 1978). Near Brean, field systems (Fig 159) survive on the Down itself, in the Bleadon area, and on Middle Hope (Isles nd, figs 1 and 8), the latter apparently Iron Age or Romano-British. Several Mendip caves have produced Bronze Age finds, though the recent report on Charterhouse Warren Cave shows that this is not all of domestic origin. That report includes a map (Levitan *et al* 1988, fig 28) of Neolithic and Bronze Age sites in north Somerset and Avon which emphasises the paucity of settlement evidence. In the vicinity of Brean (Fig 159) the only Bronze Age site is represented by nineteenth-century finds of pottery including cremation vessels from the present day Weston-super-Mare cemetery, now housed in Woodspring Museum. Some of the pottery has Trevisker type decoration and is very similar to the material in Brean Unit 5b.

A settlement and associated cemetery in the area seems a strong possibility. It would have been in a similar geographical position to the Brean site, southeast of the later Iron Age hillfort of Worlebury (J Evans 1980). A now destroyed field system is reported from here (Fowler 1978) and there is Bronze Age metalwork from the Worlebury area (Colquhoun 1978; Thomas 1983). Other permanently dry areas from which to exploit the grazing potential of the coastal Somerset Levels are limited. We might suggest the existence of a settlement in the Uphill area where there are two tumuli and a stray flat axe find (Colquhoun 1978) and an undated prehistoric sherd from the Uphill Caves (Harrison 1977). Brent Knoll is also a suitable site for occupation though nothing is known earlier than the Iron Age hillfort (Burrow 1981). Settlements may also have existed on the dune bar, where they would have been lost by erosion, or in the claylands, where Soil Pit VI suggests that they would be buried by 1–2m of later sediment, thus emphasising the difficulty, created by post-depositional factors, of reconstructing the Bronze Age settlement pattern.

A settlement on top of Brean Down, where Warre (1865) noted hut circles, is also a possibility but subsequent observers (Somerset SMR; Bothamley 1911) have suggested that he was misled by rock formations.

Burial practice

Seven barrows/cairns on top of Brean Down (Fig 3) were noted by Grinsell (1971); some were partly plundered with minimal record by J Skinner in 1819. They may well have been associated with the excavated settlement, though none is intervisible. There is also the possible Beaker burial from the basal palaeosol (Chapter 2). These were apparently not the only forms of burial practice. Human bone was found in the Bronze Age settlement (Chapter 20) as it has

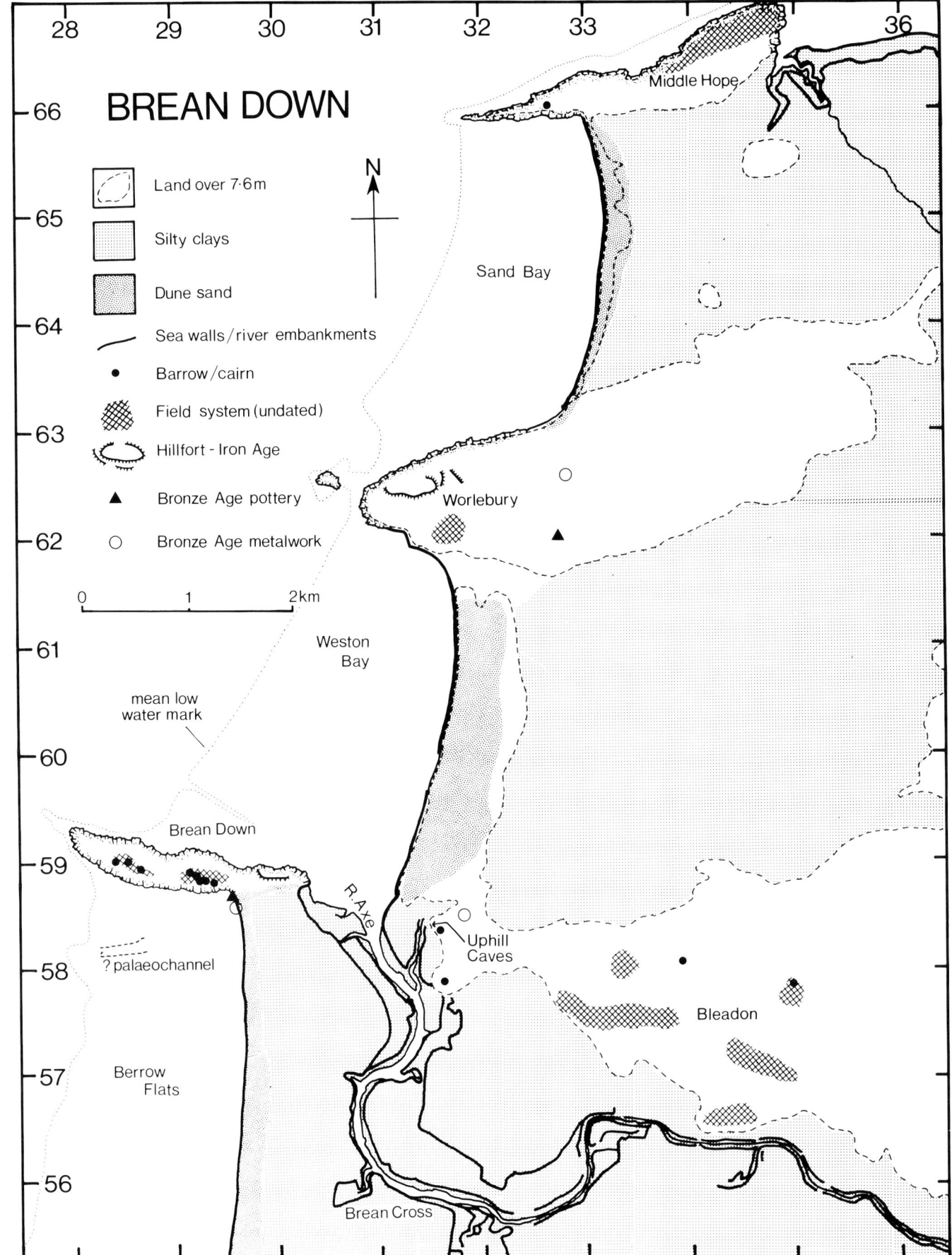

Fig 159 The archaeological and environmental context of Brean Down; the extent of field systems at Bleadon and Worlebury is approximate only (after Fowler 1978)

been on a number of contemporary settlements, eg Wallingford (Thomas et al 1986), Potterne (A Locker, pers comm), Runnymede (Longley 1980), and Stackpole Warren (Williams 1986). Some of these finds were in the midden-like deposits which suggests unceremonious disposal; see, for example, the human skull in Brean Unit 4 (Fig 55). Others, such as those in Unit 5b (Fig 142), were part of more patterned deposits associated with structures and are reminiscent of ethnographic evidence for the keeping of human bones in huts (eg Schiffer 1987, 84).

Charterhouse Warren Cave (Levitan et al 1988) shows that earlier in the Bronze Age human bones were being placed in caves. Something similar may be suggested by the undated human bones from the Uphill Caves (Harrison 1977) 2km east of the Brean settlement. Human bone may have been buried or stored in the caves and crevices on Brean Down such as the Reindeer Rift (ApSimon et al 1961), which has produced much Pleistocene bone but so far no postglacial finds. Indeed the discovery of a mammoth bone in the Bronze Age stratigraphy may relate to the transfer of bones from a cave to the settlement as part of a curation process of skeletal material as envisaged by Thomas (in Levitan et al 1988, 231) in an early Bronze Age context at Charterhouse Warren Cave.

Palaeoenvironment

In prehistory the shore would not have been the clearly defined line today represented by the sea wall (Fig 159). The vast expanse of Somerset Clay Levels to the south would have been subject to marine inundation. Soil Pit VI provided information on the sedimentary history of this area, and archaeomagnetic dating showed that the deposits were accumulating during the Neolithic and Bronze Age. They seem to have built up under brackish water saltmarsh conditions, probably partly separated from the open sea by a discontinuous dune barrier of which the sandcliff represents the landward end. The silty clay sequence in Soil Pit VI between its base at Ordnance Datum and a Romano-British surface at 5.5m OD can be correlated with the Wentlooge Formation which J Allen and Fulford (1986) have identified as the main post-glacial sedimentary unit in the Severn Estuary with its type-site in Gwent.

The considerable tidal range of the Severn Estuary, c 11m at Brean, means that these Levels, though subject to marine influence, would not have been permanently open water. The frequency and duration of their inundation would vary seasonally and according to their height relative to OD. Figure 160c shows how between 1952 and 1965 the incidence of flood conditions in three rivers in the Levels varied on a monthly basis. Figure 160a shows the range of astronomically predicted variation in high tide within a single year at Burnham-on-Sea. Today only areas below c 2m OD are inundated by every high tide, those between c 5 and 7m only by spring tidal episodes recurring on c 14 day cycles, and those above 7.16m OD are only inundated by exceptional tides resulting from meteorological conditions giving rise for instance to storm surges. Historically we know of several dramatic occasions when the sea wall was breached and widespread flooding occurred in the Levels and estuary; the best known was in 1606–7 (Williams 1970; Boon 1980). Figure 161 shows the recorded occurrence of tides above Highest Astronomical Tide at Avonmouth since the early seventeenth century. This shows that tides up to c 1m above HAT recur about every 100 to 200 years, whereas in the period since 1924, for which full records are available, tides up to 0.4m above HAT have a recurrence interval of c every 16 years. Independent statistical

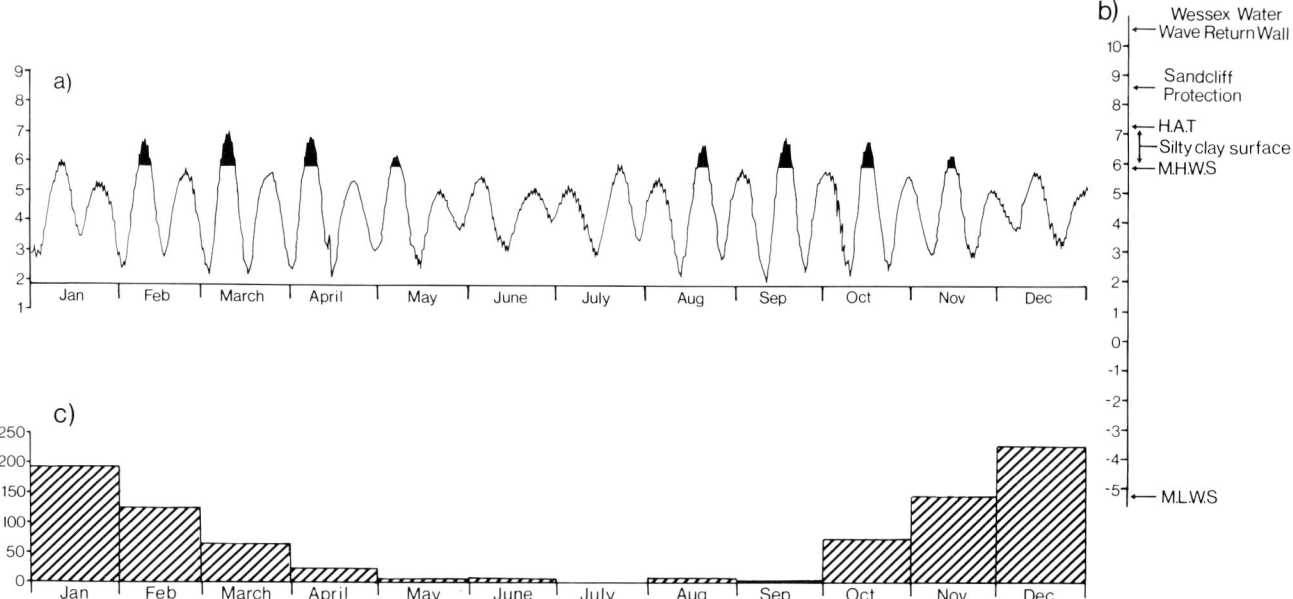

Fig 160 (a) Predicted high tide levels on OD scale for Burnham-on-Sea for 1989 from Institute of Oceanographic Sciences data; tides above MHWS accentuated in black; (b) correlation chart on the same scale as 160a showing certain tidal levels at Brean, the heights of coastal protection works, and the silty clay surface; (c) the number of days when the rivers Brue, Parrett, and Tone reached flood stage between 1952 and 1965; data from Williams 1970, table IV

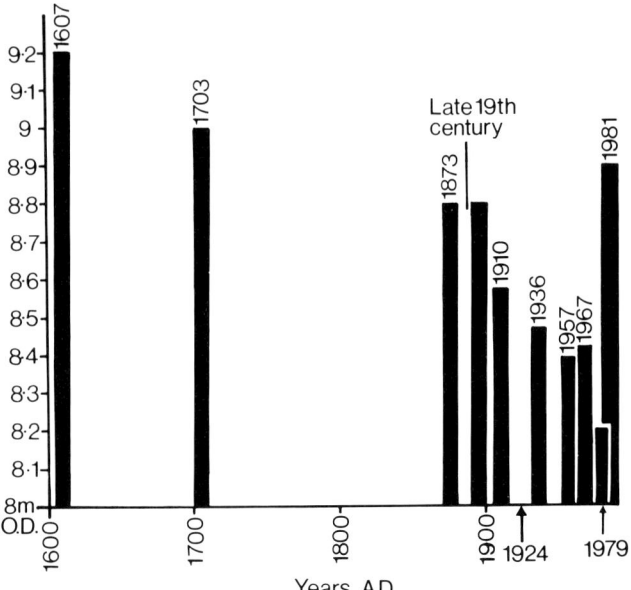

Fig 161 Records of tides at Avonmouth above HAT (8m OD) since the early seventeenth century; NB full records only available for the period since 1924 (data: City of Bristol Conservancy and Pilotage Department)

predictions of tide levels by Lennon (1963), based only on the period of detailed records, suggested more conservative figures, predicting tides up to 8.5m at Avonmouth c every 100 years and up to 8.7m c every 500 years.

Before construction of a sea wall, perhaps originally in Roman times (Leech 1981b, 29), the extent and frequency of inundation would have depended on the height to which the saltmarsh had accreted. Figure 162 shows the Mean High Water Spring Tide level calculated from the sea level curves for the Bristol Channel compared to the level of the saltmarsh surface as determined by the present project, particularly the dating evidence from Soil Pit VI. Even bearing in mind the uncertainties which attend the representation of something as complex as sea level change by a single curve (Greensmith and Tooley 1982; Kidson 1982), Figure 162 does indicate that saltmarsh accretion has taken place up to 1m or more above MHWST. The pit is, however, close to the sandcliff so the accumulation includes an as yet unquantified aeolian component.

The flats have been separated from the sea and deprived of sediment since the present sea banks were constructed probably in late Saxon times (ApSimon et al 1961, 126) when, according to J Allen and Fulford (1987, fig 1a), sea level was about 1m lower than today. Again this implies saltmarsh accretion at least c 1m above MHWST. The graph of present day high tide variation (Fig 160a) shows that a saltmarsh 1m above MHWST (ie at c 6–8m OD) would under normal circumstances only be inundated for a couple of days on between one and five spring tidal episodes a year. We can compare this with the unprotected post-medieval Rumney Surface in the Severn Estuary (J Allen and Fulford 1987, fig 1a) which has accreted to a height c 0.3m above MHWST. That surface is only inundated on between five and eleven spring tidal episodes a year and under normal circumstances is not inundated at all between the end of April and the second half of August. It follows from this reasoning and from the considerable tidal range of the estuary that much of the saltmarsh south of Brean Down is likely to have undergone only periodic inundation in the Bronze Age and would have represented a vast grazing resource. Though sensu stricto an island in the Bronze Age, Brean Down may only have been surrounded by water for a tiny proportion of the time and perhaps not at all for some months in the summer.

One uncertainty concerns the former course of the River Axe which lacks a buried channel in its present course north into Weston Bay (A Heyworth, pers comm) and must at a time of lower sea level have entered the sea south of Brean Down. There are hints of the positions of former channels (Fig 159). Brean Cross Pill runs west from the point where the Axe swings north, there are, as ApSimon et al (1961, 126) noted, traces of a former sea bank here, and this line is followed by the parish and hundred boundaries (M Aston, pers comm). If these features do indicate a fossil river course it might have survived into late Saxon times. A possible palaeochannel has recently been located by seismic survey in the intertidal area c 700m south of Brean Down but at present there is no indication of its date.

On the southern sandcliff edge we can reconstruct reasonably accurately the extent of marine influence in the Bronze Age. We know that there were deep sediments of marine origin in Soil Pit VI and an inundation was experienced in the early Bronze Age in Soil Pit V. Extrapolating from this we can conclude that inundations occurred within about 30 to 50m south of the main excavated trench. More problematic is the position of the coastal barrier to seaward. The sandcliff has been steadily eroded, its former extent being demonstrated by patches of Pleistocene sandcliff deposit which mantle the limestone cliff (ApSimon et al 1961). The foreshore peat, dated 5620±100 BP (HAR-8546), is 0.5km from the present sea wall. It was a freshwater deposit, subject to occasional marine inundation, and is likely to have lain on the landward side of a contemporary coastal dune bar. Unfortunately there is no more precise palaeoenvironmental information regarding the bar's position. Another approach is to work out possible coastal retreat from erosion rates calculated in Chapter 1 for the recent past. Table 25 attempts this, using both the lower erosion rate of 80mm per year calcu-

Table 25 Estimates of coastal retreat based on two rates calculated for the recent past

	80mm pa*	275mm pa**
Erosion since 5000 BP	420m	1375m
Erosion since 4000 BP	320m	1100m
Erosion since 3000 BP	240m	825m
Erosion since 2000 BP	160m	550m
Erosion since 1000 BP	80m	275m

* – calculated from Ordnance Survey maps over 84 years
** – calculated between 1955 and 1984

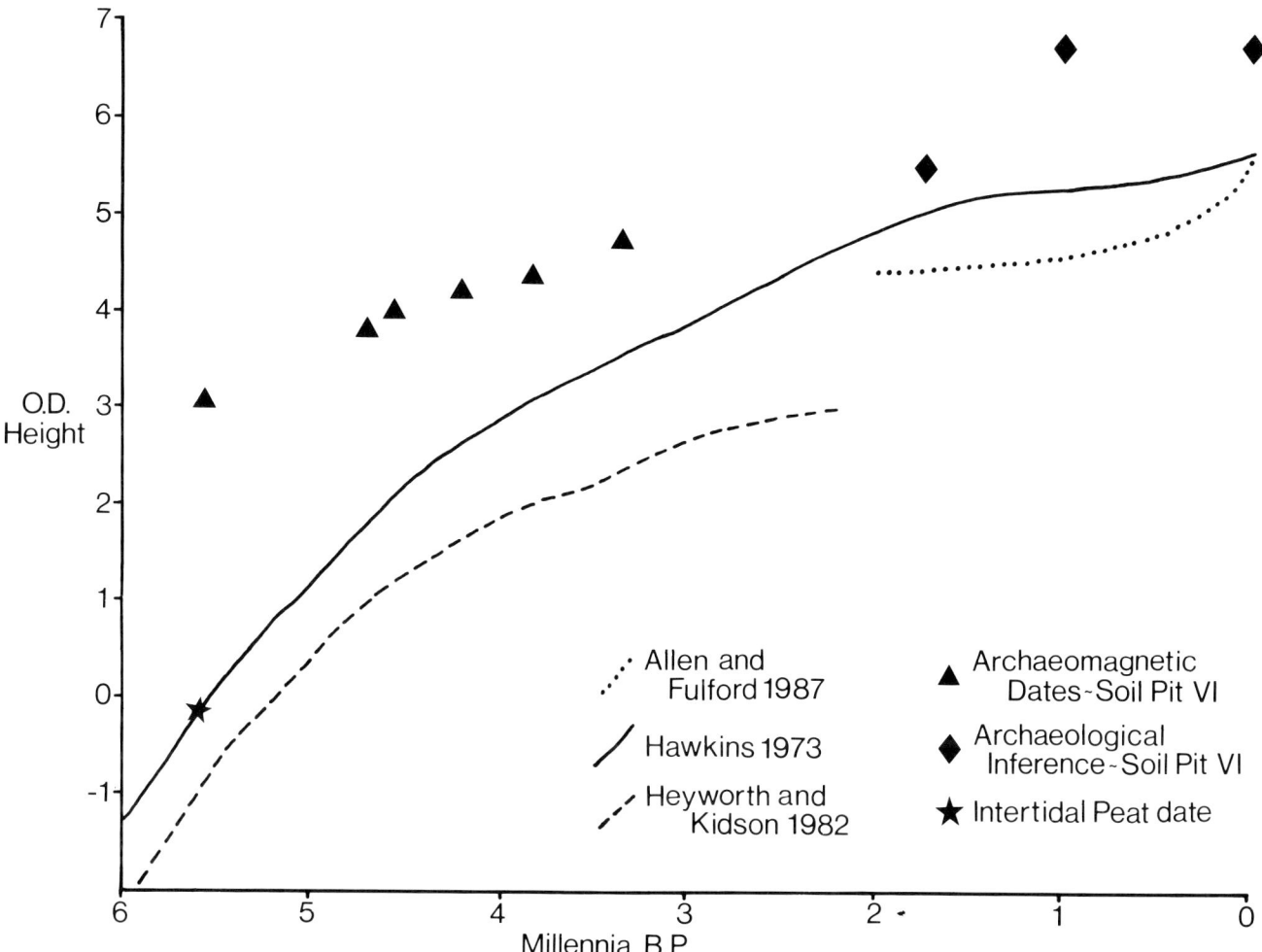

Fig 162 Comparison between the height of Mean High Water Spring Tides and the Brean saltmarsh surface in the last six millennia (sea level data from J Allen and Fulford 1987, fig 1; Hawkins 1973, fig 2; Heyworth and Kidson 1982, fig 5)

lated for Ordnance Survey maps over 84 years and the higher rate of 275mm per year based on erosion between the archaeological surveys of 1955 and 1984. If erosion rates over these short timescales are in any way representative of the last three to four thousand years, then the outer edge of the dune barrier may have lain between 0.5 and 1km to seaward. Though considerable, this erosion is less dramatic than rates suggested elsewhere in the estuary, such as the Gloucestershire Levels where 2 to 3km may have been lost since the mid first millennium BC (J Allen and Fulford 1987, 282) and the Wentlooge Levels where about 1km may have been lost since the Roman period (J Allen and Fulford 1986, 113).

As regards the environment of the Down itself, the Pleistocene relict plant community on the unstable, craggy slopes above the sandcliff suggests that these slopes have remained open throughout the post-glacial. In the reconstruction of life in Unit 5b (Fig 50) we can be reasonably confident in depicting vegetation on these background slopes as similar to that of today.

Areas of the Down with deeper, more stable soils would once have been wooded. Pollen from the foreshore peat indicates climax oak woodland with some lime, elm, and ash. By the Neolithic this was replaced on the basal palaeosol by secondary ash woodland which was then burnt giving rise to a concentration of charcoal. Micromorphology shows that this was followed by cultivation. The earliest molluscan assemblage from Unit 7 indicates lusher vegetation at the junction between the palaeosol and the encroaching very dry dunes. There are hints of limited downslope scrub invasion at this time. Thereafter the, admittedly discontinuous, molluscan sequence consists very largely of a restricted range of species indicative of dry open habitats. The sedimentary record shows that the sandcliff underwent a sequence of environmental changes involving sand deposition, colluviation, and stabilisation with occupation. These changes are not localised; the deposits extend as a series of blankets across the sandcliff implying dramatic landscape changes.

Three main colluviation episodes were involved. The earliest in the basal palaeosol (Unit 8a) during Neolithic or Beaker times is attested micromorphologically but cannot be precisely quantified in terms of its erosive effects. The second in the early Bronze Age concerned the erosion of the basal palaeosol from the upper part of the sandcliff and its deposition as Unit 6b at the base of the slope. If we calculate the probable cross-sectional area of sediment eroded at this time and divide it by the length of the contributing slope, it emerges that some 0.17m of palaeosol were eroded. In fact the section (Fig 16) shows that, on the upper part of the slope, the basal palaeosol was eroded completely down to the underlying Pleistocene breccia. The estimated figure of 0.17m agrees well with the average 0.2m depth of the surviving palaeosol where it was buried by Beaker sands (Unit 7). A third colluvial episode led to the deposition of Unit 4a sometime between c 700 BC and 400 AD. This was an extremely stony deposit derived apparently from the erosion of 0.14m depth of subsoil horizons on the craggy slope above the sandcliff. Presumably the white rockrose community survived precariously at this time on limestone outcrops. One possible scenario which might have led to extensive clearance and the creation of unstable slope conditions is the construction of the hillfort on the east end of the Down in the later Iron Age; alternatively it might relate to overgrazing. The conditions which brought about colluviation here, as elsewhere (Bell 1986a), seem to have arisen as a result of land-use factors.

More problematic, in terms of its causes, are the alternating stabilisation and sand blow episodes. Sand blow can be triggered in various ways, eg sea level change, climatic change (particularly precipitation or increased storminess), and anthropogenic factors such as overgrazing on the dune bar. Recent sedimentary studies suggest more specific possibilities. Perhaps aeolian activity was triggered by local coastal changes such as periodic breaching and re-establishment of the sandbar south of the Down resulting perhaps from changes in the course of the Axe or from storm events. Another possibility is a connection with cyclical sedimentary change in the Severn Estuary as a whole. John Allen and his colleagues (J Allen 1987; J Allen and Fulford 1986; 1987; J Allen and Rae 1987) have recently identified an estuary-wide sequence of transgressions and regressions. These are best defined and dated in the post-medieval period when the cycles of instability may have been as short as 100 years. It is suggested that further studies may produce evidence of similar oscillations in earlier formations (J Allen and Rae 1987, 228). If so this may explain the sand blow/stabilisation cycles.

Similar hypotheses have been advanced in relation to alternating stabilisation/occupation surfaces and sand blow episodes in the Older Dunes of the Netherlands (Jelgersma and van Regteren Altena 1969; Jelgersma *et al* 1970; de Jong 1971). Such changes show a degree of correlation with the transgression and regression cycles which are such an important aspect of the archaeology of the saltmarsh behind the dune barrier (Louwe Kooijmans 1974). It should be emphasised that current opinion in both the Netherlands and the Severn Estuary does not necessarily seek to explain these transgressions and regressions in terms of rises and falls of sea level. Regressions are seen as slackenings in the general trend of Flandrian sea level rise. Transgressions in the Dutch saltmarsh seem to relate to breaching of coastal barriers during episodes of increased storminess (Jelgersma *et al* 1970), higher precipitation, or more frequent westerly winds (Louwe Kooijmans 1974, 62). Similarly in the Severn Estuary J Allen (1987) and J Allen and Rae (1987) note that, while the causes of the transgression and regression cycles are unknown, they probably relate to fluctuations in the strength of waves caused perhaps by medium term climatic changes.

At Brean it is tempting to suggest that the sand blow episodes correlate with regression phases and the stabilisation episodes with transgressions. The presence of sand layers in the Soil Pit VI sequence offers some measure of support for this idea but there is no firm evidence in the form of stabilisation horizons on the sandcliff correlating with peat formation on the flats. Archaeologically it might also be argued that occupation is more likely to relate to regression rather than transgression phases. Here the critical question concerns the timescales of change. Within the Wentlooge Formation there is no conclusive evidence for transgression/regression cycles on a similar timescale to those of the post-medieval changes and to that implied by the sand dune sequence. In fact the whole Brean Bronze Age stratigraphy, including both the occupations and aeolian phases, lies within a major regression episode represented elsewhere in the estuary by peat within the Wentlooge Formation. Exposure of that peat in the intertidal area on the Gwent Levels has led to the discovery of a Bronze Age wooden roundhouse at Chapel Tump I and a further occupation site at Cold Harbour (A Whittle and S Green, pers comm). Both sites have produced radiocarbon dates indicating that they are contemporary with Brean Unit 5b with which their pottery is closely comparable. They appear to represent the extension of settlement, perhaps of a seasonal nature, out onto the peat during the regression episode.

Sometime probably in the first two centuries of the third millennium BP, just before Unit 4, the deposition of virtually sterile sand ceased. Later sands exhibit evidence of greater vegetation cover and contain rather more soil and colluvium. This pronounced late Bronze Age sedimentary change may correlate with a transgression episode represented by a silty clay of the Upper Wentlooge Formation overlying the aforementioned Bronze Age peats (J Allen 1987, 179). Evidence of a major transgression also occurs in the Somerset Levels where Hibbert (1980) reports increased flooding after c 3000 BP and Housley (1988) has identified a major marine incursion into the Axe valley leading to deposition of marine sediments as far inland as Glastonbury between c 2930 and 2500 BP. Perhaps these changes had an effect on the land-use potential of the saltmarsh and may have contributed to the final abandonment of the settlement in the late Bronze Age.

Palaeoeconomy

The site stood on the northern edge of an expanse of saltmarsh which was inundated periodically and would therefore have represented a considerable pastoral resource. The importance of grazing in the prehistoric economy of Somerset has long been emphasised (Coles 1978) and exploitation of unprotected saltmarsh for this purpose into post-medieval times is illustrated by the presence of cattle footprints in the Awre Formation (J Allen and Rae 1987, 192).

Among the Brean domestic animals cattle were the most important and ageing data indicate an annual peak of killing, whereas sheep were killed more evenly throughout the year. This suggests a logical strategy with sheep kept on the drier soils of the Down (70 ha) and cattle grazed mostly on the saltmarsh, except during inundation episodes when they must have been pastured on the Down. Reducing the cattle herd with the onset of flooding would have been a sensible strategy especially with salt available to preserve meat through the winter.

As regards crops, the macrofossil evidence includes barley, emmer, spelt, and celtic bean, together with a little processing waste which suggests that some crops may have been grown by the settlement. Most of the evidence for crops comes from Unit 5b; from the site as a whole the density is very low which could imply that crop growing was only a relatively minor aspect of the economy. The same impression is given by the total absence from the present excavation of querns, although three possible rubbing stones were found previously (ApSimon et al 1961, 120). In considering both these pieces of negative evidence we should, however, bear in mind the small area excavated. The paucity of querns contrasts with most Bronze Age sites in the south-west, eg Trevisker (ApSimon and Greenfield 1972) and Trethellan (Nowakowski 1988), including several sites on unpromising soils for arable, eg Shaugh Moor (Wainwright and Smith 1980) and Stannon Down (Mercer 1970).

Micromorphological evidence shows that tillage took place at the time of Units 8a and 6b and an associated possible stone clearance cairn has been identified in Soil Pit V. We know that as a result of these cultivation episodes the palaeosol on the upper part of the slope was truncated down to the underlying Pleistocene breccia. Once the soil at the base of the slope had been buried by the blown sand of Unit 5d there remained no possibility of arable activity in the immediate vicinity of the settlement. The fact that occupation continued intermittently on the same spot for perhaps 700 years implies that arable activity was not the settlement's main *raison d'etre*.

Crop growing on the more elevated areas of saltmarsh was a possibility. There is evidence for this in the Netherlands (van Zeist 1974) and experiments (van Zeist et al 1976; Bottema et al 1982) have shown that some crops, eg barley, can survive periodic inundation. However, at Brean there is no clear macrofossil evidence for agriculture on the flats. A more likely area for arable is on the top of Brean Down where there are two intact Celtic field systems (Fig 3) which Fowler (1975, 131) speculated were Roman or later. However, field examination suggests that the late Roman temple may sit on a level platform partly created by earlier lynchet banks. An earlier date for this field system is hinted at by the discovery of a Peterborough sherd in loam below the temple (ApSimon 1964–5, section 2). Only excavation could prove whether the field systems were in use during the Bronze Age. Even if they were, we cannot be sure that they were cultivated from the excavated settlement; they may relate to times when the sandcliff was abandoned and settlement may have migrated to the top of the Down.

It is evident from the faunal remains that fishing, fowling, and egg collecting played a part in the settlement's economy. The potential of the estuary for fishing is emphasised by the presence of post-medieval fish traps including one at the end of Brean Down (R McDonnell, pers comm) where there is also a deep pool favoured by modern line fishermen. Eels are extensively caught to this day in the rivers of the Somerset Levels. The cliffs of Brean Down, and particularly Steep Holm, would have supported large bird populations and birds from wetland habitats were exploited. It is hard to evaluate the relative importance of fish and birds because taphonomic factors are likely to have resulted in the differential destruction of more fragile bones. Bone fragments were abundant in the dog coprolites.

A further aspect of the site's coastal orientation was salt extraction and it is one of the earliest known briquetage sites in Atlantic Europe. Bradley (1975, fig 10) showed that salt extraction was a summer activity. That is the time of maximum sea water salinity, maximum evaporation, and minimum dilution by precipitation. In addition, reservoirs of water around MHWST would have been free of inundation for several weeks between May and August during much of the optimum period for solar evaporation (Fig 160a). The overall economic picture with salt extraction linked to pastoralism is as envisaged by Bradley (1975) for coastal Hampshire in the Iron Age. He suggested hide processing as an important associated activity. This was not the case in the excavated area at Brean; scrapers were few and anatomical part analysis showed that hides were processed elsewhere.

The foregoing discussion has demonstrated that the life of the Brean settlement must have been regulated to a major extent by seasonal events and within that by the regular cycle of spring tide inundations. There is no clear indication that the settlement was itself seasonal. Had it been, we would expect multiple lenses of aeolian sediment between individual activity increments and less permanent buildings. As it is, the evidence contrasts markedly with the seasonally occupied later Iron Age settlement at Meare with multiple clay floors and evidence for temporary tent structures (Coles and Coles 1986; Coles 1987). The Brean evidence suggests year round occupation concerned with the articulation of resources from the saltmarsh, the coast, and the limestone Down itself. It represents a concrete Bronze Age example of the type of site predicted by Coles' (1978) concave landscape model for the Somerset Levels with settlements at the junction between upland and the seasonally available wetland resource.

The middle Bronze Age economy of southern England has generally been regarded as a balanced mixed farming strategy (Ellison 1981, 434). That picture is derived both from the Deverel-Rimbury settlements on the chalk and the coastal sites of Cornwall and the Scillies with which Brean has a general similarity. But sites such as Gwithian (Megaw et al 1961), Trethellan (Nowakowski 1988), Halangy Down/Porth (Ashbee 1974; 1983), and Nornour (Butcher 1978) produced more evidence of arable activity, and on the first three sites the structures were set within field systems marked by lynchets. In the far south-west there seems to have been lengthy occupation on coastal sites with a mainly arable basis made possible both by a mild maritime climate and by the integration of marine resources, eg seaweed (Bell 1981) to form man-made soils. At Brean the micromorphological report suggests that silts were brought from the flats as a soil improver, but this is by no means certain and in some cases it is clear that the material was intended for structural purposes. Brean does seem to contrast with the more south-westerly sites and those on the chalkland in having a more limited arable aspect and an economy more specialised towards pastoralism and the resources of the coast and wetland. To that extent we may see the site's economy as having a distinctive Somerset Levels flavour.

Ann Woodward concludes her pottery report (Chapter 11) by noting that the 'potters of Brean Down seem to have been in contact with a wide range of other groups although the mechanisms of these contacts cannot be detailed'. Similarly the architecture has comparanda both with the timber structures of Wessex and the stone ones of the south-west. A possible mechanism for these contacts is the seasonal exploitation of grazing which would have brought together groups from a range of geographical areas around the Levels. Coles and Coles (1986) have suggested, in relation to the later Iron Age Meare settlement, that such visits played an important part in social contact and exchange. The inhabitants of Brean were in a good position to participate in exchange because they had access to salt which was not available to communities inland nor, because of reduced salinity, to those much higher up the estuary.

The extent and nature of contacts is indicated by the area from which artefacts and raw materials were obtained. David Williams' thin section analysis (Chapter 11) indicates that the vast majority of the pottery assemblage could have been locally produced. The only clear exceptions are from the collection reported originally by ApSimon et al (1961) and re-examined as part of the present study. These include sherds of felspathic tuff, for which the most likely source is Shepton Mallet 37km to the east, and a single flint-tempered sherd for which a chalkland source at least 55km to the east seems likely.

Imported chalkland flint was the main raw material used for tool production until Unit 4 when the occupants came to rely more on beach flint (Chapter 13). Of the geological specimens (Chapter 14) the vast majority were of local Carboniferous Limestone origin. There are also Pennant sandstones, shales from the Coal Measures, ?Triassic sandstones, and Oolitic Limestone for which Reg Bradshaw suggests sources in the Mendips and Clevedon/Nailsea areas. The small quantity of metalwork may also indicate exchange because, although there is a small copper vein at Brean Down and two specimens of chalcopyrite have been found, there is no evidence from the excavations that copper was worked in the Bronze Age. The gold bracelets are virtually certain to have been derived from a more distant, probably Welsh or Irish source. The shale bracelets and bracelet blanks appear to come from Kimmeridgean deposits which are known to have been worked in Dorset but which also outcrop c 55km to the east. Both the gold and shale bracelets come from Unit 4 which has not produced any briquetage, although its absence might relate to the contrasting nature of the Unit 4 activity area rather than to the cessation of salt production in the late Bronze Age.

The artefactual evidence suggests links particularly with the Mendip area to the east and north-east. It is from this area that groups are most likely to have come into contact with the occupants of Brean in the course of summer grazing on the north Somerset and Avon Levels. It is also perhaps in this area that we should look for the salt evaporation vessels which may have been traded inland. In contrast we have no clear artefactual evidence for contact with groups on the other side of the Somerset Levels in the Highland Zone, apart from the already mentioned pottery stylistic similarities in Unit 5b. The evidence we have for contacts seems much more limited than for the later Iron Age lake villages (Coles and Coles 1986) and is in line with Ellison's (1981, 434) model for small-scale, interlocking, middle Bronze Age exchange networks.

Archaeological Resource Management

Only recently has the concept of Archaeological Resource Management emerged as a clearly defined and distinctive aspect of the discipline (Darvill 1987b). The Brean project evolved through consultation with Paul Gosling, English Heritage's regional inspector, as not purely a traditional rescue excavation but very much an assessment of the nature and extent of the archaeological resource so that it would be possible to formulate proposals for its future protection and management.

As owners of the site the National Trust had, through its Archaeological Secretary, David Thackray, long been concerned by erosion of the sandcliff. Following a brief assessment of the archaeological potential in 1984 (Bell and Straker 1984) the Trust commissioned consulting engineers' reports on the problem (Taylor and Sons 1984; 1985). These established that the chief erosive factor was exceptionally high tides and storms eating at the toe of the sandcliff and causing slumping and collapse. Other factors included runoff from the Down and visitor pressure. The cost of coastal protection works to the height of the wave return wall to the south (10.5m) was estimated to be between £74,000 and £90,000. What was far from clear at this stage was whether the archaeological consequences of erosion justified such expenditure. The rescue excavation, funded largely by English Heritage, quickly established the high quality of the archaeological deposits and showed that they extended well inland. Consequently protective measures were necessary, both in the short term immediately following the excavation and on a long-term basis.

As a very short-term measure the excavation staff, thankfully assisted by a National Trust MSC team, put as much stone as possible on the seaward edge of the excavated area and behind this created a wall about 2m high of hundreds of sand-filled fertiliser sacks, behind which the excavation trench was backfilled. About a month after the excavation the National Trust MSC team emplaced about 40 1m square stone-filled wire baskets in front of the fertiliser sack wall and backfill. During this and all subsequent coastal protection work an archaeological watching brief was maintained by Michael Allen but no *in situ* archaeological deposits were disturbed. Whilst the archaeological implications were being investigated the National Trust commissioned further reports from an engineering geologist, Neil Duncan (Duncan 1985; 1986a), who showed that further protection was certainly necessary. He evaluated various options and came down in favour of a 'rip rap' of large stone placed directly against the sandcliff and rising to 10.5m OD, the same height as the wave return wall to the south. Various associated measures were also recommended, including stabilising the sandcliff with vegetation. The overall cost would be *c* £33,000–£36,000. This solution was, however, considered unacceptable by the Nature Conservancy Council which was involved because the sandcliff was a Site of Special Scientific Interest on account of the geological importance of the sedimentary sequence. The Nature Conservancy Council's terms of reference demanded that a good exposure remain visible and for this some degree of continuing erosion was necessary. Thus it was that a way had to be found of reconciling the apparently conflicting management objectives of the bodies responsible for archaeological and geological conservation. It should be stressed that, although in this particular instance there was a conflict of interests, there is in general a growing recognition of the common and complementary work of English Heritage and the Nature Conservancy Council (Darvill 1987b; Lambrick 1985).

In order to reconcile the conflicting requirements of archaeological and geological conservation Neil Duncan drew up modified coastal protection proposals (Duncan 1986b) which were implemented in February 1987. A barrier of large Carboniferous Limestone blocks was constructed directly against the excavation backfill on the southern part of the site, giving maximum protection to the Bronze Age settlement. Further north the barrier swings away and is up to 3m from the toe of the sandcliff where its north end abuts the limestone cliff face. The northern part of the barrier rises to 8.5m OD (Fig 160a), designed on a 10 year storm prediction, rather than the originally recommended 10.5m OD which would have given protection against a 100 year storm. The objective is that occasional storms will overtop the barrier and bring about a measure of continued erosion so that a good exposure of the Pleistocene sequence remains visible. Neil Duncan's ingenious solution was more costly than his earlier proposal (£50,000 rather than £36,000), but the Nature Conservancy Council contributed towards the additional cost incurred in meeting their requirements (Nature Conservancy Council 1987). The cost of all the coastal protection work was met by the National Trust with a substantial grant from English Heritage.

Though the Bronze Age settlement was now well protected, the need to allow continued erosion of the Pleistocene sequence meant that it had not been possible to give any effective protection to the early Christian cemetery in the northern part of the sandcliff. It was not even possible to encourage vegetation growth in this area in order to try to reduce erosion.

It was clear from the auger survey that burials extended at least 15m inland and would continue to erode. Consequently there remains an urgent need for rescue excavation of the burials in the most immediately threatened cliff edge area and protective measures for the remainder.

Meanwhile other factors are emerging which may have a significant effect on the site. A feasibility study for the Severn Estuary tidal barrage concluded that a suitable position for the end of a barrage on the English side is within 1km south of Brean Down (Gavaghan 1986). It was this prospect which led to some limited investigation of the intertidal area in 1986 as described in Chapter 8. In 1985 the Severn Estuary Levels Research Committee was set up to coordinate research throughout the estuarine area. In 1988 that committee was commissioned by the Severn Tidal Power Group to carry out a survey of the archaeological potential of the whole 183km of estuarine coast contained within the area of the proposed barrage.

If barrage construction does go ahead it may present severe problems for the future management of the archaeology of the area, but it would also necessitate geological surveys which would generate a tremendous wealth of data pertinent to the Flandrian sedimentary and environmental context of the archaeological site described in this report. All this serves to emphasise the conflicting pressures which, in our complicated twentieth-century world, need to be reconciled in ensuring the survival of one seemingly safe rural archaeological site on National Trust property.

Summary

Coastal erosion at Brean Down, Somerset, cut into a Bronze Age settlement site, leading in 1983 to the discovery of two late Bronze Age gold bracelets. Recording of this find suggested the existence of buildings and led to a rescue excavation of 5m of deposit comprising five distinct prehistoric occupations separated by blown sand and eroded soil.

The base of the post-glacial sequence is a buried soil (Unit 8a) containing flints and Beaker pottery. In the middle of the fourth millennium BP in radiocarbon years blown sand (Unit 7) buried the soil at the base of the slope. Some further Beaker activity took place on a stabilisation horizon within the blown sand. Cultivation of the still exposed soil upslope led to its total erosion down to underlying Pleistocene breccia. The eroded soil was laid down at the base of the slope (Unit 6b) above the blown sand and then itself overlain by ash and clay (Unit 6a) brought to the site by man. This accumulated around a well-preserved oval stone structure. The unit contained biconical urns and radiocarbon dates suggest a date in the fourth and early third millennia BP. More sand blow (Unit 5d) ensued and above this was a stabilisation horizon with two circular structures (Unit 5b) surrounded by rainwater gullies. One was almost complete and originally had wattlework walls set in a trench; there was also some stone walling and a central clay hearth. Only one third of the other structure remained and it was stone-walled. The structures contained pottery of Trevisker type and a later middle Bronze Age date in the late fourth to early third millennia BP is indicated by the radiocarbon dates. Three-dimensional artefact recording shows patterning within and around the structures which is interpreted as evidence of normal domestic tasks: cooking, food preparation, weaving, etc, in addition to a 'cottage' salt extraction industry. Sand blow resumed (Unit 5a) followed by a midden deposit (Unit 4) with much bone and pottery. There were no domestic structures but a ditch and stone wall represent field or yard boundaries. From this horizon came the gold bracelets which, together with late Bronze Age plainware pottery, imply a date in the first quarter of the third millennium BP. Sealing this was eroded soil (Unit 4a), then more blown sand (Unit 3c2) into which six graves were cut. The skeletons were east–west with the heads to the west and without grave goods, though some had stone lining blocks or markers. Radiocarbon dates confirm that they were buried in the fifth to mid seventh centuries AD and relate to the sub-Roman period; they were probably Christians. In the sixteenth and early seventeenth centuries AD occupation of a house on the sandcliff was contemporary with a dune blowout which eroded parts of the cemetery and the late Bronze Age occupation. The effects of sand blow, winnowing, faunal disturbance, and other post-depositional changes are considered throughout the report.

An auger and soil pit survey showed that the settlement extended inland and the sediments form an essentially uniform series of blankets, demonstrating that the environmental changes which gave rise to the sedimentary sequence were of a widespread nature. South of the sandcliff marine clays were interleaved with the blown sand and the chronology of these clays, most of which accumulated between the sixth and mid fourth millennia BP, has been established by archaeomagnetic dating.

The prehistoric artefacts include small collections of Neolithic and Bronze Age flints and Beaker pottery, some metalwork including the gold bracelets, shale bracelets, bone objects, and clay loom weights. Of particular interest are briquetage pedestals and trays, chemical analyses of which are presented. They come from Units 6 and 5b and with radiocarbon dates from c 3300 BP indicate one of the earliest briquetage sites in Atlantic Europe.

A notable range of environmental evidence was present. Micromorphological analysis was particularly revealing of soil and sediment histories and human activity patterns, which were further examined by a combination of three-dimensional artefact recording, and chemical and magnetic susceptibility analysis. Pollen, diatoms, and ostracods provide information on the environment of the marine clays and an associated peat deposit. Charred plant macrofossils revealed only limited evidence of cereal growing. Among the animal bones the usual domesticates predominated, and there were coastal and wetland birds and some fish. Around the Bronze Age structures were mineralised dog coprolites which contained the eggs of human intestinal parasites. Land molluscs reflect an exposed dry dune environment and marine molluscs reflect the rather impoverished fauna of the Severn Estuary.

The Down seems to have been an island in the Bronze Age but was probably only surrounded by water at high tides during spring tidal episodes. For much of the time to its south there was probably a great expanse of saltmarsh representing an important grazing resource, which, together with salt extraction, probably formed the basis of the site's economy.

Consideration is given to the causes of the alternating sequences of sand blows and stabilisations and possible links with recently identified transgression and regression episodes in the Severn Estuary.

Finally the management of this archaeological resource is discussed. Once it had been identified as probably the most well-preserved Bronze Age sequence in southern England it was protected from further coastal erosion by a boulder barrier.

The text is accompanied by a microfiche containing supporting information and an optional colour microfiche illustrating the soil micromorphological thin sections.

Résumé

L'érosion côtière à Brean Down, dans le comté de Somerset, a mis à nu un site d'occupation de l'Age du Bronze et a par la suite permis la découverte de deux bracelets en or de l'Age du Bronze tardif. L'enregistrement de cette trouvaille nous a conduits à penser qu'il existait des bâtiments et nous avons été amenés à entreprendre des fouilles de sauvetage sur 5m de dépôts comprenant cinq niveaux d'occupation préhistorique distincts séparés par des couches de sable apporté par le vent et de sols érodés.

La base des couches post-glaciaires consiste en sols enterrés (Unité 8a) contenant des silex et des vases à large col. Au milieu du quatrième millénaire en années radiocarbone, du sable apporté par le vent (Unité 7) a recouvert les sols au pied du versant. Une stabilisation dans le sable soufflé a également révélé des traces d'activité que l'on a pu associer aux peuples à vases. La culture des sols qui étaient encore à découvert, en montant le versant de la colline, a provoqué leur érosion totale jusqu'au niveau de la brèche pléistocène. Les sols érodés étaient déposés au pied de la pente (Unité 6b), au-dessus du sable soufflé, mais ils se trouvèrent eux-mêmes recouverts par de la cendre et des argiles (Unité 6a) apportées sur le site par l'homme. Ces dépôts se sont accumulés autour d'une structure de pierres ovale bien conservée. Cette Unité recelait des urnes biconiques dont la datation au radiocarbone a été estimée au quatrième ou au troisième millénaire. Un nouvel apport de sable soufflé a suivi (Unité 5d), qui a lui-même été recouvert par une stabilisation comprenant deux structures circulaires (Unité 5b) entourées par des rigoles à eaux de pluie. L'une était presque complète et était entourée, à l'origine, d'une enceinte en clayonnage plantée dans une tranchée; on y a également retrouvé quelques murs en pierres et un foyer central en argile. Il ne restait qu'un tiers de la deuxième structure et elle était entourée d'un mur en pierres. Ces structures recelaient de la poterie de type Trevisker et la datation au radiocarbone suggère une date proche de la fin de l'Age du Bronze moyen, fin du quatrième ou début du troisième millénaire.

L'étude des objets façonnés tri-dimensionnels et de leur répartition à l'intérieur et autour des édifices nous a conduits à penser que se déroulaient là les activités domestiques habituelles: préparation et cuisson d'aliments, tissage, etc auxquelles s'ajoutait une petite entreprise artisanale d'extraction de sel. Le dépôt de sable reprit (Unité 5a), puis l'endroit servit de dépôtoir (Unité 4) et est riche en os et en poteries. On n'a pas retrouvé d'édifice à usage domestique, mais un fossé et un mur constituaient les limites d'un champ ou d'une cour. Les bracelets en or proviennent de cette strate, qui recelait également de la poterie non décorée, le tout semble dater du premier quart du troisième millénaire. L'ensemble était enseveli sous des sols érodés (Unité 4a) qui étaient eux-mêmes recouverts par une nouvelle couche de sable éolien dans lequel on avait taillé six sépultures. Elles étaient orientées d'est en ouest, la tête se trouvant à l'ouest, et ne contenaient pas de mobilier funéraire: dans certaines on a néanmoins retrouvé des bornes de pierre ou des jalons. La datation au radiocarbone confirme que les inhumations avaient eu lieu entre le cinquième et le milieu du septième siècle après J-C et appartenaient donc à la période post-romaine, il s'agissait probablement de sépultures chrétiennes. Au seizième siècle et au début du dix-septième siècle après J-C, l'occupation d'une maison sur la falaise de sable coincida avec un soufflage de dune qui causa l'érosion de certaines parties du cimetière et de l'occupation de l'Age du Bronze. On examine tout au long du compte-rendu les effets du sable soufflé, du vent, des perturbations dues à la faune et autres changements postérieurs aux divers dépôts.

Un levé accompagné de forages et d'excavations a montré que l'occupation s'étendait à l'intérieur des terres et que les sédiments s'étaient déposés en une série de couches presque uniformes, nous en avons conclu que les variations dans l'environnement responsables de cette stratigraphie avaient un caractère universel. Au sud de la falaise des argiles marines venaient s'intercaler avec le sable soufflé et la chronologie de ces dépôts argileux, pour la plupart mis en place entre le sixième et le milieu du quatrième millénaire a été établie par datation archéomagnétique.

Les objets préhistoriques comprenaient de petites collections de silex du Néolithique et de l'Age du Bronze ainsi que des vases campaniformes, des objets en métal dont les deux bracelets en or, des bracelets en schiste, des objets en os et des poids de métier à tisser en argile. Des pédestals et des plateaux en argile cuite nous ont paru particulièrement intéressants et nous en rapportons les analyses chimiques. Ils proviennent des Unités 6 et 5b et remontent, d'après la datation au radiocarbone, aux environs de l'an 3300; nous sommes donc en présence de l'un des plus anciens sites avec argiles cuites d'Europe Atlantique.

On a retrouvé une importante variété de vestiges d'occupation. Une analyse micromorphologique a en particulier apporté nombre de renseignements intéressants sur l'histoire des sols et des sédiments et sur les diverses formes d'activité humaine; celles-ci ont ensuite été soumises à une étude combinée reposant sur l'examen des objets tri-dimensionnels et sur l'observation de leur susceptibilité magnétique et chimique. Du pollen, des diatomées et de minuscules crustacés nous ont apporté des renseignements sur le milieu caractéristique des argiles marines et sur le dépôt de tourbe avoisinant. Des macrofossiles de plantes carbonisées n'ont fourni que peu de témoignages de cultures de céréales. Parmi les ossements nous avons surtout trouvé des restes des animaux domestiques habituels, il y avait des oiseaux typiques des régions côtières et marécageuses et des poissons. A proximité des structures de l'Age du Bronze se trouvaient des coprolites de chiens minéralisés qui contenaient des oeufs de parasites intestinaux humains. Des mollusques terrestres témoignent de la présence d'un milieu de dune sèche découverte tandis que les mollusques marins sont un reflet de la faune assez pauvre de l'estuaire de la Severn.

Le 'Down' semble avoir été une île à l'Age du Bronze, mais cette colline n'était probablement complètement entourée d'eau qu'à marée haute au moment des grandes marées de printemps. Pendant la plus grande partie du temps, au sud, il y avait probablement une vaste étendue de marais salants qui représentaient une importante richesse pour le pâturage et qui formaient avec l'extraction du sel l'essentiel de l'économie du site.

On met à l'étude les causes de l'alternance de couches de sable soufflé et de stabilisations et les liens qu'elles pourraient avoir avec les phénomènes de transgression et de régression récemment observés dans l'estuaire de la Severn.

Pour terminer on envisage la gestion de cette richesse archéologique. Après avoir été reconnu comme étant probablement le site montrant la succession des occupations de l'Age du Bronze le mieux conservé du sud de l'Angleterre, il a été protégé contre une érosion côtière ultérieure par une barrière de pierres roulées.

Le texte s'accompagne d'une microfiche contenant des documents d'appui et, en option, d'une microfiche en couleurs montrant les minces sections micromorphologiques des sols.

Zusammenfassung

Durch Küstenerosion bei Brean Down, Somerset, wurde eine bronzezeitliche Siedlungsstelle angeschnitten. Dies führte 1983 zu der Auffindung zweier spätbronzezeitlicher Goldarmreifen. Während der Fundsicherung wurde die Existenz von Gebäuden vermutet und dies wiederum führte zu einer Rettungsgrabung durch eine 5 m tiefe Ablagerung, die aus fünf deutlich durch Flugsand und Abtragungsschichten von einander getrennten vorgeschichtlichen Siedlungshorizonten bestand.

Die Basis der nacheiszeitlichen Schichtenfolgen ist ein überdeckter Boden, der Feuersteinartifakte und Glockenbecherkeramik enthielt. In der Mitte des vierten Jahrtausends vor heute in Radiokarbonjahren überdeckte Flugsand (Unit 7) die Erdschicht am Fuße des Hanges. Einige weitere Glockenbecherspuren zeigten sich innerhalb des Flugsandes nach der Stabilisierung dieses Horizontes. Ackerbau auf dem hangaufwärts noch freiliegenden Boden führte zu dessen vollständiger, bis auf die unterliegende pleistozäne Breccie reichenden Abtragung. Der abgetragene Boden (Unit 6b) wurde am Fuße des Hanges über dem Flugsand abgelagert und dann selbst durch Asche und Lehm (Unit 6a), welche durch menschliche Einwirkung an diese Stelle gebracht worden waren, überlagert. Diese Schicht sammelte sich um eine guterhaltene Anlage aus Stein an. Die 'Unit' enthält Knickwandurnen und die Radiokarbondaten ergeben eine Datierung im vierten und frühen dritten Jahrtausend vor heute. Weiterer Flugsand (Unit 5b) folgte. Darüber lag ein Stabilisierungshorizont mit zwei kreisförmigen Anlagen (Unit 5a), die von Regenwasserrinnen umgeben waren. Eine dieser Anlagen war nahezu komplett und besaß ursprünglich in einen Graben gesetzte Flechtwerkwände; zu diesem Gebäude gehörten auch etwas steinernes Mauerwerk und eine zentrale Feuerstelle aus Lehm. Nur ein Drittel der zweiten Anlage war noch vorhanden; sie hatte Wände aus Stein. In den Alagen fand sich Keramik des Trevisker Typs und die Radiokarbondatierung weist auf ein spätes mittelbronzezeitliches Datum im ausgehenden vierten und frühen dritten Jahrtausend vor heute hin. Die dreidimensionale Fundaufnahme zeigt eine Fundstreuung innerhalb der und um die Gebäude, die als Hinweis auf normale häusliche Betätigungen gedeutet werden kann: wie z B Kochen, Nahrungszubereitung und Weberei mit Salzgewinnung im kleinen Rahmen als Extrabetätigung. Der Flugsand kehrte zurück (Unit 5a), gefolgt von einer Ablagerung häuslichen Abfalls (Unit 4), die Knochen und Keramik enthielt. Wohnbauten wurden nicht gefunden, doch weisen ein Graben und eine Steinmauer auf eine Feld – oder Hofeinfriedung – hin. Aus diesem Horizont stammen die beiden Goldarmreifen. Zusammen mit spätbronzezeitlicher unverzierter Ware weisen sie auf ein Datum im ersten viertel des dritten Jahrtausend vor heute hin. Abgetragener Boden (Unit 4a) überdeckte diesen Horizont; darauf folgte neuer Flugsand (Unit 3c2), in den sechs Gräber eingeschnitten waren. Sie waren ost-westlich ausgerichtet mit dem Kopfende nach Westen und enthielten keine Grabbeigaben. Einige waren jedoch mit Steinen ausgelegt oder hatten Kopfsteine. Die Radiokarbondaten bestätigen, daß die Grablegungen im Zeitraum zwischen dem fünften und der Mitte des siebten Jahrhunderts n Chr stattgefinden haben und in die nachrömische Zeit gehören. Sie waren wahrscheinlich christlich. Im 16 und frühen 17 Jahrhundert n Chr wurde ein Haus auf der Sandklippe zur gleichen Zeit bewohnt, als eine Ausblasung der Düne Teile des Friedhofs und der spätbronzezeitlichen Besiedlung abtrug. Die Auswirkungen von Flugsand, Worfeln, Zerstreuung durch tierische Einwirkungen und andere, nach der Ablagerung eingetretene Veränderungen werden durchlaufend in dem Bericht besprochen.

Eine mit Erdbohrern und Sondagen durchgeführte Untersuchung zeigte daß sich die Besiedlung inland erstreckte und die Ablagerungen eine im Wesentlichen einheitliche Serienreihe von Schichten bilden, wodurch angezeigt wird, daß die Umweltveränderungen, die Anlaß für die Ablagerungsfolge gaben, weitverbreitet waren. Südlich der Sandklippe war Meeresschlamm durchsetzt mit Schichten von Flugsand abgelagert. Die Chronologie dieser Schlammschichten, die sich größtenteils zwischen dem sechsten und der Mitte des vierten Jahrtausends vor heute angesammelt hatten, ist durch archäomagnetische Datierung festgestellt worden.

Unter den vorgeschichtlichen Kleinfunden befinden sich kleine Sammlungen von neolithischen und bronzezeitlichen Feuersteinwerkzeugen und Glockenbecherkeramik, einige Metallfunde einschließlich der Goldarmreifen, Armreifen aus Tonschiefer, Knochengegenstände und tönerne Webgewichte. Von besonderem Interesse sind Untersätze und Tafeln aus gebranntem Ton, dessen Chemische Analyse beigefügt ist. Sie stammen aus den 'Units' 6 und 5b und weisen Radiokarbondaten von circa 3300 vor heute auf und sind somit die ältesten Funde dieser Art aus dem atlantischen Europa.

Der Umweltbefund war erstaunlich umfangreich und variierend. Die mikromorphologische Analyse war besonders aufschlußreich hinsichtlich der Boden- und Anlagerungschronologien und der Art und Auswirkung der menschlichen Betätigung, die außerdem weiteren Untersuchungen durch eine Kombination aus dreidimensionaler Fundaufnahme, chemischer und magnetischer Analysen unterzogen wurde. Pollen, Kieselalgen und Muschelkrebse geben Auskunft über die Umweltbedingungen in den Meeresschlämmen und einer dazugehörigen Torfablagerung. Verkohlte pflanzliche Großfossilien ergeben nur beschränkte Hinweise auf Getreideanbau. Unter den Tierknochen herrschten die üblichen Haustiere vor; daneben traten Küsten- und Sumpfvögel sowie einige Fische auf. In der Umgebung der bronzezeitlichen Anlagen fand sich mineralisierter Hundekot, der die Eier menschlicher Darmparasiten enthielt. Landschnecken weisen auf eine trockene offene Dünenregion hin und die Meeresmollusken spiegeln die ziemlich ärmliche Fauna in der Severnbucht wieder.

Der Down scheint in der Bronzezeit eine Insel gewesen zu sein, die allerdings nur während der Flut bei Springtiden ganz von Wasser umgeben war. Für die meiste Zeit erstreckte sich jedoch südlich davon eine ausgedehnte Seemarsch, die ein wichtiges Weidegebiet darstellte und so zusammen mit der Salzgewinnung wahrscheinlich die wirtschaftliche Basis für die Besiedlung bildete.

Es werden Betrachtungen über die Gründe für den Folgenwechsel der Flugsand- und Stabilisierungsepisoden und so über einen möglichen Zusammenhang mit kürzlich festgestellten Transgressions- und Regressionsepisoden in der Severnbucht angestellt.

Letztlich wird die Handhabe diese archäologischen Befundes diskutiert. Nachdem er als die möglicherweise besterhaltene bronzezeitliche Siedlungsfolge in Südengland identifiziert worden ist, wurde er durch einen Damm aus Felsblocken gegen weitere Küstenerosion gesichert.

Dem Text liegen ein Mikrofiche mit zusätzlicher Information und auf Wunsch ein Farbmikrofiche mit Illustrationen der mikromorphologischen Bodendünnschliffe bei.

Bibliography

Abercromby, J, 1912 *A study of the Bronze Age pottery of Great Britain and Ireland*, 2 vols, Oxford

Alcock, L, 1971 Excavations at South Cadbury Castle, 1970, *Antiq J*, **51**, 1–7

——, 1980 The Cadbury Castle sequence in the first millennium BC, *Bull Board Celtic Stud*, **28**, 656–718

Allan, J P, 1981 The pottery, in Excavations at Southgate Cottages, Lydford (P J Weddell), *Proc Devon Archaeol Soc*, **39**, 128–35

——, 1984a *Medieval and post-medieval finds from Exeter 1971–80*, Exeter Archaeol Rep, **3**, Exeter

——, 1984b The pottery, in An excavation at 39 Fore Street, Totnes (D M Griffiths and F M Griffiths), *Proc Devon Archaeol Soc*, **42**, 79–94

Allen, J R L, 1987 Late Flandrian shoreline oscillations in the Severn Estuary: the Rumney Formation at its typesite (Cardiff area), *Phil Trans Roy Soc London*, **B315**, 157–74

Allen, J R L, and Fulford, M G, 1986 The Wentlooge Level: a Romano-British saltmarsh reclamation in south-east Wales, *Britannia*, **17**, 91–117

——, and ——, 1987 Romano-British settlement and industry on the wetlands of the Severn Estuary, *Antiq J*, **67**, 237–89

Allen, J R L, and Rae, J E, 1987 Late Flandrian shoreline oscillations in the Severn Estuary: a geomorphological and stratigraphical reconnaissance, *Phil Trans Roy Soc London*, **B315**, 185–230

Allen, M J, 1986 Magnetic susceptibility as a potential palaeoenvironmental determinant, *Circaea*, **4**, 18–20

——, 1988 Archaeological and environmental aspects of colluviation in south-east England, in *Man-made soils* (eds W Groenman-van Waateringe and M Robinson), BAR, **S410**, 67–92, Oxford

——, in prep Magnetic susceptibility variability for the excavations at Klingleberg St Viet, Austria: interpretation of site patterning via geomagnetic data

Allen, M J, and Macphail R I, 1985 Review and discussion of magnetic susceptibility and micromorphology: examples of Hazleton Long Cairn, Gloucestershire and Seaford Head Hillfort, Sussex, *Ancient Monuments Lab Rep*, **4583**, London

——, and ——, 1987 Micromorphology and magnetic susceptibility studies: their combined role in interpreting archaeological soils and sediments, in *Soil micromorphology* (eds N Fedoroff, L M Bresson, and M A Courty), 669–78, Paris

Allen, S E, Grimshaw, H M, Parkinson, J A, and Quarmby, C, 1974 *Chemical analysis of ecological materials*, Oxford

ApSimon, A M, 1964–5 The Roman temple on Brean Down, Somerset, *Proc Univ Bristol Spelaeol Soc*, **10**, 195–258

——, 1969 The Early Bronze Age of Ireland, *Ulster J Archaeol*, **32**, 28–72

ApSimon, A M, Donovan, D T, and Taylor, H, 1961 The stratigraphy and archaeology of the Late-Glacial and Post-Glacial deposits at Brean Down, Somerset, *Proc Univ Bristol Spelaeol Soc*, **9**, 67–136

ApSimon, A M, and Greenfield, E, 1972 The excavation of Bronze Age and Iron Age settlements at Trevisker, St Eval, Cornwall, *Proc Prehist Soc*, **38**, 302–81

Armstrong, E C R, 1920 *Guide to the collection of Irish antiquities: catalogue of Irish gold ornaments in the collection of the Royal Irish Academy*, Dublin

Ashbee, P, 1974 *Ancient Scilly – from the first farmers to the early Christians*, Newton Abbot

——, 1983 Halangy Porth, St Mary's, Isles of Scilly, excavations 1975–6, *Cornish Archaeol*, **22**, 3–46

Aston, M, and Burrow, I, 1982 *The archaeology of Somerset*, Taunton

Avery, B W, 1980 *Soil classification for England and Wales*, Soil Survey Tech Monog, **14**, Harpenden

Avery, B W, and Bascomb, C L (eds), 1974 *Soil Survey Laboratory methods*, Soil Survey Tech Monog, **6**, Harpenden

Avery, M, and Close Brooks, J, 1969 Shearplace Hill, Sydling, St Nicholas, Dorset: a suggested reinterpretation, *Proc Prehist Soc*, **35**, 345–51

Baart, J, Krook, W, Lagerweij, A B, Ockers, N, van Regteren Altena, H, Stam, T, Stoepker, H, Stouthart, G, and van der Zwan, M, 1977 *Opgravingen in Amsterdam*, Amsterdam

Babel, U, 1975 Micromorphology of soil organic matter, in *Soil components, 1, organic matter* (ed J E Geisking), 369–473, New York

Baker, E E, 1919 (ms) Old world gleanings: Brean Down coney warren, in Baker scrapbooks (Aug 1919), 172, in Weston-super-Mare Library

Balaam, N D, Bell, M G, David, A E U, Levitan, B, Macphail, R I, Robinson, M, and Scaife, R G, 1987 Prehistoric and Romano-British sites at Westward Ho!, Devon: archaeological and palaeoenvironmental surveys 1983 and 1984, in Balaam *et al* 1987, 163–259

Balaam, N D, Levitan, B, and Straker, V, 1987 *Studies in palaeoeconomy and environment in south-west England*, BAR **181**, Oxford

Ballantine, W J, 1961 A biologically defined exposure scale for the comparative description of rocky shores, *Fld Stud* **1**(3), 1–19

Barrett, J, 1980 The pottery of the Later Bronze Age in lowland England, *Proc Prehist Soc*, **46**, 297–319

Barton, K J, 1961 Some evidence for two types of pottery manufactured in Bristol in the early eighteenth century, *Trans Bristol Gloucestershire Archaeol Soc*, **80**, 160–8

——, 1964 The post-medieval pottery, in The excavation of a medieval bastion at St Nicholas' Almshouses, King St, Bristol, *Medieval Archaeol*, **8**, 193–211

Bascomb, C L, 1961 A calcimeter for routine use on soil samples, *Chemistry and Industry*, 1961, 1826–7

——, 1968 Distribution of pyrophosphate-extractable iron and organic carbon in soils of various groups, *J Soil Sci*, **35**, 243–50

Bassindale, R, 1943 Studies on the biology of the Bristol Channel XI, *J Ecol*, **31**, 1–29

Beer, R J S, 1976 The relationship between *Trichuris trichiura* (Linnaeus 1758) of man and *Trichuris suis* (Schrank 1788) of pig, *Res Veterinary Sci*, **20**, 47–54

Bell, M G, 1977 *Excavations at Bishopstone*, Sussex Archaeol Collect, **115**, Lewes

——, 1981 Seaweed as a prehistoric resource, in *Environmental aspects of coasts and islands* (eds D Brothwell and G Dimbleby), BAR, **S94**, 117–26

——, 1983a Valley sediments as evidence of prehistoric land-use on the South Downs, *Proc Prehist Soc*, **49**, 119–50

——, 1983b Land Mollusca from Hazleton Neolithic long cairn, *Ancient Monuments Lab Rep*, **4000**, London

——, 1984 Environmental archaeology in south-west England, in Keeley 1984, 43–133

——, 1986a Archaeological evidence for the date, cause and extent of soil erosion on the chalk, in *Soil erosion* (eds C P Burnham and J I Pitman), South-east England Soils Discussion Group, **3**, 72–83

——, 1986b Brean Down, *Curr Archaeol*, **9**, 218–21

——, 1987a Recent molluscan studies in the south-west, in Balaam *et al* 1987, 1–8

——, 1987b The molluscs, in Balaam *et al* 1987, 201–13

Bell, M G, and Straker, V, 1984 *Fieldwork at Brean Down, Somerset 1983–4*, Lampeter

Benton, S, 1930–31 The excavation of the Sculptor's Cave, Covesea, Morayshire, *Proc Soc Antiq Scot*, **65**, 177–216

Binford, L R, 1976 Forty-seven trips: a case study in the character of archaeological formation processes, in *Contributions to anthropology: the interior peoples of Northern Alaska. Archaeological survey of Canada* (ed E S Hall), **49**, 299–351, Ottawa

——, 1979 Organisation and formation processes: looking at curated technologies, *J Anthrop Res*, **35**(3), 255–73

Bonnichsen, R, 1973 Millie's Camp: an experiment in archaeology, *World Archaeol*, **4**, 277–91

Boon, G C, 1980 Caerleon and the Gwent Levels in early historic times, in Thompson 1980, 24–36

Bothamley, C H, 1911 Ancient earthworks, *VCH Somerset*, **2**, 467–532

Bottema, S, 1984 The composition of modern charred seed assemblages, in *Plants and ancient man* (eds W van Zeist and W A Casparie), 207–12, Rotterdam

Bottema, S, van Hoorn, T C, Woldring, H, and Gremmen, W, 1982 An agricultural experiment in the unprotected salt marsh, Part II, *Palaeohistoria*, **22**, 127–40

Bowen, H C, and Fowler, P J (eds), 1978 *Early land allotment*, BAR, **48**, Oxford

Boyden, C R, and Little, C, 1973 Faunal distributions in soft sediments of the Severn Estuary, *Est Coastal Mar Sci*, **1**, 203–23

Boyden, C R, Crothers, J H, Little, C, and Mettam, C, 1977 The intertidal invertebrate fauna of the Severn Estuary, *Fld Stud*, **4**, 477–554

Bradley, R, 1975 Salt and settlement in the Hampshire–Sussex borderland, in de Brisay and Evans 1975, 20–6

Bradley, R J, and Ellison, A B, 1975 *Rams Hill: a Bronze Age defended enclosure and its landscape*, BAR, **19**, Oxford

Bradley, R, Lobb, S, Richards, J, and Robinson, M, 1980 Two late Bronze Age settlements on the Kennet gravels: excavations at Aldermaston Wharf and Knight's Farm, Burghfield, Berkshire, *Proc Prehist Soc*, **46**, 217–96

Briggs, S, 1987 Buckets and cauldrons in the late Bronze Age of north-west Europe: a review (Congrès Préhistorique de France 1984), *Actes du Colloque de Bronze de Lille*, 161–87

Britton, D, and Longworth, I H, 1968 Late Bronze Age finds in the Heathery Burn Cave, Co Durham, *Inventaria Archaeologica*, Great Britain, 9th set, **GB 55**, London

Brothwell, D R, 1963 *Digging up bones*, London

Bruce-Mitford, R L S, 1956 A Dark-Age settlement at Mawgan Porth, Cornwall, in *Recent archaeological excavations in Britain* (ed R L S Bruce-Mitford), 167–96, London

Bullock, P, and Murphy, C P, 1979 Evolution of a palaeo-argillic brown earth (paleudalf) from Oxfordshire, England, *Geoderma*, **22**, 225–52

Bullock, P, Fedoroff, N, Jongerius, A, Stoops, G, and Tursina, T, 1985 *Handbook for soil thin section description*, Waine Research Pub, Wolverhampton

Burgess, C B, 1969 The later Bronze Age in the British Isles and north-western France, *Archaeol J*, **125**, 1–45

—, 1980 *The age of Stonehenge*, London

Burgess, C, and Miket, R (eds), 1976 *Settlement and economy: the third and second millennia BC*, BAR, **33**, Oxford

Burrow, I, 1976 Brean Down hillfort, Somerset, 1974, *Proc Univ Bristol Spelaeol Soc*, **14**(2), 141–54

—, 1981 *Hillfort and hilltop settlement in Somerset in the first to eighth centuries AD*, BAR, **91**, Oxford

—, 1984 Ilchester Northover, *Somerset Archaeol Natur Hist*, **127**, 21–2

—, 1985 Brean sandcliff, *Somerset Archaeol Natur Hist*, **128**, 17

Burstow, G P, and Holleyman, G A, 1957 Late Bronze Age settlement on Itford Hill, Sussex, *Proc Prehist Soc*, **23**, 167–212

Butcher, S A, 1978 Excavations at Nornour, Isles of Scilly, 1969–73: the pre-Roman settlement, *Cornish Archaeol*, **17**, 29–112

Butzer, K W, 1982 *Archaeology as human ecology*, Cambridge

Calder, C S T, 1955–6 Report on the discoveries of numerous Stone Age house sites in Shetland, *Proc Soc Antiq Scot*, **88**, 340

Calkin, J B, 1948 The Isle of Purbeck in the Iron Age, *Proc Dorset Natur Hist Archaeol Soc*, **70**, 29–59

—, 1953 Kimmeridge coal money, *Proc Dorset Natur Hist Archaeol Soc*, **75**, 45–71

Catt, J A, 1977 Loess and cover sands, in *British Quaternary studies: recent advances* (ed F W Shotton), 221–9, Oxford

—, 1979 Soils and Quaternary geology in Britain, *J Soil Sci*, **30**, 607–42

—, 1987 Effects of the Devensian cold stage on soil characteristics and distribution in eastern England, in *Periglacial processes and landforms in Britain and Ireland* (ed J Boardman), 145–52, Cambridge

Clapham, A R, Tutin, T G, and Warburg, E F, 1962 *Flora of the British Isles*, Cambridge

Clark, A J, Tarling, D H, and Noël, M, 1988 Developments in archaeomagnetic dating in Britain, *J Archaeol Sci*, **15**, 645–67

Clark, J G D, 1933 Report on an early Bronze Age site in the south-eastern fens, *Antiq J*, **13**, 266–96

Clark, R M, 1975 A calibration curve for radiocarbon dates, *Antiquity*, **49**, 251–66

Clarke, D L, 1972 A provisional model of an Iron Age society and its settlement system, in *Models in archaeology* (ed D L Clarke), 801–70, London

Clarke, D V, 1976 Excavations at Skara Brae: a summary account, in Burgess and Miket 1976, 233–46

Coleman-Smith, R, and Pearson, T (eds), 1988 *Excavations in the Donyatt potteries*, Chichester

Coles, B, and Coles, J M, 1986 *Sweet Track to Glastonbury*, London

Coles, J M, 1959–60 Scottish late Bronze Age metalwork: typology, distribution and chronology, *Proc Soc Antiq Scot*, **93**, 16–134

—, 1978 The Somerset levels, a concave landscape, in Bowen and Fowler 1978, 147–8

—, 1987 Meare Village East: the excavations of A Bulleid and H St George Gray 1932–1956, *Somerset Levels Pap*, **13**

Coles, J M, and Orme, B J, 1983 *Homo sapiens* or *Castor fiber*?, *Antiquity*, **57**, 95–102

Colquhoun, I, 1978 Bronze Age metalwork in Somerset, a catalogue of stray finds, *Somerset Archaeol Natur Hist*, **122**, 83–101

Cornwall, I W, 1958 *Soils for the archaeologist*, London

—, 1961 Appendix II: report on the soil samples, in ApSimon *et al* 1961, 132–6

Cotton, M, and Frere, S S, 1968 Ivinghoe Beacon excavations 1963–5, *Rec Buckinghamshire*, **18**, 187–260

Courty, M A, 1984 Interprétation des aires de combustion par la micromorphologie, *Bulletin de la société Préhistorique Française*, **80**(6), 169–71

Courty, M A, Goldberg, P, and Macphail, R I, in press *Soils and micromorphology in archaeology*, Cambridge

Coy, J, 1981 Animal husbandry and faunal exploitation in Hampshire, in *The archaeology of Hampshire* (eds S J Shennan and R T Schadla-Hall), Hampshire Fld Club Archaeol Soc Monog, **1**, 95–103, Salisbury

—, 1987 Non-domestic faunal resources in south-west England, in Balaam *et al* 1987, 9–29

Crabtree, K, 1984 Two gold bracelets from Brean Down, Somerset, *Antiquity*, **58**, 49–52

Crooke, W M, and Simpson, W E, 1972 Determination of ammonium in kjeldahl digests of crops by an automated procedure, *J Sci Food Agric*, **22**, 9–10

Crothers, J H, 1974a On variation in the shell of the dogwhelk, *Nucella lapillus* (L) 1: Pembrokeshire, *Fld Stud*, **4**, 39–60

—, 1974b On variation in *Nucella lapillus* (L): shell shape in populations from the Bristol Channel, *Proc Malac Soc London*, **4**, 157–70

—, 1981 Marine fauna in *Steep Holm: a survey*, Somerset Archaeol Natur Hist Soc, Taunton, 79–81

—, 1985 Dog whelks: an introduction to the biology of *Nucella lapillus* (L), *Fld Stud*, **6**, 291–360

Cunliffe, B W, and Phillipson, D W, 1968 Excavations at Eldon's Seat, Encombe, Dorset, *Proc Prehist Soc*, **34**, 191–237

Dalrymple, J B, 1969 Experimental micropedological investigations of iron oxides – clay complexes and their interpretation with respect to the soil fabrics of palaeosols, *Third International Working Meeting on Soil Micromorphology*, 583–94, Warsaw

Darvill, T, 1987a *Prehistoric Britain*, London

—, 1987b *Ancient monuments in the countryside: an archaeological management review*, London

de Brisay, K W, 1975 The Red Hills of Essex, in de Brisay and Evans 1975, 5–11

—, 1978 The excavation of a Red Hill at Peldon, Essex, with notes on some other sites, *Antiq J*, **58**, 31–60

de Brisay, K W, and Evans, K A (eds), 1975 *Salt: the study of an ancient industry*, Colchester

de Fleury, L, 1888 Les dépôts de Cendres de Nalliers (Vendée), *Rev Archéologique*, 3 ser, **12**, July–Dec 1888, 349–59

de Jong, J D, 1971 The scenery of the Netherlands against the background of Holocene geology: a review of the recent literature, *Rev Géog Physique Géol Dynamique*, **13**, Fasc **2**, 143–62

Dick, W, and Tabatabai, M A, 1977 An alkaline oxidation method for determination of total phosphorus in soils, *Soil Sci Soc America J*, **41**, 511–13

Dobson, D P, 1935 A bone point from Brean Down, *Proc Univ Bristol Spelaeol Soc*, **4**(3), 265

Doggart, R, 1985 A magnetic susceptibility survey, in *Excavations at Mount Sandel 1973–77* (P C Woodman), Northern Ireland Archaeol Monog, **2**, 98–103, Belfast

Done, G, 1980 The animal bone, in Longley 1980, 74–9

Drewett, P L (ed), 1978 *Archaeology in Sussex to AD 1500*, CBA Res Rep, **29**, London

—, 1982a Later Bronze Age downland economy and excavations of Black Patch, East Sussex, *Proc Prehist Soc*, **48**, 321–400

—, 1982b *The archaeology of Bullock Down, Eastbourne, East Sussex: the development of a landscape*, Sussex Archaeol Soc Monog, **1**, Lewes

Drury, P J, 1978 *Excavations at Little Waltham 1970–71*, CBA Res Rep, **26**, London

Duchaufour, P, 1982 *Pedology*, London

Duncan, N, 1985 *Report on protection of important archaeological site at Brean Down for the National Trust (Wessex Region)*, ms, 22 November 1985

—, 1986a *The National Trust (Wessex Region): Sandcliff, Brean Down. Cliff stabilisation and coastal protection*, ms, 14 February 1986

—, 1986b *Sand cliff, Brean Down. Cliff stabilisation and coastal protection*, ms, 16 September 1986

Ellis, P, forthcoming   Excavations at Norton Camp, Norton Fitzwarren, 1968 to 1971, *Somerset Archaeol Natur Hist*
Ellison, A B, 1975   *Pottery and settlements of the later Bronze Age in southern England*, unpub dissertation, Univ Cambridge
——, 1978   The Bronze age of Sussex, in Drewett 1978, 30–7
——, 1981   Towards a socio-economic model for the middle Bronze Age in southern England, in *Pattern of the past: studies in honour of David Clarke* (eds I Hodder, G Isaac, and N Hammond), 413–38, Cambridge
——, 1982   Bronze Age societies 2000–650 BC, in Aston and Burrow 1982, 43–51
——, 1987   The Bronze Age settlement at Thorny Down: pots, post-holes and patterning, *Proc Prehist Soc*, **53**, 385–92
Ellison, A B, and Rahtz, P A, 1987   Excavations at Hog Cliff Hill, Maiden Newton, Dorset, *Proc Prehist Soc*, **53**, 223–69
Elvère, C, 1988   La seconde découverte du bracelet en or de l'Age du Bronze de Saint-Brieuc-des-Iffs (Ile-et-Vilaine), *Antiquités Nationales*, **20**, 29–34
Evans, J, 1980   *Worlebury*, Weston-super-Mare
Evans, J G, 1972   *Land snails in archaeology*, London
——, 1979   The palaeoenvironment of coastal blown-sand deposits in western and northern Britain, *Scottish Archaeol Forum*, **9**, 16–26
——, 1983   Excavations at Bar Point, St Mary's, Isles of Scilly, 1979–80, *Cornish Stud*, **11**, 7–32
Evans, J G, and Jones, H, 1973   Subfossil and modern landsnail faunas from rock-rubble habitats, *J Conchology*, **28**, 103–29
Farrar, R A H, 1955   Archaeological fieldwork in Dorset in 1955, *Proc Dorset Natur Hist Archaeol Soc*, **77**, 131
Federoff, N, Bresson, L M, and Courty, M A (eds), 1987   *Soil micromorphology*, Plaisir
Fieller, N R J, Gilbertson, D D, and Ralph, N G A (eds), 1985a   *Palaeobiological investigations: research design, methods and data analysis*, BAR, **S266**, Oxford
——, ——, and —— (eds) 1985b   *Palaeoenvironmental investigations: research design, methods and data analysis*, BAR, **S258**, Oxford
Findlay, D C, Colbourne, G J N, Cope, D W, Harrod, T R, and Staines, S J, 1983   *Soils of England and Wales sheet 5, south-west England*, Ordnance Survey, Southampton
Fleming, A, 1988   *The Dartmoor reaves*, London
Ford, S, Bradley, R, Hawkes, J, and Fisher, P, 1984   Flintworking in the metal age, *Oxford J Archaeol*, **3**(2), 157–73
Fowler, P J, 1975   Continuity in the landscape? Some local archaeology in Wiltshire, Somerset and Gloucestershire, in *Recent work in rural archaeology* (ed P J Fowler), 121–36, Bradford-on-Avon
——, 1978   Pre-medieval fields in the Bristol region, in Bowen and Fowler 1978, 29–47
Fox, A, 1964   *South-west England*, London
Gardener, K S, nd   *Lundy: an archaeological field guide*, Landmark Trust
Gavaghan, H, 1986   Time and tide are right for the Severn Barrage, *New Sci*, 17 July 1986, 21–2
Gebhardt, A, in prep   *Studie pédologique des paléopaysages agricoles en Europe de l'ouest*, thèse à l'Université de Paris VI
Genoves, S, 1969   Sex determination in earlier man, in *Science in archaeology* (eds D R Brothwell and E Higgs), 2 edn, 429–39, London
Gibson, A M, 1982   *Earlier domestic sites: a study of the domestic pottery of the late third and early second millennia BC in the British Isles*, BAR, **107**, Oxford
Gingell, C, and Lawson, A J, 1984   The Potterne project: excavation and research at a major settlement of the Late Bronze Age, *Wiltshire Archaeol Natur Hist Mag*, **78**, 31–4
——, and ——, 1985   Excavations at Potterne, 1984, *Wiltshire Archaeol Natur Hist Mag*, **79**, 101–8
Godwin, H, Suggate, R P, and Willis, E H, 1958   Radiocarbon dating of the eustatic rise in ocean level, *Nature*, **181**, 1518–19
Goldberg, P, and Macphail, R I, in prep   Micromorphological evidence of Middle Pleistocene landscapes and climatic changes from southern England: Westbury-sub-Mendip, Somerset and Boxgrove, W Sussex, in *Proc Soil Micromorphology Workshop* (ed L A G Douglas)
Goggin, J M, 1960   The Spanish olive jar, *Yale Univ Pub Anthropol*, **62**, 1–37
Good, G L, 1987   The excavation of two docks at Narrow Quay, Bristol 1978–9, *Post-Medieval Archaeol*, **21**, 25–126
Good, G L, and Russett, V E J, 1987   Common types of earthenware found in the Bristol area, *Bristol and Avon Archaeol*, **6**, 35–43

Gouletquer, P L, 1974   The development of salt making in prehistoric Europe, *Essex J*, **9**(1), 2–14
——, 1975   Niger, country of salt, in de Brisay and Evans 1975, 47–51
Grant, A, 1982   The use of tooth wear as a guide to the age of domestic ungulates, in *Ageing and sexing animal bones from archaeological sites* (eds B Wilson, C Grigson, and S Payne), BAR, **109**, 91–108, Oxford
Gray, H St George, 1925   A gold ornament found at Castle Cary, Somerset, *Antiq J*, **5**, 141–4
Green, G W, and Welch, F B A, 1965   *Geology of the country around Wells and Cheddar*, London
Green, H S, 1980   *The flint arrowheads of the British Isles* BAR, **75**, Oxford
——, 1983   A Late Bronze Age hoard from Llarmon-yn-lal, Clwyd, *Antiq J*, **63**, 384–7
——, 1984   Flint arrowheads: typology and interpretation, *Lithics*, **5**, 19–39
Greensmith, T J, and Tooley, M J (eds), 1982   IGCP Project 61 sea level movements during the last deglacial hemicycle (about 15,000 years), *Proc Geol Ass*, **93**(1), 1–125
Grigson, C, 1982   Porridge and pannage: pig husbandry in Neolithic England, in *Archaeological aspects of woodland ecology* (eds M G Bell and S Limbrey), BAR, **S146**, 297–314, Oxford
Grimes, W F, 1938   The excavation at Gorsey Bigbury. Section III, the pottery, *Proc Univ Bristol Spelaeol Soc*, **5**, 3–57
Grinsell, L V, 1971   Somerset barrows: II north and east, *Somerset Archaeol Natur Hist*, **115** (supp), 44–137
Guido, M, 1978   *The glass beads of the prehistoric and Roman periods in Britain and Ireland*, Rep Res Comm Soc Antiq, **35**, London
Guilbert, G, 1981   Double-ring roundhouses, probable and possible, in prehistoric Britain, *Proc Prehist Soc*, **47**, 299–317
Gurney, D, 1980   Evidence of Bronze Age salt production at Northey, Peterborough, *Northants Archaeol*, **15**, 1–11
Haldane, J W, 1969   A gold bracelet from Hope Wood, Wookey Hole, *Somerset Archaeol Natur Hist*, **113**, 99–101
Hall, A R, Jones, A K G, and Kenward, H K, 1983   Cereal bran and human faecal remains – some preliminary observations, in *Site, environment and economy* (ed B Proudfoot) BAR, **S173**, 85–104, Oxford
Harcourt, R, 1979   Animal bones from Durrington Walls, in *Durrington Walls 1966–1968* (eds G Wainwright and I Longworth), Rep Res Comm Soc Antiq, **29**, 338–50, London
Harrison, R A, 1977   The Uphill Quarry Caves, Weston-super-Mare, a reappraisal, *Proc Univ Bristol Spelaeol Soc*, **14**, 233–54
Harrison, R J, 1988   Bell Beakers in Spain and Portugal: working with radiocarbon dates in the 3rd millennium BC, *Antiquity*, **62**, 464–72
Hassall, M W C, and Tomlin, R S O, 1986   Roman Britain in 1985: 2, Inscriptions, *Britannia*, **17**, 433
Hawkes, C F C, and Clarke, R R, 1963   Gahlstorf and Caister-on-Sea: two finds of late Bronze Age Irish gold, in *Culture and environment* (eds I Ll Foster and L Alcock), 193–250, London
Hawkins, A B, 1971   The late Weichselian and Flandrian transgression in south-west Britain, *Quaternaria*, **14**, 115–30, Rome
——, 1973   Sea level changes around south-west England, in *Marine archaeology* (ed D J Blackman), Proc 23rd Symp Colston Res Soc, 67–87, London
Helbaek, H, 1952   Early crops in southern England, *Proc Prehist Soc*, **18**, 194–233
Henderson, J, 1987   The archaeology and technology of glass from Meare Village East, in Coles 1987, 170–82
Hesse, P R, 1971   *A text book of soil chemical analysis*, London
Heyworth, A, and Kidson, C, 1982   Sea-level changes in south-west England and in Wales, *Proc Geol Ass*, **93**(1), 91–111
Hibbert, F A, 1980   Possible evidence for sea-level change in the Somerset Levels, in Thompson 1980, 103–5
Hillman, G C, 1981   Macroscopic remains of an estuarine flora, in *The Brigg Raft and her prehistoric environment* (ed S McGrail), BAR, **89**, 147–52, Oxford
Hinton, P, 1982   Carbonised seeds, in Drewett 1982a, 382–90
Hodgson, J M, 1974   *Soil survey field handbook, soil survey technical monograph*, **5**, Harpenden
Hook, D R, and Needham, S P, forthcoming   A comparison of recent analyses of British late Bronze Age goldwork with Irish parallels, *Jewellery Stud*, **3**
Horne, D J, 1980   Recent Ostracoda from the Severn Estuary and Bristol Channel, unpub PhD thesis, Univ Bristol
——, 1982   The vertical distribution of phytal ostracods in the

intertidal zone at Gore Point, Bristol Channel, UK, *J Micropalaeontology*, **1**, 71–84

Houghton, J, 1989 *Mollusc analysis from Worlebury Iron Age hillfort*, unpub BA dissertation, St David's Univ College, Lampeter

Houghton, W, 1879 *British freshwater fishes*

Housley, R A, 1988 The environmental context of Glastonbury Lake Village, *Somerset Levels Pap*, **14**, 63–82

Hunter, J, 1987 New discoveries on Sandy, *Archaeology Extra*, **4**, 1

Hurst, J G, 1967 The pottery, in Excavations at Old Wardour Castle (L Keen), *Wiltshire Archaeol Natur Hist Mag*, **62**, 67–78

Isles, R, nd *Avon's past from the air*, Bristol

Jelgersma, S, and van Regteren Altena, J F, 1969 An outline of the geological history of the coastal dunes in the western Netherlands, *Geologie en Mijnbouw*, **48**(3), 335–42

Jelgersma, S, de Jong, J, Zagwijn, W H, and van Regteren Altena, J F, 1970 The coastal dunes of the western Netherlands; geology, vegetation history and archaeology, *Med Rijks Geol Dienst*, n ser, **21**, 93–167

Jodlowski, A, 1975 Salt production in Poland in prehistoric times, in de Brisay and Evans 1975, 85–7

Johnson, N, and David, A, 1982 A Mesolithic site on Trevose Head and contemporary geography, *Cornish Archaeol*, **21**, 67–103

Jones, A K G, 1982 Human parasite remains: prospects for a quantitative approach, in *Environmental archaeology in the urban context* (eds A R Hall and H K Kenward), CBA Res Rep, **43**, 66–70

——, 1983 A coprolite from 6–8 Pavement, in *Environment and living conditions at two Anglo-Scandinavian sites*, (eds A R Hall, H K Kenward, D Williams, and J R A Greig), *The Archaeology of York*, **14**/4, 225–9, London

——, 1985 Trichurid ova in archaeological deposits: their value as indicators of ancient faeces, in Fieller *et al* 1985a, 105–19

——, 1986 Parasitological investigations on Lindow Man, in *Lindow Man: the body in the bog* (eds I M Stead, J B Bourke, and D Brothwell), 136–9, London

Jones, M, 1978 The plant remains, in *The excavation of an Iron Age settlement, Bronze Age ring-ditches and Roman features at Ashville Trading Estate, Abingdon (Oxfordshire) 1974–76* (M Parrington), CBA Res Rep, **28**, 93–110

——, 1985 Archaeobotany beyond subsistence reconstruction, in *Beyond domestication in prehistoric Europe* (eds G Barker and C Gamble), 107–28, London

Jones, M U, 1977 Prehistoric salt equipment from a pit at Mucking, Essex, *Antiq J*, **57**, 317–19

Keeley, H C M (ed), 1984 *Environmental archaeology: a regional review*, DoE Occas Pap, **6**, London

Keepax, C A, 1981 Avian egg-shell from archaeological sites, *J Archaeol Sci*, **8**, 315–36

Kerney, M P, 1966 Snails and man in Britain, *J Conchology*, **26**, 3–14

——, 1976a A list of the fresh and brackish-water Mollusca of the British Isles, *J Conchology*, **29**, 26–8

——, 1976b *Atlas of the non-marine Mollusca of the British Isles* Cambridge

——, 1976c Two post-glacial molluscan faunas from south-west England, *J Conchology*, **29**, 71–3

Kerney, M P, and Cameron, R A D, 1979 *Land snails of Britain and north-west Europe*, London

Kidson, C, 1977 The coast of SW England, in *The Quaternary history of the Irish Sea* (eds C Kidson and M J Tooley), 257–98, Liverpool

——, 1982 Sea level changes in the Holocene, *Quaternary Sci Rev*, **1**, 121–51

Kidson, C, Gilbertson, D D, Haynes, J R, Heyworth, A, Hughes, C E, and Whatley, R C, 1978 Interglacial marine deposits of the Somerset Levels, south-west England, *Boreas*, **7**, 215–28

Kidson, C, and Heyworth, A, 1973 The Flandrian sea-level rise in the Bristol Channel, *Proc Ussher Soc*, **2**, 565–84

——, and ——, 1976 The Quaternary deposits of the Somerset Levels, *Quat J Engng Geol*, **9**, 217–35

Kirkham, B, 1981 The excavation of a prehistoric saltern at Hogsthorpe, Lincs, *Lincolnshire Hist Archaeol*, **16**, 5–10

Kleinmann, D, 1975 The salt springs of the Salle Valley, in de Brisay and Evans 1975, 45–6

Knight, F A, 1902 *The sea-board of Mendip*, London

Kubiena, W L, 1938 *Micropedology*, Ames, Iowa

Lambrick, G (ed), 1985 *Archaeology and nature conservation*, Oxford

Langdon, M, 1986 Wembdon, Wembdon Hill, *Somerset Archaeol Natur Hist*, **130**, 151

Lanting, J N, and van der Waals, J D, 1972 British beakers as seen from the continent, *Helinium*, **12**, 20–46

Leach, P, 1982 *Ilchester*, **1**: *Excavations 1974–1975*, Western Archaeol Trust Excavation Monog, **3**, Bristol

Le Borgne, E, 1955 Susceptibilité magnétique anomale du sol superficial, *Annales de Géophysique*, **11**, 399–419

——, 1960a Influence du feu sur les propriétés magnétiques du sol et sur celles du schiste et du granit, *Annales de Géophysique*, **16**, 159–95

——, 1960b Etude expérimentale du trainage magnétique dans le cas d'un ensemble de grains magnétiques tres fins dispersés dans une substance non-magnétique, *Annales de Géophysique*, **16**, 445–93

Leech, R, 1981a The excavation of a Romano-British farmstead and cemetery on Bradley Hill, Somerton, Somerset, *Britannia*, **12**, 177–252

——, 1981b The Somerset Levels in the Romano-British period, in Rowley 1981, 20–51

Leech, R, Bell, M, and Evans, J, 1983 The sectioning of a Romano-British salt-making mound at East Huntspill, *Somerset Levels Pap*, **9**, 74–8

Leech, R, and Leach, P, 1982 Roman town and countryside 43–450 AD, in Aston and Burrow 1982, 63–82

Lennon, G W, 1963 A frequency investigation of abnormally high tidal levels at certain west coast ports, *Proc Inst Civil Engnrs*, **25**, 451–84

Levitan, B, 1984 The vertebrate remains, in *Middleton Stoney: excavation and survey in a North Oxfordshire parish 1970–1982* (eds S Rahtz and T Rowley), 108–48, Oxford

——, 1986 On-site recording and the microcomputer, *Archaeol Computing Newsl*, **8**, 15–20

——, forthcoming A method for investigating anatomical fragmentation and frequency, *Circaea*, **7**

Levitan, B M, Audsley, A, Hawkes, C J, Moody, A, Moody, P, Smart, P L, and Thomas, J S, 1988 Charterhouse Warren Farm, Swallet, Mendip, Somerset, *Proc Univ Bristol Spelaeol Soc*, **18**(2), 171–239

Lohmeyer, W, *et al*, 1962 Contribution à l'unification du système phytosociologique pour l'Europe moyenne et nord-occidentale, *Melhoramento*, **15**, 137–51

Longley, D, 1980 *Runnymede Bridge 1976: excavations on the site of a late Bronze Age settlement*, Surrey Archaeol Soc Res Vol, **6**, Guildford

Longworth, G, and Tite, M S, 1977 Mössbauer and magnetic susceptibility studies of iron oxides in soils from archaeological sites, *Archaeometry*, **19**, 3–14

Longworth, I H, and Ellison, A B, 1988 *Excavations at Grimes Graves, Norfolk, 1972–1976: the pottery*, London

Louwe Kooijmans, L P, 1974 *The Rhine Meuse Delta*, Analecta Praehistoria Leidensia, **7**

——, 1985 *Sporen in het land: de Nederlandse delta in de prehistorie*, Amsterdam

Lynch, F, 1970 *Prehistoric Anglesey*, Llangefni

Mackin, M L, 1971a Further excavations of the enclosure at Swine Sty, Big Moor, Baslow, *Trans Hunter Archaeol Soc*, **10**(1), 5–13

——, 1971b Further excavations of the enclosure at Swine Sty, Big Moor, Baslow, *Trans Hunter Archaeol Soc*, **10**(3), 204–17

Macphail, R I, 1985 *Soil report on Balksbury Camp, Hants*, Ancient Monuments Lab Rep, **4621**, London

——, 1986a *Soil report on Hazleton long cairn, Gloucs*, Ancient Monuments Lab Rep, **4897**, London

——, 1986b Paleosols in archaeology: their role in understanding Flandrian pedogenesis, in *Paleosols: their recognition and interpretation* (ed V P Wright), 263–389, Oxford

——, 1987a A review of soil science in archaeology in England, in *Environmental archaeology: a regional review*, **2** (ed H C M Keeley), HBMC Occas Pap, **1**, 332–79, London

——, 1987b The soil micromorphology of tree subsoil hollows, *Circaea*, **5**(1), 14–17

——, 1987c *Soil report on Potterne, Devizes, Wilts*, Ancient Monuments Lab Rep, **144/87**, London

——, 1987d *Soil report on the mid-Saxon floor and Dark Earth at Jubilee Hall, Covent Garden, London*, Ancient Monuments Lab Rep, **39/87**, London

Macphail, R I, and Courty, M A, 1985 Interpretation and significance of urban deposits, in *Proc 3rd Nordic conference on scientific methods in archaeology* (eds T Edgren and H Jogner), ISKOS 5, 71–84, Helsinki

Macphail, R I, Romans, J C C, and Robertson, L, 1987 The application of soil micromorphology to the understanding of

Holocene soil development in the British Isles; with special reference to early agriculture, in Fedoroff *et al* 1987, 647–56

Martin, E, and Murphy, P, 1988 West Row Fen, Suffolk: a Bronze Age fen-edge settlement site, *Antiquity*, **62**, 353–8

Matthias, W, 1976 Die Salzproduktionein bedeutender Faktor in des Wirtsschaft der früfbronzezeitlichen Bevölkerung an der mittleren Saale, *Jahresschrift Mitteldeutsche Vorgeschichte*, **60**, 373–94 (Halle/Saale)

May, J, 1976 *Prehistoric Lincolnshire*, Lincoln

McDonnell, R R J, 1979 The Upper Axe Valley, an interim statement, *Somerset Archaeol Natur Hist*, **123**, 75–82

——, 1985 *Archaeological survey of the Somerset claylands, summary report on the area north of the Polden Hills*, Somerset County Council

——, 1986 *Archaeological survey of the Somerset claylands, summary report on the area south of the Polden Hills*, Somerset County Council

Megaw, J V S, 1976 Gwithian, Cornwall: some notes on the evidence for Neolithic and Bronze Age settlement, in Burgess and Miket 1976, 51–6

Megaw, J V S, and Simpson, D D A, 1981 *Introduction to British prehistory*, Leicester

Megaw, J V S, Thomas, A C, and Wailes, B, 1961 The Bronze Age settlement at Gwithian, Cornwall, *Proc West Cornwall Fld Club*, **2**(5), 200–15

Mercer, R J, 1970 The excavation of a Bronze Age hut circle settlement, Stannon Down, St Breward, Cornwall, 1968, *Cornish Archaeol*, **9**, 17–46

Milles, A, Williams, D, and Gardner, N (eds), 1989 *The beginnings of agriculture*, BAR, **S496**, Oxford

Ministry of Agriculture, Fisheries and Food, 1977 *Manual of veterinary parasitological laboratory techniques*, Technical Bull,**18**, London

Moffett, L, Robinson, M, and Straker, V, 1989 Cereals, fruits and nuts: charred plant remains from Neolithic sites in England and Wales and the Neolithic economy, in Milles *et al* 1989, 243–61

Moore, C N, and Rowlands, M, 1972 *Bronze Age metalwork in Salisbury Museum*, Salisbury

Morris, E, 1985 Prehistoric salt distributions: two case studies from western Britain, *Bull Board Celtic Stud*, **32**, 336–79

Müller, D W, 1987 Neolithisches briquetage von der mittleren Saale, *Jahresschrift mittledeutsche Vorgeschichte*, **70**, 135–54

Murphy, J, and Riley, J P, 1962 A modified single solution method for the determination of phosphate in natural waters, *Anal Chemica Acta*, **27**, 31–6

Murphy, P, 1983 Studies of the environment and economy of a Bronze Age fen-edge site at West Row, Mildenhall, Suffolk: a preliminary report, *Circaea*, **1**(2), 49–60

Musson, C, 1970 House plans and prehistory, *Curr Archaeol*, **2**(10), 267–75

National Trust, 1982 *Biological survey of Brean Down*, ms

Nature Conservancy Council, 1987 *Earth Science Conservation*, **23**, 31

NERC, 1972 *The Severn Estuary and the British Channel: an assessment of present knowledge*

Neale, J W, 1964 Some factors influencing the distribution of recent British ostracoda, *Pubbl Staz zool Napoli*, **33**, 247–307

Nenquin, J, 1961 Salt: a study in economic prehistory, *Dissertationes Archaeologicae*, **6**, Brugge

Newman, R, and Parkin, L, 1986 Atlantic Trading Estate, Barry, *Archaeology in Wales*, **26**, 55

Norman, C, 1977 A flint assemblage from Constantine Island, north Cornwall, *Cornish Archaeol*, **16**, 3–9

Nowakowski, J A, 1988 Trethellan Farm excavations, Newquay, Summer 1987, *Cornish Archaeol*, **27**, 195–6

O'Connell, M, 1986 *Petters sports field, Egham*, Surrey Archaeol Soc Res Vol, **10**, Guildford

Oldfield, F, Dearing, J A, Thompson, R, and Garret-Jones, S, 1978 Some magnetic properties of lake sediments and their possible links with erosion rates, *Polskie Archive Hydrobiologia*, **25**, 321–31

Oldfield, F, Krawieki, A, Maher, B, Taylor, J J, and Twigger, S, 1985 The role of mineral magnetic measurements in archaeology, in Fieller *et al* 1985b, 29–53

Otlet, R L, 1975 An assessment of laboratory errors in liquid scintillation methods of Carbon-14 dating, in *Proc 9th International ^{14}C Conf* (eds R Berger and H E Suess), 256–67, Berkeley

Otlet, R L, and Warchal, R M, 1978 Liquid scintillation counting of low-level Carbon-14, in *Liquid scintillation counting*, **5** (eds M A Cook and P Johnson), 210–18, London

Otlet, R L, Huxtable, G, Evans, G V, Humphreys, D G, Short, T D, and Conchie, S J, 1983 Development and operation of the Harwell small counter facility for the measurement of ^{14}C in very small samples, in *Proc 12th International ^{14}C Conf, Radiocarbon*, **28**(2A), 603–14

Page, H, 1982 Some notes on the geomorphological and vegetational history of the saltings at Brean, *Somerset Archaeol Natur Hist*, **126**, 119–25

Patchett, F M, 1944 Cornish Bronze Age pottery, *Archaeol J*, **101**, 17–49

Payne, S, and Munson, P J, 1985 Ruby and how many squirrels? Destruction of bone by dogs, in Fieller *et al* 1985a, 31–48

Peacock, D P S, 1969a Neolithic pottery production in Cornwall, *Antiquity*, **43**, 145–9

——, 1969b A contribution to the study of Glastonbury Ware from south–western Britain, *Antiq J*, **49**, 41–56

Pearce, S, and Padley, T, 1977 The Bronze Age find from Tredarvah, Penzance, *Cornish Archaeol*, **16**, 25–41

Pearson, T, 1979 The contents of a mid eighteenth-century pit from North Petherton, Somerset, *Post-Medieval Archaeol*, **13**, 183–210

Pearson, G W, Pilcher, J R, Baillie, M G L, Corbett, D M, and Qua, F, 1986 High-precision 14C measurement of Irish oaks to show the natural 14C variations from AD 1840–5210 BC, *Radiocarbon*, **28**(2B), 911-34

Pearson, G W, and Stuiver, M, 1986 High-precision calibration of the radiocarbon time scale, 500–2500 BC, *Radiocarbon*, **28**(2B), 839–62

Pollard, A M, Bussell, G D, and Baird, D C, 1981 The analytical investigation of early Bronze Age jet and jet-like material from the Devizes Museum, *Archaeometry*, **23**(2), 139–67

Ponsford, M W, 1980 *Bristol Castle: archaeology and history of a royal fortress*, unpub M Litt thesis, Univ Bristol

Preece, R C, 1980 The biostratigraphy and dating of a postglacial slope deposit at Gore Cliff, near Blackgang, Isle of Wight, *J Archaeol Sci*, **7**, 255–65

Prehistoric Society, 1984 *Prehistory, priorities and society: the way forward*, London

Price, R, and Watts, L, 1980 Rescue excavations at Combe Hay, Somerset, 1968–1973, *Somerset Archaeol Natur Hist*, **124**, 1–49

Pryor, F M, 1980a Will it all come out in the Wash? Reflections at the end of eight years' digging, in *The British later Bronze Age* (eds J Barrett and R Bradley), BAR, **83**(ii), 483–500, Oxford

——, 1980b *Excavation at Fengate, Peterborough: the third report*, Northants Archaeol Soc Monog, **1**, Northampton

——, 1984 *Excavation at Fengate, Peterborough, England: the fourth report*, Northants Archaeol Soc Monog, **2**

Rackham, O, 1980 *Ancient woodland*, London

——, 1986 *The history of the countryside*, London

Radford, C A R, 1981 Glastonbury Abbey before 1184: interim report on the excavations 1908–94, in *Medieval art and architecture at Wells and Glastonbury*, British Archaeol Ass Conference Trans, **4**, 110–34

Radford, C A R, and Hallam, A D, 1953 Pottery in the history of Taunton Castle in the light of recent excavations, *Somerset Archaeol Natur Hist*, **98**, 81–8

Rahtz, P A, 1969 Cannington hillfort 1963, *Somerset Archaeol Natur Hist*, **113**, 56–68

——, 1974 Pottery in Somerset AD 400–1066, in *Medieval pottery from excavations* (eds V Evison, H Hodges, and J G Hurst), London

——, 1977 Late Roman cemeteries and beyond, in *Burial in the Roman world* (ed R Reece), CBA Res Rep, **22**, 53–64, London

——, 1979 *The Saxon and medieval palaces at Cheddar*, BAR, **65**, Oxford

——, 1982 The Dark Ages 400–700 AD, in Aston and Burrow 1982, 63–82

——, 1983 Celtic society in Somerset AD 400–700, *Bull Board Celtic Stud*, **33**, 82–3

Rahtz, P A, and ApSimon, A, 1962 Excavations at Shearplace Hill, Sydling St Nicholas, Dorset, England, *Proc Prehist Soc*, **28**, 289–328

Rahtz, P A, and Fowler, P J, 1972 Somerset AD 400–700, in *Archaeology of the landscape* (ed P J Fowler), 187–221, London

Rahtz, P A, and Watts, L, 1979 The end of Roman temples in the west of Britain, in *The end of Roman Britain* (ed P J Casey), BAR, **71**, 183–210, Oxford

Ranwell, D S, 1972 *Ecology of salt marshes and sand dunes*, London
Rathje, W L, and Schiffer, M B, 1982 *Archaeology*, New York
Rees, S, 1986 Stone implements and artefacts, in Whittle *et al* 1986, 75–91
Remane, A, 1934 Die Brackwasserfauna (mit besonderer Berucksichtigung des Ostseegebietes), *Zool Anz Suppl*, **7**, 34–74
Reynolds, P J, 1979 *Iron Age farm. The Butser experiment*, London
——, 1982 Substructure to superstructure, in *Structural reconstruction: approaches to the interpretation of the excavated remains of buildings* (ed P J Drury), BAR, **110**, 173–98
Riehm, K, 1961 Prehistoric salt boiling, *Antiquity*, **35**, 181–91
Roberts, M B, 1986 Excavation of the Lower Palaeolithic site at Amey's Eartham pit, Boxgrove, West Sussex: a preliminary report, *Proc Prehist Soc*, **52**, 215–45
Romans, J C C, and Robertson, L, 1974 Some aspects of the genesis of alpine and upland soils in the British Isles, in *Soil microscopy* (ed G K Rutherford), 498–510, Ontario
Rowley, R T (ed), 1981 *The evolution of marshland landscapes*, Oxford
Salaman, R A, 1986 *Dictionary of leatherworking tools c 1700–1950*, London
Saville, A, 1981 The flint and chert artefacts in excavations at Carn Brea Illogan, Cornwall, 1970–73 (R Mercer), *Cornish Archaeol*, **20**, 101–52
Savory, H, 1980 *Guide Catalogue of the Bronze Age collections*, Cardiff
Schiffer, M B, 1976 *Behavioural archaeology*, London
——, 1987 *Formation processes of the archaeological record* Albuquerque
Sheail, J, 1972 *Rabbits and their history*, Newton Abbot
Shepherd, I, 1976 Preliminary results from the Beaker settlement at Rosinish, Benbecula, in Burgess and Miket 1976, 209–20
Shimwell, D W, 1971 Festuco Brometea Br.-Bl & R.Tx 1943 in the British Isles: the phytogeography and phytosociology of limestone grasslands, *Vegetatio*, **23**,(1–2), 1–28
Shotton, F W, and Williams, R E G, 1973 Birmingham University radiocarbon dates, 6, *Radiocarbon*, **15**(1), 8
Silverside, A J, 1977 *A phytosociological survey of British arable-weed and related communities*, PhD thesis, Department of Botany, University of Durham
Simms, S R, 1988 The archaeological structure of a Bedouin camp, *J Archaeol Sci*, **15**(2), 197–211
Simpson, D, 1976 The later Neolithic and Beaker settlement site at Northton, Isle of Harris, in Burgess and Miket 1976, 221–31
Smith, I F, 1974 The Neolithic, in *British prehistory: a new outline* (ed C Renfrew), 100–36, London
Smith, I F, and Simpson, D D A, 1966 Excavation of a round barrow on Overton Hill, north Wilts, *Proc Prehist Soc*, **32**, 122–55
Smith, K, Coppen, J, Wainwright, G J, and Beckett, S, 1981 The Shaugh Moor project: third report – settlement and environmental investigation, *Proc Prehist Soc*, **47**, 205–73
Smith, M A, 1959 Somerset hoards and their place in the Bronze Age of southern Britain, *Proc Prehist Soc*, **25**, 144–87
Soil Survey Staff, 1975 *Soil taxonomy*, Agric handbook 436, United States Dept Agric, Washington DC
Sparks, B W, 1961 The ecological interpretation of Quaternary non-marine Mollusca, *Proc Linnaean Soc London*, **172**, 71–80
Spencer, P J, 1974 *Environmental change in the coastal sand dune belt of the British Isles*, unpub BSc dissertation, Univ Cardiff
——, 1975 Habitat change in coastal sand-dune areas: the molluscan evidence, in *The effect of man on the landscape: the Highland Zone* (eds J G Evans, S Limbrey, and H Cleere), CBA Res Rep, **11**, 96–103, London
Steers, J A, 1960 *The coast of England and Wales in pictures*, Cambridge
Stell, G P, and Harman, M, 1988 *Buildings of St Kilda*, Edinburgh
Straker, V, 1987 *Carbonised cereals, weeds and charcoal from the Bronze Age midden and settlement at Potterne, Wiltshire*, Ancient Monuments Lab Rep, London
Stuiver, M, and Pearson, G W, 1986 High precision calibration of the radiocarbon time scale AD 1950–500 BC, *Radiocarbon*, **28**(2B), 805–38
Stuiver, M, and Reimer, P J, 1986 A computer program for radiocarbon age calibration, *Radiocarbon*, **28**(2B), 1022–30
Swanton, E W, 1912 *The Mollusca of Somerset*, Taunton
Swinnerton, H H, 1932 The prehistoric pottery sites of the Lincolnshire coast, *Antiq J*, **12**, 239–53
Taylor, H, 1933 The Tynings barrow group, second report, *Proc Univ Bristol Spelaeol Soc*, **4**(2), 67–127
——, 1951 The Tynings Farm barrow group, third report, *Proc Univ Bristol Spelaeol Soc*, **6**(2), 111–73
Taylor, H, and Taylor, E E, 1949 An early Beaker burial? at Brean Down near Weston-Super-Mare, *Proc Univ Bristol Spelaeol Soc*, **6**, 88–93
Taylor, J, and Sons, 1984 *The National Trust Brean Down coastal protection draft report*, Plymouth
——, and ——, 1985 *The National Trust Brean Down coastal protection supplementary report March 1985*, Plymouth
Taylor, J J, 1980 *Bronze Age goldwork of the British Isles*, Cambridge
——, 1984 The Potterne gold bracelet and its affinities, *Wiltshire Archaeol Natur Hist Mag*, **78**, 35–40
Tessier, M, 1975 The protohistoric salt making sites of the Pays de Retz, France, in de Brisay and Evans 1975, 52–5
Thackray, D, nd *Brean Down, Somerset, Archaeology in the National Trust*, Warminster
Thomas, C, 1958 *Gwithian: ten years' work (1949–1958)*, Camborne
——, 1985 *Exploration of a drowned landscape*, London
Thomas, N, 1983 A decorated bronze axe-head from Worlebury Hill, Weston-Super-Mare, *Somerset Archaeol Natur Hist*, **127**, 7–12
Thomas, R, Robinson, M, Barrett, J, and Wilson, B, 1986 A late Bronze Age riverside settlement at Wallingford, Oxfordshire, *Archaeol J*, **143**, 174–200
Thompson, F H (ed), 1980 *Archaeology and coastal change*, Soc Antiq London Occas Pap, n ser, **1**, London
Thompson, R, Battarbee, R W, O'Sullivan, P E, and Oldfield, F, 1975 Magnetic susceptibility of lake sediments, *Limnology and Oceanography*, **20**, 687–98
Thornton, J, 1973 in Excavated shoes to 1600 (ed P S Doughty), *Trans Mus Assistants Group*, **12**, 2–13
Tite, M S, and Mullins, C, 1970 Electromagnetic prospecting on archaeological sites using a soil conductivity meter, *Archaeometry*, **12**, 97–104
——, and ——, 1971 Enhancement of the magnetic susceptibility of soils on archaeological sites, *Archaeometry*, **13**, 209–19
Tomalin, D J, 1982 The formal and textural characteristics of the biconical urn assemblages from Shaugh Moor Enclosure 15, in Shaugh Moor project fourth report – environment, context and conclusion (N D Balaam, K Smith, and G J Wainwright), *Proc Prehist Soc*, **48**, 228–37
——, 1983 *The origins and development of the biconical urn series in Great Britain*, unpub PhD thesis, Univ Southampton
Turner, G M, and Thompson, R, 1979 Behaviour of the earth's magnetic field as recorded in the sediment of Loch Lomond, *Earth Planetary Sci Letters*, **42**, 412–26
——, and ——, 1982 Detransformation of the British geomagnetic secular variation record for Holocene times, *Geophys J Roy Astron Soc*, **70**, 789–92
Valentine, K W G, and Dalrymple, J B, 1976 Quaternary buried paleosols: a critical review, *Quaternary Res*, **6**, 209–22
van den Broeke, P W, 1986 Zeezout: een schakel tussen West-en Zuid Nederland in de lJzertijd en de Romeinse tijd, in *Rotterdam Papers: a contribution to prehistoric, Roman and medieval archaeology*, **5**, 91–114, Rotterdam
——, forthcoming Iron Age sea salt trade in the lower Rhine/Meuse area, in *Festschrift for John Alexander, Europe in the first millennium BC*, BAR, Oxford
van Vliet-Lanoë, B, 1982 Structures et microstructures associées à la formation de glace de ségrégation: leurs conséquences, in *Proc 4th Canadian Permafrost Conf*, National Research Council, 116–22, Ottawa
——, 1985 Frost effects in soils in *Soil and Quaternary landscape evolution* (ed J Boardman), 117–58, London
van Zeist, W, 1974 Palaeobotanical studies of settlement sites in the coastal area of the Netherlands, *Palaeohistoria*, **16**, 223–371
van Zeist, W, van Hoorn, T C, Bottema, S, and Woldring, H, 1976 An agricultural experiment in the unprotected salt marsh, *Palaeohistoria*, **18**, 111–53
Vaughan, M P, 1976 *Environmental change in areas of blown sand on the western coasts of the British Isles*, unpub BSc dissertation, Univ Cardiff
Vince, A, 1977 The medieval and post-medieval ceramic industry of the Malvern region: the study of a ware and its distribution, in *Pottery and early commerce: characterisation and trade in Roman and later ceramics* (ed D P S Peacock), 257–305, London
——, 1983 The medieval and post-medieval pottery, in *The east and north gates of Gloucester* (C Heighway), Western Archaeol Trust Excav Monog, **4**, 125–61

von den Dreisch, A, 1976 A guide to the measurement of animal bones from archaeological sites, *Peabody Mus Bull*, **1**, Harvard

von Simon, K, 1988 Hornsäulen-Briquetage von Rüssen, kr Borna, *Ausgrabungen und Funde*, **33**(1), 5–15

Wagner, C W, 1957 *Sur les ostracodes du Quaternaire récent de Pays Bas et leur utilisation dans l'étude Géologique des dépôts holocènes*, 1–259, The Hague

Wainwright, G J, and Smith, K, 1980 The Shaugh Moor project: second report – the enclosure, *Proc Prehist Soc*, **46**, 65–122

Waldèn, H W, 1976 A nomenclatural list of the land Mollusca of the British Isles, *J Conchology*, **29**, 21–5

Walkley, A, and Black, I A, 1934 An examination of the Degtjareff method for determining soil organic matter and a proposed modification on the chromic acid titration method, *Soil Sci*, **37**, 29–38

Walters, I, 1984 Gone to the dogs: a study of bone attrition at a central Australian campsite, *Mankind*, **14**(5), 389–400

Ward, G K, and Wilson, S R, 1978 Procedures for comparing and combining radiocarbon age determinations: a critique, *Archaeometry*, **20**(1), 19–32

Warre, F, 1865 Brean Down, *Somerset Archaeol Natur Hist*, **12**, 65–6

Watkins, C M, 1960 North Devon pottery and its export to America in the seventeenth century, *United States Nat Mus Bull*, **225**, *Smithsonian Inst Pap*, **13**, 17–59

Wattez, J, and Courty, M A, 1987 Morphology of ash of some plant materials, in Federoff *et al* 1987, 677–83

Watts, L, and Leach, P J, forthcoming *Henley Wood: the Roman temples and a post-Roman cemetery: excavations by Ernest Greenfield and others*

Watts, L, and Rahtz, P, 1985 *Mary-le-port, Bristol*, City of Bristol Mus Art Gallery Monog, **7**, Bristol

Wedlake, W, 1982 *The excavation of the shrine of Apollo at Nettleton, Wilts 1956–71*, Rep Res Comm Soc Antiq London, **40**

Wheeler, A, 1978 *Key to the fishes of northern Europe*, London

Whimster, R P, 1977 Harlyn Bay: the excavations of 1900–1905 in the light of recent research, *Cornish Archaeol*, **16**, 60–88

Whittle, A, Keith-Lucas, M, Milles, A, Noddle, B, Rees, S, and Romans, J C C, 1986 *Scord of Brouster: an early agriculture settlement on Shetland*, Oxford Univ Comm Archaeol Monog, **9**, Oxford

Wilkinson, T J, and Murphy, P, 1986 Archaeological survey of an intertidal zone, *J Fld Archaeol*, **13**(2), 177–94

Williams, D, 1973 Flotation at Siraf, *Antiquity*, **47**, 288–92

Williams, D F, 1977 The Romano-British black-burnished industry: an essay on characterisation by heavy mineral analysis, in *Pottery and early commerce: characterisation and trade in Roman and later ceramics* (ed D P S Peacock), 163–220, London

Williams, D F, and Woodward, A, forthcoming The pottery fabrics, in Ellis forthcoming

Williams, G, 1986 Recent work on Bronze Age sites in south-west Wales, *Archaeology in Wales*, **26**, 11–14

Williams, M, 1970 *The draining of the Somerset Levels*, Cambridge

Wilmer, H, 1908 Late-Celtic remains on the coast of Brittany comparable with the Red Hills, *Proc Soc Antiq*, **23**, 207–14

Wilson, B, 1985 Degraded bones, feature type and spatial patterning on an Iron Age occupation site in Oxfordshire, England, in Fieller *et al* 1985a, 81–3

Wilson, B, and Levitan, B, forthcoming The vertebrate remains from Claydon Pike

Woodward, A, forthcoming The prehistoric pottery, in Ellis forthcoming

Worsfold, F H, 1943 A report on the late Bronze Age site excavated at Minnis Bay, Birchington, Kent, 1938–40, *Proc Prehist Soc*, **9**, 28–47

Index

compiled by Lyn Greenwood

Pages on which illustrations occur are italicised. Where illustrations fall within a run of page references they have not been indexed separately.

Acanthinula aculeata 247
Aegopinella nitidula 247
agriculture 19, 23, 27, 261–2
air photographs 104
alder 203–5
Aldermaston (Berks), pottery 140
Amberley Mount, building evidence 52
Ammonia beccarii 209
animal bones: ageing 236–7; butchery 236–7; distribution *58*, 60, 99, 101, 103, 223–5, 238–41; and economy 260–1; frequencies 225–31, 239, 241
animal burrowing 63, 65, 192, 238–9, 241, 253
Apium graveolens (Fool's watercress) 206
Archaeological Resource Management 262–3
archaeomagnetic dating 24, 103, 105, 113–16
Arctinoptychus senarius 207–8
armlets, shale 159–60
Arrhenatherum elatius (onion couch) 219
arrowheads, flint 19, 154
artefact distribution 54; Structure 59 60, 62; Structure 95 57, 60; Unit 5b 54–62; Unit 6 36; Unit 8a 23; post-medieval 86–9
artefact recording 11, *12*, 14–15
Ascaris (roundworm) 244–5
ash 193–4, 211
Aster/Bidens pollen 203–5
Aster/Cirsium (Aster/Thistle) 206
Atlantic Trading Estate, Barry Docks (S Glam), burials 80
Atriplex (Orache) 206
auger survey 15, 90–3, 104–6
Aurila convexa 208
Avena (oats) 213, 218
Avonmouth (Avon), Crooks Marsh Farm, stratigraphy 106
awls, bone 50, 160–2
Axe, River 105, 106, 233, 258, 260

badgers 63
Balea perversa 247
Baltic tellin (*Macoma balthica*) 250, 251, 252
Bantham (Devon): non-marine Mollusca 249; radiocarbon date 249
barley (*Hordeum*) 213, 216, 217–18, 219
barnacles (Cirripedia) 251, 252
barrows 255, 257
Barry Docks (S Glam), Atlantic Trading Estate, burials 80
Beacon Hill, Lundy (Dev), burials 80
Beacon Hill, Shepton Mallet (Som), pottery 133
beads, glass 82
bells, brass 84, *86*
Benbecula (W Isles), building evidence 34
Beta B clay 188–91
Bexley Heath (Kent), bracelets 146
Bilderdykia convolvulus (black bindweed) 218
birch 203–5
bird bones 223, 225, 231, 235–6
bird cherry 211
birds' eggs 252
black bindweed (*Bilderdykia convolvulus*) 218
Black Patch (E Suss): building evidence 52, 62; flints 57; plant evidence 219

blackthorn 211
Bleadon (Avon), field systems 255
blinks (*Montia*) 217, 219
Bodmin Moor (Corn), building evidence 54
bone objects *see* awls; chisels; gouges; pins; points; smoothers
bone strip 86
bones, animal *see* animal bones
bones, human 3, 70–1, 77, *81*, 238; *and see* burials; cemeteries; graves
boneworking evidence 36, 194
book clasp, brass 84, *86*
boundaries 72; *and see* cultivation evidence; field systems
Boxgrove (Suss), soil evidence 188
bracelets: Class B1 146, 149; copper 96, 150; gold *6*, *7*, 68–9, 71–2, 146–50, 262; shale 77, 159–60, 262
brass objects *see* bells; book clasp; lace-ends; pins
Bradley Hill (Som), burials 80
Brean Down Farm (Som), historical evidence 89
Brent Knoll (Som), settlement 255
Bridgwater (Som), pottery 132
briquetage 62, 170–3, 195, 218; evaporation trays 31, *168*, 169–70; pedestals 34, 57, 62, 165–9; *and see* salt production
Bristol (Avon), pottery 84
bronze objects *see* pins; wire
bronze sheet 45, 150
Brookweed (*Samolus valerandi*) 206
Buccinum undatum (common whelk) 250, 252
buckthorn 211
burial practices 255, 257
burials 7, 26, 73–80, 263; *and see* bones, human; cemeteries; graves
butchery evidence 236–7
Butser (Hants): building evidence 36, 52, 54; soil evidence 190–1

Cadbury Congresbury (Som), settlement pattern 82
cairns 1, 255, 257, 261
Caister-on-Sea (Norf), bracelets 146
calcite 175
Campylosira cymbelliformis 207–8
Candidula intersecta 248, 249
Candona caudata 208
Cannington (Som): burials 80, 82; pottery 126, 132, 139
Capsella bursa-pastoris (shepherd's purse) 219
carbon: chemical analysis 183, *185*, 186; sediment analysis *178*, 179
Carex (sedges) 217
Carychium tridentatum 247
Castell Henllys (Dyfed), building evidence 52
Castle Cary (Som), gold ring 150
cats 233–5, 228
Cat's Water (Camb), building evidence 52
cattle 63, 221, 223–8, *229*, *230*, 232, 233–7, 261
Cecilioides acicula 247, 248
celtic beans (*Vicia faba*) 213, 217, 218, 219

cemeteries 73–80, 238–9; *and see* bones, human; burials; graves
Cepaea/Arianta 248
Cerastoderma edule (cockle) 251, 252
Cernuella virgata 248, 249
Chapel Tump Farm (Gwent), building evidence 52, 260
charcoal 19, 34, 101, 103, 211
Charterhouse Warren Cave (Som), settlement evidence 255, 257
Cheddar (Som), Tynings Farm, pottery 126, 143–4
Chenopodiaceae 203–5
Chenopodium album (fat hen) 217
Chenopodium glaucum (Glaucus goosefoot) 206
Chenopodium rubrum (Red goosefoot) 206
cherry 211
chert 152
chickweed (*Stellaria media*) 219
chisels, bone 162, *163*
Cirripedia (barnacles) 251, 252
Cirsium/Aster (Thistle/Aster) 203–5, 206
clasps: brass 84, *86*; lead 84, *86*
Clausilia bidentata 247
clay objects 32, 43, 96, 174–5
clay pipes 86, 101, 103
cleavers (*Galium aparine*) 219
clover (*Trifolium*) 217, 219
cobbling 41, 47, 69
Cochlicella acuta 248, 249
Cochlicopa spp 248
cockles (*Cerastoderma edule*) 251, 252
Cold Harbour (Gwent), occupation site 260
Combe Hay (Avon), pottery 139–40
common dog whelk (*Nucella lapillus*) 250, 251, 252
common periwinkle (*Littorina littorea*) 250, 251, 252
common whelk (*Buccinum undatum*) 250, 252
computerised data 14, 18
copper alloy objects 150–1
copper sheet 82
coprolites 31, 37, 57, *58*, 60, 242–5
cores, flint 24, 152, 156, 157
Corylus avellana (hazel) 203–5, 211, 216, 217, 219
crabs 252
Covesea (Grampian), Sculptor's Cave, bracelets 150
Craig-yr-Wolf (Clwyd), bracelets 146, 149
Crataegus monogyna (hawthorn) 211, 216
cultivation evidence 19, 23, 27, 193, 195; *and see* boundaries; field systams
curse inscription 1
cuttlefish (*Sepia officinalis*) 252
Cyperaceae (sedge) 203–5
Cyprideis torosa 208, 209, 210
Cythere lutea 208
Cytheropteron nodosum 208

Dartmoor (Dev): building evidence 54; pottery 132
dating 253–5; *and see* archaeomagnetic dating; radiocarbon dating
daub 36, 48, 101
deer *see* red deer; roe deer

diatom analysis 105, 207–8
Diploneis aestuarii 207–8
Discus rotundatus 248
dog whelk (*Nucella lapillus*) 250, 251, 252
dogs 60, 223, 225, 233–5, 238
drainage 106
Droitwich (Here-Worc), salt production 172, 173

East Huntspill (Som), 36, 173
Ebbesbourne Wake (Wilts), hoard 72
economic context 260–2
Eldon's Seat (Dor), armlets 160
Eleocharis palustris/uniglumis (spikerush) 217
Elphidium gerthi 209
Elworthy (Som), pottery 132
emmer wheat (*Triticum dicoccum*) 217, 218
Ena obscura 247
environmental context 256, 257–60
erosion 6, 7–8, 258–60
Eucypris heinrichi 208
Eucythere declivis 208
Eupatorium cannabinum (Hemp agrimony) 206

fabricator/strike-a-light 157
fat hen (*Chenopodium album*) 217, 219
Fengate (Camb), salt production 172
field systems 255, 256, 261–2; *and see* boundaries; cultivation evidence
Filicales 205
Fingringhoe (Ess), plant evidence 219
Finmarchinella angulata 208
Finmarchinella finmarchica 208
fish bones 119, 213, 221, 223, 225, 231–3, 235–6
fishing 261
flakes, flint 24; retouched 157; unretouched 19, 32, 152, 153, 154, 156
flat periwinkle (*Littorina obtusata*) 250, 251
flints 57, 152–7; *and see* cores; flakes; knives; piercers; rods; scrapers
Fool's watercress (*Apium graveolens*) 206
Fore Abbey (Co Westmeath, Ireland), bracelets 146
forts, WWII 3, 84; *and see* hillforts
fowling 261

Galium aparine (cleavers) 219
geology 1, 3, 175
glass objects *see* beads
Glastonbury Abbey (Som), burials 80
Glaucus bulrush (*Schoenoplectus tabernaemontani*) 206
Glaucus goosefoot (*Chenopodium glaucum*) 206
gold objects *see* bracelets
gold strip 146
gold-coloured metal spheres 151
Gore Point (Som), ostracod evidence 210
Gorsey Bigbury (Som), pottery 119
gouges, bone 162, 163
Gramineae (grass) pollen 203–5
graves 80; *and see* bone, human; burials; cemeteries
Great spearwort (*Ranunculus lingua*) 217
Grimes Graves (Norf), pottery 132
gullies 41–2, 49–50, 62, 65, 69, 72, 96
gunflints 157
Gunwalloe (Corn), non-marine Mollusca 249
Gwallon Down (Corn), pottery 132
Gwent Levels 104, 260
Gwithian (Corn) 8–9; building evidence 52; cultivation evidence 261; field boundaries 72; non-marine Mollusca 249; pottery 133; radiocarbon date 133; stratigraphy 255

Halangy Down/Porth (Scilly Isles): building evidence 54; cultivation evidence 261
Halle-Dölauer Heide (Germany), salt production 172
hammerstones 70, 175
Harlyn Bay (Corn), burials 80
hawthorn (*Crataegus monogyna*) 211, 216
hazel (*Corylus avellana*) 203–5, 211, 216, 217, 219
Hazleton (Glos), soil evidence 188
hearths 45, 50, 59, 60–2, 113–14, 194
Heathery Burn (Dur): awls 160; bracelets 150; gouges 162
Helianthemum appenninum (white rockrose) 1, 205, 216
Helicella itala 247–8, 249
Helicigona lapicida 247
Helix aspersa 248, 249
Hemicythere villosa 208
Hemicytherura clathrata 208
Hemp agrimony (*Eupatorium cannabinum*) 206
henbane (*Hyoscyamus niger*) 217
Henley Wood (Som), burials 80 82
Heybridge (Ess), Lofts Farm, plant evidence 219
hillforts 1, 82–3; *and see* forts
hob nails, iron 77, 82
Hockwold-cum-Wilton (Norf), animal bone evidence 241
Hog Cliff Down (Dor), building evidence 52
Hogsthorpe (Linc), salt production 173
Holne Moor (Dev): boundaries 72; building evidence 51
Hope Wood (Som), bracelets 149, 150
Hordeum (barley) 213, 216, 217–18, 219
horses 221, 223, 225, 228, 233–5
houses, construction techniques 51–4
Hullbridge Basin (Ess), salt production 172
Hyalodiscus 207–8
Hydrobia 250
Hydrobia ulvae 249
Hydrobia ventrosa 249
Hydrocotyle vulgaris (Pennywort) 206
Hyoscyamus niger (henbane) 217

Ilchester (Som), burials 80
Ilyocypris biplicata 208
Ilyocypris bradyi 209
intertidal areas 103–4
iron: chemical analysis 182–3, 184; sediment analysis 179–80, 182
iron objects *see* hob nails
Irthlingborough (Northants), soil evidence 189
Itford Hill (Suss): animal bone evidence 241; building evidence 51–2
Ivinghoe Beacon (Bucks), bracelet 150
ivory strip 86
ivy 203–5

Juncus (Rush) 206, 217, 218, 219

Kimmeridge (Dor): salt trading 172, 173; shale objects 160
knives, flint 31, 156

lace-ends, brass 82
Lauria cylindracea 247
lead objects *see* clasps; curse inscription
leatherworking 36, 57
Leptocythere castanea 208
Leptocythere ilyophila 209, 210
Leptocythere lacertosa 208
Leucophytia bidentata 249
Little Bay (Scilly Isles), building evidence 34
Little Waltham (Ess), building evidence 52
Limacidae 248
limpets (*Patella vulgata*) 248, 250, 251, 252

Littorina littorea (common periwinkle) 250, 251, 252
Littorina obtusata (flat periwinkle) 250, 251
Littorina saxatilis 250
loomweights 6, 45, 57, 60, 174
loss on ignition analysis 178, 179, 181, 183, 185
Loxoconcha elliptica 208, 209, 210
Loxoconcha rhomboidea 208
Lundy (Som), Beacon Hill, burials 80
Lymnaea truncatula 249

Macoma balthica (Baltic tellin) 250, 251, 252
Macrogastra rolphii 247
Maiden Castle (Dor): non-marine Mollusca 249; soil evidence 188
magnetic susceptibility survey 197–202
mammoth bones 37, 221, 228, 257
marine silts, pollen analysis 206–7
Mawgan Porth (Corn), burials 80
Meare (Som), occupation evidence 261
Melosira westii 207
micromorphological study 26–7, 36, 99, 101, 103, 187–96, 259
middens 36, 70, 72, 255
Middle Hope (Avon), field systems 255
Middleton Stoney (Oxon), animal bone evidence 238
Minnis Bay (Kent), bracelets 150
moles 24
Mollusca: marine 59, 250–2; non-marine 246–50
Montia (blinks) 217, 219
Morvah (Corn), bracelets 146
Mucking (Ess), salt production 173
Myosoton aquaticum (water chickweed) 217
Mytilus edulis 252

Nalliers (France), salt production 171
nettle (*Urtica urens*) 217
Nettleton Shrub (Wilts), burials 80
Newport (Gwent), Chapel Tump Farm, pottery 132
nitrogen, chemical analysis 183, 185, 186
Nitzschia 207–8
Nornour (Scilly Isles) 8–9; building evidence 34, 54, 60; cultivation evidence 261
Northey (Camb), salt production 172
Northton (W Isles): building evidence 34; peat burning 36; stratigraphy 255
Norton Fitzwarren (Som), pottery 132–3, 139
Nucella lapillus (common dog whelk) 250, 251, 252

oak 211
oats (*Avena*) 213, 218
onion couch (*Arrhenatherum elatius*) 219
Orache (*Atriplex*) 206
ostracod analysis 105, 208–10
Ostrea edulis (oyster) 101, 250, 252
Overton Hill (Wilts), smoothers 162
Oxychilus cellarius 247
oyster (*Ostrea edulis*) 101, 250, 252

Paralia marina 207–8
Par Beach (Scilly Isles), building evidence 34
particle size analysis 176
Patella vulgata (limpet) 248, 250, 251, 252
Pays de Retz (France), salt production 172
peat 36, 103–4, 105; macroscopic plant remains 205–6; pollen analysis 203–5; radiocarbon date 205
Pennywort (*Hydrocotyle vulgaris*) 206
periwinkles (*Littorina*) 250, 251, 252
petrology: Beaker sherds 120; briquetage 170–1, 173; Bronze Age pottery 122–3

Petters Sports Field, Runnymede Bridge (Surr), shale objects 159
phosphates 57, 60, 62, 193–5
phosphorus, and sediment analysis 179–80, 182–3, *184*
Phragmites 203–5, 206
piercers, flint 31, 156
pigs 221, 223–8
pine 203–5
pins: bone 43, 160, *161*; brass 84, *86*; bronze 82
Pisidium 248
plant macrofossil analysis 211–19
Plantago lanceolata (ribwort plantain) 217
Plantago maritima 205
points, bone 32
pollen analysis: marine silts 206–7; peat 203–5; sandcliff 206–7
Polypodium 205
Pomoidae 211
Pontocythere elongata 208
Pool, Sandy (Beds), peat burning 36
Poor Heath (Suff), animal bone evidence 241
Potterne (Wilts): animal bone evidence 237, 241; bracelets 71, 146, 160; burial practice 257; midden 72; plant evidence 219; soil evidence 194
pottery *254*, 262
    Bell Beaker *24*, 24, 26–7, 31–2, 34, 77, 94, 99, 103, 117–20
    Bronze Age 77, 80, 94, 96, 99, 101, 121–45; distribution 45, 47, 70, 86, *87*; fabrics 7, 34, 70, 121–3; forms and function 140–4; fragmentation 140
    Iron Age 77, 80
    Romano-British 77, 80, 82, 101, 103, 106
    post-medieval 80, 84–9, *85*, *87*, *88*
    and see briquetage
pottery objects *see* spindle whorls
privet 203–5
Punctum pygmaeum 248
Pupilla muscorum 247, 249
Pyramidula rupestris 248

Quinqueloculina oblonga 209

rabbits 63, 70, 89, 223, 225, 238–9, *240*, 253
radiocarbon dates 80, 107–13; burials 77, 80; Context 66 126; Context 163 34; Context 212 77; Context 213 77; peat 104, 105, 205, 258; Structure 57 126; Structure 59 133; Structure 95 133; Unit 3c 113; Unit 3c2 255; Unit 4 71, 113, 140, 253, 255; Unit 5b 54, 112–13, 171, 253; Unit 6 126; Unit 6a 34, 112, 126, 253; Unit 6b 34, 253; Unit 6α 112, 171, 253; Unit 7 27, 112, 253; Unit 8a 24, 26, 112, 154, 253; Bantham 249; Combe Hay 133; Gwithian 133; Hogsthorpe 173; Hullbridge Basin 172; Pays de Retz (France) 172; Trevisker 133
Radyr (Glam), Lesser Garth Cove, pottery 126
Rams Hill (Berks): animal bone evidence 241; pottery 139–40
Ranunculus lingua (Great spearwort) 217
red deer 221, 223, 225, 235, 228
Red goosefoot (*Chenopodium rubrum*) 206
Reindeer Rift, Brean Down (Avon), burial practice 257
reptile bones 223, 225
research objectives 8–9
ribwort plantain (*Plantago lanceolata*) 217
Robertsonites tuberculata 208
rods, flint 156
roe deer 228
rose 217
Rosemorran (Corn), bracelets 146
Rosinish (W Isles): building evidence 34; plant evidence 253

roundworm (*Ascaris*) 244–5
Rowden (Dor), plant evidence 219
Rumex (sorrel) 217
Rumney Surface, tidal ranges 258
Runnymede (Berks), animal bone evidence 241
Runnymede Bridge (Surr): bone objects 160; burial practice 257; plant evidence 219; shale objects 159
Rush(es) (*Juncus*) 206, 217, 218, 219
Rüssen (Germany), salt making 172
rye 219

St Kilda (W Isles), biulding evidence 36
St Martins (Scilly Isles), bracelets 146
salt production 57, 171–3, 261; *and see* briquetage
Samolus valerandi (Brookweed) 206
sampling 11
sands 175, 260
sandstone 175
Schoenoplectus tabernaemontani (Glaucus bulrush) 206
Scirpus maritimus (Sea club-rush) 206
Scirpus/Schoenoplectus 218
Sclerocheilus contortus 208
Scord of Brouster (Shet), building evidence 34
scrapers: flint 24, 31, 57, 32, 154, 156, 157; shale 57
sea blite (*Suaeda maritima*) 219
Sea club-rush (*Scirpus maritimus*) 206
seaweed 217, 252
sedges: *Carex* 217; Cyperaceae 203–5
sediments, particle size analysis 176–7, 179
Sepia officinalis (cuttlefish) 252
settlement pattern 255
shale objects 159–60, 175; *and see* bracelets; scrapers
Shaugh Moor (Dev): building evidence 34, 52; cultivation evidence 261; field boundaries 52, 72; pottery 126
Shearplace Hill (Dor): animal bone evidence 241; building evidence 51–2; pottery 126; shale objects 160
sheep 221, 223–8, *229*, *230*, *232*, 233–5, 261
sheep's sorrell 219
shepherd's purse (*Capsella bursa-pastoris*) 219
Shepton Mallet (Som), Beacon Hill, pottery 133
sieving 19, 28, 37, 39, 63, 84
Skara Brae (Ork), awls 160
slate tool 47
sleeping areas, Structure 95 60
sloes 211, 216, 217, 219
smoothers, bone 162, *163*, *164*
Snail Down (Wilts), animal bone evidence 241
soil pits 15, 94–106, 114–16, 209, 247, 249–50
soil studies 187–96
Somerset Levels, stratigraphy 105, 106, 173
Son en Breugel (Netherlands), salt production 172
sorrel (*Rumex*) 217
South Cadbury (Som): bracelets 149; pottery 139–40
Sparganium 205
spelt wheat 217, 219
spikerush (*Eleocharis palustris/uniglumis*) 217
spindle whorls, pottery 158, 175
Springfield Lyons (Ess), plant evidence 219
Stackpole Warren (Dyfed): building evidence 52; burials 255, 257
Stannon Down (Corn): building evidence 32, 52, 54; cultivation evidence 261
Stellaria media (chickweed) 219
stone: objects 80, 96, 101, 158–9, 175; sources 262

stratigraphy 3, 15–16, 18, 90–3, 176–86; Iron Age–medieval 73-4; post-medieval 84
Structure 50 69
Structure 57 28, 31–4, *35*; animal bones 223, 225–8, 238–9; briquetage 34; marine Mollusca 250; micromorphology 193–4; non-marine Mollusca 247; plant macrofossil analysis 217; pottery 34; radiocarbon dates 111, 126
Structure 59 37, *38*, 39–42, 52, 54, 60, 62; animal bones 62, 223, 225–8, 238–9; artefact distribution 60, 62; briquetage 39, 41, 62, 165–73; chemical analysis 183–6; coprolites 62; flints 62; gullies 52; hearths 62; magnetic susceptibility survey 62, 197, *198*, 201; marine Mollusca 251; phosphate values 62; plant macrofossil analysis 218; pottery 62, 144; radiocarbon dates 34, 133; stakeholes 41; stone 41, 52, 54; stratigraphy 39, 41
Structure 95 37, *38*, 42–52, 62; animal bones 57, 223, 225–8, 238–9; artefact distribution 54, 57, 60; ash 45; awl, bone 45, 57; briquetage 45, 47, 48, 57, 165–73; bronze strip 57; chemical analysis 182–3; clay objects 43; cobbles 47, 52; coprolites 48, 57; flints 57; gullies 48, 52; hearths 45, 54, 57, 60; loomweights 45, 60; magnetic susceptibility survey 60, 197, *198*, *200*, 201; non-marine Mollusca 247; pebbles, shale 48; phosphate values 57, 60; pins, bone 43, 57; plant macrofossil analysis 218; postholes 48, 52; pottery 43, 45, 47, 57, 144–5; radiocarbon dates 54, 113–14, 133; scraper, shale 57, 158–9; slate tool 47; stakeholes 45; stone 45, 47, 48, 52; stratigraphy 43, 45, 47, 49–50; wire, bronze 57
Suaeda maritima (sea blite) 219
Swine Sty (Derbys), shale objects 159–60

temples, Romano-Celtic 1, 82–3, 261
terra fusca 188–91, 201
Testacella maugei 248
Thalassiosira decipiens 207–8
Thistle/Aster (*Cirsium/Aster*) 206
Thorney Down, occupation evidence 60
tide ranges 103, 105, 171, 257–9, 261
Tisbury (Wilts), bracelets 146
Tornewton (Dev), non-marine Mollusca 248
treasure hunting 8
Tredarvah (Corn), pottery 132
Thethellen (Corn), cultivation evidence 261
Trevisker (Corn): building evidence 52; cultivation evidence 261; pottery 54, 126, 132–3, 144
Trichia hispida 248
Trichuris (whipworm) 243–5
Trifolium (clover) 217, 219
Triticum dicoccum (emmer wheat) 217, 218
Triticum spelta (spelt wheat) 217, 218
Triticum (wheat) 213
Trochammina inflata 209
Truncatellina cylindrica 247–8, 248
Tŷ Mawr (Anglesey), bracelets 146, 149

Unit 1: animal bones 220, 238–9; auger survey 93; dating 255; flints 152; magnetic susceptibility survey 199, 201; marine Mollusca 251; non-marine Mollusca 248; stratigraphy 15–16, 93–4, 255
Unit 2, stratigraphy 16, 255
Unit 3: auger survey 92, 93; flints 152; magnetic susceptibility survey 199, 201; non-marine Mollusca 248; pottery 119; stones 93; stratigraphy 92, 93
Unit 3a: animal bones 220, 238–9; awl, bone 162; coprolites 244; dating 255; flints 157; human bone 77; marine Mollusca 251,

252; stratigraphy 18, 84, 253, 255
Unit 3b: animal bones 220, 238–9; stratigraphy 18
Unit 3b1, stratigraphy 84, 255
Unit 3b2: burials 77; dating 255; non-marine Mollusca 248; stratigraphy 73, 84
Unit 3c: animal bones 220, 238–9; radiocarbon dates 111, 113; stratigraphy 18
Unit 3c1: burials 73–4, 77; stratigraphy 73
Unit 3c2: dating 106, 255; ostracod analysis 209; radiocarbon date 255; sediment particle size analysis 175, 179; stratigraphy 73
Unit 3d: animal bones 238-9; armlet, shale 160
Unit 4 63–72, 86, *91*, 104; animal bones 63, 66, 70, 220, *232*, 233–6, *240*; armlet, shale 159–60; auger survey 90, 93; bone objects 70, 160, 162; bracelets, copper 150; bracelets, gold 68–9, 71–2, 146–50; bronze sheet 150; calcite 175; charcoal 66; clay objects 70, 174, 175; cobbling 69; copper alloy plate 70; coprolites 68, 244; cultivation 72; dating 253–5; ditches 66, 68, 72; flints *154*, 156–7; gouges, bone 162; gullies 65, 69, 72; hammerstones 175; human bone 69, 70–1, 238; loomweights 70, 174; magnetic susceptibility survey 199; marine Mollusca 66, 251; micromorphology 72, 187, 195; middens 70, 72; nail, iron 63; non-marine Mollusca 248; occupation deposits 195; ostracod analysis 209; pins, bone 160; plant macrofossil analysis 212, 213, 218; postholes 66, 69; pottery 63, 65–6, 68–72, 90, 93, 123, 133–40, *144*, 145; radiocarbon dates 71, 111, 113, 140, 253, 255; sandstone 175; sediment particle size analysis 73, 179, 182; shale objects 70, 159; smoothers, bone 162; spindlewhorl 69, 70, 158, 175; stones 65, 66, 68, 69; stratigraphy 18, 63, 66, 68, 69, 90, 93, 199, 253; Structure 50 69
Unit 4a 260; animal bones 220, 238–9; auger survey 90, 93; dating 255; flints 152; magnetic susceptibility survey 199, 201; micromorphology 196; non-marine Mollusca 248; occupation deposits 196; pottery 93; sediment particle size analysis 176, 179; stones 93; stratigraphy 73, 90, 93, 199, 201
Unit 4b, animal bones 238–9
Unit 5: magnetic susceptibility survey 199; stones 7; stratigraphy 18, 90, 92
Unit 5a 37; animal bones 37, 220, 221, 238–9; auger survey 92; birds' eggs 252; dating 253–5; flints 152; magnetic susceptibility survey 199; marine Mollusca 251, 252; micromorphology 187, 194–5; non-marine Mollusca 248; occupation deposits 194–5; ostracod analysis 209; pottery 37, 123, 131–3; sediment particle size analysis 176–7, 179, 182; stratigraphy 18, 37, 92, 199, 253, 255
Unit 5b 37-62; animal bones 60, 220, 223–33, 238–9, *240*; artefact distribution 54–62; auger survey 90, 92; awl, bone 50, 162; bird bones 231; birds' eggs 252; bone objects 50, 51, 162, 165; briquetage 50–1, 60, 165–73; bronze sheet 150; calcite 175; charcoal 54; chemical analysis 182–6; clay objects 173–5; copper alloy 50, 150; coprolites 50, 51, 60, 244; crabs 252; dating 54, 253–5; fish bones 213, 233; flints 50, *154*, 156, 157; hearths 50, 60,

92, 104; human bone 60, 238; loomweights 51, 165, 173–4; magnetic susceptibility survey 197, 198, *200*, 201; marine Mollusca 60, 251; micromorphology 37, 187, 194–5; non-marine Mollusca 247–8; occupation deposits 194–5; ostracod analysis 208; pebble, shale 160; pins, bone 160; plant macrofossil analysis 212, 213, 217–18; pottery 50–1, 60, 123, 126–31, *142*, *143*, 144–5; radiocarbon dates 54, 111, 112–13, 171, 253; sandstone 175; sediment particle size analysis 179–82; shale objects 160, 175; stone 50, 51, 175; stratigraphy 18, 37, 50, 90, 92, 201, 253; wire, copper alloy 50, 51, 150; *and see* Structure 57; Structure 95
Unit 5c 37
Unit 5d 37; animal bones 220, 221; auger survey 92; bird bones 231; coprolites 37, 244; dating 253–5; fish bones 213, 233; magnetic susceptibility survey 199; marine Mollusca 251; non-marine Mollusca 247, 248; ostracod analysis 208; pottery 37, 123; sediment particle size analysis 176–7, 179, 182; stratigraphy 18, 37, 92, 199, 253
Unit 6 28–36; animal bones 220, 223–33, 238–9; auger survey 92; bird bones 231; briquetage 126; charcoal 28; colluvial deposits 191–3; coprolites 244; fish bones 213, 233; flints 34, 36, *153*, *154*, 156, 157; human bone 238; magnetic susceptibility survey 199; micromorphology 191–3; non-marine Mollusca 247; ostracod analysis 208; pottery 34, 119, 123–6, *142*, 144; radiocarbon dates 126; spheres, gold-coloured metal 151; stones 28; stratigraphy 18, 28, 92
Unit 6a: ash 193–4; dating 196, 253–5; gouges, bone 162; magnetic susceptibility survey 199; marine Mollusca 250; micromorphology 36, 187, 193–4, 196; occupation deposits 193–4; pins, bone 160; plant macrofossil analysis 217; postholes 28; pottery 34, 36, 123; radiocarbon dates 34, 111, 112, 126, 253; sediment particle size analysis 179, 182; stone 28, 36; stratigraphy 18, 28, 199, 253; *and see* Structure 57
Unit 6b 260; charcoal 193; colluvial deposits 192–3, 199; dating 253–5; fish bones 119; magnetic susceptibility survey 199; marine Mollusca 250; micromorphology 187, 192–3; plant macrofossil analysis 216–17; pottery 34, 123; radiocarbon dates 111, 112; stratigraphy 199, 253
Unit 6α: animal bone 36; briquetage 31, 34, *168*, 172; clay objects 175; coprolites 31; dating 253–5; flints 31; marine Mollusca 250–1; non-marine Mollusca 247; plant macrofossil analysis 212, 213, 217; pottery 31, 34, 36, 123; radiocarbon dates 111, 112, 171, 253; stone structure 28, 31; stratigraphy 18, 31–2, 253
Unit 7 *20*, 23–4, *25*, 259–60; animal bones 23–4, 220, 221; auger survey 92; bone objects 165; charcoal 23; colluvial deposits 192–3; dating 253–5; flints 24, 154, 156, 157; magnetic susceptibility survey 199; marine Mollusca 23, 250; micromorphology 187, 192–3; non-marine Mollusca 23, 247; plant macrofossil analysis 216; pottery 24, 119, 123;

radiocarbon dates 27, 111, 112, 253; sediment particle size analysis 176–7, 179, 182; stone 23; stratigraphy 23, 27, 199, 253
Unit 8: bird bones 231; magnetic susceptibility survey 198–9; micromorphology 187
Unit 8a 19–24, *25*, 104, 259–60; animal bones 19, 23, 220, 221; auger survey 90–2; burial 26; charcoal 19, 23, 26, 211; colluvial deposits 191–2; cultivation marks 19, 23, 27; dating 253–5; flints 19, 23, 24, *153*, 154, 156; magnetic susceptibility survey 199; marine Mollusca 250; micromorphology 26–7, 187–92; non-marine Mollusca 247; plant macrofossil analysis 211, 216; pottery 23, 24, 26, 117; radiocarbon dates 24, 26, 111, 112, 154, 253; sediment particle size analysis 179; soil study 188–91; spheres, gold-coloured metal 151; stone 19, stratigraphy 18, 24, 90, 92, 199, 253
Unit 8b: auger survey 90, 92; flints 157; magnetic susceptibility survey 198–9; sediment particle size analysis 179; soil study 188; stratigraphy 198–9
Unit 9, soil study 188, 189
Unit 10a, animal bones 221
Unit 11, soil study 187, 188
Unit 12, soil study 188
Unit 12a: animal bones 221; soil study 187
Unit 13, soil study 187–8
Unit 13a, soil study 187–8
Unit 13c, soil study 187
Unit 13d, soil study 187
Uphill (Avon): burials 257; settlement evidence 255
Urtica urens (nettle) 217

Vallonia costata 248
Vallonia excentrica 247, 248, 249
Vertigo pygmaea 248, 249
Vicia faba (celtic beans) 213, 217, 218, 219
Vitrina pellucida 248

Wallingford (Berks): burial pactice 257; midden 72; pottery 140
water chickweed (*Myosoton aquaticum*) 217
water vole 24
wattle and daub 36, 48, 52
Wemberham (Avon), occupation evidence 106
Wentlooge Formation 105, 106, 257, 259, 260
West Row, Mildenhall (Suff), plant evidence 219
Westbury-sub-Mendip (Som), soil evidence 188
Weston-super-Mare (Avon), cremation vessels 255
Westward Ho! (Dev), soil survey 104
whale bones 228
wheat (*Triticum*) 213, 216, 217–18
whelks 250
whipworm (*Trichuris*) 243–5
white rockrose (*Helianthemum appenninum*) 1, 205, 216
wild cherry 211
Windmill Hill (Wilts), animal bone evidence 241
wire, bronze 150–1
wood mouse 24
Worlebury (Avon): field system 255; non-marine Mollusca 248